**Books are to be returned on or before
the last date below.**

Ethnoarcha...

Ethnoarchaeology in Action is a first and comprehensive study of what remains, despite its centrality and multiple linkages, one of anthropology's lesser-known subdisciplines. First developed as the study of ethnographic material culture from archaeological perspectives, it has expanded its scope and relevance over the past half-century. The authors are leading practitioners, and their theoretical approaches embrace both the processualism of the New Archaeology and the post-processualism of the 1980s and 1990s. The book takes a case-study approach and is balanced in its geographic and topical coverage, including consideration of materials in French and German. Three chapters introduce the subject and its history, survey the broad range of theory required, and discuss field methods and ethics. Ten topical chapters treat formation processes, subsistence, the study of artifacts and style, settlement systems, site structure and architecture, specialist craft production, trade and exchange, and mortuary practices and ideology. The book concludes with an appreciation of ethnoarchaeology's contributions, actual and potential, and of its place within anthropology. Generously illustrated, it includes photographs of leading ethnoarchaeologists in action.

NICHOLAS DAVID (http://www.acs.ucalgary.ca/~ndavid) is Professor of Archaeology at the University of Calgary and Director of the Mandara Archaeological Project in Cameroon and Nigeria. His recent work includes video programs and numerous articles on technology and society in the Mandara mountains.

CAROL KRAMER is Professor of Anthropology at the University of Arizona. Her books on her work in Iran and India are, respectively, *Village Ethnoarchaeology* (1982) and *Pottery in Rajasthan* (1997); a 1985 article in *Annual Review of Anthropology* ("Ceramic Ethnoarchaeology") is widely cited. Ongoing research interests include vernacular architecture, craft specialization, ceramics, and gender.

CAMBRIDGE WORLD ARCHAEOLOGY

The Cambridge World Archaeology series is addressed to students and professional archaeologists, and to academics in related disciplines. Most volumes present a survey of the archaeology of a region of the world, providing an up-to-date account of research and integrating recent findings with new concerns of interpretation. While the focus is on a specific region, broader cultural trends are discussed and the implications of regional findings for cross-cultural interpretations considered. The authors also bring anthropological and historical expertise to bear on archaeological problems and show how both new data and changing intellectual trends in archaeology shape inferences about the past. More recently, the series has expanded to include thematic volumes.

CAMBRIDGE WORLD ARCHAEOLOGY

ETHNOARCHAEOLOGY IN ACTION

NICHOLAS DAVID
University of Calgary

CAROL KRAMER
University of Arizona

CAMBRIDGE
UNIVERSITY PRESS

PUBLISHED BY THE PRESS SYNDICATE OF THE UNIVERSITY OF CAMBRIDGE
The Pitt Building, Trumpington Street, Cambridge, United Kingdom

CAMBRIDGE UNIVERSITY PRESS
The Edinburgh Building, Cambridge CB2 2RU, UK
40 West 20th Street, New York, NY 10011–4211, USA
10 Stamford Road, Oakleigh, VIC 3166, Australia
Ruiz de Alarcón 13, 28014 Madrid, Spain
Dock House, The Waterfront, Cape Town 8001, South Africa

http://www.cambridge.org

First published 2001

Printed in the United Kingdom at the University Press, Cambridge

Typeface Trump Medieval 10/13pt   *System* QuarkXPress™ [SE]

A catalogue record for this book is available from the British Library

Library of Congress Cataloguing in Publication data

David, Nicholas, 1937–
Ethnoarchaeology in action / Nicholas David, Carol Kramer.
    p.   cm. – (Cambridge world archaeology)
Includes bibliographical references and index.
ISBN 0 521 66105 6 – 0 521 66779 8 (pb.)
1. Ethnoarchaeology. I. Kramer, Carol, 1943– II. Title. III. Series.
CC79.E85 D38 2001 930.1–dc21   00-065127

ISBN 0 521 66105 6 hardback
ISBN 0 521 66779 8 paperback

For the
great-great-grandchildren
of those with and amongst whom
we have collectively researched.

CONTENTS

FIGURES AND CREDITS

TABLES

PREFACE

When in early 1997 we decided to start writing the book about ethnoarchaeology that we had talked about for years, we both naïvely thought that this could be achieved by little more than putting our course notes together and filling in some blanks. Our experience has been very different. We never intended to write a text for beginning students but rather a stocktaking of a subdiscipline of anthropology some 45 years after its inception, and to do this we have had to think through our understandings of the topic, and to expand them by much further reading. In this we were greatly assisted by the *Bibliography of ethnoarchaeology and related studies* (David *et al.* 1999) that Nicholas David (henceforth, except in references, ND) had been compiling and developing for several years. However, the magnitude of the task and the inevitability of our failure to do a thorough job is apparent in its accumulation, as of the day this is written, of 883 items classified primarily as ethnoarchaeology. We wished not to produce a catalogue, a collation, or an encyclopedia, but rather, via a critical reading of case studies, to guide the reader towards an informed understanding of theoretical, methodological, and substantive issues in ethnoarchaeology at the turn of the millennium. Decisions had to be made.

The first was to adopt a restrictive definition of ethnoarchaeology, one that requires the involvement of ethnographic fieldwork in elucidation of relationships between material culture and culture as a whole. The second was to seek out and use a very broad range of published materials while refraining from detailed consideration of theses and dissertations, since these cannot easily be consulted by many readers. Third, we have attempted to discuss the work of as wide a range of authors as possible, although this has meant relegating some important contributions to "Further readings" or even omitting them entirely. We are conscious that, despite our best efforts, we have not done full justice to work published in languages other than English. Fourth, and admittedly in partial contradiction to the third, we agreed not to be shy about discussing our own research, which has been conducted over a period longer than either of us cares to contemplate.

And lastly about ourselves: we are both practicing ethnoarchaeologists with extensive archaeological and ethnoarchaeological experience primarily but not quite exclusively in the Old World, Carol Kramer (henceforth CK) in Southwest Asia and India, ND in Europe and Africa. Both of us have worked at various scales from the village to the region or to cities and their hinterlands. In terms of theory, CK is more inclined to "naturalist" and ND to "antinaturalist" approaches, but neither is an ideologue. Thus our perspective embraces both the processualism of the New Arch(a)eology and (most) postprocessualism of the 1980s and 1990s. We are, as regards theory, committed to a policy, if not of synthesis, at least of cohabitation.

ACKNOWLEDGMENTS

Very many people and institutions have contributed to this work. We jointly thank colleagues and friends who have read and commented on various chapters. We have benefited from the advice of Wendy Ashmore, Cathy Cameron, Warren DeBoer, T. J. Ferguson, Kathy Fewster, Olivier Gosselain, Natalie Kampen, Jane Kelley, David Killick, Barbara Mills, Gerry Oetelaar, Pierre Pétrequin, Ann Stahl, Molly and Ray Thompson, Polly Wiessner, and several of our students, notably Charles Mather and Kim Jones, and from the thoughtful suggestions of the Press's reviewers, Carla Sinopoli and Patty Jo Watson. We also thank other distinguished colleagues who provided us with their CVs, and regret that in the end constraints of space prevented us from including thumbnail biographies of leading practitioners of ethnoarchaeology. Many colleagues have provided us with photographs of themselves or others "in action" that, taken in their entirety, constitute the beginnings of a portrait gallery of historical value. They are recognized in figure captions, but we wish to thank them here for their willingness to hunt through old files and boxes, and for looking up details of expeditions long past. Their efforts add significantly to the book. Gerry Newlands of the Archaeology Department, University of Calgary, has been invaluable in the transformation of slides, prints, and files into our illustrations. Inasmuch as documentation of the work of the ethnoarchaeologist has never been a priority and rarely a desideratum, he is to be especially thanked for transforming smudged and fly-blown slides and other media into something (at least remotely) publishable. Robin Poitras of the Geography Department constructed elegant maps of the two hemispheres. We also wish to thank Claire Allum, Nancy DeVore and Anthro-Photo, Irven DeVore, Carol Gifford, George Gumerman, Frank Hole, Kathy Hubenschmidt, C. Milo McLeod, Peter and Ama Shinnie, Matt Stolper, Bill Sumner, and Patty Jo Watson for help with obtaining photos, and Annick Geoffroy for assistance with translation. Our very special thanks to Christian Seignobos for allowing us to use his lively sketch of iron smelting at Mawasl, northern Cameroon, for the front cover.

ND thanks the National Science Foundation (USA) and the Social Science and Humanities Research Council of Canada for major support over the years of research that has qualified him to co-author a book on ethnoarchaeology. The University of Calgary granted him a sabbatical fellowship for the first six months of 1999, and the Calgary Institute of the Humanities a year's fellowship beginning in September 1999. Both offered the essential resource of time for writing, and the latter much stimulus from successive directors, Jane Kelley and Rosemary Ommer, and co-fellows. ND also thanks the responsible governmental authorities of Cameroon, Nigeria, and Ghana that have permitted him and his students to work in their countries, especially Mohammadou Eldridge and the defunct but much regretted Cameroonian Institute of Human Studies, and L. I. Izuakor and Musa Hambolu and the National Commission for Museums and Monuments of Nigeria. ND's great debt to them pales besides that he owes to the people with and among whom he has worked as an ethnoarchaeologist over the past 32 years, especially the Fulbe of Bé, the Mafa, Hide, and others of the Mokolo region of northern Cameroon, and the Sukur and their neighbors across the border in Nigeria. He pays special tribute to a succession of assistants, Souaibou Barkindo, Isa Emmanuel Kawalde, John Habga, Philip Emmanuel Sukur, Markus Ezra Mkarma, and Isnga Dalli Sukur, whose contribution to this work is inestimable.

Above all, he thanks Judy Sterner, companion, wife, and colleague, dedicating to her his part in this joint enterprise.

CK thanks the National Science Foundation, the Smithsonian Institution's Foreign Currency Program, the City University of New York's Research Foundation, and the University of Arizona's Social and Behavioral Sciences Research Institute, for their support of research in Iran and India, and subsequent data analyses. She is grateful to representatives of the governments of Iran and India who helped her obtain research permits. In India, Komal Kothari, Vijay Verma, and, especially, Manohar Lalas, her assistant, greatly facilitated her work. Many graduate students and colleagues first in New York City and later in Tucson assisted in various phases of data analysis; they are identified in the acknowledgments of her 1982 and 1997 monographs. Here, she notes her particular indebtedness to Linda Brown, John Douglas, and Glenn Davis Stone for help with the analysis of her Rajasthani data. Working with and learning from villagers in pre-revolutionary Iranian Kurdistan and potters and vendors in Rajasthan were diverse, fascinating, humbling, and formative experiences, and CK is ever grateful for the good humor, patience, and generosity shown by the many Iranians and Indians of whom she asked what must have seemed an unending series of pointless or tedious questions. Their place is, truly, empty.

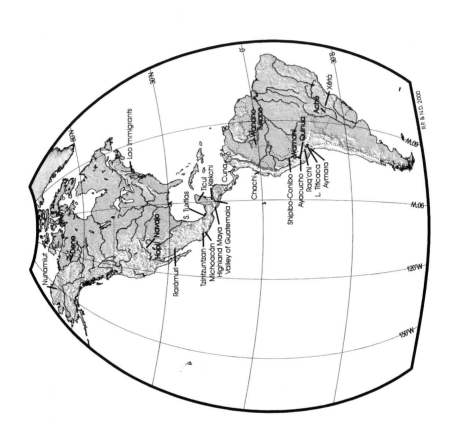

Nunámiut

Dene

Lao Immigrants

60°N

30°N

0°

30°S

Xétá

Aché

Guiná

Waorani

Shipibo-Conibo

Ayacucho

Raq'chi

L. Titicaca

Aymara

Andoke
Tukano

Chachi

60°W

Rarámuri

Hopi Navajo

S. Tuxtlas

Ticul
Kekchi

Tzintzuntzan
Michoacán
Highland Maya
Valley of Guatemala

Cuna

90°W

120°W

150°W

R.P. & N.D. 2000

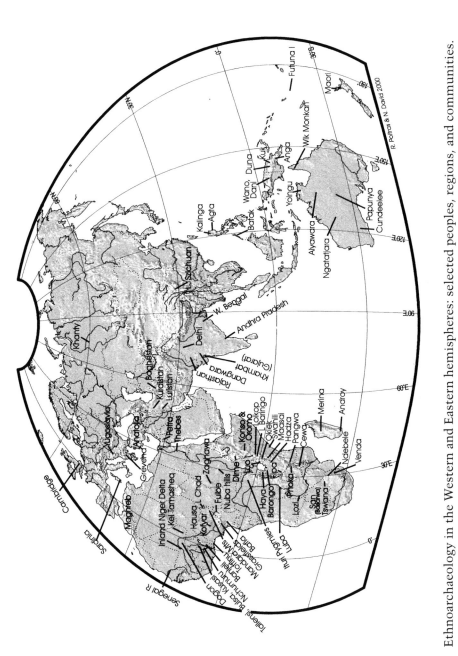

Ethnoarchaeology in the Western and Eastern hemispheres: selected peoples, regions, and communities.

CHAPTER I

ETHNOARCHAEOLOGY: ITS NATURE, ORIGINS, AND HISTORY

The problem for archaeologists, it appears, is that they are always too late . . .

(Tim Ingold 1999: ix)

Clearly a bout with ethnography is neither possible nor necessary for everyone.

(Susan Kus 1997: 209, after research among the Merina of Madagascar)

We begin by explaining why and how ethnoarchaeology came to be, and give an example from Peru as an illustration of what it is. Then, after explaining the plan of this book, we define the subject and offer a periodized history, concluding the chapter with a glimpse of what it is to be an ethnoarchaeologist.

Why ethnoarchaeology?

Archaeological interpretation is founded and ultimately depends upon analogy – a form of inference that holds that if something is like something else in some respects it is likely to be similar in others. We use it to recognize a flint flake as an artifact or, built into a long chain of reasoning, to impute a tributary mode of production to early civilizations (Trigger 1993: 45–6). Archaeologists draw upon their lives and upon everything they have read, heard about or seen in the search for possible analogies to the fragmentary remains they seek to interpret. By the mid-1950s attention was turning to a new range of questions about the past, to approaches to understanding the patterning in artifact assemblages that would lead beyond cultural chronologies and time-space systematics, the organization of cultural variety into convenient temporally and spatially limited packages such as phases and cultures (Willey and Phillips 1958). But as archaeologists turned to study cultural evolution and to the reconstruction of human behavior and past environments, they realized that common-sense reflection on their own experiences and on the wealth of historical and ethnographic information on the world's peoples could no longer be held to constitute an adequate basis for analogical inference. Why? Because the cultural range of Us was too limited for plausible analogical extrapolation to peoples living in distant times, places and contexts, and because descriptions of Others either paid little attention to their material culture or emphasized the typical,

1

whereas archaeological remains constantly confront us with variation in space and time that provides clues to past sociocultural behavior. The inadequacy of ethnographies to provide the information needed by archaeologists can readily be tested by means of an exercise suggested by Karl Heider (1961: 62) in which one first reduces "a documented living culture into archaeological remains," and then asks someone else to "develop a reconstructed culture from these remains." Such experiments, while useful in rendering apparent the analyst's assumptions, lead always to a reconstruction of the original so patchy and impoverished as to be unrecognizable.[1]

Recognition of the need for ethnographic material on which to base analogies gave rise to a new subdiscipline: ethnoarchaeology, the ethnographic study of living cultures from archaeological perspectives.[2] Ethnoarchaeology is neither a theory nor a method, but a research strategy embodying a range of approaches to understanding the relationships of material culture to culture as a whole, both in the living context and as it enters the archaeological record, and to exploiting such understandings in order to inform archaeological concepts and to improve interpretation. This is but one of many definitions. A sociocultural anthropologist might focus on a rather different aspect: ethnoarchaeology as a form of anthropological inquiry that gives a privileged position to the evidence of material culture and behavior relating to it.

An example from the Ucayali River, Peru

Warren DeBoer (Fig. 1.1) started his ethnoarchaeological work among the Shipibo and their closely related neighbors the Conibo in 1970 as part of Donald Lathrap's long-term research program on the culture history of the Upper Amazon basin. The two collaborated to write "The making and breaking of Shipibo-Conibo ceramics" (DeBoer and Lathrap 1979), in which they are primarily concerned to specify the nature of the relationship between Shipibo-Conibo behavior, especially that relating to ceramics, and its representation in the archaeological record produced in the course of the Indians' daily lives.

After briefly introducing the Shipibo-Conibo and telling us that most women make pots and that most pottery is made for domestic use, DeBoer and Lathrap give us the Indians' names for their pot types and describe their uses. The native (folk) classification is accompanied by an analytical table that shows the clays, tempers, and attributes of form, surface treatments, and size that, according to the Shipibo-Conibo, characterize different types. The authors go on to show how the raw materials for making pots are procured, clays and temper gener-

---

[1] A shorter but still instructive exercise is included in ND's (1971) paper "The Fulani compound and the archaeologist."
[2] Subdiscipline or sub-field? If archaeology, despite its philosophical divisions and multiplicity of approaches, constitutes a discipline (or subdiscipline of anthropology), then so does ethno-archaeology.

Fig. 1.1 Warren DeBoer, seen here not on the Ucayali in Peru but with an African-Ecuadorian assistant, Benito Palacios, on the Rio Santiago during an archaeological field season in Esmeraldas province, Ecuador, 1988.

ally locally but other materials, and especially pigments, sometimes from distances of several hundred kilometers. Special expeditions are not made to acquire such materials; they are obtained in the course of social visits and travel for temporary employment. Exotic materials are thus not necessarily expensive. One kind of temper consists of pulverized sherds (grog) obtained from archaeological sites, and for this reason "the presence of an archaeological midden is one factor governing settlement location" (p. 111).

Pottery manufacture is generally an individual enterprise carried out in the house or a special shed; pots are fired nearby, often singly in a bottomless pot that may be specially made for this purpose. Besides the sequence of forming, decorating, and firing, we learn that, although potters generally agree on the proportions of clays and tempers that should go into different types of vessels, there is in practice enough variation for it to be extremely unlikely that an archaeologist could use the sherds recovered from a midden to reconstruct community ideals. On the other hand, although details differ, surface finish and decoration of pots appear quite standardized, varying with vessel form.

A census carried out by DeBoer of pots in 17 Shipibo-Conibo households from five villages provides a solid basis for a study of the use of ceramics. A lack of correlation between the size or composition of a household and the number of vessels present is explained in terms of differential replacement of pots by aluminum and enameled containers, and social factors. Pots are a focus of cultural elaboration among the Shipibo-Conibo and a woman's reputation as a good wife depends in part on her having new beer "mugs" available for guests. As pots grow old, break, or are damaged, they and their parts often come to be used in different ways, for example as pot supports or as chicken coops. Pots are eventually discarded but at different rates, relatively fragile and frequently used food bowls and beer mugs having the shortest life spans. The frequencies of such types in the archaeological record will therefore be higher than their frequencies in use. The paper ends with a study of discard that reveals patterns and processes of which the archaeologist should be very much aware: the general lack of coincidence of use and discard locations, for example, and the accumulation of refuse along fences and, as middens, in areas of minimal other activity.

This wide-ranging case study nicely demonstrates that natural, economic, and sociocultural factors are all involved in the production, distribution, and consumption of material culture, and it is one of the relatively rare pieces that explicitly describes the transformation of behavior and material culture into an archaeological record. Such direct observation makes possible the generation of models for the interpretation of the typology, distribution, and other aspects of archaeological remains where the long-past behavior that produced them is unobservable and must therefore be inferred. It should also be noted that while several of DeBoer and Lathrap's observations are applicable far beyond the Shipibo-Conibo context, others are culturally specific. Deciding which analogies can reasonably be applied in a specific archaeological context and which cannot is a critical theoretical question taken up in chapter 2.

The plan of this book

It is not our aim to provide an encyclopedic account of ethnoarchaeology but rather to promote development of a critical understanding of theoretical, methodological, and substantive issues.[3] How may observations of present materials be used to construct the past? What are ethnoarchaeological data? How do we observe them; how do we choose what to record, and by what means? How should we analyze our data? Who and what have ethnoarchaeologists studied; what have they achieved? How has the subject developed? And so what? Are archaeologists making use of ethnoarchaeological insights? Is anyone paying attention? These are the themes of this book, and if they are comprehended then the reader will understand why this book cannot be a manual for the application of ethnoarchaeological results to archaeological data.

---

[3] Our coverage of research in languages other than English and French is scanty. However, ethnoarchaeology is primarily written in these languages, and especially in English.

We begin by situating ethnoarchaeology within the context of related subdisciplines of anthropology. This is followed by a historical sketch of its development that charts its relationship to larger theoretical movements within and beyond archaeology. In chapter 2 we take a theoretical view of our subject, showing how ethnoarchaeology partakes of the sciences, the social sciences, and the humanities. Consequently the range of approaches to problems that can be accommodated under the banner of ethnoarchaeology is very large. There is room both for the processualist and for the post- or anti-processualist. We show what they have in common and how different styles of ethnoarchaeology are appropriately geared to different sorts of research questions.

Different approaches require different research competencies and methodologies in order to produce valid results. Archaeologists in recent decades have at times shown themselves to be pedantically concerned with methodology and field methods, providing statistical justification of their sampling designs and specifying the mesh of their sieves to the nearest millimeter. It is remarkable how often those same researchers when doing ethnoarchaeology have been almost entirely reticent about their qualifications and methods. Our third chapter therefore deals with research design, field methods, and techniques. It also includes a discussion of ethics and of the ethnoarchaeologist's responsibility to the people with whom she or he works. Thus chapter 3 relates rather to the field component of ethnoarchaeology than to the analytical and interpretive phase; it is a necessary prerequisite to consideration of the main problem areas that ethnoarchaeologists have tackled. These form the subject matter of chapters 4 through 13 in which we begin with the most general of issues, the study of site formation processes, and proceed to ones relating to progressively more complex kinds of societies. Thus, although our treatment is by subject area, most of the material regarding foragers will appear earlier and that concerning state societies later in the book. It may be objected that, by taking a topical approach, we are in effect desystematizing culture wholes. In a sense, yes. It is sometimes necessary to parse a sentence, deconstruct a text, before it can be understood, and the fact is that ethnoarchaeology is often guilty of studying material with inadequate consideration of context. Nevertheless we intend to emphasize interrelationships and the embeddedness of material culture in peoples' economies, social lives, and systems of thought. The chapters thus reflect the constitution of the literature, but they also comment on it and in doing so may contribute to its restructuring. Most conclude with a reflection on the contributions to the topic addressed and on ethnoarchaeology's relationship to archaeology.

Our approach emphasizes critical analysis of cases, and wherever possible we contrast processual and postprocessual studies in terms of their approaches and their ability to "see" certain dimensions of the behavior they study. We append to each chapter a list of further readings. In the final chapter, rather than drawing up a balance sheet of ethnoarchaeology's successes and failures, we attempt to place it in the larger context of archaeology and anthropology, considering the extent to which it has achieved the aims of its practitioners and how those aims relate to developments in anthropology. We consider the lack of institutionalization of ethnoarchaeology, finding it no bad thing, and look into the future through the lens of recent Ph.D. theses before, lastly and reflexively, considering the impact of ethnoarchaeology on our students, on ourselves, and on the people among whom we work.

The birth and definition of ethnoarchaeology

The term "ethno-archaeologist" was coined 100 years ago by Jesse Fewkes (1900: 579) in a paper on Native American migration traditions. He used it to mean an archaeologist "who can bring as preparation for his work an intensive knowledge of the present life" of the people whose prehistory is under investigation. While it is expected that the modern ethnoarchaeologist should have mastered those aspects of the ethnography of the people studied that are relevant to the research question, it is often the case that there is no direct historical relationship between the ethnographic source and the archaeological subject of investigation. Analogies can be much broader in their scope. Bryony Orme (1974) has surveyed antiquarians' and others' use of ethnographic parallels in the period both before and after Fewkes wrote. Frank Cushing (1886) and the Mindeleff brothers (e.g., Mindeleff 1900) working in the American Southwest were ethnoarchaeologists in the Fewkesian sense. Donald Thomson's (1939) paper on "The seasonal factor in human culture" is the first that, retrospectively, can be classified as ethnoarchaeology in the modern sense of the term. Thomson showed that tools, settlement patterns, and other cultural characteristics associated with the contrasting wet and dry season adaptations of the Wik Monkan tribe of Australian Aborigines differed so greatly that archaeologists would be likely to interpret their material remains as representing separate cultures.

The formal emergence of ethnoarchaeology as a subdiscipline of anthropology is best dated to the appearance in 1956 of a paper by Maxine Kleindienst and Patty Jo Watson entitled "Action archaeology: the archaeological inventory of a living community" (Fig. 1.2). This called on "the archaeologist to take to the field of living communities with his own theoretical orientation and gather the necessary information" (p. 77). This would include data on artifact function and typological variation, butchering techniques, subsistence, social structure, and an "attempt to define where and in what degree the total non-material culture of the community could be inferred from the information gathered." Although their idea caught on, the name and nature of the subdiscipline was for a while disputed. In 1957 Joseph Bauxar had been the first to use, but in Fewkes's sense, the term ethnoarchaeology in the title of a paper (1957a and b), whereas Richard Gould (1974: 29) used "living archaeology" to refer to "the

Fig. 1.2A Maxine Kleindienst (*left*) and Susan Dunbar, students at the University of Arizona's Point of Pines field school in 1953.

actual effort made by an archaeologist or ethnographer to do fieldwork in living human societies, with special reference to the 'archaeological' patterning of the behavior in those societies." For him and others (e.g., Janes 1983: 4) ethnoarchaeology was "a much broader framework for comparing ethnographic and archaeological patterning." It is still commonly used in this sense by German scholars (see Veit 1997: 292–3), but only rarely so by North Americans (e.g., Staski and Sutro 1991: 2). Indian researchers (see Allchin 1994) also define ethnoarchaeology very broadly, some treating India's tribal peoples as representatives of relict cultures.

Fig. 1.2B Patty Jo Watson in traditional Laki garb with a Laki woman and her baby, Iran, 1959.

In the same collection, itself entitled *Ethnoarchaeology* (Donnan and Clewlow 1974), in which Gould's paper had appeared, Oswalt (1974: 6) proposed the term "archaeoethnography" for the eliciting of ethnographic information relevant to the interpretation of archaeological finds, while Pastron (1974) referred to "recording the types of data regarding living peoples that can be used as comparative material by archaeologists" as "ethnographic archaeology." Despite the unfortunate asymmetry between ethnoscience – study of the science of people who are not part of a world civilization – and ethnoarchaeology – which all agree is *not* the study of native archaeologies – the term ethnoarchaeology prevailed though with continuing disagreement as to its scope.

Ethnoarchaeology's relationships, as seen from a typically American anthropological perspective, to archaeology, ethnography, linguistics, and ethnoscience are represented in Figure 1.3, borrowed with modifications from Raymond Thompson (1991: 233). Ethnoarchaeology is seen here as a combination of archaeological and ethnographic approaches. It may be undertaken informally, involve systematic study of a single domain of material culture, or involve "the study in depth of significant parts of a living culture or even of an entire culture." Ethnoscience, partaking of ethnography and linguistics, contributes to ethnoarchaeological research by taking account of native categories and concepts. Thompson did not include physical anthropology in his diagram, perhaps because ethnographic studies that involve research into human biological characteristics are better characterized as human or evolutionary ecology even if they are highly relevant to archaeologists at a theoretical level (e.g., Hurtado *et al.* 1985).

Susan Kent (1987: 33–43), an ethnoarchaeologist who has specialized in activity area research first in the American Southwest and later in the Kalahari (Fig. 1.4), distinguishes between:

> 1 anthropological archaeology – "a holistic approach that utilizes the various fields of anthropology in order to obtain a description of an archaeological group that is as complete as possible . . . Its goals tend to be culture historical in nature . . ."
> 2 archaeological ethnography (cf. Watson 1979a) – the provision of "potentially useful ethnographic material for analogs as aids in the identification of archaeological descriptions . . . especially valuable as a source of non-ethnocentric analogies and identifications," and
> 3 ethnoarchaeology – the formulation and testing of "archaeologically oriented and/or derived methods, hypotheses, models, and theories with ethnographic data. Ideally, one starts with archaeological research interests, goes to ethnographic data for formulation and/or testing of hypotheses, models, and/or theories about these interests, and then returns to the archaeological record to implement the understanding gained from the ethnographic data."

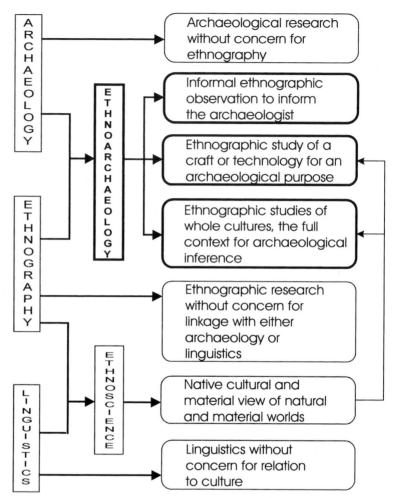

Fig. 1.3 The place of ethnoarchaeology in anthropology (after R. H. Thompson 1991: 233).

She also defines

    4 ethnographic analogy as "observations of historic groups used to identify the archaeological record," whether based upon archaeological, ethnographic or other accounts.

We regard the first three definitions as too restrictive (and the last as misleadingly phrased in that analogy is a form of inference). Anthropological archaeology is better defined more broadly as archaeology that allies itself with the social sciences rather than with science or the humanities. Kent's archaeological ethnography and ethnoarchaeology can be seen as aspects of a single research orientation, and ones that are in practice difficult to keep separate. After all we use "archaeology" to include both work in the field and subsequent analysis. While her distinction is analytically valid, when archaeological eth-

Fig. 1.4 Susan Kent with informants at Kutse, a sedentary hunter-gatherer community in Botswana, 1991.

nography provides material for ethnoarchaeology, it makes little sense to insist on the use of both terms if, in the course of a single day, field or analytical work has to be conceptualized as switching back and forth between the two modes. Rather than legislate terminology, we prefer to follow current usage, and in this book, conflating Kent's two categories, use ethnoarchaeology to mean what Robert Ascher (1962) called "ethnography for archaeology," research that includes an ethnographic component and is carried out with the analogical needs of the archaeologist in mind.[4] Such a reading conforms with the usage of the majority (see Table 1.1).

Thus ethnoarchaeology as here defined includes neither the use and application to the archaeological record of ethnographic parallels where these are drawn from the literature, nor studies of ethnographic objects in museums undertaken with archaeological aims in mind (e.g., Weniger 1992), nor descriptions of material culture or processes such as, for example, might be recorded by and for potters (e.g., Cardew 1952). Nor do we include ethnography carried out by archaeological means as in the case of William Rathje's (1978, 1985) Garbage Project. Some other studies claiming ethnoarchaeological status are better classed as ethnohistory (e.g., Adams 1973; Kelley 1982) or as ethnology (e.g., Tripathi and Tripathi 1994) or as historical archaeology, with the history

[4] MacEachern (1996: 247–50) provides a useful discussion of the range and limits of the "fuzzy set" to which ethnoarchaeology belongs.

Table 1.1 *Definitions of ethnoarchaeology*

Michael Stanislawski (1977: 379): the direct observation or participant observation study of the form, manufacture, distribution, meaning, and use of artifacts and their institutional setting and social unit correlates among living (generally nonindustrial) peoples.

Richard Gould (1978c: vii): ethnographic research for an archaeological purpose, linking material remains to the human behavior from which they resulted.

Michael Schiffer (1978: 230): the study of material in systemic context for the purpose of acquiring information, both specific and general, that will be useful in archaeological investigation.

Christopher Hanks (1983: 351): the application of archaeological methods to ethnographic data . . .

Alain Gallay and Eric Huysecom (1989: 49, our translation): archaeology's science of reference. While archaeology allows one to reconstruct historical scenarios and tries from them to deduce typological regularities, ethnoarchaeology tries to discover through observations made in the present the cause of the observed regularities by studying the mechanisms that lie at their origin.

Edward Staski and Livingston Sutro (1991: 2): the study of ethnographic or historical situations, either through firsthand observation or documentary research, to extract information useful for understanding the relationships between patterns of human behavior and material culture in all times and places.

William Longacre (1991b: 1): the study *by archaeologists* of variability in material culture and its relation to human behavior and organization among extant societies, for use in archaeological interpretation.

Rüdiger Vossen (1992: 4, 5, our translation): the connecting link between the cultural sciences of ethnology and archaeology . . . From a methodological perspective, ethnoarchaeology embraces two different research approaches: "living archaeology" and "experimental archaeology."

Farid Khan (1994: 83): study of modern (contemporary) and traditional processes which result in specific phenomena which might also be observable archaeologically.

Scott MacEachern (1994: 245): the intersection of living people and archaeological constructions . . .

Victor Fernández Martinez (1994: 137, our translation): There presently exist two definitions of ethnoarchaeology: one in a broad and the other in a restricted sense. The first includes all the connections between anthropology and archaeology . . . The second definition refers exclusively to ethnographic *fieldwork* carried out by archaeologists (or by anthropologists with archaeological training) with the same purpose as the former, that is to say to assist in archaeological interpretation . . . in practice both approaches intermingle.

Carol Kramer (1996): ethnographic fieldwork carried out with the express purpose of enhancing archaeological research by documenting aspects of sociocultural behavior likely to leave identifiable residues in the archaeological record.

frequently including the testimony of previous occupants of the site or their close relatives (e.g., Oswalt and van Stone 1967; Enloe 1993).

Often of considerable relevance to but distinct from ethnoarchaeology are some modern studies of material culture and, to a far lesser extent, cultural studies. A subset of the former is the anthropology of technical systems (Lemonnier 1986: 147), "which considers techniques in and of themselves, and not solely their material effects . . . or only the circumstances and social consequences of their application." "The stress," as Sander van der Leeuw puts it, "is very clearly on techniques as social phenomena, and is meant to encompass everything from Mauss's . . . 'ways of using the body' to industrial manufacture and all that it entails." A concept of considerable ethnoarchaeological relevance, to be discussed in chapters 6 and 7, is the *chaîne opératoire*, "the series of operations which transforms a substance from a raw material into a manufactured product" (van der Leeuw 1993: 239–40). Cultural studies on the other hand may be defined, according to the flyer for a new *European Journal of Cultural Studies*, as "interdisciplinary research . . . necessary to understand the contemporary relations between culture, power, everyday life and their material conditions." Paper titles such as "The cosmopolitanism of commerce and the allure of difference: Selfridges, the Russian Ballet and the tango of 1911" (Nava 1998), while suggesting that authors are having fun, hold little promise for the archaeologist.

Ethnoarchaeology can be subsumed within the wider category of "actualistic studies," a term used by archaeologists to refer to research aimed at providing material for analogy that involves a field or near-field component, and that is not carried out under laboratory or quasi-laboratory conditions with relatively strict control of variables. (Because experimental archaeology is characterized by such theoretically acultural and atemporal conditions it is not classed within actualistic studies, although individual experiments may transgress boundaries.) Actualistic studies encompass the replication of Clovis points by modern knappers and Glynn Isaac's (1967) field experiments directed at understanding site formation processes. Where the latter concern "processes that operate on organic remains after death to form fossil deposits" (Gifford 1981: 366) they can also be categorized as taphonomy, literally the laws of burial (see Koch 1989). Again, actualistic studies include what we might call "etho-archaeology," the study of animal behavior that can inform archaeological interpretation, the accumulation of bones by hyenas, for example, or Jeanne Sept's (1992) study of chimpanzee nesting behavior and its potential for generating hominoid archaeological sites. All the above approaches that we have characterized as non-ethnoarchaeological can and do provide analogical grist for the archaeological mill. Furthermore the logic of the application to the archaeological record of the analogies generated from them differs not at all from that which applies to analogies developed through ethnoarchaeology. If therefore we do not consider them in any detail in this book, it is on account of differences in the sources of analogy rather than in the way they are applied to the archaeological record.

A brief history of ethnoarchaeology

A bibliography of ethnoarchaeology and related studies (David *et al.* 1999) has for some years been posted in various versions on the World Wide Web.[5] As of August 1999 there were 822 ethnoarchaeology listings, 968 items from related disciplines, and 29 from the philosophy of science. The bibliography has become a tool for study of a history divisible into three main periods:

> an Initial period running from 1956, the year of Kleindienst and
>   Watson's "Action archaeology," to 1967
> a New Ethnoarchaeology period starting in 1968 and ending in 1981
> a Recent period starting in 1982 and conveniently subdivided into
>   two sub-periods: Recent 1, from 1982 to 1989, and Recent 2
>   from 1990 to 1999.

The Initial period, 1956–67

If the following discussion emphasizes ethnoarchaeology's relations to archaeology rather than to ethnography and anthropology, this reflects the concerns of its practitioners. Developments in anthropology during the sixties, for example structuralism and the symbolic anthropologies of Clifford Geertz and Victor Turner (see Ortner 1984), went unnoticed in the early years.

The first decade saw discussion of the role of "analogy in archaeological interpretation," the title of an important paper by Robert Ascher (1961), and, on a broader canvas, of the interrelationships of archaeological, ethnological, ethnographic, and historical approaches to the past. Karl Heider's (1961) "Archaeological assumptions and ethnographic fact: a cautionary tale from New Guinea" made a considerable stir because it brought home to archaeologists how poorly we were prepared to conceptualize the rich variety of life lived in very different cultures. Because "common sense" – an understanding of the world based upon ethnocentric premises – far too often misleads would-be ethnographers of the past, it is worth considering Heider's work in some detail.

In the early 1960s, Heider, then a Ph.D. candidate in anthropology at Harvard, worked for 26 months among the Dugum Dani of the highlands of Irian Jaya (or West Papua, Indonesia) (Fig. 1.5). When he first arrived, they were "not under the influence of government or missionaries," and "[e]xcept that they lacked pottery, fit the description of a typical neolithic culture" (p. 54). They traded for the ground stone blades that they hafted either as axes or adzes. Their typological distinctions tended to refer rather to the whole tool than to its parts; variations in raw materials and sizes were reflected in their classificatory

---

[5] The WWW ethnoarchaeology bibliography URL is: http://www.acs.ucalgary.ca/~ndavid

Fig. 1.5 Dugum Dani of the Grand Valley build a new compound, with a round women's house ready to thatch, Irian Jaya, Indonesia, 1963.

system only to a limited extent and in sometimes unexpected ways. The introduction of iron tools, which occurred while Heider was in the field, had no rev-
olutionary effect, or at least none that he was able to detect.

In a section on settlements, Heider noted that as a result of the reuse of materials and the digging of old house sites to make sweet potato gardens, little
would remain of individual compounds. Neither do middens form; and because
people move frequently from one compound to another, "there are at least
twice as many houses and compounds as are being used at any one time" (p.
58). Sturdy wooden fences and ditches around compounds have to do not with
defense – though the Dani raid and fight battles – but rather with drainage and
the enclosure of pigs. Again, on the subject of inter-area relations, Heider shows
how, while archaeologists could quite correctly infer the existence of an extensive trade network on the basis of the distributions of shell and stone, specific
trade relations could not be reconstructed since much of the traffic is indirect
and consists of perishable items. Despite such trade and other contacts, many
items of material culture well known to the Dani and their neighbors fail to
diffuse from one group to another.

Heider's paper reflects the archaeological assumptions of its day. How these
have changed! While we have by no means resolved all the interpretive problems posed by the Dani case, ethnoarchaeological work on lithics and classification (e.g., White and Thomas 1972), on the abandonment of households and

settlements (e.g., Cameron and Tomka 1993), on the social construction of technology (e.g., Dietler and Herbich 1998; Gosselain 1998), and on inter-group relations (e.g., Hodder 1979), has endowed archaeologists with a far larger and better-controlled analogical fund for applying to the past. On trade and exchange, another topic discussed by Heider, we used to have rather less to offer, largely because most ethnoarchaeologists work at a sub-regional scale, but this is now changing (e.g., Mohr Chávez 1991; Stark and Longacre 1993; Kramer 1997).

Heider had subtitled his paper "a cautionary tale," and the term was subsequently applied by archaeologists, sometimes dismissively, to other ethnoarchaeological case studies.[6] Perhaps they were frustrated by the continuous challenging of the assumptions on which they based their reconstructions; perhaps they were hoping for universally applicable laws or regular correlations between material and total culture. If so they remained disappointed. Cautionary tales, like other ethnoarchaeological case studies, alert archaeologists to the existence of a variety of models, and invite them to sharpen their analytical tools and develop new ones.

Ethnoarchaeology got off to a slow start in this first decade with only 1.4 publications per annum (Table 1.2). The geographical range was restricted; while Mesoamerica, with its glamorous archaeology and highly visible Indian populations at America's back door, attracted researchers, it may be that a comparatively rich early ethnographic record led North Americans to believe that ethnoarchaeological research was unnecessary. In any case that area produced no publications that meet our definition of ethnoarchaeology. The majority of papers are exploratory in nature, several discussing a range of artifact types. Raymond Thompson's (1958) monograph *Modern Yucatecan Maya pottery making* differs by juxtaposing ethnographic description and a simulated archaeological collection in an extended study of the nature of archaeological inference. Hélène Balfet's (1965) contribution to Frederick Matson's volume *Ceramics and man*, a valuable collection (despite its inappropriately sexist title), broke new ground in showing how the quality, forms, and decoration of pottery in Maghrebin North Africa varied with the mode of production. In the same volume George Foster (1965), one of whose earlier papers (1960a) on the archaeological implications of ceramic production in Mexico had initiated a long-running debate on the significance for archaeology of the differential life spans of utilitarian pottery types (see chapter 4), reflected on his research, suggesting that psychological conservatism of potters helps to account for continuity in pottery styles. Although this conclusion was later to be disputed (David and Hennig 1972), it raised, as had Balfet, interesting questions about the factors that structure material culture and the archaeological record.

---

[6] Kramer wrote (1979b: 6) of "the rather bleak level of . . . 'cautionary tales' . . ."

Table 1.2 *The distribution of Initial period (1956–67) ethnoarchaeological publications by prime topic and geographic area, based upon the David* et al. *Keyword bibliography of ethnoarchaeology and related topics as of August 1999*

Prime topic and area	VAR	M AM	N AFR	SubSah. AFR	SW ASIA	S ASIA	AUST	N	%
Theory, method	2							2	11.8
Fauna, bones				1				1	5.9
Foraging							1	1	5.9
Lithics				1				1	5.9
Ceramics		3	1					4	23.5
Other artifacts and typology		1			1	1	3	6	35.3
Org. production and learning		2						2	11.8
N	2	6	1	2	1	1	4	17	100.0
%	11.8	35.3	5.9	11.8	5.9	5.9	23.5	100.0	

    1.4 publications per annum

Note:

In these and the succeeding tables, the statistics must be regarded as impressionistic. Not all sources were available for consultation, and we have been generous in our definition of ethnoarchaeology. Thus while not every publication (monograph, edited volume, chapter, article, paper, video, etc.) that claims to be ethnoarchaeology is included, others that contain a major ethnoarchaeological component are reported in the counts.

    Geographic codes and areas are as follows:

VAR	More than one or no areas
N AM	North America
M AM	Mesoamerica and the Greater Antilles
S AM	South America and the Lesser Antilles north to Antigua
N AFR	North Africa: Morocco, Algeria, Tunisia, Libya, Egypt
SubSah. AFR	the remainder of Africa and Madagascar
EUR	Europe and the former Soviet Union east to the Urals and Caspian Sea
SW ASIA	the Near East including Turkey and Iran
C ASIA	Afghanistan and the former Soviet Union east of the Urals and the Caspian Sea to 90° east.
S ASIA	India, Pakistan, Bangladesh, and Sri Lanka
E ASIA	Tibet, Nepal, Bhutan, PRC, Japan, Korea, Mongolia, and Siberia east of 90° east
SE ASIA	Burma east to Vietnam, including the islands of the Sunda shelf
AUST	Australasia, including the islands of the Sahul shelf
OCE	Oceania

The primary topics of publications are distributed among:
Theory and method
Formation processes

Note: (cont.)
Fauna and faunal remains
Foraging, hunting and gathering
Other subsistence practices
Lithics
Ceramics
Metallurgy
Other artifact classes, including consideration of taxonomy and typology
Settlement and community patterns
Activity areas, domestic space, and architecture, including related considerations of
demography
Organization of production, apprenticeship, and the transmission of technologies
Distribution, trade, and exchange
Style and ethnicity
Mortuary practices
Ideology, systems of thought, symbolism

The New Ethnoarchaeology period, 1968–81

In 1962 Lewis Binford's "Archaeology as anthropology" ushered in the epoch of
what came to be called the "New Archeology,"[7] with its insistence that
culture, conceived of as humans' extrasomatic means of adaptation, consisted
of material remains that could be studied without reference to the ideas that
had once existed in the heads of the makers of the artifacts. At about the same
time the cultural ecological approach associated with Julian Steward, Marshall
Sahlins, Elman Service, and others was exerting an important influence on
archaeology. An overly enthusiastic adherence to Hempelian logico-deductive
positivism and to systems theory (Salmon 1976, 1978) came to underlie what
was claimed by some to be an explicitly scientific approach to archaeological
interpretation and explanation (Watson *et al.* 1971). As deduction is a form of
reasoning that extracts information from premises, it might seem to be antithetical to analogical inference, which goes beyond them – though always at
some risk of being wrong. But the New Archaeologists realized that they
required models of human behavior from which to generate hypotheses that
could be tested against the archaeological record. As CK put it in 1979:

It is assumed that some behavioral elements of sociocultural systems have material correlates; if they are incorporated in the archaeological record, such residues may be used
to develop inferences about the behaviors with which they were associated.
Observations of contemporary behavior can facilitate the development and refinement
of insights into past behaviors, particularly when strong similarities can be shown to
exist between the environments of the past and contemporary sociocultural systems
being compared. (1979b: 1)

---

[7] Often stylistically differentiated from "culture historical archaeology" by abandonment of the
old-fashioned æ ligature, a legacy retained by *American Antiquity.*

Thus ethnoarchaeology was rather encouraged than discouraged by a change in paradigm in some ways more apparent than real.

Besides the two canonical texts of the New Archaeology, *Analytical archaeology* by David Clarke and *New perspectives in archaeology*, edited by Sally and Lewis Binford, Richard Lee and Irven DeVore's edited volume, *Man the hunter*, also appeared in 1968. The combination, which expressed the New Archaeology's emphasis on adaptive systems and long-term processual change, complemented an international movement in palaeoanthropology that had found its voice in a collection edited by Sherwood Washburn (1961), *Social life of early man*. Together these stimulated the research on foragers that is one of the hallmarks of the New Ethnoarchaeology period (Table 1.3). While only 4 percent of a much larger total number of ethnoarchaeological publications were actually about foraging as a subsistence technique, initially mainly in Australia where Gould (e.g., 1967, 1969) was an early and productive exponent, research into other topics, including lithics (e.g., White 1968), was also frequently conducted among hunter-gatherers.

There is in this period a near tenfold increase in the rate of publication to 13.4 per annum, and ethnoarchaeology expands almost to its current geographical range – only East Asia and Central Asia are missing, and in both it has still scarcely begun. While state societies are poorly represented, the range of societies amongst which ethnoarchaeological work is carried out becomes much wider, to include village agriculturalists and pastoralists in a variety of environments. The modern range of topics, less only ideology, here used in the general sense to include symbolism and systems of thought, is attained. Africa, and particularly Sub-Saharan Africa, becomes the most popular area in which to carry out ethnoarchaeological research. Decolonization of the continent had led to a demand for archaeological research on later periods, and the political interests of the United States of America led to the support of much Africanist research. Work in Mesoamerica and Southwest Asia (including Iran, but among the Arab countries only isolated studies in Syria and Jordan) was similarly favored by the Americans who at this time formed the bulk of those who practiced ethnoarchaeology.

As might be expected in a recently developed subject area, a spate of theoretical articles is mainly devoted to specification of the subdiscipline and its relationships with others. In the larger bibliography there are a score of publications relating specifically to analogy, including the latter part of the Binford–Munson debate on the function of "smudge pits," and Gould's (1978a) vigorous but misjudged claim in "Beyond analogy in ethnoarchaeology" that the use of analogies would deny us the possibility of discovering new things in the past. The applicability of applying to the Pleistocene period models of the past derived from the study of modern hunter-gatherers receives special attention, and the title of Martin Wobst's (1978) paper, "The archaeo-ethnography of hunter-gatherers or the tyranny of the ethnographic record in archaeology,"

Table 1.3 *The distribution of New Ethnoarchaeology period (1968–81) ethnoarchaeological publications by prime topic and geographic area*

Prime topic and area	VAR	N AM	M AM	S AM	N AFR	SubSah. AFR	EUR	SW ASIA	S ASIA	SE ASIA	AUST	OCE	N	%
Theory, method	28	2	1			1		3			3	1	39	20.9
Formation processes	1	3	1			4		1		1	1		12	6.4
Fauna, bones	1	1				4				1			7	3.7
Foraging	1			1					1		5		8	4.3
Other subsistence	4					3	1	1		1			10	5.3
Lithics		2	2	3	2	2					13		24	12.8
Ceramics		4	1	6	1	10	1	1	1	3			28	15.0
Metallurgy						5							5	2.7
Other artifacts and typology	2		2			4				1	4		13	7.0
Settlement patterns	2	3				1		1					7	3.7
Space and architecture	1	3		2		3	1	7					17	9.1
Org. production and learning		2	1	1	1	2			1				8	4.3
Distribution, trade, exchange	2												2	1.1
Style and ethnicity				1		5							6	3.2
Mortuary	1												1	0.5
N	43	20	8	14	4	44	3	14	3	7	26	1	187	100.0
%	23.0	10.7	4.3	7.5	2.1	23.5	1.6	7.5	1.6	3.7	13.9	0.5	100.0	

13.4 publications per annum

dramatizes a supposed incompatibility of scales in archaeological and ethnoarchaeological research.

In the area of material culture, ceramics, the testing ground for so many archaeological ideas, is the most popular single topical area, with 15 percent of total publications, including the first truly ethnoarchaeological study by a non-Westerner,
"Traditional pottery technology at Krobo Takyiman . . ." by the Ghanaian Effah
Gyamfi (1980), who sadly died shortly thereafter. Ceramics are followed by lithics
with, a long way behind, other artifacts (the keyword "arti" also includes considerations of typology and classification). Artifact classes that are unlikely to
preserve in the archaeological record have been undeservedly shunned by ethnoarchaeologists. On the positive side, more intensive interrogation of archaeological sites as the loci of human activities, and in Southwest Asia the
increasingly sophisticated excavation of *tell*s (settlement mounds), was leading
to a demand for models for interpreting domestic space and architecture, and thus
to the first publications based on ethnoarchaeological fieldwork by authors such
as Patty Jo Watson (1979a, 1979b), whose monograph *Archaeological ethnography in Western Iran* appeared in 1979, and CK (1979a), and in Africa by ND (1971),
Roderick McIntosh (1974), and, in the first year of the next period, E. Kofi
Agorsah's (1982) "Spatial expression of traditional behavior . . ." (Fig. 1.6).
Another popular area, stimulated in part by the work of Michael Schiffer (1976),
and more generally by the demands of a processual archaeology for understanding the nature of archaeological components, is the study of site formation processes, of which John Yellen's (1977a) work among the !Kung San of the Kalahari
is the most sustained example. Gould (1978b) was indeed arguing that ethnoarchaeology was the "anthropology of human residues."

There were at this time no researchers who categorized themselves as ethnoarchaeologists but only archaeologists and occasional others who did ethnoarchaeology, mostly occasionally, and mostly for short periods on delimited
topics. There are only four ethnoarchaeological monographs, Watson's (1979a)
on village life in Iran, and the remaining three all on foragers: Yellen (1977a) on
the !Kung San, Binford (1978a) on the Nunamiut caribou hunters of Alaska, and
Gould (1980) on the Ngatatjara Aborigines of the Australian Western Desert.

Theoretical discussion during this period tended to focus on specific topics
rather than on broader questions (e.g., Gould 1978c). However, retrodiction of
the past through deduction from laws of culture was a major preoccupation.
Processualists (as adherents of the New Archaeology later came to be called)
hungered for general laws, and were critical of ethnoarchaeologists for not supplying them. Schiffer (1978) commented unfavorably on the particularistic
nature of most ethnoarchaeological studies, citing the following statement
from ND's work among the settled Fulbe (Fulani) of northern Cameroon as one
that conveyed the structure of a law: "The less the capital outlay or labour
required to construct a building or complex of buildings, the greater the fit
between it and its personnel over the useful life of the building. Conversely, the

Fig. 1.6 E. Kofi Agorsah with a Basia of Tutubuka, a village of the
Saramakan Maroons of Suriname, 1997. Basia is the third in the
Saramakan political ranking system after Granman and Kabiten.

more permanent the building, the less the degree of fit" (David 1971: 117).[8] It
was because of the increasing frequency of such statements that Schiffer felt
able to write in 1978 that "Ethnoarchaeology seems at last on the verge of
becoming a respectable field of endeavor within archaeology" (1978: 229).
"Already," he continued, "ethnoarchaeological findings are appreciably affecting analytical methods and leading to revised interpretations of the archaeological record." However, although ethnoarchaeologists came more and more to
consider the wider implications of their material, the hunger for laws was to
remain unsatisfied or, rather, to fade away, largely because "there simply are no
universal laws in archaeology that are neither too general nor too specific to be
of any interest" (Kelley and Hanen 1988: 232).

The Recent period

Recent 1, 1982–9
"Recent" is used by analogy to the Holocene or Recent Period in which we live,
and because the term "modern" now carries with it considerable baggage, only

---

[8] ND's pleasure at being thus singled out was tempered by Schiffer's characterization of the statement as "imprecise and probably inaccurate"!

a small portion of which we are concerned to unpack. We date the start of the period to the publication of Ian Hodder's (1982a) *Symbols in action*, a book that, in a series of ethnoarchaeological essays, explores the relations between associations of material culture items in living contexts and archaeological concepts of culture. Whereas the prevailing archaeological view of the time was that "Material culture patterning is a distorted but predictable reflection of human behaviour" (p. 11), Hodder concluded that material culture does not merely *reflect* culture, but serves actively to *constitute* it. It is in this sense that artifacts are symbols in action.[9] Although we have reservations about the field methods of Hodder and his team (see chapter 3), this was a new and tremendously exciting view of material culture – and of the role of ethnoarchaeology.

Symbols in action questioned and found wanting some of the fundamentals of interpretation, the existing archaeological concept of culture and the interaction theory of style, which held that the degree of stylistic similarity between two components or assemblages was a measure of the intensity of social interaction between them. Moreover, in treating material culture as an active element in communication – as had Martin Wobst (1977) though from a systems theory perspective – Hodder also challenged a fundamental tenet of the New Archaeology: that for heuristic purposes the human mind can be adequately conceptualized as a rational, economizing processor of information, and can therefore be ignored in the relationship between environmental stimulus and human behavioral response. The opposing view, that mental processes intervene in a more complex, transformational, manner between input and output, changes the nature of explanation by reinstating human agency as a factor in culture. Hodder was developing a new theoretical position, influenced by the ideas of a very different set of scholars from those who had inspired the processualists, most notably by Giddens's theory of structuration and Bourdieu's theory of practice, and he could and did cite ethnographic chapter and verse in its support. Two decades later, the last paragraph of *Symbols in action* makes fascinating reading:

there is a need for archaeologists to integrate theories and ideas from a wide range of studies concerned with structure, meaning and social action. The prospect is for a debate in archaeology concerning structuralism (Piaget 1971; Lévi-Strauss 1963) and its various critiques (Bourdieu 1977; Pettit 1975), post structuralism (Ardener 1978; Harstrup 1978), structural Marxism (Godelier 1977; Friedman and Rowlands 1977) and contemporary social theory (Giddens 1979; Marsh, Rosser and Harré 1978). What is meant by such concepts as ideology, legitimation, power, symbol and social structure must be argued within the archaeological literature and the concepts must be incorporated into interpretations of the past. (p. 229)

There are some names and concepts missing – most notably Michel Foucault and reflexivity – but the paragraph presages the proliferation of postprocessual

---

[9] "The word 'symbol' refers to an object or situation in which a direct, primary or literal meaning also designates another indirect, secondary and figurative meaning" (Hodder 1982a: 11).

and, in some cases, postmodern, theoretical positions that characterize "hot theory" in the eighties and early nineties.

Hodder's ideas had not been without precursors in archaeology generally and ethnoarchaeology in particular (e.g., Gould 1978d), and indeed the years 1977 through 1990 saw an ongoing debate over the definition, uses and nature of style in archaeology involving James Sackett, Lewis Binford, and on the ethnoarchaeological side notably Polly Wiessner, who was active in the Kalahari during the 1970s (chapter 7). In 1986 the publication in the *Journal of Anthropological Archaeology* of a paper by Pierre Lemonnier that featured his work on the material culture of the Anga of Papua New Guinea introduced the French "anthropology of techniques" school to Anglophone readers.

Symbols in action advanced ethnoarchaeology but scarcely resulted in an immediate transformation of the field. Processualism remains a strong force – and some "pre-processualist" papers continue to appear. An intense argument early in the Recent period between Gould and Watson (1982) and the philosopher Alison Wylie (1982) on the concept and use of analogy was effectively terminated by Wylie's magisterial "The reaction against analogy" of 1985. Otherwise theoretical debate tended to become less separate and more an intrinsic feature of papers right across the range of topics and classes of material culture treated.

The statistics for the period reveal certain trends (Table 1.4). The number of publications nearly triples to 35.5 per annum and for the first time includes a substantial number of items in French. Sub-Saharan Africa, with 29 percent of all publications, is increasingly the most popular geographic area, in large part because that continent is perceived as having the most peoples practicing "traditional" life styles, i.e., lives less obviously affected by industrialization and globalization, though Ann Stahl (1993) and Scott MacEachern (1996) – and the "Kalahari Bushmen Debate" (Smith 1996) – have warned us against accepting such views and of the dangers of essentializing the African in a mistaken search for the pure and pristine.

The most popular topical area, with 18 percent of publications, concerns domestic and community space and architecture, relating directly to interpretation of activity areas and site layouts (sometimes including their demographic implications). While Southwest Asia still dominates here (e.g., Kramer 1982a), Africa is well represented. Susan Kent begins publishing African materials in this period. Her processualist monograph *Analyzing activity areas* (Kent 1984), although set in North America rather than Africa, contrasts vividly and in a manner typical of the period with Henrietta Moore's (1986) postprocessualist *Space, text and gender: an anthropological study of the Marakwet of Kenya*, the latter being the first ethno(archaeo)logical entry in the bibliography with "gender" in its title.[10]

---

[10] We distinguish between sex (which is primarily biological) and gender (which is ideological and cultural). *Space, text and gender* is not strictly speaking ethnoarchaeology. Although Moore was

Table 1.4 *The distribution of Recent 1 period (1982–9) ethnoarchaeological publications by prime topic and geographic area*

Prime topic and area	VAR	N AM	M AM	S AM	N AFR	SubSah. AFR	EUR	SW ASIA	S ASIA	SE ASIA	AUST	OCE	N	%
Theory, method	14	3	2			2	1				1		23	8.1
Formation processes	1	2	3	1		5	1	1					14	4.9
Fauna, bones		2				2	1			1	2		8	2.8
Foraging	1	3	1	4		5				1	2		17	6.0
Other subsistence	3	2	2			2	4	6		3		1	23	8.1
Lithics		1	7	1	1						6		16	5.6
Ceramics	7	1	7	5	4	9	7	1	1	2		1	45	15.8
Metallurgy						16			1				17	6.0
Other artifacts and typology			1						2		3		6	2.1
Settlement patterns	2	2	1	1		4		3			1		14	4.9
Space and architecture	5	5	5	5	2	14		16					52	18.3
Org. production and learning		2		1		2	2		3	1	8		19	6.7
Distribution, trade, exchange						2	1			1	1		5	1.8
Style and ethnicity	1	1		1		13							16	5.6
Mortuary							1						1	0.4
Ideology	1					6				1			8	2.8
N	35	24	29	19	7	82	18	27	7	10	24	2	284	100.0
%	12.3	8.5	10.2	6.7	2.5	28.9	6.3	9.5	2.5	3.5	8.5	0.7	100.0	

35.5 publications per annum

Ceramics (16 percent of publications) is now the second most popular topical area, especially when we consider that many publications categorized in the table under other headings, for example organization of production, are in fact developed in terms of ceramics. While papers concerned primarily to describe technology continue to be published, a new range of concerns involving comparative studies and fieldwork at the regional scale is becoming evident in the literature. Gallay and Huysecom (1989) take a regional approach to pottery production and distribution in a multiethnic part of Mali. Dean Arnold (1985) writes from a comparative systems and ecological perspective on *Ceramic theory and cultural process*. In a very different mode Daniel Miller's (1985) *Artefacts as categories* relates variability in Indian ceramics to variability in society as a whole, and is a precursor to his later work on consumption (e.g., 1987) and interdisciplinary studies of material culture and cultural processes (e.g., 1998). Other publications are concerned with the functions of style, and, responding to a challenge laid down by Hodder, the generation of its content and meaning within specific cultural contexts (e.g., David *et al.* 1988).

Also detectable for the first time are the impacts of large-scale, longer-term ethnoarchaeological projects involving numbers of students and native assistants. Brian Hayden's Coxoh Ethnoarchaeology Project was based in the Maya highlands between 1977 and 1979, focusing on household variability, lithics (Hayden 1987a, 1987b, 1987c, 1987d) and ceramics (Nelson 1981; Deal 1998). It is notable for the clarity with which its methodology is specified (Hayden and Cannon, 1984a: 1–39). In the Philippines, William Longacre's Kalinga Project, begun in the 1970s, interrupted by political unrest, and reactivated in the late 1980s, has focused productively on ceramics from a variety of perspectives including the transmission of ideas, the organization of production, trade and exchange, and materials science (Longacre and Skibo 1994) (Fig. 1.7). This project's publications first become numerous in the succeeding period. In Cameroon and Nigeria, ND's Mandara Archaeological Project has since 1984 conducted seven field seasons, all but the first devoted to ethnoarchaeology and with up to seven researchers in the field at the same time, emphasizing questions of style, ethnicity, symbolism, and systems of thought (e.g., David *et al.* 1991), and including video programs among its output (e.g., David and Le Bléis 1988). The Swiss Ethnoarchaeological Mission in West Africa has been producing a substantial, and beautifully illustrated, set of publications primarily on

footnote 10 (*cont.*)
one of Hodder's students and went to Kenya to carry out ethnoarchaeological research on rubbish, she returned with an exploration of the ideological construction of gender. The book developed from her dissertation is, as its subtitle insists, an *anthropological* study. Nevertheless ethnoarchaeologists can reasonably claim residual rights; the chapter on ash, animal dung, and the organization of domestic space testifies to the ethnoarchaeological roots of the work. An interview of Mike Parker Pearson published on the Web (Giles *et al.* 1997) is well worth reading on the topic of the Cambridge class of '79, Hodder's "cogi-playgroup," and their subsequent careers. *Artefacts as categories* by Daniel Miller (1985), another of Hodder's students, occupies a not dissimilar interdisciplinary position.

Fig. 1.7 William Longacre with Kalinga potters, Luzon, Philippines, 1976.

Malian ceramics, but including historical archaeology (e.g., Gallay *et al.* 1996) and Huysecom and Agustoni's (1997) remarkable film of iron smelting among the Dogon. In part because of these programs there is a definite increase in the still relatively small number of publications that deal with the organization of production and with the distribution, trade, and exchange of artifacts.

Mention of iron working reminds us also that, in large part because bloomery techniques of smelting iron continued to be practiced very late in Sub-Saharan Africa, the subcontinent holds a virtual monopoly of ethnoarchaeological works on metallurgy (chapter 11). These begin in the New Ethnoarchaeology period (Schmidt 1980), becoming more common through time, although we should not forget the many earlier studies that are better characterized as technological or ethnological. In the 1990s interest in smelting extended, though much less than might be expected, to smithing (e.g., Robertson 1992; Childs and Dewey 1996).

It is in the Recent 1 period that, as noted above, we can begin to appreciate some broader topical trends within ethnoarchaeology. One other is worth mentioning here; categories concerned with subsistence (Fauna/Foraging/Other subsistence techniques) increase from 13.3 percent in the New Ethnoarchaeology period to 16.9 percent in this period and to 18.6 percent in Recent 2, in good part because of the work done from the University of Utah by Kristin Hawkes, James O'Connell, and their associates. Their fine-grained research among the Aché of Paraguay (e.g., Hawkes, Hill, and O'Connell 1982) and the Hadza of Tanzania (e.g., Hawkes, O'Connell, and Blurton Jones 1991) adds significantly to the range of tropical and sub-tropical foragers studied, though they would certainly label most of their work human ecology or optimal foraging research rather than ethnoarchaeology. Pastoralists become more of a focus of attention in the succeeding period.

Recent 2, 1990–8

The Recent 2 period is to be celebrated for the increasing productivity of non-Western ethnoarchaeologists. They include Kofi Agorsah (e.g., 1993) and Kodzo Gavua (1990) of Ghana, Nigerians Kolawole Aiyedun (1995), C. A. Folorunso and S. O. Ogundele (1993), the Franco-Cameroonian Augustin Holl (1993), Chapurukha Kusimba (1996) from Kenya, Sokhna Guèye (1998) from Senegal, the Franco-Algerian Hassan Sidi Maamar (Chaix and Sidi Maamar 1992), Turkey's Füsun Ertuğ (1996), India's Seetha Reddy (1991, 1997), Japan's Masashi Kobayashi (1994), and, from Szichuan in the People's Republic of China, Enzheng Tong (1990). It is curious that with rare exceptions (e.g., Eduardo Williams 1994, 1995) Latin-Americans have not been attracted to ethnoarchaeology. Almost all those named above were trained in the Western anthropological tradition and, especially as several have worked amongst peoples other than their own, most of their contributions are as yet little differentiated from those of their Western colleagues. Thus the ethnoarchaeological potential of the combination in a single individual of native and Western perspectives remains to be fully realized. However, a Master's thesis by Rowland (Caesar) Apentiik (1997), "Bulsa technologies and systems of thought," achieves precisely this synthesis.

Our statistics for this sub-period are calculated up to and including 1998 and are no doubt incomplete, as is suggested by the very minor apparent increase in the rate of publication to 37.1 items per annum (Table 1.5). Africa's excessive dominance at 39 percent of publications is also likely to be a sampling artifact though political factors are also at play, rendering parts of Mesomerica and Southwest Asia less attractive, particularly to researchers from the States. The large number of papers on theory, boosted by an important conference organized by Françoise Audouze (1992) in Antibes in 1991, includes several that deal, more or less effectively and from a variety of perspectives, with the processual/post-processual relationship. Space and ceramics remain popular subjects, and there are significantly more publications on broader and on more abstract topics. CK's (1997) book on ceramics in two Indian cities is notable for its treatment of the organization of production, distribution, and exchange in a complex society, subjects also treated in the context of Longacre's long-running Kalinga project (e.g., Graves 1991; Stark 1994). ND (1996) argues from an ethnohistoric and ethnoarchaeological perspective that the chiefdom of Sukur in the Mandara mountains of northeastern Nigeria was in the nineteenth century a "classless industrial society," and Peter Schmidt (1996a) and Michael Dietler and Ingrid Herbich (1993) discuss the nature of time among the Haya and Luo respectively.

Table 1.5 *The distribution of Recent 2 period (1990–8) ethnoarchaeological publications by prime topic and geographic area*

Prime topic and area	VAR	N AM	M AM	S AM	N AFR	SubSah. AFR	EUR	SW ASIA	S ASIA	E ASIA	SE ASIA	AUST	OCE	N	%
Theory, method	20			1		7	1		2		2	1		34	10.2
Formation processes	7	3	6	1		6	1	3	1			1		29	8.7
Fauna, bones	3			1	1	19			2					26	7.8
Foraging	2	2				3			1					8	2.4
Other subsistence	1	1	2	1		5	4	7	6				1	28	8.4
Lithics			1			3			2			1		7	2.1
Ceramics	8	0	3	3	3	19			3	1	12			52	15.6
Metallurgy	1					16			2					19	5.7
Other artifacts and typology									3		3	1		7	2.1
Settlement patterns			2	2		5	2	1						12	3.6
Space and architecture	3	4	4	1	1	12	1	9	3		1	2		41	12.3
Org. production and learning	1		1	2		8	1		3		3	1		20	6.0
Distribution, trade, exchange	1		1	2		1	1		2		2	1	1	12	3.6
Style and ethnicity	1			5		8				1				15	4.5
Mortuary				1		2	1			1	1			6	1.8
Ideology				1		16	1							18	5.4
N	48	10	20	21	5	130	13	20	30	3	24	8	2	334	100.0
	14.4	3.0	6.0	6.3	1.5	38.9	3.9	6.0	9.0	0.9	7.2	2.4	0.6		

37.1 publications per annum

Fig. 1.8 Ethnoarchaeologists gathered at the School of American Research seminar in Santa Fe in March 1985 that led to the publication of Longacre's (1991a) *Ceramic ethnoarchaeology. From left to right, front row*: Gloria London, Michael Graves, William A. Longacre, and Raymond Thompson; *back row*: Ian Hodder, Sander van der Leeuw, Margaret Hardin, Warren DeBoer, Ben Nelson, and CK.

Other developments in archaeological thought are detectable in the emergence or rapid expansion of topics. A flurry of ethnoarchaeological publications on various aspects of fauna, including several in Jean Hudson's (1993a) edited volume *From bones to behavior*, are evidence of, among other things, a desire to identify incontrovertible archaeological signatures of hominid activities and particularly hunting. Such collections of papers on special topics, for example on ceramic ethnoarchaeology (Longacre 1991a) (Fig. 1.8), abandonment (Cameron and Tomka 1993), or approaches to mobile campsites and the ethnoarchaeology of pastoralism (Gamble and Boismier 1991) have replaced the broadly based compilations of earlier years. There are also more comparative studies seeking, but not necessarily finding, underlying uniformities, for example Ben Nelson's (1991) study of ceramic frequency and uselife in cross-cultural perspective.

A newly flourishing category, that of ideology, though remaining for the moment largely African in its geographic scope, deserves special notice. While specific artifact classes and topics range from iron to calabashes, and from witchcraft to symbolic reservoirs, we are gaining new insights into the world of metaphor – "forging symbolic meaning," "pots as people" – that underlies material culture. This is a world that, while it may seem unscientific and even fanciful to some, is in fact critical to understanding how technologies are controlled and transmitted within and between generations. When such questions are related to the division of labor and modes of production, it is apparent that they are fundamental to archaeology's explication and explanation of cultural continuities, change and development.

There can be no doubt that during the Recent period there have been significant improvements in the doing and writing of ethnoarchaeology; the quickie watch-a-native-fell-a-tree kind of study is no longer acceptable. Scholars who, like the authors of this book, identify themselves more as ethnoarchaeologists than as archaeologists may remain few and far between, but the movement of individuals back and forth between subject areas is no bad thing. It would be unrealistic to claim that ethnoarchaeology has achieved maturity as a subdiscipline of anthropology – unless, as the recent history of archaeology suggests, maturity may be characterized by progressive incorporation into the discipline of a variety of viewpoints within a broadly agreed philosophical framework, a range of lively approaches to diverse subject matter, and the appearance of second-generation studies that group and synthesize individual case studies. All these developments augur well for the future.

The attractions of ethnoarchaeology

"I like to keep my archaeology dead," David Clarke once said to ND, and there is no doubt that many of those attracted to archaeology as a profession prefer to maintain a certain distance between themselves and the people they are – indirectly – studying. Some like objects, the tangible past, and there can be few of us who were not moved when they held for the first time an Acheulian handax made a quarter of a million years ago. Others, and Clarke (e.g., 1968) was a prime example, obtain a pure enjoyment, similar if not identical to that of the mathematician, in the discovery of patterning – at a multiplicity of scales – in the archaeological record. The empathetic thrill felt by the first group and the intellectual excitement of the second are both experienced by the archaeologist at a safe distance. Ethnoarchaeologists feel them too; but they also have to enjoy the in-your-face experience (the vulgarity is intentional) of interacting intimately on a day to day basis with people, usually from other cultures, from whom they have come to learn, and whose actions they do not control. This is not to say that many of us follow Karl Heider into field situations untamed by the modern world. We normally work under the protection of a state, and our research funding (however limited) usually confers upon us the power of relative wealth. Nonetheless there is an excitement to waking up in the field, not knowing precisely what one will be doing that day, being there, seizing opportunities – even if at times there is the downside of coping with frustration, boredom, physical discomfort, hunger. One is never so alive as in the field.

All research proceeds from percepts to inference of structure and process. The Inka developed a technique for permeating gold with copper and treating the alloy so that the gold showed on the surface (Lechtman 1977: 8). The surficial gold is evident; it is the task of the metallurgist to infer the structure and the processes that produced it. Ethnoarchaeologists are researchers who observe and appreciate things and the information encrusted in them, who like learning from and laughing with Others, and who delight in the discovery of patterns and explanation of the underpinnings of behavior and its material correlates. For some of us this is now an end in itself; for most the aim is to apply their findings to the archaeological record.

Many of those who practice ethnoarchaeology also enjoy digging and the pleasure of being a member of a team (usually, it should be remembered, largely composed of people of one's own culture or station in life), but there can be few ethnoarchaeologists who regret the tedious tasks of archaeology, most notably the interminable washing, weighing, counting, recording, labeling, and bagging of specimens. Unlike archaeology, ethnoarchaeology is not labor intensive, nor does it destroy data in the process of recovery, nor are its data unique. We have recursive access to artisans and other informants; archaeologists can only dig the same ground once. Ethnoarchaeology is less threatening to authorities than archaeology. So far at least, its results have been far less subject to political manipulation. Like archaeology, it contributes to the understanding of human behavior but without losing the immediacy of human interaction. For all these reasons, we expect the numbers of ethnoarchaeologists to increase and the subject to continue to flourish.

Further reading

Successive reviews of ethnoarchaeology testify to varying conceptions of the field and its development. These include papers by Stiles (1977), Longacre (1978), Atherton (1983) on Africa and MacEachern (1996) on sub-Saharan Africa, Griffin and Solheim (1988–9) on Asia, Sinopoli (1991) on S. Asia, and Allen (1996), who takes a broader ethnographic perspective, on Australia. Griffin, Solheim, and Sinopoli construe ethnoarchaeology very broadly, including many references to surveys of crafts that we would classify as material culture studies. Vossen (1992) offers a German perspective on ethnoarchaeology and Fernández Martínez (1994) a Spanish one. For a French view rich in historical insights see Coudart (1992a). The editors' introductions to the collections mentioned in the chapter also provide historical perspective.

Sherry Ortner's (1984) "Theory in anthropology since the sixties" is a perceptive and readable description of developments in anthropology coincident with that of ethnoarchaeology in the Initial and New Archaeology periods.

CHAPTER 2

THEORIZING ETHNOARCHAEOLOGY AND ANALOGY

It is particularly because human beings delegate to artifacts, to exchange and to technical acts a large part of the construction and the conservation of their social ties that human societies constitute stable frameworks, in contradistinction to the societies of other primates that – transient because they lack things – require to be continuously (re)constructed by direct contacts (touches, looks, sounds, smells), and by the physical close-ness and continuous active involvement of the participants.

(Anick Coudart 1992a: 262, our translation).

What recourse is there for the imaginatively challenged?

(Bruce Trigger 1998: 30)

The vast majority of publications on ethnoarchaeology take no explicit theo-retical position – which does not mean that they are atheoretical. In this chapter we offer the reader a basic toolkit with which to examine the theory, implicit or explicit, expressed in the ethnoarchaeological literature that we will be considering in the course of this book. For two reasons the toolkit we offer at this stage is a minimal one. First, most of us prefer to deal with theoretical complexities as they arise and in a factual context. Second, this is not the place to attempt to survey the wide web of theoretical positions taken by archaeolo-gists (and to a lesser extent ethnoarchaeologists) following an influx of theory reaching anthropology in the 1970s and 1980s from a variety of sources includ-ing the philosophy of science, literary theory, and sociology.

First however we should consider what kind of a world it is that we are attempting to understand and whether it is possible to regard ethnoarchaeol-ogy as a coherent subdiscipline of anthropology. Then, since a major purpose of ethnoarchaeology is to provide links between present and past, we turn to the question of argument by analogy. What is it? How does it work? Is there any solution to the paradox that, whereas archaeologists are interested in long-term change, the ethnoarchaeologists who desire to assist them are limited to short-term observations even of their own societies? Finally we will summarize some postprocessual developments in archaeological theory that are of particular rel-evance to ethnoarchaeology.

Explanation in social science[1]

Ethnoarchaeologists are generally mute as to their philosophical perspective. Nonetheless, all anthropological endeavor takes place in a theoretical context in which answers to the following questions are implied. What are the "things" we study? What constitutes "explanation" of our data? How do we "verify" our explanations? Are there "laws of human social life"? Realist philosophy of science in its "subtle" form provides answers to these questions that serve to orient scientific enquiry without either overly constraining its scope or forcing us into bogus intellectual gymnastics. The realist research program in social science has been conveniently set out by Guy Gibbon (1989: 142–72), from whom the following summary of what are for our purposes its essential elements is derived.

Realists distinguish between three domains:

1 the **real**: structures and processes, which are often unobservable and may be complex stratified composites (e.g., genes, migration); anything that can bring about changes in material things is real;
2 the **actual**: observable events and phenomena; compounds and conjunctures formed by the real; and
3 the **empirical**: experiences and facts generated by our theory-laden perception of the actual.

To take an example, the sun is a real thing; it is observable in many forms, as light, heat, solar winds, sun spots, etc., that we experience and record in various ways, including as photons, as changes induced on photographic plates and on our own skin, and as radio waves. Photons can be empirically recorded, but are they particles or waves? Is sunstroke a purely physical effect of exposure, or is there no such thing as a purely physical effect? Might sin or witchcraft be causal factors? Answers depend both upon how the sun is observed and upon the observer's theoretical perspective; this is one sense in which all facts are theory-laden.

Scientists are concerned to identify, define, and explain things in the domain of the real. We approach the real through our empirical reading of the actual, and according to the scientific knowledge of the day. It follows that theories about the real world, even if true, can never be proven; they are always "underdetermined" by the evidence. Herein lies the distinction between "subtle" and "naive" realism. Naive realists fail to recognize the theory-laden quality of descriptions and explanations; they believe they can have direct contact with reality and achieve knowledge that is certain.[2]

---

[1] This section is developed from part of ND's "Integrating ethnoarchaeology: a subtle realist perspective" (1992a) which appeared in the *Journal of Anthropological Archaeology*.

[2] Philosophers of science have by now advanced beyond realism to anti-realism, constructivism, and no doubt other -isms, the further implications of which for ethnoarchaeology we do not propose to explore.

Society, a concept essential for our purposes, is held really to exist as a complex structure irreducible either to its effects or to people, consisting of the sum of relations, including relations with material culture and the environment, within which individuals and groups stand. Society exists by virtue of the intentional activity of people. It can only be detected by its effects; it generates social life, is manifest in cultural behavior and its products, and is conceptualized in the experience of its bearers. The causal power of social forms is mediated by people – and by cultural things – and social forms are a necessary condition for social action. However, human behavior cannot be determined by or completely explained by reference to social forms and rules, because people are purposeful and possess intentionality and self-consciousness. Psychological and physiological as well as social reasons contribute to intentional human behavior. Thus, unlike within the closed system of a thermostat, people act in what are termed *open systems* that are co-determined by a variety of mechanisms of which the social is one. Societies are continuously being transformed in practice, are only relatively enduring, and are thus irreducibly historical.

Explanation of social phenomena proceeds by the same general process as in the natural sciences:

1 Recognition of a pattern and resolution of events into their components. Events are viewed as conjunctures, resulting from the combined effects of a variety of real things, forces or dynamic structurings of materials.
2 Redescription of events in one of the many dialects (economics, human geography, etc.) of the language of social science.
3 Creative model-building, the search for generative mechanisms that might produce the observed pattern. This is an inductive, or more precisely *retroductive*, attempt to lay out the structural conditions that must have existed for the events to be present.
4 Testing and theory construction. Candidate mechanisms are reduced to one as the reality of their postulated structures and powers is checked, in part by evaluation of each mechanism in terms of its plausibility and credibility in the light of other theories, especially those that we currently take to be beyond reasonable doubt, in part by gathering of independent evidence that will subject the theory to maximal threat. If they pass these tests, structures and their workings may then be at least provisionally accepted as explanations. But two problems must be faced. First, because of human intentionality and the openness of cultural systems, statements describing the way real social things operate must be regarded as regularities or expectations rather than as laws. Second, because societies exist as the outcome of particular historical trajectories, the boundary conditions within which such a regularity may hold may restrict its application to a very small range of societies, even limiting it to the one from which it was derived. Such expectations may then contribute to the understanding

of particular cases but be trivial from a generalizing cross-cultural perspective.[3]

5 However this may be, exploration of the stratum of reality revealed in the previous steps can now begin.

As social structures are only manifest in open systems that exist in particular historic contexts, decisive tests of theories are impossible. We may be able to explain past events precisely and accurately, but our capacity to predict remains rudimentary. While the validity of claims is subject to stringent criteria of assessment, proposed definitions of the real and theories about the nature of society and its past are ultimately accepted or rejected on the basis of their explanatory fruitfulness or power. It is this rather than predictive or, in the case of archaeology, retrodictive accuracy that decides which of a set of competing models becomes, for the time being, theory.

To this partial and abbreviated account of realist philosophy in social science, we should add a rider of great relevance. Although humans live in open systems, certain aspects of their behavior are more constrained than others and can be conceptualized in terms of, if not closed, at least restricted systems, some of which are quite simple. Much of the behavior studied by ethnoarchaeologists and archaeologists, the manufacture of tools for example or subsistence techniques, can be viewed in such terms – which does not imply that other perspectives will not also be revealing. The simpler the system and the more it approximates to the closed condition, the greater the predictability of the behavior associated with it. Thus, depending on the natures of the things and systems under investigation, different approaches and methodologies may be appropriate, and predictability greater or less.

Processual and contextual schools and styles of analysis

It is in large part because ethnoarchaeology and archaeology deal with material things and their relations to both the natural and the social environments that there is such disagreement between authorities as to what we should be doing and how we should do it. In the following discussion we follow Kosso (1991) in treating Lewis Binford and Ian Hodder, both of whom have carried out important archaeological and ethnoarchaeological fieldwork, as archetypal protagonists of the New Archaeology and "contextual" (later "interpretive") schools. Note that while the New Archaeology and processual schools are synonymous, and while the contextual school as described by Hodder (1986: 118–46; 1987b and c) in the late 1980s can be categorized as postprocessual, postprocessualism is a much broader category that accommodates a variety of poststructuralist, neo- or post-Marxist, postmodern (Jameson 1991), and other viewpoints recently surveyed by Robert Preucel (1995), some of which will be touched on later in this chapter.[4]

---

[3] See Kelley and Hanen (1988: 227–33) for a discussion of laws and lawlike statements in archaeology.

[4] Postmodernism is anti-historic and thus opposed to the aims of archaeology, though it may be said that Shanks and Tilley reflect the postmodern crisis in historicity in their more extreme

Binford (e.g., 1977, 1982, 1987b) believes that archaeology should be more like a natural than a social science and advocates the use of "middle range theory" to relate the statics of the archaeological record to the dynamics of the living, systemic context, while Hodder, who sees archaeology as historical social science, recommends a contextual approach in which context-specific structuring principles replace cross-culturally applicable middle range theories. But as Kosso (1991) has shown, there is little difference in the epistemic structure of their analyses.[5] Middle range theories relate the empirical, the perceived actual, to the real; so do Hodder's structuring principles, which may indeed be regarded as middle range theories. Both approaches proceed by working back and forth between data and theory. Where Binford and Hodder and other (ethno)archaeologists primarily differ is in

> 1 the activities, economic, cognitive-symbolic, or other, relating to less or more open, simpler or more complex, systems in which they are most interested,
> 2 their views of the real things that structure these activities,
> 3 their understandings of what constitutes explanation and verification, and
> 4 the corresponding naturalist versus antinaturalist styles of their arguments.

The terms "naturalist" and "antinaturalist," borrowed from the philosophy of the social sciences (Martin and McIntyre 1994: xv–xvi), are here used to contrast styles of analysis. Each encompasses a range of philosophical and methodological positions, and individual studies often show blends of the two. The naturalist approach is modeled after the natural sciences. Analyses are characterized by a focus on behavior and its practical effects on the world, an emphasis on the verification of hypotheses rather than on their discovery, on direct confirmation by experience, and the preferential use of quantitative approaches and statistical inference. While an earlier view that explanation consists of subsuming patternings of data under covering laws is now seen as overdeterministic, there is still a concern to obtain results that can be used in cross-cultural comparison and for generalizing about culture process. Similarly, the view that archaeologists are not equipped to study the human mind has given way to new studies of human cognitive capacities and modes; but naturalists are concerned, if at all, only with the structure of meaning.

Antinaturalist studies emphasize inductive and qualitative approaches to the

---

relativist statements in which they argue that there is no way to choose between alternative pasts except on essentially political grounds (1987: 195). True postmodernism in archaeology is to be found in the commodified pastiches of the past served up on television, whether they purport to be science (the pre-Pre-Dynastic age of the Sphinx) or entertainment (*Zena: warrior princess*).

5 Binford's philosophy of science and more obviously his rhetoric have developed over the years from logical empiricism/positivism towards the realism his practice has always tended to exhibit (see Wylie 1989). Hodder's views, approaches, and interests have changed even more rapidly. Both have written pieces they likely regret; both have contributed enormously to archaeological discourse.

study of meaning viewed in either formalist or cognitive terms. Both accept the basic structuralist assumption that, since psychic modernity was attained, human minds have worked in similar orderly ways, applying a grammar-like logic and a limited repertoire of contrastive categories to thinking about reality. Mind is therefore expressed as much in material culture as in social action or myth, and is a proper subject of archaeological inquiry (Leone 1982).[6] As Norman Yoffee and Andrew Sherratt (1993: 5) put it: "*Explanation* in postprocessual archaeology is the process of deciphering the meaning-laden constitution of material culture. As ethnoarchaeological researches have shown, adequate explanation of the parts of a cultural system depends upon the richness of contextualization within specific, long-term trajectories." Antinaturalists place more emphasis on the hermeneutic process of discovery (see below) and less on verification than naturalists. The more or less explicit criterion for verification is that of explanatory fruitfulness or power of an interpretation to contribute to understanding of a wide range of phenomena in the society or material under investigation. Some authors have on occasion taken a position of extreme relativism, denying the relevance of verification altogether: "Archaeology is not so much about reading the signs of the past but writing these signs into the present. Correct stories of the past are dependent on a politics of truth linked to the present because all interpretation is a contemporary act" (Tilley 1990: 338). However, at least in its extreme form, this postmodern position is generally rejected on the grounds that archaeological data impose evidential constraints on what can be said about them. Indeed, having failed to develop their own methodology of verification, postprocessual archaeologists often resort to processual forms that they earlier reviled.

The cultural domain

The distinction between schools can be made clearer by specification in realist terms of the cultural domain that is the object of study. This is represented in Figure 2.1, at the center of which is what Goodenough (1964: 11) termed the *Phenomenal Order*. This is a stratum of real things – activities and patterning – inferred from behaviors empirically observed in living cultures. As a soil may be represented as constituted by different proportions of sand, silt, and clay, so certain behaviors are classified as activities that may be categorized in terms of their ideological, social, and technical aspects.[7] Certain activities are responsible for that part of the material output of the phenomenal order in which archaeologists are primarily interested, that is to say artifacts or, more pre-

---

[6] Formalists study the structure of symbolic systems and consider that the meaning of an element is defined by its position in the structure. Cognitive-symbolic studies generally aim to describe how a historically situated people actually conceptualized the content of meaning embodied in one or more domains of material culture.

[7] The term "ideological" is used here in preference to the more correct "ideational" in order to avoid confusion with "Ideational Order" (see below).

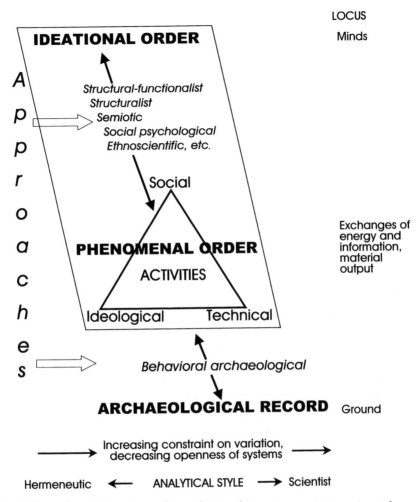

Fig. 2.1 The cultural domain and its relationship to interpretive approaches and analytical styles (redrawn from David 1992: Fig. 1).

cisely, things affected by human action and differentiated by matter, form, and context. A small portion of these is recovered as the archaeological record.

The phenomenal order exists as part of an interacting dyad, the other element of which is the *Ideational Order*. This is made up of another order of real things, unobservable ideas, values, norms, and representations, and is itself underlain by a psychocognitive order of reality, the hard wiring of the human mind. The ideational order is expressed in, though it does not determine, the activities and their patterning defined as the phenomenal order. While all ideational orders are structured by certain real things relating to the biology of modern *Homo sapiens sapiens*, they vary as a consequence of differing historical trajectories, and of varying interactions within and between the ideational and the phenomenal orders themselves, and between the dyadic complex and the environment. Furthermore, since things in the ideational order do not interact directly with the environment, they are less constrained by it than behaviors in the phenomenal order, which, particularly in its technical aspect, comprises some relatively restricted subsystems. Ideational orders are open systems characterized by some fuzziness and internal contradiction, competing representations of reality held at different times by different individuals, genders, age groups, craftspeople, ranks, classes, castes, and so on. The relations between the two orders influence actual behavior and thus its material output. It follows that one cannot reconstruct a phenomenal order without reference to its ideational correlate.

A strongly naturalist approach in ethnoarchaeology involves attempts to define cross-cultural regularities or lawlike statements derived from ethnoarchaeological and other evidence in order to apply these to the reconstruction of past phenomenal orders and their development, and hopefully to generate new regularities regarding culture change. Before these regularities can be applied to the archaeological record, they must first be reformulated, in the terminology of Michael Schiffer, as cultural (c-) and natural (n-) transforms. C-transforms are "laws that relate variables of an ongoing cultural system to variables describing the cultural deposition or nondeposition of its elements." N-transforms are laws relating to non-cultural processes of modification and decay, for example "pollen is preserved in acidic soil, but bone is destroyed" (Schiffer 1976: 14–16). Antinaturalist researchers, who instead of focusing on the causal context are concerned to understand social phenomena from the point of view of the actors (or in terms of their structures of thought), dispute the existence of most cross-cultural regularities and thus their value in prediction. To them, artifacts not only are instruments but also refer to things that exist at the level of the ideational order. They stand for concepts – in the language of semiotics, they are signifiers of signifieds (Hodder 1987b: 2–5) – with material or behavioral referents in the physical world. The meaning content of artifacts must therefore vary as a function of the ideational/phenomenal order complex, the sum of the contextual associations from which they spring. An ax means something very different to a Canadian lumberjack, a Minoan, and a "Stone Age Australian" (Sharp 1952). Antinaturalist researchers who take such a contextual approach are, as ethnoarchaeologists, concerned to describe and explain, and as archaeologists to reconstruct specific contexts and their development "from the inside" with, at least in theory, minimal appeal to cross-cultural – as opposed to cross-cognitive – regularities.

An example will clarify the difference between processualist and contextualist interests and styles of analysis. There are only a limited number of ways in which foragers can exploit a tropical rainforest and survive; the freedom to devise toolkits and even to form viable social groupings is constrained. Their religious symbolism, on the other hand, is comparatively free to vary. We have seen that the greater the constraints acting on behavior, the less open and the simpler the system, the more predictable it becomes. Thus processualists, working in a style characteristic of the natural sciences in which variables can often be strictly controlled, may quite reasonably emphasize technological hardware, economy, and ecological relations. Where, owing to the greater complexity and openness of systems, variables are much harder to control, much less quantify, it is similarly appropriate for contextualists to grapple with their materials in one of a variety of modes more characteristic of the humanities. Processualists and contextualists strive for different things, the former "explanations" that, even if no longer couched in terms of covering laws from which deductions are derived, are instantiated in the archaeological record by empiricist scientific methods. Contextualists seek "understandings" and regard laws as illusory or at best apparent only as tendencies in sets of historical conjunctions. Neither account of sociocultural life is, we suggest, complete without the other, and it may be that a new synthesis is emerging. If so it would be typified in the words of Colin Renfrew (1994: 10):

In the tradition of processual archaeology, a cognitive-processual archaeology will seek to be as "objective" as possible, while not laying claim to objectivity in any ultimate sense. The aim of producing valid generalizations remains an important goal, although to frame these as universal "laws of culture process" is now seen as impracticable. But at the same time, the claims of privileged access to other (especially past) minds, which sometimes seems implicit in the writings of the anti-processual school, are rejected. We all start off on an equal footing.

Does ethnoarchaeology need a general theory of behavior?

The preceding section serves as context and introduction to a challenging article by James O'Connell (1995) in which he categorizes ethnoarchaeologists as being

much more concerned with describing and explaining the material consequences of behavior than with understanding behavior itself. This means that while their observations can help track the past distribution of ethnographically known behavior, they generally cannot be used to interpret archaeological evidence of anything else. (p. 206)

Whether or not his inference is correct – and we shall shortly argue that it is not – his observation that ethnoarchaeologists lack a theory or theories of behavior, or at least are rarely explicit about them, is accurate. Ethnoarchaeology is, as discussed in chapter 1, primarily a research strategy, and it may well be that different kinds of behavior are best explained by different theories, but if so we should be clear about the theory invoked, whether implicitly or explicitly, in any particular account. O'Connell usefully directs our attention towards the need "to generate comprehensive, well-warranted, *ethnographically unprecedented* models of hominid behavior that might account for . . . archaeological evidence" (p. 209). To achieve this, he suggests, we require a general theory that would make possible the development of testable expectations about behavior past or present, known or unknown.

The best available candidate may be neo-Darwinian behavioral (or evolutionary) ecology
... Its basic premise is that the behavior of all living organisms is shaped by natural
selection. Its objective is to explain patterns in behavior by identifying the constraints
that underlie them, specifically those that affect differences in reproductive success. It
does this through use of formal economic models. (p. 209)

Much of O'Connell's recent work and that of his colleagues among the Hadza
of Tanzania (e.g., O'Connell *et al.* 1988a, 1988b, 1999; Hawkes *et al.* 1991) deals
with hunting, scavenging, and foraging, and their implications for human evolution. Hypothetical fitness goals are stipulated in relation to such activities,
the various strategies available are defined, and their costs and benefits calculated in terms of a currency, usually calories. This allows prediction of optimal
patterns of behavior that can be compared with those actually observed.
Mismatches lead to rethinking and revision of the model, the development of
new hypotheses and, ideally, reiteration of tests until either the match between
predicted and observed behavior is demonstrated or the model is rejected.

While the research carried out by O'Connell, Kristen Hawkes, and Nicholas
Blurton Jones on such questions can be characterized as some of the most intensive and best documented ever carried out by ethnoarchaeologists, it must be
recognized that it deals with a limited range of behaviors that (a) are subject to
significant constraints and (b) produce evident and measurable returns. The
combination of behavioral ecology and formal economic models is, as implied
in the previous section, appropriate under the circumstances. Hawkes,
O'Connell, and Blurton Jones (1997) and O'Connell, Hawkes, and Blurton
Jones's (1999) delicious overturning of the "meat for sex" theory of the evolution of *Homo erectus* in favor of a "goodies from granny" alternative, succeeds
in making the neo-Darwinian link to differences in reproductive success,
although this is not always the case, the achievement of greater success in foraging itself sometimes being accepted as a proxy measure.

The behavioral ecologists' assumption "that humans have the ability to
evaluate the reproductive consequences of behaviors subconsciously" and a
focus on "the mean fitness of some class of organisms" rather than on individuals' choices, together with the view that "the specific content of an individual's goals comes from both biological and cultural information" (Kelly
1995: 52), allow them what some might regard as an indecent – but perhaps
realistic – degree of latitude in formulating tests of hypotheses and interpretive argument. Even when dealing with economic behavior, it is often exceed-
ingly difficult if not impossible to demonstrate that improvement of
Darwinian fitness, that is to say of the propensity of members of a population
to reproduce in a given environment, better explains the data than, say, max-
imization of pleasure. In less constrained areas of behavior such as pottery decoration or mortuary practices, the linkage to reproductive success is so
indirect and distant that other theories – for example that certain kinds of
behavior are driven by a fundamental human cognitive process of personal and

social identification through comparison (see Wiessner 1984, 1997, and chapter 6) – become far more attractive.

While we may therefore disagree with O'Connell regarding the need for a general theory of behavior, we recognize the utility of optimization approaches to the interpretation of a range of constrained, primarily economic, behaviors, and especially to the development of models for the interpretation of faunal remains in the archaeological record. We take up the question of the modeling of behavior and of ethnoarchaeology's ability to assist in the interpretation of unknown behaviors in the following section.

Analogy

It is fun to find the same pattern on Aranda *tjurunga* and an Irish grave slab . . . The value of such ethnographic comparisons is just to show the funny kinds of meanings or purposes that may be attached to the queerer kinds of archaeological data. (V. Gordon Childe [1958: 4] cited by Jane Dickins [1996: 161])

The logic and practice of analogy

Ethnoarchaeology developed in order to provide better ethnographic analogies to assist in the interpretation of archaeological data. John Yellen (1977a: 6–12) defined four kinds of uses of such analogies: the general model and buckshot approaches, and the spoiler and laboratory techniques.

> The *buckshot* approach refers to the hit-or-miss use of a specific ethnographic analogy to suggest an answer to some equally specific archaeological question such as "Why are the mandibles of larger animals split open, while those of smaller animals remain intact?"
>
> The *laboratory* technique, not to be confused with experimental archaeology, involves the collection of ethnographic data in order to provide "the archaeologist with a set of controlled or 'laboratory' conditions within which he can evaluate and sharpen his own analytic techniques" (p. 11). The study of lithic classification by Duna men in New Guinea falls into this class (White *et al.* 1977).
>
> The *spoiler* technique, related to the cautionary tale, uses the relationship between known ethnographic behavior and its observable material products to "evaluate statements, models, and assumptions of a generally deductive nature" applied in archaeological interpretation, and often leads to their being discarded or reformulated. Yellen (1977b) has himself shown that patterns discerned in the form of animal bone fragments do not necessarily imply their use as tools as others had suggested, but may result from standardized butchering techniques. This is the old problem of equifinality, different causes producing similar results.
>
> *General models* "include general analogies and deductive hypotheses as well as . . . 'lawlike generalizations'," (p. 6) which Yellen

argued should be stated in the form of hypotheses susceptible to testing. As exemplified in his book, these approaches were aimed primarily towards the development of cultural transforms.

Yellen's typology is instructive, but to go further we need to understand the mechanics, the logic of analogy. In *Archaeology and the methodology of science* Jane Kelley and Marsha Hanen (1988: 44–59, 256–69) explain clearly the differences between deductive and inductive inference, the form of analogical reasoning and its role in scientific endeavor. Alison Wylie's (1985) philosophical and historical analysis of the substantial archaeological and ethnoarchaeological literature on the subject of analogy must be regarded as the prime source on the whole question, and is required reading. We make extensive use of it in the following discussion, which is intended not to summarize the arguments but rather to extract from them principles for the development and use of analogies. Only if we know how archaeologists should use analogy in their interpretations can we evaluate the quality of the models provided by ethnoarchaeologists.

"In a correct deduction the truth of the premises guarantees the truth of the conclusion" (Kelley and Hanen 1988: 44).

All birds have wings.

Aristotle is a bird.

Therefore, Aristotle has wings.

Analogy on the other hand is a form of inductive inference, and in inductive inference all the premises can be true and yet the conclusion drawn from them false, as in:

All birds have wings.

All birds have feet.

Birds fly.

Sophocles has wings and feet, and can fly.

Therefore, Sophocles is a bird.

But no! he is a mosquito. Had we considered Sophocles' lack of feathers, we would not have been so quick to infer his avian status. (And had he feathers he might still have been an ostrich.) As Wylie (1985: 80) says, "Analogical inferences are all, by definition, 'ampliative'; they inevitably claim the existence of more extensive similarities in their conclusions than has been or could be established in their premises, thus, they are always liable to be in error." But we need only reflect on how ineffably boring, because limited to the establishment of meaningless patternings, archaeology would be if we never went beyond premises, to see that, however potentially misleading, analogy is indeed indispensable. So we should learn how best to use it as a tool, and, taking an ethnoarchaeological perspective, learn also how best to design the tool for its subsequent use in archaeology.

Analogical argument takes the form:

> The archaeological *subject* X that we seek to interpret is character-
> ized by attributes A, B, D, and F.
> The known *source* of the analogy Y is characterized by A, B, C, D, and
> E.
> We can proceed by *enumerating* the similarities and differences
> between X and Y. If we are of the opinion that the former out-
> weigh the latter, we may infer that X once possessed C and E,
> and was once a form of Y. In this instance F remains an unex-
> plained component of the analogy. If on the other hand we deter-
> mine the underlying *relationships* between the attributes in the
> source and between F and other attributes in the subject, and
> can thereby explain the absence of C and E and the presence of
> F in the subject, then our case for arguing a similarity between
> X and Y is enhanced.

Analogies by enumeration implicitly assume, but do not demonstrate, the existence of underlying relationships. Relational analogies are stronger because
founded upon the causal mechanisms that determine the presence and absence
of attributes.

The excavated feature from Bé (northern Cameroon) illustrated in Figure
2.2A and the building shown in Figure 2.2B are the subject and source respectively of analogical reasoning. They have a number of characteristics in
common (positive components of the analogy) including:

> A – locations close to each other in space,
> B – attribution to a period characterized by iron metallurgy (thus a sep-
> aration in time of hundreds rather than thousands of years),
> C – round plans, defined by
> D – circular, narrow, vertical, features (walls) constructed of clayey
> earth (daub), and
> E – hard, clayey, flat, interior surfaces.

There are also negative components, subject and source differing in:

> F – interior diameter,
> G – the height of D, and
> H – the thickness of D, and
> in the absence in the excavated feature of
> I – a roof,
> J – a sunken, interior hearth,
> K – a door opening, and
> in the presence in the excavated feature of
> L – thin lenses of silt over the interior surface.

Given such evidence we have no hesitation in interpreting the archaeological feature as a room or hut. Why should this be so? First, because some of the
differences between the structures (i.e., G, H, I, and L) can be explained in terms
of minor variations in constructional techniques, and of processes of deposition
and decay (and perhaps destruction by humans) occurring before, during
and after abandonment of the feature. To investigate the possibility that the

Fig. 2.2A The remains of a structure excavated by ND at the Fulbe (Fulani) village of Bé, northern Cameroon, in 1968.

Fig. 2.2B A contemporary hut in the same village.

deposits in and around the inferred hut walls and above its floor are the products of redeposition, we might arrange for a pedological analysis. In technical language this would be termed *a subject-side strategy for establishing relevance*. The aim is to discover new aspects of the archaeological subject matter that are relevant to the drawing of the analogy. Second, while seeking to account for the discrepancies in F and J, we find that some rooms in the modern village are of a size similar to the excavated feature and lack interior hearths.

During this process – one of *expanding our source-side base for interpretation* – we also discover that other circular structures built locally of daub, for example granaries and fish-drying ovens, differ in more fundamental ways: the presence of stone bases in the case of the former, or much smaller diameters and thinner walls in the case of the latter. Thus the negative components F and J are more likely to indicate relatively minor differences in function than that the subject and source represent entirely different sorts of facilities. As regards the absence of a door opening, this may only be apparent. In modern round rooms the lowest course of mud walling is uninterrupted, forming a threshold in the area of the door, but, as the remains of the basal wall course of the excavated feature are not everywhere preserved to a comparable height, the absence of a doorway is undemonstrable. It is a *neutral* component of the analogy.

This simple example of an analogy that has both enumerative and relational elements employs the same concepts – subject, source, positive, neutral, and negative components, arguments regarding causal relationships, subject- and source-side strategies for establishing relevance – as much more complex cases. There would be no difference in principle were we to argue that Mesopotamian Ur was a city-state, although definition of the source, or better sources, would require more thought, the list of relevant attributes would be far longer and the relationships between them much more elaborate.

Such considerations lead to the following general principles regarding analogical arguments in archaeology.

1. The subject and source cultures should be similar in regard to variables likely to have affected or influenced the materials, behaviors, states, or processes being compared. Substantiating the principles of connection between variables and the establishment of relevant similarities and differences is vitally important. It is here that the analyst enters a critical area of debate regarding comparison and causality in anthropology and other relevant disciplines (geoarchaeology for example).

2. Since cultures are generally conservative, if the source culture is the historic descendant of the subject culture, there is, *always subject to the conditions of (1) above*, a greater intrinsic likelihood that similarities between the two will exist than if there is no such antecedent–descendant relationship. Unfortunately, the expansion of Europe has over much of the world resulted in major cultural disjunctions with the result that cultural descent must itself be regarded as a problematic concept (see below).

3. The range of potential source models for comparison with the subject data should be expanded by ethnoarchaeological and other means in order to obtain as representative a range as is practically possible.

4. Not merely one but several possible analogs for the subject data should be sought among the sources.

5. Hypotheses developed from these analog models should be tested by various means that may well include archaeological excavation. However, owing to the inevitable elements of inductive reasoning

and subjectivity involved in testing, deductive certainty can never be achieved.

6 Wylie (1985: 83, 100–1) emphasizes how "assessments of the relative credibility of the analogical arguments . . . can be significantly refined by upgrading the methodology and the background knowledge on which they are based." This involves "source- and subject-side strategies for establishing relevance" by "expanding the bases of interpretation and elaborating the fit between source and subject."

It is expansion of the source-side base of interpretation that primarily concerns ethnoarchaeologists, and here a paper by Ann Stahl (1993) nicely complements that of Wylie. Stahl follows Wobst (1978) in castigating both archaeologists and ethnoarchaeologists for their tendency either to assume the "pristine," unchanging, nature of forager and other societies known ethnographically, or to filter the information gathered amongst them in order to consider only that which is perceived as "traditional." Too little attention is paid to radical cultural discontinuities occurring in the period of European expansion and colonization and to their theoretical and methodological implications (Dunnell 1991; Guyer and Belinga 1995). Steadman Upham (1987: 265) has argued that "the magnitude of change that occurred during the contact period [among the Western Pueblo of the American Southwest] generally precludes the use of southwestern ethnographic information in archaeological research." And as John Chance (1996) has shown for Mesoamerica, anthropological attribution of the origins of traits and institutions to periods is often without historic or ethnohistoric justification.

Such distortion of source-side contexts, which implicitly denies both the long reach and deep roots of the modern world-system (Wallerstein 1974), and the systemic nature of culture, is obviously not the way to expand bases of interpretation. Stahl (1993: 243) welcomes the "recent reinsertion of historical concerns into anthropology" as providing some redress. Historical criticism of source-side documents and of the very concepts (such as "tribe") in terms of which we work is encouraged. Ethnoarchaeologists should make clear where, when, and how they made their observations (see chapter 3). Analogies should be grounded in specific time-space contexts: the Kalinga of Pasil municipality, Luzon, 1973–79, the Kurds of "Aliabad" in western Iran, 1975, or the Fulbe of Bé village, northern Cameroon, 1968–71.

Another way to expand source-side analogy is to develop models of behavior with which actual behavior can be compared. In this connection we have already discussed O'Connell's (1995) proposal regarding neo-Darwinian behavioral or evolutionary ecology. Gould (1980: 108–12, 140) suggests a similar procedure and that the models be generated from other general propositions about human behavior such as George Zipf's Principle of Least Effort. Gould (pp. 141–59) has tested his approach by studying the present and past utilization of different rocks used by Western Desert Aborigines for making flaked tools, and

Fig. 2.3 Richard Gould with Ngatatjara informants at Puntutjarpa
Rockshelter, Warburton Ranges, Western Australia, in July 1967.

also undertook experiments to demonstrate that – anomalously according to
expectations based upon his model – they do not always make use of the rocks
mechanically best suited to their practical purposes, and that their choice of
raw materials is, and by analogy has been, affected by social and ideological
factors. He describes as "righteous rocks" the exotic but inferior materials that
he believes were brought to Puntutjarpa Rockshelter because they were
obtained from sacred sites (Fig. 2.3). It is the departure from utilitarian expectations that allows Gould (p. 157) to conclude that: "Isotropic stones of exotic
origin thus serve as an 'archaeological signature' of a non-seasonal, risk-mini-
mizing mode of hunter-gatherer adaptation in the Western Desert of Australia
and, it is likely, anywhere else that similar limiting factors have affected
human settlement."

The "argument by anomaly," as Gould terms it, thus leads to a materialist
conclusion in which the sacred associations and inter- and intra-lineage trade
that account for the departure of observed behavior from that predicted by the
model are studied not for themselves but only as indices, "archaeological signatures," of social networks along which raw materials flow. It is the social networks rather than their meaning content – structure rather than culture – that
are projected back into the past.[8] Clearly both Gould's and O'Connell's

---

[8] As Davidson (1988: 24–6) points out in a trenchant criticism of the "righteous rocks" argument,
Gould, despite his concern with human residues, pays insufficient attention to the context of
discard. Davidson proposes an alternative model in which Aborigines collect inferior stone for
adz-making during their seasonal rounds, discarding them as exotics at Puntutjarpa Rockshelter
where they had a ready supply of superior raw material.

approaches are firmly in the naturalist mode, and could scarcely be applied to the investigation of behavior that was not significantly constrained by physical and environmental factors.

Time and the ethnoarchaeological analogy

There is a further question that we cannot pass over in silence. If the aim of archaeology is to explain change and in particular change over the long term, how can ethnoarchaeologists, whose exposure to particular cultures is usually limited to a few months – and even in the case of their own cultures only a few decades – possibly contribute significant information regarding long-term culture change? The longest-running ethnoarchaeological research program, Longacre's Kalinga project, is less than 30 years old. Does it follow that a "tyranny of the ethnographic present" (Wobst 1978) must taint all use of analogical reasoning deriving from ethnoarchaeology?

A partial answer emerges from the previous discussion of models of behavior. Ethnoarchaeology involves field study of the production, typology, distribution, consumption, and discard of material things, with particular attention to the mechanisms that relate variation and variability to sociocultural context, and to inference from mechanisms to processes of culture change. "Mechanisms" are here defined as configurations of the full range of environmental, material, and sociocultural variables that interact at one time horizon to generate patterning in material culture. In a case just cited both Western Aborigine ceremonialism and the utilitarian value of isotropic stone were elements in the mechanism invoked to produce the output of stone artifacts and waste that Gould observed in the field. "Processes" are diachronic changes in mechanisms that include their structural change, breakdown, and transformation.

Archaeologists and ethnoarchaeologists are faced with inverse observational problems. Archaeological data manifest the workings over time of cultural processes. The interpretation of a given body of archaeological data must necessarily account for continuity and change through time in terms of both mechanisms and processes. Neither are directly observable. Ethnoarchaeologists work in the "ethnographic present." While they can infer from their observations the existence of mechanisms, they lack opportunities to observe, except over very short time spans, the material manifestations of processes. It is to avoid simplistic assimilation of the past to the present (or appropriation of the past by the present) that ethnoarchaeology should emphasize the identification of sociocultural mechanisms. These, while always constituting an interplay of variables structured by a relational system that generates a (usually) material output, are not necessarily identified by reference to formal models of behavior of the type that O'Connell proposes we construct. Mechanisms may well be inferred in a less organized manner in the field. In either case inference to process then might take one of the following forms.

We could compare closely comparable developments of the same or very similar systems at different points in time. As Miriam Stark and Bill Longacre (1993) have shown in their study of social and cultural contexts of ceramic change among the Kalinga, this can be extraordinarily productive. In a case discussed in chapter 5, Yvonne Marshall (1987) combines her ethnoarchaeological observations of the mass capture of eels in New Zealand with information from ethnographic and ethnohistoric sources to project the technology back into the prehistoric period and to evaluate its significance. Unfortunately such work requires a greater degree of comparative and historical control (and often intensity of ethnoarchaeological fieldwork) than is commonly available. An alternative is to imagine the effects of changes in the value of one or more variables on output, attempting to control, as best we can, our imaginations by reference to historical documents and informants' testimony. (There is thus in fact no difference in principle between the two forms of inference.) As an example we might point to the possible outcomes under varying conditions of the socio-economic mechanism claimed by David and Hennig (1972: 26) to underlie the production of Fulbe pottery at Bé. Within an Islamic context in which male authority over women was marked and there was great desire for children but a high incidence of female infertility, the immediate factors affecting variation in pottery supply and quality were deemed to be household instability (frequency of divorce) and household income, in that these influenced the desirability and accessibility of non-pottery substitutes and the willingness of potters to enter the market. Such exercises, in which the observer's imagination interacts with informants' accounts of past events and future plans, can extend the data span to several decades while remaining anchored to the observable present. More difficult is determination of the boundary conditions under which a mechanism will continue to operate without transformative change in its nature. In the example cited, changes as different as adoption of puritan attitudes to extramarital sex or the eradication of sexually transmitted diseases would have such effects (David and Voas 1981). More difficult still is imagining mechanisms and processes that existed in the past but that have no even fairly close analogs today. This is of course not strictly the task of ethnoarchaeologists, though their contributions to the world store of analogies are a fertile source of inspiration in this area. We cite an example below.

Wobst's and Gould's objections to analogy

Both Martin Wobst's (1978) and Gould's (1980: 29–47) objections to analogy require discussion here, although Gould's is, as will become apparent, misconceived. Wobst's argument in "The archaeo-ethnography[9] of hunter-gatherers or

---

[9] Defined as "archaeological research with expectations, implications and measurements derived from ethnography" (p. 303).

the tyranny of the ethnographic record in archaeology" is that the nature of ethnographic fieldwork results in a failure to develop constructs of time, space, and human behavior that adequately model what hunter-gatherers actually do and why. Wobst is especially concerned that the local or parochial scale of ethnographic fieldwork cannot cope with the regional or greater scale of forager adaptations. Thus "if archaeologists consume ethnographically derived theory without prior testing, there is a great danger that they merely reproduce the form and structure of ethnographically perceived reality in the archaeological record." Therefore, "we have to liberate our theories from the biases imposed upon them by the ethnographic record" (p. 303). Wobst's criticisms are well taken – archaeologists are better equipped than ethnographers to study phenomena of long duration – though we may note that the ethnographic record is in fact sufficiently rich and detailed to enable Wobst to found his criticism on more than mere supposition. Perhaps this is because, rather as most archaeology is site-based and yet concerned with distributions at various larger (and smaller) scales, ethnographers also engage in regional and areal comparative studies.[10] If the historical/ethnographic record did not provide us with many of the building blocks, our ability to construct the cultural past would be much diminished. The trick is learning when and how to use them, and when and how to use other materials.

Gould's (1980: 29) objection is different: "the use of ethnoarchaeology to discover analogies to the prehistoric past is downright misleading." He fears that analogy, even when multiple analogies are employed, "cannot by itself provide a way for us to know more about the past than we already do about the present, since *we are still bound by the present as the source of these alternatives*" (p. 32, our emphasis). Whereas Wobst was suggesting that ethnographic research distorts the present, Gould (like O'Connell after him) is arguing that ethnographic research, even if it provides a conceptually appropriate and observationally accurate record, will, when used for analogical purposes, still limit the range of descriptive models. Gould is here misrepresenting argument by analogy, for, as we have seen, the analyst should be concerned not merely with the positive but also with negative and neutral components of the analogy.[11] If all we did was to apply modern patterns to past behavior, this would constitute a quite unacceptable limitation on interpretation. There is every reason to suppose that many behaviors engaged in by humans in the past are no longer practiced (far less recorded) today. It is true that the application of analogies to hominids whose psychology was very different from our own poses special problems (see especially chapters 4 and 6). What Gould is in fact objecting to is the application of analogical waffle irons to the stuff of prehistory in order to

---

[10] Not that these are without their own conceptual and methodological problems (see, e.g., papers in Holy 1987).

[11] Gould's misrepresentation and oversimplification of analogical reasoning were sharply criticized by Wylie (1982; 1985: 93).

Table 2.1 *Models of the association of lithic and faunal remains at archaeological sites in Olduvai Gorge, Bed I, and the sorts of evidence used in their evaluation by Richard Potts (1984)*

Models	Relevant evidence
Hydraulic accumulations	Geoarchaeological
"Natural" clustering of dead animals	The above, plus taphonomic, taxonomic, ecological
Carnivore dens or kill sites	The above, plus ethological and forensic
Carnivore sites visited by hominids	The above
Hominid home bases	Ethnoarchaeological plus all of the above
Hominid stone caches and fast-food outlets	All the above, plus application of the Principle of Least Effort

imprint a limited range of rigid patterns. In this he is right, as in his suggestion that analogs be used "as a basis for comparison with prehistoric patterning" (p. 35). This is precisely what Richard Potts (1984) did in a fascinating paper in which he investigates associations of lithic and faunal remains in Bed I at Olduvai Gorge. After evaluating and discarding a variety of interpretive models using many different sorts of analogies (Table 2.1), he concludes that the sites are places where protohumans cached stones.

> The time and energy spent in handling and transporting portions of meat could be minimized by taking the [scavenged] meat bones to the nearest cache, where there remained stone tools and bones from previous visits. Time spent at the cache was then minimized by processing the new material quickly to obtain whatever meat or other resources (e.g., sinew or hide) were needed. By abandoning the site immediately, hominids could probably often avoid direct confrontation with carnivores attracted to the remains. (p. 345)

Thus Potts calls up a variety of ethnographic and other analogies, tests them against the data, and infers a cultural pattern that has not existed for thousands, if not millions, of years.

In conclusion, we must accept that the value of ethnoarchaeological analogs to the study of long-term processes is limited, but that ethnoarchaeological and otherwise derived demonstrations of the workings of mechanisms can and should lead to the development of models of process involving changing material outputs over time that can be tested against the archaeological record. Second, by bearing in mind the warnings of Wobst and Gould regarding the use of analogies, analogical distortion of the past and its masking by the present can both be minimized.

This abbreviated introduction to analogy has omitted several important questions, or answered them only by implication. For example we have not discussed whether archaeologists should use analogy only for developing models in the context of discovery or also in the context of verification (the answer is both but in different ways!). The reader is now equipped with the basic understanding of analogical argument necessary for the informed appreciation of ethnoarchaeological texts and their potential use in archaeological interpretation.

Ethnoarchaeology and postprocessualism

Ethnoarchaeology has on the whole been less influenced by postprocessualism (Shanks and Tilley 1989; Preucel 1995) than has archaeology proper. Studies characterized as postprocessual have for the most part been concerned with exploring the symbolic dimensions of material culture (e.g., Hodder 1982a; David *et al.* 1988; Schmidt 1997). We postpone theoretical discussion of these and other studies to later chapters. At this stage it is more useful to introduce some postprocessualist ideas that have changed or are changing the way ethnoarchaeologists think.

By 1991 contextual archaeology had matured into "interpretive" archaeology (Hodder 1991). According to Preucel and Hodder, "The main tenets of the interpretive position are that the past is meaningfully constituted from different perspectives, that the role of agents actively using material culture needs to be considered, that there is a relationship between structure and practice, and that social change is historical and contingent" (1996: 7). The statement serves to introduce: an attitude, *reflexivity*, that relates to the theory-ladenness of data; a methodological procedure, that of *hermeneutics*; and a theory, that of *practice*.

Different perspectives

The "critical theory" associated with Max Horkheimer, Herbert Marcuse and others of the Frankfurt School and with Jürgen Habermas takes a neo-Marxist approach to the sociology of knowledge, arguing that the nature of knowledge depends upon the social constitution of society. Critical theorists are concerned to analyze *ideology*, here narrowly defined as a set of "integrated assertions, theories, and aims that constitute a sociopolitical program" (Webster's 7th Collegiate Dictionary, 1965), especially as it is used as a tool for the domination of the many by the few. The analyses (especially of Habermas) are explicitly aimed at demystifying ideologies and emancipating the masses. Feminism, in contrast, may be described as a class of approaches widely diverse in theory, but having in common the aim of redressing the androcentrism prevalent in the social sciences, a concern with gender as a factor in social and cultural life, and usually a particular focus on the role of women. Thus both critical theory and feminism constitute reflections on the nature of knowledge and thought and are associated with the deconstruction of texts – or in other words the reconstruction of the context out of which the text emerges.

Reflexivity supports but is not necessarily associated with political agendas; it is a broader term for an awareness that all research and writing, including one's own, has sociopolitical content and implications.[12] In evaluating knowledge claims one must therefore consider the position of the author in relation to her or his data and the concepts employed to work on them, and in relation to informants, colleagues, and academic and other power structures. "Our lens of perception was not a transparent window but a filter characterized by the inequities of scholarly power" (Knauft 1996: 18). The lens does not determine but strongly influences what we see; thus the theory-laden nature of data results not only from the scientific paradigm to which we adhere, but also from our political and social perspectives. In fact, and this is the point, the three are inseparable; outside mathematics and logic there is no such thing as pure theory.

Evidential constraints

It is however now generally agreed that archaeological data incorporate strong evidential constraints which, while they may not stop them being manipulated in a cavalier, crass, sexist, or even tyrannical fashion, at least restrain *bona fide* scholars from doing so, and allow their views to be challenged and corrected (Wylie 1992; 1994).

> There are . . . at least three sorts of security at issue in archaeological assessments of evidential claims: security as a function of the entrenchment or freedom from doubt of the background knowledge about the linkages between archaeological data and the antecedents that produced them; security that arises because of the overall length and complexity of the linkages; and security which is due to the nature of the linkages, specifically, the degree to which they are unique or deterministic. These are cross-cut by considerations of independence: vertical independence between linking assumptions and test hypotheses, and horizontal independence between linking assumptions and the ascriptions of evidential significance they support. (Wylie 1994: 755)

As an example of the first kind of security we can cite the certainty derived from knowledge of physics that exists regarding the half-life of radiocarbon; of the second our reasonably systematic understanding of natural and some cultural formation processes, which can be briefly and simply stated (Schiffer 1976). The third kind of security refers to cases where archaeological data could have been produced in only one way; examples are once again more likely to relate to the physical and biological world of the past than to cultural manifestations. Vertical independence between linking assumptions and test hypotheses is achieved when the data on which the test of a hypothesis is run can in no way be seen as direct consequences of that hypothesis. Thus for example it might be argued that sedentism is associated with agriculture and therefore

---

[12] A "reflexive relationship" in a related sense refers to that existing between people as conscious agents being acted on and acting upon the sociopolitical and cultural structures in which they are enmeshed. This will be discussed below under the rubric of practice theory.

that greater permanence of architecture indicates increased reliance on food production. But this would be a much weaker argument than a demonstration that, in an environment otherwise characterized by C3 plants, human skeletons from what appear to be permanent villages of the period under consideration have isotopic signatures indicative of consumption of non-native C4 plants such as maize. Lastly, horizontal independence is achieved when a number of different lines of evidence converge towards the same result. Continuing with the example of the introduction of agriculture, the argument would be greatly strengthened if, in the same period in which the change in isotopic signatures was observed, flotation produced macroscopic remains of corncobs, and pots were decorated with a motif associated with a Mesoamerican maize god.[13]

Inasmuch as ethnoarchaeology tends to be concerned more with the cultural and less with the physico-chemical and biological aspects of life, evidential constraints might be thought to be rather less than in archaeology. But this is not so, at least for the conscientious researcher, for we have recursive access to our informants and in many cases can repeat our observations or combine them with experimental archaeological techniques to strengthen our understanding of causal processes (Longacre 1992). The tissue of cultural life is tightly woven; patterns repeat; vertical and horizontal independence of assumptions and hypotheses are easier to achieve than in archaeology.

Thus, while "data represents a *network of resistances* to theoretical appropriation" (Shanks and Tilley 1987: 104), reflexivity has indirectly opened the way to feminist, native, and other so-called alternative representations of the past and present. This is not to deny that much ethnoarchaeological writing remains fixed in a naturalist and generally unreflexive mode.

Meaningful constitution

Both processualists and postprocessualists are interested in the human mind, with processualists focusing more on the prehistory and development of human cognition[14] (Renfrew and Zubrow 1994) and postprocessualists on the worlds of meaning that humans create and inhabit. It is reasonable to infer that at least some members of the *Homo sapiens sapiens* subspecies have had essentially modern cognitive abilities and psyches, and have been meaningfully constituting their presents for upwards of 40,000 years. Our ancestors thought about themselves and their environments and no doubt conferred symbolic meanings on the world around them – the moon, trees, animals, artifacts, other

---

[13] It should not be thought that interpretations that are secure in Wylie's sense will be less liable to misappropriation by interest groups of one kind or another, but only that they will be more defensible before a jury of unprejudiced philosophers.

[14] Zubrow (1994: 188) sees "a critical role for ethnoarchaeology in this endeavour. One needs to determine commonalities across cultures of the elements, the classifications and the organizing principles that are focused by sensory memory."

humans – and on their own bodies. But how are archaeologists, living in our present, to determine past cognitive capacities and reconstitute those past worlds of meanings? Needless to say, the styles of naturalists and anti-naturalists differ, but most would probably agree that "any interpretive account of the past moves within a circle, perhaps more accurately, a widening spiral, and involves changing or working theoretically upon that which is to be interpreted. . . . Interpretation thus seeks to understand the particular in the light of the whole and the whole in the light of the particular." Shanks and Tilley (1987: 104) are here describing hermeneutics, a working back and forth between theory and data whereby in this instance we come to understand our own world and those of others.

They go on to cite Anthony Giddens (1982: 12) on the distinction between the first hermeneutics of natural science which "has to do only with the theories and discourse of scientists, analyzing an object world that cannot answer back," and the second hermeneutics of social science.

The social scientist studies a world . . . which is constituted as meaningful by those who produce and reproduce it in their activities – human subjects. To describe human behaviour in a valid way is in principle to be able to participate in the forms of life which constitute, and are constituted by, that behaviour. This is already a hermeneutic task. But social life is itself a "form of life", with its own technical concepts. Hermeneutics hence enters into the social sciences on two, related, levels. (Giddens 1982: 7)

While we need not agree with Shanks and Tilley (1987: 107–8) that anthropologists who work in alien cultures are involved in a triple, and archaeologists who attempt to understand alien cultures of the past in a fourfold hermeneutic,[15] it certainly is true that both archaeologists and ethnoarchaeologists work back and forth between theory and data, building, testing, and tearing down models in order to construct improved ones that better fit what are perceived to be "the facts." Whether one prefers the metaphor of the hermeneutic circle or the dialectic, we come gradually to comprehend the part in terms of the whole and vice versa – which is not to deny that there may be a Pauline experience on the way to Damascus, sudden moments of enlightenment such as Nigel Barley (1983: 130–1, 167–8) described for the innocent anthropologist.

The theory of practice

Practice theory is or should be central to ethnoarchaeology in that it orients our approach to a world of individuals, societies, and material and sociocultural

---

[15] Giddens's second hermeneutic derives from the fact that "social life" is itself a universe that can be considered in its own terms, and that is as true for the anthropologist as for the sociologist. Inasmuch as the archaeologist has to deal with transformations of systemic behavior, it would be legitimate to regard the statics of the archaeological record as requiring a third hermeneutics for their interpretation. We prefer, rather than using this terminology, to follow the philosopher Embree (1987) who argued on similar grounds that archaeology is the most difficult of disciplines, saving one he modestly refrained from identifying!

things. It insists that we regard people not as mere vehicles through whom structures become manifest, or marionettes whose behavior is controlled by socio-cultural norms, but as active agents in society's constitution and change.

In general terms, practice emerges at the intersection between individual and collective processes, and between symbolic force and material or economic power ... On the one hand, individual practices are seen as constrained and orchestrated by collective structures of cultural logic or organization. But individuals are also seen as agents who reinforce or resist the larger structures that encompass them. (Knauft 1996: 106)

Practice theory situates individuals, ourselves and the persons we observe, in relation to cultures and societies that are conceived of in a fashion consistent with the realist view discussed above. It regards people as conscious agents capable of reflecting upon and acting on sociopolitical and cultural structures which are nonetheless overwhelmingly more powerful, and manipulated by interest groups and elites. Thus a concern with power relations and hegemony[16] has characterized the work of many who have made use of practice theory.

Marxist influence [on practice theory] is to be seen in the assumption that the most important forms of action or interaction for analytical purposes are those which take place in asymmetrical or dominated relations, that it is these forms of action or interaction that best explain the shape of any given system at any time. (Ortner 1984: 147)

But Ortner (1984: 157) reminds us that power relations are not all that are worth studying from this perspective. "Patterns of cooperation, reciprocity and solidarity constitute the other side of the coin of social being ... a Hobbesian view of social life is as surely biased as one that harks back to Rousseau." However, even in so-called egalitarian societies, individual behavior is constrained by collective structures. Thus, for example, when Hodder's (1978) Baringo tribespeople use material culture to signal changing ethnic affiliations and adhesions they are at one and the same time manipulating structures of cultural organization and acknowledging their power. It is precisely because "Technological acts ... are a fundamental medium through which social relations, power structure, worldviews, and social production and reproduction are expressed and defined" (Dobres and Hoffman 1994: 212), and because material culture assists in constituting the world of meaning, that practice theory can be of such value in orienting ethnoarchaeological research and in its assessment.

Practice theory is also related to hermeneutics. In a well-known passage Bourdieu (1977: 87) describes how a child becomes competent in its own culture,

So long as the work of education is not clearly institutionalized as a specific, autonomous practice, and it is a whole group and a whole symbolically structured environ-

---

[16] The concept of hegemony (Gramsci 1971) refers to the ability of dominant groups or classes in society to maintain their power and position not by direct coercion but by obtaining, for example through enculturation, religion, and education (i.e., through ideology in the sense that critical theorists use the term), the consent of the people to the structures on which their dominance depends.

ment, without specialized agents or specific moments, which exerts an anonymous, pervasive pedagogic action, the essential part of the *modus operandi* which defines practical mastery is transmitted in practice, in its practical state, without attaining the level of discourse.

The child is involved in a hermeneutic, trial and error process of discovering and assimilating his or her physical and social environment, learning, to use Giddens's words quoted above, "to participate in the forms of life which constitute, and are constituted by, that behaviour." Material culture is an important part of the physical environment, and the child learns to make sense of it, to read it as a kind of text (Hodder 1989a) – or, better, hyper-text. Each action and reaction teaches it more about the whole of which the child is becoming a part and about the part that the child is in course of discovering. Little by little the child develops *habitus*, "a subjective but not individual system of internalized structures, schemes of perception, conception, and action common to all members of the same group or class" (Bourdieu 1977: 86). Habitus, unthinking dispositions and basic know-how that constitute a practical cultural competence, is in large part gained through experience and unstated in words (though it can be brought to consciousness, expressed, and argued). It equips us with the strategies we need to deal with the myriad unexpected events of daily life. Linda Donley (1982) has developed an ethnoarchaeological description of the formation of important aspects of the habitus of members of the Swahili merchant class through exposure to and interaction with the division of space and the decoration of their coral block houses. As Hodder (1986: 72) notes:

The central position of processes of enculturation in Bourdieu's theory is of importance for archaeology because it links social practices with the "culture history" of the society. As the habitus is passed down through time it plays an active role in social action and is transformed in those actions. This recursiveness, Giddens' "duality of structure", is possible because the habitus is a practical logic.

Habitus is thus relevant to studies of the transmission of technologies and of the nature and work of style (Shennan 1996).

From processualist reaction . . . to possible synthesis?

Postprocessualism has not gone uncriticized by processualists in archaeology (e.g., comments in Shanks and Tilley 1989; Bintliff 1993). As to ethnoarchaeology, Miriam Stark (1993a) has commented vigorously on what she perceives as weaknesses in postprocessual, specifically structuralist and semiotic, approaches.[17] Postprocessual ethnoarchaeology "seemingly holds no place for cross-cultural comparison . . . the generalizing, empirical processual tradition

---

[17] Following Longacre (1981: 40) she offers (p. 94) a very restricted definition of ethnoarchaeology as "the testing of models relating variability of human behavior to material traces among extant groups, where the investigator can simultaneously control for both human behavior and material culture variability."

seems a foreign country to postprocessualist archaeological interpretation." But in the next breath and somewhat contradictorily she says that "Symbolic studies . . . seek to identify in ethnographic contexts generative principles and generalizations that can later be tested against archaeological data" (p. 95). She goes on to criticize postprocessualists, including David *et al.* (1988), for exhibiting at one and the same time (1) an overdependence upon informants and (2) a propensity to dismiss natives' perceptions of the material under study (p. 97).[18] Further, she notes that

of vital importance to such studies is the assumption that material culture is a "communicative medium of considerable importance . . . and as a symbolic medium for orientating people in their natural and social environments" (Shanks and Tilley 1987: 96). By unquestioningly accepting this premise, postprocessualists neatly sidestep a rigorous evaluation of their own analyses, which "processual" assumptions nonetheless receive in postprocessual hands. (p. 97)

There is an element of truth in the accusation of inadequate verification, but the importance of material culture as a communicative medium is surely what Hodder (1982a) had sought to demonstrate in *Symbols in action*, and other authors including ND and colleagues in subsequent case studies. Apparently these were sufficiently persuasive for Stark to accept their conclusion as axiomatic: "A material culture theory must recognize that material subjects constitute symbols in a complex communicative system" (p. 100).

Stark's polemic fails sufficiently to discriminate between the programmatic statements of archaeological theoreticians such as Shanks and Tilley – and Hodder in certain of his papers – who on occasion adopt a hyper-relativist viewpoint, and what Hodder and some others actually do as field ethnoarchaeologists. While a major concern of postprocessual ethnoarchaeology is to understand the worlds of meaning that material culture is active in constituting, this does not exclude the generation of law-like statements. Hodder (1982a: 85) himself has argued that in the Baringo region, "greater between-group stress has been related to more marked material boundaries." But then, and in contrast to processual studies, Hodder went on to note that the boundary conditions under which this law will hold include not only environmental and social organizational factors but also the "different meanings attached to material symbols" – which implies that their applicability will likely be restricted to a very small sample of closely related societies. Elsewhere he states (Hodder 1982b: 11): "The cross-cultural generalisations which are to be developed are concerned less with statistical levels of association in summary files of modern societies and more with careful considerations of relevant cultural contexts."

In our view the processual and postprocessual products of Yellen's buckshot, laboratory, spoiler, and general model approaches *all* have the potential, if developed with relevant boundary conditions in mind, of leading to general

---

[18] Both these questions deserve and receive much fuller treatment, the first in chapter 3 and the second in chapter 13.

models or laws, and we agree with Yellen and with Stark on the need for methodological rigor. But ethnoarchaeology should not limit itself to "the testing of models relating variability of human behavior to material traces among extant groups" (Stark 1993a: 94). In contrast to social anthropology, which privileges the Word to the virtual exclusion of the Thing, we favor an ethnoarchaeology that is the study of humans in the context of and through their works. While we must strive towards in-depth understanding of particular examples of human cultural diversity, this need not conflict with ultimate comparative and generalizing goals. Christine and Todd VanPool (1999) argue that, while postprocessualism is commonly mischaracterized as unscientific, some postprocessual approaches can indeed contribute to scientific understanding of the archaeological, and by extension ethnographic, record. Cohabitation if not synthesis is possible. Reflexivity, hermeneutics, and practice theory, and the linkages between them, can guide the practice of interpretive ethnoarchaeology and may also be considered as essential analytical tools in the evaluation of both processual and interpretive studies.

But before we can begin the process of evaluation, we must deal with what Stark (1993a: 96) rightly characterizes as a "fundamental problem . . . shared by processual and postprocessual ethnoarchaeological research: the lack of explicit methodological frameworks."

Further reading

Martin and McIntyre's (1994) edited volume *Readings in the philosophy of social science* brings together classic and critical texts on many of the issues – explanation, verification, etc. – discussed in the earlier part of this chapter. Robert Preucel's (1991) "The philosophy of archaeology" provides a compact introduction to the main philosophical schools that have influenced archaeology since the 1960s, and is usefully complemented by Bruce Trigger's (1998) "Archaeology and epistemology: dialoguing across the Darwinian chasm" which argues the case for a realist historical materialism, and, rather less cogently, for an evolutionary approach to epistemology. Mark Leone's (1982) survey of opinions about recovering mind and ideology is an admirably clear account of structuralist, neo-evolutionist, and Marxist views.

The introductory sections in Preucel's and Hodder's (1996) *Contemporary archaeology in theory: a reader* provide an excellent introduction to recent developments in postprocessual archaeological thought. Well worth reading also is the debate that appeared in 1989 under the title "Archaeology into the 1990s" in the *Norwegian Archaeological Review*. Here, after the postmodernizing Shanks and Tilley (1989) summarize the main themes in their books, their views are discussed by Scandinavian, British, and North American colleagues of various theoretical persuasions, to which Shanks and Tilley make their own response.

Gould's and Watson's (1982) "A dialogue on the meaning and use of analogy in ethnoarchaeological reasoning" covers most of the issues regarding analogy raised above, and should be followed by Wylie's (1982) commentary on the debate (see also Eggert [1993]).

The collection *Interpreting archaeology*, edited by Hodder *et al.* (1995), offers the reader wide-ranging exposure to interpretive archaeology and includes a useful glossary of concepts. Never mentioning practice theory by name, Elizabeth Brumfiel's American Anthropological Association Distinguished Lecture in Archaeology for 1992 not only presents a theoretical argument for the importance of agency – and in particular gender, class, and faction – in archaeology, but convincingly exemplifies differences this can make in archaeological interpretation.

The authors have recently become aware that complexity theory, and specifically that relating to complex adaptive systems (see e.g., Gell-Mann 1994), provides a viable architecture for a conceptualization of human society that takes account of human intentionality. Complex adaptive systems are networks of interacting components that process information and use it to develop evolving models of the world that are used to prescribe behavior.

CHAPTER 3

FIELDWORK AND ETHICS

Ethnoarchaeology . . . an excellent means of getting an exotic adventure holiday in a remote location . . . After figuring out what you think is going on with the use and discard of objects (you should never stay around long enough to master the language) you return to your desk and use these brief studies to make sweeping generalisations about what people in the past and in totally different environments must have done.

(Paul Bahn 1989: 52–3)

As archaeologists began to do ethnography in the service of archaeology, they unaccountably adopted many ethnographic techniques of gathering data.

(Michael Schiffer 1978: 234)

Experience has taught us that some consciousness-raising about the differences between archaeological and ethnoarchaeological fieldwork is necessary before young archaeologists are let loose to deal with live "subjects" in the field. This chapter does a little of that but is no substitute for a manual on research methods and the conduct of ethnographic and sociological fieldwork. Of these there are many (e.g., Bernard 1994; Babbie 1998; Berg 1998) to which we strongly recommend that all refer.[1] A second purpose is to encourage critical reading of ethnoarchaeological studies. We are here concerned to establish standards rather than to criticize particular examples, and we will comment on method in discussion of the case studies treated in later chapters. What information about the production of an ethnoarchaeological work does the reader require to evaluate its conclusions? In answering this question we will characterize different kinds of research and contrast extremes of method before considering some specifics. Advice regarding the conduct of fieldwork is offered in the process, and we draw attention to particular challenges facing archaeologists engaged in ethnography. In general, however, and *contra* Schiffer's statement above, our problems and most of our practices are substantially the same as ethnographers' even though we employ some different techniques. We conclude by alerting the reader to a number of ethical issues.

---

[1] In 1999 Sage Publications launched a new journal, *Field Methods*, with H. Russell Bernard as its editor.

Types of ethnoarchaeological research

We begin by elaborating on a point made in chapter 2: ethnographers have traditionally done in-depth fieldwork in a single community, typically for periods ranging from one to two years, occasionally returning for a restudy to monitor change. While genuine regional studies exist, it is more common for observations to be narrowly focused in space, temporally limited, rich in detail – and generalized to the larger social group, people, tribe, class, or other category, that the study has sampled. While archaeologists in many parts of the world were long similarly focused on the excavation of single or at times neighboring sites, increasingly since the 1950s they have incorporated a regional perspective into their research programs. In these respects ethnoarchaeology combines features of the two disciplines.

Although ethnoarchaeologists' concern is with material culture in relation to culture as a whole, and the focus on relations between humans and things, the principles of fieldwork differ not at all from those of ethnography. In the early years when ethnoarchaeology was often carried out by archaeologists "on the side," there was a tendency to study the production and characteristics of material culture more or less in isolation. Over the years as practitioners have become more anthropologically sophisticated and better trained, a more holistic mind set becomes apparent, although ethnoarchaeologists continue to pay much more attention to things – and especially variation in things – than most, and particularly social, anthropologists. One area, that of refuse disposal and site formation processes, is our sole preserve.

For the prospective fieldworker there is no substitute for local knowledge and an awareness of local customs and issues. Local and regional ethnographies and histories must be read, learned, and inwardly digested – and where no or only inadequate sources exist the research design must incorporate provision for gathering the information required. Time spent in learning from colleagues who have worked in the same region is always well spent, even though one may choose not to follow their methods or advice. Conditions vary so widely on a world scale that almost any generalization or counsel given will be wrong or inappropriate in some circumstances. Similarly, the reader venturing into a new geographical area must be on the lookout for unstated conventions.

Ethnoarchaeological research can be carried out during weekends by participants in an archaeological project; can result from chance encounters with potential informants; can constitute one phase of a multi-stage program of archaeological fieldwork; or can be the fruit of a systematically planned program designed to address specific questions of interest to archaeologists working locally or elsewhere. The nature of the research project will affect the ways in which observations are made and data collected, as well as the quality, quantity, and seasonality of those data.

While systematic and conscientious work can certainly be carried out by archaeologists during days away from their sites, it is likely that the archaeology during a given field season takes precedence over any time spent on ethnography. In considering such "weekend" ethnoarchaeology, one should consider whether or to what extent a research question (or "hypothesis") has been posed, whether the kinds of people and things studied are indeed appropriate to answer (or "test") it, and how they (the "sample") were selected. Because of its links to an archaeological project, such fieldwork is likely to be seasonally restricted. Indeed, whatever the research strategy, it is important to remember that different activities are carried out by different people, in different locations, and at different times of year, and to consider the possibility that, even if fieldwork spans an entire year, longer-term variations in activities and their associated material culture may exist.

Serendipitous encounters between archaeologists and potential informants, and unplanned experiences that shed light on archaeological problems, occur (by definition) in ways and in places that are unpredictable and that may be uncontrollable. One might, for example, meet an elderly woman in a town market, be told that she is or used to be a potter, and request that she demonstrate the manufacture and firing of a vessel. In this situation, it is difficult to determine how "typical" or representative she is of the entire population of potters in her community, how representative her pot is of her own repertoire and theirs, and whether her skills have improved, diminished, or remained unchanged since an earlier time when she was more vigorous and produced a larger inventory. Observation and description of such craft activities may shed light on matters pertaining to pottery production (such as clay preparation, forming technique, fuel, and firing time) but they do not necessarily have any connection with an explicit research question formulated before the chance encounter occurred. While serendipity plays a part in all research, studies that are of this or the previous kind no longer find their way into the ethnoarchaeological literature proper, instead appearing as asides in archaeological publications.

Ethnoarchaeological work that represents one aspect of a multi-stage research program may or may not have been an integral part of initial research design. ND's work (e.g., 1971) in a Fulbe village in Cameroon was anticipated before the archaeological component of the project was begun. Peter Schmidt's (e.g., 1997) ethnoarchaeological studies of the Haya and Barongo (Tanzania) form part of a long-term and multi-faceted research program of investigation of the history and prehistory of the region and of East Africa as a whole. Other ethnoarchaeological projects have been formulated in the course of a strictly archaeological field program. A case in point is CK's (1982a) study of vernacular village architecture in Iran. Here, an ethnoarchaeological project was conceived in a season of archaeological fieldwork during which village laborers frequently noted resemblances between prehistoric remains and features in their own houses. In considering such approaches to ethnoarchaeological research, one may revisit analogy, and ask whether the "direct historical approach" implied by the selection of fieldwork venue is appropriate. Had this Iranian village been situated directly atop the archaeological mound (which it was not), the source would still have been separated from the subject by thousands of years, which have seen changes in climate, land use, technology, religion, and social and political organization.

Systematic problem-oriented ethnoarchaeological research in one geographic area can be designed to address problems raised by archaeological data in another. To be sure, researchers on such projects may also have lucky encounters with potentially relevant informants, just as they may carry out archaeological survey and/or excavation during the course of their ethnographic work. The distinctive feature of this kind of research, however, is that from the outset it is organized to address specific questions of interest to archaeologists, and to do so by collecting specific kinds of information. One example of such a program is the Kalinga Ethnoarchaeological Project, initially designed by Longacre (1974; Longacre and Skibo 1994) to address questions about relationships between ceramic style, learning frameworks, and postmarital residence practices raised in the course of archaeological work in the American Southwest. Comparability of source and subject societies and the availability of ethnographic sources, notably a monograph on the Kalinga by his colleague Edward Dozier (1966), were critical factors in the choice of fieldwork venue. Hodder's (1982a) ethnoarchaeological research in several African countries, designed with theoretical questions in mind, also required certain types of society – but could have been conducted on a different continent. ND chose the Mandara region of Cameroon and Nigeria for a long-term study of the nature and workings of style on account of its unparalleled cultural and societal variety and his familiarity with the area (David *et al.* 1991).

Polar methods: participant observation and questionnaires

Approaches to data acquisition range from the "heart to heart," many long one-on-one discussions with one or a few informants, to the "horde of locusts" strategy, in which several student assistants have conversations through interpreters with many respondents, whose replies are inserted in questionnaires. Regardless of the overarching organizational framework of an ethnoarchaeological project (and the "types" outlined above are by no means mutually exclusive), all fieldworkers obtain data in a variety of ways. Most intensive and anthropologically orthodox is participant observation. What does this term really mean? First and foremost it implies being there, staying for a significant period of months rather than weeks. While any sustained period of fieldwork will inevitably begin with a round of courtesy calls, members of the host community may not uniformly or always welcome outsiders, and there may be economic or ritual aspects of local life that they are unwilling to divulge (although

Fig. 3.1 Robert Janes (*right*) and a Dene friend, Francis Baton, stretch and dry a black bear skin on a cabin roof at the Willow Lake hunting camp, May 1974. The roof is a rigid flat surface exposed directly to the sunlight and ideal for the purpose.

the fact that information is being withheld may not always be evident, at least in the short term, to the foreign visitor).The participant observer learns (or attempts to learn) the language. He or she is willing to live (more or less) according to the rhythms of the host community (Fig. 3.1). A locally hired assistant is likely to be treated as a partner or junior colleague, even junior relative. Participant observation implies flexibility – while one has a research design and a tentative schedule of work to be done, the latter can be dropped instantly as opportunities offer themselves, for example when one stumbles on a new craft practice, a funeral, or a wise and willing informant. Sampling is less formally devised than in survey work, and the researcher may come to place special reliance on an inner circle of informants. A topic is shelved, at least for the moment, when information becomes redundant and closure seems to be achieved. There are relationships of reciprocity with all informants, and when one wishes to talk about something other than the researcher had planned the participant observer is well advised to listen. Little by little the participant observer becomes incorporated into the community, not as a native member but as someone enmeshed in its network of rights, duties, obligations, privileges, expectations . . . and friendships. The ideal participant observer is of course a native, trained in and properly skeptical of texts on anthropological method, and willing to discuss his or her own community.

Participatory observation may not be essential for interpretive/antinaturalist ethnoarchaeology, but it is questionable whether the results of such research can be convincingly validated without it. Thus for example a major component of Hodder's (1982a: 125–84) Nuba study involves the documentation and interpretation of "symbolic principles which lie behind the production of material traits" (p. 126). The work was carried out mainly in 1978–9 by Hodder and a team acknowledged as "Mary [Braithwaite], Jane [Grenville], Andy [Mawson] and Sami" (p. ix), probably during Cambridge University vacations, and probably by utilizing a combination of questionnaires and structured and unstructured interviews, combined with mapping, the planning of compounds and photography and sketching of items of material culture. Verification of Hodder's interpretation of the symbolic systems underlying regional variation depends mainly upon the coherence of results over several material culture domains, underpinned by reference to Mary Douglas's (1970) theory of pollution. Despite the sophistication of the argument, the uncomfortable question remains whether Hodder's interpretation is, or is not, a Western intellectual's imposition upon the data. This is further discussed in chapter 13.

Participant observation may be complemented by the use of interview schedules or questionnaires, but such tools are sometimes used as the basis of observation. The Coxoh Ethnoarchaeological Project, directed by Brian Hayden (Hayden and Cannon 1984a), with fieldwork carried out between 1977 and 1979 in over 150 households in three Maya communities in highland Mexico and Guatemala, employed some 15 Canadian and American, mainly graduate, students, and 16 native translators, who both observed and interviewed villagers and filled out questionnaires (Fig. 3.2). Such a data collection strategy facilitates the standardization of data, enhancing the possibility of comparing information obtained in different places or at different times. The Coxoh monograph is one of very few in the ethnoarchaeological literature that describe sampling strategies in detail. Its authors are refreshingly frank in their discussion of villagers' sensitivities about particular subjects regarding which they were reluctant to provide information, and readers gain insights into the effect of such omissions on the analyses presented. Questionnaires have been used in other ethnoarchaeological studies, but, in contrast to the presentation of the Coxoh project, they are usually not published. (However, others will find Gosselain's [1995, vol. II: 363–6] lengthy questionnaire for his work on pottery a useful basis for developing their own.) Equally typically, "raw" data that readers could use either to evaluate authors' analyses and interpretations or to address different questions are often omitted. Questionnaires can provide a wealth of information about many subjects, but absence of participant observation generally precludes the recording of richly textured detail and deeper understanding of the topics studied. As fieldwork progresses and understanding grows the researcher

Fig. 3.2 Brian Hayden and members of his team in San Mateo, Guatemala, in 1979. *From left to right, back row*: Ben and Peggy Nelson, Brian Hayden; *front row*: Chuj Maya assistant Xun Xantec, and Hayden's children.

may come to realize that some questions simply don't make sense, failing to map onto the practices or the mindset of the culture studied. A Trobriander questioning an American about prestige to be gained over the Christmas season might have similar difficulties. It is thus a good idea, before finalizing a questionnaire, to apply it to a pilot sample. This may avoid the unfortunate necessity of choosing between modification of the questionnaire at the cost of comparability of data, and sticking to the original, ending up with quantified nonsense.

Whatever the main mode chosen, all projects employ a variety of fieldwork methods. Participation in and observation of activities is supplemented by many means, including the taking of household or livestock censuses and collection of oral histories relating to families or communities. Ethnoarchaeologists, more so than most ethnographers, will generally wish to obtain quantified data, for example on production and prices of artifacts, crop yields, house areas, and the like. Objects collected and maps, drawings, photographs, and video and audio tapes made in the field complement observations recorded in written field-notes. Also indispensable is information obtained from governmental and non-governmental agencies, for example archival sources, aerial photographs,

Table 3.1 *Information required for assessment of field methodology and methods*

Research context
    Location and cultural and historical context of group or groups studied
    Political context of research, including situation of the researcher, and funding
    Conditions and duration of fieldwork
    Investigator's knowledge, including linguistic competence, of the group and its
        language

Ethnographic methods and techniques
    Sampling of group or groups:
        strategies
        numbers of settlements/households/individuals
        representation of classes/ranks/statuses/roles/genders
    Research methods
        participatory observation
        interviews
        questionnaires
        other, including reenactments and experiments
    Assistants (paid)
        qualifications and relationship to informants
    Informants
        categories and how recompensed
    Records
        written materials, photographs, visual and sound recordings
        ethnographic and other material samples
        location and access

LandSat images, soil maps, and national or regional censuses and gazetteers. While it may be hard to drag oneself away from a field site that is progressively becoming more and more like home in order to undertake an often frustrating search for such materials, it is essential to do so.

Assessment of field methods

In order to assess the conditions under which an ethnoarchaeological study was produced, readers require a certain amount of information, an outline of which appears in Table 3.1. Robert Janes's (1983: 4–6) account of the methodology employed in his and Priscilla Janes's research on subsistence and formation processes among Mackenzie basin Dene is an admirable and succinct example of what is needed. Unless there is reason to preserve anonymity, readers are entitled to know the location of the research; they certainly need to know the cultural and historical context, and also the political conditions under which it was carried out. This last may often involve no more than an acknowledgment of the national and local authorities who permitted the work to proceed, and of the sources of funding. Readers may legitimately ask when ethnoarchaeological fieldwork was carried out, by whom, and in what language. Unfortunately, most publications fail to specify these things at all clearly. The fault is not always or entirely the ethnoarchaeologist's. Editorial pressures exerted on authors encourage the excision of the theory and methodology that is sometimes to be found in theses, and it is true that considerable archaeology, *sensu* Foucault, is required to unearth the methodology of many ethnographies, but there is more to it than that. Archaeologists deal with the dead and, especially before the postprocessual era, some of those turning to ethnoarchaeology reckoned that as scientists they had the right to interact with the living in much the same manner. As one senior scholar, referring to research carried out in the 1970s, said to ND, "We just went out and did it." A lack of reflexivity, if not of personal respect for Others, characterizes any ethnoarchaeologists still unaware that the term "living archaeology" dehumanizes their interlocutors.

While sampling strategies, or the lack of them, can often be inferred from a report, it is helpful if they and the means by which information was gathered are clearly specified, with indications given as to the relative amounts of effort put into different aspects of the research. Most ethnoarchaeological studies acknowledge the help of one or more individuals, some of them native to the country in which work was carried out, but rare is the author who describes the class, caste, or occupational status, and the fieldwork duties, of indigenous interpreters or assistants, the treatment of informants, and the means by which communication was achieved. In dissertations and major publications, though not necessarily in articles written while a program is in progress, the disposition of records of all kinds and the conditions of scholarly access should be described. We take up several of these matters in the following section.

Challenges

Surviving fieldwork

The most precious fieldwork resource is time. You cannot afford to be ill, and yet "anthropologists are otherwise sensible people who don't believe in the germ theory of disease" (or, one might add, other dangers), as Roy Rappaport concludes from the evidence presented by Nancy Howell (1990) in her book *Surviving fieldwork*, to which he contributed the foreword. Howell's book is required reading. Nobody should leave home, especially for poorer countries, without one of the many editions of *Where there is no doctor* (Werner 1992), nor without having physical and dental exams, nor without seeking advice, prescriptions, and inoculations from competent doctors, which may entail visiting a specialized travel clinic. Practice defensive living and driving. Opinions differ about a blanket ban on romantic and sexual liaisons; suffice it to say that they are likely to have unforeseen implications, sequelae, consequences, and even aftermaths (Bernard 1994: 156).

This discussion assumes that the field locality poses no immediate threat to the ethnoarchaeologist. However, difficult decisions about abandoning research and assisting one's local friends may be in order in such volatile and life-threatening situations as the Nigerian civil war (1967), the Iranian revolution (1979), or the genocides in Cambodia (1975) or Rwanda (1994) (Sluka 1990). A number of foreign archaeologists had to terminate fieldwork in Peru during the 1980s because of the threat of violence from the Sendero Luminoso (Shining Path) movement. Natalie Tobert (1988) suffered for and with her Zaghawa informants in Darfur, Sudan, during the famine of 1984–5. At the very least, one must always recall that one is a foreign guest (even native ethnoarchaeologists are usually strangers) who should respect local customs. Risk-taking is to be avoided, as is the naive assumption that local people will always be helpful (whether or not problems arise). Inappropriate behavior, including in some instances well-meaning but indiscreet chat with local authorities, can jeopardize friends and informants, or result in the confiscation of a camera or field notebook; at worst, one might be imprisoned or killed. Fortunately, most ethnoarchaeologists do not encounter such extraordinary disruptions. If asked by an importunate official what you have to give them, try the answer "Respect."

Language

As noted above, ethnoarchaeological fieldwork perforce involves methods commonly used by ethnographers, amongst whom it is accepted that, since direct communication with native informants is fundamental to the fieldwork endeavor, some linguistic competence is essential. In cases where there is no written language, and/or no published grammar or dictionary, ethnographers sometimes use a trade language (e.g., Swahili among Haya speakers in Tanzania) or a pidgin (as in parts of the complex linguistic mosaic that characterizes Papua New Guinea); with time, they often become increasingly competent in the local language. Ethnoarchaeologists, too, should make every effort to communicate directly. Even when such communication is feasible, ethnoarchaeologists (like ethnographers) may retain translators and/or field assistants for help in interpreting statements or actions. An often unappreciated benefit is that translation gives the ethnoarchaeologist time to think about responses and questions rather than having to devote all effort to comprehension. Such personnel deserve acknowledgment in resulting publications (unless they request anonymity). Regional studies pose special problems. In Cameroon in 1986 ND worked with speakers of six different languages, for none of which there then existed a published grammar or lexicon. His assistant, Isa Emmanuel Kawalde, spoke Mafa, the majority language, Hausa, and some Fulfulde, besides

French, in which, much interspersed with indigenous words, he communicated with ND, whose once competent Fulfulde had grown rusty since the early seventies. This array of languages proved reasonably adequate to obtain descriptive data on several domains of material culture and some basic ethnographic information (names of clans, brief descriptions of ceremonies, etc.), but the assistance of Yves Le Bléis, a linguist and ethnomusicologist then working on a Mafa lexicon, was of inestimable value when the research focus turned to the reenactment of iron smelting, involving intense interaction with Dokwaza and his family of iron workers (chapters 11 and 13). Efficiency of communication plays an important role in determining the viability of different kinds of fieldwork. Some questions are simply not worth asking if they have to pass from, say, English to Nigerian English to Hausa to the Wula dialect of Kapsiki and back, since the amount of error and misunderstanding introduced in translation cannot be evaluated. That such matters are not trivial should be clear in the following discussion.

Assistants

Field assistants are born, not made – at least in ideal situations – but sometimes they are thrust upon one and require a great deal of training. They may, for example, resent the researcher asking the same question of different people, regarding it as evidence of a lack of trust or confidence in their own ability. Worse, when translating in interview situations, they may give their own answer to questions rather than acting as a neutral channel of communication, reserving their comments until later. In our experience, there is an element of self-selection in field assistants, the researcher attracting people interested in their own societies and at the same time intellectually capable of distancing themselves from them to some extent. Such persons are quick to grasp what is expected of them and provide their researcher with inestimable support (Fig. 3.3).

Ethnoarchaeologists should be sensitive to the gender and socioeconomic status of their field assistants, as these may affect the content and quality of respondents' communications and behavior. For example, in a strongly virilocal, patrilineal society in which women are at least sometimes secluded in their homes, a young female ethnoarchaeologist may improve her chances of success in at least the early stages of fieldwork if her assistant/translator is a man. This of course has its dangers, as the male intermediary may, and not necessarily intentionally, suppress or distort women's views, and the ethnoarchaeologist may, without realizing it, assimilate a man's viewpoint – which is the common fate of all but the most reflexive male researchers, and especially those working in countries where women are less educated or less free to interact with male strangers.

If one's assistant is a member of the host community, it is well to know the

Fig. 3.3 Judy Sterner and ND with their Cameroonian field assistants,
(1989). On the left is Isa Emmanuel Kawalde, whose name (Muslim,
Christian, Mafa) is an abbreviated life history in reverse. A tailor by
trade, he had worked previously with a German ethnologist, Paul
Hinderling, and has wide experience of the region. Kodje Dadai, a
farmer and traditional healer, had also visited many mountain
communities on his own account. Although he has had little
schooling, he is an intellectual, able to see his own community,
Sirak, in comparative perspective. The photo is typical of those
taken by professional photographers in small African towns.

identity of his or her relatives, friends, and possible enemies; if factions exist,
it can be important to ascertain an assistant's status in relation to those. If, less
desirably, the assistant is a member of a different community, it is essential to
learn something of relations between and attitudes of the one towards the
other. For example, in 1984 ND hired his landlord's son, a young Wandala from
the plains, as an interpreter-guide. It soon became apparent that he regarded the

Mandara mountain peoples as risible rustics, whom he initially treated with disrespect. It can be difficult to decide whether the intensive reeducation required in such situations is preferable to the risk of having to disentangle oneself from an unsuitable or incompetent assistant who might yet be able to sway public opinion against one.

In some ethnographic settings it is important to be aware of additional particulars. There may, for example, be a history of feuding or vendetta between an assistant's family and close kin of a family in the community studied. Or one's assistant might be a member of a locally stigmatized group (such as an "untouchable" caste in India), or a member of a widely respected occupational group (such as physician, genealogist, or teacher). Whether this is advantageous or counterproductive depends on the thrust of the research.

Reciprocity and compensation

Archaeologists customarily pay laborers in local currency and at fixed rates, varying with the nature of the work and the length of time involved. In an ethnoarchaeological field setting, it may be desirable to offer monetary compensation to informants willing to discuss specific aspects of their activities and material culture. In some areas, for example Canada's North West Territories, it is expected that interviews be paid for (with the consequence that costs preclude research by students unless working on others' grants or for First Nations). Local conditions and practices apply, but one should always take care to avoid exploitation of informants, compensating them, for example, for time spent away from economic pursuits. Ethnoarchaeologists are fortunate in that the purchase of craft items can in itself be a form of repayment. However, the promise of financial reward may pit one potential informant against another, and it is not unheard of for time-consuming (and lucrative) inaccuracies or elaborate fictions to be offered up as facts of local life. Where monetary compensation is not practicable (if, for example, barter is more important than exchanges backed by currency) or is rejected by natives as an option, other kinds of reciprocity are generally possible. Personal gifts, food items, and help with transport of people, livestock, or goods are often given in exchange for information and other assistance provided.[2] Although it is sometimes done (e.g., Skibo 1999), we regard it as extremely dangerous for unqualified persons to offer medical attention other than first aid, in which all fieldworkers should receive training prior to entering the field. After a short St John's Ambulance course taken before leaving for Cameroon, Kodzo Gavua was able in 1986 to resuscitate a Mafa baby given up for dead by his parents, one of whom was a healer.

---

[2] Suitable gifts vary from context to context, ranging from salt, boxes of matches, fishhooks, oranges, and cola nuts to hand-held calculators, cologne, costume jewelry, wrist watches, blue jeans, fabric for clothing, and so on up. Collective gifts of ballpoint pens, notebooks, geographic globes (balloons), and footballs to local schools are well received in poorer communities and avoid possible jealousies. Bic lighters have rendered the once favored Zippo obsolete!

The observer's presence

It is an irony of the field situation that critical decisions have to be taken immediately upon arrival when the researcher is least able to assess the likely consequences of his or her actions. While the advice of trusted colleagues can be invaluable, and experience certainly helps, great sensitivity is always required.

The observer's presence affects what is observed, and the researcher must take account of this in evaluating his or her observations. One can influence but never entirely control how one is perceived; it may be necessary to counter local stereotypes and categorizations. Many ethnographers and ethnoarchaeologists have commented on their placement by the host community in a special category of humanity. Women researchers may well be treated in some respects as honorary men, and men allowed access to things not normally open to any but close kin and intimate friends. O'Connell was adopted by the Alyawara, and when Binford (1984: 157, 180 fn.) joined him in the field the Alyawara decided they were brothers, assigning him too to a moiety and dreaming tract.

In turn we then were expected to behave appropriately, to cooperate, to learn, and to become enculturated, at least in certain ways. To make this possible, a set of men were responsible to us, as teachers. We were quite literally enrolled in Alyawara school, with the goal of learning how to perform as an Alyawara, appropriate to the kinship-defined statuses given us.

In all such cases, one must be especially careful not to trespass on the hosts' kindness and goodwill. And while a researcher native to the area has many advantages, he or she is likely to be judged more stringently, and with less patience. The reflections of Caesar Apentiik (1997), a Bulsa working among Bulsa in northern Ghana, are of interest in this regard.

Many rural people were reluctant to divulge traditional beliefs or methods of doing things [to this sophisticated young man of their own culture]. They believed that by doing so, they may be labelled as ignorant or out of touch with the "modern world." (p. 57)
Some informants felt that as a member of the society I ought to know the answers to some of the questions put forward to them and were reluctant to respond. This was particularly common with women who believed that certain questions must be answered only by males and as a Bulsa I ought to know. Sometimes informants who strongly believed that I had knowledge on the issues raised in my discussions felt I was trying to tease them into saying things which could in the future be used against them. (p. 60)

Regardless of how unobtrusive one may try to be in a host community, it is impossible to avoid disrupting daily routines and activities, and possibly even established relationships among its members. Even the most polite, discreet, and appropriately attired stranger attracts attention and is a subject of comment and speculation, and may also experience a nearly total loss of personal privacy. Whether working alone, or with a team, it may be necessary and/or desirable to obtain housing in the host community; again, selection of living accommodation can be problematical and potentially disruptive, particularly if the community is factionalized, and the fieldworker renting from or living and eating with one household runs the risk of seeming to take sides.[3] Residence always has implications for research. For example, a family may assign their guest a fictive kinship status ("daughter" or perhaps "distant cousin"); this may have ramifications for relationships with their real kin, and for obligations to the adopting family (Briggs 1986). Reciprocity to host households is in fact as important and thorny an issue as compensation to other members of the community. One must consider one's impact on the household economy; in a society in which generosity is highly valued, the care and feeding of a resident fieldworker may deprive family members of such valued resources as water or hens' eggs. A formal arrangement involving compensation or reciprocity may be desirable, even though notions of what is appropriate vary widely. The generous are usually appreciated, spendthrifts as often despised.

Sampling

Many publications address the matters of entrée into ethnographic field settings, establishing rapport with potential informants/respondents/hosts, developing data recording tools, and designing sampling strategies (see the texts referred to earlier in this chapter, and Cohen *et al.* 1970; Honigmann 1970; Johnson 1978). Mike Deal (1994: x) provides a useful list of sampling strata suggested in the recent ethnoarchaeological literature (Table 3.2). Once an appropriate field locality has been selected, and the scope of the project determined, the sample of objects, structures, activities, and people targeted will depend in large part on their availability and the questions asked. Sampling is always an issue. For example, the rich information obtained by participant observation may well be based on work with only a few informants, and both the fieldworker and readers of his or her work should be aware of the possibility that a non-representative set of informants may bias both observations and reports. A sample greater than one is always desirable, a sample coterminous with the total population always an impossibility. Even in small- to medium-scale communities, it is rarely feasible to make observations in all households or with representatives of all a community's constituencies. A range of ages and genders should be sampled, varying information obtained from different age groups often constituting evidence of ongoing change. In a heterogeneous population, it is desirable that each component be represented. While the very heterogeneity of members of the sample will likely produce diverse information,

---

[3] In some field settings, it may be both desirable and possible to live apart from and commute to one's study community. A "commuting relationship," however, removes the fieldworker from the study locality for periods during which many interesting and relevant events can occur, and about which she or he may only learn second hand, if at all.

Table 3.2 *Sampling strata suggested in the recent ethnoarchaeological literature (from Deal 1994: x, Table 2)*

Village level strata
   Village units (pastures, neighborhoods)
   Secular/religious units (church, cemetery)
   Socioeconomic units (clans, guilds)
   Community storage and disposal units
Household level strata
   Household units (compounds, communal buildings)
   Organizational units (house/patio, garden plots)
   Construction units (house/patio, bins, pens)
   Social units (male/female, ethnicity)
   Activity units (domestic, ritual, craft)
   Storage and disposal units
Material culture strata
   General classification (native versus archaeological taxonomies)
   Spatial/temporal interrelationships
   Statistical interrelationships
Artifact level strata
   Technological classification (sourcing, manufacture, performance)
   Functional classification (morphology and formation traces: use-wear, damage, residues)
   Symbolic classification (structural rules: e.g., patterns of similarities and differences)
Ecofact level strata
   Morphology (species determination, age/sex in animals)
   Behavior (husbandry, processing, modification)
   Preservation (charring, predations)

a degree of standardization in questioning should elucidate differences between individuals, and between the categories and groups they represent.

With archaeological questions in mind, ethnoarchaeologists are likely to be tempted to ignore modern or modernizing practices. Hodder, for example, chose remoter areas for his Baringo work.

Every attempt was made to avoid localities with a non-traditional aspect such as the irrigation scheme near Marigat, and the small factory concerned with fish processing near Kapi-ya-Samaki. Compounds containing young men and women who had been to school and were wearing European dress were not studied. (1977a: 129 fn.)

Whether he was well advised to omit such localities and compounds is debatable, but he deserves credit for telling us what he did. Refusal to admit a modernizing section of the population as part of the sample may be taken to imply that the ethnoarchaeologist is attempting to reconstruct a pristine, pre-contact, condition that, as suggested in chapter 2, is in fact illusory. Moreover, by ignoring evidence of ongoing change, the ethnoarchaeologist virtually condemns her- or himself to a synchronic approach at variance with the aims of archaeology.

Lastly, we would note that too often authors provide incomplete or obfuscating information on the sample studied. We should be more careful and consistent, editors more vigilant – and readers not only critical but also compassionate, recalling that sometimes even the best-laid plans run astray, sometimes for reasons beyond one's control.

Informants' responses

Informants' responses can be problematical for a variety of reasons, some idiosyncratic and others patterned. Two potential challenges to the fieldworker are rarely mentioned: informants' providing misinformation, and the use of normative assertions. Some informants purposely mislead and the ethnoarchaeologist will certainly at some point be offered misinformation. This can consist of a straightforward lie, deliberate omission of a fact or facts considered "sensitive," or misleading information (such as the length of travel time to an important destination). There may be a taboo on specifying the number of one's children or of livestock owned. Informants sometimes make assumptions about what visitors might or might not like to hear, tailoring their responses accordingly. A straightforward lie will almost inevitably reveal itself by introducing an inconsistency into the database which can be detected and, anonymity always being preserved, checked with other informants. Misinformation is mainly a problem in the case of very brief studies; in longer ones it may be regarded as evidence in itself, a clue to understandings to be gained. A far more serious source of error is misapprehension of native concepts – for example, work, kin, time, food – which can easily lead, especially early in fieldwork, to interlocutors at cross-purposes and visitors' out-and-out misreading of the facts.

Normative statements made by anthropologists, such as "Hindus cremate their dead," pose a related problem for their readers or interlocutors. Is the anthropologist (or his or her translator or assistant) making the claim of a putative fact, or is she or he paraphrasing normative statements made by native informants? This distinction is far too rarely made. In this example, while it is true that many Hindus do in fact assert that cremation is widely (or even universally) practiced, the claim masks the fact that Hindu mortuary treatment varies within and between castes. Some members of some Hindu castes preferring cremation are instead buried, and in some castes routinely practicing adult cremation, some juveniles are buried. The normative claim about cremation is not a deceit, but a statement describing the "ideal" and most common treatment of the dead. In another example, in which the informants are neither fieldworkers nor members of the study community, members of non-potter castes in north India often claim that potters never work during the monsoon seasons.

Fieldwork with potters demonstrates that many potters do indeed work during the rains, though their routines differ somewhat from those followed in dry months. These examples point up the need for "ground truth" to substantiate descriptive generalizations with field observations, as well as the desirability of monitoring the system or community of interest during more than one season of the year.

Special techniques, practices, and methods

Some archaeological skills, the planning of sites or the classification of ceramics for example, are directly transferable to ethnoarchaeology. Several researchers (e.g., McIntosh 1977; Hayden 1979b; Vidale *et al.* 1993) have conducted "post-mortem" excavations of sites of known history, or which, as in the case of Janes's (1989) excavation of a Dene tipi, the ethnoarchaeologist had actually observed in use. Ethnoarchaeologists also conduct experiments in the field (e.g., White *et al.* 1977). However, most methods are ethnographic. Schiffer's (1978: 234) outrageous assertion that "there is no reason to believe that techniques ethnographers find useful are in any way appropriate for obtaining ethnographic data to answer archaeological questions" has been disproved by two decades of productive fieldwork, but he usefully draws our attention to alternative techniques, practices, and methods. These include Longacre's (1985) innovation of tagging Kalinga pots in order to study their uselives, in which connection Mark Neupert and Longacre's (1994) controlled study of informant accuracy in pottery uselife studies should also be mentioned. Schiffer comments favorably on a nonreactive scan sampling technique, later used by Kirsten Hawkes, O'Connell and colleagues (Hawkes *et al.* 1987; O'Connell *et al.* 1991: 69) among the Hadza, of acquiring data on activities and use of space by observers who walk specified routes at selected intervals noting down what people are doing. Hawkes *et al.* (1991: 244) also employ a "focal person follow" technique in which a researcher accompanies a hunter throughout the day (Fig. 3.4). The genealogical method so well known in anthropology from the time of W. H. R. Rivers has been innovatively applied by Kathleen Ryan and her colleagues to Maasai cattle (Fig. 3.5) in a study of herd management techniques that has implications for the interpretation of faunal death assemblages in archaeology (Ryan *et al.* 1999).

While apprenticing oneself to a specialist is not unknown in ethnography, it is rare and sometimes exotic (e.g., Stoller and Olkes 1987). Ethnoarchaeologists have on occasion more or less formally apprenticed themselves to artisans, as did Ian Robertson (1992) to a member of a guild of Wandala smiths among whom he worked in 1986 (Fig. 3.6). Valentine Roux (1989) on the other hand, in collaboration with Daniela Corbetta, has studied apprentice potters in India using the techniques of cognitive psychology (see chapter 11 and also Wallaert [1998a, 1998b]). Dean Arnold (1971) used ethnoscientific techniques to elicit

Fig. 3.4 James O'Connell, preparing to leave camp for a "focal person follow" of Magandula, a Hadza hunter, northern Tanzania, May 1986.

the ethnomineralogy of Yucatan potters. In order to better understand crafts, ethnoarchaeologists frequently commission artisans to work for them, and, where crafts are obsolescent or have fallen out of use, to engage in reenactments or reconstructions. The ethnoarchaeological study of iron smelting has been carried out entirely by the latter methods (see chapter 11).

Borgstedt's (1927) early film of iron smelting by Dime smiths in southwest Ethiopia was perhaps the first to demonstrate how moving pictures can contribute to the study of complex techniques. Films and videos expressly made for ethnoarchaeological purposes include, to choose three from different classes of material culture, Saltman, Goucher, and Herbert's (1986) *The blooms of Banjeli* on iron smelting in Togo, ND's (1990) *Vessels of the spirits: pots and people in northern Cameroon*, and Thery, Pétrequin, and Pétrequin's (1990) *Langda*, a study of the manufacture and use of flaked and ground adzes in New

Fig. 3.5 Maasai elders with Kathleen Ryan and co-author and Maasai interpreter Paul Nkuo Kunoni in Isinya, Kajiado District, Kenya, 1991. The cow, of the Noomaroro line, is a descendant of the original matriarch given to her informant (*right*) by his father when the informant was a small child.

Fig. 3.6 Ian Robertson of the Mandara Archaeological Project apprentices in a Wandala forge, Manaouatchi, northern Cameroon, 1986.

Guinea. Videography has the advantage that, at least in theory, it can be immediately played back to the artisan and thus used as the basis for a detailed
inquiry into her or his actions. In 1989 ND and Judy Sterner used video as the
basis for highly productive interviews with a master smelter and a potter in
Mokolo, northern Cameroon, but the intended series was aborted when the
television set failed.

For purposes of analysis ethnoarchaeologists have borrowed or developed
methods from a variety of disciplines including ethnobotany (e.g., Reddy 1999),
tribology or usewear studies (e.g., Kobayashi 1994), and metallurgy (e.g., Killick
1991). A critical survey of ethnoarchaeological methods is overdue and would
no doubt reveal innovations in many more areas.

Recording practices

Imaging and recording techniques are evolving so rapidly that we see no useful
purpose in discussing equipment. Few texts consider in any detail the diverse
ways in which ethnographers record the information they acquire and the processes by which observations are transformed into assertions of fact on a
printed page. Sanjek (1990) is the prime reference on this essential topic; see
also Bernard (1994: 180–207).

Ethnoarchaeologists differ in their recording practices, and so they should. By
way of example, when working in Sukur, a Nigerian village accessible only on
foot some 8 kilometers from and 500 meters above the end of the motorable
track, ND refused to take a computer into the field in part for technical reasons,
but in part also because (as a compulsive editor) he feared he would tinker with
his records, revising files and thus risking obscuring the evidence of his strug-
gles to gain understanding and of differences between informants' accounts
which, when analyzed, are some of the richest sources of information. The
many versions of the Sukur list of chiefs reveal systematic political biases. At
any one time ND maintains:

> A pocket-sized field notebook, into which in greatly abbreviated form
> – jottings, names and numbers, lists, and the like – goes every-
> thing that will, that evening or certainly no later than the next
> day, be fully reported in the following:
> a large notebook in which fieldnotes are written up, provisional inter-
> pretations made, syntheses attempted, and addresses and other
> important information copied; this may also contain documen-
> tation of ethnographic and any other samples collected,
> a large notebook devoted to language which includes wordlists,
> phrases, songs, prayers, and the like, including names of places,
> a folder containing plans, maps, sketches, tables, and genealogical
> charts,
> a wall calendar, very useful for planning and later an easily accessible
> record of activities,
> a notebook containing

> a catalogue of photographs taken by roll and frame number, date and subject matter,
> a similar catalogue of groups of video shots,
> a similar catalogue of the contents of audio cassettes,
> an account book, and
> a book of receipts.

He does not keep a daily journal, though his colleagues CK and Judy Sterner do, and these frequently prove invaluable, providing background information on what people are doing from day to day, and specifics on who went where and did what when. In the past he has used duplicate notebooks, and mailed the carbon copies to himself, but this messy solution is now obsolete because of the wide availability of copying machines.[4] But do make at least two copies of your fieldnotes and, before starting the long journey home, leave one behind in a place of security. Security requires thought.

In the foregoing sections we have no more than touched on a range of topics; it bears repeating that ethnoarchaeological fieldwork is not merely the continuation of archaeology by other means, but that it requires an interest in and empathy for living others, and an additional set of skills, that set it apart. If that is fully realized, the battle is half won, and the rest can be gained from listening to colleagues and by careful and critical reading.

Professional ethics and the ethnoarchaeologist

Archaeologists are often primarily if not exclusively concerned with recovering, recording, and preserving ancient remains. They deal with a host of ethical challenges, but until recently many have tended to ignore the living peoples among and often with whom their work is carried out. Increasingly, however, the focus on recovery, protection, and management of heritage resources has sharpened, and with it has grown a concern with the role of such resources in native belief systems. Discussion and debate about cultural and intellectual properties are ever more common and intense, and the subject of repatriation, in particular, is now often on the programs of professional meetings.

Archaeologists, ethnographers, and ethnoarchaeologists alike must be alert to an array of ethically challenging matters. These include avoidance of plagiarism and conflict of interest; eschewing deception; defense of informant confidentiality; maintenance, where appropriate or requested, of informants',

---

[4] It is essential to have good light for writing up one's fieldnotes. Pressure lamps are one solution; generators are expensive, polluting, and noisy. In Nigeria ND used a solar panel that fits in a suitcase to provide, via a 12 volt car battery, enough power to run two 40 watt fluorescent lights (special 12 volt ballasts required) and charge flashlight and videocamera batteries. Gerhard Müller-Kosack subsequently used the same equipment to run a laptop computer.

communities', and sites' anonymity; adherence to established professional codes of ethics;[5] avoidance of exploitative relations, sexual or other, with informants; and documentation of purported statements of fact.

Ethnoarchaeology is not an evil enterprise. Fieldwork is carried out by well-meaning scholars in situations that most of its practitioners regard as unusual interludes, on the whole pleasurable, perhaps exotic, but basically normal given their career choice. Many Westerners paradoxically are not, though they should be, aware that it is their privileged position *vis-à-vis* most of the rest of the world that constitutes, generally speaking, the most important ethical problem that faces them as individuals and as representatives of a discipline and academic tradition that purports to serve humankind (see Leone and Potter 1992 for a succinct exposition of relevant critical theory). While one is far too often exposed to suffering and death, most ethnoarchaeologists will never be faced with extreme circumstances that call for extraordinary conduct. In what follows, while not ignoring exceptional circumstances, we emphasize the importance of ethics in everyday interaction in the field and at home.

Hosts

Ethnoarchaeologists have particular professional relationships with three rather different groups of people, and responsibilities to them may sometimes be in conflict. The first group consists of our informants and host societies. We must be mindful of their needs and wishes regarding such ordinary matters as scheduling of interviews and activities, and of their reluctance to share with us or allow us to disseminate information which is personally or culturally sensitive. Also important are matters of cultural relativism: how are we to behave in the face of practices like genital mutilation, infanticide, or child labor?

Permission to carry out fieldwork must be obtained not only from the host community,[6] but at other levels as well; in many places, national ministries or bureaus issue a formal permit (which may also be needed to obtain a visa), and representatives of state, district, towns, or tribal land where fieldwork is done may also grant formal permission. In some places, government or indigenous representatives accompany the fieldworker, who may also be expected to have a formal affiliation with an academic or other public institution in the host

---

[5] Even fieldnotes can if necessary use pseudonyms or code numbers for houses and/or informants. The American Anthropological Association, the Society for American Archaeology, and other such bodies publish codes of ethics.

[6] A number of North American Indian Tribes and First Nations, and Australian Aborigines, and no doubt others elsewhere, require anthropologists to obtain permits before conducting research on their lands. These often make specifications that may conflict with common academic notions regarding the conduct of research and intellectual property rights in information obtained and research products (see Greaves 1994; Brown 1998). Accommodations have to be made, and while in some cases conditions set may be unacceptable, in general we believe that such developments are to be viewed as opportunities rather than as impositions.

country to which periodic progress reports must be sent and at which lectures are given and collaborative relationships developed. A requirement to deposit fieldnotes with agencies of the host government presents a potential ethical dilemma regarding anonymity and other issues. Sending publications is usually less problematical since these are in a sense censored documents, but raises the related question of to whom they should be sent. While nothing should be published that can reasonably be expected to harm the host community or its members, this does not relieve the scholar of the responsibility to keep the host community, through its representatives, up to date on the progress of research, nor does it excuse a wishy-washy refusal to deal with difficult topics that are nonetheless academically significant.

Anonymity is an ethically complex issue that, more and more, is negotiated between the researcher, ethics committees, and peoples and persons studied. When working in, or subsequently writing about, areas subject or potentially subject to political turmoil, ethnoarchaeologists may be well advised, as CK in Kurdistan (Kramer 1982a) and Dorothy Hosler (1996) in the northern Andes, to disguise the location of research. But in most situations the community and its artisans take pride in their history and their achievements, and wish to be named. They may gain political and economic benefit from the presence and writings of their ethnoarchaeological guests. Ethnoarchaeology may well involve the recording of oral traditions. In such situations the names and affiliations of the persons who supplied the information establish the authority of the accounts. Having obtained the verbal agreement of his informants,[7] Scott MacEachern requested the permission of a University of Calgary ethics committee, which took advice from several sources, to publish such data in his dissertation (1990) on processes of montagnard ethnogenesis in the northern Mandara mountains of Cameroon. There being no reason to envisage that publication could harm the informants in any way, permission was granted. Meanwhile strict anonymity should be retained in describing the ethnographic background, for example in reporting disputes the resolutions of which so often serve to clarify problematic issues.

Some of the thornier problems raised by relationships with host communities may be subsumed under the term "expert witness." Both archaeologists and ethnographers sometimes serve as expert witnesses in litigation involving indigenous peoples with whose customs they are familiar. One recent example is the acrimonious dispute over Hopi and Navajo tribal lands; both tribes claim long histories in the southwestern United States, both claim rights to particular tracts of land, and both brought expert witnesses to court to provide documentation and other support for their claims. In such cases, the anthropologist may have confidential – though not legally privileged – information, whether

---

[7] Verbal agreement because his informants were illiterate and, not unrealistically given their experiences with colonial and national authorities, regarded the signing/marking of documents as a risky business.

personal or sacred; she or he may have to walk a fine line between providing information and betraying confidences by revealing, for example, the names and locations of sacred places, or materials used secretly in ritual or political activities. As an anthropologist working with living people, the ethnoarchaeologist faces the same dilemmas. In extreme cases the only ethical resorts may be to stop taking or to destroy notes, maps, and photographs to preclude their confiscation or theft, to postpone publication, or not to publish. In taking such a radical step, the fieldworker can be left without some of the very documentation that supports the claims made by those with or for whom she or he is working. Fortunately, ethnoarchaeology deals with less immediately or obviously sensitive matters than, say, political anthropology, and such cases are, if not unheard of, at least extremely rare.

In our view the value of ethnoarchaeological, as other anthropological, research, not so much for the discipline as for the people one is studying and their descendants, often outweighs any potential benefits of direct political action by the researcher. Documentation of a society and culture at a certain stage in its history will retain, indefinitely, evidential value. But there are times when, always considering the risks to which any such action might expose the people that he or she is concerned to assist, the researcher is no longer able to hide behind such beliefs, and has to stand up and be counted. Anthropologists have been active in advocating the rights of the indigenous peoples of, for example, Amazonia and Kurdistan, both of which have long been under intense pressure from powerful economic and political interest groups. Massacres and forced relocations characterize the twentieth-century history of these and many other indigenous peoples, and anthropologists have in some cases joined forces with human rights groups to urge their own governments to consider such human rights abuses when reformulating foreign policy. The American Anthropological Association often debates and votes on resolutions pertaining to perils threatening native peoples, though for various reasons information about such profession-wide decisions is not as accessible to non-members as are other sources.[8]

Lastly we should note that obligation to the host community does not cease when the researcher leaves the field, nor when the research is published. Keeping up communications is in fact difficult once one is reinserted into a quite different world with its own multifarious demands. (Infinitely worse is when political events render *any* form of communication potentially dangerous for one's informants.) After long-term or intensive studies, contact is likely to be maintained, usually to the mutual advantage of the researcher and the community and involving various forms of reciprocity, throughout the former's academic career – and sometimes well into retirement, even to the next generation.

---

[8] *Cultural Survival Quarterly* is a good source of information about indigenous groups' trials and tribulations, and about the roles played by anthropologists.

Sponsors

The second group of people with whom ethnoarchaeologists have relationships that may involve ethical problems are sponsors of research, commonly national or non-profit private funding agencies, but sometimes universities, museums, and private benefactors. While neither ND nor CK has ever received an unto-wards demand, a sponsor might request that informant confidentiality and ano-nymity be breached; they might demand that "raw" data be stored with them at the termination of the project, or rights of first refusal on publication (of, for example, photographs taken with equipment and film purchased with agency funds). In accepting financial support for research, ethnoarchaeologists should not agree to do anything that they cannot publish or disseminate freely, nor to do anything that might compromise informants' confidentiality. Many young scholars are unaware of the unsavory reputation bestowed on anthropology as a result of US government-sponsored espionage carried out in Chile and Thailand, some of it by persons merely posing as anthropologists (Wakin 1992). Even now, social scientists working abroad are sometimes suspected of acting as agents in the service of government or business. This happened to ND in 1968 though the misapprehension was soon corrected. Under such circum-stances, gaining the trust and confidence of potential informants becomes even more challenging. We know of archaeologists and ethnographers who, after their return from fieldwork in potentially volatile areas, were approached by US federal agents asking them to divulge information about members of polit-ical factions, to identify leaders of such groups, and to describe their activities. When such requests are couched in terms of national security interests, the fieldworker committed to maintain informant anonymity faces a personal crisis of conscience and a professional ethical dilemma.

Colleagues and students

The third group of people with whom ethnoarchaeologists (as well as archaeol-ogists and ethnographers) regularly interact comprises colleagues and students. Several ethical problems can arise in dealing with both constituencies. Much research is predicated on obtaining financial support from funding agencies, which base their decisions, in part, on a peer review process that involves (anonymous) external scholars evaluating and ranking a pool of formal research proposals (whose authors' and associates' identities are usually known). Reviewers are in the unique position of having access to unpublished ideas and data, and when confronted with such opportunities must at all costs avoid pla-giarizing or satisfying personal grudges. Most funding agencies specify circum-stances constituting potential conflicts of interest, and ask that reviewers remove themselves from the process if they consider themselves in potential conflict.[9] Fortunately, in our experience a spirit of collegiality and cooperation reigns! Other areas in which ethical problems can arise in relationships with colleagues and students involve the use and dissemination of data. Research entails the acquisition and sharing of knowledge; when that knowledge has been obtained from other researchers, it is necessary to acknowledge their work and their generosity in sharing their findings. (If it is unpublished, one needs their permission to refer to such work.) If such shared data appear problematical, one can be unexpectedly thrust into the role of "whistle-blower" or "gatekeeper"; how and to whom should one entrust the perception that the research has produced questionable or patently false information?

While student members of ethnoarchaeology teams will likely be expected to conduct their research more or less independently, certainly less closely supervised than archaeological colleagues, they should be able to count on the logistic, moral, and legal support of the project director, most especially in difficult circumstances. If a student is responsible for gathering a body of data while acting as a team member (rather than as a casual employee), it is normal that she or he be entitled to publish it (with appropriate acknowledgments) under her or his own name, and that in the case of joint work the form of co-authorship be a matter for discussion, and, hopefully, generosity on the part of the senior researcher. Team research raises a variety of questions – ownership and long-term storage of records, for example, or reimbursement of expenses – that different projects deal with in different ways. It is in student members' interest to sort out such matters with the project director before going into the field. Otherwise the latter's view is likely to prevail – and views can change with time.

We have refrained from discussing specific cases, but note that the *Anthropology Newsletter* published by the American Anthropological Association has a regular column titled "Ethical dilemmas," and we encourage readers both to consider those dilemmas, and to imagine and discuss with others hypothetical situations or conflicts facing ethnoarchaeologists in the field or at home. We cannot emphasize enough that ethnoarchaeology is not merely archaeology with live informants. The human beings with whom we live and interact, and whose words and actions we hope will help us make more sense of complexities in the archaeological record, must be treated with respect and tact, and their persons and communities protected from any harm that association with fieldworkers might bring. Ethnoarchaeologists face the same ethical dilemmas and challenges that confront ethnographers, and it would be fatuous to claim immunity because one is really "just an archaeologist."

---

[9] Examples of relationships involving conflict of interest include co-author, dissertation advisor or advisee, spouse or relative, close personal friend, consultant on one's own research project, competitor for the same research permit, and in some cases institutional colleagues. ND insists on being identified when evaluating colleagues' projects and post-doctoral applications, and encourages others to do the same.

Further reading

The texts on qualitative and quantitative methods cited above render it unnecessary to suggest further reading in those areas. Vicarious experience of fieldwork and insights into writing it up can be gained from such works as Elenore Bowen's (Laura Bohannan) (1954) pioneering *Return to laughter*, Stocking's (1983) *Observers observed*, Peggy Golde's (1986) collection of accounts by *Women in the field*, and, most recently, James Skibo's (1999) account of his initiation into ethnoarchaeological fieldwork among the Kalinga. A debate between Roy D'Andrade (1995) and Nancy Scheper-Hughes (1995), followed by comments and responses, takes up the issues of anthropological advocacy and moral engagement. Ethical issues, anthropological and archaeological, are the subject of several collections including: *Conflict in the archaeology of living traditions* (Layton 1989), *Ethics in American archaeology* (Lynott and Wylie 1995), and *Plundering Africa's past* (Schmidt and McIntosh 1996).

CHAPTER 4

HUMAN RESIDUES: ENTERING THE ARCHAEOLOGICAL CONTEXT

If . . . by observing the adaptive behavior of any living society, we can derive predictions about that society's discards, we are doing living archaeology.

(Richard Gould 1980: 112)

Household no. 1 collected their domestic refuse, including tin cans, in a large duffel bag which was later transported by canoe to a lake about 19 km from the residential camp.

(Robert Janes 1983: 32).

We start the chapter by introducing relevant concepts and ideas of middle range theory, especially those concerned with processes relating to the transfer of materials from the systemic to the archaeological context (S–A processes). We then survey their application to deposits and sites and consider the effects of processes such as curation on the archaeological record. A processual and a postprocessual case study relating to residues are presented and critiqued, and the chapter concludes with a consideration of the ethnoarchaeology of abandonment.

Middle range theory from S to A

Some regard "the reconstruction of prehistoric lifeways in the form of prehistoric ethnographies to be an appropriate goal for archaeology," while others consider rather "that we should be seeking to understand cultural systems, in terms of organizational properties," as Binford (1981b: 197) argued in his "Pompeii premise" paper. Many take an intermediate view:

To analyze archaeological units without referring back to where they came from and to what they represent is to divest such units of most meaning. It leaves archaeologists free to make assumptions pertaining to meaning and equivalency of such units without ever having to demonstrate the accuracy of those assumptions. It is only by following a material system through its several transformation phases (from Pompeii-type contexts to utter destruction) that archaeologists will be able to clearly understand what their units mean and how comparable they are. (Hayden and Cannon 1983: 118)[1]

---

[1] This appears to have become Binford's view also, although in 1981 he was arguing for his second alternative. See for example the chapter on "People and their lifespace" in *In pursuit of the past* (Binford 1983a: 144–92) and his interpretation of Neanderthal life at Combe Grenal reported by Fischman (1992) in *Discover* magazine.

Most would agree that the archaeological context is not merely a filtered version but a transformation – if not necessarily a distortion – of the behavioral systemic context. Michael Schiffer (1976, 1987) is one of the main theoreticians of the processes involved, the inventor of the cultural and natural transform terminology to which reference was made in chapter 2. Let us reemphasize that Schiffer conceived of these transforms not as formation processes but as law-like regularities regarding formation processes that could be applied to relate the statics of the archaeological record to the dynamics of the systemic context. As such they constitute elements of what Binford (e.g., 1977: 1–10; 1981a: 21–30) calls "middle range theory," but which is better termed formation theory (Shott 1998: 311).[2] Richard Gould (1978b: 815) proclaimed that, "Since discard behavior and residue formation, like language, are universal human characteristics, their patterning can be studied in a manner akin to grammar in languages." Unfortunately the linguistic analogy does not hold. There are no discard phonemes or morphemes that are strung together according to residue syntax, and in any case Gould's analogy does not take account of semantics, that part of linguistics concerned with the generation of meaning. As Edward Sapir (1949 [1929]: 162) said many years ago, "No two languages are ever sufficiently similar to be considered as representing the same social reality." Nevertheless we may reasonably expect that within any one society discard behavior and residue formation exhibit some systemic qualities, and that there are also, besides unique forms, cross-cultural commonalities for ethnoarchaeologists to discover and document.

Many natural and many cultural processes contribute to the formation of an archaeological site. We are here concerned not with natural processes (for a survey of which see Schiffer 1987), including the taphonomic (Gifford 1981), or with non-ethnoarchaeological actualistic or experimental approaches to the cultural (of which Toth and Schick [1986] give several examples relating to humankind's first million years), but only with ethnoarchaeological approaches to a limited subset of the cultural.

At any one time a site is a component of a settlement system and as such is likely to be functionally differentiated from some other contemporary sites. The various activities practiced at a site will result in particular combinations of material remains, a buffalo jump kill site for example typically being characterized by huge quantities of bone but by few and specialized formal artifacts. As John Yellen (1977a) showed in his monograph on the !Kung, the organization of space and activities at a site and the duration of its occupation contribute to the patterning of the archaeological remains that may eventually be recovered. These subjects are discussed in later chapters. Here we are primarily concerned with simpler relationships between the living (systemic) and

---

[2] To distinguish it from middle range theory in the original sense of the sociologist Robert Merton, "a theory of substantive phenomena, of human behavior in its cultural and social context . . . rather than a theory of how to infer structure or behavior" (Shott 1998: 303). Optimal foraging theory is middle range theory in Merton's sense.

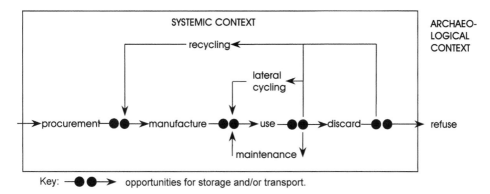

Fig. 4.1 Flow chart for durable elements (redrawn from Schiffer 1976: Fig. 4.1)

archaeological contexts, transformations involved in the formation of deposits that contain archaeological remains, in the discard of artifactual and other materials, and in the generation of refuse. Our focus on naturalist approaches to these topics reflects the great preponderance of processualist studies in the literature, but we also discuss works that show that there are symbolic aspects even to putting out the trash.

Schiffer (1976: 27–41) has again provided us with a useful terminology for describing cultural formation processes, together with flow models for durable and consumable elements. In the case of durable elements (Fig. 4.1), materials are procured, manufactured into artifacts, and used.[3] Use may be followed by:

1 episodes of *maintenance* during which an artifact's form may be progressively modified while its function remains essentially the same, as for example when a stone ax is repeatedly resharpened by flaking,
2 *lateral cycling*, in which the artifact passes from one user to another without modification or change in its use,
3 *secondary use* of the artifact by the same or a different user for a different purpose but without extensive modification of its form, as when a grindstone is incorporated into a wall, and
4 *recycling*, in which an artifact is transformed into a new product before a new and different period of use whether by the same or a different user. Thus for example potsherds may be ground to produce grog for tempering a new generation of pots, or a broken bone point reworked into an awl. The welding and reforging of worn-out iron tools is a form of recycling of a valuable material that probably accounts for the rarity of all but tiny rusty fragments in most African Iron Age archaeological assemblages.

It should be noted that in ordinary parlance "recycling" is often used to refer to all but the first of these processes.

---

[3] Consumable elements are prepared and consumed rather than manufactured and used, but otherwise the flow model as presented by Schiffer (1976: Fig. 4.2) is very similar.

Whatever the sequence through which an object may pass, and this may be short and aborted or long and complete, eventually it will become refuse – at which time it passes from the systemic into the archaeological context, though not necessarily for ever. Michael Shott (1989: 17–19) has distinguished six discard processes: breakage in production, abandonment during or after production, loss or breakage in use, abandonment in use, depletion during cycles of reuse and maintenance, and (inappropriately) recycling. Loss constitutes an unintentional form of discard, while caching (Binford 1979) and disposal of the dead, the latter to be discussed in chapter 13, constitute special forms each with its own modalities.[4] Schiffer (1976: 30) also provides us with a terminology for refuse; if material "is discarded at its location of use, it forms *primary refuse*, and if away from its location of use, *secondary refuse*." There are numerous categories and stages of secondary refuse, from the trash collected and temporarily housed in your kitchen to New York City's Fresh Kills landfill site, the world's largest man-made monument. As Binford (1983a: 190) points out, what really matters is not the formal distinction of categories but "understanding the organizational relationships among items from the site [which] depends on teasing out structural patterns in the observed data . . ." A third Schiffer (1976: 33) category, *de facto refuse*, is defined as consisting "of the tools, facilities, and other cultural materials that, although still usable, are abandoned with an activity area."

Thoughtful observation of one's own culture and behavior leads to the identification of cultural formation processes. Useful if often simple c-transforms can be generated, for example relating probability of loss to the size and salience of discarded items. Valuable and noticeable items like coins are less likely to be discarded or permanently lost than cigarette butts, which since they are small and valueless only too often end up on floors as primary refuse rather than being disposed of as secondary refuse in the containers provided. Very large objects, for example the concrete tank traps constructed on British beaches to slow down a German landing during the Second World War, are more likely to end up as de facto refuse than smaller items less localized in their utility, for example pistols of the same era. Other, more complex, c-transforms have been proposed, for example "that the larger the population of an activity area, and the greater the intensity of occupation, the larger the ratio of secondary to primary refuse produced" (Schiffer 1976: 31).

It would seem reasonable to expect that, by the description of cultural formation processes unknown in our own cultures and by the formulation of

---

[4] Caching implies that objects buried or otherwise put aside are intended for further use, as presumably were European Bronze Age hoards of damaged axes and other items that were buried but never reclaimed by their owners. Another special category of discard is represented by intentional disposal of often valuable items, for example the burial of a composite jade jaguar mask at La Venta or offerings of gold plates tossed into the *cenote* at Chichen Itza. Such items can scarcely be described as refuse.

c-transforms, ethnoarchaeologists would have contributed a great deal to the understanding of discard and refuse. In fact, ethnoarchaeologists have generally concentrated much more on procurement, manufacture, and use, the earlier phases of the Figure 4.1 flow chart, than on discard and entry into the archaeological record. Nor is it necessary that observations of cultural formation processes always be formally expressed as laws, whether universal or probabilistic, of the form, "Under specified conditions Z, if A then B in x per cent of cases." (If the law is universal then x equals 100, if probabilistic then a lesser figure.) But implicit statements of this general form underlie any and all attempts to use ethnoarchaeologically observed formation processes as models to be applied to or tested against some part of the archaeological record. A hypothesis is, after all, a candidate law – although boundary conditions may greatly limit its applicability.

Deposits and sites

Ethnoarchaeological contributions to understanding cultural formation processes generally relate to the artifactual contents of deposits and not to the deposits themselves, the analysis of which, even if they are in the process of becoming, is more properly the task of geoarchaeologists and of experimental archaeology. The latter's contributions, ranging from the reconstruction and destruction of houses, to experimental earthworks, and the transport and erection of megaliths (Coles 1973: 55–97), includes Freide and Steel's (1980) experimental burning of Nguni huts in South Africa.

A study by Anne-Marie and Pierre Pétrequin (1984) of the habitat of Toffinu villages built on and around Lake Nokoué in Bénin, West Africa, spans the uncertain boundary between c- and n-transforms. It was undertaken with the aim of improving and controlling interpretations of housing in prehistoric European alpine and other lacustrine habitats. Variations in architecture and community plans are set in their geographic, cultural, sociopolitical, and economic contexts, and close attention is paid to differential processes of "fossilization" of structures and features in relationship to their dry-land, liable to flooding, emerging at low water, and fully aquatic situations. As might be expected given the marked cultural contrasts between the ethnographic source and the archaeological subject, this study's major contribution is to the understanding of the archaeological expressions of human behaviors tightly constrained by their unusual lacustrine environment. Brian Dillon (1984) has provided comparable information on the building of islands for settlement by the Cuna of Panama.

Roderick McIntosh (1974) made careful observations of mud and wattle-and-daub wall decay in a West African village in a study explicitly designed to assist in the excavation and interpretation of features at a nearby site. Although he is able to suggest a number of subtle indicators of walling – for example "anomalous concentrations of the small lateritic concretions that form on the surface of heavily weathered walls" – these did not, perhaps on account of prevailing soil conditions, prove particularly useful in site excavations nearby (pp. 166–167). Another reason may be practices common in West Africa: of repuddling old wall materials to build new structures, and of farming abandoned house sites to take advantage of their exceptional fertility, in the course of which walls are incorporated into the soil and other architectural features either broken up or obliterated (David 1971: 119). McIntosh (1977) was later to conduct sophisticated experimental excavations of mud structures of known history, thus anticipating Pawel Gorecki's (1985a) demonstration of the value of "post-mortem" archaeological inquiry to complement ethnoarchaeological work.

Gorecki, working in association with Jack Golson's (1982) archaeological research on early agriculture in the highlands of Papua New Guinea, mapped a 6 square kilometer area of Kuk settlement in the course of a study of domestic structures and farming practices. His methods included mapping, planning, observation, and interviews, supplemented by use of documentary evidence and air photographs. He then excavated a number of sites abandoned less than five, five to fifteen, and over fifteen years previously. He identifies a variety of successive disturbance and disappearance processes that are active in the first fifteen years after abandonment (Table 4.1), after which a site becomes more or less stabilized, there being, Gorecki suggests, little difference between a site abandoned 15, 400 or even 10,000 years ago (p. 187).

But will that site survive? Gorecki draws attention to the massive impact of these dry-land subsistence gardeners on the ground surface:

On the basis of the ethnographic observations . . . I think the whole 6 square kilometres was the subject of severe disturbance over the last 20 years of occupation. With a 3.4 square kilometres area . . . where more detailed observations were carried out, gardening activities alone have resulted in the moving of at least 121,500 cubic metres of subsoil (i.e. basal clay), and a minimum of 267,000 cubic metres of top soil was turned over at least once . . . Thousands of features were dug, often new ones destroying old ones. . . . Given the stratigraphic context, one must once again emphasize that all cultural material (organic and inorganic) . . . is found mostly within a disturbed deposit, only 30 cm thick in drylands, which may have been the subject of cultural activity and artefact deposition lasting more than 30,000 years. (p. 187)

As ethnoarchaeologists we should note that Gorecki's observations on the small and large (site and landscape) scales result in quite different and yet complementary and important inferences. Archaeologists should be aware that such situations are far from atypical; the long-term activity of even small, low-density, human populations is likely to impinge on the environment and the human sites within it. Under many circumstances the archaeological sites that do survive may well constitute an unrepresentative sampling of the past cultures from which they derive.

Table 4.1 *Processes intervening after house site abandonment at Kuk, a Kawelka tribal holding in the Wahgu valley, New Guinea highlands (adapted from Gorecki 1985a)*

Short term (1–5 years)
  Immediately after abandonment
    Children's play (a randomizing factor)
    Plundering/scavenging of site by children and adults
    Lateral cycling and recycling of useful materials
  Next few months
    Rooting and wallowing by pigs
    Potential erosion/sealing up of the site
  Up to five years after abandonment
    Progressive disappearance of "driven-in" features such as postholes (but survival
      of features dug-in to basal clay)
    Substantial decay of organic remains

Short to medium term
    Possible building of agricultural earthworks across the site

Medium term (5–15 years after abandonment)
    Vegetation regrowth, damage to dug-in features by roots of woody plants (but not
      by grasses)
    Total loss of driven-in and some smaller dug-in features
    Disappearance of any remaining organics
    Stabilization of inorganic artifactual remains

Cycling, curation, lifespan

A point noted by McIntosh (1974) was that building practices that make use of earth (mud, pisé, daub, adobe, etc.) from the immediate vicinity of the new structure, usually involving the digging of pits, will almost inevitably result in the incorporation of older artifactual materials into the fabric of the new building. This – what Schiffer terms an A–S (archaeological to systemic context) – process has implications for the interpretation of typological sequences and results in the blurring of cultural boundaries between successive phases and cultures represented at the site.

  Several ethnoarchaeologists have explored the implications of various kinds of cycling and curation for the archaeological record. Lee Horne's (1983a) study of recycling (*sensu lato*) in an Iranian village makes the point that objects in contemporary use may in fact have been manufactured over a very long time span. The ground stone tools include "smoothly worn handstones . . . small flattened rubbing stones, large polished ovoids, mortars and pestles" (p. 18) that are no longer made, but which have been retrieved, perhaps generations previously, from archaeological sites in the area that may be a thousand or more years old. For some, like the mortars and pestles, use is or appears to be effectively unchanged; other types, like the querns reused as door sockets, take on new functions that result in significant modifications to their original form (see also Watson 1979a).

Curated artifacts are generally manufactured with a view to future use on several occasions; they are kept, transported from place to place, and if necessary maintained for considerable periods of time. "Expedient" tools, on the other hand, are manufactured as need arises, utilized on the spot, and discarded after use. The extent to which their differential discard affects the nature of the archaeological record has been the subject of considerable debate. In 1973, Lewis Binford (1973, 1976), whose views had been shaped by fieldwork among the Nunamiut Eskimo of Alaska, argued that the contrast between upper and middle paleolithic assemblages could in part be explained by the curation of upper paleolithic toolkits versus the expedient nature of the tools made and used in the middle paleolithic. Curation was deemed to result in there being little correlation between where a tool was used and the place of its eventual deposition. Thus, in Binford's view, the assemblages relating to particular cultural phases of the upper paleolithic of Western Europe are relatively homogeneous compared to those of the Mousterian. Brian Hayden (1976) took up the question, arguing that a polarized view of curated versus expedient toolkits is misleading. Acheulian handaxes of the later lower paleolithic are likely to have been curated and repeatedly resharpened. He also notes that the Nunamiut toolkit includes many industrially manufactured items such as guns that, in contrast to even the most carefully worked stone spearheads, are virtually infinitely curated. Some handmade metal artifacts, for example spears carried by Loikop men and their East African cultural relatives are also curated over long periods (Larick 1985).

Lithics, as Hayden had observed them among the Aborigines of the Australian Western Desert, cycle rapidly from manufacture to discard, curated items such as adzes used on hardwoods in some cases actually having fractionally shorter average uselives (28 minutes of use) than expediently manufactured chopping implements (29 minutes). Hayden concluded that in the case of lithic toolkits curation will have only a very minor effect on inter-assemblage variability: "the major determinant of how many tools are deposited . . . [is] . . . the lifespan of the implement in relation to the length duration of the activity" (Hayden 1976: 54).[5] But this depends in part upon the definition of the concepts in terms of which the argument is phrased. "Lifespan," according to Hayden (p. 59), "is equated with the total time during which the tool was actively being used, and does not include rests, interludes or other periods when the tool was not in use." What then is the "lifespan" of a gun? And how does lifespan relate to curation?

How many lithics might archaeologists expect to be discarded per person per

[5] Binford (1979) was later to show that a considerable range of other factors relating to technological organization affects inter-assemblage variability.

annum? On the basis of direct but intermittent observations, Gould (1980: 133) estimated that almost 19 kg of lithic raw material (excluding quarry waste) were needed per *man* per year by the Western Desert Aborigines that he studied. In the late 1960s they were still making extensive use of stone tools although they had obtained from the Warburton Ranges Mission steel axes, knives, at least one rasp, and bottle glass from which they made other tools. Hayden's (1976: 49) estimate, based largely on informants' statements and relating to the number of retouched stone tools replaced per *person* per year, is rather higher (156 "implements" versus 40, but there are problems of definition). It would seem that in both studies the lithic contributions of women to annual discard were less well controlled than those of men, although they are likely to be smaller (Gould 1980: 132), so this cannot explain Hayden's higher estimate. In any case both computations must underestimate the amount of stone that would have been required in pre-contact times before any metal tools were available. Perhaps this is why no one, so far as we know, has yet attempted to apply appropriate modifications of these ethnographically derived estimates to the interpretation of lithic assemblages elsewhere.

Regarding grinding equipment, perhaps the most important result of attempts at estimating uselives is the realization that, while it may be possible to make estimates in particular instances, variation in raw materials (e.g., vesicular basalt versus granite), the forms of the grinding surfaces and the contact between them, and materials ground (e.g., dry grains of sorghum versus wet maize kernels) preclude any broader generalizations (David 1998).[6]

Differential lifespans and the archaeological record

The effects of differential lifespans of artifacts on the formation of the archaeological record have received considerable attention over the years. Starting with George Foster's (1960b) study in Tzintzuntzan, Mexico, the focus has been largely on utilitarian pottery. Foster suggested that basic strength, function, mode and context of use, and pottery costs all affect life expectancy. ND (1972) calculated that in the Fulbe village of Bé in northern Cameroon pots in current use had median ages varying from 2.7 years in the case of small bowls and cooking pots to 12.5 years for storage jars of 40–60 liters capacity. He went on to point out that the relative frequencies of pot types – or of other tool types – in an archaeological horizon depend upon their frequencies relative to each other in the systemic context, their different lifespans, and the length of the period during which the horizon formed. This seemed to raise (yet another!) serious question about the validity of seriation for the chronological ordering

---

[6] Estimates of uselives can be misleading; Detlef Gronenborn (pers. comm. to ND) now regards as highly questionable the inflated estimates for the uselives of handstones and querns obtained for him by a Kanuri assistant and published by him (1995) as part of research undertaken to assist in interpretation of materials from his excavations in northeast Nigeria.

of assemblages, and about the use of frequency data to reconstruct activity patterns and establish cultural relationships. However, Warren DeBoer (1974), using data from the Conibo Indians of the Upper Ucayali valley in eastern Peru, soon showed that the problem was less acute than ND had supposed. As time goes by the frequencies of vessels in use at time zero become insignificant in proportion to the total number of vessels in use and in the archaeological context, and the relative frequencies of the different pot types become progressively more stable. "In the Conibo case, it is unlikely that any seriation based on the relative popularity of vessel forms would be seriously affected given midden samples occupied longer than 5 yr" (p. 337). Nevertheless, since the relative frequencies of vessels in the archaeological record represent a transformation of the relative frequencies of vessels in use at any one time, simplistic reconstruction of activities based upon such data will indeed be seriously in error. DeBoer (pp. 337–8) therefore devised a formula for converting the limiting (in practice after 100 years) percentage representation of a type in archaeological context to its representation in the systemic context.[7] Longacre (1985) conducted censuses of Kalinga pots in order to calculate minimal uselives and found that, amongst other factors, economic expectations influenced replacement rates. A member of his team, Masakuzu Tani (1994), related pot breakage to household size. Shott (1989) took up the issue from a theoretical perspective, arguing that ceramic uselives are related to elementary properties such as size and weight, whereas in stone tools "use life is related most strongly to manufacturing cost and curation rate, an archaeological measure of which is proposed" (p. 9).

Subsequent cross-cultural analysis by Nelson (1991) of eight case studies from around the world, including his own among the Highland Maya (undertaken as part of Hayden's Coxoh project), reveals wide variation in vessel uselives and frequencies per household, not all of which is he able to explain. However, it would appear that different fieldwork techniques tend to produce different results, with interviews recording shorter uselives than pottery census techniques (Neupert and Longacre 1994), and that factors such as differential stockpiling of vessels may obscure similarities in uselives that are measured in terms of use episodes rather than the total span of time between manufacture and breakage. Anne Mayor (1994), in another cross-cultural study of samples of ceramics from 38 villages in the inland delta of the Niger river in Mali, has taken a quantitative approach to identification of the factors responsible for differential lifespans (Fig. 4.2). She shows that life expectancy varies: (a) by formation technique, pots formed by pounding in a concave mold (press-molding) having shorter life spans than those made by other methods; (b) by exposure of the pots to fire, as when they are used for cooking; and (c) by size, this being a proxy variable for mobility and frequency of manipulation of vessels.

---

[7] DeBoer's constant should be used with caution and in the understanding that, with longer average uselives, it will take longer for the relative frequencies to approximate their limit values.

Fig. 4.2 Alain Gallay and Anne Mayor draw pottery in the Inland Niger Delta village of Kirchamba, occupied by Peul (Fulbe) and Songhai, Mali, 1989.

We have made three important points in the preceding paragraphs: first, we have again shown that the archaeological context is a transformation of the systemic; second, that the factors responsible for such transformations are likely to be many and complex; and third, that cross-cultural comparisons even of data collected by ethnoarchaeologists and limited to a particular domain of material culture are, as Nelson demonstrated, likely to be subject to biases and problems inherent in the acquisition of datasets under different research designs and using different methodologies. This is not to say that comparisons are not desirable and should not be attempted, merely that they should be approached with appropriate circumspection. Mayor's study is based on data gathered by members of the same team over a limited period. Although the results achieved regarding the influence of pot function and size on life expec-

Fig. 4.3 Dimtivey, a casted potter, prepares to decorate a spherical vessel made by beating it out with a ceramic tamper on the wooden concave mold on which it sits, Sirak, near Mokolo, northern Cameroon, 1986. Sirak potters produce work of exceptionally high technical quality.

tancy cannot be regarded as particularly new, they are well established, and the information relating technique of manufacture to lifespan is original, interesting, and provocative. The research question that immediately comes to mind is whether the apparent inferiority of press-molded pots is intrinsic and due to the technique, to the interaction of other factors studied (might they all be small pots used for cooking?), or to socioeconomic or other factors that result in the potters that use this method of forming being less technically competent. In the Mandara mountains of Central Africa where the same technique is very commonly employed, especially by the female members of a caste of potters and smiths, local people and ethnoarchaeologists recognize considerable variation in the abilities of potters of different communities and in the quality of their pots (see David *et al.* 1988) (Fig. 4.3).

Similar conclusions regarding the factors influencing the content of the archaeological record could be derived from any other major class of artifacts and also non-artifactual materials, including faunal remains (see chapter 5).

Natural garbage and discarded meanings

We turn now to consider more directly the nature of the discard process itself. In an account of the archaeologically near-invisible Willow Lake Dene of Canada's North West Territories, Robert Janes (1983: 34) noted:

There is one simple conclusion that can be drawn from the Willow Lake data on refuse disposal. That is, the Willow Lake Dene do not live among their garbage any more than we do. Obvious as this may seem, much of archaeological thought is, or used to be, based upon the tacit assumption that the locations of artifacts (read refuse) in a site correspond to their locations of use. To begin with, much of the material record in the form of refuse simply does not survive the intentional disposal methods of the Willow Lake Dene . . . Excavating only in areas where the artifacts are most abundant may be more stimulating, but one can only do this by ignoring the increasingly contradictory observations emerging from ethnoarchaeology.

So what is the archaeologist to do? Brian Hayden and Aubrey Cannon's (1983) study of refuse disposal in the highlands of Mexico and Guatemala gives a partial answer. It is a classic example of the naturalist or processualist style of ethnoarchaeology and was conducted using the Coxoh project's interview-cum-observation methodology described in chapter 3. The authors emphasize the importance to archaeologists of models regarding the generation of refuse and contexts of abandonment for application to archaeological data, and for "the identification of principles that appear to guide choices and decisions made by people everywhere" (p. 118).

Their sample consists of three "traditional" Maya villages in which most compounds consist of a single main room, sometimes with separate kitchen and storage structure, set in a fenced garden. About 50 households were studied in each settlement, allowing the effects of variation both within and between villages to be analyzed. The data are summarized in the form of a large table (Table 4.2) and village plans provide overall context and information on compound size, and show the locations of some street and neighborhood dumps. A plan of an idealized Maya compound is also included.

Hayden and Cannon find that "effort, value, and hindrance largely determine how refuse will be sorted and where it will be dumped" (p. 119). Thus house sweepings and ashes, like other refuse with little value or hindrance potential, are mainly deposited in the compound garden, though they may be taken to fertilize the household's fields or, if the compound is very small, removed to a neighborhood dump. "Clutter refuse" comprises objects having some value or hindrance potential, broken pots that are potentially recyclable besides worthless items that await final disposal. While fragments of glass are disposed of quickly, sometimes in pits or ravines, many large refuse items undergo several

Table 4.2 Overall percentage frequency distribution of locations used for refuse disposal, by village and refuse type (slightly modified from Hayden and Cannon 1983: Table 1)

Refuse type	N	Compound area (unspecified)	Around house	Near fence or hedge	On sweatbath	Discrete place on house site	Over fence	Street	Dump	Stream or ravine	Old house site	Field	Misc.
Chanal													
Ashes	21	67				5						29	
House sweepings	21	67				5	5					24	
Inorganics	13	23				8		54	8	8			
Pottery	35	9	3	3				51	9	9	3		
Rock	26					4	14	58	12	23	4		
Bone	21	14 + 19*	5					43	5	5		9	
Aguacatenango													
Ashes	7	29	43			29							
House sweepings	10	50	20			10			20				
Inorganics	59	36	3			10	2	3	5	29			3
Pottery	34	15	9			6		18	3	32	9		3
Rock	5	20				20		40		20	15		
Grindstones	1	100											
Glass	12	25		8									
Bone	3	67 + 33*						17		17	17		17
San Mateo													
Ashes	26	50			12			4	12	15		8	
House sweepings	3	67										33	
Inorganics	52	19		4		8		6	10	48			
Pottery	10	40	10			20				30			
Rock	34	9	24	3		15			9	41			
Grindstones	5	40	20					20	20				
Glass	14	7				29		7	20	29			
Bone	18	56*	28*8	21		5 + 5*				5			
Total	430												

* Percentage generally stated to have been removed by dogs.

stages of provisional discard, often at the margins of activity areas, for example along fences and under eaves where they are subject to a variety of attritional processes (weathering, children's play, retrieval for recycling, etc.), or, within the house, in corners and under beds. Hayden and Cannon make the point that because activity areas themselves are generally kept clean, their best archaeological indicators are likely to be micro-debitage and other minuscule inorganic and organic by-products (primary refuse) of the activities performed.

Under normal circumstances, but not in the case of abandonment, most clutter refuse is eventually carted away, though there is considerable variation in the amount allowed to accumulate, and, interestingly, refuse disposal within the compound is not correlated directly with compound size within villages. Moreover, compounds are larger in Chanal than in the other two villages, but their inhabitants are *less* likely to dispose of refuse within them, and this despite regulations against dumping in the streets. The reasons for this are not made clear here, but have to do with the relationship of Chanal to its surrounding area. Elsewhere (Hayden and Cannon 1984a: 6) we learn that the village is set in a humid depression with better soils while the fields around it have to be fallowed for long periods. The villagers are thus maximizing their use of the best land.

While only a sampling of Hayden and Cannon's results, the foregoing paragraphs give a fair indication of what naturalist research comprises, and of its very considerable potential for assisting archaeological interpretation. The data are presented in considerable detail, and statistical tests are used in their analysis. The authors claim (1983: 154) to have determined the factors influencing compound-associated refuse (Fig. 4.4), and to have perceived

a basic, underlying structure involving refuse disposal in the Maya study area. The principles which create this structure are economy of effort, temporary retention of potentially recyclable materials, and hindrance minimization. These principles interact with specific situations and types of refuse to produce the actual disposal behavior responsible for archaeological assemblages.

But perhaps one might ask, if this is true, and if the structure is generalizable, why then could it not have been established in Canada in the houses of Professors Hayden and Cannon? Is it worth taking a team to Mexico and Guatemala merely to put cultural clothes, which are in any case not those of the classic Maya, on a mannequin who lives in all our houses? To such a criticism there are several answers. First, we are often blind to our own cultures; it is easier to detect principles and structures in cultures other than one's own precisely because they are less taken for granted. Second, as archaeologists we do indeed need to learn about others' cultures and not merely about behavior. Although research in our basements and studies might very well reveal similar patterning of clutter refuse, reflection on that and the weekly placing of a trash can at the kerb are insufficient preparation for excavating Tikal or La Madeleine.

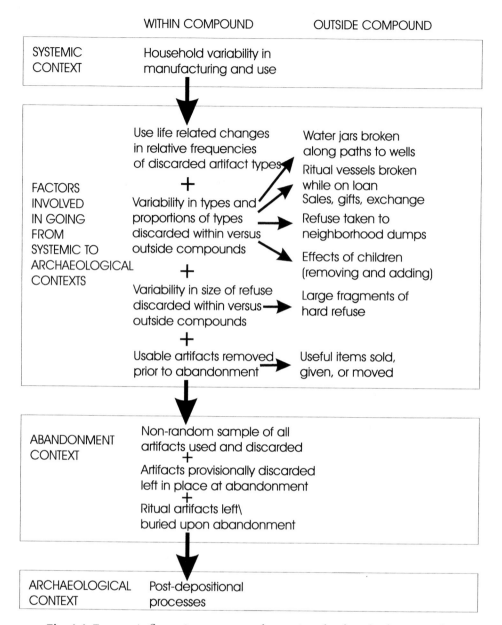

Fig. 4.4 Factors influencing compound-associated refuse (redrawn with minor modifications from Hayden and Cannon 1983).

But one can also contend that Hayden and Cannon's scientism is inadequate both in its own terms and because it fails to take account of what is going on in Maya heads. Table 4.2 purportedly sets out the results of interviews and observations made in about 50 households in each village. But if so why was ash disposal only reported in seven Aguacatenango households, in less than half of those in Chanal, and in only 26 in San Mateo? Why in the statistical sections of the paper are samples of households nearer 30 than 50 per village? How comparable were the interviews conducted in each village? We are told that the questionnaire evolved during the course of the study. Do differences in the data reflect variation in Maya behavior or are they in part the artifacts of differential recording by observers working through interpreters in a language (or languages) that some spoke less than perfectly? Coherent patterning in the data indicates that, although there may have been some problems in the translation of Maya thought into data, the ethnoarchaeologists were indeed recording a large measure of reality. Sometimes they may have made mistakes. Hayden and Cannon comment on the relative rarity of refuse disposal in pits, whereas "Trash-filled pits are common in Maya archaeological sites" (1983: 141), and they suggest that changes in patterns of storage, especially of maize, may be in part responsible. But perhaps here they are misled, for the apparent abundance of pits on archaeological sites may be a function of the inability of archaeologists to locate them precisely in time. In fact for their 150 households Hayden and Cannon record 18 artificially dug pits used for refuse disposal, a not inconsiderable number that, one might argue, could well correspond with the number open at any one time in a similar-sized classic Maya sample.[8]

We raise these questions not to diminish an original and important piece of work, but to make two points. First, well-conducted naturalist research such as this contains the elements that allow its conclusions to be contested and sometimes even contradicted. It is in this sense transparent. Second, it may be relatively shallow. The Coxoh team had little in-depth knowledge of Maya culture, its systems of thought, its cosmological beliefs, and, being of the processual school, were not particularly interested to inquire. Thus we learn, but only in passing, of ritual items buried as offerings, and "attitudinal considerations" are acknowledged as having minor effects on disposal patterns, but the Maya are otherwise portrayed, like Binford's Nunamiut, as rational consumers untroubled by any symbolic connotations of the items that they are recycling or discarding.

This can certainly not be said of the Ilchamus as described in Ian Hodder's (1987a) "The meaning of discard: ash and domestic space . . ." The Ilchamus (the Njemps of Hodder 1982a) are cattle pastoralists who also practice agriculture, and who live in dispersed family compounds south of Lake Baringo in Kenya. Hodder begins by throwing down his antinaturalist gauntlet, stating

---

[8] Given Nacirema (Miner 1956) and Naidanac concern for body ritual, it is somewhat surprising that the reader is not specifically informed whether or not the Maya dig latrine pits.

that there "can be no general theory and no universal method for measuring and interpreting activity residues, except in relation to physical, non-human processes of decay and deposition" (1987a: 424). His approach is thus diametrically opposed to that of Hayden and Cannon. In his view "action cannot logically be separated from culture since 'to act' involves intention and thought which are dependent on background and perception." Behavior is not controlled by cultural norms, nor does it consist merely of responses to the environment; rather it is "creatively and actively adaptive" (p. 425). We agree, although this does not, we think, imply the impossibility of general theory. But Hodder is quite right to insist on the importance of *cultural* context: "I need to discuss women and their roles in society because it is largely women who produce and discard ash. I need to discuss the meanings of the color white because ash is described as white . . . of the color red because ash is often contrasted with red soil" (p. 425).

Hodder's paper appears in a book that otherwise consists almost entirely of work in the naturalist mode, and he is concerned to advocate a contextual approach allied to the human rather than the natural sciences. We focus here on that part of the paper that deals with discard and specifically the meaning of ash from domestic hearths, which is not disposed of outside the compound with the general rubbish but is discarded by women behind their huts within the compound surround (Fig. 4.5). The reasons for this are complex and appear to be perceived differently, in part according to the gender, age, and status of informants but in part also according to individual personalities. Hodder shows that domestic ash is associated with the compound, with the color white, with women, milk, healing, and, somewhat tenuously, fertility (one might argue for sterility in the hygienic sense). But when taken outside the compound by men, the associations are very different. Ash then becomes associated with cursing and with death. White ash is also contrasted with the red color of the soil as inside to outside, as domestic to wild, as milk to blood, and, amongst other contrasts, as male elders to the young warriors who live for long periods in the bush. Hodder goes on to show that, while women are associated with domestic life within the compound, the compound is in fact founded upon a core of patrilineally related males, and that the women in it are in a sense strangers: either mothers and wives who have come to it from outside, or sisters and daughters who will themselves in due course marry out. Thus by a curious inversion women are both quintessential insiders and at one and the same time outsiders more similar to the wild warriors than to the elders to whom they are married.

We have come a long way from the ash deposited behind the women's huts, and indeed the paper's primary topic is not discard but the identification of the nature of male–female relationships and their expression in the ordering of domestic space. Nonetheless Hodder has revealed the existence of a dimension of variability in the archaeological record, that of the effects of symbolic

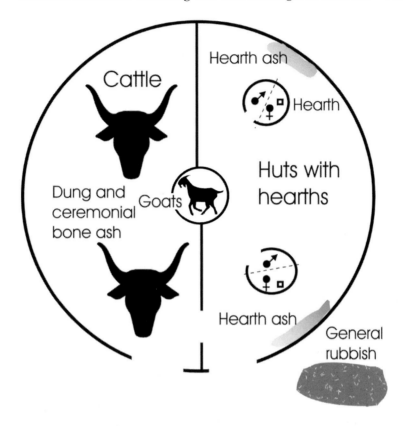

Fig. 4.5 Discard in an Ilchamus compound (after Hodder 1987a: Fig. 9.1).

thought and behavior, that was effectively ignored by Hayden and Cannon. And that is something that archaeologists must bear in mind even though it is highly improbable that they would be able to reconstruct more than a small part of the complex web of meanings that Hodder claims to have discovered.

Before leaving this topic it is worth contrasting the methodologies and databases of the two studies. We have seen that Hayden and Cannon employed questionnaires and observations to produce a quantified dataset that can be studied using statistics. Hodder speaks of that kind of ethnoarchaeology being "quick, non-participatory, and from the outside" (a fair description, it would seem, of his and his students' work among the Nuba) as opposed to the kind of research exemplified in his paper which starts "not with theoretical predicted linkages between variables, but with a concern to seek in the data for relationships, similarities, and differences," and which is of necessity therefore "long-term, participatory, and from the inside" (pp. 443–4). But of what do his data actually consist? It is by no means clear how long he actually spent in the field, how he communicated with the Ilchamus, or how much variation (if any) there may be in disposal patterns or hut plans. For the most part it would seem that his data consist of statements, texts, that he subsequently analyzed at his leisure to produce a fascinating reading of Ilchamus life, but one that readers cannot confirm or refute by reference to his material.

The Ilchamus paper was, we suspect, intended as much to provoke as to document, but it was for his lack of concern with verification that Patty Jo Watson chose to pillory it in a paper (Watson and Fotiadis 1990) to which Michael Fotiadis added a thoughtful comment. Watson claims that he "expresses a particularistic perspective so thoroughgoing that it would seem to rule out any hope of obtaining knowledge of the past, or at any rate knowledge of the only sort he believes to be interesting and worthwhile about the human societies the archaeological record represents" (p. 619). The Ilchamus paper and others like it, she continues, are counterproductive to Hodder's stated goal of correcting the weaknesses of processual archaeology while building on its strengths "because they leave the reader with the strong impression that the author has gone native, has lost his analytical perspective, having come to believe that the only true understanding of a particular society is in the minds of its creators and participants" (p. 620). And, she says, Hodder is "not only walking the razor's edge that separates far-extended inference about the past from imaginative formulations free of empirical contact or content, but also slipping off it into the realm of ingenious but non-empirical and archeologically irrelevant literary exercises" (p. 621). This is strong stuff, passionately expressed by a theorist of the New Archaeology, who is yet sympathetic to the expansion of archaeological inference. But, while Hodder's description of Ilchamus treatment of ash is unlikely (and unintended) to be of immediate practical utility to an archaeologist digging a tipi ring in Saskatchewan, we do insist on its importance in raising questions about factors structuring the archaeological record beyond economy of effort, provisional discard, hindrance factors, and the like.

Abandonment

If in the earlier parts of this chapter we have mainly considered processes of discard and deposition in ongoing occupations, we should remember that sites are themselves "discarded" in the process of becoming archaeological, and that abandonment is a process best regarded as lying at one end of a continuum of types of use. Rather than being a simple concept, it embraces various scales from the intra-site to the regional, and constitutes a family of processes that archaeologists need to understand and regarding which ethnoarchaeologists can contribute both theory and data (Cameron 1993). The ethnoarchaeological literature on abandonment goes back at least to Robert Ascher's (1968) "Time's arrow and the archaeology of a contemporary community," in which he drew lessons from an American automobile yard and abandoned Seri Indian sites on the Gulf of California, Mexico. The latter part of John Yellen's (1977a) monograph on the !Kung depends on a database consisting of plans of abandoned camps, although Yellen was mainly concerned with the spatial analysis of human residues and the reconstruction of activities. Binford (e.g., 1980) contributed by pointing out some of the archaeological implications of abandonment forming part of the normal course of settlement, most especially in subsistence-settlement systems based on foraging. The subject has gained momentum in the Recent period and is currently most readily accessed through a volume edited by Catherine Cameron and Steve Tomka (1993) in which a selection of ethnoarchaeological and archaeological papers, naturalist in approach and wide-ranging in geographical and societal coverage, demonstrates the complementarity of the two subdisciplines.

We will not attempt to synthesize in a few paragraphs the conclusions of these and other works that readers can explore on their own and to which we draw their attention below. In part because the topic of abandonment in ethnoarchaeology received less attention than it should in earlier periods, its development in recent years provides an instructive example of how advances are made – and not only in ethnoarchaeology. First comes the recognition that abandonment is not a simple concept, not an either/or phenomenon but one end of a continuum of which the other is full-time residence. It comprises a range of processes that operate at different scales. Aridification usually affects a broad area; warfare may devastate regions or sites; disease sometimes drives people from particular locations or environments. The smaller the unit of settlement, region, locality, site, activity area, the more and the more adventitious the factors that may be involved in its abandonment.

Next we require a terminology in order to be able to discuss the variation perceived. The following are some of the types of abandonment distinguished by authors in Cameron and Tomka's edited volume: catastrophic, gradual, permanent, episodic, seasonal, punctuated, and agricultural. Whether there is in fact an archaeological difference in kind between the episodic abandonment of the seasonal residences of Bolivian agro-pastoralists described by Tomka (1993) and the perhaps more regular punctuated abandonment of those of the Rarámuri (Tarahumara) of Mexico (Graham 1993), who are also agro-pastoralists transhumant over short distances, is doubtful. Similarly Kent's (1993a) terms "actual mobility" and "anticipated mobility," though useful concepts, are confusing in that they refer rather to actual and anticipated *immobility*, the lengths of time a settlement has been occupied and that it is planned to occupy it. As a subject matures an initially exuberant terminology commonly requires pruning.

The third important step is the contextualization of abandonment processes and the identification of the factors involved and conditioning their variability. Numerous such processes and factors have been identified: delayed curation (the curation of materials at an unoccupied site) and caching of items, dismantling of structures, interruption of normal discard patterns, scavenging, and dumping are a few of the processes, several of which were observed in Gorecki's

Table 4.3 *Percentages of artifact categories found in abandoned residences of Bolivian agro-pastoralists by type of abandonment (data from Tomka 1993: Tables 2.1–2.3)*

Artifact categories	Expedient	Improvised	Craft	Industrial	N artifacts	N residences
Abandonment type						
Seasonal	13	28	28	31	819	9
Episodic	17	24	26	33	440	10
Permanent	48	21	13	17	52	9

study discussed earlier. Speed of abandonment and the degree of planning possible, anticipated (im)mobility, distance moved, seasonality, and ritual and ideological factors are among those identified. Contextualization involves demonstration of the operation of these factors and processes in particular cases, and, as Glenn Davis Stone (1993a: 79) points out, what we find are "organic, structural linkages between agricultural [and other economic] tactics, residential mobility, social organization and ideology." This step has clearly been achieved in abandonment studies, and scholars have been successful in demonstrating correlations between factors and patterning in artifact distributions or characteristics of structures. For example Tomka shows how in a Bolivian context the numbers of artifacts found in permanently abandoned residences is much lower than in those to which return is planned. The proportion of expedient artifacts is substantially higher and those of craft and industrial items correspondingly lower, while that of improvised artifacts (e.g., can lids used as sheep shearing knives) remains relatively unchanged (Table 4.3).

Whether one can proceed from here to systematic articulation on a cross-cultural basis of the relations between behavior before and at the time of abandonment and resulting patterns in the archaeological record is much less certain. As Tomka and Stevenson (1993: 191) remark of the papers collected by Cameron and Tomka (1993): "the cross-cultural similarities evident . . . are strong indications that processes of abandonment are not culture or region specific. Rather, it appears that the contextual milieu (e.g., environmental, technological, sociocultural factors) within which site abandonment takes place contains the factors conditioning abandonment processes." Which when one gets right down to it means that universal cross-cultural regularities are going to be blindingly obvious, and that the better one knows a particular context the easier it is to appreciate that abandonment behavior within it is (a) eminently sensible in its terms and (b) on the whole quite similar to patterns found elsewhere! This at first sight is not a great deal of use to an archaeologist faced with the interpretation of material overlying a house floor. But in fact it is.

Ethnoarchaeologists are alerting archaeologists to a wide range of processes and factors, which are reasonably predictably likely or unlikely to apply to materials from the archaeologist's own region and period. Thus while the hindrance factor may be regarded as a near universal, punctuated abandonment and its artifactual expressions are unlikely occurrences in Iraqi Early Dynastic *tell*s. Dumping in unoccupied structures is, on the other hand, very probable at least in parts of nucleated and urban sites. Ethnoarchaeology also contributes to research design, for example in deciding the necessary scale of a project. Joyce and Johannessen's (1993) research at a small, recently abandoned, domestic site in Mexico showed that in this instance the numbers and patterning of artifacts in only one of four buildings was consistent with the prediction that, where abandonment is gradual and possible return planned, *de facto* refuse will cluster in caches away from use locations. They conclude that "abandonment of multistructure sites can result in differing treatment of structures creating complex patterning in the archaeological record," and that therefore "broad areal sampling at archaeological sites is crucial to control for abandonment processes" (p. 151).

It would seem that ethnoarchaeological research on abandonment from McIntosh (1974) to the present should provide the resourceful archaeologist with numerous leads towards definition of the conditions of abandonment in specific cases. But, as Tomka and Stevenson (1993: 193) conclude, similar conditions may well result from different causes. Explanation of abandonment remains a problem for archaeologists, while, for ethnoarchaeologists "Abandonment studies . . . are likely to be ultimately unrewarding and perhaps even misleading if we do not use our knowledge to address larger cultural or theoretical questions." This is of course true for all work regarding formation processes. Their analytical control is the means to avoidance of distortion in archaeological interpretation occasioned by their transformation of the systemic context.

Concluding remarks

In order to address the interpretation of the archaeological record – or even to recognize its existence – archaeologists require a body of theory that guides inference relating archaeological statics to the dynamics of once living systems, and a store of analogies on which they can draw in order to develop models appropriate to and hopefully testable against their data. As this chapter has shown, ethnoarchaeologists are contributing in both areas, whether their work tends more towards that of Binford, Hayden and Cannon, and others, who develop concepts and replicable methods that are transferable to archaeological cases, or towards that of Hodder and his followers (e.g., Moore 1982), who show that the passage of the systemic into the archaeological involves not merely natural and utilitarian cultural transforms but also symbolic

Fig. 4.6 Augustin Holl plans a recently abandoned Shuwa compound in the Extreme North province, Cameroon, 1988.

transformations. It is equally satisfactory that archaeologists are benefiting from a variety of ethnoarchaeological insights in the interpretation of site formation. To cite just three examples from recent work, Augustin Holl (1987) makes use of McIntosh's (1974) and Agorsah's (1985) research into mud wall collapse, besides taphonomic and experimental studies, to reconstruct mound formation processes around Lake Chad in Central Africa (Fig. 4.6). A particularly sophisticated application is Mark Varien and Barbara Mills's (1997) development of ethnoarchaeological information on ceramic uselives to model accumulation rates and infer site occupation spans in the American Southwest. Lastly, Susan Kent (1999a) has studied the patterning of artifact inventories of trash and activity areas among sedentary Botswana San, and devised statistical characterizations that she has herself applied to differentiate storage from trash areas in an Anasazi Pueblo in the American Southwest. It is significant and encouraging that in three out of four of these instances ethnoarchaeological insights are being applied on continents different from those in which they were first formulated.

Further reading

Michael Shott (1998) provides the most recent discussion of formation theory, situating it in relationship to middle range theory in social science, and decrying its marginal status in academic practice. Jean Sept's (1992) research on chimpanzee nests offers an alternative approach to understanding the patterning of the Plio-Pleistocene record. McIntosh's (1974) research was extended by E. Kofi Agorsah (1985, 1988), who studied house construction and community patterning among the Nchumuru of modern Wiae, Ghana, and applied his findings to reconstruction of Old Wiae.

Thomas Killion's (1990) work in Vera Cruz complements Hayden and Cannon's analysis by relating site structure and refuse disposal to agricultural practices (see chapter 5). Edward Staski and Livingston Sutro's (1991) collection of short papers on refuse disposal also contains several that extend either geographically or topically those discussed in the body of this chapter. While neither we nor William Rathje (1985) consider his Garbage Project to be ethnoarchaeology, it has generated many insights into formation processes (e.g., Wilson *et al.* 1991).

FAUNA AND SUBSISTENCE

. . . successful farmers have social relations with one another while hunter-gatherers have ecological relations with hazelnuts.

(Richard Bradley 1984: 11)

. . . as the choice of food species is a cultural phenomenon, techniques themselves are the result of choices made by a culture. These choices are made in accordance with goals it has set itself, but also in accordance with all sorts of social representations which, although some way removed from techniques, partly determine the local ways and means of acting on the environment.

(Pierre Lemonnier 1993: 680)

Beginning in the 1950s archaeologists such as Grahame Clark (1954) at Star Carr in England began the systematic recovery of faunal and plant remains in order to reconstruct prehistoric subsistence. Clark (1952) himself had sought material for analogy in European folk practices, and, both then and now, archaeologists have turned for assistance to a rich ethnographic, experimental, ethnobotanical, and historical literature. Merely to give an indication of the range of such sources, and limiting ourselves to North America, we might cite Wilson's (1917) *Agriculture of the Hidatsa Indians*, Wright's (1993) simulated use of experimental maize grinding tools, Nabhan's (1985) *Gathering the desert*, and Crader's (1984) use of historical sources in her study of the zooarchaeology of Thomas Jefferson's residence at Monticello. So rich and varied indeed is the literature that, when ethnoarchaeologists have undertaken studies of subsistence, they have done so with very particular archaeological questions in mind. In this chapter we review two areas of ethnoarchaeology relating to subsistence. Considered first are studies concerned primarily with hunters' acquisition, processing, and distribution of mammals. These are especially notable for the linkage of subsistence practices to formation processes and inference from the representation of skeletal parts in archaeological assemblages. The second part of the chapter samples other innovative ethnoarchaeological research of recent years relating to subsistence.

116

Fauna and their remains

Faunal remains supply direct information on several topics of interest to the archaeologist. While there have been ethnoarchaeological contributions to the study of reptile (Rybczynski *et al.* 1996) and fish (Stewart and Gifford-Gonzalez 1994; Belcher 1998) remains, most papers deal with the exploitation of mammals. The range of species found in an archaeological site is generally indicative of site environment and of its occupants' subsistence. Butchery practices differ, and provide evidence of economic and social differentiation. It is for such reasons that archaeologists interested in the Stone Age, and particularly in the lifeways of early hominids, have expended immense energy and ingenuity in the study of bones. Our ability to infer subsistence practices from fauna is contingent upon understanding of their passage into the archaeological context. This is subject to transforms comparable to those affecting artifacts, although the circumstances under which bones are brought to a site, are there modified and eventually either are destroyed or enter the archaeological context are more complex and problematical to reconstruct (Fig. 5.1). Numerous publications on taphonomy and experimental and actualistic studies describe the many processes whereby faunal remains selectively arrive at sites, are there redistributed and discarded, and, with further modification by humans, carnivores and other agents of destruction and decay, enter the archaeological context. The ultimate aim of many authors is to define the archaeological "signatures" of particular scavenging, hunting and other practices and the types of site associated with them.

Among the actualistic studies are ethnoarchaeological ones conducted for the most part among groups whose subsistence includes a significant hunting component, although their foraging is usually combined with other practices: pastoralism as among the Khoi-khoi (Hottentots) of South Africa (Brain 1967, 1969), agriculture or a degree of dependence on agriculturalists as among the Pygmies of the African equatorial forests (e.g., Fisher 1993), or obtaining food and other goods from missionaries or other representatives of the industrialized world as among the Alyawara of central Australia (Binford and O'Connell 1984). The influence of other groups and technologies on these communities introduces further complications, rendering even more difficult such aims as interpreting Plio-Pleistocene scavenging in the light of modern Hadza practices (O'Connell *et al.* 1988a). Such problems are always faced by those wishing to reconstruct an earlier, perhaps hypothetical (see Stahl 1993), period during which behavior was pristine and uninfluenced by groups at significantly different levels of socioeconomic integration. It is particularly acute when the intended subject of the analogy dates to a time preceding agriculture – and perhaps even the development of human psyches that are recognizably modern. What are required are theoretical approaches and methodologies that allow the

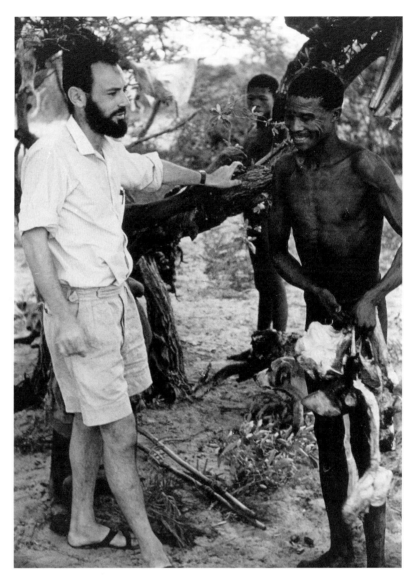

Fig. 5.1 Richard Lee, who with Irven DeVore led the long-term Harvard University Bushman Studies Project, talks with a !Kung San who is holding part of the cow described in Lee's (1971) "Eating Christmas in the Kalahari," Botswana, 1965.

Fig. 5.2 View of the Nunamiut village of Anaktuvak Pass with a meat
drying rack in the foreground, wall tents of Lewis Binford's
expedition on the left, and the Brooks Range in the background,
Alaska, 1971.

broader implications of a study to be distinguished from its specifics, and then
to be applied to the archaeological record.

Lewis Binford's Nunamiut studies

Lewis Binford has been a major contributor in this field as in several others.
Nunamiut ethnoarchaeology (Binford 1978a) and *Bones: ancient men and
modern myths* (Binford 1981a) were the first monographs to deal, respectively,
with the meaning of the within and between site representation of body parts
and with bone taphonomy. They lay the foundation for much later actualistic
and archaeological research. *Nunamiut ethnoarchaeology* describes research
undertaken by himself and students between 1969 and 1972 that focuses on the
Eskimo community of Anaktuvak Pass in inland north Alaska (Fig. 5.2).
Binford's publications do not specify duration of research (although seasonality
can be partly reconstructed from the texts), data recovery and recording strategies, or, while they are named, the attributes and activities of student assistants or informants, among whom some, specifically acknowledged, were

Fig. 5.3 The 1971 University of New Mexico field crew and Nunamiut
assistants at Anaktuvak Pass. *From left to right*: Jack Snyder, Jane
Rulland, Jean-Philippe Rigaud (a French Palaeolithic archaeologist),
Johnny Rulland (one of Binford's main informants), Caroline
Reeves, Catherine Cameron, Weber Greiser (*sitting*), Clint Binford,
Lewis Binford, and Rodney Rulland.

clearly more crucial than others (Fig. 5.3). It must be assumed that English was
the field language, but while Binford often specifies the sizes of samples (or raw
numbers for specific components thereof) and the bases of often complex calculations, he provides no sample questionnaires, if indeed these existed. The
bases for normative statements are not always explicit. On the other hand it is
a somewhat unexpected pleasure in a naturalist work to find extensive quotes
from native informants explaining Nunamiut practices and ideas; while it is
unclear how these interviews were conducted or recorded, they represent a
form of multivocality more usually associated with postmodern writers.

The 21 resident households of Anaktuvuk Pass are heavily dependent upon
caribou for their subsistence, exploiting migratory herds at various passes in
the Brooks ranges and engaging in hunting in all seasons of the year. Binford
sets out to demonstrate that "much variability in the archaeological record . . .
is directly referable not to differences between systems, but to *differing states
of a single system*" (1978a: 4). Rather than culture and mental templates deter-

mining what faunal remains in what frequencies will be deposited at a particular site, he argues that adaptive systems incorporate functional variability resulting from the application of a body of knowledge to environmental circumstances that change from day to day, season to season, and year to year. (This view is in effect very close to that of practice theory though individual agency is not made explicit.) As the argument can be extended to artifacts, Binford's intention – "My strategy has been to seek a toe in the behavioral door [*sic*] through fauna" (p. 453) – is to mount a frontal attack on the "Custom is King" assumption of traditional culture historical archaeology, and in this he is successful, even if his portrayal of the Nunamiut as supremely rational, pragmatic empiricists is an exaggeration dictated by his philosophical approach (see specially pp. 452–8), though contradicted here and there (e.g., p. 413) by the existence of skull shrines and other forms of special treatment of body parts.

Before Binford can conduct his analysis he has to develop a system of measurement. This requires study of the economic anatomy of caribou and sheep and the elaboration of measures of the utility of different body parts in terms of their meat, marrow, grease, and other values. (In *Nunamiut ethnoarchaeology* there is a salient and poignant description of Binford's awakening to the realization that out of respect for local custom and beliefs about the proper butchering of animals he would have to modify his approach to data acquisition.) Lengthy passages of densely argued text with accompanying graphs and statistical tables lead up to the definitions and justifications of a general utility index (GUI), a drying utility index, and numerous other such indices that are subsequently applied to the materials recorded on more than 275 prey animals at kill, initial field and secondary field butchering sites, caches, and processing sites. Variation in Nunamiut hunting, processing, sharing, and consumption patterns throughout the year is exhaustively described, and we learn a great deal about Nunamiut strategies and decision making. Throughout, Binford is concerned to develop middle range theory that models the relationships between the dynamics of living systems and the statics of the archaeological record. And, in part because the Nunamiut practice, in an environment characterized by marked seasonality, a "logistical" hunting strategy in which task groups go out from seldom-moved bases to obtain resources, and in which storage is extremely important, he must attempt to identify complex and seasonally varying patterns of decision making. He speaks, for example, of different spring and fall systems, which generate different patterns of bone discard. But while the ethnographer can identify patterns and trends, the number of interacting variables is such that characterization of gross categories of sites – kill sites, residential sites – in terms of their fauna must be so general as to be of limited analogical value, while "reverse engineering," the identification of the precise complex of interacting factors that produced a particular assemblage, is in most cases impossible. This kind of conclusion to an ethnoarchaeological study is by no means uncommon, the ethnoarchaeological contribution to archaeology being very often enhancement of our ability to conceive a range of possible interpretations rather than formulae that can be applied to particular archaeological cases.

Binford insists (overly pessimistically as it turns out [see Boyle 1993]) that the specifics of the Nunamiut case are not comparable or applicable to, say, a study of paleolithic Aurignacians, but goes on to say (in typical Binfordese) that, "The citation of unique properties for empirical cases in no way places in contention general propositions that such cases may be cited as exemplifying" (p. 452). The book and especially its final chapter is full of such propositions: "all kill sites fit some negative form of a utility index regardless of season" (p. 459) is one of the simpler and more obvious, while his statement that "Evaluating the utility of faunal elements against known anatomical scales (of value) may permit the recognition of a strategy, but the teleology may not be evident" (p. 477 [original in italics]) indicates both the possibilities and the limitations of the kind of approach advocated. Binford's outstanding achievement is methodological, the development of replicable methods for studying hunters that are transferable to archaeological cases, enabling "the meaningful analysis of patterning in assemblage characteristics, location, and responsiveness to general system change" (p. 482). And since he is interested in understanding system properties and behavior rather than in applying presentist Nunamiut analogies to archaeological materials, it matters not at all that the Nunamiut are not "pristine" hunters but make a living using rifles, telescopes, and, besides dog teams, also snowmobiles.

While *Nunamiut ethnoarchaeology* is heavy going, and Binford's indices are unnecessarily complex (K. T. Jones 1984, cited by O'Connell 1993: 171), it is extraordinarily rich in data and ideas, a milestone in faunal analysis that has stimulated much later work (e.g., Speth 1983). However it deals only incidentally with patterns of bone modification by human and non-human agents. This is the topic Binford takes up in *Bones: ancient men and modern myths* in which he again uses, in addition to other materials, his and his students' data gathered among the Navajo (Binford and Bertram 1977) and Nunamiut, some ethnographic, and some ethological, regarding the behavior of dogs and wolves. His object is once again to use actualistic studies to generate middle range theory that can underpin studies of the relationship between behavior, whether of humans or animals, and its archaeological consequences. Only when causes are linked to their diagnostic effects can one begin to interpret patterning in the archaeological record. The undesirable alternative is to use *post hoc* accommodative arguments, for example Perkins and Daly's (1968) "schlepp effect" model, for explaining specific archaeological observations. These, Binford (1981a: 184–5, 244) complains, are grounded not in research but only in the imagination. Such "myth making" is what Binford wishes to move beyond. Unfortunately, while it "would appear that we can make strong uniformitarian assumptions about nonhominid predator-scavenger behavior as a cause of redundant patterning in faunal assemblages ... No such limitation seems operative with respect to tool-using man viewed in a generic sense" (p. 238). Indeed "our current knowledge of variability as generated by man appears almost overwhelming in its diversity" (p. 237). Nonetheless Binford is able to go a very considerable distance in establishing "differential patterns of association stemming from the behavior of Man versus that of Beast." In the penultimate chapter these insights are applied to materials from Olduvai Gorge. The argumentation, involving the use of factor analyses, is complex, with results that, put at their simplest, indicate that the assemblages register complex interactions of natural, animal, and hominid factors, and that the hominids were scavenging animal carcasses rather than hunting and killing prey, sometimes transporting animal parts to protected locations (but not base camps) mainly to break them up with hammers in order to extract bone marrow for individual (and not shared) consumption. This somewhat unflattering view of our earliest hominid ancestors is a far cry from the noble big-game hunter image of earlier years, but it has been enormously influential. For present purposes we should note that, "This view was made possible by the application of a *methodology* to a body of applications ... When a methodology is the basis for statements about the past, it is possible to research the methodology itself and to uncover its weaknesses and perfect its strengths" (p. 294). Glynn Isaac's (1983) thoughtful review begins this process.

Recent developments

Both works of Binford described above have, as is generally acknowledged (e.g., Ringrose 1993: 136), contributed significantly to theory and methodology, and to our understanding of the past. Katherine Boyle (1993), combining study of anatomical element representation and butchery marks in order to detect structural properties of the archaeological record, in this case contrasting upper paleolithic procurement and processing strategies in southwest France, exemplifies the productivity of Binford's ethnoarchaeological contributions to faunal studies. Both of Binford's themes, the representation of skeletal parts and the taphonomy of vertebrate faunal remains, have also been taken up in more recent actualistic research of which Jean Hudson's (1993a) edited volume *From bones to behavior* offers several excellent examples.

Proportional representation of skeletal parts
In classifying archaeological sites into types by reference to the proportional representation of skeletal parts in bone assemblages,

The guiding principle ... has been that because different parts of carcasses provide variable sources of nutrition, past human groups who were confronted with carcass transport constraints would have selected for transport to their camps for subsequent consumption those parts that provided the best nutritional yield in meat and marrow and caused the fewest transport problems. (Bunn *et al.* 1988: 412)

The decisions that have to be taken regarding butchery and transport once an animal has been slain, or its body encountered by scavenging hominids, depend upon a wide variety of environmental and other factors of which only a few are represented even in so detailed a study as *Nunamiut ethnoarchaeology*. Gifford-Gonzalez (1993: 185) has culled the following list of factors from the literature relating to foragers:

1. size of the animal relative to that of the human processors;
2. number of animals requiring immediate processing;
3. distance of the animal from the destination of its products;
4. number of persons in carrying party;
5. condition of the carcass at the time encountered;
6. time of day.

[Other factors relate to processing and consumption:]

7. gear at hand to effect field processing;
8. processing technology available at destination site;
9. ultimate form or forms the animal products will take.

Lengthy as this may be, this is not a comprehensive listing. For example, Bartram (1993) indicates that the potential for sun drying of meat may influence skeletal part profiles, though his conclusion that "The technology required for efficient meat drying is present in Oldowan assemblages" (p. 133) surely applies only to the hardware required. Oldowans lacked the intellectual capacity to develop and benefit from such food storage techniques. Many other factors could be added, including the representation of ages and sexes in the foraging party and in the larger risk and obligation sharing group.

Rather than attempt to survey a very technical literature, let us focus on a debate between teams of scholars led by Henry Bunn (1993; Bunn *et al.* 1988, 1991) and James O'Connell (1993; O'Connell *et al.* 1988b, 1990). Both groups studied the formation of bone assemblages among Eastern Hadza foragers of northern Tanzania but with apparently very different results. Why this should be so is of considerable theoretical and methodological interest.

Bunn sets out the dilemma as follows:

[My] group concluded that in transporting carcasses of all but the largest animals (i.e., giraffe, elephant) from kill sites to base camps the Hadza typically (1) try to carry entire carcasses in field-butchered units, (2) abandon mainly axial units at kill sites when circumstances warrant, and (3) consequently accumulate the entire range of skeletal elements in approximately natural anatomical frequency but with a notably high representation of limb bones . . . [O'Connell's] group concluded essentially the opposite pattern for the same people by suggesting that the Hadza typically (1) try to reduce the energetic costs of transporting skeletal elements, (2) consequently abandon limb bones at kill sites after defleshing them and extracting and consuming the marrow from inside them, and (3) preferentially transport and accumulate mainly axial and girdle elements at base camps. (Bunn 1993: 156–7, with references omitted)

The Bunn and O'Connell teams' initial conclusions were based on data gathered among the same Hadza groups studied consecutively. The O'Connell team were in the field for 144 days between September 1985 and October 1986, while Bunn and his group's 73-day field season began as O'Connell's ended. During these periods O'Connell, Hawkes and Blurton Jones (1988b) obtained data on 43 medium and large animals acquired by hunting and a further 11 by scavenging. Bunn, Bartram and Kroll (1988) record the procurement of 29 carcasses. In order to obtain a larger sample, Bunn's team later returned to the field to document a further 81 carcasses. Their results, even when pooled with the O'Connell sample, generally confirm their earlier findings, "the Hadza typically transport essentially entire field-butchered carcasses of all but the largest taxa, while abandoning mainly some axial elements at kill sites" (Bunn 1993: 158–9). However, they observed that the limb bones of the alcelaphine antelopes, hartebeest and wildebeest, were often discarded in the field, in part because their marrow, while more abundant, is of lower quality than that of zebra, which is highly valued as a food for children. The earlier Bunn study had failed to note this effect, in part because it grouped animals by size classes rather than species. Thus, as Binford had earlier noted among the Nunamiut, and as Emerson (1993) elaborates in a related paper, while transport constraints must always be considered, the nutritional benefits of body parts are not constant but vary according to the specific needs of the human group and its individual members. Fat and bone grease may be particularly important at one time of year, lean flesh at another. Different body parts may be brought back to camp at different seasons or for different purposes.

It is possible that a high representation of antelopes in the O'Connell team's sample, which was grouped by species for analytical purposes, may have led them to attribute an alcelaphine pattern to the assemblage as a whole. Other factors may be involved, conceivably even differential interaction between the Hadza and the two teams of anthropologists. O'Connell (1993: 172) criticizes Bunn for attempting to characterize a "typical Hadza pattern" of body part transport, preferring "to explore alternate explanations for observed variation in carcass processing and transport within a single ethnographic case." In our view both scholars are concerned to discover the variables involved and their interactions, but, as it will clearly be impossible to define archaeological signatures for each and every combination, it remains useful to determine the patterning likely to be dominant at, for example, Hadza base camps as opposed to kill sites. While this debate is probably far from over, it is worth emphasizing (1) the dangers of small sample sizes, (2) the value of repeated observations of the same group at different times, and (3) the advantages of documentation sufficiently standardized for Bunn to be able to combine both team's samples for purposes of analysis. In order to evaluate data on forager behavior, which is typically modified to a greater extent than that of food-producers by the presence of observers, themselves likely to be perceived as a potential resource (cf. Yellen 1977a: 56–63), especially precise information on methodology is required.

Taphonomy of vertebrate faunal remains

To the very considerable literature on the natural and biological modification of bones following their discard by hominids (see Koch 1989), ethnoarchaeological studies have made a limited but significant contribution. While there is a taphonomic component in many papers, Jean Hudson (1993b) has paid particular attention to the impact of domestic dogs, as has Susan Kent (1993b) in a paper on a sedentary Kalahari community in which she shows that mode of cooking is a relevant variable. Cooking, and this time hyenas rather than dogs, are also considered in a paper on the Hadza by Karen Lupo (1995). Nonetheless, Gifford-Gonzalez (1993) is right to argue that, as a consequence of a predominantly androcentric view of human foraging, the effects of the social subdivision of animal foodstuffs and culinary processing on the production and discard of faunal remains have received far too little attention, although Yellen (1991a, 1991b) has studied !Kung utilization and discard of small mammals. Presumably because *Australopithecus* didn't cook and archaic *Homo* only barbecued, researchers have tended to ignore an aspect of human life that has long been recognized as especially rich in meaning. This is certainly an area deserving of much further research. One wonders whether the relative lack of consideration of faunal remains in the archaeology of societies more complex than hunter-gatherers is not due in large part to the absence of ethnoarchaeological models for their interpretation.

Symbolic behavior and faunal assemblages

A notable feature of the literature on fauna is its strong naturalist bias. In part because the primary interest of many researchers tends to be interpretation of the archaeological record of early hominids who had little in the way of language and symbolic thought, symbolic behavior relating to faunal remains evidenced by the source societies goes generally unnoticed or is ignored. And yet it exists. In 1989 a special number of *Anthropozoologica* devoted to the material manifestations of religious practices involving animals included an ethnoarchaeological component (e.g., Sidi Maamar 1989; Beavitt 1989). Chaix and Sidi Maamar (1992) describe variation in the sacrifice, butchery, distribution, and processing of sheep and goats by Muslims in Algeria, Egypt, and France. The differences can be attributed to ritual and social, as well as economic, factors. They fail however to demonstrate that one concern of ritual butchery is to "objectivize the division of the world in terms of animal topology" (p. 272, our translation). Hodder (1982a: 155–61) describes the differential treatment of cattle and pigs as regards butchery, consumption, and bone disposal among peoples of the Nuba hills, Sudan. Jaws and skulls are hung up in or in front of granaries in order to provide the grain with symbolic protection. According to Hodder, pigs, associated with women and dirt, and cattle, associated with men, are caught up in a complex discourse regarding fertility and pollution (see chapter 13). Among the Mesakin Qisar the bones of pigs and cattle are kept separate and stuffed into crevices in the rocks some little distance from the compound. Symbolically charged treatment of faunal remains and especially skulls is widespread and of long duration – as anyone who has wondered at hunters' trophies, pet cemeteries, or Egyptian cat mummies can testify.

Subsistence

We now turn to ethnoarchaeology's other contributions to the analysis and reconstruction of diet and of subsistence practices. Information on subsistence is incorporated into many ethnoarchaeological works. Here we consider only a small sample of those in which it is a major component, and even in this we are selective. Kristen Hawkes and James O'Connell at the University of Utah are the nucleus of a larger team of scholars the core of whose research among the Hadza of Tanzania and the Aché of Paraguay, better characterized as behavioral or evolutionary ecology than ethnoarchaeology, falls outside the scope of this book (see Hurtado *et al.* 1985; and Hawkes, O'Connell, and Rogers 1997). Aspects of their research, notable for its rigorous methodology of observation[1] and contribution to knowledge of scavenging and its potential for contributing to hominid subsistence, were discussed above.

Some other reports provide straightforward descriptive accounts of subsistence practices and, while written for an archaeological audience, are essentially works of ethnography. One example is Gould's (1967) "Notes on hunting, butchering and snaring of game among Ngatatjara and their neighbours . . ." Elsewhere Brian Dillon (1988) challenges the notion that the ancient Maya were essentially vegetarian by investigating modern Maya hunting and taming of peccaries and their contribution to the diet. He advances an "agricultural commute hunting" model for the ancient Maya, a variant of the "garden hunting" model proposed by Olga Linares (1976) for the forests of Panama. But rather than attempt to survey the range, we prefer to focus on particularly interesting and novel examples.

Maori: the rich sweet flavor of eel flesh

The Maori mass capture of eels during intermittent summer and autumn runs from inland swamps to spawning grounds in the ocean is well documented in the ethnohistoric and early ethnographic record. Eels were an important resource over most of New Zealand, but are scarcely represented archaeologically. Yvonne Marshall (1987), dissatisfied by the untested explanation that eel bones, being soft, do not preserve, decided on an alternative approach, and

---

[1] The authors exemplify a naturalist style of field research that, despite apparently close relationships with their hosts, emphasizes etics over emics, and fieldworkers' observations over informants' statements.

Fig. 5.4 Members of the Baker family, Maori of the North Island, New
Zealand, attending their eel-weir in 1984. When the stream is high,
conical multi-part nets are attached to the weir to capture migrating
eels. The eels are then stored alive for periods of up to a year in the
flow-through storage boxes, their up- and downstream ends closed
by grills, seen in the picture.

collected ethnoarchaeological data to inform her reading of the ethnographic
and ethnohistoric sources. Her aim, inspired by historical linguistics, is to
"reconstruct the pathways by which a cultural artefact," in this case the eel
fishing complex, "changes from one form to another." In this manner, she continues, "extrapolation back into the prehistoric becomes an informed rather
than an *ad hoc* process" (p. 56).

The capture of migrating eels requires the construction of eel weirs, nets for
the actual capture, and storage boxes in which eels survive for extraordinary
lengths of time (Fig. 5.4). These Marshall documents in detail on a tributary of
the Kawakawa river on the North Island, recording present and, from oral testimony and written sources, past variations in form and materials over New
Zealand as a whole. The material of the nets has changed and eel-pots, once
made of flexible local plant material, are no longer made. In general it may be
said that, while modern eel fishing equipment does not correspond exactly
with that described in ethnographic accounts, there are no elements that lack
ethnographically recorded antecedents. "Contemporary [weir] design is in

accordance with this principle, synthesizing elements of many different styles into a new form in which maximum efficiency of capture is combined with minimal upkeep, while retaining the [main posts] as the central points" (p. 63).

The same trend towards improving efficiency through lowering costs of upkeep is found in the modern preference for storing eels in wooden boxes through the ends of which water flows through a wire mesh. Some proto- and prehistoric structures found are likely to have fulfilled the same function, although under past conditions of seasonal movement of residence more effort was expended on preservation, usually by cooking and drying. Marshall summarizes her arguments for a prehistoric origin for eel-weir fishing by pointing out that the documented practices relating to storage, preparation, and consumption of eels imply that the deposition of eel-bone middens is unlikely. The eel-weir assemblage, manufactured in locally available materials and varying styles, is widely distributed in the historic period, and is thus presumably old. When change does occur it first takes the form of substitution of materials, with forms changing only later. This pattern is characteristic of other Maori artifact classes including fishhooks, bird spears, and adzes.

In later sections of her paper, Marshall applies her approach to estimation of the potential returns of eel fishing, which were very great, to a consideration of the organization of production and distribution, to the social dynamics involved, and to the implications of this resource for sociopolitical development. "[T]he judicious use of kin-based and non kin-based gifting of eels would have been an important source of sociopolitical influence, and a major contributor to the underpinning of the distinctive form of complex sociopolitical organisation which emerged in northern New Zealand" (p. 76).

Marshall's article is a first-class example of the way in which an ethnoarchaeologist can define mechanisms, configurations of the environmental, material and sociocultural variables that interact at one time horizon to generate patterning in material culture, and then proceed by judicious use of historical evidence to reveal the nature and workings of processes, diachronic changes in mechanisms that include structural change, breakdown, and transformation.

One aspect, however, that she does not consider is the manner in which the eel weirs and cages express Maori social and symbolic relations. As is emphasized by the anthropology of techniques school (discussed in chapters 6 and 7), humans do not engage things directly but indirectly through ideas, mental representations that are social and cultural constructs, whence the term "social representation." Coincidentally, the clearest application of this perspective to material culture is Pierre Lemonnier's (1993) demonstration of how social relations and ancestor myths are incorporated into the manufacture of eel traps among the Ankave-Anga of Papua New Guinea, which embeds layers of meaning in this at first sight entirely utilitarian device. Representation conditions behavior, including the manufacture of artifacts, and neither real objects nor the behavior associated with them can be fully comprehended without reference to the associated mental object or representation.[2]

India: the mute threshing floor speaks

Ethnoarchaeologists working as or with ethnobotanists are also providing archaeologists with useful information, as for example Kolawole Aiyedun's (1995) catalogue of "Aesthetic, domestic, and nutritional use of plant resources in Niger state . . .," Füsun Ertuğ-Yaraş's (1996) study of contemporary plant gathering in central Anatolia, and Wendy Beck and colleagues' (1998) description of Aboriginal Australian processing of the carbohydrate-rich but toxic seeds of cycads.

A more analytical approach involves the development of crop processing models that can aid in the paleoethnobotanical reconstructions typically undertaken after recovery by flotation of plant materials from archaeological deposits. Building on a model of plant processing originated by Robin Dennell (1974), Glynis Jones (1983, 1984) and others have sought "to develop research models and methodology through ethnographic observations and data analysis to facilitate stronger and more reliable interpretations of archaeobotanical materials" (Reddy 1997: 169). Seetha Reddy's exemplary study combines ethnoarchaeological analysis with application of the results to archaeobotanical remains from Harappan sites. She documents the processing of millet (*Panicum miliare*) grown by opportunistic flood retreat agriculture in Andhra Pradesh, southern India, and of sorghum and pennisetum cultivated during the summer monsoon in Gujarat, western India. Crops require different processing depending upon their biological characteristics (e.g., small versus large seeds), harvesting methods (which may or may not result in the incorporation of weeds), and subsequent processing. The sequence is complex because even within the same culture there are, depending on crop maturity and quantity, and ephemeral conditions (e.g., wind velocity at the time of winnowing), a variety of processing pathways for any particular crop. Each stage produces a crop product and a crop by-product, the by-products being of most interest in that they are more likely to be retrieved as part of the archaeological record. However, their preservation depends on a variety of factors including their subsequent trajectory, for example as fodder for animals, and the likelihood of their exposure to fire and charring. Reddy's diagram (Fig. 5.5) of the processing pathway of *Sorghum bicolor* harvested by cutting the stalks at the base is complex but certainly less so than the phenomena it represents. Such analyses permit signatures of different processes to be defined, for example "*Sorghum bicolor* rachillae with

---

[2] Over much of sub-Saharan Africa, iron workers' representation of the furnace as a fecund bride is intrinsic to the smelting process (chapter 11). In Western consumer societies, advertisers, religions, and politicians are the prime purveyors and perverters of representations. Social representations include elements of habitus besides consciously held ideas (see Lemonnier 1992: chapter 4, for an extended discussion).

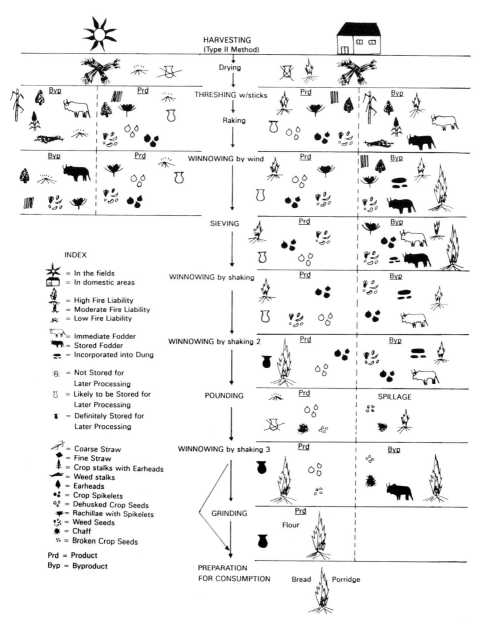

Fig. 5.5 The complex processing pathway of sorghum harvested by cutting the stalks at the base.

spikelets occur in significantly dominant frequencies only in the sieving byproduct" (p. 179), and to be used as models for archaeological interpretation.

Reddy's application of her results to intensively sampled Harappan sites in Gujarat allows her to identify the macrobotanical assemblage of Oriyo Timbo as indicative exclusively of later stages in the processing of summer crops, while another, Babar Kot, produced evidence of both summer and winter crops at all processing stages (Fig. 5.6). Furthermore, her conclusions help to answer larger culture historical questions, showing that "There is little evidence to suggest that the Late Harappan in Gujarat witnessed a simple increase in pastoralism and a corresponding dichotomy between pastoral and agricultural economies" (p. 185).

Comparable research is being carried out in Ethiopia on pulses (Butler, Tesfay, *et al.* 1999), and the same project is also taking a broader approach in which, besides study of seasonality and crop processing, domestic settings are investigated from the perspective of their potential for the preservation of plant remains (D'Andrea, Lyons, *et al.* 1999). A different kind of processing is investigated by Seona Anderson and Füsun Ertuğ (1998) in "Fuel, fodder and faeces . . .," a study of dung cakes (see also Reddy 1999). The new fusion of ethnoarchaeology and ethnobotany is responding quickly and effectively to the interpretive challenge presented by improved archaeobotanical retrieval. Thus far these studies have been processual in nature. While the existence of cultural variants is admitted, it is generally assumed that the prime determinants of crop processing and treatment are biological and environmental. This is unlikely to be the whole truth. The extent to which social representations influence cultural practice remains to be determined.

A note on pastoralists

In a quite different mode, Kathleen Ryan and colleagues (1991, 1999) have studied changing herd management practices among the Maasai of Kenya. Since these affect herd demography and death assemblages they are of direct relevance to archaeological interpretation. Susan Smith's (1980) ethnographic research into the environmental adaptation of Kel Tamasheq (Tuareg) camel and goat herders in the Malian Sahel zone, undertaken with archaeologists in mind, contains much information on subsistence and other matters (see chapter 9). An interesting and essentially ethnographic study by archaeologists is summarized by Kent Flannery, Joyce Marcus, and Robert Reynolds (1989) in *The flocks of the Wamani: a study of llama herders on the punas of Ayacucho, Peru.* Flannery collected data on herd composition; he had previously worked with Richard MacNeish on the fauna from Ayacucho, and his interest in prehistoric fauna extends back to graduate student days with Robert Braidwood in the Middle East. Marcus has long been interested in integrating ethnohistoric and archaeological data and, like Flannery, her geographic interests extend

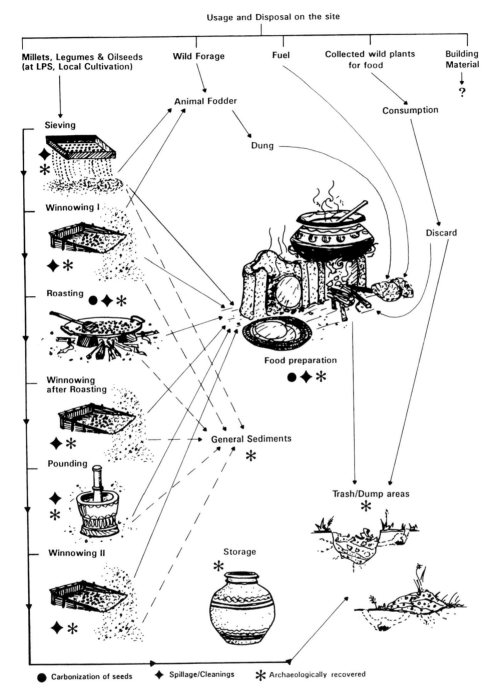

Fig. 5.6 The analysis of processing pathways applied to the site of Babar Kot, Gujarat, India.

south of Mesoamerica. Reynolds created computer simulation models of herd growth, permitting his co-authors to consider some of the relationships between demographic features of livestock, the humans controlling them, and change. Flannery and Marcus worked in five communities between 1970 and 1972, and their study intermittently includes maps of features and sites. This is not an explicitly archaeologically oriented work, but it does stress the need for historically based longitudinal ethnographic work. This and Ryan and her colleagues' research should be compared with an article by Mary Martin (1987), a member of the research team in which Horne (1994a) participated, that considers variations in herd composition in relation to the uses to which their human handlers plan to put the animals.

Activities centered on livestock are usually carried out under the sky rather than the built roof, and tangible remains of domesticated animals present are often sparse, particularly in warmer climes. Sometimes they can be inferred from troughs. More perishable organic evidence – fragments of wool or hair, animal hides, dung or fodder on floors, and milk residues on vessels – may not be looked for, and, further, may not survive.

Farming and intensification

Several researchers have described agricultural practices. A collection edited by Ian Farrington (1985) contains papers with ethnoarchaeological content by Alba González-Jacomé (1985), an ethnohistorian, on home gardens in central Mexico, and by Graham Connah (1985) on farming on the *firki* (black cotton soil) plains south of Lake Chad in Nigeria. Pawel (Paul) Gorecki (1985b) documents the rapid development of large drained field complexes in Kuk, near Mount Hagen in Papua New Guinea. These involved the construction of major "public works," such as the canalization of creeks and the digging of large and small drainage ditches, by cooperating tribesmen. A companion paper by Jack Golson and Axel Steensberg (1985) discusses the tools of agricultural intensification in the same area. These two volumes contain other actualistic papers of interest including one by Clark Erickson (1985) on experiments with raised fields near Lake Titicaca in the Andes. For Oceania, A. Di Piazza (1990) describes irrigated taro gardens on Futuna as a prelude to the interpretation of an archaeological layer with small pits dug into the subsoil.

Evidence of agricultural intensification may be expressed in "perimetric," boundary-marking features, as is shown by Glenn Davis Stone (1994), citing examples from northern Nigeria. Thomas Killion (1990) approaches intensification through study of the relationship between house lots and infields in the Sierra de los Tuxtlas, Vera Cruz, Mexico. His sample is intentionally "skewed to generally poorer, subsistence-oriented families, who live in the periphery rather than the core . . . of the settlements examined" (p. 195). Intensity of cultivation is here defined in terms of the frequency of cropping (measured by the formula C/C+F, where C represents crop and F fallow years). Whereas outfields are up to five hours walking distance from the house lot, infields are no more than 40 minutes away, contrasting with gardens in which plants are individually tended, in that the crops are managed in bulk. Killion demonstrates statistically that as the intensity of infield cultivation increases, so does the size of the Clear Area (patio), the area kept clean around the house (Pearson's r = .73; P <.001; N = 40). The rationale is that most of the tasks associated with infield agricultural production, including crop processing, maintenance of tools, and storage, take place in the house lot, whereas for outfields these are carried out away from the settlement. Killion uses data from the 35 households at or below the .5 level of cultivation intensity (i.e., with infields cropped no more than every other year) to derive a formula that could potentially be applied archaeologically: Infield intensity = .013 + .001 Size of Clear Area.

Unthinking use of such an estimate would however be extremely unwise since only 53 percent of the variation is in fact explained by the correlation established. Environmental variation between the northern and southern parts of the sierra contributes to the variance observed. Other factors must surely include the political situation, which affects nucleation of settlements, as does population density, and the absolute and relative sizes of infields, gardens, and outfields, technology, and probably also family size, stage in the domestic cycle, and the length of occupation of house lots. Killion's research, in its early stages at the time his article was written, will no doubt take more factors into account as analysis continues. By showing that there is "linkage between the material record of the residential area and features of the agricultural system" he may not actually provide "a methodological foundation for archaeological investigations of the nature and effect of agricultural production" (p. 192), but he demonstrates an innovative approach to the development of such a methodology that deserves to be applied elsewhere.

Conclusion: the importance of ethnography

Ethnoarchaeology is contributing both substantively and methodologically, and in innovative ways, to the interpretation of fauna and other evidences of subsistence in the archaeological record. The complexities revealed suggest that, as is also the case with settlement, we need to refine our typologies of and approaches to ancient subsistence strategies and settlement patterns. People in the past were not always either hunter-gatherers or farmers (sometimes they were both), and when such subsistence specializations exist, they may involve different groups, sometimes "ethnic" in character, with a long history of cooperative interaction, as for example the Marka and Bambara farmers, Fulani herders, and Bozo and Somono fishers of the inland Niger delta of Mali described by Susan and Roderick McIntosh (1980: 338–44), or Barth's (1961) nomadic Basseri pastoralists with their attached gypsy tribe of tinkers and smiths, and settled land owners and farmers in southern Iran.

The value of information gathered over periods much longer than the average ethnoarchaeological study is evident in cases discussed above. Binford benefited from Nicholas Gubser's (1965) ethnographic, and particularly John Campbell's (1968) earlier ethnohistorical, work among the Nunamiut, and Stone from that of his project director and later colleague, Robert Netting (e.g., 1968). The value of detailed longitudinal data is especially obvious in the latter case. Similarly, Longacre's Kalinga project relied on earlier ethnographic research by Dozier (1966) and others, and John Yellen's on previous studies of the !Kung, notably by Lorna Marshall (e.g., 1965) and Richard Lee (e.g., 1965). The productivity and quality of ethnoarchaeological research is greatly dependent upon the ethnography that precedes it. Where there is little or none, ethnoarchaeologists have no alternative but to undertake basic ethnography and ethnohistory themselves, as was the case with ND and Judy Sterner at Sukur in Nigeria (David and Sterner 1995, 1996; Sterner 1998). Thus, rather as much of methodological significance can be inferred from acknowledgments, so it is good practice in evaluating an ethnoarchaeological text to turn to the references to see on what ethnographic foundation it is constructed.

The concept of social representation introduced in this chapter is explored in later chapters in relation to technologies as varied as iron working and the cultivation of fig trees for bark cloth. Meanwhile, we may note that the extent to which social representations influence cultural practice in matters of subsistence has received much less attention from ethnoarchaeologists than from sociocultural anthropologists.

Further reading

Binford's (1987a) paper, "Researching ambiguity: frames of reference and site structure," links the study of fauna to site structure. There is much of value on which we have been unable to touch in Jean Hudson's (1993a) important collection of papers, including John Fisher's study of the material expressions of interaction between Pygmy Efe and Bantu Lese at elephant processing sites in Zaire. This is one of a number of recent papers on Pygmies that includes one by Hudson (1991) herself on the expression in faunal remains of non-selective small-game hunting strategies. In the same volume, Fiona Marshall (1993; see also 1994) shows how social relationships, personality, hunting success, and animal size affect body part representation in Okiek hunter-gatherer households on the western Mau escarpment, Kenya. A set of papers by Karen Lupo (1994, 1995, 1998) focuses on different aspects of hominid and other scavenger activity, including their distinction in archaeological contexts.

Patricia Anderson's (1999) edited volume, *Prehistory of agriculture: new experimental and ethnographic approaches*, contains several examples of the kinds of cross-cultural literature reviews and experimental archaeological studies commonly used by archaeologists studying subsistence in the Old World.

CHAPTER 6

STUDYING ARTIFACTS: FUNCTIONS, OPERATING SEQUENCES, TAXONOMY

A spade is a spade is a spade.

(Gertrude Stein)

A spade is never so merely a spade as the word spade would imply.

(Christopher Fry)

If [archaeologists] are to realize their avowed aim of reconstructing past decision making, they will have to stop looking back from their present position in time, trying to recognize in the past patterns that are observed in the present. *They will have to travel back* in time and *look forward* with those whom they study.

(Sander van der Leeuw 1991: 13)

Archaeological and ethnoarchaeological approaches

Ethnoarchaeologists have contributed by providing descriptions of ethnographic specimens – archaeological ethnography (*sensu* Kent) – to the identification of archaeological artifacts and, through ethnoarchaeology, to interpretation of many aspects of their significance. We shall discuss examples, but need first to answer two not so simple questions: what are artifacts and what do archaeologists hope to learn from them? An artifact is something culturally fashioned, arranged, or substantially modified by humans, for example a basket, a circle of unworked megaliths, or the mark of a plough on a buried land surface. Although the concept covers machines and facilities – airplanes, traps, buildings, and the like – we are concerned in this chapter rather with small, transportable objects, tools, weapons, clothing, and decorative items. We will emphasize those, especially pottery and lithics, that tend to survive in the archaeological record, and those that are produced by non- or part-time specialists or by household industry (van der Leeuw 1977: 70). Appropriately questioned, artifacts provide information on how humans coped with their environments, on their social arrangements, and on their systems of thought, or, put another way, how they acted on the world, on each other, and on themselves. These categories of course correspond with Binford's (1962, 1965) famil-

Fig. 6.1 Michael Dietler takes notes on Luo pots at Oriang market, South Nyanza, Kenya, 1982.

iar technomic, sociotechnic, and ideotechnic subsystems – or interpenetrating domains – of culture.

Archaeologists, confronted by the discarded end-products of behavior, must use the formal properties of artifacts for purposes of classification and seriation (ordering their materials in terms of similarity). By these and other means they define toolkits and infer sociocultural entities, processes, and relationships in space and time. How is it that artifacts come to carry such information? Archaeologists account for the formal characteristics of an artifact in terms of stylistic, functional, and material attributes. We shall not recapitulate here a lengthy archaeological debate on the meaning of style (see Conkey 1990 for a thoughtful introduction), nor anticipate style's role in marking social boundaries (see chapter 7), but shall adopt an approach founded on that of James Sackett (1990). Style inheres in a polythetic set of attributes distinctive of a particular production system; thus we may speak of Luo pots (Fig. 6.1), i.e., pots that are stylistically Luo because, despite variations in shape, size, decoration, and other attributes, certain characteristics appear repeatedly throughout the set even though no single one is necessarily present on or diagnostic of all pots made by Luo (Dietler and Herbich 1994). Although artifacts may function in all three cultural domains, utilitarian, social, and ideological, when archaeologists speak of functional attributes they usually mean those that relate to the artifact's ability to perform its intended utilitarian or technomic role(s). Sackett's (1977) first and most basic contribution was to see that style and function are not mutually exclusive. A characteristic of an artifact can be *both* functional *and* stylistic. Thus the elegant parallel flaking of a predynastic Egyptian flint knife contributes to its instrumental function of cutting, slicing, carving, and gashing various materials, but also marks it as the product of a specialist manufacturing tradition with defined spatial and temporal coordinates. On the other hand, painted decoration on a pot has no technomic function, and is sometimes therefore referred to as "adjunct" form. We have much more to say about style in the next chapter.

Attributes are incorporated into artifacts in the course of their production, a process that involves a series of technical decisions that are "embedded in and conditioned by social relations and cultural practice" (Dietler and Herbich 1998: 235).

Displacing predominantly craft-based production in which skilled laborers exercised substantial control over their conditions of work, Fordist production entailed an intensified industrial division of labor; increased mechanization and coordination of large scale manufacturing processes (e.g., sequential machining operations and converging assembly lines) to achieve a steady flow of production; a shift towards the use of less skilled labor performing, *ad infinitum*, tasks minutely specified by management; and the potential for heightened capitalist control over the pace and intensity of work. (Rupert forthcoming)

The Model-T Ford did not merely revolutionize transportation in North America; it both rested on and contributed to a transformation of social and economic life. In a particularly clear ethnoarchaeological case, Dorothy Hosler (1996: 82) has shown how, in a northern Andean community where potters make copies of archaeological artifacts,

Upper and lower *barrio* [ward] stratification or status distinctions and gender role differences are enacted in technological behavior, specifically in firing and construction procedures. Status differences are also expressed in the relative prices of the artefacts that are the products. The technological styles characterizing the two *barrios* reinforce and create the social and economic differences between these two sectors.

Chosen techniques are applied to raw material in sequences, and particular combinations of raw materials, techniques, and sequences are known as *chaînes opératoires*,[1] a concept first employed by André Leroi-Gourhan in the 1950s (Lemonnier 1992: 25) and adopted by Francophone scholars (see especially Lemonnier 1992: 25–50; also 1976; Pelegrin *et al.* 1989) interested in *technologie culturelle*, roughly translatable as the anthropology of technology (Pfaffenberger 1992) or of techniques. Olivier Gosselain's (1992a) study of ceramic technology among the Bafia of Cameroon, and Michael Dietler and

---

[1] Sometimes translated as "operating sequences" which fails to capture the nuances of the French. A better translation would be "enchainments," with the dual implication of linked operations and involvement of other spheres of life; but anglicization is, as in the case of tuyère, probably the best solution.

Ingrid Herbich's (1989) paper on Luo ceramic technology and style exemplify ethnoarchaeological uses of the chaîne opératoire approach.

Michael Schiffer and James Skibo's (1997) theoretical framework for investigating formal variability in the design of artifacts can be considered a recasting of Francophone ideas in the terminology of behavioral archaeology. Their proposal usefully identifies many of the factors and their interactions that influence artifact design: performance characteristics, capability of the artisan, and a wide range of situational factors (procurement of raw materials, manufacture process, transport, distribution, use, storage and retrieval, maintenance and repair, reuse, curate behavior, and disposal). However, it sets forth an unrealistic and ethnocentric image of artisan as engineer-handyman adjusting design in the light of feedback regarding any or all activities on an artifact's "behavioral chain" in order to attain weightings of performance characteristics that approximate a culturally determined ideal (or, in socially heterogeneous contexts, ideals). Their archetypal artisan is in fact a projection of Schiffer and Skibo busily engaged in the Laboratory of Traditional Technology in a program of reverse design engineering that does indeed have the potential to act as a control and reality test of the type of explanation that, without reference to technological or utilitarian factors, attributes formal variation to such causes as gender competition and asymmetries in social power.

This paper provides experimental archaeologists with an agenda, and a careful reading will certainly assist the ethnoarchaeologist in designing research on ceramics or any other artifact class. Ethnoarchaeologists have an extraordinary advantage over archaeologists in that they can watch the unfolding of chaînes opératoires, demarcate what is determined by raw materials and physico-chemical constraints versus the areas of potential cultural choice, and document the integration of the technomic, sociotechnic, and ideotechnic domains, for to observe the forming of a pot or the smelting of iron, even the flaking of an adz, is to be offered simultaneous access to all three, though to greatly varying degrees. Observation of the classification, distribution and exchange, use, and discard of artifacts offers similar opportunities. While archaeologists must engage in a painful process of reconstruction, ethnoarchaeologists have available to them, though they rarely if ever take full advantage of, privileged access to the full range of interpenetrating cultural domains expressed in material culture.[2] However, whether even the most committed ethnoarchaeologist can achieve the high standard of explanation advocated by Schiffer and Skibo (1997: 43) is extremely doubtful.

---

[2] Naturalist students of material culture, now it would seem mainly German (e.g., Weingarten 1990; Hahn 1991), are primarily interested in documenting material culture for its own sake and as an index of cultural relationships. (In a more theoretical paper that aims to link material culture studies to ethnoarchaeology, Hahn [1996a and see also 1996b: 1–25] proposes that ethnicity be studied by taking a semiotic approach to material culture.) Art historians may have similar agendas; a fine example is Barbara Frank's (1998) comparative study of technological styles in Mande potting and leather-working as evidence of regional history.

In constructing an explanation [of design variability], the investigator must argue not merely that specific factors affected a design, but also demonstrate that others did not. Apparently, one cannot resolve problems of equifinality without controlling for the influences of all *potentially relevant* causal factors.

Lastly we may note that, as Schiffer and Skibo (1997: 44) themselves recognize, "explaining design variability is only one of many social issues surrounding technology . . . Explanations of [quantitative, relational, and spatial dimensions of] artifact variability clearly require other bodies of theory." Thus their suggestion that we should "discard some of our most cherished theoretical and analytical categories – style and function, utilitarian and symbolic causes, technological and cultural factors, and so forth" (p. 28) is misguided.

Identification of artifact functions

Ethnoarchaeology is rarely essential in the identification of the functions of archaeological artifacts; this is usually achieved by some combination of ethnographic, ethnohistorical, and other means including of course the accounts of early travelers from Herodotus on. James O'Connell's (1974) identification of the functions of *yilugwa*, distally and laterally retouched quartzite blades that he had collected during a survey in Central Australia, depends on critical readings of ethnographic descriptions, the testimony of Alyawara Aborigines, and observations of use-wear. He concludes that these tools, which a Europeanist would likely describe as endscrapers or *limaces*, were in fact used as women's knives, for light scraping, and as spoons for eating baked or roasted tubers. Similarly, in a study of the functions through time of Maya vessels with appliqué spikes, Michael Deal (1982) combines his ethnoarchaeological observations with the evidence of Maya codices, monumental art, and the archaeological record. He confirms the ritual use of these vessels, but concludes that they served a wider range of functions than previously supposed. Also combining sources of evidence in order to investigate the function of lithic assemblages, Brian Hayden (1977, 1979b) found that in Australia the vast majority of flaked stone tools were used for wood-working activities. Use of chipped stone tools for processing vegetable foods was very rare; wooden clubs and digging sticks were and are used to procure small animals, while the killing and butchering of larger game, kangaroos and emus, might require only a single flake. The Western Desert groups among whom he worked did no skin processing. Small wonder that these Aborigines, with their particularly impoverished inventory, were little interested in stone tools. More morphologically distinct functional types are found elsewhere in Australia (e.g., Cane 1988), including well-made knives and bifacial points (e.g., Jones and White 1988). On the whole, Aboriginal stone toolkits appear generally closer to paleoindian than to style-rich and varied European upper paleolithic inventories – which may limit but certainly does not deny their analogical potential.

African landscapes are frequently littered with boulders and slabs that have on them numbers of artificial depressions (Fig. 6.2) that are commonly referred to as grinding hollows. Almost all appear to have been abandoned before records begin and detailed accounts of their functioning are non-existent. In 1996, ND (1998) carried out a study in the Mandara mountain community of Sukur, Nigeria, that combined ethnoarchaeological and field archaeological approaches to understanding this class of artifacts. He began by obtaining information on all the grinding and related activities carried out presently and in the recent past using stone tools. There are two mains sets of equipment: (a) flat querns (grinding slabs, metates) and handstones (manos) primarily used for grinding the staple millets, and (b) grinding hollows on small blocks that are now used with either rounded or elongated pestles as mortars for a variety of crushing, pounding, grinding, and other functions including the threshing of small quantities of beans or grain, as troughs for domestic livestock, and at times as altars. The original form of their hollows, shaped like a longitudinally cut piece of a hard-boiled egg, is frequently modified by internal channeling or rounded depressed areas that testify to lengthy secondary use. Such "grindstone-mortars" are obviously ancient and are believed to be have been made by God.

Arguing that the same broad division of functions could reasonably be extended back in time, and utilizing oral testimony regarding recent use of some hollows in iron production and a field census of 182 hollows and complexes of hollows, ND developed a classification of grinding hollows and their probable uses:

> Basin hollows, ovoid: grinding grain
> Mortar hollows, rounded: as grindstone-mortars (with threshing and crushing sub-types)
> Fining hollow complexes, multiple, small, irregular, rounded: for breaking up iron blooms produced by smelting (such complexes often being superimposed over other types)
> Informal facets and complexes, shallow, sometimes multiple: miscellaneous grinding functions (in some cases early stages of basin hollows)
> Grinding groove complex, multiple narrow grooves: for forming stone axes (one very ancient example).

The functioning of the basin hollows was elucidated by further reference to ethnoarchaeology. In all the many Sukur compounds visited, wives are equipped with a grinding stand of daub and rubble construction into the top of which are set one, two, or occasionally three querns, pairs and triplets having surfaces differentially pecked to enable coarser and finer grinding. The flat surfaces of the querns and handstones, which are carefully maintained, achieve maximum attrition and grinding efficiency. In contrast, ovoid basin hollows are deeper at the broader end, conforming to the expectation that a person grinding will bear down more heavily and with more lateral freedom at the start of the thrust. This is confirmed by the consistent positioning of the deeper end of hollows

Fig. 6.2 Grinding hollows on a granite block at Sukur, Nigeria, (1996); note that the larger hollows' deeper ends are near the edge of the support. Besides the larger hollows, inferred to have been used for grinding millets, there are also informal facets besides pitting resulting from the crushing and breaking of iron blooms. Field assistant Isnga Dalli Sukur acts as scale.

nearer the edges of their supports. Their conformation renders it impossible to maintain good contact between them and any shape of handstone, and moreover they are frequently located on bedrock outcrops and boulders that would have been difficult to protect from the elements. Thus they would appear technically less efficient than modern grinding stands. The latter maximize convenience of use and contact between upper and lower grinding surfaces; they also represent a form of economic intensification, since they facilitate the production of fine flour, rendering more nutrients available than from the same weight of coarsely ground groats. Such considerations enabled ND to devise a classification of basin hollows into four technological stages that were shown by field archaeological evidence to correspond to a historical development that culminates in the flat querns of the present.

ND's study was informed by other ethnoarchaeological, archaeological, and experimental research (e.g., Roux 1985; Hayden 1987c; Horsfall 1987; Wright 1992, 1994; Adams 1993, 1996), and indeed there is in this area a productive synergy between the three approaches. It could have been improved by better recording techniques and by analytical and experimental work on grinding and wear patterns. Nevertheless it begins to systematize understanding of a phenomenon widespread in Africa, and has implications also for other continents, for the history of landscape, and even, ND argues, for prehistoric demography.

Hayden's (1987d) paper on stone tools in the Maya highlands is concerned with present and inferred prehistoric uses besides the relationships between traditional tools and industrial replacements and other topics. He shows that lithic cutting tools have been replaced by metal ones, and proceeds to investigate the range of functions of cutting tools and then look for artifacts in the archaeological record that might be capable of fulfilling them. A surprising inference is that hardwood billhooks would appear to have been used for a lot of bush cutting. Other examples of ethnoarchaeology contributing to the understanding of artifact function include Robert Carneiro (1979) on tree felling with a stone ax among the Yanomamö, J. Desmond Clark and Hiro Kurashina (1981) on the work of a tanner using obsidian scrapers in Ethiopia, and Ramon Silvestre's (1994) unique ethnoarchaeological study of basketry, carried out in the Philippines. Ethnoarchaeology can also assist in the identification of architectural and other features, as for example M. K. Dhavalikar's (1994) use of modern housing to interpret chalcolithic sites in India's Maharashtra state. But the citing of such cases, if not invidious, is at least potentially misleading since concern for function pervades ethnoarchaeological research, as it does other studies of material culture.

Techniques of manufacture

Techniques mediate between things and society and it is precisely for this reason that the ethnoarchaeological study of technologies leads in so many directions, towards apprenticeship and craft transmission, the organization of production, trade and exchange, style and the expression of social boundaries, gender, and ideology – to name only some – which we treat in later chapters. Here, while recognizing that there is no such thing as a purely technical question, we will concentrate on material aspects of technology. Archaeologists want to know how things are made because the answers have consequences for the design and execution of fieldwork, for classification, and for interpretation. To take a simple case, features of sherds from Iron Age ceramic series from Phalaborwa in South Africa led Richard Krause (1984) to believe that some potters might have formed the middle part of the pot before the rim and the base. His subsequent observations provided ethnographic examples of a modeling technique that does precisely that, starting with the formation of a cylinder of clay made out of one or more "straps" or flattened coils. A more complex example might involve the discovery of a sherd on a dig. Once identified as stoneware this would imply an achieved firing temperature of about 1200° C, requiring a kiln, and suggestive of other forms of advanced pyrotechnology such as metal working and a complex division of labor, or an alternative means such as trade of acquiring such items, or both.

While more "scientific" information comes from materials science and experimental archaeology than from ethnoarchaeology, and variables are harder to control and monitor, field studies almost always produce data that are unexpected and of significance for archaeology .

Ceramics

Because ceramics are, at least in the form of sherds, virtually indestructible, and because they offer almost infinite potential for cultural expression, they are, as indicated in chapter 1, the class of artifacts most intensively studied by archaeologists in general and ethnoarchaeologists in particular (Kramer 1985). There was already a considerable ethnographic and ceramicist literature on pottery manufacture in various parts of the world, from Frank Cushing (1886) on the Zuni to Michael Cardew (1952) and William Solheim (1952) on Nigerian and Oceanic pottery respectively, before the publication of Anna Shepard's (1956) *Ceramics for the archaeologist* in the year that ethnoarchaeology was born. This book served as the standard archaeological text on ceramic analysis until the appearance of Prudence Rice's (1987) *Pottery analysis: a sourcebook* three decades later. Owen Rye's (1976) seminal study of materials and manufacture of Papuan pottery was carried out from a perspective closely resembling that underlying the chaîne opératoire, with the intention of providing archaeologists with etic data to complement and counteract the "cultural determinism" of traditional archaeological analyses of ceramics. Rye's research, which combined field and experimental work in a broad comparative framework, continues to inform and influence ethnoarchaeological research on ceramics.

Here we contrast the work of two authors, Richard Krause, with whom we are already acquainted, and Olivier Gosselain, a Belgian ethnoarchaeologist. Krause (1978, 1985: 38–62) had developed a formal account of "Iron Age Bantu potting practices" on the basis of his study of materials from Phalaborwa. His purpose in his 1984 article and in a monograph (1985) entitled *The clay sleeps* is to compare his formal model, predictions based on his reading of the archaeology, against ethnographically observed cases. To do this he chooses (we are not told how) three women, representing the Ndebele, Venda, and Tswana ethnic groups, with each of whom he spends about seven to eight days, describing in considerable detail their manufacture of pottery. (Despite processualist jargon and the use of a descriptive notation derived from formal logic, Krause's descriptions in "natural language" are readable and clear.) He uses two thermocouples to measure temperatures during the firings (incorrectly described in terms of "furnaces" and "kilns"; open bonfire and pit firing are the appropriate terms). He then compares the formal account and the ethnographic practices, finding that

the archaeological model of ceramic manufacture predicted the kinds and distributions of acts reasonably well. To be sure it lacked some of the detail supplied by ethnographic observation . . . The greatest disparity lay, as expected, in the domain of decoration . . . Despite these differences, however, both ancient and modern potters confined primary designs to precisely the same decorative environments. (1985: 144)

What are we to make of this? First, let us discount Krause's rhetoric regarding prediction. If the potters had made their pots differently, would that have disproved his reconstruction of Iron Age practice? Of course not, though it might be inaccurate. More probably such an outcome would have indicated that different potting traditions were being practiced in the past and the present, for any or several of a variety of reasons relating to population replacement or other forms of culture change. Second, we are invited to assume that each tribal group has its own tradition of potting and that the work of any potter within that group is equally representative of it. This may not be the case; the study of variation within and between entities is a hallmark of good ethnoarchaeology – although we recognize that Krause's fieldwork was constrained by limited money and time. Third, while we learn some native terms, the descriptions of potting practice are almost entirely from the outside.

The second ring was placed atop the first before [Mutshekwa] knelt, threw the weight of her body back on her heels, and began to weld the two cylinders together. To accomplish the weld, she started from the outer surface of the bottom ring and pulled upward with the first three fingers of her cupped right hand. (p. 92)

We enter the compounds of Emma and her sisters but little into their minds and the processes of decision-making. We learn that bad clay is distinguished by tasting salty, and get an occasional glimpse into the world of technological metaphor. Clay and water are mixed, and "Emma explained that during the night the clay sleeps, adding that the clay was like a woman, the water like a man . . . 'If the clay is good and the water strong the clay will take the water in and the union will be fruitful' " (p. 68). But for the most part video surveillance could have substituted for the human observer.

Fourth and last, there is a very real value in formal descriptions of manufacture (though to the best of our knowledge no one has adopted Krause's system of notation) in that they facilitate the definition of similarities and differences between materials. This is a prerequisite for the study of change, for unless we know precisely what is different we cannot begin to explain it (van der Leeuw 1993). We return to this point at the end of the chapter.

Rather than treating his informants as icons of techno-ethnicity, Olivier Gosselain (1992a, 1994, 1995) employs a chaîne opératoire approach incorporating scientific analyses that assist in determining the extent to which material and environmental factors determine the potter's behavior, and which decisions express "free" cultural choice. In his thesis and elsewhere Gosselain (1995, 1998) describes the work of 82 potters drawn from 21 ethnic groups speaking languages of two families, and distributed in a broad band across southern Cameroon in environments ranging from upland savanna to rainforest. In this section, rather than with his inquiry into the relationship of technology and ethnicity, and the exploration of symbolism in ceramics, we are concerned with the constrained cultural manipulation of the materials and forces of nature that constitutes the chaîne opératoire.

There is cultural choice even in the selection of clays; the Bafia, for example, reject clays that nearby groups would happily use in favor of materials that, not being too wet or sandy, are suitable for near immediate use, only requiring pounding to render them workable. As Gosselain (1992a: 567) demonstrates through field use of a Thorvane shear device, the pounding reduces excessive initial plasticity to a relatively standard workability. The pots are then built up by one of the very many variants of the coiling technique known from Africa and elsewhere (Fig. 6.3). When Gosselain gives a Bafia potter a different clay prepared by a Banen potter, whose own practice is to form pots by drawing from a lump, the former has no difficulty in shaping it into a pot. As Gosselain (1994: 105–6) demonstrates elsewhere for his entire sample, "the successfully exploited clays have an extreme granulometric and plastic variability for the same potting techniques and pot functions. Second, there is no clear correlation between the use of different techniques . . . and the selected clays." The existence within southern Cameroon of a wide range of manufacturing techniques that are little if at all constrained by the kinds of clays available is indicative of considerable freedom of cultural choice and an absence of environmental determinism.

And yet, beyond selecting from standard ranges of forms and decorative treatments, potters very rarely make a conscious decision to employ a particular forming or decorative technique. The choice, made at some time in the past by

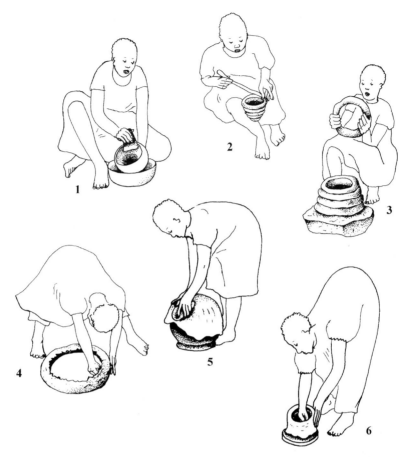

Fig. 6.3 African techniques of forming pots according to Olivier Gosselain:
1, pounding in a concave mold; 2, coiling (numerous variants); 3,
superimposition and drawing of large rings; 4, drawing of a ring-
shaped lump; 5, molding over a convex mold; 6, drawing of a lump.

a social, though not necessarily an "ethnic," group, is reaffirmed and inculcated
through apprenticeship. Indeed, Gosselain (1992a: 572) states that "all the
potters I was able to interview, among Bafia as among other groups, are convinced that there are no possible alternatives to their shaping technique." This
may represent an extreme set of cases, or oversimplification by the potters for
the benefit of an importunate visitor, for elsewhere when groups come into
contact potters are often aware of and sometimes able to demonstrate alternative forming techniques.

The shaping of rims and handles, and surface finish and decoration are, even
if channeled by cultural tradition, prime exemplars of cultural choice, but the
drying of pots is required to expel the water of plasticity contained within the
pot fabric lest firing turn it explosively to steam. Drying, therefore, while it

may be influenced by placement of the drying pot in the shade or sun or near a fire, is strongly influenced by meteorological conditions. Firing on the other hand allows for much greater expression of cultural choice, from the simple bonfires used by the Bafia to the extraordinary variant of pit firing described for the Bamileke (Gosselain 1995: 229) during which the removal of palm fronds supporting the pots causes them to tip into a pit. But in contrast to the close correlation of a potter's forming techniques with membership of the group into which she was enculturated, in the firing of pots economic and individual decisions are more in evidence, and, perhaps because firing is more obviously public, potters seem often to follow local practice even if they originally learned another. Thus not only are the different stages in the manufacture of pottery associated with different degrees of cultural, economic, and environmental determination but cultural constraints on choice are themselves correlated with different sociocultural groupings. All of these factors render the chaîne opératoire an extraordinarily complex and sensitive record of patterned human behavior. Its information potential for the archaeologist is correspondingly great – if only it can be deciphered. This is an area in which precise measurements in the field and study of causes and effects in the laboratory are of special value.

Relations with experimental archaeology and laboratory studies
In 1992 Longacre described the "essential joining of ethnoarchaeology and experimental archaeology" as "the perfect marriage" and gave several examples from the work of his team among the Kalinga. These include James Skibo's (1992) and Masashi Kobayashi's (1994) work on use-alteration of pots,[3] and Aronson and colleagues' (1994) study of comparative performance characteristics, perceived and actual, of vessels from different villages and their relationship to factors such as pot thickness and clay constituents (see also Schiffer, Skibo *et al.* 1994). Maurice Picon (1992) provides other examples relating to ceramics from Morocco.

Archaeologists and others have attempted to infer firing temperatures from characteristics of pot fabric (see Rice 1987: 426–35 for a critical review), and even to use inferred firing temperature for classificatory purposes. Field studies are rare. Keith Nicklin (1981) used pyrometry to measure the firing temperature of pottery among the Ibibio of southeastern Nigeria, and Gosselain (1992b; 1995: 256–83) used from three to twelve thermocouples in a varied set of firings (Fig. 6.4). These revealed extraordinary variation in maximal temperatures in different parts of the same firing and even of the same pot, between firings done

---

[3] A Master's thesis by J. N. L. Smith (1993) combines field study of use-wear and alteration in two villages in the Democratic Republic of the Congo (*ex* Zaïre) with application of the results to an archaeological sample of Colono ware, hand modeled, low-fired pottery made by African slaves in parts of the southeastern United States. However, it remains to be demonstrated that successful elucidation of use alteration and breakage patterns on archaeological ceramics will result in consequential new insights into the past.

Fig. 6.4 Olivier Gosselain replaces fuel on a Banen potter's bonfire after inserting thermocouples to monitor variation in temperature during the firing, Ndikinimeki, southern Cameroon, May 1991.

by the same potter, and between firings by different potters using the same procedure. On the other hand when his and others' data were combined, major overlap in the temperature ranges associated with different types of firing was found (Fig. 6.5). It is remarkable that in southern Cameroon, and by implication elsewhere under domestic modes of production, very different rates of heating (from 10 to 140°C/minute), maximum temperatures (400° to 950°C), and durations of firing (14 to 64 minutes) are *not* associated with careful selection of clays. Reconstruction of firing temperatures is shown by Gosselain's study to be both problematic and of very limited use for the drawing of technological inferences. One might add that the genius of the domestic potter lies in her ability to produce, using a simple technology, viable products from varied materials that full-time specialist potters would unhesitatingly reject as substandard. The same is true of African smelters of iron (chapter 11).

Lithics

The flaking of stone tools is a rarity today, sometimes surviving as among the Lacandon Maya (Clark 1991) as a tourist art, or practiced for the benefit of visiting anthropologists as among the Xêtá Indians of Brazil (T. O. Miller 1979). Hayden and Nelson (1981) found core tools being used for the manufacture of

TEMPERATURES (° C) RANGE

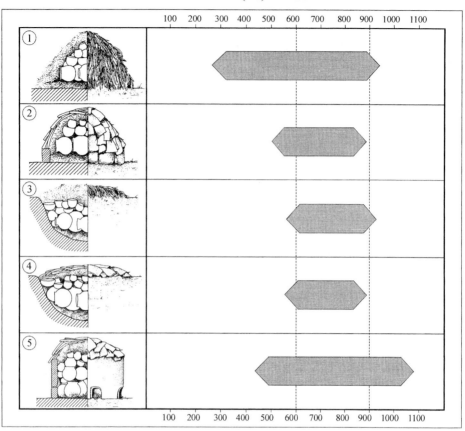

Fig. 6.5 Temperature ranges for five kinds of firing, based on thermometric data. 1, open firing; 2, open firing with sherds covering the pots; 3 pit firing; 4, pit firing with sherds covering the pots; 5, updraft "kiln" firing. The shaded temperature ranges for each type of firing comprise over two thirds of the data. In Gosselain's (1992b) article sample sizes were 27, 18, 12, 4, and 26 respectively.

grinding equipment (manos and metates) in the Maya Highlands, and industrial glass being flaked to make a variety of finishing tools and others for curative and ritual bloodletting. In 1978 Richard Gould (1981) studied Fred Avery, whom he believed to be the last of the knappers of gunflints at Brandon, England. Some Gurage, Konso, and other Ethiopian leather workers still manufacture scrapers (Gallagher 1977; Brandt 1996; Brandt and Weedman 1997), but if not the only African knappers these are the only ones studied by ethnoarchaeologists. In parts of Australia a broader range of artifacts continued to be made at least into the early 1970s (Gould 1968a, 1968b, 1980: 121–37; Gould *et al.* 1971), but by the mid-1930s all Aboriginal groups had reliable access to steel axes (Hayden

1979b: 5), and thus all the properly ethnoarchaeological studies of flaking have a strong flavor of reenactment. In Papua New Guinea, White (1967, 1968) and White and Thomas (1972) reported on the manufacture of stone flakes by the Duna in the 1960s, but, since they did not retouch their products but only chose from among them, these papers are of limited technological interest for the many archaeologists who, mistakenly, characterize as tools only those cores, flakes, and blades that are either retouched or burinated. It is unfortunate for archaeology that none of the peoples who have been observed manufacturing flaked stone tools have evinced much interest in this aspect of their culture, far less elaborated their knapping in the manner of, for example, the European Solutreans. Perhaps the closest are the Yolngu (Murngin) of Arnhem Land, whose quarrying of quartzite, core reduction, and flaking of points and other forms are described by Jones and White (1988). These are genuinely "righteous rocks," *sensu* Gould (1980: 141–59), imbued with "spiritual essence," and in part for that reason were widely traded.

The most sustained of the Australian studies is that of Hayden (1976, 1979b) carried out mainly at Cundeelee, southern Western Australia, and Papunya near Alice Springs in the Northern Territory. However, as noted above, his informants had little expertise in knapping and frequently appeared to be attempting to reconstruct the process from memories of an older generation. The 1979 monograph includes reports of post-mortem excavations of old camp sites that are of interest in regard to site formation processes and activity areas. Binford and O'Connell (1984) describe a day spent with Alyawara men at a stone quarry in Australia's Northern Territory about 250 km northeast of Alice Springs. While this was a reenactment performed at their request, they found, as have other ethnoarchaeologists in similar circumstances, that the men did more than they were asked (Fig. 6.6). They "were acting out past situations, in a nostalgic mood triggered by the events of the day and their interest in the place" (p. 406). The observers especially noted:

1 the kneeling or squatting rather than sitting postures of the men while flaking, which would influence the distribution of waste materials,[4]
2 a specific technique of core production and flaking that produces an end product commonly represented in the Australian archaeological record, and
3 the "organization of technical options."

The men produced blade blanks at the quarry but also a core that they brought back to camp. The blade blanks were to be used for men's fighting knives (see Binford 1986) and they wanted, before leaving the quarry, to be sure they had just the right pieces for these curated artifacts, while the core would be used to produce a number of expedient cutting and woodworking tools, the forms of

[4] Diltjima, a Yolngu whose flaking is described and photographed by Jones and White (1988: Plates 3, 4, and 6), sits cross-legged and flakes cores held well off to his left side.

Fig. 6.6 Lewis Binford, as participant observer, assists Alyawara men in quarrying a quartzite block, Northern Territory, Australia, June 1974.

which mattered much less. The authors conclude that the staging of manufacturing sequences among different sites requires archaeologists to think of the organizational factors that contribute to assemblage variability.

While ethnoarchaeology has made limited but nonetheless real contributions to the functional and technological analysis of flaked stone, archaeology has probably learned more from the experiments of such well-known knappers as François Bordes, Jacques Tixier (e.g., 1980, 1984), Nick Toth (e.g., 1985) and Don Crabtree (e.g., 1968, 1972), and from use-wear analyses (Hayden 1979a). There are even fewer ethnoarchaeological accounts of the manufacture of ground stone tools,[5] but some, since they describe actual rather than remembered and reenacted behavior, are of considerable value, including Homer Aschmann's (1949) brief study "A metate maker of Baja California." A major source is Hayden's (1987a) edited volume *Lithic studies among the contemporary Highland Maya*, which contains informative papers on manufacture using stone tools (Hayden 1987c) and on the quarry sites (Nelson 1987a, 1987b), and one by Gayel Horsfall (1987) entitled "Design theory and grinding stones" that by establishing functional and material constraints on form looks forward to a chaîne opératoire treatment of the topic.

[5] Papers by J. Mark Kenoyer and colleagues (Kenoyer *et al.* 1994; Vidale *et al.* 1993) that describe the organization of production and the techniques of stone bead manufacture in India are discussed in chapter 11.

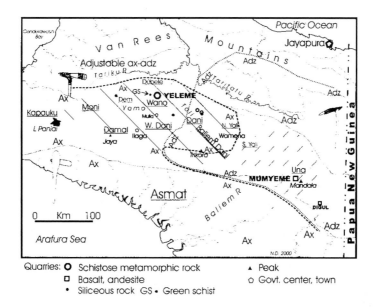

Fig. 6.7 Simplified map of east-central Irian Jaya (Indonesian New Guinea)
showing the Highlands and Van Rees mountains (shaded), main
peaks, major rivers, and some government centers. Selected quarries
are indicated, together with the main areas of distribution (hatched)
of rock from the Yeleme and Mumyeme quarries, and the areas of
distribution of axes, adzes, and, to the north, adjustable ax-adzes
(*haches à pince et tête pivotante*). Names of ethnic groups are
underlined. Data from P. Pétrequin and A.-M. Pétrequin (1990) and
other sources.

Multiple chaînes opératoires are evident in accounts by Pierre and Anne-
Marie Pétrequin (1990, and see also 1992, 1993) of two ancient traditions of
ground/polished stone tool use in east and central Irian Jaya (Indonesia). Axes
are the prime woodworking tool in the western part of this region, but are
locally being replaced by adzes, the tool long favored in the east (Fig. 6.7). To
the northwest an ax-adz, with a hafting system that permits changing the
blade's angle of attack, is used, though in practice rarely as an adz. The considerable typological variety within the two main traditions cannot be correlated
with environmental zone (highland or lowland), type of agriculture, practice of
specific techniques – for example canoes are made using both axes and adzes –
or linguistic or cultural groups. However there appears to be a relationship
between mean blade length and the state of the humanly transformed environment, smaller blades, whether hafted as ax or adz, being adequate to cope with
the vegetation of areas of higher population density. Within each tradition
variant chaînes opératoires are practiced. Basalt and andesite raw material
occurring in stream beds in the eastern Mumyeme area in areas of low population density is first broken by thermal shock and flaked at the quarry into crude

Fig. 6.8 Anne-Marie Pétrequin with Wano men in a rockshelter close to the Yeleme ax quarries and a day's walk from their village of Ye-Ineri, Irian Jaya, 1985. It is evening and they are relaxing around a fire that also serves to dry carrying nets and the meat of arboreal kangaroos hung on a wooden rack.

roughouts. These are then brought back to nearby villages where they are given almost final form by specialist knappers, often lineage heads, using hard and soft hammers. These require little polishing to produce a 20 cm blade in a total of about three hours. The process is documented in a film (Thery *et al.* 1990) that shows the manufacture by the Langda sub-group of Una of basalt adzes and their use for tree felling and a variety of more delicate functions.

In the western zone an alternative strategy is used by western Dani and other groups who travel to quarries in rockshelters and streams in the Yeleme territory of the northern Wano in order to obtain blue-green schistose metamorphic rock for making axes (Fig. 6.8). These tough and resistant raw materials are first broken up using thermal shock and then crudely blocked out by flaking on an anvil and subsequently with a hard hammer to produce a roughout with a more or less symmetrical lenticular section. The workers are not specialists and there is much breakage. The roughouts are then carried back to the village, which may be several days' walk away, and given their final form with very little further flaking but by lengthy polishing, requiring about 20 hours to produce a 20 cm blade. Thus, in contrast to the Una and other adz-makers who live close to the Mumyeme quarries and have invested in craft skills, the western Dani first invest in social relations, either by gift giving or by forming quasi-military expeditions to gain access to raw materials, and then invest labor in the simple but time-consuming task of polishing.

These very different chaînes opératoires are not associated either with the form of the final product or with the raw materials used in their manufacture. The northern Wano who live in the area of the Yeleme quarries are expert knappers, making regular preforms that require little polishing. Technical knowledge tends to decrease as a function of distance from quarries, while polishing of the blade, which helps to reduce breakage in use by better distribution of shock waves, increases with distance. A third, black siliceous, raw material is often not flaked at all. Cobbles of suitable shape are selected from stream beds and then ground and polished into shape directly.

It is clear even from this simplified account that cultural strategies play far greater roles than any supposed technological imperatives in determining the chain of techniques used to manufacture axes and adzes in Irian Jaya. The interrelationship of the ax and adz traditions is further considered in chapter 12 in the context of exchange.

Other types of artifact

With the exception of studies of metallurgy (to be considered in chapter 11), ethnoarchaeological contributions to understanding the manufacture of weapons and tools other than ceramics and flaked stone are rare, although considerable information on woodworking is incorporated into primarily lithic research (e.g., Hayden 1979b; Gould *et al.* 1971). Hester and Heizer (1980, 1981) have described the manufacture, using metal drills, of alabaster vases in Egypt, and Belcher (1994, 1998) has written on fishing technology and especially nets in the Indian subcontinent, but archaeologists who wish to find out more about the manufacture of these and other classes of artifacts are best advised to turn to the extensive ethnographic and other literature on material culture.

Taxonomy, emics and etics

Taxonomy, based on its OED definition "Classification, especially in relation to its general laws and principles . . .," is the term here employed to refer to the class of procedures that includes classification, typology, and other forms of categorization.[6] Archaeologists are experts in the development of typologies for analytical purposes.

[6] This is the OED's (Compact Edn 1971) definition of taxonomy. Hayden (1984: 80) maintains that the term is best reserved for typologies intended to express historical relationships between units of study (but uses it in the more general sense three pages later). Classification, he says, "refers to virtually any system used for grouping objects together," for example by size or age. Typology, on the other hand, "should properly refer to systems of categorization which . . . reveal something about the nature of human behavior in relation to artifacts, whether this information is by nature evolutionary, functional, technological, temporal, social, or other."

Typologies can be devised to resolve problems of temporal relationships, cultural affiliation, and tool use; to identify individual manufacturing styles . . .; to identify community styles, trade, and technological processes; to estimate interaction between
communities . . .; to monitor recycling and status differences; to help interpret religious
structures and beliefs; to distinguish between egalitarian . . . and hierarchical . . . social
organizations; or to deal with any other specific interpretational problems of interest.
(Hayden 1984: 82)

Typologies can be evaluated according to a number of criteria of which the most
important is how well they succeed in their intended task.[7]

Contrasting with devised typologies are the folk classifications that we use
in our daily lives and to which ethnographers and ethnoarchaeologists are
exposed in the field. These "are used by the common people, have multiple
authors (usually unknown), are transmitted informally from generation to generation, and change through time" (Kempton 1981: 3). Whether or to what
extent folk classifications and typologies discriminate in the same manner
between artifacts, and whether their categories correspond, are questions over
which a lot of archaeological ink has been spilled (see Hayden 1984: 82–3 for a
summary history, and van der Leeuw 1991 for an innovative perspective).

It is useful here to distinguish "etic" versus "emic" standpoints for the
description of behavior (Pike 1954). The typologist's etic view is that of the cultural outsider who must painstakingly discover structure in data, defining, tab-
ulating, and analyzing variables and attribute states and their combinations,
before arriving at one or more of a number of possible classifications. The
ethnoscientist's emic approach on the other hand involves an attempt to understand and describe behavioral systems – such as folk classifications of color –
in their own terms as structures that have meaning within the cultures studied.
By extension the classes recognized in folk classifications are often referred to
as "emic categories" or even "emic types."

Folk classifications are obviously of the greatest relevance to the emically
inclined postprocessualist, while we might expect processualists, etically concerned with typologies, to ignore them. But the situation is not quite so simple.
Hayden (1984) provides a useful introduction to the question in which he points
out that there is limited understanding of the conditions under which and the
manner in which folk classifications are elaborated, that people are generally
unaware of and unable to explain the principles upon which the folk classifications they use are founded, and that, since in many societies much learning
occurs by imitation rather than through verbal instruction, the full complexity
of an artifactual domain – an element of habitus – may well not be expressed
in the range of native terms that applies to it.

Folk classifications, embedded in social life, also vary along social lines

---

[7] The criteria suggested by Hayden (1984: 82) are: testability, parsimony, the extent to which
observations fit hypotheses derived from the typology, the different types of data that fit such
hypotheses, compatibility with generally accepted theories, internal consistency, power, and
scope.

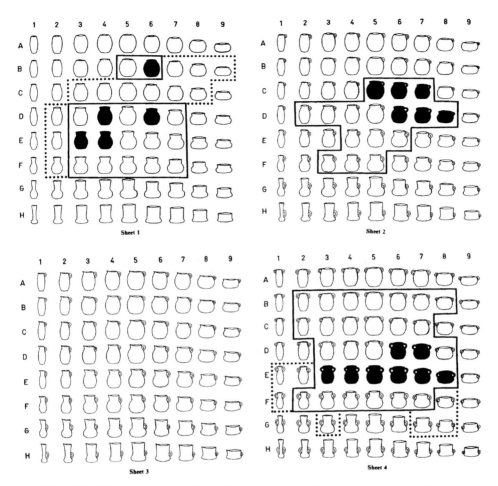

Fig. 6.9 *Olla*, a pot for cooking beans, as identified to W. Kempton by a 28-year-old Mexican woman, 1981. She classed the drawings shown with black fill on three of the sheets as "the best examples of *olla*" (one of which may be the prototype), those within the solid line as *olla*, and those within the dotted line as "sort of *olla*." The shapes illustrated include but extend beyond the range of pots actually made; note that the *olla* category includes pots with and without handles.

within the same culture. Willett Kempton's (1981) research – cognitive anthropology of considerable relevance to archaeologists and ethnoarchaeologists – demonstrates this very nicely. He develops a prototype and extension model for describing folk classifications and applies this in an extended study of Mexican folk classification of household ceramics (Fig. 6.9). Potters' and consumers' categories differ, and males' categories, he finds, emphasize vessel shape, while those of women, who more often use the pots, pay more attention to handles. Kempton's prototype concept has a resemblance to the "mental template," the cultural ideal that, in the bad old days when culture was supposedly shared rather than participated in, artificers were supposed to be aiming at when they made an artifact. But the resemblance is superficial inasmuch as different subcultural groups – experts, potters, women – define not only prototypes differently but also their extensions.

Peter White, Nicholas Modjeska, and Irari Hipuya (1977), an archaeologist, a social anthropologist, and (one supposes) an assistant from among the Duna people of Papua New Guinea, set out in 1973 to investigate the mental template concept as it applied to the categorization of Duna flaked stone tools. Their experiment involved asking about a dozen men in each of five parishes (settlement areas) separately to classify a sample of stone flakes made by men of one of the villages. Their selections were then compared in terms of the between parish variance in the metrical attributes of the samples selected, and secondly the degree of agreement between the selections of men in the same local group. The results are consistent with Kempton's prototype and extension model, and it is interesting, but in the light of practice theory not unexpected, that the prototype would appear to be a "covert category" that is not linguistically accessible. Given the rudimentary nature of the stone tools, which had already been largely replaced by steel knives, and the Duna lack of interest in classification this is perhaps not surprising. It would be interesting to repeat the experiment with more highly characterized artifacts in a different context, perhaps one in which potters' terminologies for vessels are based on volumetric variation, which may or not be related to vessel functions.[8]

To return to the question of taxonomy, Dorothy Washburn and Andrea Petitto (1993) show that weavers and nonweavers among southern Lao immigrants to New York State classify their embroidered skirts differently:

Weavers use more technical knowledge to classify the skirts than do women who do not weave and must buy the skirts to wear. In contrast, we found that southern Laotian women's categories of textile function involve adherence to social mores and cultural values and are based on general criteria used by both weavers and nonweavers. (1993: 157)

Weavers' and nonweavers' "categories of identification" differ, though both base them on technology, the kind of weaving, rather than on the decoration. But the two groups are similar in their "categories of function," which are based on different though overlapping criteria relating to which kinds of skirts should be worn on what occasions. This study of textiles, an ethnoarchaeological first, is also of methodological interest. By asking their respondents to sort and discuss color photographs and black and white Xerox copies of skirts, and to construct decorative patterns from colored paper, they were able accurately to determine which attributes were salient for which group of women. This is a

---

[8] The only other ethnoarchaeological paper with template in its title is Ian Robertson's (1992) study of hoes and metal (sic) templates made in northern Cameroon (see chapter 11).

paper that can be categorized as "cognitive processual" (Renfrew 1994), in that we learn what distinctions are emically significant to the Laotian women, but not what they mean to them at a deeper level.

Other processual explorations of emic categories include Dean Arnold's (1971) paper on the ethnomineralogy of the Maya potters of Ticul in Yucatan, which demonstrates that the folk classification of minerals reflects scientifically measurable characteristics of raw materials that have real implications for pottery manufacture. Other communities of potters categorize their materials differently (though it seems likely they are using similar if not identical principles). In his concluding section Arnold (1971: 38) claims that

> this paper indicates that the discriminations and contrasts which people make are reflected in the physical world of artifacts. It should be theoretically possible then, to build emic categories and perhaps emic strategies (combination of categories) out of physical discriminations and contrasts *without relying on ethnographic analogy for this reconstruction.* (1971: 38 [our emphasis])

Remembering the Shipibo-Conibo case in which DeBoer and Lathrap (1979) found that although the potters shared ideal recipes for mixing clays and temper, actual pots showed much variation from the ideal, we find it unlikely – and hard to demonstrate! – that emic mineralogical categories can be reconstructed from sherds, even though several archaeologists (e.g., Raymond *et al.* 1975; Hodder 1982a) appear to have achieved the logically comparable construction of "grammars" of prehistoric decoration (in some cultures the proper execution of decoration is subject to firmer prescription than the preparation of pottery clays). Let us ask instead why Arnold should regard the purely archaeological reconstruction of emic categories as important? Because if (a) ethnologists or ethnoarchaeologists could "link up descent rules, prestige formulations of stratification, ideal moral imperatives, and all other subjective actor-oriented ethnographic categories with the durable and verifiable material conditions of sociocultural systems" (Harris 1968: 361 quoted by Arnold), and *if* (b) archaeologists could apply c- and n-transforms to the remains of those systems, they could then (c) interpret the whole of past cultural life! Unfortunately, as we have indicated in chapter 4, because cultures are complex and emergent from long and individual histories, and because similar products may result from diverse causes, such working backwards from effects to causes is impossible. On the other hand, Arnold's analysis could well be integrated into a chaîne opératoire approach.

To what extent, given the preceding examples, has ethnoarchaeology contributed to archaeological taxonomy? Not, perhaps, a great deal, although Herbich and Dietler's (1991; see also Dietler and Herbich 1994) boiling down of Luo regional pottery variation into one "global repertoire" is certainly of interest. It can reasonably be argued that it matters not at all whether a particular typology corresponds to a folk classification unless it is specifically designed to do so (cf. Hill and Evans 1972). Hayden (1984: 89) asks whether there are any benefits for the archaeologist in studying folk classifications, and concludes, citing examples from his own work, that

Emic functional categories . . . can help archaeologists enormously when archaeologists are interested in dealing with functional problems in their assemblages. This approach is especially useful in cases where it is appropriate to use the direct historical approach . . . On the other hand, if an archaeologist's primary concern is to establish cultural-historical groupings, such emic categories would be of limited, or perhaps no, use.

This is true but not the whole truth, for folk classifications and, in the case of material culture, the corresponding sets of artifacts relate to each other as sets of categories, a topic which we take up in the following section.

Artifacts as categories

The theoretical position we have just presented is consistent with practice theory (see chapter 2) and is exemplified by Daniel Miller's (1985) monograph *Artefacts as categories*. Note the similarity to the chaîne opératoire approach in his introductory statement.

The central aim of this study is to explore the factors underlying variation in artefacts. The major proposition is that artefacts, as objects created and interpreted by people, embody the organisational principles of human categorisation processes.[9] Through the intensive study of a specific corpus of contemporary artefacts – the earthenware pottery in an Indian village – it is intended to investigate the manner in which these organisational principles generate variability in material forms. The variability of objects is significant as a major source of evidence for the study of society, the artefactual environment being one of the main products of social action. It is anticipated, therefore, that an understanding of the forces which create artefactual variability can also contribute towards an understanding of the social. (1985: 1)

Miller's data were collected in Dangwara, a village in Madhya Pradesh, in two periods of fieldwork between 1979 and 1981 that "covered most of the yearly cycle, apart from the monsoon and the preceding high summer [May through September?], when activities such as potting are comparatively restricted" (p. 17) (Fig. 6.10). The village is predominantly Hindu with a population in 1971 of 1537, in which 30 castes are represented. Caste is a fundamental institution in Hindu life, "a structure within which the guiding principle of hierarchy gives meaning to the individual elements of society by reference to the wider whole which it informs" (Miller 1982b: 91, paraphrasing L. Dumont). Castes are in most cases associated with a traditional occupation, and they and local (sub)castes are ranked on a scale of purity and pollution. During Miller's fieldwork there were seven households of the potter caste, six of them practicing potters with whom he worked intensively. He names two Indian research

---

9 The process of categorization, in Miller's sense, includes the manufacture of artifacts and the transformation of natural substances into cultural categories, as for example when certain natural items are classed as inedible or edible (Miller 1982a: 17).

Fig. 6.10 Daniel Miller (*left*) with Dangwara villagers, Madhya Pradesh, India, 1980.

assistants and states that his "own linguistic competence was sufficient for conversations about pottery and for following the gist of other conversations" (p. 17).

The wheel-thrown ceramic assemblage of Dangwara is rich – a reference list gives 51 named types. The average number of pots per Hindu household is 21.3 and there is a strong association between the numbers of pots per household and three main dimensions of household variability: position in the caste hierarchy, wealth, and number of adult members. This can in part be explained by the importance of transactions involving food for marking the relative hierarchical positions of castes, and of the extension of the symbolic associations of food and water to the vessels in which they are stored, cooked and consumed, and kept from members of lower-ranked castes. Pots play an important role in rituals, and indeed ceramic, and to a lesser extent metal, containers are involved in all aspects of life. Miller treats the pottery assemblage as a symbolic framework, a set of categories that relates to other sets of categories including those of caste and social position, "the creation of a meaningful dimension, a set of categories, from clay is a process of objectification by which the medium is turned by its makers and consumers into an instrument for potential representations of the nature of the world and society" (1985: 142) Ceramics becomes not a language, but a medium of discourse in which expression of caste differentiation is made possible through the production of numerous variant forms to serve a limited number of functions. Village households express their caste status in their ceramic inventories rather as North Americans situate themselves in society in part through their choice of automobiles (the academic Volvo, bourgeois Buick, daycare worker's rusty Ford, lawyer's Lexus, farmer's GMC 4x4, etc.). Nor is the situation static. While one's caste is fixed at birth, the members of local subcastes can change their behavior, their material culture, ritual, and ideology to approximate those of a higher caste, creating the basis for a subsequent claim to a higher status in the local hierarchy than they traditionally enjoyed. This process of emulation in pursuit of upward movement in the caste hierarchy (known as "sanskritization") acts, Miller argues, as a dynamic for ceramic change as upwardly mobile lower castes order pots associated with those above them, and members of higher castes demand innovation from their potters in order to maintain the distinctions. Thus, given the propensity to emulate and the symbolic importance of pottery, it becomes a condition of the maintenance of the set of categories that constitutes caste that there be changes within it! We have here a dynamic for change in artifacts which would seem unrelated to efficiency, only indirectly related to the economic sphere, and (*pace* O'Connell's general theory of behavior) very distantly to reproductive success.

We have necessarily ignored Miller's rich ethnographic description and documentation of the manufacture, typology, forms, decoration, functions, and distribution of the pottery in order to focus on his theoretical approach, and his forcefully presented argument for a particular view of objects and their role in constituting society. It is an original work that not everyone found compelling at the time of its publication. A reviewer of the processual school complained that "Virtually no data are presented that would permit independent verification of Miller's calculations or the results of his analyses" (Graves 1987: 194). Nonetheless, despite a difficult style and some incompleteness and ambiguity in the presentation of data, acceptance of his viewpoint has been favored by changes in the theoretical climate, in particular towards concepts of verification that emphasize explanatory fruitfulness. Support for his ideas on categorization is also found in later research in other societies and material domains, for example on the ceramics of the Mafa of northern Cameroon (David *et al.* 1988), or on the evolving architecture of Annapolis (Leone and Potter 1996). As Miller (1982a: 23) phrases it, "Categorisation processes mediate and organise the social construction of reality, and may be our best means for understanding and interpreting the remains of material production."

Does this mean that if archaeological typologies can be designed to correspond as closely as possible with emic categories they will prove effective tools in the analysis of the areas of culture to which they relate? Hardly so, since Dangwarans deny the relationship between pottery and society that Miller is concerned to propose (p. 192), though this did not lead another processualist reviewer (Kramer 1986) "automatically [to] presume that Miller is wrong and the Dangwarans right." The problem of demonstration of complex claims about such matters is taken up later in this book (and see the *Current Anthropology* treatment of David, Sterner, and Gavua [1988]). In the meantime we may answer the question posed above by saying that, while the approach may be fruitful, such disagreements, taken together with Hayden's cautions noted above, indicate that the answer is certainly not an unqualified yes – quite apart from the impossibility of demonstrating correspondence of types with emic categories in archaeological contexts.

Many questions and problems remain. Where ceramics are a focus of elaboration, as in Dangwara and among the Mafa, archaeologists should from their study be able to gain considerable, albeit imprecise, insights into the nature of their societies. However where, as among neighbors of the Mafa such as the Sukur (David 1996), far less skill and artistic attention is invested in pots, their lack of distinctiveness will likely render this impossible – even though they are still, unostentatiously, engaged in similar forms of discourse. It would seem that archaeologists require a certain degree of elaboration in a class of material culture to be able to interpret it in the manner of Daniel Miller. It would for example surely be futile to attempt to relate the impoverished lithic assemblages of Australian Aborigines to the sets of categories represented in their flourishing arts or complex social structures. But the reasons why different material culture classes are elaborated in closely related societies are varied, being subject to multiple historical contingencies, and are unpredictable, and even in some ethnographic cases inexplicable. Another question is how to link a set of material culture categories to a set of social categories. How particular is the linkage? Or do different material culture classes all inform from different perspectives upon the same social structures? Lastly let us note that, while phrased in terms of categories, Miller's argument could equally well have been couched in terms of style, the topic of the following chapter, or indeed chaînes opératoires.

A note on change

If in this chapter we have considered artifact change only incidentally, this is for two reasons. Change does not occur independently but is always related to other aspects of life, emulation, stylistic expression, economic efficiency, organization of production, and so on, and is therefore best treated in appropriate later chapters of this book. Second, and this is more serious, ethnoarchaeologists and archaeologists have conceptualized change poorly. Van der Leeuw (1977) points out that if we are to study change then we must first decide what constitutes change. On the basis of data drawn from ethnography, ethnoarchaeology, and archaeology he argues that, in the case of ceramic vessels, the three critical dimensions, in his words the "conceptual 'anchors'," of any potting tradition are:

1 topology – how the potter conceptualizes the shapes and transformations of shapes with which she or he deals,
2 "partonomy" – an ugly neologism referring to the potter's perception
   of the basic parts (coils, segments, handles, decorative bands, and the
   like) of which pots are made, and
3 sequence – how the many steps involved in the manufacture of pots
   are ordered.

He then applies these concepts to ethnographic datasets from the
Philippines, South Africa, and Mexico, and to archaeological sequences from
medieval northern Europe and the Mississippian of the southeastern USA,
revealing continuities and discontinuities in space and time that might well
have gone unrecognized and thus unquestioned in traditional typological analyses. This is an approach that deserves to be widely adopted and developed by
ethnoarchaeologists and archaeologists alike.

Further reading

Pierre Lemonnier's (1992) *Elements for an anthropology of technology* is basic
reading for anyone interested in the anthropology of techniques. Dobres and
Hoffman's (1994) "Social agency and the dynamics of prehistoric technology"
provides a critical and (relatively) accessible perspective on its application to
archaeological materials. See also their recent (1999) collection, *The social
dynamics of technology: practice, politics, and world views*, and especially
Dobres's paper on chaînes opératoires. Dietler and Herbich (1998) review the
French and Anglo-American traditions and advocate the incorporation of practice theory into the study of technology. Françoise Audouze (1999) sets the
chaîne opératoire in historical context and updates its development in upper
paleolithic studies.

In addition to Rye's Papuan study, he and Evans (1976) produced a major
monograph on the "ethnotechnology" of pottery in Pakistan that contains
much of value for archaeologists. Gosselain's (1992a) research on potters' clays
is usefully complemented by Arnold's (1972) mineralogical analyses of materials from Quinua, S. Peru, and by Arnold *et al.* (1991) on compositional analysis of pottery in the valley of Guatemala.

Prudence Rice (1987: 274–88) discusses a variety of typologies and folk classifications of pottery in her *Pottery analysis: a source book*. Gosselain and van
Berg (1991–2), the latter a Europeanist archaeologist, carried out an interesting
experiment in which, with considerable success, van Berg set out to identify
the work of individual potters in Gosselain's Bafia series. A.-M. and P. Pétrequin
(1990) relate variation in New Guinea arrows to a variety of ecological and
social factors, developing hypotheses that they apply to French neolithic materials (see also Giligny and Sidi-Maamar 1990).

The study of ceramics plays such a quantitatively and qualitatively important role in ethnoarchaeology that it deserves a book to itself. Our coverage is necessarily limited, and we regret the inevitable decision to exclude extended treatment of some of Dean Arnold's publications that combine cultural ecology with aspects of ethnoarchaeology, for example his *Ceramic theory and cultural process* (1985) and *Ecology and ceramic production in an Andean community* (1993).

CHAPTER 7

STYLE AND THE MARKING OF BOUNDARIES: CONTRASTING REGIONAL STUDIES

The concept of style is a bad concept, as it is commonly used by archaeologists.

(Lewis Binford 1986: 561)

Without style we have little or nothing to say.

(Margaret Conkey and Christine Hastorf 1990b: 2)

. . . we remain a thousand leagues from a theory of material culture as an ensemble of signifying traits.

(Pierre Lemonnier 1986: 173)

This lengthy chapter is divisible into two parts. In the first we tackle the definition of style and discuss where it resides, how it is produced, its function as a medium of information exchange, and its behavioral basis. In the second, we present critical analyses of four studies of manifestations of stylistic behavior on scales greater than that of a single community, three of which are genuinely regional in their scope. Why devote what might seem disproportionate space to this topic? Because there would be no archaeology if archaeologists did not regard the form of artifacts as in some manner informing on the culture that produced them. In 1912 when the Abbé Breuil (1913) delivered his classic address he relied on morphological differences in a variety of bone and stone tool types to distinguish cultural subdivisions of the European upper paleolithic and as a basis for inferring their evolutionary relationships. A characteristic European neolithic decorative tradition defines the "Linear Pottery culture," and so on. Style, "a highly specific and characteristic manner of doing something . . . always peculiar to a specific time and place" (Sackett 1977: 30), is an abstraction from form. For many years archaeologists implicitly made use of an "interaction theory" of style in defining cultures and other cultural entities. Its basic proposition can be simply formulated as follows: the degree of stylistic similarity between two components or assemblages is a measure of the intensity of social interaction between them. Thus if two assemblages are very similar they will be assigned to the same phase and culture; if more different, to separate phases of the same culture or to different cultures.

This approach has proved extremely useful and effective in developing time–space systematics (establishing the spatial and chronological relationships of assemblages to each other), but it has to be qualified. Warfare can be considered intense interaction but is unlikely to lead to stylistic resemblances between the opposing parties. More likely it will lead to functional convergence combined with stylistic differentiation (Sackett 1982). The interaction theory also ignores dynamics internal to society. Do modern teenagers wear the same clothes as their parents? Probably not; they are concerned within certain limits to differentiate themselves from the parental generation. But in ten years Japanese teenage boys may well find themselves wearing dark suits to work and young women comparable "power clothes," very like those their parents are wearing now. Were we living not in the twentieth century but in Shang China or the Natufian village of Beidha, our similarity in dress to our parents at the same age would be very close indeed, even though dress and other domains of material culture are used to mark differential status, rank, class, and roles. However, in the process of discard and site formation, a community's internal stylistic variation becomes jumbled together, so that in the archaeological record the stylistic difference between two assemblages is usually a pretty good measure of cultural relationship whether through space or time or both. Such relationships are one of the things that typologies are designed to measure.

Because style and social dynamics are interrelated, style also offers the archaeologist access to the social and ideological realms. It is therefore not surprising that the concept and functions of style should have been the subject of intense debate in the Anglo-American archaeological and ethnoarchaeological literature since 1977, a seminal year in which James Sackett proposed a general model of style and Martin Wobst that style is a mode of information exchange; Heather Lechtman introduced the notion of "technological style," and Ian Hodder (1977a) published the first of his essays on the material culture of the tribes of the Baringo district in Kenya. Developments in France, where a year previously Pierre Lemonnier (1976) had written "La description des chaînes opératoires . . .," were proceeding independently along similar lines. Only quite recently, as we saw in the previous chapter, has there been cross-fertilization of the Anglo-American and French intellectual traditions.[1]

Below we define style and show how ethnoarchaeologists have contributed to understanding how it is produced and how it works. We reserve to a later chapter (13) discussion of its connections to ideology and systems of thought. As debates over style have frequently been hampered by misunderstandings over terminology, we begin by providing a glossary for the convenience of the reader.

---

[1] "White (1993: xviii) muses," notes Miriam Stark (1998b: 7), "that, had translations of this French [culture and technology] literature been available twenty years earlier, we might have avoided the *style vs. function* debate altogether!" The remark underscores the (decreasing) unwillingness of American and French scholars to read in other languages.

Style

The definition and terminology of style

Influential authors' definitions of style and associated concepts are given below. Note that while these are expressed in terms of artifacts, style is expressed in all forms of cultural behavior.

Martin Wobst

Style: "that part of the formal variability in material culture that can be related to the participation of artifacts in processes of information exchange" (1977: 321).

James Sackett

Style: "a highly specific and characteristic manner of doing something . . . always peculiar to a specific time and place . . . the perfect complement of function . . . style and function together exhaust the potential of this variability, save for the . . . role post-depositional agencies may play in modifying the form of artifacts" (1977: 370).

Adjunct form: "variation that is added on and supplemental to the utilitarian *instrumental* form involved in [an artifact's] manufacture and functioning as an item in the techno-economic realm" (1990: 33), for example painted decoration on a pot or a manufacturer's hallmark on a wrench.

Isochrest-ic, -ism: literally "equivalent in use," a term coined by Sackett (1982: 73) for an approach, that taken in this book, that recognizes that style resides in the formal consequences of any cultural choice made by an artisan, including a choice between two functionally equivalent forms.

Icon-ological, -icism: an approach "that restricts style solely to those aspects of formal variation [especially decoration] that artisans purposely invest with symbolic content . . ." (1982: 59). A strict iconologue would not regard the form of a water pot as having stylistic qualities unless it was demonstrably non-functional in the utilitarian sense.

Active style: intentional signaling in the stylistic mode, often deemed to "constitute ethnic 'messaging' generated by what is essentially self-conscious, deliberate, and premeditated behavior on the part of artisans" (1990: 36). A view aligned with iconicism and which regards most if not all stylistic behavior as being of this nature.

Passive style: style that is "latent, inherent in the isochrestic choices which lie behind [artifact] manufacture" and deemed not to constitute intentional messaging. "The notion of passive style differs from active style . . . in that it regards making choices and assigning meaning to those choices as two distinct kinds of behavior" (1990: 36–7). Thus for example an observer may interpret a feature of an artifact as a marker of ethnicity even though the artisan never intended to invest the artifact with that message. A view aligned with isochrestism, and one that regards the bulk of stylistic behavior as being of this nature.

Vernacular style: "passive style with a vengeance . . . [consisting] of the bedrock design notions artisans of any given group inherit and in turn perpetuate as the agents of that group's craft tradition, notions that are as deeply and unconsciously embedded in their behavior as their motor habits, the dialects they speak . . . these design notions constitute a kind of substratum to the group's style . . . [which] might be viewed as a kind of stylistic genotype . . ." (1990: 39).

Deep style: "the realm of patterning that unifies and provides congruence to the vernacular styles" (1990: 41).

Heather Lechtman

Style: "the formal, extrinsic manifestation of intrinsic pattern . . . the manifest expression, on the behavioral level, of cultural patterning that is usually neither cognitively known nor even knowable by members of a cultural community except by scientists" (1977: 4), that is to say by scholars adopting an etic standpoint to advance their emic interests.

Technological style: the format or "package" defined by the relationships of "the many elements that make up technological activities – for example, by technical modes of operation, attitudes towards materials, some specific organization of labor, ritual observances – elements which are unified nonrandomly in a complex of formal relationships" (1977: 6). The crucial importance of cultural choice is implied by the nonrandomness, as it is in Lechtman's characterization of technological style as "expressed 'emic' behavior based upon primarily 'etic' phenomena of nature . . ." (1977: 7).

Polly Wiessner

Style: "formal variation in material culture that transmits information about personal and social identity" (1983: 256).

Emblemic style: "formal variation in material culture that has a distinct referent and transmits a clear message to a defined target population . . . about conscious affiliation of identity . . . Most frequently its referent will be a social group . . ." (1983: 257).

Assertive style: "formal variation in material culture which is personally based and which carries information supporting individual identity" (1983: 258).

Ian Hodder

Style: "the referral of an individual event to a general way of doing" (1990a: 45).

Where style resides

In the preceding chapter we suggested that when in the course of manufacture an artificer makes a cultural choice between two or more different ways of proceeding, the formal characteristics that the piece acquires as a result of the process can be regarded as stylistic. We may define style as *a potential for interpretation residing in those formal characteristics of an artifact that are acquired in the course of manufacture as the consequence of the exercise of cultural choice*. The term is however frequently employed in a loose sense to refer to the patterns of formal characteristics that give rise to the interpretive potential. Certain outcomes of the choices, for example between two rim forms varying in their degree of eversion, may be presumed to be functionally equivalent, whence the coining by Sackett of the term "isochrestic," equivalent in use, to refer to the approach advocated here. Archaeologists cannot in practice know that the resultant artifacts are indeed equivalent in use, a weakness in Sackett's argument that laid him open to attack by Binford (1989). Whether or not the outcomes of choices are strictly functionally equivalent is not, however, critical to the present argument. What matters is that patterns of cultural choices, themselves subject to selective pressures of various kinds, are evident in, and serve to differentiate, assemblages of material culture. Our view of style and Heather Lechtman's (1977: 6) concept of "technological style" (see above) deal with the same cultural reality from slightly different perspectives.

To be cultural a choice does not have to be made consciously each time it is exercised; indeed in chapter 6 we have seen Bafia potters denying to Gosselain the existence of alternative methods of forming pots, although they had consciously to learn their technique in the first instance and it is unlikely that none is aware of others. After first being learned, most choices, like that of shaking hands with the right hand, become habitual and rarely reach surface consciousness. A choice that is determined by the characteristics of a raw material is not cultural, although the choice to use that raw material generally is. Thus where in flint working the physical characteristics of the stone require the knapper to apply blows of a specific force and angle to a precise spot on the striking platform in order to remove a flake, cultural choice is considerably constrained – although the choice of different techniques of flake removal, hard or soft hammer or pressure flaking, may be regarded as largely cultural, and the form of even so banal a tool as an endscraper is imbued by style. There is far more potential for choice in the plastic medium of potters' clay, and far more again in its decoration, whence the intensive study of archaeological ceramics as vehicles of stylistic expression.

Thus style in material culture resides in the formal residue of cultural choices, conscious and unconscious, expressed in the actions of artificers and later users and modifiers of the artifact. While sometimes, as with advertising logos, form is added with the express purpose of transmitting a message, style is very often latent, existing in things as an unintended potential that must be realized by an act of observation. In this way the faunal analyst can read style and recognize ethnicity or other referents in butchering practices (Binford 1981a: 91–2; Chaix and Sidi Maamar 1992). The meaning of style is in fact always constructed by the observer, who may well misinterpret a message, or read meaning into formal variation when none was intended by the maker. (Artificers are of course observers of their own and others' work.) "Messages are far more often read than deliberately sent," writes Sackett (1990: 37).[2]

The production of style

Style is defined by the art historian Whitney Davis (1990: 19) as a polythetic set of attributes present by virtue of "common descent from an archaeologically identifiable artifact-production system." Note that the "potential for interpretation" that forms an essential part of our earlier definition of style is implicit in his phrase "archaeologically identifiable." Rembrandt's contemporaries were as concerned to differentiate his works from those of lesser artists as are art historians today. From mass production to unique works of art, formal variation first and foremost informs upon itself, upon the production system that resulted in its generation, a point neatly brought home in Hélène Balfet's (1965) study of pottery manufacture in the North African Maghreb. In this she showed that the pots housewives are accustomed to make on one annual occasion are richly decorated but of poor technical quality. In contrast, part-time "elementary" specialists work "often enough to ensure a certain skill and even a certain routine, which leads to a work rhythm and often to a quality apparently at variance with the crudeness of the means employed" (p. 170). Much less effort is spent on the surface finish and decoration of their products. In a third Maghrebin production system, "technical uniformity and . . . aesthetic standardization . . . characterizes the work of the specialist-artisans . . .[but] . . . does not exclude either change or progress" (p. 169). In this case – as in material culture generally – "techno-stylistic characteristics show certain kinds of techno-economic relationships" (p. 171). It follows that before an archaeologist can usefully explain patterns of formal variation in sociocultural or indeed other terms, she or he had better attain a good understanding of how they were produced. Inferences to American culture based on a Model-T Ford and made under the assumption that it was the unique product of a twentieth-century Leonardo da Vinci would be egregiously in error.

Ethnoarchaeological studies of the production of style from the perspective of the transmission of the knowledge and techniques required to produce stylistically competent results are few and far between. David and Hennig (1972) showed that Fulbe potters in Bé village in northern Cameroon produced pots in the local style even if they had learned to make them in a town or village where a different decorative range was practiced. They attributed this to the marginality of the potters, poor old widows for the most part, who by signaling their

---

[2] This can be disputed on the grounds that deliberation is a somewhat ambiguous concept, and that people express in style things they are unable to in words (P. Wiessner, pers. comm. to ND 1999).

Fig. 7.1 Ingrid Herbich with women of a Luo potting community at the Pap
Nyadiel clay source, Siaya District, Kenya, 1981.

membership of the community were stating a claim to be treated and supported
as kin. Another potter, a non-Fulbe though previously married to a Fulbe of low
status, while retaining her accustomed coiling technique of forming pottery,
had entirely given up the decorative style she had learned as a child in order to
produce for Fulbe consumers vessels finished in their local style. Whereas these
women had made individual decisions to produce in the local style, Ingrid
Herbich (1987) has described how Kenyan Luo women married into the rare
potters' households are taught to pot by their mothers-in-law and co-wives.
Communities of potters clustered around a clay source (Fig. 7.1) produce a
selection from the range of Luo forms, and each community's wares, distinguishable from those of others by minor technological, morphological, and decorative features, constitute a micro-style within the larger Luo tradition. These
develop because, in a situation of patrilocal post-marital residence combined
with polygyny, a new wife comes under the authority of her husband's father's
wife (or senior co-wives) "until she is considered ready to assume her role as
the proper mistress of her own house in the homestead. During her apprenticeship under the mother-in-law, she will be tested and expected to learn and
conform" (p. 200). Interaction with potters in other homesteads and at markets
helps to prevent the micro-styles from remaining entirely static or diverging
indefinitely from each other. Both the David and Hennig and the Herbich

studies warn against the common assumption that mother to daughter transmission of ceramic technology is the norm (see also Stanislawski 1977, 1978a, 1978b). Post-marital socialization of women married at a young age may have very general effects on stylistic behavior.

DeBoer (1990) describes the learning of the elaborate Shipibo-Conibo art style by girls – and by boys up to about age eight (see chapter 11). The degree of similarity in designs between teacher and pupil, and between the work of individual potters at different stages of their lives, is extremely variable, though all these artists produce work that is unmistakably Shipibo-Conibo. Factors operating at different scales are responsible for this situation. The Shipibo-Conibo style is a potent, religiously sanctioned, marker of ethnic affiliation, but it "encompasses an astonishing amount of variability. No two artists ever produce identical designs. The style is complex enough to ensure endless novelty" (p. 103). It provides the artist with the means of expressing, within overall constraints, her feelings regarding her place in society and individual experience. In sharp contrast to the conformity in ceramic production imposed by Luo mothers-in-law on wives marrying in to the homestead, micro-styles are unlikely to develop or to endure among the Shipibo-Conibo even though the compound is normally made up of matrilineally related households.

The Kalinga of the Philippines were chosen by William Longacre for study precisely because they lived in nucleated settlements, were described as practicing matrilocal residence, and in some villages most women were seasonally engaged in making pots. Thus the transmission of ceramic styles might be expected to parallel that in presumptively similarly organized prehistoric households of the American Southwest, where Longacre (1970) had earlier attempted to infer aspects of social organization from the distribution of ceramic designs. However, Michael Graves's (1981, 1985, 1991) research on materials collected in 1975–6 showed that despite the usual pattern of daughters learning to pot from their mothers or grandmothers, when it came to decoration the factors most affecting the structure of a potter's designs were her birth cohort (younger potters tending to apply more bands of decoration) and the size of the vessel produced.

The context of consumption

In considering the significance of the distribution of styles, understanding of the context of consumption is as important as the context of production. One of the most fascinating aspects of the research of the Kalinga Ethnoarchaeological Project is that during the interval when the project was interrupted the contexts both of production and of consumption of pottery changed (see chapter 12). The materials considered in this chapter generally relate to economies in which markets, if they exist, constitute only one form of exchange. The classes of artifacts discussed are produced either by household members or by part- or full-time specialists within the community. It is for the most part in the context of such societies that ethnoarchaeologists have struggled with the concept of style and its role in marking social boundaries. In doing so they have focused on traditional material culture, largely ignoring "modern" industrial items introduced through markets from the wider world. This is understandable but unfortunate; there is a considerable literature (e.g., Miller 1987, 1998; Bocock 1993) on consumption, part of it concerned with self-definition of groups or individuals by this means (e.g., Spooner 1986). Yet no ethnoarchaeologist has thought to investigate whether the aluminum cauldrons made by Alucam are used by Cameroonian tribes or other social categories to define themselves.

The importance of considering the context of consumption even in a society traditionally characterized by a segmentary lineage system is well brought out by Dietler and Herbich (1994) in a sequel to Herbich's study on production. Nowadays most Luo pottery is sold in markets which are commonly near the borders of tribal and sub-tribal territories and often serviced by potters from several communities. Each market is characterized by a different blend of the microstyles produced by potter communities of one or more tribes or sub-tribes, and, there being no preference among consumers to purchase the pots made by members of their own group, this blend extends over the territory of the market. "The result in the context of consumption is [in one instance] a homogeneous style zone centered on the market of Luanda, composed of a mixture of . . . two microstyles and having no relation to any social or cultural entity other than the habitual users of the Luanda market" (p. 466). Despite a strong tribal and sub-tribal sense of identity, ceramic style is not used by the Luo to mark social boundaries. "Processes of distribution linking producers and consumers necessitate a change of context and of meaning; and the eventual spatial distributions of ceramic styles . . . tend to override and obscure the meaning of style within the context of production" (p. 469). In a cultural context in which ceramics do serve as ethnic markers and decoration is of symbolic significance, David *et al.* (1988: 377–8) found that pots that cross ethnic boundaries, usually through a market, are regarded by their purchasers in a secular manner in terms of their quality, utilitarian function, or aesthetic appeal. Why the Luo should not use and did not in the past use their pots to carry messages of social identification is unclear; it is not simply due to the influence of markets. This is an instance of one of the more recalcitrant problems faced by ethnoarchaeologists, to explain why certain artifact classes are chosen in particular contexts to carry certain messages and others are not.

In reading the succeeding sections the importance of the contexts of production and distribution should be borne in mind. We may, for example, suppose that the differentiation, described by Wobst (1977), of Yugoslavian ethnic groups by male headdresses was achieved through strategies of consumption, while in the case of the ornamental features of shirts that marked particular villages the contexts of production and consumption were the same.

Style as a medium of information exchange

Formal variation, much of it stylistic, is the material basis upon which typologies are erected, and typology, as CK (1985: 88) has argued, reinforces principles of social structure, including gender and power relationships, and reifies other aspects of world view. This was evident in Miller's (1985) treatment of ceramics in Dangwara as a set of categories that model and reinforce other sets of categories relating to caste and social position. Much of this chapter will be devoted to ethnoarchaeological exploration of this perspective, but we should first consider the assumption upon which it and examples earlier discussed are implicitly based, that style is indeed a medium of information exchange comparable to speech or, for example, semaphore. What sorts of information are likely to be communicated in the stylistic mode and to whom?

Wobst's information exchange approach to style

It is Martin Wobst (1977) who first addresses these questions in a systematic manner.[3] He begins by castigating the then current archaeological treatment of style either as a negative category – that which is not functional – or as one that is "unmanageably multidimensional," relating to those aspects of artifact variability adjudged characteristic of certain areas, time periods, or groups. The latter is of course associated with the interaction theory of style introduced above. Above all, for Wobst was at this time strongly influenced by systems theory, he is concerned to show that style articulates with other cultural variables and is more than "a strangely self-contained, a-cultural, a-systemic variable within the system that is culture" (p. 318). To this end he "equates style with that part of the formal variability in material culture that can be related to the participation of artifacts in processes of information exchange" (p. 321). While this is like defining a train as "that which pulls cars along a railroad," and leaves open the question of whether there exists and if so what to call formal variability that does not have this function, his formulation

avoids the semantic muddle of counterposing "style" and "function" by explicitly acknowledging that much stylistic behavior does have functions, at least in the sense of articulation with other variables in the cultural and ecosystem; it also invites investigation into the adaptive advantages style may convey. (p. 321)

Wobst reasons that if human beings "avail themselves of the option to transmit messages in the artifact mode," this must have an adaptive function and be efficient in certain circumstances and not in others. He identifies the following as some of the advantages of stylistic messaging through artifacts:

---

[3] His paper was first drafted in 1969, as he informs us in a recent retrospection on the topic of style (Wobst 1999: 118).

1 The human emitter of a message, by realizing it in the form of an artifact, allows it to broadcast its (almost always visual) message even in
   the absence of receivers; conversely the message can be received in
   the absence of the emitter. Since artifacts are often portable they can
   broadcast widely.
2 Messages change more slowly than in other communication modes,
   and thus require more of a commitment to the content of the message
   on the part of the emitter.
3 Messages in artifact form are more costly in energy and matter to
   produce than speech, thus making it easier to monopolize and control
   information exchange.
4 Once the message is encoded in an artifact, it requires little or no
   maintenance, and the relative longevity of signals (combined with
   item 3) facilitates standardization.
5 The more frequent the message event in which an artifact is utilized,
   the lower the cost of emission and reception relative to other modes
   of information transfer.

There are also disadvantages:

6 If messages are highly variable, the cost of emission of each message
   becomes prohibitively expensive in the stylistic mode.
7 If the message is complex, the cost of emission and decoding may
   become prohibitive (pp. 322–3).

Given these potentials and constraints, messages emitted in the artifact
mode are likely to be limited to "simple invariate and recurrent messages" (p.
323), falling for the most part into the categories shown in Table 7.1.
Constraints on content and the requirement that most stylistic messages be
seen in order to be received lead Wobst to the inference that, relative to other
modes of communication, style is most effectively and economically used as a
communication medium not among those close to the emitter to whom he or
she can speak, and for whom the messages would be redundant, but to socially
distant "potential receivers [who] have little opportunity to receive the
message otherwise, but nevertheless are likely to encounter it and are able to
decode it." The larger the number of people in this category the more efficient
it becomes to transmit the message through style. Thus we would expect more
use of stylistic messaging in complex societies, and conversely "it is not surprising to find that certain aspects of band society material culture show so
little evidence of 'stylistic' elaboration" (p. 326). This statement reflects the
face-to-face nature of small-scale societies (and by its use of the phrase "aspects
of" admits that style can be used for other communicative purposes). The prime
function of stylistic messaging is, Wobst suggests, to render social intercourse
more predictable; "it broadcasts the potential advantages or disadvantages to
be realized from a more intimate encounter, before such encounter has taken
place . . . Style helps to mark, maintain, and further the differences between
[socially differentiated] groups at little cost" (pp. 327–8).

Table 7.1 *Message content in stylistic behavior (after Wobst 1977: Table 1)*

Type of information conveyed	Example of message	Example of American material culture which shows this behavior
1 Identification (a) "emotional state" (e.g., state of bereavement)	I am in mourning	black armband, flag at half mast
(b) social or economic class affiliation or occupation	I am a nurse I am (or wish to be regarded as) married	nurse's dress wedding band
(c) position along ranked scale	I am wealthy	display of late model luxury car, mink coat, platinum jewelry
	I am a general	number of stars on epaulets
2 Ownership	This key belongs to the last motel you slept in This cow belongs to rancher X	unwieldy attachment to key cattle brand
3 Authorship	We the Shakers manufactured this chair This is brand X by company Y	distinctive form of Shaker chair logo, distinctive packaging
4 Prescription	Walk here	zebra stripes on road
5 Proscription	Danger, keep off! Stay away ye evil spirits!	skull and crossbones Pennsylvania Dutch hex sign
6 Religious or political objectification	Jesus Christ is watching over you	crucifix
7 Deictic	LOOK!	Goodyear Blimp Exaggeration of messages 1 through 6

Earlier in the paper Wobst had very interestingly proposed that the evolution of signaling in the artifact mode is likely to be punctuated rather than gradual, and that in prehistory various categories of material culture were progressively switched on as vehicles for stylistic communication. He proceeds to offer a number of predictions of obvious relevance to archaeologists:

1 "the less an artifact is visible to members of a given group, the less appropriate is it to carry stylistic messages of any kind. Classes of artifacts which never leave the contexts of individual households . . . are unlikely to carry messages of social group affiliation" (p. 328),

2 "sets of material culture which potentially are visible to all members

of a given social group are much more likely to show a society specific expression of stylistic form . . . Examples include . . .outer layers
of clothing and the outer surfaces of living structures" (p. 329), and

3 "We would expect to find social-group-specificity of stylistic signals
particularly in those instances where all members of a social group
potentially encounter a given stylistic message, *and* where this
message enters into contexts of boundary maintenance" (p. 329).
This is likely to apply to only a small subset of the material culture
inventory.

These predictions (or hypotheses or expectations) are then tested against the
evidence of the traditional dress of Yugoslavian males, of which Wobst has
some personal knowledge (Fig. 7.2), although he draws most of his data from
the rich literature relating to the period 1919–39. In the light of recent horrors
afflicting that part of the world, we should scarcely be surprised that headdresses, worn in all seasons and identifiable from beyond gun shot range,
should have signaled affiliation to the largest social group with which an
individual identified (e.g., Albanian-speakers, Vlach herders, Serbs), nor that
Muslim Serbs, previously allied with the former Turkish rulers, did not label
themselves in this manner. According to simple visibility principles (see Carr
1995a), progressively less conspicuous (or less continuously worn) items like
coats, pants, gross ornamental features of shirts, and small decorative features
are correlated with a descending scale of increasingly restricted social units: the
general area, sub-region, valley, or village, down to the individual.[4]

Wobst's paper was, and rightly remains, influential, but it is neither above
nor has it escaped criticism. By 1985 Wobst (pers. comm. to ND) had himself
recognized that he had misjudged the range of likely targets of stylistic communication. When, before an evening out, a woman perfumes herself – an
example of olfactory stylistic signaling – it is evident that her message is
intended for a very restricted range of persons, perhaps only for a partner, possibly only for herself. Style can, as Wobst's Yugoslavian data indicated, be effectively utilized as a medium of communication at all social distances. In a paper
entitled "Who is signalling whom? . . .," Judy Sterner (1989) made this point
effectively by showing that among Sirak, and indeed some other, montagnard
groups of the Mandara mountains of northern Cameroon, the most elaborately
decorated pots are stored, hidden away under granaries, and brought out only
for familial ceremonies. And yet, she argues, these pots, which are manufactured by women of the smith-potter caste, often of the same clans as the users,
reinforce the Sirak sense of community. "The decoration of pottery partakes of
ritual . . . and, as [Edmund] Leach (1976: 45) reminds us, 'We engage in rituals
in order to transmit collective messages to ourselves'" (Sterner 1989: 459).
Signaling to outsiders constitutes only one part of the marking of community

---

[4] Similarly in Rajasthan (north India) CK has observed that men can, at considerable distances,
identify each other's caste and sometimes subcaste affiliations on the basis of differences in
turban fabrics and style of wrapping.

Fig. 7.2 Martin Wobst, aged eighteen, in the white shirt of a German youth
group (with a home-made shirt of Russian fabric underneath), and
wearing the characteristic Serbian fur hat that he was later to
describe as a medium of information exchange, 1962.

or ethnic boundaries; internal reinforcement is at least as important (see also Hodder 1982a: 54–6).

Wobst was also led by his view of the adaptive value of style to assume that artifacts are intentionally imbued with style. Like Lathrap (1983) he speaks disparagingly of the artificers imagined by archaeologists to learn a style in their youth and ever afterwards to apply it mechanically, calling them "Skinnerian [behaviorist] automatons" or, in Lathrap's terms, photocopy machines. Style in Wobst's view is active, intentional signaling in the stylistic mode, and he takes what Sackett (1982: 59) was later to describe as an "iconological" approach to style, one "that restricts style solely to those aspects of formal variation [especially decoration] that artisans purposely invest with symbolic content." This was indeed the view taken, though rarely explicitly, by most archaeologists of the time, and especially those who worked with ceramics. For some it seemed almost as if the analysis of ceramic style variation could be regarded as analysis of social organization itself, but they assumed that formal variation that did *not* have as its primary function the symbolic expression of social information was *not* stylistic. Sackett on the other hand is an archaeologist specializing in the European upper paleolithic and his special expertise lies in the analysis of flaked flint tools that have no decorative features. Their forms are determined by the application of a particular series of shocks[5] to a range of sizes and shapes of more or less variable raw materials. Thus an endscraper has no decorative attributes, none that cannot be described as functional, and yet when you place a set of Aurignacian endscrapers side by side with examples from the Gravettian they appear very different: in the types of blade they are made on, in the shape and angle of the scraping edge, and in characteristics of the retouch used to form that edge. Given that, even in favored French Aquitaine, early upper paleolithic Aurignacians and Gravettians lived at vanishingly low population densities, and for hundreds, perhaps thousands, of years may never have come in contact with each other, it is in the highest degree unlikely that they consciously invested their endscrapers with stylistic information or intentionally signaled social boundaries with these everyday tools. Indeed such signaling is doubtful among modern San hunter-gatherers of Botswana and Namibia (see below). Surely they were much closer in attitude to the Bafia potters, and would likely have denied the existence of alternative manufacturing norms. This is an example of what Sackett (1990: 36–7) has described as passive style, style that is "latent, inherent in the isochrestic choices which lie behind [artifact] manufacture," and is deemed not to constitute intentional messaging. "The notion of passive style differs from active style . . . in that it regards making choices and assigning meaning to those choices as two distinct kinds of behavior."

---

[5] These shocks have patterning over the series as a whole and thus can be said to constitute a particular technology of stone working, or, in Heather Lechtman's terminology, to exhibit a certain technological style.

Sterner's (1989) work is again of relevance here in that she shows that, in the Mandara region, it is not decoration but the eminently functional form of water-carrying pots and beer jugs and even the way they are carried on the head or shoulder that broadcast to Wobst's "receivers intermediate in social distance" information about community membership and ethnicity. "Decoration is simply at too small a physical scale, too inconspicuous, to be able usefully to broadcast information of such a nature" (p. 454).

Wobst's analysis has also been criticized for its assumption that humans would always practice economizing behavior in stylistic signaling as in other parts of life. Wiessner (1984: 193; 1985: 162) points out that stylistic, and especially identity, displays are sometimes extravagant. This could however be interpreted in a number of ways. Perhaps the anthropological observer or the emitter of the message has misjudged the strength of signal required, or, as Pharaoh Chephren knew when he built his pyramid, conspicuous consumption sends its own message (Trigger 1990). Why do people pay millions of dollars for a Van Gogh, or for a baseball? The point is surely that economic activity always takes place in a cultural frame, and that cost and value cannot be considered independently of context.

In summary, Martin Wobst's analysis of the place and role of style in cultural systems laid down a solid foundation for incorporating stylistic studies into processual archaeology, and testing of his predictions constituted an agenda for ethnoarchaeologists. However, recognition that style is efficiently used for communication over a wide range of social distances, including to oneself, and the realization that much style is passive rather than active, are important revisions of his interpretation, even if a close reading of his work suggests that he was wrestling with such questions in the 1970s. Later work on style has consistently acknowledged Wobst's influence even as it has advanced into new areas. We now review some of the more important of the later ethnoarchaeological studies and the debates they stimulated.

The behavioral basis of style

In the 1970s Polly Wiessner carried out extensive ethnographic and later ethnoarchaeological research among the San of the Kalahari desert in Namibia and Botswana (Fig. 7.3). While her paper on San arrows (Wiessner 1983) was written from the ecological perspective evident in earlier works (1977, 1982a), after she became associated in 1981 with the Max Planck Institute of Human Ethology, her theoretical concern turns, in a paper on beaded headbands (1984), towards study of "a fundamental human cognitive process . . . personal and social identification through comparison" (1984: 191), a theory in social psychology particularly associated with the school of Henri Tajfel (e.g., 1982). Indeed she argues that this is the behavioral basis for style, and comparison the mechanism underlying stylistic development and change. Material culture is

Fig. 7.3 Polly Wiessner and two !Kung San (Ju/'hoansi) women talking about beads at //Aru, Namibia, 1999.

mobilized as a medium in the comparative process. Theories of social comparison and of emulation, as described by Miller (1982b, 1985) and discussed in chapter 6, clearly have much in common.

The 1983 paper on San arrows elicited a reply from James Sackett (1985), complimenting her on the quality of her fieldwork but critical of her conceptualization of style. Below we summarize the thrust of Wiessner's argument, interspersing it with comments deriving in large part from Sackett's reply, and conclude by briefly considering aspects of her (1985) response to Sackett.

Wiessner begins by pointing out how limited is our understanding of (a) what items and variables carry social information, (b) the conditions that stimulate the use of material culture to transmit messages about inter-group relations, and (c) how patterns of stylistic variation in space correspond to social groupings. She characterizes style in a manner comparable to Wobst as "formal variation in material culture that transmits information about personal and social identity" (1983: 256). But what is formal variation that does *not* transmit information about personal and social identity? Some, we later discover, appears to relate to rote learning and practice of a craft, but this hardly exhausts the range. Is there, besides direct observation in the present, any way of discriminating between formal variation that does transmit such information and that which does not? Apparently not. Wiessner's concept of style is thus more limited and limiting than that adopted in this book. She also distinguishes between two broad categories of style. "Emblemic" style is

> formal variation in material culture that has a distinct referent and transmits a clear message to a defined target population . . . about conscious affiliation of identity . . . Most frequently its referent will be a social group . . . Because it has a distinct referent, emblemic style carries information about the existence of groups and boundaries and not about degree of interaction across or within them. (p. 257)

A national flag is the obvious example.[6] In contrast "assertive" style is "personally based and . . . carries information supporting individual identity" (p. 258), for example pierced ears. Apart from uniforms which emphasize emblemic style, style of dress is generally assertive, as is the manner in which bourgeois North Americans decorate their houses. There is some blurring of the categories, and objects can transmit both emblemic and assertive messages, as do the dresses worn by Herero and Tswana women, the former's always being long rather than knee-length, but nonetheless variable in details of cut and fabric (p. 259).

Emblemic style carries a distinct message and may be expected to undergo strong selection for uniformity and clarity. Assertive style is likely originally to have developed in association with the desire to create a positive self-image and stimulate others to engage in reciprocal relations. It supports individual identity and is more likely to diffuse across social boundaries, offering archaeologists a potential measure of interpersonal contact. Natural, functional, and social properties of objects affect their suitability to carry messages. Wiessner suggests for example that "Artifacts that are quickly made and discarded soon after use draw little notice and would be expected to be poor indicators of contact" (p. 258). Sackett (e.g., 1982: 102) would certainly disagree that this is necessarily or always true.

What items are likely to repay stylistic analysis? Wiessner presents alternative views: (a) that items that are for some reason important to social identity will be chosen to carry stylistic messages, and (b) that the longer the sequence of transformational stages an item goes through, the greater its chances of bearing social information. The chaîne opératoire approach holds that the second alternative is necessarily true, though it does not follow that more complex items will necessarily be actively used for stylistic communication. The unique importance to social identity of the San poisoned arrow, which has a short uselife and is quickly made, is based upon its role in the procurement and sharing of meat. Arrows are a significant theme in myth and folklore. They are frequently exchanged between *hxaro* partners, members of different bands who offer each other mutual support, these exchanges enhancing the visibility of weapons that are normally carried in a quiver, poisoned tip down. It would

---

[6] Wiessner also uses emblemic in a different, subsidiary, sense to refer to the use of symbols to carry messages of prescription and proscription. Traffic lights enforce boundaries.

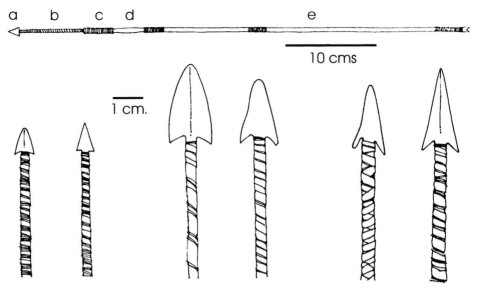

Fig. 7.4 A Kalahari San arrow and pairs of examples of, from left to right, arrowheads made by !Kung, !Xo, and G/wi . The parts of the arrow are (a) metal point; (b) poisoned shaft, of same piece of metal wire as the point; (c) stem joint; (d) link of giraffe rib or wood; (e) main shaft.

seem reasonable that they should constitute a vehicle for stylistic communication, a proposition Wiessner is concerned to test.

The San studied included the !Kung, G/wi and !Xo bands who at the time of Wiessner's study still depended primarily on foraging for their livelihood, although gun and spear were rapidly replacing bow and arrow. San men make their small arrowheads for hunting animals by cold and hot hammering of heavy gauge fencing wire, and while there are some who are particularly skilled, all but a few can make their own (Fig. 7.4). They vary mainly in size, shape of the barbs and the tip, and body shape. Wiessner's detailed study of arrowheads belonging to several !Kung men and bands, and of 129 arrowheads distributed over six band clusters/linguistic groups revealed

1 limited but not marked variation between !Kung men and between sets of arrowheads made by the same individuals at different times,
2 no significant differences between sets of arrows collected from different !Kung bands, nor between !Kung band clusters (although there seem to be differences at the level of the dialect group), however
3 G/wi and !Xo arrowheads are significantly different, the points being twice the size of those of the !Kung;
4 the arrowheads of the two !Xo band clusters differed in body shape, and
5 those of the Gw/i and !Xo differ in tip, body, and base shape, rendering them easily distinguishable.

Wiessner proceeds to argue that San arrows express both emblemic and assertive style. Since, as Sackett (1985) points out, men have difficulty in recognizing even their own arrows after the interval of a year, they can scarcely be
regarded as in the forefront of assertive fashion! However, all informants recognized differences between !Kung, Gw/i, and !Xo arrowheads even though
they might never have seen such forms before, identifying them as foreign
rather than attributing them to named groups. Thus these arrowhead types do
serve to mark boundaries.[7] However the most potent factor in establishing
what boundaries are marked appears to be access to resources. Thus in the
resource-poor south, where the favored strategy among the !Xo is to maintain
almost exclusive territorial rights, boundaries are first evident at the band
cluster level, whereas in the richer north among the !Kung, where resources are
highly localized and variable and risk is best minimized by the maintenance of
varied ties over broad areas, band clusters are poorly developed and it is
between dialect groups that differentiation of arrowheads first occurs. Does
this constitute proof of emblemic style? While boundaries are indeed marked,
Wiessner adduces no substantial evidence to demonstrate that San consciously
invest their arrowheads with style for this purpose – indeed the G/wi and !Xo
claim to exchange arrows (p. 268) – but only that the differences can be raised
to consciousness.

Since many San are only vaguely aware of the existence of San others who
make different kinds of arrowheads, the differences in arrowheads are not being
produced in order to mark boundaries *vis-à-vis* competing groups. Instead style
unites the larger population (whether band cluster or dialect group) that pools
risk. This risk-sharing strategy indeed militates against the assertive investment of style in arrows, directing personal expression into other channels such
as beaded headbands. As in the case of Sterner's Sirak, the San are communicating with themselves. The form of each group's arrowheads is the product of
a particular, quite recent, historical development that, in the absence of selective pressures favoring other attributes, is maintained in the course of the transmission of the technology from one generation to another and within
generations via *hxaro* exchanges. The arrowheads are indeed emblemic in that
they have a distinct referent and carry information about boundaries, but the
stylistic message is not consciously emitted nor can it be said to transmit a
clear message to a defined target population.

In her response to Sackett's criticisms (incorporated above but avoiding the
use of his isochrestic terminology), Wiessner (1985: 161) makes the valid point
that "Social and stylistic comparison and corresponding choices can be made
at very different levels of consciousness and intent" but she persists in

---

[7] It is hard to estimate what happens to style differences at linguistic boundaries since these are
now mostly in farming territory. Wiessner notes that "Because many wounded animals are not
pursued, animals shot in one area may die in another, bearing the arrow of the hunter. The !Kung
do discuss this possibility and maintain that if foreign people with different arrows are hunting
nearby, eventually they would find out" (p. 261).

contrasting "stylistic" and "isochrestic" variation, largely, it appears, because she is under the impression that Sackett regards certain cultural choices as being fixed once and for all during the learning process.[8] Indeed his concept of "vernacular" style (see above) comes very close to this. However it is clear from his reply that he perceives the craft tradition as being socially bounded, and the matrix of cultural choices, while possessing considerable inertia, as nonetheless subject to change at both the individual and group levels through the same mechanism, social comparison, that Wiessner herself invokes (see especially Sackett 1985: 158). She also introduces new evidence of formal variation in quiver-carrying devices, mortars, and men's loin cloths, that does not correspond to that exhibited by arrowheads. These differences are attributed (p. 163) to "history of social relations, both internal and external, trade networks, availability of materials and other factors." But are these factors not equally significant in the case of the arrowheads? Not in her view, for she maintains (pp. 163–4) that the San "manipulated style in arrows to obtain certain desired effects, whether or not individuals could be said to be fully conscious of the intended effects." Despite her claim that "style is often used to make statements that cannot be made verbally," one is left to wonder whether for her the difference between stylistic and isochrestic behavior is not simply that the former is intelligible in the light of her approach and the latter is not.

The beaded headbands that she treats in her second paper (Wiessner 1984, published after Sackett had written his critique of the first) are examples of assertive style to which an iconological approach is entirely appropriate. These headbands decorated by women constitute a running commentary on social life and interrelations, responding sensitively to different social situations. We grasp the nature of the discourse even if not the full content of the headbands' messages. It is in this paper that Wiessner insists that style is founded upon a fundamental human cognitive process of comparison and that an understanding of that process is a prerequisite for developing a general theory of style.

Wiessner's studies are particularly remarkable for their large spatial (about 150,000 km^2) and social scale, which allowed her, avoiding one aspect of Wobst's "tyranny of the present," to tackle questions of stylistic variation through space that are of the greatest importance for archaeologists, and to demonstrate the polyvalence of attributes and the complexity of the factors involved in the signaling of social group affiliation and interrelationships. Information about group affiliation expressed in arrowheads is not consistently carried by the same attributes, size being of importance in some contexts, and shape in others. And, as in the case of Herero women's dresses, different attributes of the same artifact may carry different messages, emblemic and assertive. Wiessner's establishing of identity formation through comparison as a behav-

---

[8] Wiessner's clearest statement on this issue appears in her 1984 paper (p. 194) in which she states that style is generated by the negotiation of identity relationships while isochrestic variation represents the rote passing on of ways of doing things.

ioral basis for style would seem to have become generally accepted,[9] although since (a) such comparisons can apparently "be made at very different levels of consciousness and intent," and (b) not all stylistic expression (as we have defined it) is implicated in social comparison, it is questionable whether it provides us with much analytical leverage. Although in archaeological instances one might hope that context would provide clues, Wiessner offers no way other than through ethnographic or historical research of distinguishing between formal variation in material culture that is or is not related to social comparison. But she does not claim this is the only source of stylistic behavior, and would certainly agree that something more was involved in the building of Chartres cathedral.

Her contribution to understanding of style is considerable, but, as she herself recognizes, "these approaches will certainly not make stylistic prediction and interpretation less complex" (1983: 273). The reasons why stylistic variation should not exhibit similar structure across domains of material culture are indeed complicated. Conceptualization in terms of practice theory and the agency of individuals and groups acting over time in particular historical circumstances, as is nicely shown in the headband study, leads almost inevitably to the conclusion that, while we will never be able to formulate precise predictive rules, there are likely to be certain fairly common tendencies, one of which is that items so critically important to a culture as arrowheads to the San or money in the West are likely to be subject to considerable constraints in their stylistic expression, leaving other realms freer to vary.

Style at work

Symbolic boundaries

While Wiessner was searching for cognitive underpinnings and a behavioral basis for style among the San, Ian Hodder had been conducting ethnoarchaeological research among Nilotic groups living around Lake Baringo in the Rift Valley of northern Kenya, over an area of about 2,300 km² (Fig. 7.5). The Ilchamus (or Njemps), Tugen, and Pokot are tribes without chiefs who live in dispersed compounds and whose subsistence combines pastoralism and farming in varying proportions, the Tugen doing more farming and the Pokot depending most upon their livestock. His early work there involved visiting 187 seemingly traditional compounds and collecting 400 life histories. Records of material culture included sketch plans of the compounds and of individual huts, and measurements and other details of pots, basketwork, wooden containers, stools, items of personal adornment, weapons, and other tools and

---

[9] Style, conceived by Hodder (1990a: 45) as "the referral of an individual event to a general way of doing," involving a theoretically endless dialectic between event and referral, is at bottom a process of comparison.

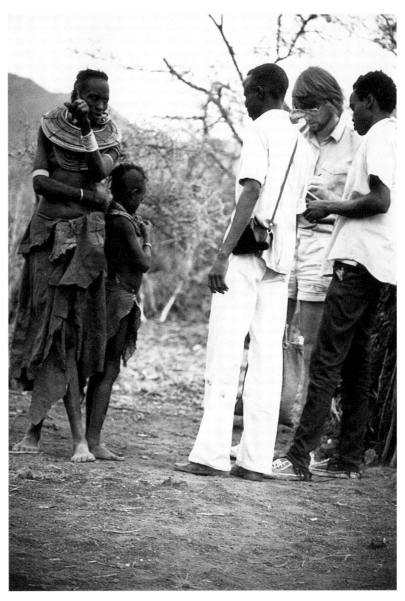

Fig. 7.5 Ian Hodder and field assistants interview a Pokot woman near Lake Baringo, Kenya, late 1970s.

furnishings (Hodder 1977a, 1977b). Hodder's initial aim was like Wiessner's in that he was concerned to study the factors responsible for structuring artifact distributions. His research constituted a test of interaction theory and of the reality of archaeological "cultures." Comparative study of type distributions (rather than of the artifacts themselves) showed that while the Ilchamus were clearly differentiated from the Tugen, the Tugen/Pokot boundary was much less distinct.

How to explain this contrast? With regard to the Ilchamus/Tugen border, Hodder (1977b: 259) notes four characteristics of the distributions likely to draw the attention of archaeologists:

1 some items have mutually exclusive distributions on either side of the boundary,
2 traits tend to move across the boundary more from east (Ilchamus) to west (Tugen) than vice-versa,
3 male and female associated items differ in their tendency to cross the boundary, and
4 up to 30 to 40 years previously traits appear to have crossed the border more frequently.

The first characteristic might suggest lack of interaction across the border, but on the contrary it is intense and frequent as people freely cross for social reasons and to go to market. Other explanations that might occur to an archaeologist appear equally unfounded; the border cannot be explained in terms of different environments or economies since these are little differentiated, or in terms of a language barrier, since communication presents little difficulty. There are fewer marriage moves across the border than within tribal areas, but although most such moves are by women it is male-associated items that are more likely to "transgress" the boundary. The few women who do marry across boundaries tend quickly to adopt the material styles and customs of their new home. Hodder, remarking that the boundary has been maintained for at least 70 years, suggests "that the most important reason for the existence of a boundary in this case is that, without clear central authorities, the whole functioning of society, its laws and rules, are dependent on the force of public opinion" (p. 261). Thus conformism in material culture might be seen as an expression of a more general need to assert tribal identity.

The tendency for items to move across the border from east to west cannot be explained in terms of marriage movements or of a trade bias. Hodder suggests that social pressure to conform is stronger in Ilchamus society, inhibiting the adoption of Tugen items, and that the Tugen, envious of the Ilchamus' greater wealth in cattle, are readier to copy their neighbors. The easier movement of male-associated traits cannot be explained in terms of marriage movements, since marriage is virilocal, nor as a consequence of men having much wider contacts than women, but should rather, he argues, be attributed to a patriarchal regime that insists on great conformity for women. The fourth characteristic, that traits once crossed the border more easily, can be explained in terms of a higher degree of interaction in the period before the colonial regime began to stabilize the border and to prohibit raiding for cattle. Nonetheless the border was then quite clearly marked. As to the Tugen–Pokot border, these tribes are more closely related in language and "consider themselves as belonging to the same Kalenjin group of people" (p. 266). It would seem that this results in less pressure to differentiate themselves through material culture.

In the conclusion to this early paper, Hodder (1977b: 268–9) argues that

the type of explanation which has been found most relevant concerns the pressures to conform to tribal identities . . . [T]raditional archaeological explanations . . . are of little importance or value in this instance . . . The major factors which maintain group distinctiveness are . . . the importance of public opinion and censure in a society without centralized control and authority, the resulting necessity overtly to conform, and the position of women in society.

This explanation represents an intelligent and thoughtful reading of the material evidence, and one that, notably, considers gender a relevant variable, but in which the supposed cause is inadequately documented. The greater pressure on the Ilchamus to conform is, for example, here simply asserted.

A paper that appeared a year later benefited from an enlarged database of 400 compounds, now extending east of the lake, and a noticeable deepening of Hodder's knowledge of the areal ethnography and history. Ilchamus conformity is now, following Spencer (1965), attributed to a greater degree of gerontocracy and an age-set system that prevents men from marrying until a relatively late age. Competition and the incidence of inter-tribal conflict are recognized as relevant factors. "[A]s competition over resources and conflict between groups increase, there are greater advantages in groups overtly stressing their differences" (p. 51). A family's livelihood and security depends upon the wider group; thus the wearing of Ilchamus costume and use of Ilchamus material items constitute a claim on Ilchamus support systems, and most immediately on Ilchamus warriors to retrieve one's stolen stock. Blurring of the border between the Kalenjin Pokot and the Maa-speaking Ilchamus immediately east of Lake Baringo cannot be attributed, as had been the interpenetration of Tugen and Pokot material cultures west of the lake, to the existence of a wider cultural grouping, but is explicable in terms of lack of economic stress in that area. Further to the east where there is competition between these groups the material cultures are distinct. Competition over resources also characterizes the more densely populated area to the south and west of the lake where Ilchamus and Tugen are in contact and where the material culture boundary is most clearly marked. This means not that there is no migration across the borders, but rather that when a person settles with the other group he or she rapidly adopt local styles of material culture, assimilating to Ilchamus or Tugen as the case may be. The cultural membrane dividing the tribes is permeable by people but much less by things. An earlier period in which the border between the styles was less marked can be attributed to a greater degree of symbiosis in the earlier part of the century.

Hodder has shown how practically feeble and logically unsound are many of the types of explanation commonly invoked by archaeologists, and has gone on to link a particular configuration of society and economy to patterning in material culture. While the truth of the statement that "The maintenance of distinct overt identities is a necessary part of any between-group relationship that involves negative reciprocity" (p. 58) is questionable,[10] this is an important achievement, as is the finding that "Much archaeological material may have been part and parcel of the symbolizing or signalling of identities" (p. 58). Hodder cites Leach (1976: 10) to the effect that patterning in all the non-verbal dimensions of culture incorporates "coded information in a manner analogous to the sounds and words of a natural language," and that it is therefore meaningful to talk about "grammatical rules which govern the wearing of clothes" or other domains of material culture. Hodder is moving towards a position in which material items are conceptualized as not merely reflecting culture but as actively and symbolically contributing to its very constitution. This is the perspective of the book we have chosen as marking the beginning of the Recent period in ethnoarchaeology (Hodder 1982a).

Symbols in action consists of a connected series of essays describing the work of Hodder and his students among the Baringo tribes, Dorobo hunter-gatherers and Samburu pastoralists in Kenya, the Lozi of western Zambia, and the Nuba of Sudan. In the chapters on Baringo Hodder goes considerably further than in the papers just discussed to emphasize the active nature of material symbols: "Especially in the border areas where there is greatest tension and competition, material culture of many forms is used to justify between-group negative reciprocity and to support the social and economic dependencies within groups" (p. 56). Thus Pokot warriors' justification for raiding Ilchamus cattle is that they come from Ilchamus compounds – which is not of course why the Ilchamus built them that way. But, as we saw in chapter 2, Hodder is not prepared to argue that greater between-group stress will always be expressed in marked material boundaries. Indeed some of his most interesting work deals with artifacts that transgress the tribal limits. Spears, mostly made by three smiths, one a Tugen, the others from outside the region, are the insignia of the warrior.

The spear types are similar over wide areas when other things are very different between tribes because the young men of all tribes wish to demonstrate their prowess and readiness for elderhood and their opposition to the older men. (p. 68)

---

[10] An oppressed group might well strive to conceal any characteristics that distinguished it from its oppressors. Jews did not voluntarily don yellow stars under the Third Reich.

The decorations that each woman incises on her calabashes exhibit a quite different pattern of distribution, with some widespread motifs and others that are localized, relating to the women's local community contacts and relationships. Such decorations are beneath men's notice and therefore

appropriate for use as a medium for silent discourse between women. In contrast to the overt, controlled symbols of dress by which women demonstrate their conformity and the tribal dichotomies, women use calabashes to disrupt the boundaries in opposition to the older men and to form their local independence. (p. 69)

From the various patterns of distribution Hodder infers that

Whether an artefact does or does not "reflect" a particular type of interaction or information flow depends upon how it comes to be used as part of the strategies and ideologies of particular groups . . . In other societies . . . there may be no relationship between inter-group competition for scarce resources and marked material boundaries. (p. 85)

Thus he refuses to attribute lawlike status to his Baringo findings except within tightly specified boundary conditions.

We may wish to question some of his interpretations that appear to lack evidential support. But his reading of the spears is backed up by observations regarding their use and association with warriorhood and virility. Moreover his inferences are broadly confirmed by Roy Larick's (1985, 1986, 1987a, 1987b) detailed and fascinating studies of spears and their relationships with age-sets among the Ilchamus-related Loikop (see chapter 12). We are given much less reason to accept Hodder's reading of the calabash decorations; this appears in *Symbols in action* to be little more than an assertion. However after further fieldwork in 1983, Hodder (1991) provides a much richer and more fully documented account (also in chapter 12) that tends to substantiate his earlier insight.

In an interesting meeting of the British and French schools, Hodder's Baringo work was criticized by Pierre Lemonnier (1986: 180), who argues that both ethnoarchaeology and the anthropology of techniques

must avoid considering as "demonstrated general laws" what are at best powerful hypotheses. An anthropologist of techniques can only be astonished at the facility with which Hodder . . . considers verified his hypothesis – sometimes perfectly worthy of being entertained – of the reinforced marking of ethnic identity through material culture in situations of intergroup tension . . . Even were such a result established, and it doubtless is in numerous cases, there would be the necessity of bringing out the specificity of it, or risk transforming it into a dangerous and useless recipe for a careless archaeologist.

We have demonstrated that this criticism is unjustified, and that Hodder (1982a: 85; 1979) takes care to contextualize his findings and not to proclaim them as general laws. Can we use Hodder's research in order to predict? At the broadest level we would agree that much "material culture acts as part of an ideology of control" (p. 85), a point brought out in Hodder's chapter on the Lozi state, and we have been alerted to the probability that where there is domination, there we may anticipate resistance. But should we always expect to find women's household crafts subversively undermining a male-dominated *status quo*? As we have seen, it appears unlikely that this is the case for the pottery painted by Shipibo-Conibo women whose designs combine assertive with emblemic characteristics (DeBoer 1984: 550; 1990). What are the Western equivalents of the Baringo warriors' spears? We should indeed avoid transforming ethnoarchaeological inferences into recipes, using them instead as food for archaeological imagination.

Log odds on Dangtalan

Wiessner's work among the San made use of descriptive statistics and tests of associations by chi-square; Hodder (1982a: 52) employed the *I* coefficient of spatial autocorrelation to investigate whether artifact attributes were dependent upon their spatial locations. Michael Graves's (1994, and see 1991) analysis of material culture boundaries among the Kalinga applies more sophisticated statistical measures to a large database consisting of almost 1000 pots recorded by Longacre in 1975–6 (of which over 200 were purchased for intensive analysis). These pots, produced on a household basis, came from all three villages in Dangtalan community and from the village of Dalupa in the community of Dalupa-Ableg.[11]

Pots are more common in Kalinga than in Baringo households, but, before the explosion of new types in the 1980s, they do not appear to have been greatly more varied in form. Longacre (1991b) provides a description of their manufacture and a typology. The three most common types, each of which is made in various sizes, comprise a water storage jar, a rice-cooking pot, and a pot used for cooking vegetables and, rarely, meat. These are all restricted vessels, the most obvious differences between them being the relative height and the size of the mouth, water storage vessels being taller and narrower-mouthed, vegetable/meat pots squatter and with wider mouths, and rice-cooking pots having intermediate characteristics (Skibo 1992: 60). Graves (1994: 20–1) studies the decorative bands that are impressed around the upper body and shoulder of all

---

[11] The nature of Kalinga settlement is important for understanding Graves's results, but the terminology is confusing. Graves (1994) refers to households, agglomerated settlements or villages, and "regions" which are largely endogamous groupings of one to ten settlements that establish and enforce peace pacts with other such units, generally comprising populations varying from a few hundred to a maximum of less than 4000. Stark (1994: 170 fn.) writes of households, *sitios* (neighborhoods, often kin-based), settlements, and villages or communities, the latter pairing more or less corresponding with Graves's "region" though she places less emphasis on its political function. Combining these two terminologies, we refer to agglomerated settlements as *villages* and to the groupings of allied settlements as *communities*. It should be emphasized that while population densities are high, ranging from 48 to 183 persons/ km^2, community territories are very small, neither Dangtalan nor Dalupa-Ableg exceeding 5 km^2, and the largest, Lubuagan, being only 23–30 km^2. Municipalities, sub-provinces, and provinces are much larger units imposed by the Philippine state.

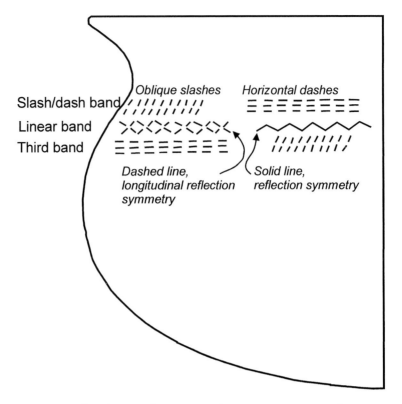

Fig. 7.6 Decorative bands on Kalinga pots, showing variation in designs (after Graves 1994).

three types (Fig. 7.6). He is concerned "to estimate the degree of design difference, homogeneity and distinctiveness" within and between the ceramic assemblages from which his sample is drawn.

Difference refers to the extent to which the distributions or proportions of design attributes within a given class in two samples are separable or otherwise unlike each other . . . Homogeneity . . . is a quality of diversity. Diversity can measure both richness and evenness of counts across a set of attributes . . . Whereas measures of difference compare two samples, measures of homogeneity or diversity are applied to single samples that can then be compared. By combining both homogeneity and difference measures, it is then possible to estimate the distinctiveness of design systems with respect to some spatial referent . . . [villages and communities]. (p. 21)

Graves (p. 21) makes use of multivariate statistical analyses, involving cross-classification of design features, including numbers of decorative bands and designs, by vessel size, community, and date of production ($\leq$1970 or $>$1970) which were then analyzed using log-linear methods based on chi-square.[12]

[12] This enables him to choose the model that best fits the data from among several in which various combinations of these factors are cross-tabulated. He uses log odds ratios and other statistics to present the results of comparisons. As an example of the former, he takes the

Table 7.2 *Decorative features characteristic of the Kalinga potters of Dangtalan*

1 On what is usually the top (slash/dash) band of decoration, consisting of either oblique slashes or horizontal dashes, they are over three times as likely to use oblique slashes; furthermore their preference for slashes becomes more marked through time, as does Dalupa's preference for dashes.

2 On what is usually the second (linear) band of decoration, they are more likely to use a dashed line, whereas the Dalupa potters use a solid line nearly exclusively.

3 As in Dalupa, this band is more often characterized by reflection symmetry than longitudinal reflection symmetry; however this is more marked at Dangtalan.

4 In both communities larger vessels are more likely to be decorated with more bands of decoration; however, Dangtalan potters are nearly twice as likely to apply two or three bands of decoration.

5 Whereas only 12 percent of the pots are either undecorated or bear three bands of decoration, the Dangtalan potters are twice as likely to produce pots with these features.

6 Whereas a single band of design is the most popular whatever the size of vessels, Dangtalan potters are more likely to decorate their large vessels with a single band of design.

7 In contrast they are less likely to decorate medium and small pots with only the slash/dash band; thus the effects of vessel size differ between the two communities.

8 Dangtalan potters are much more likely to apply the linear design whatever the vessel size.

9 If the slash/dash band is absent, there are similar log odds that potters in the two communities will apply a linear band. However, if the slash/dash band is present, Dangtalan potters are more, and Dalupa potters less, likely to apply a linear band.

10 Over time potters in both regions have made less use of solid linear designs, but the two communities remain distinct from each other because Dangtalan potters have consistently used this design less frequently. However, if horizontal dashes are used in the slash/dash band, then a solid line is much more likely to be used in the linear band; if oblique slashes are used, the choice of line in the linear band is much more equivocal.

From Table 7.2, which shows the majority of the results, it is clear that we are dealing with minor differences of decorative emphasis, and that inter-community differences are more marked than temporal ones. Graves notes that result 9 is particularly important since it suggests that the two communities are consciously differentiating themselves with respect to the bulk of their output, the pots that receive the slash/dash band. With respect to result 10, he says that potters in the two communities are

(continued from p. 196)
appropriate model, and uses the expected values to calculate the odds on the occurrence of design X and design Y on large and medium–small pots at Dangtalan and Dalupa; the odds are then converted using the natural logarithm. If this seems "relatively intricate," it is. See Graves 1981 for a detailed explanation of the statistical analyses.

emphasizing somewhat different classes of design when they make pottery with two bands of design. Dangtalan potters use the oblique slash . . . in virtually all the cases (95 percent) in which two bands of design are produced. Dalupa potters use the solid line . . . in most of the cases (90 percent) in which two bands of design are produced. (p. 39)

Graves also shows that inter-village differences within the Dangtalan community are always much less than the inter-community differences. Thus he can reasonably claim that the two communities are different in respect to decoration. Using other statistics, he shows that as one moves up the scale from village to community the homogeneity of the design system decreases, but that Dangtalan potters "certainly are not characterized by a heterogeneous design system" (p. 44). Thus, combining the evidence of difference and of homogeneity, Graves can assert that community

design systems are highly distinctive relative to one another . . . One can pick up a vessel of any size or use-class, and in the vast majority of cases can identify the production locale. Kalinga women do this all the time, even relatively novice ethnoarchaeologists can acquire the ability. (pp. 44–5)

Community endogamy, circumscribed learning frameworks, and pressure to conform to the design system in use in each community, combined with a desire to differentiate themselves from potters in other communities, are identified as the factors responsible for the patterned differences identified. The case is strong that Kalinga potters are using style to signal their community affiliation and to mark boundaries as against other communities. Furthermore, despite very considerable differences between the Baringo tribes and the Kalinga in population density, kinship organization, and economic base, this signaling occurs in a situation of competition for resources, among the Kalinga primarily regarding access to land suitable for irrigated rice agriculture.

Can, Graves asks, his results be used "productively to organize prehistoric cultural variability or to explain aspects of the archaeological record? My answer," he writes, "is a qualified yes" (p. 49). He continues

Knowing that the Kalinga organization is predicated on strong community differentiation and that this is reflected in aspects of pottery production, archaeological analyses can then ascertain to what extent community homogeneity and intercommunity differences are comparable to those among the Kalinga. In this way both archaeological and ethnoarchaeological approaches are critically evaluated and enhanced. (p. 49; with substitution of "community" for "region" and "regional" in Graves's text)

And he has indeed attempted such comparisons (Graves 1982). It should however be noted that the ethnographically documented pattern will *not* characterize Kalinga archaeology. This is because through time communities are liable to segment, merge, or annex territory; "until the 1930s, dynamic processes (e.g., population growth or decline, agricultural success or failure, and limited warfare and raiding) ensured that there would be constantly shifting numbers of communities and sets of intercommunity allegiances and rivalries" (p. 16, with same substitutions). Owing to the operation of these processes, archaeologists would, we suspect, be unable to detect Kalinga communities but only a much larger (and in this case undefined) grouping – much as David and colleagues (1991) suggest would be the case for the Mandara mountains (see below).

Graves claims that his analysis is superior to that of Wiessner's (1984) head-band study in that she inadequately considered variability within areas, and the extent to which diversity might be a function of sample size, and also that in comparing areas she failed to control for the effects of exchange and thus to "separate production-based variation in design usage from variation created by exchange networks" (p. 47). Similarly, Hodder's Baringo research

suffers from a decided lack of documentation . . . in no instance does he combine an analysis of interregional or intercommunity differences with an analysis of interregional or intercommunity diversity. Consequently, there is no way to know if there is sufficient distinctiveness in the spatial distribution of the material culture samples he has collected that would render them exploitable for information transmission by the people who make or use the objects. Again, Hodder assures us that people do use material culture to transmit messages. Unfortunately, his analyses of material culture variation are insufficient to confirm his hypotheses . . . We cannot assume that, simply because interareal differences are statistically significant, symbolically encoded information transfer has been documented. (pp. 47–8)

While right on their specific failings, Graves's judgment could well be wrong. The reason for this lies in the contrasting styles of analysis. Graves has treated his material as if it were archaeological. It is unclear from the 1994 paper whether he ever visited the Kalinga. (He did so briefly in 1985.) His inference regarding pressure on Kalinga potters to conform to community design standards is based (a) on the results of his analysis, and (b) on Longacre's (1981; 1991c: 102–3) observations, confirmed by tests, regarding the ability of potters to recognize each other's work. No cases are adduced in which a potter was encouraged to apply decorative bands in her community's style or sanctioned for not doing so. In contrast Wiessner talked in !Kung to her informants and Hodder and his team interviewed large numbers of Tugen, Pokot, and Ilchamus, both providing anecdotal evidence to support their arguments. Whether that evidence is sufficient is a matter for debate; it would certainly have been advantageous for Wiessner and Hodder to have carried out similar statistical analyses, but it should be remembered that they worked on more than one domain of material culture. The contrasting patternings that both found in different artifact classes contribute substantially to their overall interpretations. Wiessner and Hodder might justifiably counterclaim that their analyses are superior to Graves's in that he entirely fails to consider, let alone explain, whether other artifact classes manufactured by women show a similar patterning to that evident in pottery, and whether artifacts made by men show the same or other distinctions, and why. What, for example, of the tattoos on the arms and chests of elderly Kalinga (Trostel 1994: 216)? Are these related to designs on pottery? In the one Kalinga project paper that deals with another artifact class, Ramon Silvestre (1994) describes their basketry. This is made by men, the simpler forms being within any man's competence while more complex types are manufactured by specialists. Their typology is considerably more complex than that of the pottery of the 1970s, and there are indications in his preliminary study that different factors structure basketry design.

The naturalist style of research that reaches its apogee in Graves's 1994 study and the humanist (yet in the Baringo chapters scarcely antinaturalist) style of Hodder both have advantages and disadvantages. Given the impossibility under foreseeable funding conditions of acquiring the resources necessary to collect data on a regional scale and to carry out on them both naturalist and antinaturalist analyses – and given the improbability that any one project director could combine the virtues of a Longacre and a Hodder – it seems likely that, while remaining critically conscious of their achievements and failings, we must content ourselves with ethnoarchaeological studies that favor one or the other approach.

Ensembles of signifying traits

We turn now to the first of two research programs that are more aligned with Hodder's interpretive than Longacre's and Graves's processual approach. Pierre Lemonnier's criticism of Hodder was noted above; we will now consider his treatment of quite comparable data from Papua New Guinea (Lemonnier 1986). Lemonnier's intellectual ancestry goes back to André Leroi-Gourhan and beyond to Marcel Mauss, whose paper on the techniques of the human body showed that the utilization of this, the most fundamental of human tools, was strongly under the influence of culture and society (Mauss 1935). Leroi-Gourhan's (1943) two-volume work *Evolution et techniques* presented "a classification of techniques intended as universal, derived from the kinds of actions on materials which they employ . . . [and] established a theoretical framework which remains indispensable to anyone who would examine the nature of the discontinuities observed in material culture" (Lemonnier 1986: 150). Attempting to understand the interrelations of social phenomena and technological evolution, Leroi-Gourhan found it necessary to develop a terminology that included the concepts of tendency and fact.

By "tendency," Leroi-Gourhan meant that characteristic of technological evolution by which, independent of any direct connection, processes and tools appear that make use of the same forces and exhibit the same mechanical, chemical, and other properties, in response to technological problems posed in identical terms. It is what causes roofs to be peaked, axes to have handles, and arrows to balance at a third of their length from the head. (Lemonnier 1992: 82)

A "fact," on the other hand, is the material expression of a tendency, the product of its realization by cultured humans using the materials available in their environment: an ax, a bow, a roof. But "ethnic groups produce objects whose morphology or mechanical properties differ to the degree that the observer is meticulous in observing them" (p. 83), and there are thus

"degrees of the fact" . . . steps by which a classification of a given technology becomes more and more detailed. Thus, the first degree of the fact corresponds to the main function of a given technology, and can be identified with the tendency . . . The subsequent degrees of fact correspond to secondary physical aspects of the technology in question. The last degrees of fact correspond to the last branches of a tree diagram. They are those details having little or no physical efficiency . . . they . . . correspond, therefore, to the realm of what is today called style. (p. 84)[13]

So, by a curious irony, it would seem that this proponent of the chaîne opératoire approach does not himself recognize the stylistic potential inherent in each and every cultural choice but rather aligns himself with those iconicist Anglo-American scholars who regard style as separate from function! This is not quite the case as "the line between stylistic (communicative) and functional (linked to physical action) is hard to draw" (p. 86), but nonetheless while Lemonnier is mainly interested in the social representations that underlie material cultures, his position on what is actually designated stylistic is closest to Wiessner's.

Lemonnier worked among the 60,000–70,000 Anga who live in an area of 18,200 km^2 that encompasses varying elevations from highlands to coastal plain, and rainforest and savanna ecosystems (Fig. 7.7). They are primarily horticulturalists, combining different mixes of crops with hunting and, except in the lowlands, the raising of pigs. Their societies, lacking chiefs, are characterized by patrilineal clans, although marriage arrangements vary. Their languages are more closely related to each other than to those of their neighbors, and their subdivision into twelve "tribes" is based on linguistic criteria. Lemonnier is concerned in his 1986 paper to advocate to an English-speaking audience the superiority of an anthropology of techniques viewpoint to that of Anglo-Saxon ethnoarchaeology, using as his vehicle the exploration of differences between the technical choices underlying the material culture inventories of the various Anga tribes (Tables 7.3 and 7.4).

Regarding his fieldwork, and specifically that seen in Figure 7.7, Lemonnier (pers. comm. to ND, 2000) writes:

In New Guinea comparative studies are often "calf-killers" involving strenuous hiking; 42 days "on patrol" have taken us through Watchakes territory and across the mountain spine of the island, from the Markham to the Tauri basin. Seen at a distance, nothing resembles a garden, a hut, or a cassowary trap more than another garden, hut, or cassowary trap. However, from one valley to another, sometimes even on opposite banks of a stream, customs can change entirely. Systematic visits to neighboring tribes are the only means of spotting the variation in objects, chaînes opératoires, and knowledge that are the subject matter of the ethnology of techniques. Planning gardens,

---

[13] Leroi-Gourhan's "dernier degré du fait" and Sackett's (1990: 34) sibylline description of style as "function writ small" have a lot in common.

Fig. 7.7 Pierre Lemonnier, accompanied by assistant Iwadze Nguye, visits the Ankave Anga hamlet of Piabae, located on a ridge above the Kogan River, Papua New Guinea, and tapes notes on the plants in a household garden, August 1990.

describing chaînes opératoires, together with censuses of the human, pig, and dog populations of villages are all necessary parts of the painstaking routines of fieldwork. Days off, or when it is either raining or very hot, are times to write up tape-recorded notes made while traveling. Dozens of visits spread out over nearly two decades are required to appreciate the ebb and flow of human settlement, the relocation of gardens, or the peaceful but ineluctable pressure exerted by a dominant clan on the territory of its neighbors.

Because they are culturally related and occupy a continuous geographic area, the discontinuities in Anga material culture are ideally suited for study of the "relative arbitrariness of these choices and to measure in what ways and how they are compatible with other aspects of Anga societies" (Lemonnier 1986: 159). Technical traits at varying degrees of generality, varying from whether houses have single or double walls to details of skirt forms, have discontinuous distributions, though there is a substantial degree of coherent patterning that Lemonnier does not emphasize (Table 7.4). Belts of rattan versus those of orchid fiber apart, a northern group consisting of tribes A–F rather consistently assort together (in some cases we lack evidence from C), as does a southern group of tribes J–L (Fig. 7.8). Only three tribes, G–I, themselves geographically contiguous (and in one instance a detached part of F), vary in their affiliation to either

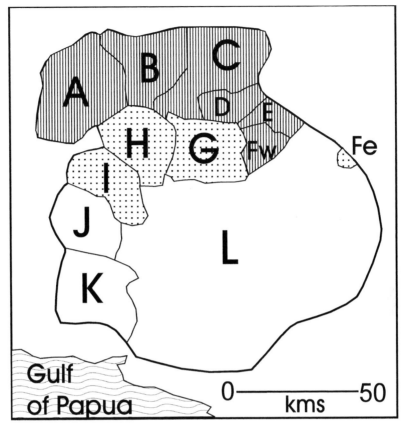

Fig. 7.8 Northern, intermediate, and southern groups of Anga tribes
according to Lemmonier's (1986) data on distributions (see text).

the northern or the southern set. Lemonnier demonstrates that these differences cannot be explained in terms of functional links between the technical
traits, nor are they determined by environmental factors, nor can random variation be invoked; they represent real cultural choices. How then are we to
explain the observed patterning? He finds it unsatisfactory to suggest that the
various Anga groups are using technical traits to mark their ethnicity. For him
the question is rather, what are the inter-group differences in question and why
are they marked in the manner they are?

We do not get an answer to this question, unless it is that "there are still
representations of technological phenomena underlying these technological
differences, and the physical consequence of this is far from being neutral"
(Lemonnier1992: 66). Interpretive archaeologists would at this point turn to
history for answers, but there is little historical evidence available (though oral
traditions assist in explicating the atypical distribution of rattan belts). Instead,
Lemonnier considers a structuralist approach: "The simultaneous presence in

Table 7.3 *The Anga tribes distinguished by Lemonnier (1986) and divided here into three categories according to the distributional data (see Fig. 7.8)*

Northern group
A   Simbari
B   Baruya
C   Watchakes
D   Yoyue
E   Kawatcha
Fw   Western Langimar, separated by L from a much smaller eastern block (Fe)

Intermediate tribes
Fe   Eastern Langimar
G   Menye
H   Kokwaye
I   Ankave

Southern group
J   Ivori
K   Lohiki
L   Kapau, the group in the south and east distributed over by far the greatest area

Table 7.4 *Technical traits and their association with Anga tribes according to Lemonnier (1986)*

Technical trait	Tribes	Technical trait	Tribes	Notes
Barbed arrows	A–Fw	Unbarbed arrows	G–L and Fe	
Single walled house	A–H	Double walled house	I–L	
Bows with oval cross-section	A–G	Bows with non-oval cross-section	H–L	
Skirt attached at neck	A, B, D–I	Skirt attached at waist	J–L	C unknown
Skirt form triangular	A, B, D–I	Skirt form sub-rectangular	J–L	C unknown
Skirt voluminous	A, B, D–H	Skirt flat	I–L	C unknown
Belt of rattan	A, B, K	Belt of orchid stalks	C–J, L	

one or several groups of a series of techniques not functionally linked would then 'simply' reflect the application, most often unconscious, of one or several classifying principles" (Lemonnier 1986: 171). But to identify these principles and their mode of functioning is easier said than done. There is a sense in which, in any one culture, techniques form a system (p. 154) with some degree of coherence in that they are underlain by a relatively coherent body of knowledge (e.g., genetics and chemistry are related disciplines that depend upon each other), and are apprehended according to one or a limited number of paradigms (e.g., scientific versus creationist cosmologies). Technical "signs" may be said to participate in a signifying system that produces meaning.[14] One function of these signifying systems may be to mark differences between and within groups at various scales, but "replacing in their context the lines cited at the beginning of the present [chapter] . . . we remain a thousand leagues from a theory of material culture as an ensemble of signifying traits" (pp. 172–3). The best that can be done at present is to bring to light some of the underlying relationships between real objects and the mental objects (social representations) that refer to them. Lemonnier provides an example. The Anga wear skirts or capes of beaten bark, normally made in the case of women of a particular wild fig species, while men's are of cultivars. However, when the wild species is the only fig tree available, it is "'defeminized': the women no longer have access to it for making their skirts and the men use it only when cultivated" (p. 178). Thus bark and its cultivated or wild origin are being used to express differences between men and women – and in lowland tribes where the hierarchy of the sexes is less marked there is also less distinction in dress materials.

The trouble with most of Lemonnier's article is that the Anga appear frozen in time and isolated from their neighbors. The several distribution maps look like nothing so much as successive slices through the organs of some vast beast preserved for forensic investigation. And when this reveals very little, Lemonnier's first reaction is to turn to structuralism, another approach that freeze dries its mental subject matter and denies agency to human bearers. It is precisely when he allows us to look into the bowels of the living creature (usually revealed, we infer, by his own fieldwork) that we glimpse the nature of Anga material discourse – as with the last example, or when we are shown the Baruya (group B) trading their salt for a variety of items including some that are available to them on their own lands, or changing their orchid stem belts for ones of rattan as they move into conquered territory. When we learn that tribes F and L are mortal enemies as are G and F, but that H, G and L did not fight among themselves (pp. 174–5, 182), the distribution maps begin to take on new meaning.

Despite their differences, Lemonnier and some "Anglo-Saxon" ethnoarchaeologists have a great deal in common. Some of Hodder's (1982a) essays in *Symbols in action*, for example the chapter on the Nuba provocatively titled "Dirt, women and men . . .," and elsewhere (including the paper [1987a] on the meaning of discard discussed in chapter 4), involve searching for "functioning principles of technical systems as signifying systems" (Lemonnier 1986: 174), though there are good theoretical reasons (differences in group interests) to deny that entire technical systems could ever be coherently represented as complex social representations within a culture. Some ethnoarchaeologists, less ambitious than the structuralists, have instead employed the concept of

---

[14] At least this is part of what we think Lemmonier (pp. 172–3), elsewhere critical of others' formulations, intends to mean in a difficult passage invoking Lévi-Strauss, myth, and bricolage.

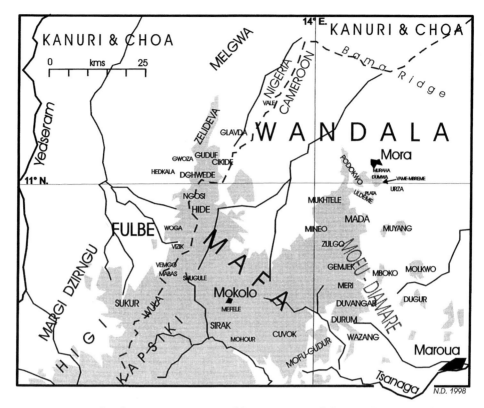

Fig. 7.9 Ethnolinguistic groups and larger towns of the northern Mandara
mountains and nearby plains, Nigeria and northern Cameroon, 1980s.

the symbolic (or conceptual) reservoir to interrelate the diverse material
expressions of cognate groups.

Symbolic reservoirs

The concept of symbolic reservoir was introduced to African archaeology by
Roderick McIntosh (1989: 77): "Art becomes a lens on the process by which different subgroups in society dip into a long-held reservoir of symbols, myths,
and beliefs in order to extract, craft and visually display a legitimating tradition
to serve their own sectional interests." The symbolic reservoir thus links cultural tradition with human agency and for this reason has been applied by some
members of the Mandara Archaeological Project (MAP) – the primary concern
of which has been to understand stylistic behavior – to the material cultures,
and not merely arts, of the highly diverse, though culturally and linguistically
related, groups living in the northern Mandara mountains of northern
Cameroon and northeastern Nigeria and in the plains at their feet, a study area
of about 7000 km² (Fig. 7.9). A thousand years ago the peoples of this area all
spoke languages of the Biu-Mandara branch of the Chadic language family

(Barreteau and Jungraithmayr 1993). During the course of the second millennium AD the region became progressively embroiled in the economy and politics of the southern part of the Lake Chad basin. The states that developed on the plains were perennially hungry for two products that their montagnard neighbors could provide, slaves and iron. Thus began a long, asymmetric, and on the plainsmen's side largely predatory, commerce that led in one instance to the division of the speakers of one Chadic language into two sharply differentiated cultures. The interests of the Wandala, on the plains at the northern feet of the Mandara mountains, became allied to those of the northerners and eventually led to the development of a state on the Sudanic model. Meanwhile the Mura (Muraha), located in the mountains and inselbergs at the northeastern tip of the chain, retained their montagnard character despite continuous and multifaceted interaction with their plains cousins (Barkindo 1989).

Since at least the sixteenth century, under pressure from the Wandala and expeditions from Borno, the Kanuri state located south and west of Lake Chad, and later from Bagirmi to the east, individuals, families, and groups from the plains have sought refuge in the mountains. The linguistic and genealogical evidence is indicative rather of progressive incorporation of plainsmen into montagnard societies than of wholesale resettlement of plains communities in the mountains. In the early nineteenth century the Fulbe *jihad* initiated by Usuman dan Fodio of Sokoto in Nigeria led to the founding of an eastern province of his caliphate that challenged Wandala and Bornoan supremacy in the region but resulted in little change for the montagnards, now exposed to Fulbe exploitation and raiding. Thus, through much of the nineteenth century, Fulbe, Bornoans, and Wandala disputed control of the plains and of the non-Muslim Chadic-speakers still resident there, while independent groups held out in their mountain fastnesses. There immigration, combined with the need for labor to support intensive agriculture and for defense, had in a few centuries resulted in the achievement of high population densities, recently in the range of 100–200 persons/km^2, in regions that required the laborious sculpting of mountainsides into agricultural terraces in order to produce sufficient crops to sustain life on an ongoing basis. Most montagnards make their living by the farming of staple millets and numerous other crops, now including some grown for cash, the labor-intensive husbandry of small numbers of cattle, sheep and goats, and poultry, and for the last half-century by the export of seasonal labor.

Several seasons of ethnoarchaeological fieldwork led ND and his colleagues to an appreciation that the surface variety expressed in montagnard material culture was underlain by common themes (David *et al.* 1991). An indication that these themes might be very ancient came from continuities in ceramics, both general and specific, for example the red ware tripod vessels and black ware food bowls that could be traced back to the earliest Iron Age of the region, now known to date to the mid-first millennium BC (MacEachern 1996). The Mandara team asked what was being signified by the variations in material culture, especially as these related to group identity, and sought to identify the mechanisms responsible for generating that variety in the present and recent past. A third major aim, which despite a different vocabulary is not very different from Lemonnier's, was to understand the symbolic roots of the styles observed. Given that they were dealing with a wider range of cultural groups than Wiessner, Hodder, the Kalinga project, and even Lemonnier, with much larger populations, and with rich material culture inventories, their approach to research was bound to differ. Since an attempt even to sample the material culture of the whole region would have led only to superficial results, some members of the team worked on the ethnoarchaeology of particular communities while others researched the technologies most likely to be represented archaeologically, as practiced by different groups.[15] Research methods varied in detail but combined participant observation with unstructured interviews.

The "ethno-linguistic groups" shown on the map (Fig. 7.9) have some cultural reality but also represent the imposition of foreign or at least non-montagnard categorization processes operating for purposes of administrative convenience. Let us describe the ethnographic present of 1901, the last year of the precolonial period in a part of Africa that subsequently experienced a complex political history (Kirk-Greene 1969). In the southwest, among the Mafa and their neighbors, a settlement comprising members of several patrilineal descent groups is the most common political entity (Martin 1970). Such political authority as exists resides in the elders of the several descent groups and a priest-chief whose authority rests on a special relationship with the main spirit of the place. A small but more complex chiefdom, with a strong industrial base in iron making, exists at Sukur (Smith and David 1995; David 1996). Among the Mofu of the southeast there are also chiefdoms, the largest however with a population barely over 10,000 (Jouaux 1989; Vincent 1991), founded on a sociocultural base almost identical to that of the Mafa (David and Sterner 1999). In the northeast, culturally similar groups are organized into more fragmented sociopolitical units. Among the Mura, Plata, Uldeme and their neighbors, small, exogamous, co-resident, patrilineal descent groups exist in a web of traditional relations of alliance and opposition, many sharing historical traditions of migration from a common place of origin (MacEachern 1990). These political arrangements still survive in attenuated forms in the context of provincial/state and national institutions.

[15] The groups studied by members of the MAP team included Muslim Wandala, Shuwa and descendants of montagnards living in enclaves around an inselberg north of the main Mandara chain (Lyons 1989, 1992, 1996), a guild of Wandala smiths (Robertson 1992), Plata, Uldeme, and other montagnard groups in the northeast (MacEachern 1990, 1992, 1994, 1998), several southwestern groups (David 1990, 1992b) including intensive study of a Mafa community by Kodzo Gavua (1989, 1990) and of Sirak by Judy Sterner (1989, 1992) and, across the border in Nigeria, of Sukur and neighboring communities by David and Sterner (1995, 1996; David 1995, 1998; Sterner 1998). The southeast (Mofu-Diamaré groups, Mofu-Gudur) of the northern Mandara mountains and its northwestern horn (Zelideva, Dughwede, etc.) remain ethnoarchaeologically unstudied. The very little anthropological work carried out in the latter area is sufficient to show that, while institutions may vary, its peoples belong to the same northern Mandara mountains cultural whole (Müller-Kosack 1996).

Then and now the montagnard man or woman identifies in different circumstances with a number of social groups. These include the household, patrilineal descent groups of varying inclusiveness (usually referred to as lineages and clans), a less well-defined and much less studied grouping of kin related through women, a community varying from a co-resident patrilineage to a chiefdom that is localized in space, and a group comprising the speakers of a language. The latter may vary in size from a single community with a few hundred speakers to much larger linguistic entities, such as the Mafa, now numbering over a quarter of a million but divided between many, and in precolonial times for the most part independent, community polities. (It is doubtful whether Mafa ever had a sense of membership in a larger Mafa-speaking community until after independence when politicians began to mobilize the language in their favor.) Shared ceremonies sometimes link otherwise independent communities. In the southern part of the area two endogamous castes, of farmers on the one hand and of male smiths and female potters on the other, constitute another type of social category. Montagnards, who are often bi- or multi-lingual, quite frequently operate not merely *in* but *as* members of two or more cultural communities, sometimes in the course of a single day. An individual's social identity is rather a process than a state.

How does material culture engage with this complex reality? In the 1991 article ND and his colleagues used the term "ethnicity" to refer to what to the outsider appears "as a polythetic set of cultural behaviors explicable in terms of shared membership in an identifiable multi-purpose social group" (p. 171), and they admitted the possibility of multiple referents. This was a mistake; ethnicity is a much contested concept (Fardon 1987, 1996), and it would have been preferable to omit the label while remaining focused on the expression in material culture of social affiliation at several scales.

Stylistic expression in material culture of group affiliation is variably expressed at all levels above that of the family, and also, especially during ceremonies, in the context of categories such as male initiates or parents of twins. For example, and limiting ourselves to domains of material culture that might well preserve archaeologically, only the chiefly clan at Sukur has a right to place a lintel across the entrance to their compounds (residences, usually walled, containing several rooms [huts], subsidiary structures, courtyards, and the like). The compounds of different communities and sometimes of larger groupings are characterized by distinctive plans (Seignobos 1982). Amongst the Mafa around Mokolo the typical compound takes a spiral form with a particularly important sequence of conjoined rooms leading from the entrance room, which is also the male household head's bedroom, to the first wife's bedroom, to a room holding granaries and shrines, and ending in the first wife's kitchen (Figure 7.10). These are curled around a central stall for small stock. In most of these Mafa settlements the spiral turns clockwise, but in others counterclockwise. The spiral relates to a gesture used in prayer when the officiant turns an offering three times around his head. Granaries, always a focus of ritual in

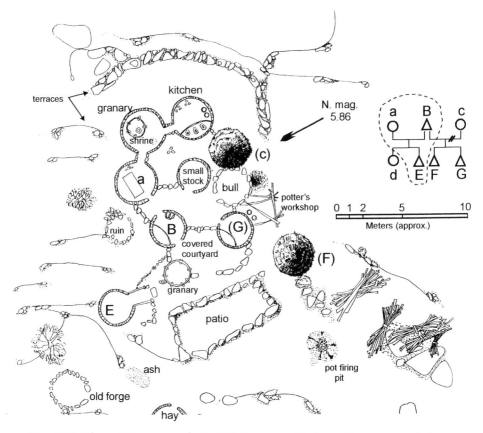

Fig. 7.10 Plan of the compound of Dokwaza, a Mafa smith, near Mokolo, northern Cameroon, 1986. Most roofs are removed to show interior features. The kinship diagram shows only those members of his family represented by structures. One wife (c) is divorced, and children d, F and G have married and moved out. Their rooms are now mainly used for storage. Daughter d slept in her mother's room before marriage.

this region, are also differentiated stylistically, variation relating generally to the community or linguistic group.

The Sirak and other neighboring speakers of Mefele make quite large pots by beating them out on a concave mold, coiling only the neck and rim. This gives them a distinctively spherical shape. The Mafa beat out only the bases of restricted vessels, coiling their upper parts. The range of Mafa and Sirak types, of which there are very many, is remarkably similar, though there are detailed differences in the forms of pots serving closely comparable functions. The Mafa pot representing the creator, Zhigile, is usually represented with a stylized beard, pellets for hair, and a single raised left (though sometimes right) arm. In Sirak an almost identical pot represents the spirit of a disease with symptoms like those of epilepsy, and is named Shetene, presumably from the Arabic form of Satan (Sterner 1992). While the pots of the Mafa and Sirak are of very high quality, those of the Wula, who live only a few kilometers to the west and use the same techniques, are coarser, heavier, and not so finely finished. The remarkable elaboration of Mafa and Sirak ritual vessels diminishes among the Wula and is virtually absent among the Sukur, although their technologies, beliefs, and ritual practices are very similar.

In the northeastern subregion there is no smith-potter caste. Some crafts, such as iron working, are carried on by, though not explicitly restricted to, particular descent groups, while others are generally practiced, for example potting by most women. Ethnolinguistic groups are less distinguishable by their pottery than among the Mafa and their neighbors. Instead we find ceramic complexes that characterize the Plata and groups to the north of them versus the Uldeme and others to the south and east (MacEachern 1998: 119–22). Spheres of movement of women in marriage, themselves based in part upon degrees of linguistic similarity and in part on other historical factors, are implicated in such patterning, which is now also influenced by markets. Thus the ceramic complex of the Plata and their neighbors is spreading southwards, while paradoxically the Plata themselves are becoming more willing to accept identification with their southern neighbors, the Uldeme. Over the region as a whole it is possible to distinguish a northern ceramic tradition marked by coiling without use of a concave mold, and a smaller and different range of forms from those of the Mafa and their neighbors to the south. The pottery suite of the Gemjek, located at the frontier, is allied to the northeast in terms of its forms and decoration, but is more characteristically southern in its functional range and diversity.

Iron making in the Mandara mountains is discussed in chapter 11. Here it suffices to note that large smelting furnaces appear to have differentiated the Mafa from other groups, but that it is unclear how details of form and decoration are associated with linguistic groups, communities, descent groups, and individual smiths. In Sukur somewhat taller (male) and shorter (female) versions of the same furnace type (Fig. 7.11) were constructed according to the sex of the iron master's first child! Patterning in forges on the other hand appears to be much more closely associated with ethnolinguistic groups, although variation within the large Mafa block is ethnoarchaeologically uncontrolled. The same is true of hoes, the blades of which are often distinctive, although as population has increased, iron has become cheaper, and suitable wood has become harder to find, more and more hoes, whatever the shape of their blades, are now made with a tang instead of a socket.[16] Women's pubic aprons made of iron plates, chains or spikes, or fibers, tend to differentiate groups at a scale larger

---

[16] The latter requires a shaft made of a suitably angled branch and part of the trunk (or of a larger branch) of a tree, which is harder to find than the straight shaft that is all that is needed for a tanged hoe.

Fig. 7.11 Mandara furnaces are of a rare type in which the tuyère hangs more or less vertically down the shaft, the bellows being situated above and behind a shield. Magnetite ore and charcoal are charged through a hole in front and near the top of the shaft. The example illustrated is a "female" furnace from Sukur, Nigeria, probably last used in the 1950s. It was cleared and photographed in 1992, and is reconstructed in the diagram.

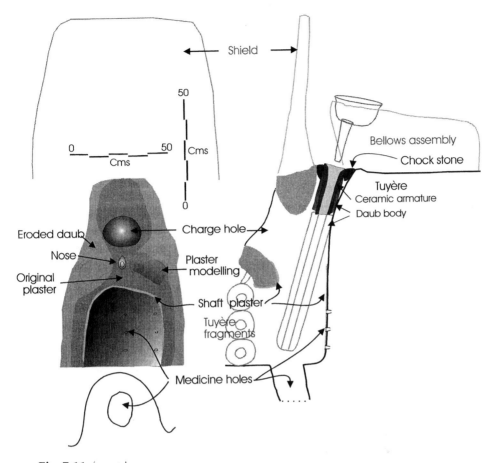

Fig. 7.11 *(cont.)*

than the community. The range of other iron tool and weapon types, axes, arrowheads, amulets, and the like, appears remarkably similar throughout the area and not to be used to signal affiliation at any scale. Moreover, over the whole region and beyond, twisted iron bracelets designate twins, other unusual births, and the parents of twins.

Even with the reservation of mortuary practices to chapter 13, it is evident from the above that a rich material culture is a medium for a great variety of messages, many assertive and some emblemic, though none, so far as we can see, so consciously expressed as a national flag. There is a fairly strong tendency, especially in the southeast, for reasonably distinct material culture sets to be associated with communities and language groups. An anthropologist with experience of this sub-region and a sensitivity to its material culture could be parachuted into it and hope to recognize by a combination of material clues – costume, compound layout, roof construction including details of the binding of the thatch, forge plans, pots – in which language group and even sometimes in which community she had landed. In the northeast she could make similar though grosser distinctions.

However, as David *et al.* (1991) point out, it is in the highest degree unlikely that in either area this differentiation in space would translate into an archaeological record of distinct cultures. This is not merely because so much stylistic expression takes forms that do not preserve, but because over time, as among the pre-1930s Kalinga, communities are not stable entities. Though some have very deep roots, they are, on a time scale of generations and centuries, constantly dividing, budding off daughter communities, declining, recombining, and disappearing. Sirak was, for example, formed by the coming together of six clans from at least three, culturally differentiated, directions; not one claims autochthony. The undated ruins of Kova-Mondossa, now in Mafa territory but not claimed by the present inhabitants as their own, testify to a presumably more complex society that once lived there (Seignobos 1982; Gerhard Müller-Kosack pers. comm.). The Mofu-Diamaré chiefdoms frequently changed their boundaries as they gained or lost territory and people. Examples could be multiplied indefinitely (Sterner 1998). Nor did communities once established retain stable populations. Unlike the Kalinga, communities are far from endogamous. Vincent (1991) describes the many small-scale migrations from the plains that contributed to the development of the Mofu-Diamaré chiefdoms. Müller-Kosack's (1991) study of the Mafa villages of Guzda and David and Sterner's (1999) research at Sukur reveal a similar pattern of multiple small-scale migrations, stimulated by famine, drought, intra-group conflict, need to escape the wrath of spirits or human oppressors, or the search for new farmland. Such movements are indeed documented in all the ethnographies of the region. Even the boundary between the Wandala state and the montagnards was indistinct (Bourges 1996; Lyons 1996).

The population build up in the mountains in recent centuries and consequent competition for land and labor might be expected, on the pattern of the Baringo tribes and the Kalinga, to have stimulated stylistic differentiation of montagnard political communities. It would indeed be hard to account for the diversity observed in any other way, but those communities' constant rise and fall and changes in their personnel appear to have militated (though statistical proof is lacking) against the development of material culture suites to serve as consistent emitters of emblemic style. (No one who has attended the same ceremony in the same community more than once can fail to have been impressed by the variety of its expression, and indeed by the extent of negotiation of procedures required to carry out any public ceremony in the first place.) Nor perhaps were vehement emblemic statements much needed since, again in contrast to the Baringo tribes though more like the Kalinga, people moved around very little under normal circumstances, would have had no difficulty in recognizing the menace of a Wandala cavalier, and could no doubt read very subtle expressions of similarity and difference in interactions with montagnards on the next massif, with whom they occasionally fought but also married and exchanged goods and services.

In any community in which material culture is produced by non-specialists who either regularly assist each other in making and doing things, or have multiple opportunities to observe each other as in the case of rope making, woodworking, or preparation of skins, convergence of practice is likely to develop unless the artifact being produced is adopted by individuals or groups as a vehicle for assertive style. We may also reasonably ascribe the tendency to intra-community consistency in certain aspects of material culture, for example architecture, to the emulation by more recent arrivals of longer-established and therefore senior clans, and perhaps other low-grade pressure to conform. It is interesting to note that members of different communities may indeed claim that their compounds are the same as those of their neighbors even though the ethnoarchaeologist can observe systematic differences, as for example the more spacious layout of Kurang as against Sukur compounds. The contrast between the Zhigile and Shetene pots of the Mafa and Sirak on the other hand partakes more of a Sirak comment (possibly idiosyncratic) on a neighbor's practice, one that recognizes its potency while displacing its referent. Members of northern Mandara communities are conscious of and frequently comment on the customs of their neighbors. Fads, for example in 1986 the placing of neem tree leaves above doors to guard against sorcery, spread, virtually instantaneously, through the area, and soon disappear. Material culture is actively utilized in the process of personal and social identification through comparison at many scales and in both horizontal and, as in the case of chiefly residences, vertical social dimensions (Smith and David 1995).

Other factors reinforce homogeneity in material culture, most notably the smith-potter caste among the southwestern montagnards. Caste members are disproportionately responsible for the production of material culture, including metal goods and ceramics, and commonly also disposal of the dead and a varying range of other specialties. Because they are relatively few in number (usually 2.5–5 percent of the population), they intermarry more frequently across community and language lines than do farmers, and, as divorce is quite frequent, a potter is likely to practice in several communities during her lifetime. Male smiths change residence less often but are regarded as important resources who are likely to be encouraged, in the past sometimes forcibly, to relocate to communities lacking their services. In earlier times their skills ensured they could travel between communities more safely than farmers, and they did so in order to obtain ore or metal, to sell their wares, and also to practice divination. The farmers' attitude towards the smith-potters, often characterized in the literature by terms like "despised," is in fact ambiguous, marked by elements both of disdain and respect, modeled in part upon relations between the genders (Sterner and David 1991). Here, caste is an imposed anthropological concept and there is in fact a gradient in attitudes expressed from the almost complete endogamy of smith-potters in casted societies to farmers' hesitance to marry them among the nominally uncasted Mofu-Diamaré (Sterner and David in press; Sterner 1998: chapter 8). So it may well be that overall contrasts between the material cultures of the south and north-east are in part the result of an interaction between smiths' and potters' transcendence of boundaries and their ability as specialists to vary their products to conform to community standards. On a larger scale, state-induced stresses on the peoples of the Mandara mountains increased rates of population mixing within the region, generating, whether directly or indirectly or both, pressures leading towards a growing together of local styles.

In their 1991 paper ND and his colleagues argued that the broad-scale similarities in material culture which characterize the northern Mandara mountains are produced both by the integrative social processes discussed above and by the workings of their mental counterpart, a symbolic reservoir. Some components of this reservoir include belief in a creator God and in the existence and potency of spirits attached to particular places, a belief in the existence of a spiritual counterpart of the individual that forms part of a complex of ideas related to ancestors and to the dangerous potency of twins, a widespread metaphor of containment and release that applies to spirits, bulls, and the dead (explored in the film *Vessels of the spirits* [David 1990] and by Sterner [1998]), a concern with annual purification, beliefs in the possession by certain individuals of powers over nature, ideas about witchcraft, the assimilation of pots to people, the association of odd numbers with males, of smelting with both procreation and warfare, and much more. Not that any of these concepts is peculiar to the Mandara mountains – indeed many are widely distributed in Africa south of the Sahara – but their combination and the forms in which they are expressed in behavior and material culture are distinctive. The symbolic reservoir that they represent is drawn upon like a well of pure water by individuals and groups, but in different ways. Thus for example among the Mafa and Sirak the typology of ceramic vessels can be said rather precisely to model relations between the worlds of the living and of the spirits, while among the Sukur, where there is a greater division of ritual labor, very similar beliefs are held and expressed in ceremonies even though ceramics are and were unelaborated, often being acquired from other groups. The animated discussions regarding procedure to be observed on the occasion of, say, a burial, represent in part the invocation and negotiation of elements in the symbolic reservoir. In this manner also, while endowed with massive inertia, the contents of the reservoir change and the character of the reservoir as a whole is modified. Tripod pots – the number three is significant as is the common resemblance of tripod legs to the horns of bulls – provide material evidence that this has happened. They are everywhere special, being used by Mafa men, and not by women, for cooking meat and other rare high-protein foods, and also pierced and with legs broken off to cover the burial of a boy baby's placenta. Although rarer in the north today, though common at times in the past (Wahome 1989), among some northern groups they are used for preparing medicines, and a Mura example collected by Diane Lyons from Doulo was used in twins' ceremonies.

David *et al.* (1991: 175) concluded their paper by saying that:

> For the archaeologist oriented towards ecological and economic questions, it probably matters very little that she will be unable to reconstruct neat, bounded ethnic groupings, but only the larger cluster that drew on the same symbolic reservoir. For this is surely the significant unit for understanding economic process on a macro-scale. Archaeologists whose interests are rather in the re-construction of frameworks of meaning must on the other hand be prepared to take an interpretive and probably generative (see Barth 1987) approach that can cope with multiple, polythetic and varied expressions of prehistoric ideas.

While this may be true also of Kalinga archaeology, it remains to be added that one member of the team, Scott MacEachern (1994), subsequently challenged the symbolic reservoir concept, preferring to substitute that of "symbolic sets." This disagreement mainly reflects Western archaeologists slipping up in their own hydraulic metaphors, but it is worth insisting that one of the reservoir's primary characteristics is that its contents are mixed even though the mixture may vary from one basin to another, whereas symbolic sets show internal coherence but no necessary relationship with other sets similarly conceived. In the northern Mandara mountains the interpenetration of symbols and concepts is very marked, to the point that it is impossible to isolate a ceremony for analysis without taking account of its relationships to other ceremonies and to behaviors in societies where the ceremony does not recognizably exist (Sterner 1998). MacEachern does not lay out details of symbolic sets but we would argue that where they can be isolated they are likely to prove foreign and not fully integrated into Mandara ways. The titles that are commonly bestowed on certain elders even in the simplest montagnard societies are an example. These have been borrowed at different times from the surrounding states, but in the process of transfer and repeated borrowing have become dissociated from their original functions. They serve instead to embellish variants of a concept of chieftaincy that, itself an element in the symbolic reservoir, has been differentially elaborated by montagnard societies.

Another question raised by MacEachern (1994: 215) relates to the social boundaries of the symbolic reservoir. The presentation above hopefully clarifies the concept, but it is indeed true that boundaries are by no means always clear. Whether the Margi living on and around outlying portions of the Mandara mountain chain, many of whom say that their ancestors came from Pabir-Bura country to the west, draw on the same symbolic reservoir as their Sukur neighbors is uncertain (cf. Vaughan 1964, 1973). Certainly they share many elements of culture, and the claim by the Margi of Gulak that their ruling family is of Sukur origin is undisputed. The research required to find out more might well lead to better definition of the reservoir, but in truth the concept is intended to assist in visualizing broad patterns of cultural variety rather than as an analytical tool. On the other hand there are instances where the social boundaries of the reservoir are sharply defined. The Hide who walks down the mountain and into Fulbe Madagali is crossing much more than an international frontier; he is entering a different symbolic reservoir, its boundary still distinguished by styles of architecture, clothing, and other material domains, though far less clearly so than in the early years of this century when Madagali's ruler, Hamman Yaji, was aggressively raiding the montagnards (Vaughan and Kirk-Greene 1995). At that time we might have said, as does DeBoer (1990: 102) of the Ucayali basin, that "ethnic boundaries . . . are highly permeable with respect to bodies but almost inviolable with respect to style."

On one occasion in 1986 ND was working with Diane Lyons in Doulo and chatting to a Wandala whose compound she was planning. He asked him what languages he spoke and was surprised that Mafa was included. That man's parents were Mafa slaves purchased by the Sultan of Wandala as children and brought up in his palace to serve him. They had married and taught their son their language, but in all other respects he appeared a Wandala, to the extent of sporting Wandala tribal marks. His parents had crossed a style boundary and from one symbolic reservoir to another. Does this mean that the boundaries of symbolic reservoirs are always also stylistic frontiers? Surely if material culture plays a significant role in constituting culture, the answer must be yes. We would expect stylistic differentiation between reservoirs in most if not all domains of material culture. But the reverse is not necessarily true. In the Ucayali case the stylistically distinguished ethnic groupings defined by DeBoer are unlikely to relate to different symbolic reservoirs. Data are lacking, but it would appear that in this case the pattern of similarities and differences across language families and ecosystems might appropriately be handled in terms of symbolic sets, some of which are borrowed across ethnic boundaries in a process of emulation, while others, differentiating the people of the interfluves, "are viewed more appropriately as desperate, and often futile, stylistic expressions on the part of kidnapped, pillaged, and otherwise tyrannized peoples" (DeBoer 1990: 103).

Conclusions

We have looked in some detail at five regional studies of style particularly as they relate to the marking of sociocultural boundaries at various scales. The chapter has dealt almost entirely with the expression of social differentiation in relatively egalitarian societies, with what we might term horizontal uses of style. Other examples and uses of style, not necessarily labeled as such, are found throughout the rest of this book. In later chapters we are also concerned with uses of style to express rank and class differences, the vertical dimension of society, and with the questions of where style comes from, the relationship between material expression and underlying belief, between signifier and signified.

What have we learned? Style is defined in many ways but is best understood as a relational quality, the potential for which resides in those formal characteristics of an artifact that are acquired in the course of manufacture as the consequence of the exercise of cultural choice. It is on account of its rooting in cultural choice that style opens the door to inference regarding the social and ideological characteristics of prehistoric cultures. The interaction theory of stylistic similarity exploits one aspect of style, that, in the mass, it constitutes "a highly specific and characteristic manner of doing something . . . always peculiar to a specific time and place," in order to detect and order temporal and spatial patterning in bodies of material culture. However, this ignores the role of style in communicating within and between individuals and social groups. In order to probe the internal workings of past societies it is necessary to achieve an understanding of the various systems responsible for artifact production and consumption, and to theorize the functioning of style as a medium of communication. Arguing from a systems theory perspective, Wobst showed that style has adaptive functions and can be used to transmit a range of simple messages cheaply and effectively. He developed theoretical expectations regarding the contexts in which signaling "in the artifact mode" were likely to be efficient, and conducted a partial test using ethnographic data. Despite the adoption of an iconicist view of style that blinded him to certain of its manifestations and lesser failings, his 1977 paper prepared the ground for future work.

Polly Wiessner's research among the San documented the workings of the cognitive process of personal and social identification through comparison and introduced two terms, emblemic and assertive, that remain useful. The subsequent debate between her and James Sackett went a long way towards clarifying the difference between the iconicist view of style and his isochrestic approach which, while allowing the importance of active signaling, regards passive style as far more pervasive; more messages are indeed read than sent.[17] Wobst had attempted a general theory of style as a medium of communication and Wiessner offered some guidance as to what kinds of artifacts are likely to repay stylistic analysis: those that are important to social identity and those that pass through several stages of manufacture. This has not proved particularly helpful. Wiessner supplied a behavioral basis for certain kinds of stylistic expression, but it is clear from the concluding pages of her 1984 paper on San

---

[17] Unfortunately Sackett's own message was expressed in terms that not everyone found easy to understand; he talked, for example, of "ethnicity" versus "activity," when he was really speaking of ideo- and sociotechnically versus technomically related variability in material culture. By ethnicity he does not refer necessarily to a quality associated with tribes, peoples, and groups of substantial size; if a family has a special way of doing something their neighbors do differently, that would be an ethnic distinction in Sackett's terms.

beadwork that, while striving towards a general theory of style that will be of predictive value to archaeologists, she recognizes the unlikelihood of its ever being achieved. First, she realizes that her concept of style fails to cover the full range of formal variation. Second, the Wobstian assumption that efficiency, judged in neoclassical economic rather than psychological terms, guides the use of style is flawed, and this fatally weakens the predictive power of the information theory approach. Development of general theory is also inhibited by the historically contingent nature of stylistic expression which, amongst other things, renders it difficult to predict which domains of material culture will be elaborated. Style is too flexible in use, raising the "problem of how to interpret the nature of relationships created by certain stylistic strategies, particularly since a single strategy can be used to create not one, but several, kinds of identity relationships" (p. 227).

Several of these points are reiterated in Ian Hodder's research, which reveals the inadequacies in relation to the Baringo database, and by implication many prehistoric ones, of many of the kinds of explanation frequently employed by archaeologists to account for variation within and between archaeological cultures. Hodder emphasizes the importance of competition between groups in stimulating stylistic differentiation, but he also shows, as does DeBoer for the Ucayali, that people can and do adopt different tribal styles depending upon their changing social affiliations. By 1982 he had consolidated his position that style actively contributes to the constitution of culture, and that items of material culture can indeed be regarded as symbols in action. But he also shows that, far from stylistic expression covarying with cultures, artifact classes are manipulated in different ways to different ends by different groups. While Hodder's documentation of the role of inter-group competition in stimulating stylistic differentiation has proved influential, he himself has been careful to specify the boundary conditions within which this tendency is likely to be realized. We remain far from a general theory of style that can be readily applied to archaeological materials even if Hodder's ideas have advanced our understanding of the workings of style and stimulated archaeologists to test a variety of models, some suggested by ethnoarchaeology, against the various parts of their databases.

Graves's research on Kalinga materials is utterly different. At the same time as it sets high standards for the documentation of differential patterning in material culture, its impact is weakened by the narrowness of its focus. It appears unlikely that the advantages of the naturalist and antinaturalist approaches can be successfully combined, in part owing to the context of research funding but in part also to the tendency of researchers to subscribe to and practice particular styles of research.

While the authors so far considered are concerned with style as an index of sociocultural phenomena, Lemonnier is equally interested in the functional aspects of technology. But he recognizes that the mental image, the social representation, interacts with functional requirements to constrain designs even in societies that pride themselves on their scientific approach (see especially his discussion of arbitrary choices in airplane designs [Lemonnier 1992: 66–77]). It is here that his interests and those of Hodder converge. Lemonnier is also a useful, though at times erratic, critic of others' work, asking important questions. Why is social identity expressed in certain ways, in certain artifact classes, and not in others? How does variation in material culture relate to systems of meaning? "Without explaining how the context (namely, the particular social representations held by a human group) determines the choice of a particular trait to express some social relation, no generalization is possible" (Lemonnier 1992: 88). Another nail in the coffin of general theory, even though he hopes one day to reach the "functioning principles of technical systems as signifying systems" (1986: 174).

Lemonnier's interpretation of variation in material culture among the Anga suffers from a concept of style derived from Leroi-Gourhan that approaches the iconicist (but which can yet regard a design as "merely . . . an aesthetic feature"! [1992: 88]). Much of the material was gathered by others, which partially explains the absence of chaîne opératoire analyses. His analysis is also hampered by a lack of historical data. Thus the apparent arbitrariness of the adoption or refusal to adopt technical traits most probably derives from our threefold ignorance of their chaînes opératoires, social representations, and the historical circumstances that have differentially affected Anga groups. Various clues, clearly deriving in large part from Lemonnier's own fieldwork, suggest that despite environmental and cultural differences Anga and Baringo tribespeople react to similar stimuli in comparable ways, and that they are similarly drawn to represent aspects of the human condition, such as gender, in material terms.

The theme of social representations is taken up, though using a different vocabulary, by members of the Mandara Archaeological Project team who, in their studies of stylistic variation in and around the northern Mandara mountains, come to the conclusion that a great variety of stylistic expressions in many different communities may be considered a polythetic set linked by their common derivation from a shared symbolic reservoir, or in Lemonnier's terms a common fund of social representations. The integrated nature of the symbolic reservoir and the limited number of its "prime concepts" is a theme insufficiently emphasized and explored in their work. Internal and external pressures have led in this region to what we might regard as stylistic play conducted under reservoir rules, those rules themselves being modified through time through the operation of mechanisms such as micro-migrations and institutions such as caste within a cultural whole that responds more or less as an entity to major changes in the natural, economic, and political environments. Once again, while their findings support the antinaturalist contention that such pressures will always be mediated through culture, itself a complex

Fig. 7.12 Shipibo-Conibo designs, unlike those of the Chachi, are often
applied to multiple media, as here to (a) the human face, (b) cotton
textiles, and (c) ceramic vessels, in this case two examples of the
relatively rare *joni chomo* (human jar) form; Ucayali region, Peru,
1970.

historical construct, and thereby deny the possibility of achieving what was in fact their original aim, the development of a predictive theory of style, they provide archaeologists with food for thought about the nature of the entities they discern in their materials. Interpretation of prehistoric materials stands to benefit not only from their redefinition of what some archaeological cultures may represent, but also by the testing of hypotheses regarding the nature of inferred entities against competing models: the overall coherence of material culture suites derived from symbolic reservoirs versus the more diversified products of the interaction of internally coherent but differentiated symbolic sets. It is possible that such distinctions underlie DeBoer's (1991) intriguing characterization of Shipibo-Conibo decorative organization as "pervasive" and "multi-mediated," occurring across a wide range of material media (Fig. 7.12), versus Chachi "partitive" organization, in which decoration shows significant differences from one artifactual medium to another. If only things were that simple!

Further reading

We have allotted little space in this chapter to the concept of technological style which Terry Childs (1991) applies to iron smelting furnaces in Africa. Her paper should be read with the relationship of technological style to chaînes opératoires and the anthropology of techniques in mind. *The uses of style in archaeology*, edited by Conkey and Hastorf (1990a), is an important compilation of papers, several by ethnoarchaeologists (including Wiessner), on various aspects of style. A recent paper by Wiessner (1997) takes an evolutionary approach to further development of her ideas on the behavioral basis of style. Michelle Hegmon's (1992) paper "Archaeological research on style" is a useful survey. Christopher Carr (1995a) has attempted in a massive paper, more cited than read, to develop "A unified middle-range theory of artifact design." Papers in Miriam Stark's (1998a) *The archaeology of social boundaries*, including one by Hegmon, also deal with topics discussed in this chapter, in some cases from the perspective of the transmission of technologies, an issue we take up in chapter 11.

CHAPTER 8

SETTLEMENT: SYSTEMS AND PATTERNS

... none but the largest !Kung dry-season camps would be found by the future archaeologist.

(John Yellen 1977a: 80)

Some of these sites were surprisingly large.
(Lewis Binford 1983a: 133 regarding Nunamiut activity areas)

... mobility among foragers is not only the result of techno-economic decisions or energetic variables ... it is also the consequence of a myriad factors, psychological, social, historical and ideological.
(Gustavo Politis 1996: 500–1)

This chapter is concerned with ethnoarchaeological contributions to understanding of subsistence-settlement systems, the broad patterns of interaction between demography, economic adaptations, and the environment that result in distribution across the landscape of interrelated sites of varying importance and function. We take a traditional (but not evolutionary) approach, treating studies of hunter-gatherer settlement before ones relating to pastoralists and cultivators. The chapter concludes by discussing contrasts and the concepts of mobility and sedentism.

Settlement patterns and subsistence-settlement systems

Settlements often leave substantial tangible remains on landscapes, and evidence of what their occupants cultivated, gathered, hunted, bred, and ate is also often preserved. It is on the basis of site types and associated remains of plants and animals that archaeologists make provisional identifications of subsistence adaptations, which are often subsumed under such overly broad categories as "hunter-gatherer" or "farmer." Archaeologists are interested in the closely interrelated matters of subsistence and settlement for many reasons. Beginning in the latest Pleistocene, long-term and possibly irreversible changes in subsistence adaptations in several parts of the world, and the subsequent development of specialized subsistence strategies and techniques, led to new demands for labor and to concomitant changes in household size and organization, to alterations in inheritance patterns, and within a few thousand years to such

225

labor intensive but increasingly productive "inventions" as irrigation. Human societies were transformed. Subsistence and settlement are also often, although questionably, linked with forms (or "levels") of socio-political organization – the bands, tribes, chiefdoms, and states of neo-evolutionary theorists. Such linkages raise questions (or mask assumptions) about causal relationships between subsistence and other aspects of sociocultural organization.

The term "settlement pattern" has had diverse meanings. In one influential publication (Chang 1958), it refers both to the internal organization of individual settlements and to the distribution and interrelationships of multiple settlements on a landscape. It is in the latter sense that we use it here. Community pattern, the organization of individual settlements, is considered with activity areas in chapter 9. Archaeologists have long been interested in documenting patterns of and changes in settlement; in the vanguard, Willey's work (1953) in Peru's Virú valley was soon followed by regional studies of diachronic change in settlement morphology and location in relation to posited economic and sociopolitical transformations. Notable examples are the work of Adams (1965, 1981; Adams and Nissen 1972) in Iraq, and Parsons (1971) and Blanton *et al.* (1993) in Mexico. These studies all demonstrate that while subsistence and settlement are tightly linked, settlement patterns are the complex products of, in addition, social and political relations.

In the late 1960s and 1970s, archaeological work focusing on subsistence and settlement was influenced by concepts derived from General Systems Theory. Numerous publications consider the interrelatedness of ancient subsystems and the ways specific variables can, through positive and negative feedback, assume "causal" roles, affecting the trajectories of other variables within systemic contexts (e.g., Flannery 1968). Advocates of a systems approach sometimes used diagrams to illustrate schematically the ways in which subsystems might interact, and in which variables might contribute to either stability or change. Elizabeth Brumfiel (1992: 552–3), referring to a flowchart devised by Charles Redman (1978: 230) that purports to show positive feedback relationships leading to class stratification in Mesopotamia, has castigated such attempts for ignoring social actors and social dynamics:

The boxes in [Redman's] flowchart . . . are activities rather than agents, functions rather than performers. . . . the ecosystem theorists' reliance upon natural selection as the mechanism of systemic change determines the nature of the connections between systemic components. The connections between boxes are either functional responses to population needs . . . or necessary consequences of one variable for another . . . These connections are stimulus response or input–output relationships.

In systems theory approaches the absence of human agency is also frequently associated with an absence of concern with rates of change. It is possible, for example, to posit and compare likely causal variables and their interrelationships in plant and animal domestication in Southwest Asia and Mesoamerica, but this provides no basis for identifying the overall duration of such a process, or for explaining the rates of such transformations there and in other parts of the world.

Archaeologists cannot observe systems, and even patterns are inferences derived from the numbers, associations, and spatial distributions of the surviving residues of the range of activities carried out over the course of time at different places in a landscape. Ethnoarchaeologists can, on the other hand, observe a sample of such activities directly, and more easily infer from them the nature of the subsistence-settlement system. General systems theory and the desire to develop bridging arguments linking patterns and systems were important stimuli in the development of ethnoarchaeology in its New Ethnoarchaeology (1968–81) period. As discussed in chapter 1, much early ethnoarchaeological work focused on subsistence and settlement. Seminal research was done among hunter-gatherers in Alaska, Australia, and Botswana, besides significant studies of agriculturalists and pastoralists carried out in Iran and elsewhere. The research carried out among hunter-gatherers was, and remains, wildly disproportionate to their numbers, although, given their fragile, rapidly changing, and jeopardized status, the bias is understandable. It is also reasonable, since for so much of the human career we were foragers and collectors, and since so much methodologically and theoretically influential archaeological work focuses on the reconstruction of paleolithic subsistence and settlement, contributing importantly to understandings of activities and site structures. Ethnoarchaeological research on hunters and gatherers is also more immediately relevant for the archaeology of the last 40,000 or so years than it is for earlier periods, when there were substantial differences in the structure and organization of hominid brains, their psychology, and potential communicative and motor abilities, that remain matters of contention. It should, however, be remembered that all ethnoarchaeological research on hunter-gatherers has been conducted in colonial or postcolonial settings that strongly influence many aspects of human behavior. Thus for example the hunter-gatherer label is applied to the Alyawara, who are dependent on seasonal work and government welfare and obtain no more than 25 percent of their food by hunting and gathering (O'Connell 1987).

In this chapter we characterize several subsistence adaptations – hunting and gathering, pastoralism, and agriculture – and their spatial correlates, drawing on selected case studies with a view to identification of their archaeological signatures. We recognize that most living peoples combine these subsistence practices in various ways, and happily acknowledge that researchers generally recognize the complexity of such combined strategies. Farmers are for the most part tethered to their land although Martha Graham (1993, 1994), one of Binford's students, in her ethnoarchaeological study of the Rarámuri of Mexico, describes a system in which agriculturalists are quite mobile. Ertuğ-Yaraş (1997) documents sedentary Turkish farmers' extensive reliance on collected wild plants. As these examples indicate, a landscape can be utilized in

Fig. 8.1 In a mongongo grove in the Kalahari desert, John Yellen interviews
!Kung San about kill sites, Botswana, 1968.

different ways by people who, though they may spend more time and energy
in one part than in others, will use a variety of places for a variety of reasons.
No community is functionally or spatially limited to a single site, and even in
one locality or subregion land use almost always varies seasonally. With
knowledge of ranges of variations, archaeologists should be able to modify and
refine their research designs by allowing them to incorporate specific expectations about the material remains and spatial organization associated with particular subsistence adaptations, and we would expect increasingly nuanced
approaches to sampling and data recovery.

Hunters and gatherers

!Kung masters of cleverness

Arriving in 1968 as a member of the Harvard University Bushman Studies
Project directed by Irven DeVore and Richard Lee, John Yellen spent over two
years working with !Kung San in the Kalahari desert, during which he acquired
sufficient linguistic competence to allow him to dispense with an interpreter
(Fig. 8.1). After completing the manuscript for his (1977a) book, he returned in
1975 for another year's work, leading to further publications (1991a, 1991b;
Gould and Yellen 1987, 1991). Of his first fieldwork, Yellen says:

In essence, my goal was to obtain plans of a large enough series of campsites to permit statistical analysis, and to obtain relevant information about how long each site was occupied, who lived at each, and what activities occurred there. The latter data I collected [often with DeVore] primarily by after-the-fact interview, although in some instances I was present or nearby throughout an occupation. . . . In retrospect, it also became clear that I had allowed my own presence to affect !Kung informants more than I might have wished. In the text that follows, I take pains to point out just where such transgressions have occurred. (1977a: xiii)

Yellen's treatment of the arrangement of people and activities within individual camps is considered in the next chapter. Here we are concerned with his views on the nature of !Kung bands and detailed study of the Dobe band and their yearly cycle of movement.

In the relatively harsh and highly variable Kalahari desert environment, small bands of kin and affines concentrate around permanent water sources during the dry season, splitting up into smaller groups to exploit parts of a loosely defined band territory during the rains. While bands, which have a core of close kin who are acknowledged "owners" of the territory, show a considerable degree of continuity through time, for both economic and social reasons there is a high turnover in individual membership, no less than 80 percent in the Dobe band (22–25 adults) between 1964 and 1968. This allows the population to distribute itself over the landscape in an orderly but nonetheless flexible manner, enabling it able to cope with year to year and shorter-term variation, some of it highly unpredictable, in rains and other resources. Binford calls this "mapping on" to resources (see below). Bilateral inheritance of territories and the practice of arranging children's first marriages with persons from distant areas contribute to band and individual security, Wiessner's "pooling of risk," by extending mutual obligations and widening residence possibilities.

When asked about group membership the !Kung regularly make normative statements to the effect that individuals are assigned to specific bands. Yellen (pp. 50–1) suggests that "to deal with complex situations a society may adopt simple rules and then allow great leeway in their application" – with interesting consequences. If a rule is violated 20 percent of the time, by the fifth generation only a third of the population will neither have violated the rule themselves nor have violators in their ascendance. Such social arrangements underlie the different stylistic patterns discussed in chapter 7. There is much less movement of persons between bands among the resource-poor !Xo, where arrowheads assort by band clusters, than among the !Kung, where such stylistic differentiation is first evident at the level of the dialect group (Wiessner 1983). The !Kung refer to people who are flexible, and who excel in maintaining and choosing between a number of alternatives, as "masters of cleverness," and Yellen argues that this quality has had a strong positive selective value in hominid evolution.

As Yellen's fieldwork was coming to an end he realized that "our data [on

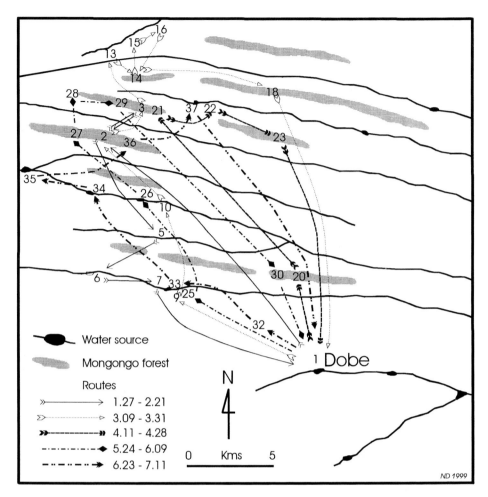

Fig. 8.2 Routes taken and camps occupied by two brothers and their
families, members of the "core Dobe group" of !Kung San, which
consisted of about 20 adults and their children, on five successive
expeditions between 27 January and 11 July 1968 (after Yellen 1977:
Table 3 and Maps 5–7). It is likely that they had made one previous
eight- to ten-day trip in January, but they went on no further
extended trips until the next rains (in October or November 1968)
(Yellen 1977a: 59).

camps] also documented the movements of a hunting and gathering group over
the major part of the year" (p. 59). In particular he had a complete record of the
movements of two brothers and their families who, with a varying cast of other
band members, had camped together during the heavy rains, autumn and the
first half of winter (Fig. 8.2). Yellen, concerned about bias, notes that on two
occasions he drove the group back to Dobe, and that they probably stayed there
longer than they otherwise would as they were able through relatives to obtain

milk from Bantu herders at a nearby water source. He is right to note this although, as we saw in chapter 2, it would be mistaken to suppose that it is merely the presence of himself and his Landrover and of Bantu with their cattle that prevents !Kung behavior from being "traditional."

The pattern produced by the cyclical movements of the hunter-gatherer group may be characterized as one of tethered nomadism, the main Dobe camp being the tether both because it is the only water source during much of the dry season and because it is the center of the band's social life. Groups move out from Dobe during the period when standing water is available in pans (localized depressions) and "By frequent movement these units can then adjust to minor changes in resources, game distribution, and varying food preferences" (p. 39). Mongongo nuts and other plant foods are collected, and game sought especially around the salt pans in the north (Table 8.1). The map (Fig. 8.2) seriously underestimates the density of coverage of the region since it shows only camp to camp movements and not the radial foraging out from and around those sites (that are more than overnight travel camps) of mainly women gatherers and, over greater distances, of mainly male hunters. Even so, the overlay of the routes of the five trips clearly demonstrates the systematic manner in which, in the course of the rainy season, autumn, and early winter, the group quarters the area of the band's territory that they have chosen to exploit. While their knowledge of their environment is less than perfect, there cannot be much that escapes their attention. Had we comparable maps for other subsets of the Dobe band, this kind of coverage would no doubt be evident for the territory as a whole.

Yellen draws a number of other inferences from these data. If overnight way station camps are excluded, there are complex relationships between season, size of group, and length of stay, dependent in part upon the changing availability of water, but also upon the more varied diet that will be obtained by and shared between members of a larger group. Thus for the period covered and for camps away from Dobe there are low $(r \leq .57)$ but significant correlations between group size and season and between season and length of occupation. As to the camps themselves, Yellen shows that while subsistence activities practiced in them vary by season and by environment, manufacturing activities are much less predictable. Thus the inventories of material discarded will vary considerably and in relation to manufacturing debris erratically, a point that is perhaps of less concern to the archaeologist than it might be since Yellen is of the opinion that only the largest dry season camps are likely to be identifiable archaeologically. We return to the remarkably documented camps of the !Kung in chapter 9.

Willow smoke, dogs' tails, and beyond

While Yellen worked among the !Kung, Lewis Binford was conducting the research among the Nunamiut discussed in chapter 5. He later (1980) wrote

Table 8.1 *The succession of camps occupied by two !Kung brothers, their families, and various others, during the main rains, autumn and early winter of 1968 (data compiled from Yellen 1977a, especially Table 3 and Maps 5–7)*

Camp and location	Environment	Distance to camp (km)[a]	Days of occupation (arrival date)	Type of site	Seasons
1 Dobe	permanent water	N/A	?	base camp	main rains
2 n/on/oni ʔtoa	nut grove	18.1	7 (1.27)	new camp	
3 ʔtum ʔtoa	nut grove	2.6	8	new camp	
4 return to 2	nut grove	2.6	2	reoccupation	
5 /tanagaba	inter-dune	6.5	2	new camp	
6 /twi /twama	inter-dune, seasonal water	4.4	3	new camp	
7 n!abesha	inter-dune, seasonal water	3.7	2	new camp	
8 return to 1	permanent water	10.4	17 (2.21)	return to base camp	
9 n!abesha	inter-dune, seasonal water	8.9	5 (3.9)	new camp	
10 shum !kau	inter-dune	5.4	2	new camp	
11 return to 2	nut grove	5.6	2	reoccupation	peak rains
12 return to 3	nut grove	2.6	2	reoccupation	
13 hwanasi	near salt pans; herds of large game in rains	3.5	3	new camp	
14 chu!ko n!a	nut grove	2.0	2	new camp	
15 /twi !ka hwanasi	near salt pans; herds of large game in rains	2.0	1	overnight camp	
16 /twi !ka hwanasi	near salt pans; herds of large game in rains	1.9	1	overnight camp	
17 return to 14	nut grove	3.0	2	new camp	

18 !gum ?toa	nut grove	8.0	2	new camp	end main rains
19 return to 1	permanent water	15.7	11 (3.31)	return to base camp	rains ending
20 Dobe ?toa	nut grove	5.6	1 (4.11)	overnight camp	autumn (brief)
21 ?tum ?toa	nut grove	12.0	3	new camp	
22 //gakwe ?dwa	inter-dune, seasonal water	2.4	12	new camp	
23 !gausha ?toa	nut grove	4.4	1	overnight camp	
24 return to 1	permanent water	13.1	26 (4.28)	return to base camp	
25 n!abesha	inter-dune seasonal, water	9.2	5 (5.24)	new camp	winter starts
26 shum !kau	inter-dune seasonal, water	5.7	1	overnight camp	
27 n/on/oni ?toa	nut grove	5.0	5	new camp	
28 ?tum ?toa	nut grove	2.2	3	new camp	coldest period starts
29 ?tum ?toa	nut grove	2.4	1	overnight camp	
30 Dobe ?toa	nut grove	13.0	1	overnight camp	
31 return to 1	permanent water	5.9	14 (6.9)	return to base camp	
32 north of Dobe	other	4.1	1 (6.23)	overnight camp	
33 n!abesha	inter-dune, seasonal water	5.4	1	overnight camp	
34 shum !kau	inter-dune, seasonal water	7.0	6	new camp	
35 mokoro	inter-dune, seasonal water	4.1	2	new camp	
36 n/on/oni ?toa	nut grove	6.1	1	overnight camp	
37 //gakwe ?dwa	inter-dune, seasonal water	4.1	8	new camp	
38 return to 1	permanent water	16.3	(7.11)	return to base camp	coldest period continues

Note:
[a] Direct distances estimated from Yellen 1977a: Maps 5, 6, and 7, and Tables 3 and 4. Inconsistencies render these data approximate.

what has turned out to be the single most influential paper on subsistence and settlement among hunter-gatherers, "Willow smoke and dogs' tails," a romantically titled think piece based largely upon his Nunamiut experience and upon Silberbauer's (1972) and Yellen's (1977a) research among the San. In this paper Binford actually presents very little ethnoarchaeological data as he develops expectations of the archaeological records likely to be produced at the two ends, characterized as foraging and collecting, of a graded series of hunter-gatherer subsistence-settlement systems. The foraging pattern, modeled on the San, is described as entailing "high residential mobility, low-bulk inputs, and regular daily food procurement strategies" (p. 9), with frequent forays around and, in the case of male hunters, beyond the vicinity of relatively briefly occupied campsites in search of food, which tends to be obtained on an "encounter" basis. Thus the settlement patterns of foragers are characterized by (a) residential bases (presumably including the !Kung way station camps), (b) "locations," places where they carry out extractive tasks, and (c) occasional overnight camp sites occupied by men on longer hunting trips (Table 8.2). The assemblages likely to be found at such sites will vary according to the nature and variety of tasks performed and their seasonality, and upon the density and abundance of resources through time. For example, "Under low-bulk extraction or low redundancy in localization, the archaeological remains of locations may be scattered over the landscape rather than concentrated in recognizable 'sites' . . . So called 'off-site' archaeological strategies are appropriate to such situations" (p. 9). This conforms to Yellen's view.

In contrast, "collecting," characterized not by "mapping on" to resources but by a "logistic" strategy, is modeled on the subsistence practices of the Nunamiut, who

supply themselves with specific resources through specially organized task groups . . . composed of skilled and knowledgeable individuals. They are not groups out "searching" for any resource encountered; they are task groups seeking to procure *specific resources* in specific contexts. (p. 10)

Collectors like the Nunamiut hunt fewer species and engage in comparatively fewer extractive episodes; however, these often bring in large quantities of animal or other foods that are systematically processed and sometimes cached until needed. Thus in addition to the site types found among foragers (which under a logistical regime show rather different characteristics), collectors create field camps, stations, and caches (Fig. 8.3). The assemblage contents of the various types of collector sites is complicated by the factor of curation, but, says Binford, arguing in the language of systems theory:

Logistically organized systems have all the properties of a forager system and then some. Being a system, when new organizational properties are added, adjustments are made in the components already present such that residential mobility no longer plays the same roles it did when the system had no logistical component. Given basically two strategies, "mapping on" and "logistics," systems that employ both are more complex . . . It

Table 8.2 *Site types and activities associated with foraging and collecting strategies, and their archaeological characteristics (after Binford 1980)*

Strategy	Site types	Activities	Archaeological characteristics
Foraging	Residential base, frequently moved	Processing, manufacturing, maintenance	Medium visibility, higher if critical resources are of localized availability; considerable range of tool types; relatively "coarse-grained" assemblage[a]
	Location	Extractive	Frequent, but low visibility; aggregates of (often expedient) artifacts, lacking structure; palimpsests likely
	Overnight camp	Processing, manufacturing, maintenance	Rare, low visibility; assemblage fine-grained
Collecting	Residential base, infrequently and seasonally moved	Processing	High to medium visibility, wide and structured range of tool types; coarse-grained
	Location	Extraction	Visibility varying from high (e.g., buffalo jumps) to low; varied toolkits, likely specialized; grain variable depending upon redundancy of occupation
	Field camp, briefly occupied perhaps on a seasonal basis	Temporary operational center; processing, manufacturing, maintenance	Medium to low visibility; possibly specialized toolkits; grain variable
	Station, e.g., hunting stand, observation post, ambush	Information gathering, maintenance, some manufacturing	Medium to low visibility; varied toolkit; grain variable
	Cache	Storage	Low visibility, few artifacts

Notes:

[a] By "coarse-grained" Binford means that archaeological remains cannot be attributed to specific events with any degree of precision ("the resolution between archaeological remains and specific events is poor" [p. 17]).

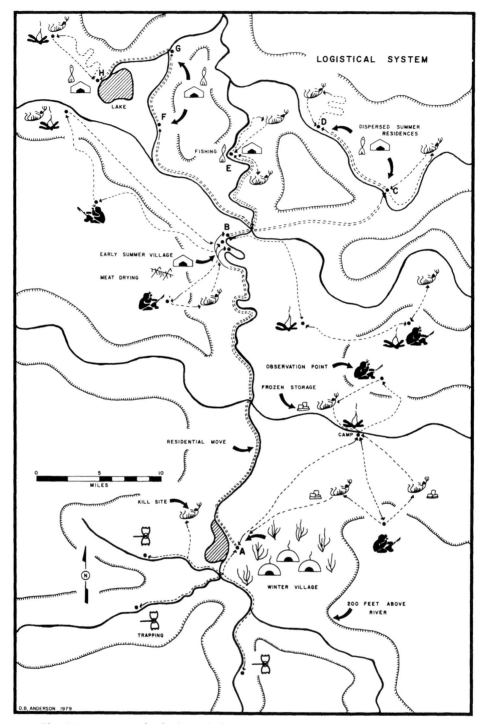

Fig. 8.3 Lewis Binford's (1980) characterization of a logistical subsistence-settlement system associated with collectors.

should be clear that, *other things being equal, we can expect greater ranges of intersite variability as a function of increases in the logistical components of the subsistence-settlement system.* (p. 12)

In the latter part of the paper he goes on to argue, using Human Relations Area Files[1] data, that "the differing strategies are responsive to different security problems presented by the environments in which hunter-gatherers live. Therefore, given the beginnings of a theory of adaptation, it is possible to anticipate both differences in settlement-subsistence strategies and patterning in the archaeological record through a more detailed knowledge of environmental variables" (p. 4). Numerous laws (presented as above in italics) are proposed.

It is unfortunate that Binford's arguments are not explicitly supported (except in one minor instance) by the presentation of field data, but only exemplified in imagined and polarizing characterizations of the two types of system.[2] His representation of the forager round and his implication that they are "just out looking for food on an encounter basis" suggest that he underestimates the knowledge and planning required for successful foragers that are evident from Yellen's description and can be inferred from Figure 8.2. Nonetheless, Binford undoubtedly provided theoretical underpinning for numerous projects archaeological and ethnoarchaeological. For example, while it is more about hunting and processing practices than a subsistence-settlement system, James Savelle's (1995) unique ethnoarchaeological study of Inuit beluga whale and narwhal harvesting is Binfordian in its approach and makes extensive use of concepts developed in this and other of his Nunamiut studies.

In a response to Binford, Polly Wiessner (1982b) took him to task for failing to take into account that (as Yellen had emphasized) even among hunter-gatherers social relations are as much determinants of settlement patterns as subsistence techniques and environmental factors. She argues that "strategies for reducing risk . . . require the most extensive cooperation and thus have a marked influence on social organization" (p. 172). Such strategies include:

1 "centralized pooling," the prevention of loss by various means, including rituals and allocation of land rights,

2 transfer of risk or loss, as by potlatching among the Kwakiutl and other groups of the Northwest Coast of North America, or, negatively, by raiding as formerly among Bedouin Arabs,

3 storage, whereby risks are covered by previous accumulation, as among the Nunamiut, and

---

[1] The HRAF were created by George Peter Murdock. This complex compendium makes accessible highly edited and reorganized portions of ethnographic accounts published by scholars working in different culture areas at different times; the authors whose works are included had, or have, different sorts of training, different research agendas, and come from different colonial experiences. Archaeologists have often availed themselves of these databases, sometimes wisely and sometimes to produce tabulated nonsense (see chapter 13).

[2] Binford had plenty of data, some obtained by direct observation and more through interviews with Nunamiut informants (see e.g., Binford 1983c: 379–86), but there is still an element of imaginative reconstruction in Figure 8.3.

4 pooling of risk, whereby small daily "losses" occurring in the course of sharing resources are compensated by accumulation of credit in the form of others' obligations to reciprocate.

The Kalahari San, as do most foragers, rely primarily on the pooling of risk, while collectors more commonly rely on the first three strategies. All have implications for subsistence-settlement patterns, and, as was seen in chapter 7, the marking of social boundaries.

Wiessner goes on to develop the implications of these strategies in relation to internal site structure, distribution of faunal remains within sites, intersite variability, and other dimensions, including implications for change. She suggests, for example, that groups who in order to cope with the risks rely on private storage are the most likely to make the transition from hunting-gathering to food production. Insights gained from ecology and among the San lead her to insist that settlement patterns among hunter-gatherers are not simply determined by demography, technology, and the environment, but that they are also influenced, as had long been recognized in complex societies, by the workings of human agency in the form of social, cultural, and political relations. No more than that of Brasilia is the location of the Anaktuvuk Pass settlement strictly determined by economics and the environment.

Before leaving the Nunamiut, we should draw attention to Binford's (1983b: 379–86) paper on longer-term "land use which I recovered from five old Eskimo men regarding what they 'expected' to happen if their lives had not changed drastically from the 'traditional' life of inland Caribou hunters" (p. 382). This reconstruction has the band moving within an "extended annual range" for approximately nine years before moving on to another such range "as things get used up and the place gets full of flies, then people start to fight" (p. 383). Binford and his informants envision a cycle of such moves within an "extended territory" during which sites in one annual or extended annual range may be reused for different purposes by band members resident in another part of the extended territory. This is likely to give the archaeological "appearance of considerable change. *It would occur, however, not as a consequence of change in the organization of the system, only in its positioning within the region*" (p. 384). And we might expect the cycle to continue over the medium term, leaving successive deposits at sites that represent different kinds of base camp, location, and other types of occupation.

By use of his informants' memories and knowledge of their culture, Binford is able to transcend the limitations of the duration of his own fieldwork and reconstruct what we would rather call a medium- than long-term pattern of cycling land use. Over the longer term, the unstable nature of Arctic and other simple environments results in resource booms and busts that test and in extreme cases likely exceed the capacity of the hunter-gatherer system to adjust. In boom times the system reproduces itself through population increase and the budding off of new groups, while catastrophic population declines in the worst times may lead to cultural collapse, and, after a period of population build up, the appearance of a new archaeological culture (David 1973). Such long-term cycles may extend beyond the span of human memory, but ethnographic and ethnoarchaeological research contribute to understanding of the mechanisms and processes responsible for the formation of an archaeological record that may preserve material evidence of a variety of shorter and longer, regular and irregular cycles.

Pastoralists

Formal ethnographic studies of pastoral adaptations rarely if ever consider their archaeological implications, but East African cattle-keeping groups, and Andean herders (for example), utilize landscapes in differing ways and leave differing material traces (e.g., Hodder 1982a; Flannery *et al.* 1989; Kuznar 1994). Subsistence strategies centering on domesticated mammals (sheep, goat, cattle, and Old and New World camelids) often involve substantial mobility, since the livestock must often be moved as grazing becomes available. (Pigs and water buffalo can be more readily accommodated in fully sedentary settlement systems.) In several geographic areas, settlement patterns organized around livestock are characterized by marked mobility, but some of these systems involve facilities for both humans and animals, and cyclical or at least repeated visits to any given campsite. Thus, while the human and animal occupants are comparatively ephemeral, and artifactual remains comparatively few, there may in some cases be distinctive signatures of this kind of land use. One of the important findings to emerge from the few ethnoarchaeological studies of pastoralists is that they leave residues different from those of other such mobile populations as hunter-gatherers (Gamble and Boismier 1991). Another is that they often do not situate their camps in locations more typically selected by either hunter-gatherers or agriculturalists. With information on criteria used in site selection, archaeologists can better select areas in which to look for their remains. Ethnoarchaeological studies also provide information about salient features of the material culture of nomads. Like hunter-gatherers, they travel light, but some leave substantially altered landscapes and built structures.

True nomads: optimization and instability

Roger Cribb's study (1991a) of nomads in archaeology reviews some of the differences between hunter-gatherers and pastoralists, and provides a useful survey of the literature on Old World pastoralists. Its major contribution, however, is its description of migratory herders in Cilicia (southeastern Anatolia), including plans and photographs of campsites. In this region, herders utilize continuous linearly organized tribal ranges, returning to particular localities on a seasonal basis. The settlement pattern is predicated on relatively predictable changes in temperature, precipitation, and accessibility of vegetation for livestock.

Cribb worked with sheep and goat pastoralists at comparatively high elevations marked by rugged terrain and seasonal inaccessibility. Even in that part of the Middle East migration routes are not necessarily linear and seasonally repetitive (and hence predictable), and constant communication between groups camping in different localities is an essential factor in decision-making. Surface water and pasture, for example, vary seasonally as well as annually, as do size and composition of flocks (and human groups), so it is crucial to have up-to-date information. In situations in which large groups of animals are led to pasture daily by an adult shepherd or child apprentice, it may be important to know exactly where milk can be obtained, or animals shorn. It is unwise to consider traditional non-Western subsistence adaptations as if they either are writ in stone or involve decisions made by individuals in information vacuums. Social and political organization – and politics – are integral features of decisions, and hence outcomes, of subsistence and settlement practices. Cribb's study points to some of the salient features of their interrelationships.

In 1973, Frank Hole had the opportunity to travel with an Iranian graduate student, Sekandar Amanolahi-Baharvand, who had tribal affiliations in Luristan (Fig. 8.4). They joined the annual migration from winter to summer pastures, and Hole (1978, 1979, 1980) later wrote up his experiences, noting observations of relevance to archaeologists. In addition to thoughtful comments about interviewing strategies, he provides evocative descriptions of camps and suggests that, at least in the mountainous Middle East, nomads select sites with level land, pasturage, and water; in the winter, they situate their tents so that prevailing winds batter the structures' shorter rather than longer ends, and they seek localities warmed by the morning sun. As in Anatolia, tents in western Iran are often clustered in linear patterns, and idiosyncratic deposits reflect the presence of controlled (if not necessarily always corralled) animals. Such observations can help locate ancient sites.

In contrast to Binford (e.g., 1983a), who considers differences between hunter-gatherers in different environmental settings, Hole is interested in how hunter-gatherers – in general – differ from pastoralists. Since both subsistence strategies are organized around animals, and both involve considerable mobility and diversity in locations and sometimes sizes and contents of sites, this is a subject of interest to archaeologists in Southwest Asia who want to discriminate among remains left by late Pleistocene foragers and early post-Pleistocene food producers, some of whom counted animal husbandry among their new specializations. In considering this crucial change in relationships between humans and the animals on which they depend, Hole briefly discusses differences in site location, duration, use, and contents. Finally, and importantly, Hole notes that, as is the case in Luristan, for climatic and other reasons vegetation in a given area may change over time; modern botanical communities

Fig. 8.4 Frank Hole (*left*) next to Murad Khan, leader of the tribe of Luri nomadic pastoralists with whom he traveled during their spring migration in the mountains of Luristan, western Iran, April 1973. Murad Khan is preparing kebabs of a sheep that has just been slaughtered.

are not necessarily analogous to those of earlier periods, but are often impacted and altered by land use. Since human and animal exploitation of particular biomes is likely to change through time, it is important that archaeologists use modern base-line environmental data prudently and cautiously in reconstructions of the past.

The work of Cribb and Hole shows that pastoralists' camps are preferentially situated in relation to pasturage, water, slope, and aspect (exposure to the sun). Unlike some arid zone hunter-gatherers (Brooks and Yellen 1987), herders may camp comparatively close to water sources; in Southwest Asia, they do not have to compete with nocturnal carnivores for scarce and highly localized water. The scale of the nomadic operation is also more substantial than is the case with most hunter-gatherers. They travel in comparatively large groups, and camp in tents that they carry with them. Other studies (see Kramer 1982b) show that mobile peoples often camp in a circular pattern, but in at least some parts of the Middle East, tents are arrayed in linear configurations, or rows, reflecting, in part, kinship and other social relationships. The number of tents may be a function of flock size and the availability of human labor to manage livestock – which in turn relates to status and power. As in the case of hunter-gatherers, pastoralists' settlements (if not necessarily their seasonal movements, which may be constrained by groups using pasturage before and after them) are highly flexible. This is in marked contrast to the more permanent settlements of most agriculturalists. Cribb notes that such factors, as well as the dispersion of tents and other features, such as corrals, across a landscape, create interesting archaeological sampling problems. He makes specific and useful suggestions having to do with tent dimensions and orientation, and observes that tent sizes and spatial relationships can reflect not only seasonality, but differences in household size, economic status, and kinship relations. Larger tents reflect greater wealth, and proximity to the headman's tent, while often signaling closer kinship, may also indicate servitude and/or dependence. And because, as elsewhere (see Nelson 1981), wealthier households do more entertaining, their tents are associated with larger ash dumps.

In the region of Turkey Cribb describes, shallow and extensive sites place unusual constraints on archaeological sampling and recovery. The same is, of course, true for sites left by hunter-gatherers in many parts of the world. However, many nomadic pastoralists who build and use structures occupy them repeatedly, even if intermittently. They are often constructed with durable materials, such as stone, used in tent footings. Second, many hunter-gatherers use perishable building materials for structures such as huts and hunting blinds, and while they often return to the same location, they do not necessarily camp on the remnants of their former structures, partly to avoid vermin infesting organic residues. In both cases, archaeologists run the risk of encountering palimpsests created by repeated occupation over long periods. Because of the lack of building materials that might produce mounds, and particularly in areas with serious erosion and deflation, there is a good chance that multi-component sites will become stratigraphic blurs difficult to decipher chronologically and hence functionally. In Binford's terms, they are likely to be coarse-grained.

Cultivators plus[3]

Contrary to stereotypes of subsistence-settlement adaptation, while swidden (slash-and-burn) farming generally involves settlement relocation at varying intervals, some herders and hunters, and especially hunter-fishers, are comparatively sedentary, occupying substantial built habitats for much of any year and for many years, as in parts of the Northwest Coast of North America. But it is generally true that the habitation sites of most cultivators are occupied for

---

[3] Not all who cultivate the land have farms, at least not in the Euro-American sense; some are horticulturalists and tend plants more or less individually; others are agriculturalists and tend fields. Some keep livestock and others do not. Intensification, production, and productivity vary. In this section we use the terms "farmer," "agriculturalist," and "cultivator" interchangeably, specifying details of economic orientation as necessary.

longer periods than are those of either hunter-gatherers or pastoralists. While some hunter-gatherers and herders build fixed and semi-permanent facilities for habitation, storage, and stabling, agriculturalists typically live in more substantial and, often, more aggregated structures made of more durable materials, which are thus more likely to be preserved archaeologically. However, our first case study from Mexico treats mobile cultivators. Another on which we focus (Watson 1979a) involves Iranian peasant farmers practicing a mixed economy – one based on both agriculture and livestock management – who are sedentary for most of the year, occupying substantial built habitats. Elsewhere in Iran, Horne (1994a) describes relationships between farming and pastoralism. The Kofyar of our last example have migrated to new lands on which they have established themselves on a permanent basis, which is not to say that some movement of families does not take place (Stone 1992).

Rarámuri: seasonally mobile farmers

In the New World, describing a system exploiting both domesticated plants and animals, Martha Graham (1994) provides detailed information on the relocations of traditional Rarámuri (Tarahumara) farmers of northern Mexico, and variations in their residences, corrals, and settlements (Fig. 8.5). Using a sample focusing on 14 households in one community, Graham, who made comparative visits to others, monitored movements over a 14 month period during 1987 and 1988. Her monograph, which includes maps of nine residential compounds, provides rich detail on activities and site structure, as well as on activities focused on subsistence. Rarámuri farmers cultivate the classic Mesoamerican trio of corn, beans, and squash in dispersed land holdings, and raise diverse Old World livestock (sheep, goat, cattle, and pig); they also have chickens and (New World) turkeys, as well as dogs. In the community best known to Graham, they move at least twice each year, from warm to cold weather residences. Warm weather residences are on or near a valley floor; cold weather dwellings are upland, in rockshelters or on low knolls.[4] As is the case for at least some nomadic pastoralists, settlement decisions are sometimes based on a potential site's aspect, as well as slope and availability of water. As elsewhere (Stone 1996), the scheduling of productive activities is closely related to the possibility of enlarging the labor force, with people coordinating their schedules and working in cooperative supra-household groups. One of the contributions of Graham's study is its attention to the roles that kinship and social organization, in addition to seasonality, play in decision-making in relation to settlement. And one of her observations most relevant – and perhaps most vexing – to archaeologists is that

---

[4] The opposite of agro-pastoralists in the Alps who move all or parts of their families and herds up into the mountains in summer to exploit upland pastures.

Fig. 8.5 Martha Graham in Rarámuri costume including the muslin shawl
slung on her back that women use for carrying burdens and babies,
N. Mexico, 1987.

Mobile agriculturalists share organizational aspects with both agriculturalists and hunter-gatherers. These organizational similarities reflect commonalities in the way space is organized and used under conditions dictated by aspects of the subsistence-settlement system. (p. 97)

She concludes that such mobile farmers as the Rarámuri present archaeologists with a unique opportunity to reconsider their limited and restricting terminological baggage and, perhaps, even the methods they use in observing and describing socio-cultural systems that may leave ambiguous archaeological remains because they reflect integrated, complex patterns played out in multiple locations. For us, the question remains: how can archaeologists know that two or more morphologically different sites presumed to be contemporaneous are the remnants of a single group? This is not a frivolous question if we wish to disarticulate complex systems and start to identify them, rather than assume that we are looking at contemporaneous palimpsests, some comprised of farmers and others of pastoralists. In addition, if each site is presumed to represent a separate group, population estimates might be substantially inflated. We return briefly to Graham's study in chapter 9.

Dr. Watson's clues to Iranian prehistory

Farmers and pastoralists are also the subject of Patty Jo Watson's (1966, 1979a) pioneering work in Iran. As a graduate student, Watson excavated at neolithic sites in the Middle East and was encouraged by Robert and Linda Braidwood in her desire to put flesh on the bones of the archaeological sites the University of Chicago had been exhuming in the decades immediately following World War II. Watson, who worked in three (pseudonymous) communities on the borders of Kurdistan and Luristan in western Iran at intervals during the period November 1959 to June 1960, devotes most of her book (1979a) to the most sedentary, Hasanabad. The study, completed by 1970, has proved a model for subsequent work and is organized topically, beginning and ending with discussions of "archaeological ethnography." Each chapter contains detailed descriptions of, for example, land use, activity areas, and kinship relationships within the village, and some include and/or conclude with brief sections on possibly analogous archaeological remains in the prehistoric Middle East. Compared with more recent ethnoarchaeological studies, this volume may, because of its straightforwardness and attention to descriptive detail, strike some as theoretically unsophisticated, but at the time the manuscript was completed it was truly breaking new ground, and it stands as a key statement from one of the founders of the subdiscipline. The rich documentation of the communities, Hasanabad, Shirdasht, and Ain Ali, allows the reader to use Watson's data to address questions different from those she was asking when she did her fieldwork. Watson "worked without an interpreter. I had previously studied Iraqi Kurdish . . . but was by no mean proficient in either Persian or the local Laki

[Kurdish] dialect . . . when beginning work at Hasanabad" (p. 9). She specifies the times she was in the field, permitting readers to consider her data on subsistence in relation to seasonality, and she also makes it very clear that her fieldwork was carried out during a period of famine. As we note in relation to other case studies, such important information is not often made available.

Watson's study is among the few to provide scale maps both of houses (24) and of an entire village, and almost unique in providing a map of agricultural holdings. Hasanabad, a village of 207 sharecroppers in 43 households, is near enough to a large provincial center for occasional interactions and influences, but in many respects it was, in the 1960s, a very traditional, and quite endogamous, community. The same would appear to be true of the two other communities Watson visited briefly, Ain Ali, a village of about 85 houses with an economy based on mixed farming, and Shirdasht, a village of recently sedentarized sheep/goat pastoralists. The seasonal cycle of Shirdasht villagers includes a spring migration into the neighboring mountains. Like Cribb, Watson notes that the herders' families reoccupy their tent sites and use the same animal pens each year. Maps and photographs reveal linear alignments similar to those reported by Cribb, and areas adjacent to tent clusters are distinctly discolored, suggesting that their function as corrals and trash dumps might be identified through soil analyses.

Watson cautiously considers the extent to which twentieth-century communities are relevant to reconstructions of prehistoric settlements, concluding that there are enough parallels to warrant some comparisons. Among the features that she considers particularly relevant in making such comparisons are (a) annual per capita cereal grain requirements for human sustenance, (b) aspects of the care and exploitation of domesticated animals, (c) relationships between agriculturalists and pastoralists, and (d) technologies related to both architecture and subsistence. Watson's empirical documentation of variations among these three communities neatly highlights ranges of variation in subsistence-settlement practices within a single geographic region.

Like Cribb and Hole (whose fieldwork post-dated hers), Watson discusses the temporal primacy of agriculture and pastoralism, a debate dating back at least to V. Gordon Childe (1951) and pursued by Robert Braidwood and others concerned to elucidate relationships between settled village life and domestication. Like Braidwood, we doubt that such questions, important though they are, can be answered solely through ethnoarchaeological research, but agree that ethnoarchaeological observations can both suggest new interpretations of existing datasets, and guide us in formulating future research agendas.

Baghestani agro-pastoralists

Lee Horne's work in the Khar o Tauran region of northeastern Iran was carried out during three summers (1976–8), under the auspices of a multidisciplinary

Fig. 8.6 Lee Horne wearing *chador* (body veil) in Baghestan, northeastern Iran, 1977.

UNESCO-sponsored project focusing largely on desertification and directed by Brian Spooner, a social anthropologist. She was thus in the field in the period between the last shah's land reform (1962) and the Islamic Revolution (1979); it is difficult to know how or to what extent these important events affected the people with whom she worked. Fluent in the local dialect of Persian, she appears to have been at home in the field (Fig. 8.6). Horne (1994a) focuses on a single village, Baghestan, which she compares with 12 other villages in the plain, providing a comparatively large sample, which is one of the strengths of this thoughtful study.

Like Watson, Horne found seasonal variations in settlement location and configuration that center around differences in plants' and animals' seasonal distributions and abundance. Baghestan is a community whose subsistence is characterized by a complex combination of farming and herding, and which maintains a number of morphologically different and locationally discrete facilities relating to both plants and animals. Some of this morphological variability is related to seasonal variation in land use. Livestock graze in a variety of locations. Long-range transhumant pastoralists find winter pasture for their flocks in the Baghestan area. Some locally owned flocks graze at (constructed) sheep stations away from the village throughout the year; others, with more goats than sheep, winter in villages and spend summers at milking stations; and still others graze on village commons, usually returning home for the night but sometimes in summer staying out to graze. More than with natural water sources, the locations of sheep and goat grazing and enclosures vary with flock size and composition, topography, and vegetation.

Horne's study strongly suggests that a more than passing knowledge of key animal domesticates' behaviors (and of the main ways in which humans utilize those species) is required to enable archaeologists to predict where they might find sites and other remains of different economic activities. As in Anatolia (Cribb 1991b) and western Iran (Watson 1979a), some areas relating to livestock (as well as some designed to enhance agricultural activities) are characterized by built structures that are ephemeral, while others are comparatively substantial. Many of these structures, however, are at some distance from residential sites that possess architecture likely to become either mounds, or deflated surfaces with abundant cultural debris. They are therefore at risk of being omitted from archaeological surveys designed to identify sites on the basis of comparatively prominent features on landscapes.

Kofyar: living together to farm together

Glenn Davis Stone's (1991, 1992) research into the dynamics of settlement among the Kofyar of Nigeria is human geography of the greatest relevance to archaeologists. Stone was a student of Robert Netting (1968), whose work on Kofyar cultural ecology goes back to the 1960s, his data providing Stone, whose fieldwork was undertaken between January 1984 and March 1985, with precious historical and census information. The Kofyar were long confined by threats of raiding and slaving to the hilly southern edge of the Jos plateau, where they lived in densely populated settlements in which each compound was surrounded by its intensively worked fields. Under the colonial regime, from the 1930s onwards, they began to settle on previously unoccupied land in the plains north of the Benue river. Stone's goal was to reconstruct the evolution of a settlement system on land that approximated the geographers' idealized, uniform plain, and to explore how settlement change related to the Kofyar practice of farming.

Stone's research involved the census of over 800 households, for each of which he and his wife Priscilla reconstructed settlement histories. Air photographs taken in 1963, 1972, and 1978 enabled him to locate nearly 800 settlements on

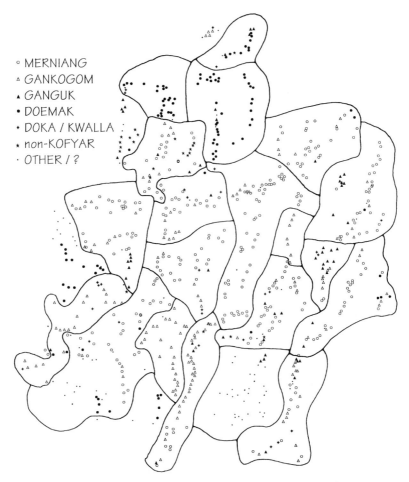

○ MERNIANG
▵ GANKOGOM
▲ GANGUK
● DOEMAK
✦ DOKA / KWALLA
★ non-KOFYAR
· OTHER / ?

Fig. 8.7 Kofyar farmstead settlement pattern in Namu district, Plateau state, Nigeria, 1985. Neighborhood (*ungwa*) boundaries appear as solid lines. Symbols represent different homeland village affiliations, with small dots indicating that these are unknown. The linear arrangement of farmsteads along paths and dirt roads is very evident, as is the tendency for neighborhoods to be settled by migrants from particular villages, and for the "encystment" of farmsteads of minorities. (See Stone 1992, 1996.)

the ground, to relate them to compounds subsequently established, and to investigate those that had been abandoned. His maps are remarkable, showing the linear arrangement along paths and dirt roads of compounds grouped into *ungwa*, neighborhoods of 20–50 farmsteads (Fig. 8.7). Rather than farms occupying circular or hexagonal cells, they occur as ragged strips in which are set compounds spaced 100–150 m apart, maximizing proximity between neighbor farmsteads and facilitating communication between them. But what attracts a Kofyar migrant to settle in a particular neighborhood? Stone develops statistics based on the affiliations of each farmstead's nearest two neighbors, and that are manipulated to yield an "attraction coefficient." He demonstrates that migrants are attracted to other migrants from their village and from other villages in the same historic military alliance (*sar gwat*). In the hills these alliances show tendencies towards endogamy but this is less the case on the plains.

Attraction, as measured by the affiliation of nearest neighbors, is generally stronger at the level of the village, especially for the hill villages which have high levels of social propinquity. Attraction as measured by spatial concentrations of members of particular social taxa is strongest at the *sar gwat* level, although there are some village-level concentrations. Some large *sar gwat* concentrations include several *ungwas*, while small sub-*ungwa* concentrations, or encystments, occur among settlers socially distant from surrounding farmsteads. (1992: 163)

Stone goes on to argue that where kin relations are relations of production, there are good economic reasons to settle next to kin. Indeed in the early phase of settlement this was demonstrably more important than settling on optimal soils. Among the Kofyar, cooperation in farming is the paramount consideration, and this takes the form, common in Africa, of agricultural work parties. Stone's statistics demonstrate that 97 percent of trips to participate in such parties are undertaken within the neighborhood, mostly to farms 700 m or less distant, and preferentially to work with people from one's own original village. The settlement pattern, with its strip farms arranged perpendicular to communication routes, minimizes the distance that farmers have to walk to work with their kin and village mates. Other factors are also at play. Whereas in the initial phase of settlement the desire to minimize labor costs resulted in easy access to water being a more important factor in settlement choice than soil type, as suboptimal soil types became exhausted and competition for land increased, farmers quickly moved to occupy large and productive plots even if water had to be carried considerable distances. Some areas were largely abandoned. Thus the balance between three critical factors of production, human labor, water, and soils, shifted through time.

Ethnoarchaeologists can learn a great deal from Stone's research and analytical methods, and his finding that "Social relationships can both affect and be affected by spatial organization" (1992: 169) must be accepted as a guiding principle of settlement archaeology. But his work is not strictly ethnoarchaeology in that, in contrast to the article (1994) on boundary-marking features mentioned in chapter 5, the material expression of social relationships is not described in a manner that allows a linkage to be established between the sociocultural and material records that might later be drawn on to interpret potentially analogous archaeological contexts.

Concluding contrasts, mobility and sedentism

While ethnoarchaeological studies focusing on settlement at a scale greater than the site are relatively few, they include some that are substantial, influential, or both. Yellen and Binford have both had a major impact on archaeological approaches to and the conceptualization of hunter-gatherers. After a very slow start, ethnoarchaeological research on pastoralists took off in the 1990s with over a dozen publications appearing during that decade, more than in all previous periods put together. There is considerably less strictly ethnoarchaeological research on the settlement patterns of farmers, but of course there are other literatures, those of human geography and rural sociology amongst them, on which archaeologists can draw.

In the topical areas of settlement and site structure (discussed in the next chapter), there is an obvious and marked contrast between ethnoarchaeological studies of hunter-gatherers and of all other peoples. Those engaged in hunter-gatherer research are primarily interested in behavior and the development of laws or expectations regarding it, while those who have worked with pastoralists and cultivators show themselves more interested in culture and the accumulation of analogical materials. We have previously alluded to this difference; paleolithic archaeologists know that there are no direct historical analogies available to them and require principles on which to base their interpretations; students of later periods, like Grahame Clark (1952) before them, hope that in the folk cultures of the Middle East and elsewhere they will find cultural clues to the interpretation of prehistoric sites. This characterization exaggerates the differences, and in other topical areas they are less marked or even absent – the Kalinga project, for example, is concerned with behavior more than it is with culture – but they are nonetheless real.

The scale of land use documented ethnographically gives archaeologists a basis for formulating sampling and research design; locational preferences suggest where archaeologists should begin to look for the kinds of sites that interest them. Any site is part of a larger system. The number and diversity of settlements within any one system indicates that archaeologists should always be thinking in terms of congeries of sites used during the same period at different times or seasons, and for different purposes by members of the same social group. Both hunter-gatherer and other ethnoarchaeological research suggests that many sites are small, and their archaeological visibility sometimes nil. Building materials, their recycling, and environmental circumstances militate against the preservation of all but a small number of sites that, although once parts of larger systems, are likely to be atypical. Whether regarded as a structuring principle or a form of distortion of the archaeological record, this has not, in our view, been sufficiently taken into consideration.[5]

---

[5] Another aspect of settlement systems and subsistence practices is the modification of land surfaces themselves, which though sometimes requiring intermittent or regular modification or repair, and though rarely immutable, can both reflect and affect settlement locations and resource exploitation. Examples include weirs and dams, irrigation canals, wells, water traps or check-dams, and terraces. Integration of members of one community and articulation of related communities in construction, maintenance, and repair of such features involve sometimes complex decision-making, scheduling, negotiating, and deployment of laborers and maintenance of facilities. Archaeologists would welcome ethnoarchaeological study of, for example, communities of differing demographic and areal size arrayed along a canal system fed by a larger river.

Another generalization emerging from ethnoarchaeological work is that, as the Politis quote introducing this chapter indicates, settlement systems cannot be explained simply in economic and energetic terms. Other humans are, and not only as mates, essential informational and social resources. During the rains, !Kung are drawn back to Dobe not by need for water or the promise of milk from Bantu herds, but because they get bored and want company. One of the contributions of Graham's study is its attention to the roles that kinship and social organization, in addition to seasonality, play in decision-making in relation to settlement.

Politis's (1996) paper does not in fact emphasize the non-economic aspects of subsistence-settlement systems. Rather he is concerned to show how the Nunak of the Colombian tropical forest "move to produce." They relocate their camps very frequently and before their occupation places any significant strain on locally available resources. During their brief stays they modify the immediate environment of their camps by cutting down vegetation without destroying the canopy and by introducing seeds of useful plants in such a way that they leave behind them "wild orchards," patches of future resources. Their manipulation of their environment has important implications both for processes of plant domestication and indeed for tropical forest ecology. This study is part of a larger program of anthropological research on a group of Indians whose regular contacts with Colombian colonists began only in 1988, and it is to be hoped that, together with recent studies of Pygmies (e.g., Fisher and Strickland 1989; Laden 1992), it signals a revival of ethnoarchaeological interest in hunter-gatherers inhabiting complex, wetter, environments. The !Kung, Hadza, Australian Aborigine, and Nunamiut studies that have had such an impact on archaeologists are not particularly informative regarding the early human career over large parts of the earth's surface, including, for example, much of that trod by *Homo sapiens* when first journeying from Africa to Australia.

Perhaps this is because there are fewer archaeologists working in tropical and subtropical forests than elsewhere, or perhaps it is because tropical hunter-gatherers tend to be in more obvious contact with other peoples, often engaging in trade and sometimes in cultivation, and therefore more difficult to conceptualize as Stone Age survivals. However this may be, it is unfortunate for, as a paper by James Eder (1984) demonstrates, they have much to teach us. Eder, an ethnographer unusually writing for archaeologists, uses his research among the Batak, a Negrito group of Palawan Island (Philippines), to problematize the concepts of mobility and sedentism. The Batak presumably once lived by hunting and gathering alone, but have progressively incorporated trading (perhaps for a millennium), shifting cultivation (probably for centuries), and, since 1900, wage labor into their economy. To achieve this they divide their time as indicated in Figure 8.8 between a house in a settlement, a swidden field house, and temporary forest foraging camps and wage labor camps. In the 1920s the government encouraged them to establish "permanent" settlements, and

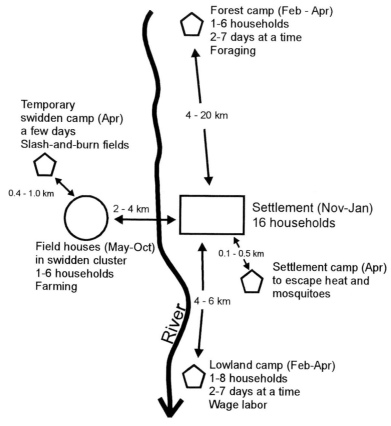

Fig. 8.8 Batak local group settlement, Palawan Island, Philippines, in 1981, showing types of sites (after Eder 1984: Fig. 1). While a single permanent settlement is home to most individuals from November to January, and while families tend to live in field houses in swidden clusters for most of the May through October cultivation season, the period February through April is one of great individual and family mobility between temporary camps.

these they have maintained for part-time living, and on occasion relocated in the face of an advancing front of colonists. But the Batak are also highly mobile, probably more so than in the past, and individuals shift residence as many as 90 times a year. At the same time their settlements are rarely if ever entirely unoccupied, and it can be argued that sedentariness has increased.

Eder points out that some archaeologists regard sedentism as relating to settlement permanence, others to settlement size, some speaking of degrees of sedentariness, others treating it as either present or absent. It cannot be treated as a continuous variable since seasonality is a factor, there being a real difference between two populations, one of which lives for six months at one settlement before moving to another, the other alternating between two sites every two weeks. Should we therefore regard sedentism as a threshold, one that the Batak may be approaching? Similarly one may ask what archaeologists mean by mobility. Is it best conceived as a continuous variable relating to individuals, perhaps in terms of numbers of locations slept in or as kilometers traveled in the course of a year, or does it relate to stability of residence? Hitchcock (1982: 258) distinguishes between residential mobility relating to the co-resident group, and the logistical mobility of producers or task groups ranging out from a residential base. Eder's article, which has received less attention than it deserves – especially since the Batak case is by no means unique – addresses the implications of these questions and suggests answers. But our purpose here is simply to follow Hodder (1982a) in underlining the value of ethnoarchaeology as a tool for the exploration and interrogation of archaeological concepts.

Further reading

While the adaptation of hunter-gatherers to the humid tropics has received less attention than it deserves, the works of Estioko-Griffin and Griffin (1975, 1981) and Griffin (1984, 1985) provide an account of the Agta of Luzon, Philippines, one of the least acculturated Negrito groups of Southeast Asia. As indicated above, expressions of mobility vary. Natalie Tobert (1988) in a wide-ranging but somewhat unfocused monograph describes the contrasting seasonal movements of male and female members of the despised Zaghawa *hadahid* (blacksmith) caste in northern Darfur, Sudan, and their material consequences. Subsistence, settlement, and intrasite patterning are the primary topics of Lawrence Kuznar's (1994) short monograph, designed primarily for beginning and intermediate undergraduates, on transhumant goat pastoralism in the Andes of southern Peru. While this is of undoubted analogical value for the detection and interpretation of Andean sites, it is rather "living archaeology" than ethnoarchaeology, for the anonymous Aymara herders are kept so much in the background that we gain little understanding of their society or lives, but only of their sites.

CHAPTER 9

SITE STRUCTURES AND ACTIVITIES

Analyses and interpretations of [site structure] patterns have until lately been based on three assumptions: (1) that activities are spatially segregated . . .; (2) that activities typically produce characteristic co-variant sets of artifacts and other refuse in proportion to the frequency of performance; and (3) that artifacts and other refuse associated with a particular activity are deposited at or very near the place of performance.

(James O'Connell 1987: 74)

There can be no general theory and no universal method for measuring and interpreting activity residues . . . we cannot look to ethnoarchaeology to provide the answers.

(Ian Hodder 1987a: 424)

In this chapter we discuss living space and activity areas of peoples, focusing especially on hunter-gatherers and others who do not produce substantial built structures. When approached archaeologically, such situations require that both the living context of the remains be inferred and the activities that took place within and around it. Where there are architectural remains (see chapter 10), artifacts and other debris can be directly related to structures and the spaces between and around them. We begin by sampling the ethnoarchaeological literature on the site structure of hunter-gatherers, the latter term requiring somewhat liberal interpretation, and proceed to survey evidence relating to peoples practicing other subsistence strategies. The chapter ends, rather than concluding, with discussion of studies that consider the extent to which gender is associated with activities, and whether these are likely to be archaeologically identifiable.

Archaeologists' interest in identifying activity areas and interpreting the nature and internal organization of sites (their "structures") has a long history, and one whose subject intersects with studies of subsistence and settlement patterns. Recognition of site types (e.g., kill or butchering sites, less often plant processing sites) is prerequisite to the identification of settlement patterns. Sites have been analyzed in terms of component activity areas, very often according to the assumptions listed in the O'Connell quote at the head of this chapter. At Pincevent, for example, Leroi-Gourhan and Brézillon (1972) attempted to identify knapping stations, and *foyers* (hearth and/or tent areas) which they thought represented individual families within a larger Magdalenian encampment. Archaeologists often believe they can locate areas at which craft activities were carried out; and others have attempted to identify remains of gender-differentiated activities (Voigt 1983; Gero and Conkey 1991; Crown 2001). In seeking to identify and interpret such locations, archaeologists can benefit from ethnoarchaeological studies of sites' structures and activities carried out in particular kinds of places. Activity areas relate to economic activities and diversity; they comprise minimal elements of settlement systems. Site structure, as well as site size, may relate to duration of occupation, degree of sedentism, and population size; these and other factors (some related to changes in subsistence economy) are of direct relevance to studies of the so-called neolithic revolution, marked in many areas by growing reliance on and extended occupation of built habitats. For decades, archaeologists have attempted to distinguish between multipurpose and special purpose sites (e.g., Binford and Binford 1966). Such distinctions are based on artifact types and diversity in relation to their contexts. Diversity measures, in turn, have been cited to support arguments about number of activities at a site, duration (and anticipated duration) of a site's occupation, number of activities carried out at a site, and site size. We return to some of these issues below.

A note on sources

In this and the succeeding chapter we are forced by the nature of the material available to depart somewhat from our policy of sampling the widest possible range of geographic areas and authors. While there are a considerable number of ethnoarchaeological publications on the closely interrelated topics of site structure and architecture, these are poorly distributed geographically, with 60 percent relating to either sub-Saharan Africa or Southwest Asia (Table 9.1). Not only are the analytical categories indistinct, with site structure and activity areas grading into use of domestic space and architecture, but several important monographs and some less substantial works deal with all these areas, some indeed also covering settlement pattern and/or other topics. Yellen's (1977a) *Archaeological approaches to the present* is a good example. Many of the publications categorized in the WWW ethnoarchaeology bibliography in the "spac" (space and architecture) category would fit equally well under site formation processes (e.g., Agorsah 1985; Brooks and Yellen 1987), fauna (e.g., Binford 1987a), the organization of production (e.g., Arnold 1991), ideology (e.g., Donley 1987), or other headings. Thus the material to be covered in chapters 9 and 10 is at one and the same time concentrated, in that many of the more significant works take the form of monographs, and diffuse, in that the subject matter relates variously to, and is sometimes covered in, other chapters.

Between the two areas in which the relevant studies are concentrated, there are definite differences in focus. In sub-Saharan Africa more work has been

Table 9.1 Tabulation of publications in ethnoarchaeology relating to (a) site structure and activity areas, (b) domestic space and architecture, and (c) combined. Keyword revisions, additions and omission of items primarily relating to population estimates account for minor differences between these statistics and those categorized under "Space and architecture" in Tables 1.3 through 1.5

PERIOD	VAR	N AM	M AM	S AM	N AFR	SubSah. AFR	EUR	SW ASIA	S ASIA	E ASIA	SE ASIA	AUST	OCE	N
(a) Site structure and activity areas														
New E-A 1968–81		2		1			1	2						6
Recent 1 1982–9	4	4		1	1	10		3			1	6		30
Recent 2 1990–8	1	1	5		1	8		5	1					22
N	5	7	5	2	2	18	1	10	1		1	6		58
(b) Architecture and domestic space														
New E-A 1968–81				1	1	2		3						7
Recent 1 1982–9						3		10	2					15
Recent 2 1990–8		3				7		4				1		15
N		3		1	1	12		17	2			1		37
(c) Combined (a + b)														
N	5	10	5	3	3	30	1	27	3	0	1	7	0	95
%	5.3	10.5	5.3	3.2	3.2	31.5	1.1	28.4	3.2	0.0	1.1	7.4	0.0	100.2

done on site structure, especially of hunter-gatherers who are in some cases more or less sedentary or in process of settling down (e.g., Hitchcock 1987); publications on architecture tend to include a strong component of ideology. In Southwest Asia the emphasis is reversed; while studies of site structure often concern pastoralists, the demands of archaeological interpretation lead to a particular focus on architectural indices of socioeconomic variability (e.g., Kamp 1982; Kramer 1982a). Also notable is the contribution by French scholars, Olivier Aurenche in particular, whose work tends to be highly descriptive. This is best seen in Aurenche, Bazin, and Dadler's (1997) study of a cluster of Kurdish villages in southeastern Turkey that can be described as salvage ethnoarchaeology. The architecture was recorded in photographs and a rich diversity of maps and floor plans while colleagues were excavating Cafer Höyük, which, like the villages, was scheduled to be inundated as a result of dam construction on the upper Euphrates. Given a rare opportunity, Aurenche and his team questioned villagers about where they might move, and the kind of housing they would like. Complementing information incorporated in the floor plans, this beautifully produced tome also includes photographs of villagers carrying out mundane domestic tasks in a variety of locations.

Hunter-gatherer studies

The Mask site, and man as the measure of all things

Though not a monograph, one of the most influential publications on activity areas was Binford's (1978b) account of a Nunamiut hunting stand, which considered some of the ways in which small "off-site" locations away from settlements were used and configured. As with some of his other work in Alaska, this piece suggests where in a landscape archaeologists might begin to locate special-purpose non-residential sites. It is also important in its consideration of the spacing of sites, and its discussion of which objects might be left at a site as seemingly ephemeral as a hunting stand in expectation of reuse, and those which would be removed. Such subjects reflect earlier interests aired in the Mousterian debate. However, the most important contribution of the paper on the Mask site relates to site structure. Using sketched (and, we infer, highly schematized or normative) bird's eye views of activity areas, Binford implied that the structure and interrelationships of features such as hearths and so-called drop and toss zones may reveal, in their scale and content, the number of participants and their activities. While accompanying text suggests that the number of observations of such activities was few and seasonally limited, this article is widely cited, and was evidently inspirational to many archaeologists in the 1980s. Binford (1983a: 144–92) himself draws on this and other Nunamiut data besides comparative ethnoarchaeological materials from the San and elsewhere in an important chapter "People in their lifespace," in which he uses these findings to develop models of working around a hearth, of sleeping areas, and of butchery areas that, "because of the way in which the size and basic mechanics of the human body affect patterning in the archaeological record" (p. 160), can be applied to archaeological cases, including, in this instance, the sleeping area model to Magdalenian Pincevent and Aurignacian and Perigordian VI layers at the Abri Pataud (France).

Although we may legitimately doubt whether the archaeological record at these two sites is sufficiently fine-grained to support his interpretations, we must admire Binford for once again performing a signal service by forcefully bringing to our attention the notion that the human body and its mechanics constitute a relatively constant factor in the creation of activity areas and site structure (and there is a great deal more to the chapter than this). Binford's insight can be read into studies of site structure that both precede and succeed his own, but once again we should note that he treats human behavior as a response to external stimuli – heat, cold, light, and the like – paying little attention to human assignation of meaning to these stimuli and to the place in which they are felt. A !Kung will do things rather differently in the presence of his mother-in-law, and an Anglican attending a service in frigid Ely cathedral will refrain from huddling over an altar candle.

Yellen's ring model

Perhaps the most remarkable feature of Yellen's (1977a) *Archaeological approaches to the present* is its appendix B, consisting of 90 pages of ungrouped data from 16 !Kung camps keyed to large-scale plans. The camps were treated like archaeological living floors, grids being laid out, and features and other material remains described and plotted to the nearest centimeter. Besides detailed information about cultural, plant, and faunal residues left on the sites' surfaces, this rich lode of data on abandoned camps specifies length of stay and often day by day accounts of the occupation, social relationships of the occupants, and vegetable and animal foods consumed. Yellen mines this lode in his chapters on intracamp patterning, but does not exhaust it, making explicit his desire that the data be explored by others.

The arrangement of huts in a !Kung camp tends towards a ring (Fig. 9.1). The huts, each with its surrounding nuclear family area and hearth, encircle a communal area in which dancing and meat distribution take place. The nuclear family areas are the sites for a variety of activities including sleeping, cooking and eating, and the manufacture of tools and ornaments. Outside the hut circle is another communal area in which messy activities such as skin drying take place, and where shade trees may at certain times of day attract activities that would otherwise be carried out elsewhere. Thus the communal versus nuclear family and general versus special activity contrasts, together with social context, messiness, space required, and time of day, are the factors that

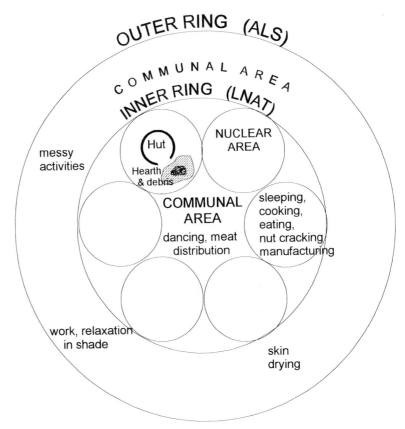

Fig. 9.1 Ring model of a !Kung camp showing nuclear and communal areas and a selection of the activities that take place within them (after Yellen 1977). Each nuclear area, normally associated with a nuclear family, contains a hut and a hearth. (ALS = absolute limit of scatter; LNAT = limit of nuclear area, total.)

determine where activities will be carried out in the camp and its immediate surround. In contrast to archaeological expectations of the time, there is little spatial segregation of the activities that occur in nuclear family areas and which leave material traces. Anvils used to crack mongongo nuts and splinters of bone from a family meal are found together but relate not to the same *activity* but to the identical *social context*, that of the nuclear family, in which the activities with which they are associated took place. Yellen argues that this is likely to be generally true of societies with simple technologies and lack of craft specialization, and that

the !Kung pattern I have observed is not limited to one time, place, or environment . . . [Thus] the archaeologist may move directly from scatters of debris to questions of basic social organization. Paradoxically the seemingly easier step of reconstructing basic activities . . . may prove more difficult and not serve . . . as a necessary step or building block for more abstract kinds of speculation. (p. 97)

The work of Robert Janes (1983) among Mackenzie basin Dene who depend on hunting and gathering for a good portion of their subsistence tends to confirm this insight (see chapter 10), although their camp is not organized on a ring model. As Wiessner (1982b) has observed, hunter-gatherer camps with layouts that allow mutual surveillance are likely to be associated with the sharing of risks and benefits, and this panoptical arrangement no doubt assists in maintaining the sharing, egalitarian, ethic.

Yellen proceeds to examine quantitative relationships between area of site debris, resident population, length of occupation, seasonality, and activities. In order to investigate the relationships between variables, he defines a number of measures, including the "absolute limit of scatter" (ALS) of occupation debris, the "limit of most scatter" (LMS), and the "limit of nuclear area, total" (LNAT). Many correlations are established, and the following regression equation (p. 130) gives an example of the kind of results achieved: the number of days a !Kung camp has been occupied = 0.1 (ALS − LMS) + 1.87. This relates to the finding that the "inner ring area correlates closely with group size and . . . the size of the outer ring is time dependent" (p. 129) rather than being dependent on group size. The specifics of the !Kung case are historically contingent, and, as Gould and Yellen (1987, 1991) have themselves shown, the existence of other variables in other contexts forbids the simplistic application of Yellen's correlations and regressions to archaeological contexts. Some critiques contest his reliance on a group of diversity measures drawn primarily from the ecological literature, while others, taking up his invitation to explore the data for themselves, have used them to question his inferences. For example Robert Whallon's (1978) review disputes his contention that "the probability of any particular maintenance activity's taking place is purely a function of length of occupation." Nonetheless, many archaeologists have been inspired by, and elaborated on, Yellen's work (see, e.g., Hietala 1984), which for its coverage of analogy, settlement, and site structure, must be regarded as one of the leading contributions of the New Ethnoarchaeology period.

Other ethnoarchaeological studies of African hunter-gatherers suggest that increasing sedentism and expectation of long occupation are associated with both larger and more internally differentiated structures (Hitchcock 1987; Kent and Vierich 1989). Construction materials may not be notably less durable (or more perishable) than those used in buildings of agriculturalists in similar habitats (Parkington and Mills 1991), so that differentiation of the archaeological remains of farmers and gatherers may need to focus on other classes of material culture and botanical and faunal remains. Studies such as these have implications for the interpretation of residues left by late Pleistocene and early post-Pleistocene gatherers in, for example, Southwest Asia. There, built habitats in the Natufian and subsequent aceramic periods of the ninth and eighth millennia BC suggest substantial investment of time and energy in both construction and remodeling of (probably residential) structures with stone foundations

(Byrd 1994). Natufian sites have not yielded indisputable evidence of either domesticated plants or animals, though breeding and cultivation experiments were likely carried out. The point is that ethnoarchaeological observations permit a more nuanced appreciation of the combined architectural, botanical, and faunal data than existed previously, and move us beyond simplistic arguments about the chronological primacy of domestication versus sedentism.

Alyawara: hunters on welfare

O'Connell's (1987) study of Alyawara site structure makes a nice contrast to Yellen's. The central Australian Alyawara were first contacted by Europeans in the nineteenth century. Their former hunting and gathering way of life progressively gave way to participation in a local economy characterized by sheep and cattle stations, and by the 1970s most lived in large semi-permanent settlements located near European homesteads or on reserves. Some were seasonally employed but most depended on cash and "rations" provided by government welfare, although up to 25 percent of the diet still came from hunting and gathering. O'Connell's discussion is based on his observations made over a period of ten months during 1973–5. He lived in and focused on one settlement, Bendaijerum, in which he "conducted regular censuses and kept a continuously updated site map" (p. 76), collecting additional data in six others. Archaeological field crews under his supervision made surface collections in abandoned settlements including ones studied a few years previously by an ethnographer, W. W. Denham. Like Yellen, O'Connell takes a naturalist approach and makes much use of quantitative analysis.

Settlements are relatively large with populations ranging from 20 to 200 and averaging about 90, and with areas of about 1 to something over 10 hectares, over which households are distributed either uniformly, as in small settlements, or in clusters. While settlements do not approximate to the ring form characteristic of the !Kung, the positioning of households, generally located some 25–50 m apart, is a function of social, and particularly kin, relationships. Most households are nuclear, sometimes polygynous, but up to a quarter may be women's households typically organized around a core group of widows. A third type of household (3–20 percent) consists only of men, often linked primarily by friendship. Most activities take place in household activity areas, consisting of a circle of cleared ground up to 20 m in diameter and containing a main shelter. Subsidiary shelters, windscreens, sun shades, and dog shelters also occur (Fig. 9.2). Special activity areas include shady spots away from household activity areas where people congregate, automobile repair areas adjacent to household activity areas, roasting pits located to avoid fire hazards on their margins or between them, and defecation areas at the edge of the settlement. Hearths, varying in position by season, are numerous and found both in and outside the main shelter. Multiple regression analysis shows that "where the span of the occupation is held con-

Fig. 9.2 Topsy Jones, an Alyawara woman, prepares to roast two red kangaroos by covering them with embers, Northern Territory, Australia, 1974. Note the scatter of refuse across the area, her household camp in the background and the sunshade in the upper left. This is early in the sequence of occupation and the household activity area has not yet been swept.

stant, the size of the [household] activity area increases with household population but at a declining rate . . . Similarly, where household population is a constant, the activity area should grow at a slow, steadily decreasing rate through time" (pp. 80–1).[1] Refuse disposal zones, varying with length of occupation from the few scattered items to encircling middens, flank the household activity area which is swept clean every few days. The location of activities within household space is highly variable, being affected by changing weather conditions from hour to hour and, over longer periods, by household composition (subject to frequent change in single sex households), by size, and by the compatibility of other activities going on at the same time.

Although settlements are occupied for long periods, there is considerable movement within them. Thus for example at Bendaijerum over an 11 month period 43 of the 45 households present for over six days occupied a total of 135 shelters at 133 different locations. This movement, much of it *within* the settlement, is occasioned by

---

[1] Size of household activity area = 1.67 (number of days occupied)$^{.645}$(total household population)$^{.765}$. Multiple r = .73.

1 death (35 percent), the importance of the move depending on that of the deceased
2 changes in settlement population (30 percent)
3 domestic strife within and between households (< 5 percent)
4 weather (seasonality), proximity to water being more important in summer
5 deterioration of the main shelter, it often being easier to build a new shelter close by rather than replace the old (shelters made of grass or leafy boughs are occupied for about 90–120 days before becoming fire hazards)
6 refuse build-up, leading to moves that are often short, and, as in the previous type, to dumping of secondary refuse in the household area being abandoned.

Alyawara behavior leads to a number of consequences that affect refuse distribution through time and space. As among the !Kung, social context rather than activity is initially responsible for the association of most artifacts and other debris, although away from the household activity area there may be closer relations, as for example between ash and roasting pits. But, because household activity areas are occupied much longer than San hunting camps, refuse is swept and tossed into secondary accumulations. Detailed analysis of refuse at a men's household shows marked size sorting of materials, larger objects (11 cm and up) including soft drink cans mostly ending up in toss zones and middens, while smaller ones, including soft drink pull tabs, similarly sized tabs from chewing tobacco tins, and double-edged razor blades, remain in the central portion of the site where they were either dropped directly or discarded and moved a short distance by sweeping. The contrast between primary and secondary refuse is very marked, and it is of interest that razor blades, salient because of both their metallic shine and capacity to wound, are not accorded special treatment. The Alyawara did not simply overlook them; O'Connell appears not to have found a single coin at the site!

O'Connell also considers the evidence relating to auto repair, a special activity that because it requires considerable space and time might be expected to result in discrete scatters of discarded parts. However, this is very little the case as (a) "auto repairs . . . move in response to the same situational considerations that affect the location of other activities" (p. 96), and (b) "it may be that the spread results in part from the post-depositional activities of children, who frequently redistribute refuse during play, often moving items between or away from disposal areas" (p. 98) (cf. Hammond and Hammond 1981). Auto parts are particularly salient items, however, and it may well be that other, more traditional, special activities carried out adjacent to or at some distance from household activity areas might produce more clustering of functionally associated artifacts.

But even this is not necessarily true, since we have not considered the full implications of the frequent movements of household activity areas into, around, and away from the settlement. This results in redeposition of refuse as new household activity areas are cleared, and large-scale blending and smearing of debris such that clusters of facilities and refuse begin to coalesce. What is more, "this process may occur within a relatively short time, no more than a few months after a site is first occupied" (p. 91). Some archaeological implications are immediately obvious. On the one hand, definition of nuclear and activity areas is most likely to be possible at sites occupied for periods of days rather than months, and at the edges of sites occupied for longer periods. On the other, we may need to rethink interpretations of paleolithic and other hunter-gatherer sites likely to have been occupied intermittently, repeatedly, and/or over much longer time spans.

Comparative studies

O'Connell (1987) ends his paper on the Alyawara by comparing his findings with those of Yellen on the !Kung and Binford on the Nunamiut and considering archaeological implications. We summarize very briefly and comment. While all three groups concentrate domestic activities in household areas and nearby special purpose areas, underlying similarities between Alyawara and !Kung are obscured by longer mean duration of Alyawara occupations, leading to secondary refuse deposition, and larger household size. Responses to marked seasonality of climate, bulk food processing, and storage all help to differentiate Nunamiut household areas, in which there may be greater segregation of activities, while refuse resulting from special activities is often deposited in secondary disposal areas that may be quite distinctive in content. O'Connell also deals with the issue of spacing between households, on average 5–7 m apart in !Kung camps and 25–45 m apart in the Alyawara case. This he suggests is likely due to the absence of predators in Australia and the much lesser importance of food sharing among the Alyawara. More recent research suggests that predators are unimportant but that the very fact of (relative) permanence of settlement encourages spacing on the principle that "Good fences make good neighbors."[2] In any case, before we are tempted, in an essentialist manner, to attribute the contrasts to basic differences between !Kung and Alyawara, we should remember that the !Kung camps recorded by Yellen were occupied by a self-selected group of close relatives. A fairer, but not necessarily more instructive, comparison would surely have been between Bendaijerum and Dobe, which we may be assured is not laid out in the stereotypic circle associated with Plains Indians, but more probably resembles Bendaijerum. Indeed the similarities between that site and the permanent, primarily San, settlement of Kutse in Botswana are obvious (Kent 1995a: especially the plan, her figure 2).[3]

---

[2] For more on the issue of spacing, readers are directed to the debate between Gould and Yellen (1987, 1991) and Binford (1991), to Hayden and Gargett (1991), and to Kent (1995a).
[3] The degrading impact on the !Kung of the wider world over a period of decades is portrayed in Marshall and Miesmer's (1982) film *N!ai, story of a !Kung woman*.

While the Yellen of the late 1960s can of course be accused of the search for the mythical pristine, this does not detract from the value of what he did record, and if anyone, remembering the relevant passage in Kent Flannery's (1982: 273) "Golden Marshalltown" paper, might be inclined to think that because the Alyawara drive jalopies they are of little relevance to prehistory, let them consider two of O'Connell's (1987: 104) concluding statements:

Patterns in site structure will be identified only in relatively large scale exposures, at or beyond the largest now undertaken in hunter-gatherer sites . . . the data most likely to be informative with respect to [patterns in site structure] are very small refuse items, such as chipping debris, small bone fragments, and plant macrofossils, which will often be found in primary context. [original in italics]

Binford's insights into the ways the nature of human bodies contributes to structuring the archaeological record, Yellen's demonstration that social context more than function is responsible for the association of artifacts in household areas, and O'Connell's findings relating to the effects of duration of occupation – none of these or any other of their results can be formulaically applied to archaeological sites, but all of them can and have been intelligently utilized by archaeologists to whom historic sources such as Flannery's Old Timer envisaged for a sixteenth-century Arikara site in South Dakota are simply impossibilities. The wise archaeologist takes account of culture *and* behavior!

Nomadic pastoralists

Cribb (1991b) has noted that Anatolian nomads' tents are often divided along lines of division of labor by sex, but that these areas are movable, and he prefers to think of spaces used by men and women as adjustable and overlapping "domains." Activity areas shift, but men and women tend consistently to carry out distinctive and engendered activities. Based on his own work in Anatolia, and on a review of the literature on pastoralists, he compiled schematic plans of a number of camp sites, suggesting that linear arrangements are common and that tent openings are oriented in relation to the sun. Kinship and other social relationships between tents' occupants are not discussed at any length but one may infer from the literature that such factors affect the locations of tents within sites, as well as the scheduling and location of sites along migration routes.

Cribb's study provides a wealth of data on activity areas and site structure. In addition to two regional plans, his book includes fifteen plans of sites, and about the same number of plans of nomads' tents, evidently similar in many details to those described (but not illustrated) by Hole (1978, 1979). Cribb has published some fine photographs of camps and tent interiors. As among African hunter-gatherers, each residential structure typically has a hearth in front of it; there is often a smaller interior hearth as well. In contrast to Central Asian yurts, Middle Eastern tents are rectilinear. In cases where there are stone tent footings, such distinctions might be recoverable archaeologically and be useful in localized cultural-historical studies.

Susan Smith (1980) provides information and sketch plans of camps of Kel Tamasheq cattle and camel nomads in the sahel zone of Mali. The Kel Tamasheq (Tuareg) comprise five distinct social categories: nobles, vassals, marabouts (Muslim clerics), slaves, and artisans. Camps are ephemeral in the wet season but tethered to water sources in the dry. They house from 10 to over 100 people, size depending largely on whether nobles with a retinue of vassals and retainers are present, although other factors such as the temporary absence of slaves on wild-grain collecting expeditions also come into play. Camps are said to be "as a whole vaguely crescent- or U-shaped" (p. 481), with camels on the inside (possibly for reasons of defense) and cows, sheep, and goats on the outside (Fig. 9.3). Smith's statement that "Within the camps there appears to be no pattern regarding the placement of tents other than personal preference" (p. 481) is contradicted by both her plans and text. The chief or most senior man is first to choose his site, and others follow "apparently in order of seniority." Thus presumably the relationship of nobles' tents to each other expresses kinship and other social relations. Families who have herds in common camp near each other. There is a tendency towards linear arrangements of tents that are generally oriented with their long axis approximating north–south. Privacy may be a factor. Slaves responsible for the camels pitch their tents to the east of their masters, and those responsible for the cows to the west. Artisans camp together, also to the west. All in all it would seem that a Kel Tamasheq could read a great deal about social relations and status, and something of ideology, from camp layout, but that virtually nothing would be left for the archaeologist, except perhaps some concentrations of refuse at the more permanent dry season camps.

Mobile populations with domesticated animals

Martha Graham (1994) documented use and reuse of sites in a very different setting, that of the seasonally mobile Rarámuri, who practice a mixed farming economy and, as noted in the previous chapter, move between compounds and rockshelters located at different elevations. Focusing on a single settlement (Rejogochi), she discusses others visited and provides scale plans of seven "residences" (which we refer to here as "compounds" since more than purely residential space is involved).

These compounds include residential structures, barns, animal pens, ash and trash scatters, wood piles, rock piles, looms, and miscellaneous activity areas (including, presumably, grinding, since the location of portable grinding stones is noted). To judge from the plans with scales, Rarámuri compounds visited by Graham range in size from about 180 m^2 to approximately 950 m^2. With such

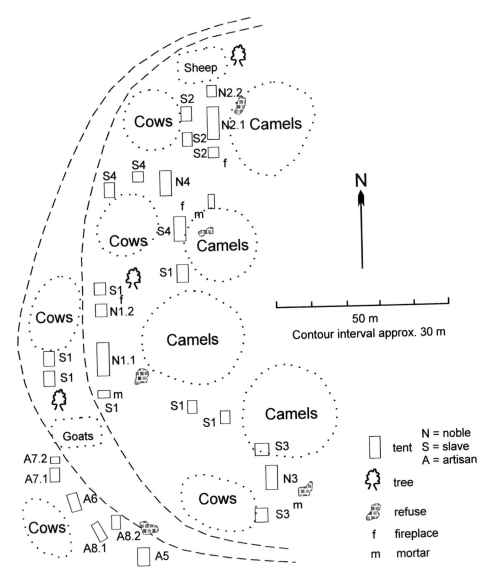

Fig. 9.3 Disposition of a typical Kel Tamasheq camp on a sand dune during the wet season (after S. Smith 1980: 482, Fig. 19.3). Numbers refer to households; thus S1 refers to a slave family associated with the chief, whose tent is N1. Artisans appear to be associated with the camp rather than with particular noble families.

a small sample it is scarcely meaningful to consider average sizes, but we can note parenthetically that mean area is about 440 m². Some of these compounds are occupied seasonally, some by different households from one occupation to the next, and some by a single household whose composition and size changes from one occupation to the next. One of the few "patterns" suggested by the compound plans is that the area immediately surrounding residential structures is comparatively clear of trash or objects related to specific activities. Presumably this relates to these locations, as for some courtyards, patios, and similar spaces elsewhere, being used for the practice of a succession of activities (cf. DeBoer and Lathrap 1979; Deal 1985, 1998; and Hayden and Cannon 1983). It is, though, difficult to detect any general patterns in these Rejogochi data. This may be due in part to variability in both seasonality of occupation and household composition. Activity spaces are described as "generalized" (p. 4), and landholdings include small fields which are dispersed and inherited bilaterally.

Horne's (1994a) study of village spaces in northeastern Iran is based largely on her research in Baghestan (see chapter 8) where some village members are, like Rarámuri, seasonally transhumant. In Iran and northern Mexico, many communities' economies are based on a complex combination of livestock breeding and herding, and seasonally varied tending of domesticated plants. Wild animals and plants can also play important roles, and they do so in both Graham's and Horne's study populations, as well as those discussed by Watson (below). In the setting Horne describes, however, villagers typically spend most of their annual round in their settlements, which are visited seasonally by pastoralists. Control of livestock, and processing of their products, are important activities, and are reflected in a variety of artifacts as well as built structures. That number, complexity, and location of such structures varies cross-culturally is suggested by a comparison of the accounts of Graham and Horne, and Claudia Chang's (1981) discussion of Greek sheep pens. Graham describes a situation in which domesticated animals seem fewer and of less economic importance. Ethnographic and archaeological measures of "importance" can be problematical, and they can be diverse and sometimes at odds with one another, but we suggest that this is another arena in which ethnoarchaeological observations can contribute to larger archaeological endeavors.

One of the chief contributions of Horne's study is the description of idiosyncratic features that distinguish "off-site" productive activities from those routinely carried out in villages. Perhaps more elaborate than most of the structures reported for Inuit and Rarámuri (and certainly the result of greater energy expenditure), some of those created by villagers in northeastern Iran (and elsewhere in the Middle East, South Asia, and parts of the New World) include low-walled step terraces and check dams, irrigation ditches, water storage ponds, and other built structures. In addition to structures directly related to human and animal shelters, and features in fields and gardens, villages have threshing floors and cemeteries. Some also have public bath houses, religious buildings, schools, and government buildings. As elsewhere, public places with access to water can be important loci for such comparatively intangible activities as food preparation, laundering, bathing, and the exchange of banter and social and economic information (Kramer 1982a). While archaeologists may not typically seek out such locations, which may not often provide rich artifactual lodes, such sites may offer clues to scales and patterns of interactions within communities.

Horne's discussion of Baghestan has important implications. Access to, and use of, arable land and pasture are affected by kin and other social relationships. Many economically important activities are carried out far from sites likely to be identified as such by archaeologists. Herding and milking stations are among these; they are well documented by Horne, and they exist elsewhere. In considering probable locations of flocks, she suggests that vegetation rather than drinking water is the key constraining variable. Livestock are also sometimes kept – seasonally – in built structures or excavated subterranean areas. Personnel, equipment, structures, and activities are differentially distributed, depending on animals' needs, household economics, and subtle variations in the physical environment. She also demonstrates that arable land is not necessarily owned by those residing in the villages nearest them, and that not all adjacent architectural areas belong to a single household.

Cultivators

Iranian studies

One of the many contributions of Watson's (1979a) Iranian monograph discussed in the previous chapter is its floor plans of 19 Hasanabad houses showing the locations of specific objects and areas in which specific activities are carried out. Not all rooms in any given compound were mapped, and so, as in other ethnoarchaeological studies of activity areas, it is difficult to know which activities may occur in areas not represented in the illustrations. The trade-off is the richness of the information provided. A plan of Hasanabad identifies rooms in relation to the households owning and using them, and shows activity areas at the village perimeter (dung heaps and dung cake manufacturing areas, dirt quarrying pits, ash deposits). Photographs also provide details, for example of village middens (on which, in one case, a dog contemplates a dead sheep), and village walls are shown clearly. One important category of activity area is devoted to the stabling of sheep and goats, and, as elsewhere in Southwest Asia, there are underground stables. In the warmer months, important off-site activity areas are devoted to the care of flocks, as in the case of Horne's study, in areas unlikely to be explored by archaeologists and, in any case, probably fairly poor in structures, artifacts, and even such ecofacts as animal dung and bones.

In 1975, CK spent five months in (pseudonymous) Aliabad, a Kurdish village in western Iran (Kramer 1982a). With moderate competence in colloquial Persian, CK retained a respected (senior male) villager to help with translation from Kurdish to Persian (closely related Indo-European languages), and with explaining her research objectives and gaining entrée to village homes where she might converse with their occupants, and sketch and photograph. His wife was a village midwife, a wonderfully gracious and humorous person, and a great help in the research project. Mapping of the village, in which 67 houses were occupied by 83 households (Fig. 9.4) was an extended project, much enhanced by a visiting architect, Claus Breede, then of the Royal Ontario Museum. The work investigates relationships between house size and spatial organization, and composition and economic organization of the households occupying residential structures. Frequently kin occupy adjacent houses, the preferred residential pattern being extended patrilateral households, adult sons and their families residing with their parents. To a great extent, the real reflects the ideal.

Data on the location of activities are provided. For example, manufacture of dung cakes, and threshing of harvested cereal grains, are carried out beyond the limits of the village, while weaving of rugs typically occurs within house compounds. Members of extended family households often prepare and eat food together, and often work together in such activities as shearing sheep or whitewashing walls. In a setting in which adobe architecture tends upon disintegration to form mounds, archaeologists have traditionally explored these obvious features of landscapes, and have paid comparatively little attention to "off-site" areas. This is despite the fact that an uneven but fairly rich ethnographic record shows that many important economic and social activities are carried out beyond settlements' built perimeters, for example at water sources. As in the puebloan American Southwest, roofs also constitute important activity areas (particularly for provisional storage and seasonal plant processing), and thus may play a role in constituting stratigraphically distinctive signatures.

Detailed architectural plans of four houses were drawn (Fig. 9.5). CK and Breede reviewed the plans and asked villagers to enlighten them on functions of rooms which, for a variety of reasons, they were unable to inspect personally.[4] CK's discussion of village architecture suggests that rooms' attributes, including features like bins and plastered depressions in floors, and surface treatments of both floors and walls, can be reliable indicators of rooms' functions, though, like David (1971) and Horne (1983a), she notes that rooms are

---

[4] CK had typhoid while Breede was assisting her, and although she took him to the village and made what she considered appropriate introductions, she was unable to accompany him during all stages of his mapping, particularly those involving work on rooftops. Breede, an easy-going and friendly man who had spent some time in Iran but spoke neither Persian nor Kurdish, was evidently accepted by most villagers, many of whom asked solicitously about him after his departure. The only areas which he could not visit were houses that were locked because of owners' temporary absences or recent familial deaths, and some villagers suggested that he not map the cemetery.

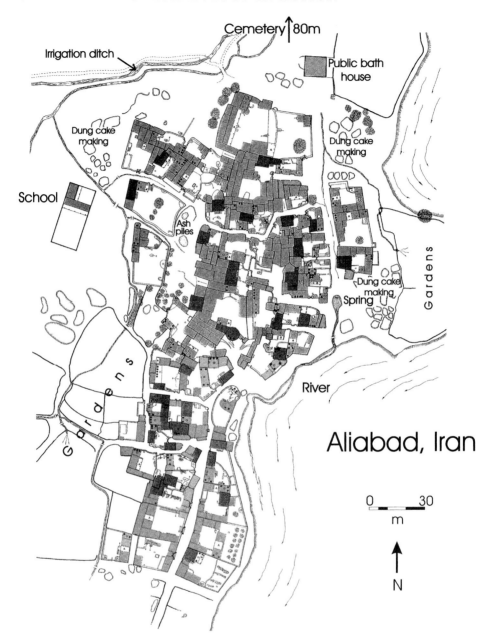

Fig. 9.4 Simplified map of Aliabad village, Iranian Kurdistan, in 1975, after that compiled by CK and Claus Breede (Kramer 1982a: Fig. 2.1). Abutting a seasonal river, as the village of about 400 people grows it cannot expand to the east, and since land to its north is occupied by its cemetery and by the fields of a neighboring village, the possibilities of adding new houses at the north end of the settlement are limited. Labor-intensive gardens and orchards are at the west, and some are being used for new residential structures.

recycled as their functions change, with concomitant addition, deletion, or camouflaging of morphological features. Aliabad's residents claimed that all houses had two stories, to catch cooling breezes in the summer; in fact, only about half did. Many villagers also asserted that all houses had storage bins; at least five did not (Fig. 9.6). Informants are not always to be believed; people have axes to grind or agendas to push or follow. The existence of local faction-alism may be something people want to hide from outsiders (or even neighbors), and both anthropologists and the kind of people among whom they work and live may nourish "normative" or idealized notions of on-the-ground circum-stances that more accurately reflect what is desired or believed to be appropri-ate than what is actual.

Craft specialization

CK's later study (1997) is different in scale and focus, but it, too, includes dis-cussions of activity areas. Working with traditional urban potters in Rajasthan (northwest India), she found that while potters often work within the confines of their residential compounds, the areas in which they carry out their craft responsibilities are marked by numerous idiosyncratic features and artifacts (Fig. 9.7). Both men and women are involved in ceramic production, although men rather than women throw on the wheel. Women are involved in all other aspects of craft production (preparation of clay, inclusions, and pigments; surface treatment of vessels; firing; distribution; sales). This division of labor by sex might seem to have implications for archaeologists but in at least this setting the location of tasks also varies seasonally. For example, a potter's

Caption to Fig. 9.4 (*cont.*)
Outdoor activities evident on the map include ash-piling and dung cake manufacturing areas. Villagers prefer two-storey homes (darker shading) and use the second floor during the summer, when they can enjoy light breezes. Examination of genealogies in conjunction with the village map shows that close kin tend to reside with or near one another, and allows a tentative reconstruction of the relative chronology of particular houses and blocks of houses. For archaeologists working in the Middle East, and other places where abandoned settlements become mounds, such a map can suggest ranges of variation in architecture, relative chronology of structures within a single site, and the processes by which a living settlement becomes an archaeological site.

   This map is a good example of challenges facing the ethnoarchaeologist when publishing hard-earned data. On the reverse side of the original is a genealogical chart of the inhabitants of Aliabad. As is evident from the much reduced version seen here, legibility required publication in a large format, but since stitching into the binding was deemed too costly, it was inserted loose (soon to be lost from library copies).

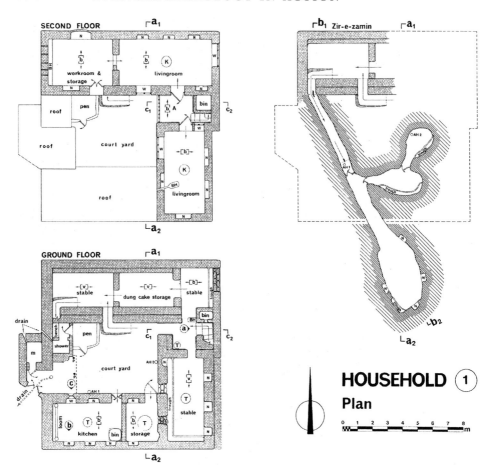

Fig. 9.5 Floor plan of a two-storey house in Aliabad, Iranian Kurdistan, 1975. The ground floor has thick walls (some added since the initial construction) to support the upper storey. Below and extending beyond the house (*right*) is an underground stable used, during the coldest months, for sheep and goats, which in more clement weather occupy pens in household courtyards. This house is occupied by an ageing couple, their sons, and their sons' families. Its owner told CK that he had built the work and storage room on the second floor specifically to create a wall in which he could install beehives (BH). Abbreviations on the plans represent oven (T), floor hearth (K), wall niche (N), air hole for the oven (AH), window (W), ceiling beam (b), vaulted brick ceiling (v), and wooden post (P).

Fig. 9.6 Aliabad women standing beside a grain bin built by the woman of the house (spinning wool) and decorated by her with appliqué versions of the "Tree of Life," considered an auspicious image in much of Southwest Asia, 1975. Grain or flour is poured from the top into the bin, which is then covered with a flat unbaked clay disk on which miscellaneous small household items are placed in temporary storage; the contents are removed through a small hole at the bin's base, which is sealed during the period of active storage.

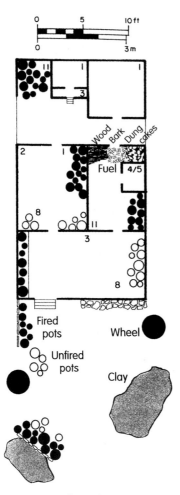

Fig. 9.7 Home and workshop of two married Udaipuri brothers, Rajasthan, India, 1982–3. The house was partitioned after their father's death. The younger son, who inherited their father's wheel, occupies the left side of the house, the older son the right half, and their elderly mother, who paints their pottery, is housed in the living room (top). The younger brother uses the potter's wheel and clay at lower left, those at the lower right being his brother's. Homes of rural potters are typically larger than those of city dwellers, but in either setting most have areas set aside for a wheel, for raw materials (clays and fuels), for tools, and for storage of both leather-hard and fired vessels.

wheel moves from a shady courtyard spot (preferred in summer) to a warm sunny spot, sometimes on a roof, in winter (Fig. 9.8). As the wheel is relocated, so too are laborers of either sex. Children and other kin, and hired laborers, may also participate in various activities, but may well be lost to the archaeological record because their activities are ephemeral and spatially dispersed.

Fig. 9.8 A middle-aged potter in Jodhpur, Rajasthan, India, throws small
vessels off the hump. Because it is winter (1982) and the roof is
sunny, he has made it his base of that season's operations; during
warm weather, he works downstairs in a cool, dark room in his
house. Stacks of the same vessel form are at the rear, in storage
until they are sold. The stick with which Rajasthani potters
typically rotate the wheel is beneath his right elbow.

However, there are numerous attributes by which the work places of ceramic
specialists may be identified, both ethnographically and archaeologically. Floor
plans of Rajasthani potters, both urban and rural, suggest that spaces for raw
materials (particularly clay and fuel) and for drying leather-hard vessels, especially in the rainy season, are crucial. Few of the many potters interviewed by

CK specified that these were key elements in the spatial organization of their domestic and work compounds, but a few did offer observations, and some agreed – when asked – that it was an issue they considered. It is important to note that before CK began her fieldwork (with a pilot project during the summer monsoon), various Western scholars (none of whom had worked with potters, though all had done ethnographic work in India) asserted that potters work throughout the year. Such normative claims by non-specialists (and by Indians peripheral to but claiming awareness of the system) reinforce our view that ethnoarchaeological research can provide more realistic assessments of "on-the-ground" situations than casual observations or unsystematic and undocumented experiences.

Rafters and roofs, as others have noted elsewhere, can be important storage places for Rajasthani potters, as can spaces within residential areas (under beds, or on shelves) and in rented localities separate from potters' homes or shops of vendors of earthenwares. Thus, were a Pompeii to be inflicted on the communities described by CK, it might be possible to identify areas used by potters and vendors of utilitarian pottery, but it would be difficult if not impossible to move to a microscopic scale and specify the areas connected with particular potters and vendors. Such a distinction would be made even more difficult to sustain because many potters also sell their own (and sometimes others') wares, some from their own residential compounds, some from rented space at some remove from their homes, and some in both kinds of places. In addition, some vendors sell imported pots manufactured up to several hundred kilometers away; they and many other vendors sell vessels made in several out-of-town places.

In another study in South Asia, J. Mark Kenoyer *et al.* (1991, 1994; Vidale *et al.* 1993) describe the layouts of workshops and the deposition of debris associated with carnelian bead production (see chapter 11). In this very labor-intensive craft situation, the final product goes through a series of manufacturing stages, each associated with specific byproducts and specific locations. This is "reconstructionist" ethnoarchaeology, in that researchers were seeking information that would allow them to determine how beads associated with the Harappan civilization had been made. Besides the detail provided about the chaînes opératoires of bead production, there is information on the nature of activity areas in which specialized tasks are performed, and characteristic residues left. One of the lessons of this work is that the scale of research units (such as test trenches) and of recovery techniques (such as sieves and their screen sizes) should be closely pegged to the questions asked and the anticipated scale of items to be recovered.

Engendered activities, engendered spaces?

Very few ethnoarchaeological studies discuss sex or gender explicitly. Even fewer address the question of engendered activity areas. We suggest that this is not because such areas do not exist, but because much ethnoarchaeology has been done by men who have, at least until recently, shown themselves comparatively uninterested in matters relating to gender.[5]

O'Connell, Hawkes, and Jones (1991) consider refuse-producing activities at seven camps of the Hadza (Tanzania) visited during a period extending over 14 months during 1985–6. They define three types of sleeping groups (nuclear families, older women, and same sex adolescents), and three kinds of activity areas (household, communal, and specialized). Households are "often arrayed in a roughly circular pattern" (p. 68) reminiscent of the !Kung, and locations of individual household areas express kin relationships between their members, with proximity reflecting relatively closer kinship ties. One camp mapped (p. 65) shows households only a few meters apart and several communal areas. Surprisingly, communal areas, which are periodically swept clear of refuse, are "used for essentially the same range of activities as household areas, but [are] not associated with any particular household or sleeping group" (p. 67). Behavioral scan sampling (walking through the camps at selected times and noting what each and every person present was doing) resulted in some 25,000 individual observations, 1000 of them from nine scans conducted over 14 days in March–April 1986 at a camp called Umbea B. The results show very marked differences in the performance of different categories of refuse-producing activities by gender of actor, and according to whether the activities are performed in peripheral communal areas, associated mainly with men (Fig. 9.9), or in central communal and household areas where there is a more even distribution of activities by gender (Table 9.2).

These data show interesting contrasts with !Kung and Alyawara, who both perform a much higher proportion of tasks in household areas. The archaeological implications, always assuming that each category of task leaves distinctive residues, are that activities associated with males would only be distinguishable in peripheral communal areas, where refuse associated with women's activities is absent. But why Hadza and !Kung use of communal areas should be so different remains a puzzle. The findings of O'Connell and colleagues demonstrate that ethnoarchaeological research can provide data supporting gender-based differences likely to leave archaeological signatures, and that reconstructions based on archaeological evidence should make use of such data rather than simply asserting that such differences exist.

Some of the obvious arenas in which women and men are spatially segregated in carrying out their respective activities pertain to domestic work, including food preparation, food consumption, and child care, as well as entertainment of guests, and sleeping. We ourselves have seen, but not systematically

---

[5] Hodder and some of his students consider gender and power, and while Hodder himself has written about relationships between gender, ideology, and material culture, those of his students who have focused on such matters are all women (Mary Braithwaite [1982], Linda Donley [1982], Henrietta Moore [1982], and Alice Welbourn [1984]) (see chapter 13).

Fig. 9.9 Hadza men in a communal area on the periphery of a camp, northern Tanzania, 1986. The man on the left uses a ballpeen hammer to flatten metal to make an arrowhead; the man third from left shapes an arrow shaft, and the man fourth from left sews a bag.

documented on any meaningful scale, differences in the ways in which males and females are treated at birth, puberty, marriage, and death (to name the most obvious critical points in the life cycle). As we and others have noted, important craft activities are sometimes gender-segregated and, usually, spatially segregated as well. One example of spatially restricted activity areas in which gender plays a key role is the Middle Eastern harem. Traditionally, when wealthy Muslim men have numerous wives and concubines, these women are restricted to enclosed architectural areas. In some elite contexts, their activities are organized and facilitated by both women and men (some of the latter are, as was the case in the Ottoman empire, eunuchs). In non-elite situations – such as peasant villages – women's quarters are often in comparatively remote parts of residential compounds. In some cases, a male intruder would have – almost literally – to run a gauntlet to reach the women's quarters. If specific activities, such as weaving, are associated with women, then artifacts associated with such activities might be anticipated in comparatively inaccessible domestic locations.[6]

---

[6] Information about gender-related craft activities may be obtained from, among other sources, the Human Relations Area Files (HRAF). One of Murdock's publications (Murdock and Provost 1973), which focuses on gender-related activities, is a potentially useful introductory resource for ethnoarchaeologists interested in activities and activity areas.

Table 9.2 *Refuse-producing activities at a Hadza camp by sex of actor and type of area (data from O'Connell et al. 1991)*

Activity category: actors	Men	Women	Total
Weapons maintenance	129	0	129
Clothing maintenance	4	10	14
Tool maintenance	1	10	11
Food processing	2	42	44
Totals	136	62	198
Activity category: area type	Communal	Household	
Weapons maintenance	118	11	129
Clothing maintenance	11	3	14
Tool maintenance	9	2	11
Food processing	33	11	44
Totals	171	27	198

One of the earliest ethnoarchaeological studies of activity areas was set in the American Southwest. Working with a small group of Navajo (9), Spanish-American (3), and Euroamerican households (3), Susan Kent (1984) considers the organization of domestic space in relation to (among other things) gender roles within households and ideological underpinnings of spatial organization. She presents her observations in normative descriptions of "typical" days in her informants' lives. Kent provides 12 maps of houses (some drawn by their inhabitants, which we consider a useful data-acquisition strategy, particularly when complemented with photographs and plans drawn to scale), and several maps of their immediate surroundings. While she specifies some of the ways in which children and adults, and males and females, use domestic space, she concludes that activity areas "are not universally sex specific" (1984: 225).[7] In summarizing some of the salient differences between the groups she worked with, she notes a greater frequency and diversity of artifacts, and more monofunctional activity areas, among Euro- and Spanish-Americans, and comparatively fewer of both among Navajos, some of whom use different areas within traditional residential structures (hogans) according to gender (and age). Socioeconomic status is not discussed at length, nor is degree of sedentism considered in detail; rather, "ethnic" or "cultural" affiliation and ideology are treated as centrally causal factors in spatial behavior. Kent's study is essentially ethnographic and was of comparatively short duration. Klara Kelley's work on Navajo land use (1986), incorrectly described as an ethnoarchaeological study, is in fact largely ethnohistoric and archaeological. However, it too contains a

---

[7] Kent writes throughout of sex rather than gender.

number of photographs and plans of house sites (though not plans of individual houses), and it is an informative complement to Kent's volume.

In comparing her sample households, Kent considers gender-specific activity areas as well as diversity of functions in activity areas (both greatest among Euroamericans). Robert Hitchcock (1987) also considers the diversity of activity areas, though in the context of sedentarizing populations in the Kalahari Desert, an area to which Kent was soon to turn. Both Hitchcock and Kent (Kent and Vierich 1989) suggest that internal organization and complexity of sites is, in part, a function of anticipated duration of occupation: the longer the anticipated stay, the more complex the site. Patricia Draper (1977) has also commented on San sedentarization, changes in residential structures (which become increasingly private), and in gender relationships (with, in some cases, increasing restrictions on women's mobility, and increasing spousal abuse). It seems clear that occupational duration is a significant factor in determining the diversity and number of activity areas, and the internal organization of settlements. However, as Hitchcock notes, sedentism may not immediately affect site size, but may be linked both to increasing occupational specialization and complexity of activities, and to increased attention to and construction of storage or other facilities. With preparation of foods for storage, special activity areas may be established to separate detritus associated with food processing from other living and working spaces. Like others, Hitchcock comments parenthetically about the siting of activity areas in relation to prevailing winds, and notes that among sedentary groups space is differentiated on the basis of age, gender, and status, in ways not typical of mobile populations.

Concluding remarks

It is evident that the ethnoarchaeology of site structure has been essentially naturalist – a more postprocessual tone is sometimes apparent as the topic shifts towards architecture – and that the greatest analytical effort has been expended on hunter-gatherer studies. This is not to say that research on food producers, sedentary or nomadic, is devoid of analytical insights; far from it. Correlates are often established, but the aim in such cases is usually to use ethnoarchaeology, usually with more than a whiff of direct historical analogy, for interpretive reconstruction of archaeological sites. In contrast, those who specialize in hunter-gatherer ethnography service an archaeological clientele that, faced with a far poorer archaeological record, is hungry if no longer for laws then for expectations, interpretive principles, and models. As we noted above, but it bears repeating and is emphasized by continuing debate and ongoing search for causes, there are no ethnoarchaeological keys to the interpretation of prehistoric site structures. We can on the other hand offer quite sophisticated suggestions concerning the variables that are likely to be structuring the data in particular contexts, and, at the very least, point to questions that need to be answered before any interpretation of social arrangements can begin.

Further reading

Susan Kent's (1987) introduction to her collection *Method and theory for activity area research: an ethnoarchaeological approach* was mentioned in chapter 1. The book is a prime source for activity area studies in the processual mode and contains several ethnoarchaeological chapters. Kent's paper (1999b) on the archaeological visibility of storage usefully supplements the information on San and applies it to an Anasazi pueblo in Colorado. In a major paper, "When the going gets tough, the tough get going . . ." Binford (1991) provides more information on Nunamiut camps and their relationship to settlement and social organization than can be accommodated within the confines of this chapter. This paper appears in Gamble and Boismier's (1991) edited volume, which brings together a varied set of papers on the mobile campsites of hunters, horticulturalists, and pastoralists from all over the world. Holl and Levy's (1993) edited volume *Spatial boundaries and social dynamics* contains material of interest on food-producing societies.

CHAPTER 10

ARCHITECTURE

> The most urgent requirement at present is for detailed case studies that mediate between the ethnographers' structural models and the technologists' models of structures.
>
> *(Nicholas David 1971: 128–9).*

In this chapter we revisit some ethnoarchaeological studies, and introduce others that suggest ways in which archaeologists might think about architecture. Some of the topics we explore have to do with relationships between vernacular and other (especially state-run) building enterprises; relationships between built habitats and household size, organization, and economic status; the importance of sampling, and the "production" of space. We note that some ethnoarchaeological discussions of architecture consider gender, and a (very) few consider the building trades as crafts involving specialists. Most, but not all, of the accounts below are firmly in the processualist mode. One we will not consider, but which is suggestive of what might be done in postprocessualist mode, is Bourdieu's (1973) reading of the Berber house, an archetypal study of the Structuralist (with capital S and definitely not *post*structuralist) school. This is hardly ethnoarchaeology, but rather a model distilled from the author's ethnographic experience.

"Vernacular" architecture

Archaeologists are drawn to architectural remains largely because they are sometimes comparatively substantial and well preserved. As such, they provide physical and humanly constructed contexts for artifacts and their spatial and chronological distributions. We draw a distinction between "vernacular" and other sorts of built habitats, by which we mean that vernacular architecture is (a), though built to cultural standards, not usually physically standardized, (b) reflects inhabitants', and often the builders' own, needs, and (c) is not typically the product of designers or construction workers who have no intentions of occupying their handiwork. When changes in the domestic cycle alter perceived needs, modifications can often be made to accommodate those changes (see Goody 1971). Another important aspect of much vernacular – and other – architecture is that, unlike most artifacts, it doesn't move. We do not discuss tents or yurts here; while these are important forms of shelter, they are comparatively ephemeral, although sometimes leaving remains (see chapters 8 and 9). The same can be said of huts, windbreaks, tipis, wickiups, and similar structures of organic materials, like those reported for many hunter-gatherers.

When archaeologists examine architectural remains, they tend to consider building materials, scale, patterns of circulation, and location. They also consider the numbers, associations, and spatial distribution of objects, features, and facilities within structures (such as hearths, grain bins, painted walls, platforms covering burials, caches of skulls, terrazzo floors, niches, platforms, and stelae). These assist in formulating hypotheses relating to, for example, variation in the functions of built habitats, or in the economic statuses of households within a settlement. Of course, architecture at many archaeological sites is not well preserved, with walls often only the merest stubs or represented by foundation trenches or a line of postmolds, so it is impossible to know what arches, windows, and the like might have formed part of their upper reaches.

Most ethnoarchaeological studies of architecture are set in non-industrial societies in which buildings are constructed of locally available materials and vary one from another. The sort of standardization seen at such a comparatively early site as Kahun (modern Lahun), a workers' village in Middle Dynastic Egypt of the mid-second millennium BC (Kemp 1989), is unusual in the context of the larger ancient world. However, by Greco-Roman times some towns had what we would describe as apartment buildings, as in Ostia in Italy, and in Classic Mesoamerica urban Teotihuacan had neighborhoods organized along ethnic and class lines, characterized by different sorts of structures. Like the ticky-tacky houses of Pete Seeger's greater San Francisco, residential units in the prehispanic Americas were sometimes strikingly similar, and some regularities in house form may have been encouraged by state or other authorities. Architectural standardization is a phenomenon often associated with complex societies, bureaucracies, and indeed urban centers. But, as Hillier and Hanson (1984) have shown, even in the absence of *regulations*, a few simple rules can generate extraordinary *regularities* and the appearance of planning. It is however more common for conjunctures of rules and expectations to be materialized in constrained architectural variety. As ND (1971: 117) wrote of the Fulbe compound:

Given a household of known size and kinship configuration, and of which the wealth, status and professional specialization, if any, of the head is known, the numbers and kind of huts in the compound may be predicted with some degree of accuracy. Regularities exist that the ethnographer can formulate into a housing code, but which the archaeologist must decipher from excavated remains.

Such regularities have been related by Anick Coudart (1992b) to group solidarity. Using data gathered by four French anthropologists, she compares variation in housing within two Anga tribes (New Guinea). The Baruya (B on Fig. 7.8), a conquering group numbering about 2500, practice long collective initiations. In each village of 150 to 200 people there is a men's house, and there are plenty of other markers of strong, indeed oppressive, social cohesion, including frequent suicides (6.2 percent of deaths). In contrast, the Ankave (I on Fig. 7.8), a tribe of about 900 people who have been pushed into the lowlands, hold short initiation ceremonies for males only, and their small hamlets of 30 to 50 individuals are occupied irregularly and generally lack men's houses. There are no suicides, but murders constitute 6 percent of deaths. Given these data we are not surprised to find that Baruya houses, all with conical roofs on cylindrical bases and built in a day by work groups, show little variation (Table 10.1), whereas Ankave houses, constructed mainly by a man and his wife over a period of a month or two, are extremely variable in plan, roof form, and other characteristics, such that there are *no* items in the left-hand column of the equivalent Ankave table (not reproduced here), 15 in the second column listing features with two to four options, five in the third (five to six options), and four in the fourth column (random variation). Coudart notes that within Baruya villages some optional traits are standardized while others are not, but that standardization increases towards the margins of Baruya territory "as if the cohesion of the group has to be advertised where it is most menaced" (p. 438, our translation). This conclusion is obviously very much in line with Hodder's interpretation of Baringo data.

Coudart's analysis was undertaken "to discover rules of correspondence between degree of architectural variation, house transformation and cultural durability ([in the] Danubian Neolithic [of Europe]), and between degree of architectural variation and a group's social cohesion" (p. 410). She applies the same method of classification to Danubian longhouses. She also, in a pair of remarkable figures, models the evolution, the cultural durability, and the rhythms of transformation of the house in relation to the different levels of variation of its architectural components. Her paper is of methodological interest, and testimony to the fine-grained recording of field data by Pascale Bonnemère, Maurice Godelier, Pierre Lemonnier, and Jean-Luc Lory.

Why the Willow Lake Dene build log cabins and tipis

Our next case study describes the combination of architecture, some substantial and some less so, with extreme flexibility of use, and also addresses the question of round versus rectangular structures. In 1974 and 1975 Robert and Priscilla Janes spent a total of 22 weeks with Slavey Dene, who live much of the year at Fort Norman in Canada's Northwest Territories, moving out in the late winter or early spring for four to six months to live in residential camps used as bases from which to launch a variety of hunting, fishing, trapping, and gathering expeditions. In contrast to the Nunamiut, these forest Dene are not classic collectors in the Binfordian sense, though their trapping and fishing

Table 10.1 *The different levels of variation of architectural traits of the Anga Baruya house (from Coudart 1992b: table 3, our translation)*

First level Uniformity Collective representations Cultural identity	Second level Minor variation tending towards uniformity (2–3 options)	Third level Variation in typology with 5–9 options	Fourth level "Random" variation Contingencies and "individual" identity
1 plan (circular)	1 hearth base: 3 options (box, conical basket, suspended in net)	1 exterior wall covering: 6 options with 2 dominant (covering or band of bark, bands of bamboo, planks, pandanus leaves, mat, absent)	1 storage platform (often 3 bamboo trunks running through the house along the axis of the door; numerous variants: impossible to develop a typology
2 roof (conical)	2 initial roof construction: 3 variants (4 poles, 2 superimposed rings, 1 piece of bamboo)	2 threshold: 9 options of which 6 are variants of one type	2 door or equivalent (formerly war shields)
3 floor (raised)	3 number of sticks at summit of roof (4 or 5)	3 internal wall covering: 5 options of which 2 are combinations of 2 types	
4 wall structure (separate planks)	4 floor (3 options)		
5 structure supporting the floor	5 exterior join between floor and wall (3 options)		
6 stones and form of the hearth	6 interior join between floor and wall (3 options)		
7 entry (where ground is highest)	7 interior join between wall and roof (4 options, 1 rare)		
8 summit of roof (small sticks)	8 exterior space: 2 options (drain, no drain)		
9 roofing material (grass brought by women)	9 joining of floorboards: 3 options (knots, running stitch, nails)		
10 men's space (opposite entry and higher than women's)	10 division of interior space: 2 options (division by sex, + antechamber)		
11 end of construction marked by moralizing speech			
12 end of construction marked by collective meal			

certainly fall under that head; they also undertake considerable encounter hunting, typical of "foragers," of moose, woodland caribou, and sometimes bear. The Janes's lived for 16 weeks in the months of March–June with seven related families at their camp on Willow Lake. There, working in English, they collected a remarkable amount of detailed information on site formation processes, male and female activity areas and patterns – their work constitutes the earliest significant ethnoarchaeological consideration of gender – special purpose sites, tool manufacture, and, of special concern here, variation in structures and in their use. In the course of archaeological survey in the area, Robert Janes (1983) had been struck by the "potential immensity of the gap which could and does develop between the results of field archaeology and the richness of a living culture" (p. 1), particularly in an area characterized since time immemorial by a "mobile, unencumbered hunter-gatherer way of life . . . [in which] much of the prehistoric technology was made of perishable materials such as bone and skin, and the rapid deterioration of archaeological remains caused by the acidic subarctic soils" (p. 3). Noting "the failure of archaeologists not only to recognize, but also to deal with the true complexity and variability which characterized past human affairs" (p. 2), he is concerned therefore to record the material manifestations of a changing way of life in which many "activities, such as hunting, meat processing, land travel, hide processing, cooking, water travel, shelter construction and gathering, represent forms of adaptive behavior that appear to be only superficially altered since Euro-Canadian contact" (p. 16).

His monograph, which deserves to be better known, culminates in no less than 77 "expectations" to be borne in mind by archaeologists, and not only by those working in the north. To give something of the flavor of the Janes's work and of Dene life, we sample (from pp. 105–9) expectations in several major categories:

Sites Features and artifacts such as clustered pits with food contents, highly compacted soil horizons, and faunal assemblages exhibiting variation in modification may . . . result from the activities of dogs.

Refuse There is little meaning in assigning household ownership to individual refuse pits or surface accumulations, as these features may be used exclusively by individual households, be shared by households, or be communal.

Structures Seemingly non-portable objects such as log cabins have complex use histories involving construction, use, disassembly, relocation, reassembly and reuse, and renovation and reuse. Curation is not restricted to easily transportable objects.

Activity areas Log cabins and tipis are not functionally distinct activity centres, as all the activities that occur within tipis can also occur within cabins, including cooking, eating, tool repair and manufacture, sewing, meat and fish processing, hide and fur processing, communal feasts, and sleeping.

Male and female activity patterns The fact that activity areas within the residential camp are nearly all multifunctional, and the fact that most activities are shared among the sexes there, preclude the existence of sex-specific space within the residential camp.

Special-purpose sites and features Repeated use of the same hunting camp cannot be

Fig. 10.1 Robert and Priscilla Janes take a break during the installation of a spruce bough floor in their tipi with the children who taught them the proper technique, Willow Lake camp, North West Territories, Canada, May 1974.

used as a principle of settlement patterning, because even though an area is used repeatedly, the hunting camps . . . need not be. Several factors are relevant to the selection of a specific site, including the availability of game, ice conditions, and the need to eat and rest.

Willow Lake Dene households all make use of at least one log cabin (or, as a stop gap measure until a cabin can be built, a substantial canvas tent of similar plan) and a tipi; other structures include raised platforms used for storage and in hide working, temporary hide-smoking facilities, and recently introduced outhouses. Log cabins and tents are of Euro-Canadian origin, and are rectangular. Tipis are (with one exception) round and, with a mean diameter of 4.48 m, now smaller and less squat than those used in the past when they sometimes housed more than one family. Their poles are left standing throughout the year (Fig. 10.1) and covered as required with a variety of materials including spruce boughs, plastic, and burlap in any combination; caribou skins are no longer used. Janes notes very considerable variety in the construction of log cabins – there are at least three methods of making the corners – which he attributes to the Slavey Dene principle of minding one's own business and not offering "suggestions or assistance even to someone incapable or ignorant of the correct procedure in a task or activity . . . This diffident behavior has obvious adaptive value in allowing individual interests and expression to coexist with group cohesiveness" (p. 44). One may indeed wonder to what extent correct procedures and group cohesiveness exist. The range of cabin forms is also likely associated with the quite varied geographic origins of the Willow Lakers (as they refer to themselves).

By means of cabin and tipi plans, some of the same structures on different days, Janes demonstrates an extraordinary flexibility in the occupants' use of interior space. He also raises the question of why the tipi should persist as an important part of Dene domestic architecture. He considers Rosalind Hunter-Anderson's (1977) thesis that rectangular structures are associated with more complex adaptations, and that a causal relationship between content housed and house form hinges upon three variables: the numbers and variety of roles of the occupants, the heterogeneity of the activities performed within the house, and the volume of associated materials and facilities. Higher values of the variables are associated with rectangular structures (as round vessels are suitable containers for undifferentiated water or grain, whereas mechanics keep arrays of specialized tools in rectangular boxes equipped with multiple levels and compartments). The Willow Lakers score low on the first two variables and tolerate the successive performance of a wide variety of activities, and not always in the same places, in their highly multifunctional structures. Why then do they use rectangular structures? Not, Janes believes, because of a post-contact increase in the volume of their material culture inventories, since equipment and supplies are frequently stored on platforms outside the house, but perhaps, as Hunter-Anderson also suggested, because of a relationship between "the certainty of procurement of large amounts of resources and the amount of effort invested in facilities" (1983: 58). More permanent facilities require less maintenance, and in these coniferous forests are most easily, when steel axes and chain saws are available, built of logs and in rectangular shapes. Tipis are, Janes argues, "retained for ideological, aesthetic and functional reasons" (p. 58). They are valued as part of Dene heritage, are appreciated for freshness of the air in contrast to the stuffiness of cabins, are needed for the drying and smoking of meat and fish, and are preferentially though not exclusively utilized for a variety of other messy activities. Log cabins are not furnished with often-to-be-replaced spruce-bough floors, and are easier to keep clean and require less maintenance, adjustments, and repairs. Thus a great variety of factors including "low population, minimal role differentiation, the storage of materials outside dwellings, historical precedent, culture contact, and the constant availability of bush resources" (p. 58), but also ideology and comfort besides the characteristics of available building materials, account for the Willow Lakers' continued use of rectangular and round structures that, although their functions overlap to a very great extent, have different advantages and disadvantages.

Before leaving the Willow Lakers, we should note that Robert Janes (1989) returned there in 1984 to conduct a post-mortem excavation of one of the tipis in order to develop an ethnoarchaeological model for the identification of pre-historic tipi remains in the Boreal forest. On the basis of this excavation he suggests the following as potentially diagnostic attributes: "a central hearth [with contents relating to a late stage in tipi use], a hard-packed, sloped floor, ostensibly complex stratigraphy, rodent disturbance, subsurface tepee [*sic*] furniture, subterranean storage facilities and a circular zone of debris . . . [and a] roughly circular configuration of stones used to hold down tepee coverings" (p. 137). Fossorial rodent and insectivore disturbance is a major factor since, as meat, fish, and hide-processing debris filters down through the fragrant carpet of spruce, it attracts insects, whose eggs and larvae, together with scraps of meat and seeds, are in turn eagerly seized on by mice, voles, and shrews. Not a pretty picture, but what a basis for metaphor!

Architecture in the Islamic world

Several papers and monographs treat architecture in the Islamic world from a variety of perspectives. One aspect of life in the Muslim Middle East often commented upon is the spatial segregation of women in various contexts. Only one component of *purdah*, this tradition has been interpreted in many ways by both natives and outsiders, but it results in men and women carrying out their various activities in different areas. Lois Beck (1978) has commented on some of the ways in which women manipulate their spatial isolation to their own advantage (and that of their men), and cross sometimes permeable boundaries to achieve various goals. The most extreme example of the spatial isolation of women is the "Oriental" harem where Muslim women, producers of sons, are considered property, and may indeed be shut away for life. This inverse form of conspicuous consumption by males is, however, a rarity in Islam, where it is associated with the marking of special status. We know of no ethnoarchaeological studies of such situations, although Donley(-Reid) has commented on the architectural correlates of elite women's status in Lamu, an island off the north coast of Kenya, noting that three women "born within the walls of the house . . . only left it to be buried" (1982: 67). This fascinating and provocative study leaves us, as do her other publications that deal with this topic (Donley 1987; Donley-Reid 1990a, 1990b), with unanswered questions. One has to do with methods of data acquisition and sample size and composition (not trivial, since the author draws a distinction between females who are slaves and other women, and comments on toilet facilities for women of various statuses though, again, their number and location are not made clear). Perhaps her research among the Swahili is better described as oral history (though the historians or interlocutors are not identified) than ethnoarchaeology. This is one case – among many – that points to the need to be explicit about dates and circumstances of fieldwork, modes of data acquisition, and sample size and composition.

Baghestan: structures of inheritance

Archaeological structures' shapes are, for obvious reasons, most typically evaluated on the basis of their floor plans, rather than on the basis of their roofs.[1] In Baghestan Lee Horne (1994a) carried out one of the most comprehensive and explicitly archaeologically oriented studies of contemporary dwelling spaces published to date. About 150 villagers make up 32 households; they and some of their livestock occupy 170 rooms on about 1.9 hectares. While much of Horne's work details "man"–land relationships, discussed in chapters 8 and 9, it is the aspect of her study dealing with residential architecture that we consider here. The village plan (Fig. 10.2) is broken down in a number of maps highlighting rooms' differing functions (such as storerooms, straw storage rooms, animal rooms, and living rooms), and in detail in nine figures in an appendix. In her meticulous "etic" account of her systematic and quantified observations, articulated with villagers' "emic" accounts of their architectural ideals, Horne describes the criteria by which building sites are selected, how building materials are obtained and prepared, the costs involved in construction (in terms of both labor and money), and the functionally different units said to comprise an ideal residence. Aspects of this local ideal are Islamic in character. For example,

There are entrances that are offset to block direct line-of-sight into private spaces, courtyard walls, low or windowless building walls that cannot overlook another's courtyard, blank facades and embellished interiors, and a historical need for fortification . . . values said to underlie these architectural forms are ritual, privacy, and the seclusion of women. (p. 115)

Horne's further observation that courtyard walls do not always block outsiders' views of compounds, but instead reflect local etiquette by marking acceptable boundaries, is a useful reminder that anthropologists should be cautious in imposing associations and presumptions based on their own cultural backgrounds on sometimes quite different Others. Horne is one of the few authors describing architecture who notes the existence and role of specialized builders, some of whom come from other settlements to help with construction. This is a little-studied form of craft specialization, one that might be detected in such archaeological traces as bricks of standardized size or the degree of perpendicularity of walls in rectilinear structures, and, possibly, identifiable fingerprints left in plaster or paint. Horne also usefully provides a detailed account of the quantity of raw material (most of it local dirt) used to build a house, and the volume of earth comprising village structures that might erode into an

---

[1] In parts of Southwest Asia, including northeastern Iran, some structures with rectilinear floor plans have curvilinear roofs.

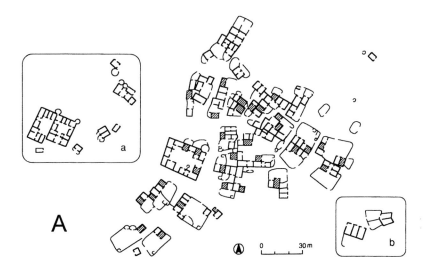

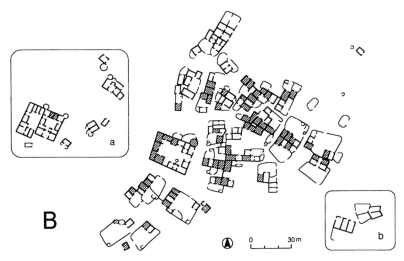

Fig. 10.2 In Baghestan (Iran), Lee Horne found that room functions
sometimes change seasonally. The upper plan indicates the
distribution of summer "living rooms" (shaded areas). Such rooms,
used for a variety of domestic activities during most of the year, are
often used during summer months for storage. The lower plan
shows the locations of storerooms (shaded). At some distance from
the village, insert "a" represents a decaying but still imposing fort,
built to protect the villagers in earlier times; "b" is another fortified
dwelling. When Horne did her fieldwork, neither was occupied by
residential households, but both were used occasionally for straw
storage and as stables (Horne 1994a: 95).

archaeological mound of a certain size.[2] This is archaeologically oriented ethnography indeed! For archaeologists, perhaps the most "confounding" (p. 160) observation made in Baghestan is that rooms owned by a single household may be spatially dispersed within the village, contiguous rooms sometimes being owned by people who are not immediate kin. Horne explores this phenomenon elsewhere (1982), showing that it relates to local patterns of marriage and inheritance. In this small community located in a region of dispersed settlement that is characterized by village endogamy, women as well as men have, and exercise rights to, heritable built structures. This results in heirs to buildings and their siblings having more housing options than in other parts of the Islamic world where first-born males are traditionally the main inheritors.

Aliabad: architecture and wealth

Elsewhere in Iran, CK (1982a) considers the ways in which vernacular village architecture may reflect differences in households' size, composition, and wealth. She is one of the few ethnoarchaeologists who documents households' use of space, noting that while residents repeatedly insisted that they – and their houses – were all alike, in fact there was diversity in household capital and income, or "wealth." In the 1970s, villagers throughout the country reckoned wealth mainly in terms of traditional resources, land and livestock. This poses methodological problems, as wealth is difficult to quantify when largely measured in land of varying quality and in livestock whose species and numbers vary annually. Arable land can be assessed in terms of slope, but also in terms of the number of oxen (or other animals) available to draw a plow. The price of animals varies (e.g., horses are far more expensive than donkeys). To assess other aspects of household wealth, both CK and Horne also assigned monetary values to such portable possessions as bicycles and radios. Even with such comparatively crude measures, it was possible to assign a wealth value expressed in currency to each household, to group households by wealth – for example into quartiles – and to consider wealth in relation to house size. In developing a variety of estimates of wealth, CK learned that some villagers had owned the land on which their houses were built, while others were relative newcomers, who had purchased their land under a different governmental protocol introduced in 1962, one allowing sharecroppers (some of them immigrants) to purchase their houses and land on an installment basis. A measure of

---

[2] Of the village as a whole Horne (1994a: 163) writes, "if all this mud and straw construction (including courtyard walls, paving, and features as well as buildings) contained in the central residential area were consolidated, I estimate the resultant cube would measure nearly 20 meters on each side, or about 8,000 cubic meters of deposit. Or if, instead, the consolidation were evenly deposited across the occupied area, the resultant deposit would be about 0.4 meter deep, a significant quantity of mud. Organic matter (especially ash, straw, grains, and human and animal urine and feces) is also present in large quantities. Because much organic matter is routinely removed to fields or wasteland outside the village, the buildup inside the village is slower than might be expected, given the quantities produced."

Fig. 10.3 An Aliabad villager plasters a wall, summer 1975. The horizontal crack at the level of his knees reflects drying between the end of one day and when work began the next. Specialist builders can be found in the Middle East, but, as elsewhere, many "vernacular" structures are designed and built by their occupants.

wealth applicable to two rather different historic and ethnographic situations had to be created to allow groups with different residential histories in the village to be compared with one another. CK returned to the variables constantly mentioned by villagers, land and livestock, and used the market values obtaining during the period of her fieldwork as the basis of her estimates.

As in Baghestan, Aliabad's buildings are constructed of local materials (earth and stones) (Fig. 10.3) with the occasional addition of plaster or cement purchased in nearby towns, some of these imported materials signaling greater household wealth. In extended family households, constituent nuclear families usually sleep in different rooms but prepare and consume food in shared common areas, a kitchen and living room (sometimes one and the same). As elsewhere in Southwest Asia, roofs and unroofed courtyards are important activity areas; roofs are used for the transitory storage of organic materials such as roofing beams, prepared foods destined for consumption in later months, and drying crops. Courtyards often have such built-in features as animal pens and troughs, and ovens.

CK's architectural data clearly show that habitation areas differ from animals' pens and stables in distinctive ways, and that architectural areas designed for human use have idiosyncratic signatures, many of them likely to be preserved archaeologically. For example, sleeping rooms may be white-washed, but roofed areas designed as stables are not. However, as is the case in another Iranian village described by Horne (1983a) and in Bé in Cameroon (David 1971), rooms initially intended for one purpose are often reused in different ways. Such changes are sometimes a function of alterations in household size and composition as the domestic cycle (Goody 1971) evolves; others may reflect more radical reorganizations within households and larger kin units and the settlements they inhabit. This was the case at the Hopi site of Orayvi (Oraibi), Arizona, studied by Catherine Cameron (1993). While her research cannot be described as ethnoarchaeological (because the communities she discusses had either dissolved or reconstituted themselves before her work began), it is a fine example of the integration of longitudinal data obtained from archaeological, ethnographic, and photographic documentation.

Both Horne and Kramer carried out their fieldwork in the 1970s, before the Iranian revolution that overthrew the last monarch. Both found positive correlations between household wealth (measured in similar ways) and house size, though the associations are not overwhelming in either case. One reason for this is that household size, composition, and wealth may change over time more rapidly than architecture decays or is modified, so that some structures observed relate not directly to the present household but to a previous more populous or affluent phase. This is in marked contrast to ND's study of Bé, in which he showed that relative impermanence of structures combined with low building costs facilitated annual remodeling of the compound to adjust to changes in household composition and other circumstances. This led him to propose what Schiffer was later to call David's law (see chapter 1).

Architectural recycling and decay

Two ethnoarchaeological studies that discuss architectural reorganization and recycling were published by David (1971) and Horne (1983a). One of the expectations that emerges from many ethnoarchaeologists' observations, some less systematic than others, is that residential spaces can be, and often are, transformed into such less lofty functions as stables and storerooms, whereas stables and storerooms are very rarely converted to human habitations.[3] ND (1971: 119) claimed that "In any one culture the precession of uses is such that we may speak of a devolutionary cycle," but while both this and the previous expectation may commonly be true, they clearly do not apply to housing for

---

[3] In one unusual case, an Iranian village house was rented by T. Cuyler Young, Jr., director of the Royal Ontario Museum's Godin archaeological project, in which CK participated. The stable, scrubbed and replastered, was converted to a dormitory for Western bachelor members of the project, but retained an enduring olfactory ovicaprine aura.

the very poor in major urban centers. Perhaps we might enunciate a law on laws: "The truth value of the preceding expectations are inversely related to the value of built space."

Not strictly ethnoarchaeological in their original intent, two additional studies are worthy of notice. One, by Bienkowski (1985), resulted from a brief survey (May–June 1983) of Bedul Bedouin habitations in cliff dwellings at the Jordanian site of Petra prior to their relocation by the government, then developing Petra as a tourist attraction. Bedul tribespeople occupied caves carved into Petra's sandstone cliffs by Nabataeans in the fourth century BC. Bienkowski's text is accompanied by three floor plans; clearly, these sites are quite different from the open-air camps of pastoralists described by Cribb (1991b), Hole (1978, 1979), and Watson (1979a), but their existence in caves suggests that a comparison with Ralph Solecki's (1979) account of seasonal occupants of Shanidar Cave (Iraq) might be in order. Of particular interest is the modification of cave interiors. Thus, while caves cannot be considered architectural structures, they are sometimes modified in important ways, can yield archaeological evidence of human habitation, and are often the loci of spatial recycling by successive inhabitants. This is certainly true, for example, of the Abri du Cro-Magnon in Les Eyzies (Dordogne, France), once the home of some of the earliest fully modern *sapiens* yet known from southwest France, but in recent years the garage of a multi-starred hotel much appreciated by Glyn Daniel and other hungry archaeologists.

Georges Castel (1984) has published a fascinating study, more ethnohistoric than ethnoarchaeological, but noteworthy both for its content and for its integration of various sources of data. In a series of superb floor plans, he documents the alteration of residential space in Egypt's Nile valley, where housing is at such a premium that the vacancy rate must be a negative figure. Many ancient Egyptian sites are occupied by what some would term "squatters," people taking advantage of uninhabited areas possessing walls and roofs. In the case Castel describes, over the period 1840–1973 several generations of a family occupied a pharaonic structure in the necropolis at Thebes. By 1971, the "house" had about 50 rooms and courtyards, divided among seven households comprising approximately 90 people descended from one ancestor. In accompanying figures, Castel indicates blocked doorways and bonded walls; such clues are here and elsewhere evidence of the reappropriation of structures, and not always by lower strata of the population. Archaeologists should pay as much attention to past inhabitants' reconstruction and rearticulation of structural features as they typically do to the excavation and reconstruction of the original architectural forms.

Sukur: the chiefly production of space

The inhabitants of the three Iranian villages described by Horne, Kramer, and Watson share an egalitarian ideology, and while it is clear that there is

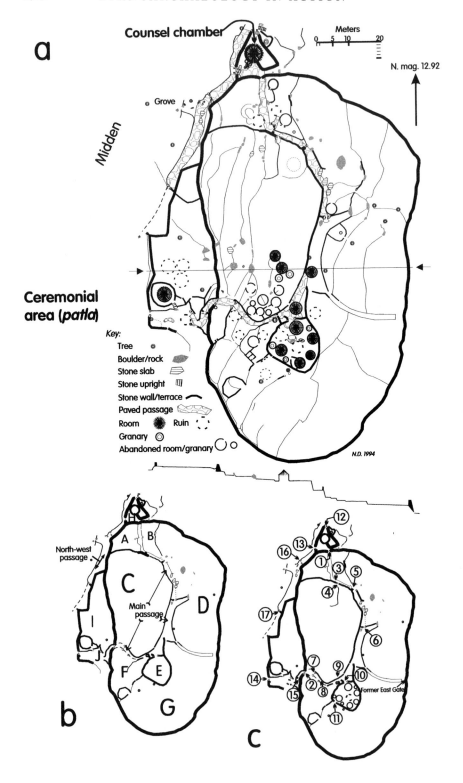

economic variation among households in these communities, and some architectural variation within them, there is no glaring case of distinctive or
"special" residential structures. In contrast to these studies, Adam Smith and
ND take a postprocessual approach to architecture in their study of the compound or "house" of the chief of Sukur in the Mandara mountains of northeastern Nigeria (Smith and David 1995). Drawing on the theoretical perspectives of
Harvey (1989), a postmodernist geographer, and the Marxist philosopher and
sociologist Lefebvre (1991), they aim to show how the chief's residence, built
largely of broken granite blocks, is "produced" as the material inscription of
social relations. Set in an ethnographic context recorded by Judy Sterner and
ND, the latter's plan of the complex (Fig.10.4), observations of its ceremonial
and other uses, and discussions, especially with a son of an important former
chief, constitute a database relating to its utilization and history that permits
the development of a gross relative chronology of its various sectors and identification of their functions and of numerous shrines.

Unlike some other Mandara montagnard chiefs, those of Sukur often acceded
to office through violent coups, and their power and privileges had constantly
to be negotiated and reinforced by various means. The chief's compound,
locally believed to have been constructed by supernatural beings in a single
night but more probably in fact by work parties of initiates and others no earlier
than the sixteenth century AD, can be conceptualized as an instrument for generating and maintaining chiefly power. Several strategies are employed. The
strategy of inclusion and the manipulation of proximal relations are exemplified by the building next to the main enclosing wall of the northern enclosure, with its large round room once used as a courtroom and still on occasions
as a counsel chamber. It is in this area and sectors A and B that initiates are

Fig. 10.4 (a) Plan and east–west section of the compound (house) of the chief
of Sukur, Adamawa State, Nigeria, 1993 (vertical scale of section
approximate); (b) sectors of the complex: A, now in ruins, the
quarters of the chief's sons between leaving their mothers' rooms
and marriage; B, now in ruins, a gate-keeper's room, bull and goat
pens, also stabling for the chief's horse, and the place where he is
dressed before certain public appearances; C: terraced fields adjacent
to the western wall, and a large flat area where the majority of
former chiefs' wives and small children were housed (most
structures now decayed); D: mainly fields, but with some structural
remains, said to be the rooms of old women taken in by the chief; E:
the inner house, where the chief lives with the wife who cooks for
him; F: ruined storerooms and other buildings, and terraces; G:
mainly fields, but with some structural remains that included
housing for wives; and, external to and later than the preceding
sectors, H: northern courtyard and counsel chamber; I: guest
accommodation, and J: west entrance features; (c) main gateways of
the complex. Plan by ND, modified after Smith and David 1995:
Fig. 4.

brought to be addressed by the chief and blessed by his "chaplain." Sector I, in which long-distance traders and other important visitors were housed, represents the extension of the chief's power into the economy and regional and national politics. The multiple gateways (see Fig.10.4c), many associated with shrines, are evidence of a strategy of exclusion, whereby entrance to and circulation within the compound were controlled by both physical and ritual means.

The chief lives with a single "cooking" wife in sector E, other wives formerly being housed in sectors C and parts of G. It is especially remarkable, given the Sukur and universal Mandara association of higher with superior, senior, and male, not only that the chief's residence is overlooked by others on nearby hills, but that his personal quarters are below those formerly inhabited by wives, and that visitors entering the main enclosure by either the western or northern gate descend paved passages to his audience chamber. Indeed the chiefly compound, once overflowing with wives, livestock, and other wealth, reverses rather than elaborates the features of the standard Sukur compound, metaphorically representing him as the "wife" of Sukur and nurturer of his people. By this third strategy, "the house simultaneously reifies real relations of inequality in spatial practice and obscures exploitation through ideological representations of space. Thus it both structures cultural production and ensures cultural reproduction" (p. 457).

Smith and David conclude by emphasizing four theoretical points: (1) the specific forms of landscape and built space are contingent upon historical developments; (2) space not only is defined by the exercise of power, but also recursively constrains and conditions power's further exercise; (3) general principles of spatial analysis such as exclusion and proximity lack significance outside particular cases; and (4) spatial practice is not simply a matter of architecture but also, as the metaphor of chief as wife indicates, of culturally conditioned perception. With increasing anthropological and archaeological interest in space and landscape evidenced by edited volumes such as Bender's (1993) *Landscape: politics and perspective* and Rossignol and Wandsnider's (1992) *Space, time and archaeological landscapes*, it will be interesting to see whether and how Smith and David's approach, certainly open to criticism for its heavy focus on power relations, will be taken up and developed.

Conclusions

The ethnoarchaeology of architecture is limited in volume and range, although, as Coudart demonstrates, archaeologists are quite capable of making good use of ethnographic – and other – data for interpretive and analogical purposes. We conclude this chapter with reflections on the ethnoarchaeology of architecture and its development, taking as our vantage point the conclusions to an early example of the genre, ND's (1971) paper on "The Fulani compound and the archaeologist." In that study, undertaken in a village where land was virtually a free good and the median life of cheaply built, daub and thatch, cone-on-cylinder huts was only about ten years, architecture was shown to express cultural norms and expectations and historical changes in village society quite precisely. This is not unlike CK's findings in Aliabad, except that variation from the cultural code is produced by opposite effects: impermanence and cheapness of structures at Bé, the Fulbe village, and higher costs and longer use of buildings in Kurdish Aliabad. Similar effects make it difficult, perhaps most markedly in Horne's Baghestan, to identify households, recognition of which is, ND argued, prerequisite to inference of higher-order social groupings – though perhaps not of broader social categories. The cost of buildings and even more of land upon which to build are prime factors in determining whether structures are built to suit people or people are forced to fit into structures.

Processual studies of architecture have been useful in identifying principles that underlie the relationship between people and their built environments. Some of these are local (e.g., the negative correlation at Bé between diameter of hut and expected intensity of white ant infestation), while others are likely to be more or less universally active though subject to varying cultural expression. These include devolutionary cycles of recycling, and the tendency for architecture to relate both to essentialist concepts about the nature of men and women and to ideas about status and role. It is clear also that there are some systemic biases in the household architectures of most cultures. While the existence of a household generally signals a male household head, and granaries or other features can be said to represent the family as a whole, men are associated with less domestic architecture, and often fewer artifacts, than women, and children go for the most part unrepresented in architectural terms. It is paradoxical that the androcentrism of most archaeology is associated with a material record that, in the domestic sphere, is most closely associated with females. It is in the public and ceremonial spheres that male dominance is most dramatically expressed, but Smith and ND's analysis of the house of the chief of Sukur is the closest ethnoarchaeology has yet come to studies of temples, stadiums, palaces, and government buildings.

Postprocessual ethnoarchaeological studies of architecture that look, for example, at the symbolism of architectural forms are few and far between.[4] Peter Dawson's (1995) paper on the symbolic violence done to Inuit family values in the Arctic by the imposition of Euro-Canadian housing falls in this general category, as does Nick Gabrilopoulos's (1995) MA thesis on the Tallensi compound (Ghana) in which he takes an approach informed by structuration theory, and Seamon's (1980: 157–9) concept of the place ballet, "a fusion of many actors' space–time routines in terms of place" (p. 120), arguing that social

---

[4] Linda Donley-Reid's (Donley 1982; Donley-Reid 1990b) and Diane Lyons's (1998) postprocessual research on Swahili houses and the expression of intimate relations in Mura architecture in northern Cameroon are briefly considered in chapter 13, as is Herbich and Dietler's (1994) paper on the Luo homestead as representation of the principle of complementary opposition.

engineering begins in the home, and that compound layout expresses social logic. The compound epitomizes defensible space, but vigilance directed to the exterior is also turned inward. The inward gaze of a hierarchy of watchers, ancestors at the top, elders for their own political ends, and so on down to the wife in her courtyard, keeps the inhabitants under surveillance, exerting moral force on their behavior.

There remains considerable room for more ethnoarchaeological studies of architecture, both processual and postprocessual.

Further reading

Richard Wilk (1983) usefully questions the value of common correlates for relating dwellings and their resident households, and shows how among the Kekchi Maya of Belize membership of and position within a household cluster is a significant variable. Diane Lyons, besides considering the expression of gender in architecture (1992), has also written on the politics of house shape in a small multi-ethnic town in northern Cameroon (1996). Roe and Siegel (1982) take a life history approach to study of a Shipibo compound. CK (1980) and William Sumner (1979, 1989) develop architectural and settlement area data for purposes of estimating prehistoric populations. While not ethnoarchaeology, Suzanne Preston Blier's (1987) *The anatomy of architecture: ontology and metaphor in Batammaliba architecture expression*, is a superb example of an antinaturalist approach to vernacular architecture.

CHAPTER 11

SPECIALIST CRAFT PRODUCTION AND APPRENTICESHIP

Craft specialization has long been recognized by Marxists and non-Marxists as a factor of significant weight in the development of complex societies.

(Maurizio Tosi 1984: 22)

As usual in archaeology, pottery provided the key . . .

(William Adams in Adams and Adams 1991: 101)

After introducing the topic of craft specialization and presenting typologies of the phenomenon, we discuss learning of crafts and apprenticeship, focusing on research in India that combines ethnoarchaeology with cognitive psychology. Most of the ethnoarchaeological literature on craft specialization relates either to ceramics or to metallurgy. As ceramics are extensively treated elsewhere in this book, we here limit ourselves to citing a range of studies relating to forms of craft specialization in pottery manufacture. We then present two contrasting approaches to the analysis of agate beadmaking that have conflicting implications for the interpretation of Harappan archaeology. The larger part of the chapter relates to the ethnoarchaeology of metallurgy. Iron smelting in Africa is emphasized, but we also consider blacksmithing and brasscasting.

Specialist craft production

The rise of craft specialization has been tied to numerous factors, including ranking and power structures . . . the rise of urbanism . . . elite and/or ritual goods . . . restricted access to raw materials . . . trade and exchange systems . . . and elite control of markets and allocation of resources . . . It has often been tied directly to metallurgy . . . Nevertheless although most scholars agree that specialization is part and parcel of the rise of social complexity, there is no consensus on the precise mechanisms involved in the rise of this phenomenon. (Rosen 1997: 112, references omitted)

The division of labor takes many forms and there are many kinds of specialists. In prehistoric periods most, including ritual (e.g., priests), medical (e.g., doctors, midwives), managerial (e.g., rulers and bureaucrats), and specialists in physical coercion (e.g., warriors and police), left only indirect or ambiguous evidence of their organization and activities. In many instances, this evidence includes the products of craft specialists. Thus we may infer the existence of architects from

303

arrangements of stone blocks, the work of masons, and of European Bronze Age elites from gold torcs and other jewelers' creations found in tumuli. For such reasons the identification of artisans practicing complex crafts and of those producing in bulk is a matter of particular interest to archaeologists hoping to develop a chain of inference leading from products, through the mode of production, to relations of production, systems of distribution, social organization and structure, and thus to the developmental processes that dynamically interrelate the many factors and institutions noted above by Steven Rosen.

Many social scientists, including ethnologists and sociologists, are interested in specialists, though generally less in artisans than in those whose expertise lies in the manipulation of information and people. When discussing crafts they tend to focus on those of major economic importance, on the social and economic organization of craftspeople, broad patterns of distribution of their products, and their articulation with society at large. They write about castes of specialists in West Africa, but are not particularly interested in the techniques employed or the material culture produced (e.g., Tamari 1991). Art historians, ceramicists, and metallurgists, on the other hand, focus on objects and techniques from their own specialized perspectives. Thus scholars in none of these disciplines provide the information archaeologists most need: data on the material correlates of different patterns of craft production and on their broader cultural significance. It follows that an interdisciplinary opportunity is wide open for ethnoarchaeologists to play their part in establishing linkages between such aspects of material culture and society. We are qualified to document the range and nature of craft specializations, including those, for example the making of manos and metates (Hayden 1987b), unlikely to receive attention from other social scientists. We can inquire into the scale of specialization, and into whether and why specialists work full-time, seasonally, or part-time, into how specialist knowledge of materials and techniques is encoded, and how it is controlled and transmitted within and between generations. Such inquiries lead to understanding of the causes of standardization and variation in the output of various crafts. Ethnoarchaeologists can also seek to show how patterns of distribution of material items result from the interaction of certain modes of specialist production with particular means of distribution and consumption, and how such patterns relate to sociocultural entities of various kinds. In preceding chapters we have touched on several of these matters, on Balfet's (1965) demonstration that pot quality and decoration covary with mode of production in North Africa for example, or Dietler and Herbich's (1994) argument that Luo style areas, rather than representing Luo sub-tribes, correspond to areas served by trans-tribal markets in which the differentiated products of potter communities become mixed and their stylistic variety homogenized. We treat several of the above questions, but are constrained by existing biases in the literature. The overall paucity of sources can be explained in large part by the youth of the discipline and the need for practitioners to understand and describe basic techniques of manufacture and types of product before beginning to work at a larger scale.

Organization of craft production

Several archaeologists have formulated typologies of production that cover the range from elderly women working at home to proletarian masses toiling in factories. Some, with a view to facilitating archaeologists' interpretations of the materials they recover, attempt to identify archaeological attributes peculiar to specific forms of organization. Three of the most widely cited typologies are by van der Leeuw (1977), Peacock (1982), and Costin (1991). The first two relate specifically to ceramics. Van der Leeuw's (Table 11.1) is largely based on ethnoarchaeological data, some gathered by himself. The characteristics of the examples cited should be regarded as illustrative rather than diagnostic of the various types, and the typology says nothing about who controls production. Peacock's sub-title is "an ethnoarchaeological approach," but his book is primarily a study based on data from the Roman world, prefaced with descriptive comments drawn from a diverse literature. To the dimensions of scale and intensity (as in van der Leeuw's), his classification adds the degree of elite or governmental participation. Similarly, Costin (1991: 8–9), noting Earle's (1981) distinction between independent specialists and those attached to an elite, and Sinopoli's (1988) categories of independent, centralized, and administered specialists, has suggested that four parameters – degree of elite sponsorship, concentration in space, scale, and intensity – characterize the organization of production, and she has produced an eight-part typology that draws on a variety of archaeological and, to a more limited extent, ethnographic and ethnoarchaeological literature. Her categories and their approximate van der Leeuw equivalents are set out in Table 11.2. While such studies can alert archaeologists to relevant variables, they dwell if at all only momentarily on the nuanced ways in which social relationships between artisans affect craft production, nor can they explain how changes from one to another of these generic modes might occur.

Like Prudence Rice (1987), Costin and others have argued that (regardless of kinship relationships among artisans) craft specialization may be recognizable in the archaeological record when product standardization can be documented. We discuss this below in relation to Roux's (1989) research in India. Longacre (1999) is among the few ethnoarchaeologists to have collected data on standardization who also considers the sociological relationships among potters. In important early work, Margaret Hardin (1977, 1983a) discussed the identification of motifs, designs and design structure, kin-based work groups, and the influence of kinship and personality on the transmission of designs on painted pottery in Michoacán, Mexico.

Thus far it is the crafts of ceramics and metallurgy that shed most light on

Table 11.1 *Typology and characteristics of modes of production, with selected examples drawn from ceramics, modified after van der Leeuw (1977)*

		Household production	Household industry	Individual industry	Workshop industry	Village industry	Large-scale industry
	Primary examples →	Kabyles (N. Africa)	Fulbe, Gisiga, Lame (northern Cameroon)	Ladakhis (W. Tibet)	Farnham (UK)	Tzintzuntzan (Mexico)	Wedgwood (UK)
Economy	*time involved*	occasional	part-time	full-time	full-time	part/full-time	full-time
	persons involved	one	one or few	one	several	several	many
	gender	women	women	men	men	men, women	men, women
	organization	none	none	none	(guild)	certain	certain
	locality	sedentary or itinerant	sedentary or while visiting	itinerant	sedentary	sedentary	sedentary
	hired hands	none	none	none	some	some	labor force
	market	own use	group use	regional	village/town	region	region/export
	raw materials						
	clay	local	local	local	neighborhood	neighborhood	neighborhood/distant
	temper	local	local	local	neighborhood	neighborhood	neighborhood/distant
	water	local	local	local	local	local	local
	fuel	local	local	local	neighborhood	neighborhood	neighborhood/distant
	investments	none	none	few	some	some	capital
	seasonality	production as needed	season without other work	all year except winter	all year/good weather	all year/good weather	all year
	labor division	none	none	none	some/considerable	some/considerable	detailed

	high amateur	high semi-specialist	medium specialist (many techniques)	medium-low specialist	medium-low specialist	low specialist (few techniques)
time per pot						
status	high amateur	high semi-specialist	medium specialist (many techniques)	medium-low specialist	medium-low specialist	low specialist (few techniques)
Technology manuf. techns.	hand/small tools	hand/small tools	hand/small tools	mold/wheel	mold/wheel	wheel/cast/press
tools/facilities						
settling basin	none	none	none	when needed	when needed	needed
wheel	none	none; rotary support	turntable	var. kinds	var. kinds	kickwheel or similar
drying shed	none	none	none	needed	needed	needed
firing/kiln	open firing	open firing/impermanent	impermanent			
raw materials						
clay	wide range	wide range	wide range	narrower range	narrower range	narrow range
temper	wide range	wide range	wide range	narrower range	narrower range	narrow range
water	any	any	any	any	any	any
fuel	wide range	wide range	wide range	narrower range	narrower range	narrow range
range of pottery	narrow	narrow or wide	wide	narrow or wide	narrow or wide	narrow or wide
range of functions per pot	wide	narrower	wide	narrower	narrower	narrower
Reference	Balfet 1965	David and Hennig 1972	Asboe 1946	Brears 1970	Foster 1965	

Table 11.2 *Comparison of Costin's and van der Leeuw's typologies of specialist production*

Costin (1991)	van der Leeuw (1977)
individual specialization	household production and industry
dispersed workshop	workshop industry
community specialization	village industry
nucleated workshops	workshop industry (aggregated)
dispersed corvée	household or village industry working on a part-time basis for an elite or governmental personage(s) or institution
individual retainers	individual industry, but attached to an elite or governmental personage(s) or institution
nucleated corvée (part-time labor recruited by a government institution, working in a special-purpose, elite, or administered setting or facility)	no precise equivalent
retainer workshop (working for an elite patron or government institution)	something less than large-scale industry

the relationship between gender and craft production. In a number of geographic areas, perhaps most notably in India and Africa (see chapter 7), there are endogamous specialist groups. For example, among the Bambara of the Inland Niger Delta of West Africa, women potters marry smiths; Fulbe potters, also women, marry weavers, shoemakers, and coopers (Gallay *et al.* 1996). Natalie Tobert's (1988) monograph describes casted Zaghawa and other specialists in Darfur, focusing on the women's ceramic output, and there is a considerable literature on the work of casted smith-potters in the Mandara mountains of Cameroon and Nigeria (Sterner and David 1991). In such instances, as in much of India, the acquisition of skills (discussed below) runs along caste or caste-like lines. That is, an occupational specialty is learned and shared within endogamous groups which often have distinctive names and sometimes live in circumscribed areas within settlements. None of the typologies of production mentioned earlier in this chapter pays adequate attention to this form of specialization which, in various contexts around the world, spans the van der Leeuw range from household to workshop and village industry.

In the case of Indian potters, as elsewhere where pottery is wheel-thrown, men make almost all the vessels. Their mothers, wives, sisters, daughters, and daughters-in-law, however, are active participants in every other stage of production: processing clays and pigments, decorating vessels, assisting with firing, and distributing the final products (Kramer 1997). It may be noted par-

Fig. 11.1 A female member of India's potter caste paddles a lid, using the spherical base of a broken water jar as a mold, Rajasthan, 1982. This is one of the rare situations in which women in India form vessels, although they routinely participate in most other aspects of ceramic production.

enthetically that, while in this strongly patrilineal and virilocal society men tend to learn from male kin, their in-marrying wives, who may have been apprenticed as children or adolescents in their natal communities, must sometimes adapt to new craft traditions when they move to their husbands' homes (Figs. 11.1, 11.2). Pre-adaptation to working as a potter is discussed briefly by David and Hennig (1972) in a study of a multi-ethnic community in Cameroon, and is also remarked on in Mali by Gallay *et al.* (1996).

In South Asia, where pottery is hand-made it is, as in Cameroon, Amazonia, and many other areas, produced by women. Dean Arnold (1975a 1975b, 1984a, 1985, 1993) has emphasized the roles of ecology and scheduling in such decisions, though one may be forgiven for suggesting a simple rule: if a craft is dirty and doesn't pay much but can be undertaken on a flexible schedule and at no great distance from the household it will be the domain of women; should it become profitable men will take it over. There is much work here for ethnoarchaeologists.

Fig. 11.2 The 11-year-old daughter of a Hindu potter in Udaipur, Rajasthan, paints her father's pots during the first season of her apprenticeship, 1982. Young painters, all female, are typically observed, criticized, and praised by their maternal kin, whether older sisters, mothers, or paternal grandmothers. When girls marry into the homes of potters, they sometimes receive additional training from female in-laws.

Learning and apprenticeship

The manner whereby craft skills are transmitted and learned affects continuity and change in cultural traditions. Ethnoarchaeological texts on crafts commonly include a brief statement regarding the route or routes of transmission of the technology. For example Michael Stanislawski (1977: 395–401), in questioning assumptions underlying early attempts by Longacre (1968) and Hill (1968) to reconstruct kinship from sherds, provides data on the relationships of some Hopi potters and their pupils. Ingrid Herbich's (1987) discussion of the context in which Luo potters learn their trade is already familiar from our discussion of style, and we have mentioned Hardin's work on design structure and transmission. Chapurukha Kusimba (1996: 391–3), describing the apprenticeship of smiths on the Kenya coast, summarizes the six stages of training and ritual through which they have to pass before graduating to their own forges. Such information is valuable but tells us little of the cognitive and psychomotor *processes* of acquiring skills. Warren DeBoer (1990) has studied how girls learn the Shipibo-Conibo art style (Fig. 11.3), and, after describing eight cases of transmission, summarizes his results diagrammatically (Fig. 11.4).[1] The picture is far from simple for, while "settlement size and the social origin of artists do not appear to have any stunningly significant impact on the fidelity of stylistic transmission," their particular family situations and psychological states clearly do. While the optimist may regard these data as supporting a "largely imitational mode of design acquisition . . . a skeptic . . . might be very uneasy with any theory that accounts for only two-thirds of all observations" (p. 100)!

Hayden and Cannon's "general model"

In 1984, Hayden and Cannon, concerned about the combination of untested assumptions and lack of actual studies that underlay the interaction theory of style, attempted to systematize the fragmentary ethnographic information on the relationship between craft learning and intracommunity interaction. They devised a set of six learning modes – Family-Centered, Corporate, Kin-Extensive, Minimally Structured, Formal Schooling, and Specialist – distinguished by the social distance between teacher and learner and the "number of learning sources that individuals are exposed to" (1984b: 327). Each mode is associated with expectations that in retrospect appear simplistic and overformalized, especially as the authors tend to regard stylistic elements as if they were genes subject to particulate inheritance.

While their constructs have not been incorporated into the canonical literature, Hayden and Cannon (1984b) used Coxoh project data to describe learning

---

[1] Unfortunately a lengthier paper (DeBoer 1975) on children's art was never published.

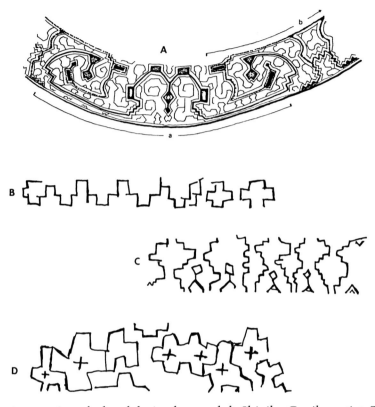

Fig. 11.3. A: a portion of a band design by an adult Shipibo-Conibo artist. The design is painted in black (solid) and red (stippled) pigments over the white-slipped upper body of a beer mug; "a" and "b" refer to two major motifs that are repeated to complete the band. B–D: designs painted by 7-year-olds from a different (B–C) and the same (D) village. Note the prominence of either isolated or concatenated cross-shaped elements. (DeBoer 1990: Fig. 9.3.)

frameworks in the three Maya communities studied. These societies are characterized by weak-to-moderate development of corporate groups, and are

internally nonstratified peasant communities, with little or no hereditary ranking, although individual differences in wealth, social rank, and influence in decision making are present . . . The economies are dominated by marginal subsistence agriculture which generally requires a substantial network of cooperative relationships. (p. 341)

Such institutions, networks of social interaction, and economic integration are associated with the Kin-Extensive learning mode, perhaps in this instance shifting, owing to increasing wage labor and "rudimentary specialization," towards the Family-Centered mode. Hayden and Cannon necessarily rely primarily on questionnaire data from 154 households. Their results are of value in documenting (a) the number of crafts practiced, 30 in all and mainly, one infers,

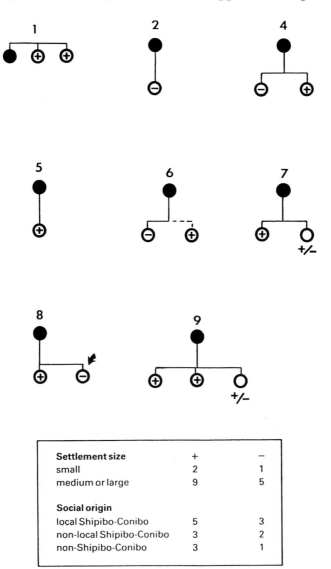

Settlement size	+	−
small	2	1
medium or large	9	5
Social origin		
local Shipibo-Conibo	5	3
non-local Shipibo-Conibo	3	2
non-Shipibo-Conibo	3	1

Fig. 11.4 Diagrammatic summary of eight cases of design transmission among the Shipibo-Conibo. Solid circles refer to teachers, open circles to students. A plus sign indicates a student whose art closely resembles that of her teacher; a minus sign lack of such resemblance. Plus/minus refers to a student who shifts styles, alternately producing art that resembles, or differs significantly, from her teacher's. The arrow in case 8 indicates that the student did not learn art primarily from her mother, but rather from unidentified outside sources. The table at the bottom plots the frequency of cases of resemblance or dissimilarity against settlement size and social origin of the artists. (DeBoer 1990: Fig. 9.15.)

Table 11.3 *Distribution of teachers of all crafts in three Mesoamerican villages. Each record represents one instance of craft learning. Recalculated from Hayden and Cannon (1984b: Table 5)*

	Family of orientation	Extended family	Friends	Others	Self-taught	N
n	470	81	45	74	107	777
%	60.5	10.4	5.8	9.5	13.8	100

on a part-time basis, ranging from broom making and weaving to construction wood manufacturing, and radio repair, and (b) that while by far the most learning of crafts takes place in the family, teachers may also come from the extended family, friends, and others, and a not insignificant proportion (13.8 percent) of crafts were claimed to be self-taught, including 38.1 percent of hunting, and a surprising 22.6 percent of construction wood manufacturing and 45.5 percent of furniture manufacturing (Table 11.3). Hayden and Cannon show that the more frequently a craft is practiced in the household of orientation, the more likely is learning influenced by the family, rarely practiced crafts being more frequently taught by persons outside the family. Though not unexpected, this is well worth stating. However, it is certainly untrue "that pottery, and perhaps most crafts, will only be learned from mothers when the volume of production is considerably above the needs of the household" (p. 350). What, for instance, about the household production and consumption of Shipibo-Conibo pottery, and what about sewing? Other factors, cultural and ideological as well as economic, are involved.

The authors' tabulations fail to specify the genders of teacher–learner dyads, and indeed we only learn incidentally that certain crafts are associated with a particular gender. On the other hand, males and persons of higher economic rank are shown to be more likely than females or the poor to learn from a teacher outside the nuclear or extended family. Learning is in this respect an aspect of and influenced by general interaction patterns.

Learning patterns of the Kin-Extensive mode should produce "a relatively random distribution of styles within communities and a greater variety of styles within individual households where more than one craftsperson is present" (p. 357). This is exemplified by reference to a single attribute, the body form of *ollas*. There are problems with this argument and indeed with the whole approach in that style is too simply viewed as reflecting the strength and character of cooperative interaction within and between social units, and, it would seem, as being generally transmitted like genes from teacher to learner.[2]

---

[2] Though not entirely, since we are told that some potters may copy from purchased pots, others only from certain kin, others from pots they saw and liked in a variety of contexts. More surprisingly, "others don't like the forms their teachers make" (p. 357).

Thus, for example, one of the principles enunciated in the conclusion of the article is that "strong, residential corporate groups will tend to maximize cooperative interaction between members . . . [creating] very discrete learning pools which have the greatest potential to produce stylistically different crafts" (pp. 359–60). This ignores the variable internal dynamics of social units (which might stimulate or repress stylistic variation), relations between social units, and larger-scale factors that can affect communities or society at large, at times reducing the range of sanctioned stylistic variation, as Hodder (1982a) argues is the case in the context of inter-group competition among Baringo tribes, at times allowing more variety to flourish.

Hayden and Cannon's (1984b) paper is less successful than "Where the garbage goes . . ." (1983) in part because of theoretical weaknesses, in part because questionnaire data are simply inadequate, even when complemented by a little observation, to investigate the learning of crafts, especially when the investigator's knowledge of the culture is limited. Discard practices, more easily observed, sampled, and quantified than craft acquisition, are more effectively studied by the methods employed by the Coxoh project team, although, as discussed in chapter 4, even in this area naturalist approaches have their limitations. Subsequent research on learning crafts, discussed in the following section, focuses on particular cases of craft specialization, and there have as yet been no second tries at achieving the overall synthesis that Hayden and Cannon were bold enough to attempt.

In concluding this section we should note that there exists a literature on situated learning and cognition that forms part of the anthropology of knowledge. Charles and Janet Keller's book *Cognition and tool use: the blacksmith at work* (1996) is an example of special interest to ethnoarchaeologists in that Charles Keller, an archaeologist, obtained a large part of the data by participant observation, apprenticing himself to a blacksmith in the United States. Ethnoarchaeological sources in this area are rare and have, to our knowledge, only been carried out by Francophone researchers who have engaged in experimental field studies, sometimes facilitated by technological advances that permit the use of accelerometers and other equipment outside the laboratory. Hélène Wallaert's research (1998a 1998b), combining psychology and ergonomics in a study of the impact of left and right handedness on teaching and learning procedures among potters in northern Cameroon, takes an original approach, but has as yet seen only preliminary publication. Its demonstration of the influence of societal values on the transmission of technical skills and the varied forms that apprenticeship can take in societies at a comparable level of social complexity should be borne in mind when considering the following case study.

Fig. 11.5 Valentine Roux arrives at a potter's workshop in Uttam Nagar, New Delhi, 1986.

A transcultural definition of specialization?

Is it possible to arrive at an objective measure of craft specialization that can be applied to archaeological data? This is the question that Valentine Roux, an ethnoarchaeologist of the Francophone logicist school (Fig. 11.5),[3] sets out to study in collaboration with Daniela Corbetta, a cognitive psychologist specializing in the development of children's psychomotor skills. As so often, the general question is approached through ceramics. Roux (1989, 1990) notes that in the area of the Harappan civilization there are, during the fourth and third

---

[3] Roux (1989: Fig. 20) provides a logicist diagram of the first part of her study. Alain Gallay's foreword to the book is a clear statement of the logicist ethnoarchaeological agenda.

millennia BC, developmental changes in pottery. Wheel throwing appears and a gradual mastering of the technique is expressed in an increase in the maximum size of vessels. At the same time throwing replaces coiling. Roux relates these archaeological data to her ethnoarchaeological observations in Uttam Nagar, a suburb of New Delhi, and in nearby Haryana state. There boys, starting at age eight to ten and continuing into adulthood, pass through a locally recognized series of stages of apprenticeship during which they learn to throw progressively larger pots. This for Roux constitutes craft specialization, which to her is defined by the acquisition of difficult psychomotor skills that can only be achieved during a prolonged apprenticeship.[4] The coiling technique is here traditionally applied only to tandoori ovens, made by males, and to cooking hearths and small granaries, which are made by females (with fancy jars as a modern introduction). The skills required for building the ovens, the most difficult to make, are achieved in about a year after an apprenticeship starting in adolescence. Roux does not regard these workers as specialists.

Roux hypothesizes that the progression seen in the archaeological record and the stages of apprenticeship are in some ways comparable, suggesting that society was changing during the fourth and third millennia in ways that favored investment in specialist skills even though this delayed the returns on labor that would otherwise have been expected from maturing children.[5] Her working hypothesis is that the relationship between wheel throwing of pottery and craft specialization can be established by comparing the learning processes associated with wheel throwing on the one hand and coil building on the other. The results of her ethnographic comparisons, based on observations, video recordings, and interviews, of artisans employing wheel throwing and coiling techniques are summarized in a comparative table (Table 11.4). But Roux and Corbetta also carry out a series of experiments that test the performances of sets of apprentices at various stages and of non-potters at comparable ages in surrogates for the psychomotor tasks associated with making wheel-thrown pottery (Fig. 11.6). The results of these tests convincingly demonstrate that over the course of their apprenticeship potters acquire psychomotor skills associated with throwing pots that differentiate them from non-potters. Inasmuch as these skills are common to wheel throwing of pots everywhere, the relationship between wheel throwing of pottery and specialization should be valid transculturally.

In order to be able to relate these findings to archaeological materials, Roux needs to establish the material signatures of the different stages of apprenticeship. This she achieves by performing a typological analysis on a corpus of

---

[4] Roux (1989: 5) formally defines craft specialization as "the takeover by part of the population of a craft activity, the products of which are consumed by the community," but this is inadequate and by no means the sense she gives the phrase in the body of her work.

[5] Inasmuch as apprentices carry out a considerable variety of useful tasks around the workshop, it would seem that the actual cost of apprenticeship, reckoned as the difference between the value of their production while working as apprentices and their potential earnings in other jobs, including oven-making, is likely to be quite small.

Table 11.4 *Traits which distinguish the wheel throwing technique from the coiling technique (slightly modified from Roux 1989: 70, Table 4)*

Wheel throwing technique	Coiling technique
Actions on clay mediated by wheel	Actions performed directly on clay
Potter is still (squats) while clay turns	Potter moves around motionless clay
Operations of potter consist in successively transforming a single mass of clay	Operations of potter consist in successively assembling pieces of clay
An unsuccessful operation cannot be corrected	An unsuccessful operation can be corrected at any point
Success of one operation determines that of the next	Success of each operation is independent
Mastery of the technique requires development of specific motor abilities	Mastery of the technique requires no particular motor ability
Apprenticeship is by trial and error	Apprenticeship is scaffolded*
Apprenticeship is long and arduous	Apprenticeship is short and easy

Notes:
* By scaffolding is meant that the teacher is involved in every phase of construction, the pupil being left on his or her own only after acquiring the requisite know-how. The pupil is saved from failing even with the first items made.

ethnographic material made by the apprentice potters. Statistics shown to be significantly related to the stage of apprenticeship include the absolute height of vessels (only apprentices in the third and last stage manufacturing pots over 22 cm high) and the height : thickness ratio. Other measures serving to differentiate stages of apprenticeship include indices of regularity of manufacture and or standardization – all based, it should be noted, on characteristics of pots that are observable in the archaeological record.

In a second phase of research Roux develops a taxonomy that expresses the degree of difficulty of throwing restricted and unrestricted vessels of various forms. After defining a series of forms related to those found in the chalcolithic of the Indus basin, she arranges to have these manufactured by three sets of potters of different degrees of competence. She then elaborates a techno-morphological taxonomy relating to the degree of difficulty of manufacture of the various forms that is based upon the potters' own evaluations. This is then checked (a) against the corpus of pots manufactured by the potters and observations made during the course of their manufacture, and (b) by seeking the opinions of French wheel-using potters, who, by and large, agree with the opinions of their Indian counterparts. Theoretically then, her results could be applied to archaeological ceramics, and particularly those of the Indus valley chalcolithic, with a view to reconstructing in precise detail the history of the

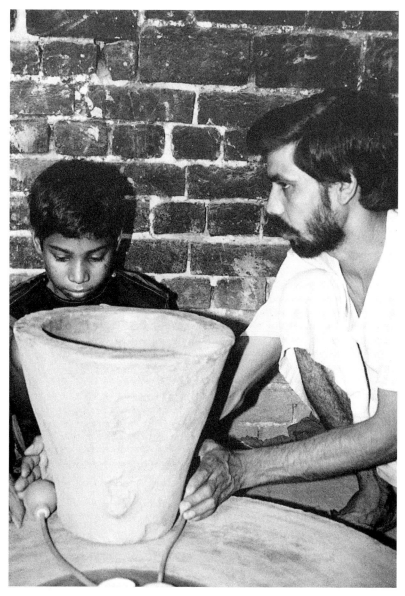

Fig. 11.6 An apprentice is instructed by Har Kishan, Roux's assistant and an accomplished potter, in preparation for a test of his ability to maintain identical left- and right-hand pressure for a period of five seconds on bulbs of Jaquet manometers, Uttam Nagar, 1986. The experiment simulates the bimanual skills required to center a lump of clay on the wheel. The low wheel is larger than that used by apprentices and it is for this reason that the flower pot is placed near its outer edge.

mastering of this specialization, and ultimately inferring from such a recon-struction broader conclusions regarding the changing nature of Indus society.

That her results have not been, to the best of our knowledge, so applied requires some explanation. While the approach is logically impeccable, the utility of the results is questionable on two main grounds. First, in this part of India the range of vessel forms that are made by coiling or throwing alone is very limited. For example, large wheel-thrown rough-outs are characteristi-cally completed by paddling. Thus the potters studied can be considered repre-sentative neither of wheel throwing nor of coiling potters generally, nor even of those of the Indus region during the chalcolithic. Second, her techno-morphological taxonomy is (a) extremely complex (one of her figures shows 44 restricted and unrestricted vessel forms graded in order of increasing difficulty of execution [1990: Fig. 26]), (b) applicable only to complete or reconstructable vessels, and (c) immediately applicable only to Harappan ceramics, whereas what most archaeologists would appreciate more is a grosser taxonomy that can profitably be applied to wheel-thrown sherds anywhere.

In summary, Roux and Corbetta's work succeeds in establishing transcultu-ral standards in terms of which a particular kind of specialization can be defined, one involving the acquisition over an extended period of difficult psychomotor skills, and in relating these standards directly to material signa-tures. But, owing to (a) the limited range of vessels formed by throwing and coiling in this part of India, and (b) problems in extending to archaeological series the derived sequence of difficulty of execution, it is much less clear that Roux has developed a viable methodology for the detection and measurement of this kind of specialization in the archaeological record. (One might wish that she had chosen to work in Pakistan, where potters throw a wider range of forms [Rye and Evans 1976].) It would surely be worth following up and confirming Roux and Corbetta's results among other wheel-using potters, not to mention attempting to develop similar measures among those making pottery by coiling, press-molding, and other techniques, some of which in our experience require a considerably longer apprenticeship than for those practicing coiling in Haryana and New Delhi.[6] As yet however, while Roux and colleagues have taken a similar approach to the reconstruction of production of Indus stone beads (see below), no one appears to have followed her lead in the field of ceramics.

With appropriate modifications Roux's approach to ceramics and beads is potentially applicable to other domains of material culture, including the forging and casting of metal, carpentry, and stone masonry. However, for her method to yield valid results it is essential that the artifact (or at least well-

---

[6] But what are we to make of the difference between the superb pots made by Gobway of Sirak (seen in the film *Vessels of the spirits* . . . [David 1990]) and the heavier and cruder pots of very similar forms made by the Wula a few kilometers away? It is interesting that Nancy Benco (1988) found that the standardization of coil-built pots made by "domestic potters" in a Kalinga village in the Philippines was as great as that of wheel-thrown pots from Islamic Basra (Morocco).

defined and recognizable stages in its manufacture) be the work of a single individual. It could not be appropriately applied in a situation where apprentices prepared rough-outs to be completed by a master or mistress whose work obliterated the traces of their activity. It is particularly unfortunate that nowhere in the world is a substantial range of lithics still being knapped in Stone Age mode – but even in the absence of ethnoarchaeological data, Roux's approach can be of value in guiding research, as for example in the study and interpretation of Magdalenian lithic chaînes opératoires. Lastly we should also remember that there are behavioral packages that we would not hesitate to characterize as craft specialization that do not require the development of particular psychomotor skills. Smelting, where the skills reside in the head rather than in the hands, and where the apprentice's work is part and parcel of the master's, is a good example. Thus Roux and Corbetta's research gives us only a partial key to decoding the mysteries of specialization. But it is a fine beginning.

Examples of craft specialization

Ceramic studies

Kramer (1985), Arnold (1984b), and Eggert (1991) have surveyed the field of ceramic ethnoarchaeology, overall the ethnoarchaeologists' most popular topic for research, in part from the perspective of craft specialization. In this and previous chapters and in greater or lesser detail we have discussed several ceramic cases relevant to the topic, notably DeBoer's (e.g., 1984, 1990; DeBoer and Lathrap 1979) work on household production among the Shipibo-Conibo, and two studies of household industry, one by David and Hennig (1972) in northern Cameroon, the other, on a wider canvas, by Gosselain (e.g., 1992a, 1995) in the south of that country. Miller (1985) described workshop industry practiced by casted potters in an Indian village. (Kramer's [1997] research into the same type of organization of production which she studied on a much larger scale in two Indian cities is discussed in the next chapter in relation to distribution and exchange.) Village industry is represented by the research of Longacre's Kalinga team (see Longacre and Skibo 1994), and we paid special attention in chapter 7 to Graves's (1994) analysis of inter-village and inter-community stylistic variation. Balfet's (1965) research among the Kabyles spanned household production and household and workshop industry and was an important element of the database available to van der Leeuw for the development of his typology. Workshop industry specialization is also reported for potters in southern Egypt (Nicholson and Patterson 1991). Here, about 400 miles south of Cairo, male potters produce only one vessel type, an amphora-like water jar. Individual potters, who claim to be able to identify their own vessels on the basis of slight variations in rim form, depend on middlemen to distribute their wares. The claim to be able to identify one's own work, seemingly a recurring theme

Fig. 11.7 Kuldeep K. Bhan and J. Mark Kenoyer document heated beads at a workshop in Khambhat, India, 1989–90 season.

among potters (and likely other artisans), has not been documented in detail, but seems worthy of further study. A range of archaeological questions center on archaeologists' ability to identify individual craftsmen (Hill and Gunn 1977), and ethnoarchaeological studies of micromotor variation and change in performance with age could be informative.

There are, so far as we know, no ethnoarchaeological studies of large-scale industry whether ceramic or other.

We list selected studies of ceramic production under further reading below, but, inasmuch as ceramics are already sufficiently covered elsewhere in this book, have chosen to subject another specialist craft, that of agate beadmaking in India, to closer scrutiny, before turning to a discussion of metallurgy.

Khambhat beadmaking: socioeconomic and activity analysis approaches

A team of scholars led by J. Mark Kenoyer and interested primarily in the archaeology of the Harappan civilization of the third and second millennia BC has investigated the production of agate beads in India (Fig. 11.7). They are dissatisfied with a concept of craft specialization that they perceive to be "in its operational usage . . . a *state of being* that is achieved in the course of technological and social evolution" (Kenoyer *et al.* 1991: 46). Instead, they see craft specialization as an adaptive process, continuous in both space and time, and have turned to ethnoarchaeology as a means of developing models of craft specialization that can be applied archaeologically in the absence of written records or a rich iconography. Where these are lacking, they propose to

develop models to investigate the control [of] production by a limited number of individuals and to develop a ranking of crafts, both in terms of a scale of production and the socioeconomic importance for the overall economy. This ranking can be attempted through a careful evaluation of several factors: the raw material availability; the technologies used to produce specific objects; the degree of economic interconnection of a given production cycle with the other industrial cycles; and the patterns of distribution of those commodities. (Kenoyer *et al.* 1991: 48)

Stone beadmaking was once widely practiced in the Indian subcontinent, but in India is now largely restricted to a single center, the city of Khambhat in Gujarat, western India. Its beadmaking industry is the source of the analogy that they apply to the Harappan subject.

The several stages of beadmaking from mining to finished product are summarized in Table 11.5 and do not require further discussion. The production of beads was for a long time and is still in large part subject to the control of a varied but powerful elite group of Khambhat merchants. Mining is undertaken by laborers working for mining contractors, some with hereditary contracts with Khambhat merchants, and some agate nodules are collected and stockpiled by middlemen, but from that point on a small number of well-connected Hindu, Jain, and Muslim merchant houses are in direct control of most of the production. They rigidly supervise the work of full- and part-time beadworkers, some toiling in the merchants' own centralized workshops while others undertake piecework at home or in dispersed, smaller workshops. The industrial power of the merchant family houses has depended primarily on their control, by political and other means, of labor. This has been undermined in the past generation or two by the introduction of electrical machines that grind, drill, and polish beads many times more quickly than traditional hand techniques. Small entrepreneurs have seized on the possibility of substituting capital for labor and have taken over a part of production on their own accounts. As with production, so with distribution: while small-scale traders, pilgrims, and others trade and otherwise distribute beads, the merchant houses act as wholesalers, controlling the main lines of distribution throughout the Indian subcontinent and beyond to Nepal, Tibet, China, Afghanistan, Iran, the Arab countries, Africa, Europe, and the Americas.

The archaeological signature of this highly centralized production system was investigated by both ethnographic observation and post-mortem excavation of beadmaking workshops.[7] Such is the degree of control over those employed on piecework in dispersed workshops that they are required to report

---

[7] While other sources mention these excavations, Vidale *et al.* (1993) offer the fullest account.

Table 11.5 *The production of beads in Khambhat, Gujarat, India. Data for this necessarily simplified representation from Kenoyer et al. (1991, 1994). Inferences by the authors of this book and lack of data are marked by queries*

Production stage and techniques	Tools and materials	Product	Labor	Period	Archaeological traces	Comments
mining by tunneling	simple	agate nodules	casual labor (men, women, children)	dry season pre- and post-monsoon	tunnels, tools	In Gujarat (laborers from Bhil tribe) and Baluchistan
quality control by test flaking	?nodules	selected agate nodules	? as above	as above	scatters of cortex flakes and reject nodules	? transport cheap therefore no blocking out/dressing blanks
collection and stock-piling	? none	selected agate nodules	? as above	? as above	? none	as above
transport from mines to Khambhat	trad. boat, oxcart; more recently railway, trucks	selected agate nodules	?	?	? none	
drying by exposure to sun next to house or workshop, on roofs	? none	selected agate nodules	beadmakers and their families, employees	March–May	Scatter and loss of some lower-quality materials	location chosen to protect better-quality stone from theft
heating by baking for up to three days (pots), one day (kilns)	pots, sawdust; pit kilns (permanent kilns in larger workshops), rice husks	agate nodules ready for chipping	specialist beadmaker; skilled kiln supervisor in larger workshops	April–?	pots, kilns, kiln ash with spalled and broken nodules	drying and heating to change color and flaking qualities
sawing of large nodules to conserve materials	trad. with copper/iron saw and emery abrasive	sawn nodule fragments	? specialist beadmakers in centralized workshops	before or after chipping	sawing detectable on flakes later removed	electric saws now used
chipping by inverse direct percussion	pointed iron stake, wood or horn hammer	bead roughouts	? part and full time beadmakers in dispersed and centralized workshops	? full time in larger centralized workshops	scatter of mainly small and micro flaking debris; or (temp.) dumps	recycling and dumping produces characteristic patterns

Process	Technology	Labor	Product	Timing	Material evidence	Notes
recycling and sale of rejected nodules and debitage	? none	beadmakers, merchants	selected debitage, later flaked into small bead roughouts	? occasional	scatter of rejected material, and of mainly small and micro flaking debris	see above
repeated secondary heating (up to 10)	small pots, ash, kilns; sawdust, cow dung	specialist beadmaker; skilled kiln supervisor in larger workshops	roughouts transformed into carnelian, etc.	? non-seasonal, dependent upon labor availability	pots, kilns, kiln ash, cracked beads	kiln waste provides evidence of scale, quality, bead types
grinding	trad. on sandstone or quartzite grindstone	? part and full time beadmakers in dispersed and centralized workshops	ground beads	? as above	various types of grindstone, agate dust, some broken beads	
drilling (may be before or after polishing)	diamond tipped metal drills, wooden vise, water pot, thread and wire device drops water on to bead for cooling	farmers working part-time in dispersed localities	ground (or polished) and drilled beads, agate powder for polishing	not in farming season; ? any time in larger workshops	metal drill bits, pots, wire	green jasper drills used prehistorically
polishing	trad. bow lathe, wheel with emery or corundum powder set in resin (lac); tumbling of beads in leather bag (modern polishing drum) with abrasive	? full and part time beadmakers in dispersed and centralized workshops	polished beads	depending on availability of labor and demand	microfacets on bead surface	electric lathes and mass tumbling of beads now used, greatly speeding up the process
repeated heating of carnelian beads	?small pots, ash, kilns; sawdust, cow dung	kiln supervisors in centralized workshops	deep red-orange carnelian beads	?	?pots, kilns, kiln ash, cracked beads	

to their employer with both the product and the byproducts of their labor, for example the bead roughouts they have chipped, together with pieces broken in manufacture and associated debitage, in order for their output to be weighed and checked. As a consequence, "types of semi-finished items from each stage of production are represented in the archaeological record in or around the merchant's house/workshop" (p. 57). Conversely, archaeological evidence of bead-making is sparse (though might we not expect to find the grindstones used in bead manufacture?) in the dispersed workshops of the largely part-time bead-makers to whom the merchants farm out piecework. Combined with other indications such as the physical segregation of stages of production and their characteristic byproducts in larger workshops, and evidence of the distribution of highly standardized products over wide areas, such patterning might well serve as a signature of this mode of production in archaeological contexts. As small-scale entrepreneurs may only undertake certain stages in the production process, or make specialized items, their workshops are also potentially identifiable.

Vidale *et al.* (1993) also discuss the interrelationship of, on the one hand, Harris's (1979) approach to conceptualizing and recording stratigraphy and, on the other, the chaîne opératoire, and their applicability to Khambhat beadmaking, which they show is characterized by discontinuities in time and space, intersections of production cycles, and the interchangeability of some production stages (see Table 11.5 for examples). In this paper they suggest some subtler archaeological indicators – for example the presence in larger workshops of similar numbers of polished and unpolished beads broken during perforation – of a segmented production process, which they regard, though quite why is unclear, as "generally characterized by hierarchical relationships" (Vidale *et al.* 1993: 192).

Kenoyer and colleagues conclude their 1994 paper by arguing that the archaeological evidence from the Harappan sites of Chanhudaro and the Moneer area of Mohenjodaro is suggestive of the highly centralized and controlled mode of production at the former site, and of wealthy merchants closely connected to the elite of this site and of Mohenjodaro. In the Moneer area, on the other hand, the evidence seems rather indicative of short-term agate bead production by entrepreneurs. While the authors insist that their work is in its initial stages, and it is clear that they have not completed the program laid out in the passage quoted above, they have accumulated, by ethnographic and archaeological techniques, a rich and varied database, and have besides:

1 described a form of capitalist industry so controlling and exploitative that, were it not for the absence of physical constraints on the workers, it might well be designated the "sweat shop" mode of production,

2 described the material signature of this mode in terms sufficiently precise for it to be recognized in the archaeological record, and

3 described significant variations from the dominant pattern in the form of small-scale entrepreneurship and its material consequences.

This is a substantial achievement; however, given the imperial British and later independent Indian political contexts in which the Khambhat beadmaking industry has been developing in recent centuries, one must wonder at the improbability of their finding avatars of these same two modes in the Harappan.

Luckily we are able to expand our source-side base for interpretation by referring to the work of another team led by Valentine Roux that has also been studying Khambhat beadmaking, in part from the cognitive psychological viewpoint familiar to us from her work with potters (Roux *et al.* 1995). We will consider here only a recent paper by Roux and Pierre Matarasso (1999) which offers a very different perspective on craft specialization. Their aim is to "reconstruct the technosystem of Harappan stone beads . . . by interpreting archaeological data in the light of quantified ethnoarchaeological observations ascertained through the method known as *activity analysis* . . ." (pp. 46–7). Activity analysis (Koopsman 1951) is an economist's version of the chaîne opératoire approach that emphasizes the constraints and alternatives that underlie the organization of complex production systems (technosystems). Roux and Matarasso take a global approach, focusing

on the complementary factors existing among major technical classes of bead production and not on micro-organizational factors constituting small-scale craft enterprises. This perspective . . . is best suited to the archaeological constraints that we typically confront, which (more often than not) do not permit detailed consideration of past socio-economic structures. (p. 49)

It is apparent from the above that their bead-focused studies are fundamentally different from Kenoyer and colleagues' socioeconomic approach to the industry. Roux and Matarasso are concerned with "elementary technical operations [that] are considered cultural invariants and the quantitative data obtained about them, [which are considered to be] cross-cultural" (p. 47). The description of their fieldwork relates only to their methodology, which involves quantifying each elementary activity, for example drilling or polishing a certain kind of bead, in terms of inputs and outputs. No information is provided in this short paper as to how and in which kinds of workshops this was actually achieved. Technical sequences are then developed for each bead type – 16 are recognized – and standardized by assuming that each successive task is carried out by 1000 workers. This allows for the calculation of a variety of statistics, amongst others the annual number of beads per worker by type, annual sales and expenditures per type, and profit margins. The results are then applied, allowances being made for differences in techniques, to Harappan archaeology.

In Harappan times techniques of grinding and polishing/shining beads using grindstones and not bows are thought to have been used. These techniques are the most time-consuming and least productive, the (theoretical) full-time worker being assessed as making 337 long (7–12 cm) or 723 short (1.5–3 cm) beads of superior quality per annum. The authors proceed by estimating, by means we need not consider here, the total number of beads recovered from Harappan sites and the percentage (1 percent) that this represents of the parent population. They thus arrive at an estimate of total production, which when divided by 500 (2500–2000 BC) gives figures for annual production of, remarkably, only 100 large, 1000 medium, and 10,000 small beads of superior quality. With specialists reckoned as working 6 hours/day, 26 days/month, and 10 months/year, the manpower required to achieve this output consists at any one time of only 0.49 knappers, 0.40 perforators, and 15.11 workers engaged in grinding, shining, and polishing.

We shall not presume to adjudicate between the Kenoyer and Roux interpretations of craft specialization in Harappan beadmaking. Suffice it to say that they are incompatible. However, far from being regarded as a failure of the ethnoarchaeological approach, it should rather be seen as testimony to the discipline's vitality and capacity for self-correction. We now require integration of the two ethnoarchaeological approaches and development of new subject-side strategies for establishing relevance. Given the quality of the ethnoarchaeological research this would constitute a particularly fine example of the approach to analogical inference advocated in chapter 2.

The ethnoarchaeology of iron smelting in Africa

The people follow the habits of a life which, measured by our standard, would be termed savage, yet the existence of an industry such as is herein described removes from them this stigma. (Bellamy 1904: 99)

Archaeology's tendency to describe and explain the development of culture in terms of leading technologies, as evidenced by the Three Age System, helps to account for the interest in iron smelting in Sub-Saharan Africa, the only part of the world in which traditional smelting by bloomery techniques still survived, though very patchily, into the second half of the twentieth century.[8] Locally smelted iron is no longer produced, having everywhere been replaced by industrially manufactured stock and scrap. There was here an extra incentive to study surviving smelting traditions since iron played a role in one of the world's great colonizing movements, that of the Bantu-speaking peoples who, especially during the first half of the first millennium AD, were rapidly expanding over central, eastern and southern Africa.

The ethnoarchaeology of metallurgy is almost entirely limited to the smelting and smithing of iron. In Africa, Asia, and other parts of the world, gold, silver, copper and its alloys (bronze and brass) are still worked by smiths using

---

[8] Indian scholars have described bloomery iron smelting in Bihar (Agrawal, Prasad *et al.* 1998) and Orissa (N. R. Srinavasan 1998) but in the context of attempted revivals, using some non-traditional elements, of former industries. See also Tripathi and Tripathi (1994).

non-industrial techniques but, with the exception of Lee Horne's (1983b, 1994b) research on South Asian brasscasters (see below), there have been no ethnoarchaeological studies.[9] Even were there no bias in the literature towards smelting, we would be bound to focus upon it. It is the most sophisticated of prehistoric technologies, making the most demands on ethnoarchaeological observers, who must develop collaboration with metallurgists while at the same time taking pains to ensure that they understand the relationship of the practices they observe to the technology under investigation. Reflexivity is, more than ever, important. For these reasons smelting warrants the extended treatment it is given below. Furthermore, because the principles of smelting are not part of anthropological common knowledge, it is necessary to provide a brief introduction to the subject.

Over the past five centuries a Eurasian tradition of iron making based upon blast furnaces has spread around the world, progressively replacing, where they existed, bloomery furnaces. Blast furnaces, in which preheated combustion gases are forced through the charge, generate temperatures high enough to melt the metal produced, which can be tapped from the furnace to run down into a system of channels, likened to a sow with piglets, where it solidifies as "pig" iron, a form of cast iron. This, with >2.0–5.0 percent or even more carbon, is not suitable for forging as, though very hard, it is brittle. In the industrial context pig iron is refined to produce metal with the particular characteristics desired. In bloomery furnaces the iron does not become sufficiently liquid to flow but forms a "spongy" mass of metal, the bloom, that normally consists of a mixture of ferrite, which contains <0.1 percent carbon, and steel with 0.1–2.0 percent carbon. Ferrite, which when forged is known as wrought iron, is relatively soft and malleable, suitable for ornamental iron work. Steel, harder but still forgeable, is preferred for most tools and weapons. Although bloomery furnaces survived to 1900 in North America, these were sophisticated industrial types, hugely more productive than those studied by archaeologists (Gordon and Killick 1993). They can hardly serve as analogies to assist in understanding the furnaces used in antiquity.

What happens in the bloomery furnace? Iron is obtained from various oxides of iron, ores in which metallic iron (Fe) is bonded to oxygen (O). For example, the mineral hematite is Fe_2O_3 and magnetite Fe_3O_4. The ores used in smelting also comprise a variety of other minerals, mainly silica (Si) and aluminum (Al). The smelter's task is to separate the atoms of metallic iron from oxygen atoms, a process known as reduction, and from other associated materials. This is done by heating the ore to temperatures of around 1300° Celsius while it is in close contact with charcoal, which is almost pure carbon. Heat breaks the molecular bonds between the iron and the oxygen atoms, and the oxygen released combines with carbon to produce carbon monoxide gas (CO), which by reduction

---

[9] Sharada Srinavasan's (1998) study of the making in Kerala of bronze bowls with high tin content is rather ethnometallurgical than ethnoarchaeological.

of iron oxide becomes carbon dioxide (CO_2) that, together with inert nitrogen (N) from the air, is vented from the furnace. Meanwhile the silica, aluminum, and other impurities, melting at lower temperatures than metallic iron, drip down to the base of the furnace in the form of slag, leaving an iron bloom to grow above by coalescence of iron particles. The process, in its simplest form, may be summarized as follows:

$$Fe_2O_3\ Si_xAl_x\quad + C\qquad + (N+O)\ >>> \qquad (CO + CO_2 + N) + \ Si_xAl_x + Fe$$

Ore (hematite   + charcoal   + air   *is converted to*   gases,   slag,   and metallic
and sand)   iron

When we consider that the necessary heat energy can only be generated by introducing more of the element, oxygen, that must be *removed* for reduction to take place, and learn that slag is not mere waste but in certain phases plays a vital role in protecting metallic iron particles from re-oxidization, we begin to gain an appreciation for the difficulties that smelters face.

The forms of African furnaces are extremely variable, from simple bowls dug in the ground to short shaft furnaces with pits to receive the slag, to short shafts from the bases of which slag may be tapped, to much larger furnaces, 3 m or so tall. Air is caused to enter them in one of two ways, each of which is highly variable in detail. In *forced* draft furnaces, the air is blown into the shaft by bellows through tubes called tuyères (Fig. 11.8). In *induced* draft furnaces, generally but not always tall, the relationship between the vent at the top of the furnace and the openings of tuyères inserted at its base is such that the furnace draws like a chimney (Fig 11.9). The smelter controls the flow of air by opening and closing tuyères and vent.

Iron blooms always contain some slag and charcoal, and, given the impossibility of maintaining constant conditions in the furnace, the iron produced is of variable quality, consisting mainly of ferrite and steel, sometimes with small quantities of cast iron. The discovery that some African smelters were intentionally producing cast iron and decarburizing the metal to steel in the forge resulted from ethnoarchaeological research (David, Heimann, *et al.* 1989).

Studies of smelting in Africa have a long history that pre-dates ethnoarchaeology by half a century. The best early description is C. V. Bellamy's (1904) account of village industry smelting at a Yoruba village in southwestern Nigeria (see Table 11.6). Besides describing a smelt in technical and quantified detail and the subsequent smithing of the steel produced, Bellamy, an engineer, was at pains to provide contextual data, and to seek information on a master smelter's perception of the process. He also gathered samples that were later subjected to metallurgical analysis. Although not undertaken with the interests of archaeologists in mind, he provided precious information on the division of labor (everyone in the village was involved in smelting in one capacity or another), on the relations of production (each furnace was run on a share system) and on the distribution of the iron to several major centers over an area of hundreds of square miles. Unfortunately Bellamy's work lay forgotten for

Fig. 11.8 A Haya smelt in progress in a low shaft furnace constructed of blocks of slag and mud, W. Tanzania, 1976. The forced draft is supplied by eight sets of bellows. Donald Avery is taking a temperature reading.

many years, and one finds few studies of comparable scholarship mentioned in Walter Cline's (1937) invaluable compilation *Mining and metallurgy in Negro Africa*, or indeed until very recent times.

Ethnoarchaeologists[10] concerned to study African metallurgy confront a technology that involves complex and non-obvious physico-chemical processes, and that calls for mobilization of substantial material and human forces of production, and an equally vigorous engagement with the supernatural. This threefold challenge to explain the physical, the social, and the cognitive and symbolic aspects demands theoretical and methodological sophistication. While valuable work can be done by materials scientists acting more or less on their own, for example Judith Todd's (1979, 1985) research on Dime (or Dimi) smelting in Ethiopia, and by ethnologists, for example Yves Moñino's (1983) study of smelting by Gbaya in the Central African Republic, such accounts generally fail to integrate the technical with the social and cognitive-symbolic aspects of smelting. Integration we regard as the ideal; it is not surprising that

---

[10] The field research described below has been carried out by a variety of researchers, all with the intention of applying its results to the interpretation of metallurgical history and prehistory. We treat such work as ethnoarchaeological even though its authors may have regarded themselves as practicing ethnology, archaeometallurgy, or history.

Fig. 11.9 A tall induced draft furnace built for a reconstruction of smelting at the Cewa village of Chulu (Malawi) organized in 1982 by van der Merwe and Avery (1987). Note the tuyères at the base and the ladder used for charging the furnace with ore and charcoal. Donald Avery has inserted a thermocouple into one of a series of holes bored through the wall of the furnace and is reading the temperature. (He is wearing "hot, scratchy, and wholly inappropriate" bark cloth that he paid the villagers to make and wear. In former times they sensibly worked naked.) Information from David Killick.

Table 11.6 *Selected examples of African smelting observed by ethnoarchaeologists and others. The nature of specialization refers to the period before the decline of smelting, and even when specialization was full time, smelting was often seasonal*

Group	Country	Date smelting abandoned	Years smelts observed	N smelts	Furnace types	Nature of specialization FT = full time PT = part time	Primary references and their nature MS = materials science ET = ethnological EA = ethnoarchaeological
Traditional smelts							
Yoruba	SW Nigeria	post-1903	1903?	1	Induced draft	FT village smelting industry	Bellamy 1904 MS
Mafa	N Cameroon	late 1950s	1953	2	Forced draft vertical tuyére	FT casted iron workers	Hinderling 1955 ET; Gardi 1955 ET+MS
Hausa	S Niger	c.1976	1965, 1967	2	Induced draft	FT casted iron workers; cooperative smelting	Echard 1968, 1983, 1986 ET
Dime (Dimi)	SW Ethiopia	1973 or after	1973	1	Forced draft	FT casted iron workers	Todd 1979, 1985 MS
Reenactments							
Gbaya-'bodoe	W Central African Rep.	1943	1977	2	Forced draft	PT smelters	Moñino (1983) ET
Mafa	N Cameroon	late 1950s	1986, 1989	2	Forced draft vertical tuyére	FT casted iron workers	David et al. 1989 EA+MS

Table 11.6 (cont.)

Group	Country	Date smelting abandoned	Years smelts observed	N smelts	Furnace types	Nature of specialization FT = full time PT = part time	Primary references and their nature MS = materials science ET = ethnological EA = ethnoarchaeological
Plata	N Cameroon	1950s	1989	1	Forced draft vertical tuyére	Iron working lineages; PT smelters, some FT smiths	David 1995 EA, and unpublished MS
Barongo	NW Tanzania	c.1951	1979–84	9	Forced draft	FT multi-ethnic work association of smelters and smiths	Schmidt 1996b
Fipa; Pangwa	WC and S Tanzania	early 1960s; before late 1960s	1990–1; 1995	3; 2	Two-stages: induced draft + forced draft	PT smelters	Barndon 1996a, 1996b EA
Reconstructions							
Haya	NW Tanzania	c.1925	1976–84	9	Forced draft	PT smelters	Schmidt 1997 EA+MS
Cewa of Chulu; Phoka	C and N Malawi	c.1930; 1930s	1982, 1983	1; 2	Two-stages: induced draft + forced draft	FT/PT; PT smelters	van der Merwe and Avery 1987; Killick 1990 EA+MS
Bassari	Togo	early 1950s	1985	2	Induced draft	FT Village smelting industry	Goucher and Herbert 1996; Saltman et al. 1986 EA

the research that comes closest to it has been carried out by teams that, *while in the field*, combine ethnoarchaeological and metallurgical expertise.

A further circumstance of ethnoarchaeological work on iron smelting must be made explicit. Unlike Bellamy, Todd and, in Niger, Nicole Echard (1968, 1983), *no ethnoarchaeologist has ever observed a smelt carried out in earnest to obtain iron*, but only ones arranged for the benefit of Western researchers or as semi-folkloric attractions.[11] Ethnoarchaeologists have commissioned iron making in the form of reenactments (smelts carried out by master smelters some two to three decades after they had last made iron) and reconstructions. The latter term is used when any master smelter still living is too feeble to take full responsibility and the smelt is in part improvised by former apprentices and others (not always excluding the ethnoarchaeologist) on the basis of prevailing technological dispositions, fading memories of particular techniques, and trial and error (see Table 11.6). It should therefore be no surprise that the majority of reenactments and reconstructions of smelting in Africa have been qualified failures. Under all such circumstances the social and economic context of smelting obviously differs from that of earlier times. The technical and magical aspects are also likely to have changed, and since humans, if suitably compensated, are quite prepared to put on a performance, the visitors have also to ensure that the smelt, so far as may be possible, is representative of the former technology. For example, when ND and Yves Le Bléis, a linguist and speaker of Mafa, were negotiating with Dokwaza, they had as guides not only René Gardi's (1954, 1955) superb photographs of Mafa smelting, but also Paul Hinderling's (1955) timed log of a Mafa smelt conducted in 1953.[12] ND's knowledge was sufficient to convince Dokwaza, who had on occasion carried out mini-smelts for the benefit of tourists, of the seriousness of the enterprise. In the event the course of the 1986 smelt corresponded closely to that recorded 33 years earlier. The Dogon smelters filmed by Eric Huysecom and Bernard Agustoni (1977) were motivated less by money than by the opportunity to demonstrate their skills to a generation ignorant of their past achievements. These may be ideal circumstances, but they are nonetheless insufficient on their own to guarantee (illusory) authenticity.

Given the uncertainties of such field situations and of control of personnel, of other variables, and in general of an occasion that risks becoming a carnival (Fig. 11.10), it might be argued that we can learn more about ancient and traditional metallurgy by experimenting under laboratory conditions than through reenactments and reconstructions in the field. David Killick (1991), an archaeometallurgist with field experience in many parts of Africa (Fig. 11.11), argues strongly for the complementarity of the two approaches. Much information

---

[11] Hamo Sassoon's (1964) brief but valuable study of iron smelting at Sukur in Nigeria in 1962 is a partial exception.

[12] Although smelting was still being practiced at this time, this was a short smelt, lasting only 6½ hours from the time the furnace was lit to the breaking of the shaft seal and removal of the bloom mass. It may well have been commissioned by Gardi and Hinderling.

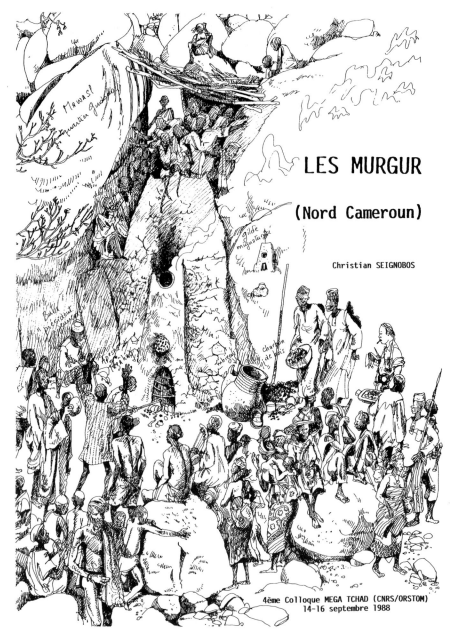

Fig. 11.10 A smelt reenacted by the Mofu of Mawasl, northern Cameroon, in January 1983, was organized and sketched by Christian Seignobos, a human geographer, seen on the right side of the picture. The illustration, which perfectly depicts the atmosphere on such occasions, was used as the cover of the paper presented by Seignobos (1991) at the fourth International Mega-Tchad Colloquium in which this and other reenacted smelts are described.

Fig. 11.11 David Killick selects charcoal for dating from the base of a furnace at the site of Juude Jaabe, on one of the levees of the Senegal River, Senegal, January 1993.

about technological process is potentially available in the contents and microstructures of archaeological metals and slags, but to interpret these correctly one must have analogical standards with which to compare them. Sophisticated experiments can do what ethnoarchaeologists cannot, controlling variables in order to establish dependable links between cause and effect. However,

professional metallurgists and engineers have a scientific understanding of metallurgy that their prehistoric counterparts could not have possessed. This knowledge is essential . . . but it inevitably acts to constrain the choice of materials, apparatus and procedures in the *design* of experiments . . . Metallurgists are necessarily conditioned by their education and their professional experience to favor certain possibilities and to dismiss others. (Killick 1991: 47–8)

Theory-laden European experiments have, for example, made use of valved bellows or a motorized blower to introduce air into the furnace, whereas African forced draft furnaces invariably employed valveless bellows which provide a rapidly reversing, turbulent air flow that produces different distributions of oxygen and temperature in the furnace. Ethnoarchaeological studies contribute both by providing contextualized accounts of smelting and materials for metallurgical analysis, and by informing and improving the design of experiments.

In what follows we discuss a sample of ethnoarchaeological studies of smelting carried out by multidisciplinary teams. We pay special attention to methodology and to the question of whether the cultural and metallurgical aspects of such research inform upon each other – for if not they might as well be studied separately – and conclude by commenting on the range of types of specialization relating to smelting in particular and to iron working in general in sub-Saharan Africa. Some further consideration of the systems of thought that underlie iron working is found in chapter 13.

Malawi: the materialist and the missionary positions

Nikolaas van der Merwe and Donald Avery (1987) are impressed by the universality of the association of "magic" – "the combination of ritual and medicines" – with smelting in Africa and the repeated presence of certain themes: propitiation of supernatural forces, the contribution of technical and magical knowledge to the special status of smelters, and sexual symbolism and taboos. The authors, an archaeologist and a metallurgical engineer biased, in their own words, towards technical explanations, undertook to investigate the relationship between the technical and magical aspects of iron production through their analysis of reconstructions, after a gap of half a century, of smelting among the Cewa and Phoka of Malawi. Their paper contrasts the "materialist and the missionary positions" on magic and ritual. Where not simply dismissive, materialists propose a functional explanation, interpreting the magic and ritual component of smelting as a means of maintaining monopolistic control over the technology. Those more interested in belief systems, the "missionaries," are prone to downplay smelting's technical aspects and to emphasize the supernatural work, the invocation and coordination of magic and spirits, through which the smelter achieves success. Neither approach satisfies van de Merwe and Avery.

The two groups studied and their two-stage smelting process, involving partial reduction of ore in tall induced draft furnaces (Fig. 11.12) followed by the making of blooms in small forced draft furnaces, are set in historical and technological context.[13] In both societies iron used to be produced on a small scale by part-time smelters for their own and local consumption. As the traditional task group comprising master smelter and family, plus pupils who paid to acquire the techniques, no longer existed, local chiefs and others were involved in the selection of people to carry out the smelt. The researchers participated in rituals and bound themselves to observe the same taboos as the

---

[13] The metallurgical analyses are published in Avery et al. 1988.

Fig. 11.12 Van der Merwe (*right*) and Avery watch as Cewa smelters, 114 hours after firing the furnace, remove 91 kg of "sintered sponge," imperfectly reduced material, parts of which were subsequently resmelted in a small forced draft furnace to form a bloom, Malawi, 1982.

smelters (with whom they communicated, via an interpreter from the Antiquities Department, in their own languages [D. Killick, pers. comm. 1999]). The smelting cycles from construction of the furnaces to resmelting of the product in the smaller furnaces are succinctly described, and an account is given of Cewa and Phoka ritual and magic, the latter for the most part taking the form of applications to the smelters and the furnace of "medicines," so-called because most are of plant origin and have pharmaceutical uses. Appendices describe the medicines, giving their botanical and local names, and their placement in relation to the furnace. Given that the Cewa used 27 and the Phoka 56, these are impressive documents in themselves.

In addition to the empirical account of smelting and its attendant magic, van der Merwe and Avery also draw attention to interrelated metaphors of human reproduction and heat/danger that are particularly evident in the practice of Phoka smelting. Their concluding discussion denies the validity of either the materialist or the missionary position, and specifically the "contention that the ritual component of smelting is of secondary importance, at most a type of trade union secret" (p. 164). Nor in the cases observed did magic "provide an organising force . . . [in that] a sequence of rituals may order a technical process.

. . . the rituals merely punctuate the successful completion of various prepara-
tory phases" (p. 165). The authors incline to the view that magic relieves
anxiety in the face of the unpredictable:

Our perceptions of the importance of the magical evidence in smelting increased substantially as we were progressively introduced to its mysteries. The investment of time
and effort in smelting magic is large and the expertise required is extensive: it is a technology in its own right, with its own body of knowledge and network of personal and
commercial relations. We did not find that magic has a scientific contribution to make
to iron smelting technology, but nevertheless concluded that smelting could not be conducted without it, because it is too important to the smelters. (p. 144)

This fine piece of work may be considered deficient in two respects. First, as is
too often the case, the authors' brief exposure to the Cewa and Phoka prevents
them from fully situating smelting in its former social and cultural contexts.[14]
Second, and partly as a consequence, the technical and magical aspects of
smelting are treated as separate domains between which there appears to be
only limited linkage, mainly at the level of metaphor, smelting and human
reproduction being perceived as similar processes. The scientists offer a coherent technical account, but their knowledge is insufficient to attempt the same
for the magical aspects. Thus their rags and patches conclusion regarding the
magic may be correct but remains undemonstrated until the possibility has
been investigated that it is systematically linked to technical practice.

Cameroon: approximation of operating sequences via comparison

In 1986 and 1989 ND organized reenactments of smelting in the northern
Mandara mountains. Team members collaborated to compile a detailed
written, photographic, and videographic record. Numerous samples of ore, clay,
charcoal, slag, and bloom were collected, but no metallurgist was present.
Samples were subsequently analyzed by metallurgists David Killick and
Michael Wayman and by Robert Heimann, a ceramicist. These were published
in a detailed account that, while it sets Mafa smelting in social and historical
context, barely mentions its magical and ritual elements (David *et al.* 1989).[15]
In 1989, when Dokwaza conducted a second smelt, Killick was present in the
field to make his own observations, including of furnace temperatures by use
of thermocouples. Full accounts of this and of a smelt conducted in the same
year among the Plata under similar conditions await publication (the Plata
smelt, smithing scenes from Sukur in Nigeria, and laboratory analysis of slags
and metal are shown in the film *Black Hephaistos* [David 1995]). The Mandara

---

[14] Van der Merwe and Avery's work at Chulu is however substantially complemented by David
Killick's (1990) doctoral thesis, a work that combines ethnohistory, ethnoarchaeology, and
archaeometallurgy in a study of the technological and economic, social, and ideological aspects
of the iron industry.

[15] A video, *Dokwaza: last of the African iron masters* (David and Le Bléis 1988), documents the
building of the furnace, the smelt, the fining of bloomery iron, and the forging of a hoe.

project's study of smelting, smithing, and the distribution of metals is a work in progress, and we consider only selected aspects below.

In chapter 7 we described the caste system existing in parts of the Mandara mountains. Dokwaza was a member of the specialist smith-potter caste, and well known as a diviner and healer. His wife, Demagay, was an accomplished potter. (Both died in the early 1990s.) In the northeastern extension of the Mandara mountains where the Plata live, smelters and smiths are not casted but iron working tends to be the specialty of particular lineages. Ajokfa, the Plata master smelter (also now deceased), was not casted, and while he and other members of his lineage had been active smelters, he had never worked as a blacksmith. Throughout the mountains smelting was carried out by task groups based on the family. Caste members would invite kinsmen and affines to assist, and at Sukur, where everybody, farmers and smith-potters, men and women, was involved in smelting, families of close neighbors would sometimes pool their labor.

Were ND today to be describing the three smelts observed he would certainly wish to use the chaîne opératoire as an analytical tool. Such an explicated sequence of choices is a richly informative record, but we should not underestimate the commitment required. Terry Childs' (1991) paper on furnaces in Bantu-speaking Africa brings out very clearly the number of factors, and therefore the number of choices, involved even in the building of a furnace (Table 11.7). An operating sequence of a complete smelt would certainly demand monographic treatment, and it is not surprising that no one has described such a chaîne opératoire in full. To do so would call for an intensity of interaction between researcher and specialist artisans that is rarely achieved. A possible, if partial and imperfect, alternative to the detailed analysis of particular sequences of choices is the critical comparative analysis of different sequences whether of the same artisan at different times or of different ones working under similar conditions. We will not develop such an analysis here, but will highlight certain elements of comparison.

Furnaces in the Mandara mountains are characterized by the use of a single tuyère hung vertically down the shaft and through which air is blown by bellows located on a platform above (Figs. 7.11 and 11.13). They probably developed for the efficient smelting of magnetite ore in the form of sand-sized particles eroded from local granites, and are found nowhere else.[16]

The elegance of the Nigerio-Cameroonian vertical design [of furnace] in which the oxidizing zone [and the reducing zone around it] is confined to the very centre of the furnace, inheres in its ability to use very high grade ores that produce relatively little slag. Where pure magnetite ores were used elsewhere in furnaces with horizontal tuyères, as at Phalaborwa [in South Africa] . . . quartz sand had to be added to *lower* the grade of ore. (David *et al.* 1989: 204)

---

[16] Some furnaces in the Cameroon Grassfields region appear to have been similar. However, despite important ethnohistorical work on the economy of that area (Warnier and Fowler 1979), we lack a technical description of smelting.

Table 11.7 *Influences affecting furnace building (extracted with modifications from Childs 1991: 341, Table 1)*

Choice	Influences	Referent
Furnace location	Access to resources	None
	Environmental factors (e.g., wind, shade)	None
	Political constraints and group dynamics	Villagers
	Ideology	Villagers
	Access to spirits	Villagers, spirits
Resource selection	Accessibility	None
	Technical qualities	None
	Labor	None
	Transport	None
	Symbolic references	Villagers, spirits
Pit diameter	Iron yield	None
	Labor	None
Medicine orifices	Ritual	Spirits
Furnace walls	Technical needs	None
	Iron yield	None
	Labor	None
	Space for symbolic expression	None
Wall height	Method of air draft	None
	Raw materials	None
	Labor	None
	Ideology	Villagers, spirits
Wall shape	Technical aspects	None
	Labor	None
	Group identity	Ethnic group
	Ideology	Villagers, spirits
Wall holes (chimney, shaft, tuyère, peep, etc.)	Technical aspects	None
	Ideology	Villagers, spirits
Furnace decoration	Group identity	Ethnic group
	Ideology	Villagers, spirits

Mafa furnaces have especially tall shafts and contrast with the much smaller furnaces, blown through slighter tuyères, typical of most other montagnard groups, including those of the Sukur (Fig. 7.11) and the Plata. Both types of furnace use the same ore and the same or similar charcoals are preferred. It is smelting practice that differs. After about two hours' smelting in the smaller furnaces, the shaft is opened, a coherent bloom weighing around 2.5 kg is removed, the red hot charcoal is shoveled back in, the shaft is again blocked up, more charcoal and ore are added, and the cycle recommences, producing another bloom an hour or so later. Tuyères are replaced as their tips melt and they become too short. When smelting was regularly practiced, one of these fur-

Fig. 11.13 The start of a reenacted Mafa smelt near Mokolo, northern Cameroon, 5 June 1989. The master smith, Dokwaza, is pumping the bellows. His eldest son stokes the furnace through the charge hole; to his right another relative squats, breaking up lumps of charcoal. The group of women and children sitting to the left of the furnace are family, and thus caste, members; other spectators keep their distance. Two God (Zhikile) pots on the furnace platform to the left of the shield have already been consecrated and will later receive the blood of two sacrificed cocks.

naces would, when properly served, in the course of a day produce nine or more small blooms that could be broken up and forged directly (cf. Sassoon 1964; Vaughan 1973; David 1996). This is known as the *batch* process.

In the *continuous* Mafa process, a thin clay wall (shaft seal) supported by bent sticks closes off the tall shaft. As the smelt progresses the reduction zone moves upwards as the tuyère is consumed, contributing to the formation of slag that is tapped through vents that are cut progressively higher and higher in the shaft seal as the smelt proceeds. This promotes the buildup within the shaft of a heterogeneous bloom mass, consisting of iron with some slag and unburned charcoal. In earlier practice the smelt would not end until, 24 hours or so later, the bloom mass had filled the shaft. The advantage of the continuous process lies in reduced heat loss and thus the ability to maintain higher temperatures conducive to the production of the cast iron identified, together with ferrite and steel, in the product of Dokwaza's 1986 smelt. The disadvantage of a bloom mass as against the more coherent blooms produced by the batch process is that many of the iron fragments are small and have to be welded together in the forge, a process the Mafa achieve by the use of crucibles. Dokwaza performed this welding without difficulty, mixing cast with lower-carbon iron to obtain steel.

Although in this section we have not considered the nature of Mafa and Plata technical choices from an emic perspective, their comparison allows us to begin to evaluate the relations between the cultural and physico-chemical factors that influenced the choices made by iron masters in the Mandara mountains. The decision to use tall furnaces suited to the continuous smelting process rather than the smaller ones used for batch processing, while affected by economic factors, is certainly cultural. Once this decision is made many other features and practices, for example vent cutting in the continuous process, follow, while other aspects, of decoration for example, or of the placement of charcoal and ore before charging, are much freer to vary. However, such freedom is more evident to the observer than to the artisan constrained by traditional practice and its symbolic code. Thus comparative analysis of technological behavior within a geographic region can go some way towards providing the account of the culturally embedded nature of technologies sought by the anthropology of techniques.

Tanzania: Haya reinvention and Barongo reenactments of smelting

There is one example of a study that, although it does not use the terminology of the anthropology of techniques, is close to it in spirit. This is Peter Schmidt's and his colleagues' – notably Terry Childs, primarily responsible for the ceramics aspects, and the metallurgical engineer Donald Avery – long-term research among the Haya of northeastern Tanzania, the fullest account of which is given in Schmidt's (1997) monograph *Iron technology in East Africa: symbolism, science and archaeology.* This is complemented by and contrasts with the same trio's work among Barongo – a category of specialist iron workers of multi-ethnic origins – who live further south (Schmidt 1996b). Schmidt's multi-disciplinary research among the Haya combines studies of oral tradition, politicoreligious history, archaeology, historical ecology, and ethnoarchaeology. The work of concern here was carried out between 1976 and 1984 and involves no less than nine smelts, not including two experimental ones carried out at Brown University in 1975 (Childs and Schmidt 1985).

The Haya, among whom smelting had been a part-time specialization, had not smelted for half a century, and the team included very old men who had smelted, practicing smiths who at least knew how to pump the bellows, and younger men. "Thus, the organization of work bore no relation to past circumstances, when each individual smelter [one of a team of eight under a master smelter] used to be responsible for gathering, in a communal work group, the iron ore and charcoal that he would need for a given number of smelts"

(Schmidt 1997: 53). Schmidt emphasizes the experimental nature of the process – which he characterizes by the Lévi-Straussian term *bricolage* – as the Haya (re-)invent a smelting tradition in both its technical and ritual aspects (Fig. 11.8)

Schmidt provides a full and frank account of his relations with the smelters. They communicated mainly in Swahili, the Tanzanian lingua franca. Although Schmidt (pers. comm. to ND 1999) understands much of the related Haya language, he relies on Dr. M. M. Mulokozi, a Haya scholar, to assist in the interpretation of the esoteric and often bawdy songs sung during the smelts. Aware that the presence of the observer influences the behavior of the observed, particularly when the latter are the former's employees, he and Avery resist the temptation to direct. This is sophisticated work, giving a rich account of technical, social, and ideological process, particularly of the first, unsuccessful, smelt. The Haya smelters' failures in furnace and tuyère construction and the unfortunate effects of damp charcoal – examples could be multiplied – not only help to define the limits of cultural choice but also stimulate ritual activity. Disputes between the Haya master smelter, the smiths, and other Haya authorities are informative, and the insightful description of social and ritual matters is integrated with that of the technical process. The team's account of the latter includes detailed quantitative and qualitative data. The reader cheers when the last of six smelts conducted in 1976 produces over 4 kg of bloom, a success to be bettered in 1979. Schmidt proceeds to develop a model of the Haya bloomery process based upon analyses of ores, charcoals, tuyères, temperature readings, slags, and blooms, and he attempts a structuralist interpretation of the symbolism. The Haya certainly win the prize for sexual content, overt and covert, in smelting, and the dominant metaphor evident in songs and other acts is of the impregnation of the furnace which is assimilated to a fecund womb.[17]

A gap of just over a quarter of a century had intervened between the cessation, forced by the colonial administration, of regular smelting by the Barongo and 1979 when Schmidt (1996b) initiated a further series of nine smelts that can be described as reenactments. He notes important differences between Haya and Barongo smelting and its social representations, with an overarching metaphor among the Barongo that links the themes of reproduction and transformation to young women's puberty rites. During the course of the nine smelts the iron workers never achieve their former levels of production,

but their bricolage shows a remarkable conjunction of ritual and technological fabrication that is richly interwoven and that leads to empirical solutions, illustrating that any attempt to analytically separate the two domains is meaningless and misses the point: experimentation is both ideological and procedural. (p. 119)

While the last phrase is entirely justified, it does not necessarily follow that analytical separation of the two domains is meaningless. Is there evidence that

---

[17] A scene in the film *Tree of Iron* (O'Neill and Muhly 1988) that shows Schmidt peering up a furnace vent through an optical pyrometer led ND to turn to his neighbor and whisper that Schmidt was in truth the Dr Kinsey of metallurgy.

Haya and Barongo objects and social representations influence and cause modifications in each other in the manner that (as seen in chapter 7) Anga representations of gender cause wild fig trees to be cultivated in parts of their territories? This question is taken up indirectly in chapter 13.

Conclusions on smelting

The most important substantive lesson learned from studies of smelting in sub-Saharan Africa is that in situations of widely varying labor and raw material availability an extraordinary variety of social and technical arrangements were devised to manufacture iron. Correlations between these and factors such as environments, ores, population densities, and social types remain underdeveloped. The advantages, under conditions of low labor availability and very poor ores, of two-stage smelting in tall, induced draft, followed by small, forced draft, furnaces, and of Mandara mountain down-draft furnaces where rich magnetite ore and plentiful labor are available, seem evident. But why among the populous Yoruba of Nigeria did full-time specialists use induced draft furnaces while most Gbaya, living at very low population densities in the Central African Republic, employed forced draft shaft furnaces – even as other Gbaya did not? The variety observed in African smelting has to be explained in the light of particular conditions and historical trajectories, and it is more properly the task of ethnologists than ethnoarchaeologists to investigate these and other matters, such as the varying division of labor and social status of iron workers. It is however worth noting that, while some iron workers are casted and others associated with ruling houses, no African smelters can be described as attached specialists. Rather they worked on their own account even when the scale of smelting reached the level of village industry.

The very variable success of the smelts observed by ethnoarchaeologists cautions against the characterization of reenactments as representative of former practice, against overinterpretation of the data gathered, and generally against their incautious use for analogical purposes. Nonetheless they provide some limited basis for estimates of production in the past. The evidence of Dokwaza's 1986 smelt and oral testimony indicate that in former times a smelt could well have provided sufficient iron to make 16 of the metal handled hoes preferred by the Mafa of this region, with a total finished weight of about 10.5 kg. When integrated with data on consumption, estimates of this kind serve to provide a context for the interpretation of evidence of iron working on a regional basis, and for the drawing of further inferences regarding societal and economic implications.

To what extent is the African tendency to associate smelting and other technologies with ritual paralleled elsewhere? The ethnographic record suggests greater ritualization of technology in sub-Saharan Africa than elsewhere even though intensification of production is demonstrably associated with increasing secularization (Rowlands and Warnier 1993; David 1996). But in earlier times a similar association might have characterized other world areas. The question remains open. The African data are of importance in that they express a very different attitude towards technology and progress than that which has come to characterize the capitalist West. It is simplistic, when contrasting the 1.27 tonnes of bloom produced in a day by a 1900 American bloomery with the 8.2 kg achieved by a Cewa furnace, to portray this (and other) African technologies as primitive. After all, African smelters successfully produced metal from iron oxide deposits that economic geologists would not even classify as ore (Gordon and Killick 1993: 259).[18] They had different priorities, and are usually denied credit for maintaining industries that were environmentally friendly and sustainable – until forced to respond to new circumstances brought about by climatic or sociopolitical change.

Smelting and the other examples of crafts considered in this chapter can be generalized to show that the symbolic, ritual, and magical aspects of complex technologies have several functions: creating and relieving the stress of a demanding enterprise, conceptualizing and managing complex and sometimes highly variable processes, serving to channel and control the transmission of knowledge, and legitimation of artisans' status. It is a common misconception that ritual has the effect of fossilizing technological procedures. Ethnoarchaeologists have shown that this is not the case and that ritual and technical innovation may go hand in hand. They have also provided much technical data and food for the imagination that can be applied to the reconstruction and interpretation of ancient smelting.

Blacksmiths and brasscasters

The ethnoarchaeological sources on smiths are disappointingly sparse, are geographically limited to sub-Saharan Africa, and, since many specialists combine smelting with smithing, show considerable overlap with the materials discussed in the previous section. Ian Hodder's (1982a: 59–68) treatment of the stylistic variation of spears in the Baringo district formed part of our discussion in chapter 7, but it should be noted that only one practicing smith resided in Hodder's research area. Thus his study was effectively limited to the explanation of consumer preferences, which were little differentiated despite a strong tendency on the part of purchasers living in areas of inter-tribal competition to buy from smiths of their own ethnic group wherever possible. The far greater variation in spear form among the Loikop (Samburu) and its relation to age grading and ethnicity has been studied by Roy Larick (see chapter 12), but only in his 1991 paper is there a brief discussion of smiths' responses to colonially

---

[18] Figures on productivity are also calculated from data provided by Gordon and Killick. And, by the way, let not the African ability to make something of inferior resources lead to overstated claims, again couched in Western terms, for technological sophistication.

induced changes, and of their strategy of settling at social and environmental borders.

Nor do other papers that deal with the products of the smiths, for example Childs and Dewey's (1996) comparative study of the symbolic roles of axes through time among the Luba of the Democratic Republic of Congo (former Zaïre) and the Shona of Zimbabwe, have much to say about the smiths themselves. As these authors point out, "there has been little investigation of the specific smithing techniques and processes . . . by which indistinct metal pieces are rendered into recognizable objects and are given function and meaning in prehistoric [or for that matter recent] societies" (p. 145) – though see Keller and Keller (1996) and references therein cited for information on blacksmithing in the West. Indeed, the literature deals for the most part only peripherally with the material corollaries of specialization, exchange, and trade, focusing more on the ethnology of smiths, on their position in society and economy; alternatively it is largely devoted to straightforward description and classification. We take brief note of contributions in each of these categories before considering in more detail a paper on competition between two African iron industries.

Jean Brown (1995: ix) makes "no apology for an old-fashioned ethnographical approach" taken in her monograph on *Traditional metalworking in Kenya*. To make this survey, conducted between 1964 and 1974, she visited and observed smiths of 37 of Kenya's 39 "tribes,"[19] recording and classifying their workshops and tools, products and techniques, and documenting the heredity, training, status, and death of smiths. Her analysis leads to the definition of two technological "streams" each divisible into a number of "industries," whose affinities Brown sets in historical context. The work thus provides much "raw material for analogy for archaeologists" but is more material culture studies than ethnoarchaeology.

In the ethnological category we can cite de Maret's (1980, 1985) papers on the place of the smith in Central African and especially Bantu society. Drawing on a wide variety of ethnographic, historical, and archaeological sources, he assembles useful social and economic data and shows how over most of this culture area smiths are highly regarded and associated in fact and symbol with chiefs and rulers. In a more sociological mode, Chapurukha Kusimba (1996) has written on the social context of iron forging among several Swahili-speaking ethnic groups on the Kenya coast. He visited 30 villages, finding 29 master smiths, 18 of whom, representing all four groups identified, agreed to act as informants (Fig. 11.14). It is worth noting that the remaining 11 declined to be interviewed by their fellow Kenyan, "citing illness, bad timing, death in the family, or distrust of my intentions" (p. 389). Of particular interest are sections on the smith's life cycle and apprenticeship, and on social ambiguities and

---

[19] There is limited correspondence between the "peoples" located on a map of Kenya (p. xii) and the "tribes" assigned to the streams and industries in the table on p. 160.

Fig. 11.14 Chapurukha Kusimba (*center*) interviews Kalume wa Masha wa Chai, a Giryama master smith while assistant Kaingu Kalume Tinga tapes the interview, Mkaumoto, Kilifi District, Kenya, January 1992.

ritual power, in which areas the similarities seem to lie more with Sudanic than with Congo basin smiths. Another section on competition and the future describes how traditional smiths are facing tough competition not only from imports but from "an informal industrial sector called Jua Kali. Jua Kali are an expanding community of semi-skilled artisans who work in different service crafts, including panel-beating, welding, shoemaking . . . [and many] others" (p. 401). The Jua Kali – possibly a modern equivalent of the Barongo? – and the nature of their community and products are prime subjects for ethnoarchaeological research.

Consumption, competition and change in northern Cameroon

A fundamental difference between the smithing of locally smelted iron and of the largely scrap metals that Third World smiths use today is that formerly the welding of bits of metal was at the core of the technology. Smithing is now subtractive rather than additive. Minor differences in industrial iron alloys prevent them being welded together, and, since the smith's raw material comes from a variety of sources, welding is so rarely possible that it may fast be being forgotten as a technique. Consequently the chisel, used for cutting tool rough-outs from wheel rims and iron sheets, rails, and bars, has come to play an ever more important role in the work of the forge.

We mentioned in chapter 4 the consequences for site formation processes of the change in the technology. In earlier times iron was everywhere expensive and regularly recycled. In the 1940s, when smelting was still actively practiced by the Mafa, three handfuls of bloomery iron, enough for a single hoe, were exchanged for a medium-sized goat. In 1989 such a hoe was worth 550 CFA (then about US$2.30) and a goat about 9000 CFA ($37.50). Other testimony confirms that in the old days iron was some 15 to 20 times more expensive in real terms (ND 1989 fieldnotes). When a hoe blade wore down its owner took it back to the smith to have a new one attached. Iron was rarely discarded except as small pieces, for example the tangs of tools like arrowheads, as special depositions, for example as grave goods, and as lost items, which are in any case unlikely to become part of the archaeological record. Nowadays, on the other hand, the combination of cheaper iron and the difficulties of welding result in very different patterns of discard. Although a worn out hoe could be reforged into a knife and a worn out knife into an arrowhead, the cheapness of metal prevents this becoming regular practice.[20] Compounds are littered with fragments of iron, worn out tools not considered worth recycling as smaller items, and the tips outside smiths' forges are full of cut scraps. This is surely the case in other parts of the world where local smiths with access to a variety of raw materials still compete successfully against the products of industry.

We actually know very little about the consumption of iron. Various Mafa elders were consistent in holding that, in the first half of the twentieth century, there used to be many fewer people and fewer hoes owned per person. Today every adult has at least two hoes, one for initial cultivation of a field, the other for weeding. In the old days people cultivated less and diet was supplemented more by gathering and hunting. There was perhaps on average one hoe per person, but some did not even have that or were forced to cultivate with worn out tools that would be thrown out today. An assistant's mother remembers using a hoe made of ebony. Hoes were also smaller in size. Axes were rare; some households had none and had to borrow. Adults all owned a sickle, the indispensable everyday tool, and every woman possessed the small sickle-awl used in basketry. Knives were rare and heavy picks very rare. Multi-barbed spearheads were handed down from generation to generation, as were presumably the typological fusions of throwing knives and sickles used ceremonially at dances, and seen hanging from the furnace shield in Figure 11.13. Besides wooden clubs, men's main weapons were bows and iron-tipped arrows. A small amount of iron was used for women's pubic shields, musical rattles and bells,

---

[20] The technical difficulties of maintaining carbon content (decarburization being the normal consequence of reforging) may also be a factor, for although cold hammering of low carbon iron can greatly increase hardness it also reduces ductility, rendering the tool liable to breakage if it strikes a hard object.

and small items, for example tweezers and strike-a-lights, besides ornaments and amulets. All in all the household inventory was very limited.

In 1986 ND made a non-exhaustive census of the iron objects in the house of a Mafa man in his sixties with one wife and no resident children (Table 11.8). The statistics suggest that this particular couple would even today purchase less than one kilogram of tool iron forged by local smiths (nor did the household possess a bicycle or any Western metal items beyond two alloy spoons). Although the estimate of 765 g tool iron purchased by this family per annum is impressionistic, it is evident that even in the mid-1980s Mafa household purchases of locally forged iron were quite limited, though substantial when multiplied by the approximately 35,000 households in the Mokolo subprefecture. The figure must have been a great deal lower in former times when recycling was much more intensive; we doubt that in 1930 an average family would have consumed more than 500 g of tool iron in a year or around one kilogram of impure iron direct from the bloomery. The estimate is comparable to one calculated by ND on the basis of data gathered in 1967–9 of 740 g of tool iron purchased per annum by a settled Fulbe family of five at the village of Bé on the plains further south, children accounting for very little demand. Such a figure may reasonably serve also as an estimate for the amount bought annually by families of Wandala and other plains dwellers further north who were in contact with montagnard producers.

The preceding data serve to introduce David and Robertson's (1996) study of competition and change in two northern Cameroonian iron industries. Mandara montagnard smiths are dispersed among the settlements in familial production units. Amongst the Muslim Wandala, they are members of a guild with its own rules and responsibilities, into which there is recruitment by formal apprenticeship. There are two major production centers; Manaouatchi, situated 12 km southeast of the Wandala capital of Mora, is the larger. The hereditary chief of the Wandala blacksmiths resides there, and there were in 1986 about 30 active blacksmiths.

Up to the 1940s and early 1950s, most of the iron consumed in the region was locally smelted by montagnards who, since the ore originates in the mountains, had a logistic advantage. Wandala smiths, whose position in society may be described as ambiguous, were, even in times of conflict, able to maintain access to the mountains where they traded for iron blooms and sometimes ore. By the early 1950s, the influx of imported iron was putting montagnard smelters out of business. While neither on the plains nor in the mountains have Western industrial products made significant inroads in the farmer's toolkit, the flow of metal has reversed. Larger towns, predominantly Muslim and all except Mokolo situated on the plains, became entrepôts of iron stock and scrap. Muslims acquired a near monopoly of iron supply and Wandala smiths were quick to exploit the newly favorable terms of access.

Montagnard smiths have on the whole persisted in their traditional roles.

Table 11.8 *Partial census (see text) taken in 1986 of iron objects in the house of a Mafa man and his wife, both aged in their sixties and with no resident children*

Tools, weapons, and ornaments	N	Est. uselife (yrs)	Est. weight range for similar items (g)	Est. mean weight of type (g)	Est. no. replaced annually	Est. tool iron purchased per annum (g)
"Dog's head" hoe (with integral neck and socket)	5 (various states of wear)	2–3 (formerly new blade welded on every 2–3 years)	365 (much worn)–650	500	0.1 (may never be replaced)	50
Tanged hoe	2 usable; 6 worn out	2–3	250–415	340	0.8	272
Socketed hoe	1 worn out	2–3	230–365	290	0.5	145
Ax	2	10+	250–300	275	0.2	55
Tanged adz (reworked by smith from worn out hoe)	1	?	150–220		replaced from existing stock of hoes	0
Socketed billhook	2	10+	300–400	350	0.1	35
Sickle	2	2–4	100–200	175	0.7	122.5
Basketry sickle + awl	1	10	10–20	15	0.1	1.5
Dance sickle	1	25–?	300–400	350	0.05	17.5
Mafa knife with metal handle	2	3–10	uncertain; now a rare item	60	will be replaced by Muslim types	0
Muslim butcher's knife (tang in wood handle)	1	3–10	100–150	125	0.15	18.75
Muslim men's knife (blade often decorated; tang in wood handle)	2	3–10	50–75	65	0.3	19.6

| Arrowhead | c.20 | 1–20 (variable loss) | 8–15 | 12 | 2 | 24 |
| Small items (tweezers, ornaments, etc.) not counted | | | | | | 4 |

Total tool iron required per annum: 764.85 g

Mafa types not noted in this household

spearhead	15+	160–250	180
large tree-felling ax	10+	700–900	800
pick	10	500–650	575
amulet	10+	10–25	15
bracelet	10+	35–50	40
pubic shield	10+	?80–120	100

Note: of the bloom entering the smithy rather less than half by weight is lost in the forging of tool iron.

Nevertheless the reversal of the flow of iron and the establishment of the modern market system have placed their products in direct competition with those of Muslim smiths. In the south, largely owing to the presence of Mokolo as a secondary entrepôt, montagnards still obtain the majority of their iron goods from blacksmiths of their own group, but this is less and less the case in the north. Wandala smiths have shown remarkable technical and managerial initiative in responding to increased opportunities offered by improved access to raw materials and by a more open national society. Individual smiths vary their products according to their age and abilities, and to changing patterns in the supply and demand for apprentices, assistants, and metal. The potential for increased sales accompanying market centralization has been realized through the adoption of improved smithing and marketing techniques including the use of metal templates. Approximately half the local markets have a significantly non-Muslim, ethnically diverse, clientele. Shoppers are offered a wide range of products, some targeted towards specific ethnic groups (Robertson 1992). Wide sales territories are now serviced from Manaouatchi by two smiths who act as ironmongers, distributing finished products to the various markets.

The organizational and technical advantages of the Wandala smiths include their ability to act as a unit to obtain the best prices for raw materials, and to plan production in such a way as to maximize output while minimizing internal competition. Most montagnard smiths engage in other specialist activities and until recently were prepared to reproduce the complete toolkit to order. Owing also to their more primitive forging equipment, the montagnards are less efficient blacksmiths than the Muslims. Heavy forging is conducted with massive (about 6 kg) boulder hammers, wielded either by an assistant, or, especially when a tool is being made to order, by the client. Montagnard forges generally require a third worker to pump the bellows. In contrast, Wandala smiths normally, and always when manufacturing the better quality of hoes, work in pairs. The apprentice or mate works the bellows and he and the smith collaborate in forging. Because they are colleagues, as montagnard smiths are not, and because they tend to specialize in certain products, technical innovations occur and spread more easily. An example is the addition, within the memory of practicing smiths, of imported sledge hammers to the traditional repertoire of forging equipment. The energy expended by the Wandala striker is much less than that of his montagnard counterpart, as is the time in which a hoe can be forged to shape. Tool production is further streamlined through the use of highly standardized and efficient ways of cutting up stock into tool blanks. By such means they are capable of manufacturing 20 hoes in a day, while a traditional montagnard forge with a greater input of labor can produce only about 12.

Montagnard responses to Muslim initiatives are various. Several montagnard groups no longer have *any* practicing smiths to serve them. Perhaps because of their relative ease of access to Mora and Mokolo and on account of the importance of the Mayo Plata market, the Uldeme smiths appear to be the only north-ern montagnard iron workers still in full production. But their 20-odd forges are unable to satisfy local demand, and so even this their home market has been invaded by goods from Manaouatchi. The acceptance of a dependence upon others, even upon Muslims, for basic tools is thus one response to changing circumstances. However, some montagnard smiths are reducing the range of their activities and attempting to retain market share by investing in new tech-nology (especially sledge hammers) with a view to increasing productivity and reducing labor costs.

ND and Robertson conclude with generalizations of potential use to prehis-torians confronted with technological successions in the archaeological record. First, context is crucial. In this case the factors that set the stage for the com-petitive success of Muslim technology are economic, the reversal in the tide of iron; sociological, the special status of the Wandala smiths that allowed them continuous contact with montagnards; and political, the colonial pacification. More proximately, the organization of production plays a critical role; another factor is that the two technologies are in genuine economic competition. The artisans of the expanding system innovate by expanding the stylistic and func-tional ranges of their products in the hope of attracting a wider clientele, while the craftsmen of the threatened group make changes in their technology, usually towards that of their rivals, in order better to compete. Conversely, ND and Robertson suggest, were one society dominant over the other and impos-ing its technology, the disappearance of one school of craftsmanship would be accompanied by substantial stylistic continuity in the products of the other.

Archaeologists frequently observe evidence of processes such as those described above, and indeed technological successions are *par excellence* the phenomena in terms of which cultural entities from stages to phases are defined. However, it is only by undertaking regional studies that ethnoarchae-ologists can contribute to such questions.

Itinerant Indian brasscasters

Lee Horne's (1983b, 1994b) regional study of brasscasters in West Bengal began when Sri Haradhan Karmakar of the Dariapur Artisans Cooperative came to Philadelphia to demonstrate his craft as part of a Festival of India tour. In a pre-liminary report, written after a brief visit to Dariapur and West Bengal, Horne introduces the Malhar artisans and their techniques of lost model (wax or resin) brasscasting, and sketches the manner in which these formerly itinerant spe-cialists are adapting to settled life in their own caste hamlet, and to changes in the cost and availability of raw materials that affect their traditional markets and force them to seek new ones. After further fieldwork involving other itin-erant specialists, all of whom claim descent from one, centrally located, found-ing group, but who are now divided into endogamous subcastes speaking different languages and practicing different religions, her interests came to focus on the ways in which such social units might consciously differentiate themselves from each other through their techniques and in other ways. Behura (1978: xiii, cited by Horne 1994b) reported this to be the case among potter sub-castes in Orissa, saying "The pottery techniques of each of the potter subcastes have a unique configuration that varies independently of social structure and language." Thus for Horne (1994b: 271),

The task for this project is to see whether the variations in production techniques cohere into what might be called sets of techniques, and if so, how these sets are related to particular brasscasting groups, and ultimately, whether they serve a functional role in maintaining group cohesion and identity.

Preliminary indications are that there are indeed sets of techniques associated with particular groups (Table 11.9), but whether the differences are consciously used to distinguish groups one from another remains to be demonstrated.

Horne, whose research problem would seem perfectly suited to a chaîne opératoire approach, is making an original contribution to ethnoarchaeology by tackling the topic of itinerant craftspeople. Frederick Matson (1965: 212) long ago drew attention to the interest such groups hold for archaeology, but as Horne remarks "No existing study I know of has considered these [or other] mobile groups as communities that extend beyond any particular settlement, nor how the groups maintain communications, solidarity, and social order in the face of their dispersion" (p. 278). Nor indeed, we would add, do we have any knowledge of the archaeological correlates of such an organization of production, but inasmuch as metal artifacts hold within them much of the history of their manufacture they would seem to be perfectly suited to such an analysis. There is a caveat; metal artifacts are frequently reforged or recast, deleting evidence of their original morphology and techniques of manufacture, and leaving only a garbled signal relating to the ore bodies from which they derived.

Concluding remarks

Ethnoarchaeological studies of craft specialization are limited in topical range and scope. Even for ceramics there is insufficient coverage of the more complex and developed forms of specialization likely to have supplied ancient civilizations and other complex societies. Nonetheless ethnoarchaeological studies are of value for their demonstration of the wide variety of types of specialization and for having explored at least some of their material consequences. What are the overall trends evident in classes of material culture as the scale and intensity of specialization increases? They would seem to include greater standardization with initially some loss of variety, though we know that the range of types may increase as industry develops, for example in the output of the Wedgwood or Delft industrial potteries. There is also greater investment in

Table 11.9 *Variations in selected variables among lost-model brasscasters in West Bengal, eastern Bihar, and northeast Orissa states, India (after Horne 1994b: Table 1, with modifications and additions from her text)*

Variables	Particularly associated with Malhar, Burdwan district, W. Bengal	Particularly associated with Jadu Patua, Dumka district, Bihar	Known variations (these and other groups)
Social and spatial variables			
Group name	Malhar	Jadu Patua	Mal, Mal Parahia, Sekra
Language	Malhar, "Farsi"	Bihari	Maral, Halbi, Hindi, Bengali
Religion	Hindu	Muslim	Hindu/Muslim combined
Surname	Karmakar		Lag, Nag, Jana, Mhanta, Das, Naik, Ure Kamar
Degree of mobility	Presently settled	Itinerant	From settled to totally itinerant
Material variables			
Metal			Aluminum, brass, bell-metal
Model material	Resin	Beeswax	Tar, paraffin, mustard oil
Temper			Ash, dung, charcoal
Mold construction	Vented, crucible at rim	Sealed, crucible at base	
Tools	(Tubular press)*	Tubular press	Wire brush, file
Kiln type	Above ground	Below ground	
Fuel			Wood, coal, dung, palm fronds
Products	Small Lokki Saj figurines	Dance jewelry, rings	Measuring bowls, containers, ladles, anklets, large religious images, "tourist" items
Surface finish			Motifs, degree of wire thread smoothing, polishing, filling
Economic variables			
Distribution			Village hawking, weekly markets, yearly fairs, shops, middlemen/agents, government co-ops, commissions
Forms of payment			Rice, scrap metal, cash, credit
Consumers			Village households, tourists, Indian emporia shoppers, overseas customers, shrine patrons
Other occupations			Snake catcher, bird catcher, tinker, magician, musician, craft demonstrator, exorcist, middleman, beggar

Note: * In Dariapur the tubular press technique for pressing out threads of beeswax was recently learned in development workshops.

facilities, workshops, settling basins, kilns, and the like. In some areas, as for example in African iron smelting, craft specialization is accompanied by increased ritual activity, although intensification of production leads to routinization and secularization of the technology. This appears much less the case in other crafts, and perhaps other continents, although the gender of the observer may be a factor in recording, and we have no ethnoarchaeological studies of, for example, medicine, a technology in which ethnographic sources indicate considerable ritualization.

While archaeologists can learn a great deal about crafts from other sources, ethnoarchaeological studies demonstrate that social relationships have important implications for craft specialization, with considerable implications for the typological variety of the products. A cross-cultural analysis focused on such effects would be of great value. Another area in which more research is needed is that of apprenticeship. Given the importance of typological sequences for the elaboration of time–space systematics in archaeology, it is surprising how little research has been undertaken on the learning, rather than routes of transmission, of crafts. Probably this is because a genuinely productive approach to the subject requires an expertise in cognitive psychology that few anthropologists command. Teamwork such as Roux and Corbetta's offers a solution, but more is needed.

Lastly we would note that craft specialization is intimately bound up with the distribution, exchange, and marketing of its products. These are discussed in the following chapter.

Further reading

The large, ceramic-focused, output of the Kalinga project team includes several studies of particular relevance to the study of craft specialization. Stark (1991, 1995) and Stark and Longacre (1993) are especially important in that they deal with specialization and change. Another set of their papers (Longacre 1999; Longacre et al. 1988; Kvamme et al. 1996), to which we should add Benco's (1988) Moroccan study, take up the issue of standardization and its relation to craft specialization. Michael Deal's (1998) *Pottery ethnoarchaeology in the Central Maya highlands* deserves more comprehensive treatment than we have been able to accord it. Also on ceramics, the set of papers by Margaret Hardin (1977, 1979, 1983a, 1983b, 1984; Hardin Friedrich 1970), essential reading on the topic of decoration and its transmission, should be read in conjunction with Dean Arnold's (1970, 1983, 1984a) studies of society and ceramic design in Quinua, Peru. Beatrice Annis's (1988) "Modes of production and the use of space in potters' workshops in Sardinia" is the most recent of her varied papers (e.g., Annis 1985) on the Sardinian industry.

Haaland and Shinnie's (1985) *African iron working* and Childs and Killick's (1993) survey "Indigenous African metallurgy: nature and culture," although both by now somewhat dated, provide convenient entries into the varied literature on African metallurgy. Nambala Kanté's (1993) autobiographical account of learning to be a Malinke smith in Mali and to fulfill the wide range of functions carried out by caste members is a unique, though not ethnoarchaeological, document.

Hester and Heizer's work (1980, 1981) on the manufacture of stone vases in Egypt extends the limited topical range of ethnoarchaeological studies of craft specialization.

CHAPTER 12

TRADE AND EXCHANGE

Specific types of exchange and interaction are characteristic of various levels of sociocultural complexity.

(Kent Flannery 1972: 129)

To avoid the chaos that would result if they were obliged to redistribute all materials to all of the populace at feasts, the elites developed market institutions.

(Brian Hayden 1993: 405)

We left Sirjan for Kirman yesterday on a truckload of dried limes . . . going to Tehran and had to change over to a truckload of stovewood . . . We searched the bazaar and found plenty of large still-fresh muskmelons, in form and size much like those that are sent from Kabul to India, but these are sweeter. They are a common item of the fruit trade in the capital, and every Tehrani will accordingly tell you that the country's best musk-melons come from Isfahan. Anyone who has ever been in Khorasan will have quite a different opinion.

(Walter N. Koelz 1983: 18, 48)

In this chapter we consider ethnoarchaeological studies of trade and exchange, processes repeatedly implicated by archaeologists in the development of complex societies and societal evolution. Of the limited number available we choose five for special attention. These cover a wide range of socioeconomic complexity.

Exchange, trade, and distribution

Let us use "exchange" as a general term for the transfer of goods and services between people, reserving "trade" for forms that involve at least part-time specialists. Exchange and trade distribute raw materials and artifacts across space through a variety of physical and institutional mechanisms, and, as items move, information and energy, sometimes in the form of armies, move with them. The desire to rationalize trade is frequently implicated in the spread of state forms of polity and the development of empires. The contexts in which objects move from producer to consumer that are most familiar to archaeologists are markets, a type of institution for which there is no evidence in many ancient contexts.

Merchants existed in ancient Mesopotamia, for example, but the mechanisms by which their wares were distributed are poorly understood. In other cases where written records complement archaeological data, such as the Aztec and Inka empires (Brumfiel 1992), observers' reports suggest that indigenous populations – both before and after the Spanish conquest – may have been forced to adapt to radically different models of distribution. Here, we consider ethnoarchaeological studies that include descriptions of markets, but also other mechanisms of distribution including gifting, exchange between friends, allies, kin, and members of different age-sets, and formal exchange partnerships between members of unrelated families over the course of generations. In India's patron–client (*jajmani*) relationships, already mentioned in chapter 6, different goods and services are exchanged, usually on specific occasions. All these are suggestive of the variety of non-market forms of exchange existing in the past.

Loikop spears: circulation and meaning

In 1983 and 1984 Roy Larick (1985, 1986, 1987a 1987b, 1991) worked for "an extended period" with a number of presumably local assistants among the Loikop (related to the Ilchamus/Njemps studied by Hodder), cattle pastoralists then numbering approximately 66,000 and living in Samburu district in northern Kenya. He made a particular study of their spears, which, carried by males from the age of about seven into old age, constitute their most indispensable accouterment. Like many other pastoralists in this part of Africa, the Loikop have a system of male age-sets and grades, named sets (or cohorts) representing males born over an approximately 14-year period who pass through a series of grades: boy, junior and senior warrior, and junior, intermediate, and senior elder (Table 12.1). There are two intakes approximately seven years apart into the junior warrior grade, but at about the same time as the first intake of the following cohort is initiated, those sets already in place move up to the next grade.[1]

---

[1] Larick, in his 1987 and other publications, provides information of two kinds regarding passage through the grades. The first (e.g., 1987a: Table 2) is normative in that it is based on a cohort span of 15 years, but it also gives the actual spear types carried by members of the various (here unnamed) grades. The second (e.g., 1987a: Table 3) gives the names of cohorts, the span of years of their (presumably junior) warriorhood, and the type or types of spear carried by them during that period. Unfortunately we are not told what spears they were carrying in 1984, nor is this clearly evident from figures or other data. Thus it is impossible to reconcile the two sets of information with any certainty. Cohort spans have in fact varied in the past between 12 and 16 years as against Larick's standard 15 years. A more serious discrepancy is that the first set of information suggests that there is only one warrior grade, each intake of which carries different spears, whereas the second set would seem to indicate that there are two grades of warriors, that at the time of Larick's fieldwork the first intake of a new cohort of junior warriors (Kiroro) had taken place, and that the Kishili cohort constituted the senior warrior grade of the time. Reference to Spencer's (1965) ethnography clarifies the picture; progression from warrior to elder is accomplished individually through the act of marriage. Thus at certain transitional times – including it would seem during Larick's fieldwork – there are two grades of warriors, and at others only one. While the interpretation represented in Table 12.1 and Figure 12.1 may be mistaken in detail and some spear types misattributed, the overall structure of the system of circulation is correct.

Table 12.1 *The state of the Loikop age-grade system on 1 January 1984;*
information from Larick 1987a: Tables 1 and 2, as interpreted by ND (see
text for explanation)

Grade	Cohort name and intake	Cohort span	Cohort (intake) age limits	Midpoint of cohort (intake) age span in years
Elders				
senior	Kileko 1 and 2	1921–36	62–77	70
intermed.	Mekuri 1 and 2	1936–48	50–62	56.5
junior	Kimaniki 1 and 2	1948–60	38–50	44.5
Warriors				
senior	Kishili 1 and 2	1960–76	22–38	30.5
junior	Kiroro 1	1976–84?	15–22	18.5
Boys				
older	(Kiroro 2 to be)*	1984?–90?	11–15	13
younger	as yet unnamed		7–11	9

Note: * Larick's 1987a: Fig. 7 suggests that this group was being initiated while he was
in the field.

Between cohorts and grades there is both cooperation and competition. As
the first intake of a new cohort enters warriorhood its members choose the
style or styles of spear that will identify the cohort, and the reasons behind particular choices are complex (Larick 1985).[2] Spear styles are borrowed from
neighboring groups and invented or modified in response to functional needs
and political circumstances. For example, lighter spears were developed for
dealing with enemies equipped with firearms, and others were made with
tapering blade bases so that they would fall more easily from wounded (and
poached) big game. Fears of renewed inter-group warfare led the warriors initiated around the time of Kenyan independence to choose a spear of a style
adopted from the Turkana, who are perceived as dangerous (and less than
human). Thus styles of spears are in part the dynamic product of changing historical circumstances. Together with ways of speaking and dancing, and other
material items, they are actively manipulated as symbols of identity by the
Loikop.

However, the meaning of spears does not simply depend upon the choices of
particular cohorts; it is also generated by frequent and patterned exchanges of
spears (Fig. 12.1). Spears are purchased for stock or cash from a small number
of specialist smiths, about one for every 600 spear-owners. The purchasers
are for the most part senior warriors and junior elders, men who have full

---

[2] Interestingly, not in every case does the intention appear to be differentiation of the cohort. Thus
when the Mekuri cohort (1936–48) entered warriorhood they adopted two of their predecessors'
three preferred spear types.

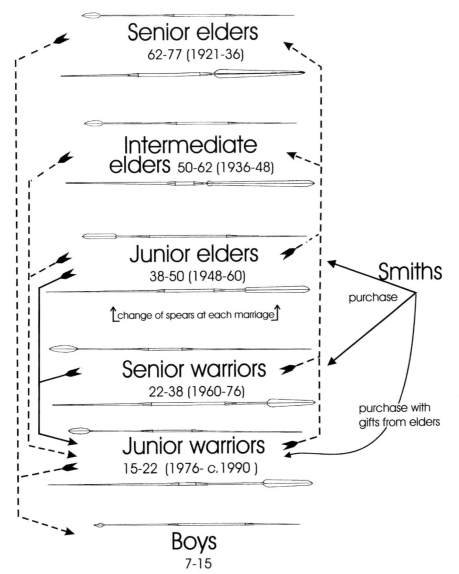

Fig. 12.1 Main inter-grade circulation as of 1984 of new (solid line) and used and worn (dotted line) spears among the Loikop of northern Kenya, starting with the purchase of spears from smiths and continuing with repeated exchanges between members of different age-grades. The years during which cohorts of each grade entered warriorhood and the approximate ages of members in 1984 are indicated. A typical spear adopted by the cohort at the time of its initiation into warriorhood is shown below each grade with tip to the right, and a spear type frequently carried by members of the cohort in 1984 is shown above, tip to the left. Exchanges of spears within grades are not indicated. Data from Larick (1985, 1986, 1987a, 1987b); spear types after Larick (1987b).

managerial control over herds. Young men entering the junior warrior grade may be given money to purchase spears from smiths or they may be given the worn, morphologically modified, spears passed down by members of age-grades senior to themselves. (Spear fashion is likely set by a small number of young men in the first intake of a new junior warrior cohort, those of high-ranking clans who have been given money, allowing them freedom to choose a style for their spears.) Senior warriors and junior elders tend to carry the heaviest and most impressive spears (or in some cohorts pairs of lighter spears), while as men progress through intermediate to senior elderhood spears become less important to their image and they carry lighter, worn specimens of a variety of original forms. Senior elders own small, light spears, and the smallest and lightest are carried by boys.

The choice of cohort styles is only one of three factors that can be said to underlie the patterning of stylistic variation in Loikop spears. The second relates to spears as material items subject to use-wear. As frequent polishing and sharpening of the blade reduces its size and modifies its shape, a spear ages faster than its owner. The third factor is circulation. Since spears are modified by use and since there are expectations regarding basic characteristics, especially size and weight, of the spears appropriately carried by men of different grades, they become frequent objects of exchange (lateral cycling). Elders change their spears each time they marry, but age-group transitions are the most important mechanism for the circulation of spears. The main flows of their initial exchange and subsequent inter-grade circulation, from smiths to senior warriors and junior elders and then both upwards to senior grades and downwards to junior warriors and boys, are diagrammed in Figure 12.1. This circulation is as important as are the other two factors in generating the complex stylistic patterns that Loikop are capable of deciphering, to the extent that:

Herders (men and women) are able to identify the social age (age grade and generation) of a male by viewing the otherwise ethnic traits of his spear . . . More subtle patterns of size and shape may reflect the owner's more personal attributes: sequential position within his age set, physical stature and strength, sequence within his father's line of sons, responsibility within his mother's house, and prestige as a warrior. (1987a: 147–50)

The precision with which Loikop are asserted to be able to identify a man's social persona by his spear in fact remains somewhat mysterious, much depending on a variety of other stylistic – speech, dress, comportment – and physiological clues.

What would this pattern look like archaeologically? Larick (1987a) documented over 600 exchanges of which "all but a few" were between members of the same patrilineal clan, most often within segments of the clan. Thus, as "members of any one segmentary unit, up to the level of clan, tend to reside closer to each other than to members of any other unit at the same level . . .

Social proximity serves to limit the spatial scale of circulation in weapons, in that men most commonly pass weapons to brothers, parallel cousins, and father's brothers" (p. 159). One might therefore expect locality, inasmuch as it tends to be correlated with clan kin relations, to constitute a fourth factor, one that crosscuts the pan-tribal factors noted above, in determining the range of styles present in any part of Loikop territory. But there are extra-clan relationships that lead to exchanges of weapons: from mother's brother to sister's son, between mentors (chosen from among initiates' fathers' non-kin friends) and initiates undergoing circumcision, and between non-kin "oath partners" of an outgoing warrior cohort and initiates entering warriorhood. Marriages also generate exchanges of weapons and other goods between affines, often over long distances as marriages are commonly contracted between persons residing in different environmental zones. Such exchange relationships, some lifelong, complicate stylistic patterning, but it seems doubtful that they obscure the effects of the patrilineal localizing tendency. Nonetheless, it seems certain that, combined with a certain amount of noise in the system (attributable to individual taste, persons for whatever reasons taking more or less time to change their weapons, and similar small-scale factors), they result in a loss of focus in the patterning that would render it forever uninterpretable archaeologically – even if, in response to some hypothetical Pompeiian imperative, the Loikop one day laid down their spears and walked away.

Whereas spears rust, are resharpened, laterally cycled, and recycled, and are unlikely to enter the Loikop archaeological record as identifiable spears, Larick insists that comparable patterns of circulation exist for other items, some of which are likely to leave a stronger archaeological trace.

Weapons constitute only one component of a diverse set of material items, services, and information that constantly flows among kin, with only an indirect accounting of value. The spatial and social pattern of exchange is unplanned, and the observed result, circulation, is an abstraction. (p. 155)

Despite its uncertainties, the Loikop case clearly demonstrates the role played by patterns of circulation (abstractions of which actors may be unaware) in structuring the archaeological record. It also reminds us that the normative constructions of ethnographers only imperfectly represent the complex realities that exist on the ground and that are, as imperfectly, conceptualized by members of the culture under analysis.

Irian Jaya: axes from Yeleme, adzes from Mumyeme

P. Pétrequin and A.-M. Pétrequin's (1990) chaîne opératoire approach to the manufacture of axes and adzes in Irian Jaya (see chapter 6) is part of a project carried out over an area of about 100,000 km² that started in 1985 and required five missions (of unspecified duration) to complete. A second aim was to document and explain the movement and exchange of ground stone and other items within and between the highland and lowland zones and especially from quarries in the Yeleme and Mumyeme localities. The Pétrequins give no information regarding their field techniques but state that the use of polished stone tools ended between 1960 and 1968 in this part of the world. Thus their work might better be characterized as ethnohistory than as ethnoarchaeology, were it not that the project's film *Langda* (Thery *et al.* 1990) demonstrates that knapping and related skills were at that time far from forgotten, and we infer that stone tools continued to play a role in social exchanges.

Large numbers of Yeleme ax blades are transported up to 170 km from their quarries of origin, with isolated pieces going as far as 230 km (see Fig. 6.7). They are widely exchanged over central Irian Jaya, being the most common materials used by the Dani of the Baliem valley (the Grand Valley Dani), 150 km to the southeast, though less frequent in the Paniaï lakes basin some 180 km to the WSW. Their extended distribution through the area of highest population density expresses linguistic and cultural relationships between neighboring highland groups: including, from east to west, the northern Yali, the Dani, Wano, Moni, and Kapauku. Despite the use of similar tools, an environmental and linguistic frontier inhibits north–south movement of blades from the Yeleme region into the northern lowlands, and where this occurs, as among the Dubele, it is on account of recent population movements. Nor do Yeleme blades reach the southern lowlands. Two to three days' walk south of the Yeleme quarries the southern Wano live in a valley through which ax roughouts must pass on their way to the Dani of the Yamo valley. They are thus in a better position to exert control over the transit of blades than the less populous northern Wano who occupy the land around the quarries. Warriors in groups of 20 to 25 sometimes risk forcing the passage but most western Dani prefer to establish long-term relations with the southern Wano, exchanging women, pigs, salt, and cowry shells for access to the quarries.[3] The quarries are in fact mainly exploited by western Dani warriors, mostly 20–30 years old, who seek once or twice during their lifetimes a rapid way of paying their bridewealth by mounting expeditions that take up to a week to reach the quarries. Each man brings back with him five to ten crude roughouts of which some are exchanged for pigs on their return.

The western Dani add value to the roughouts by polishing them on local outcrops of high-quality sandstone, and traders ("commerçants") originating in this area carry axes and salt to the densely peopled Baliem valley.[4] They also

---

[3] Whether women should be included in this list is problematic; bridewealth (in French "le dot") is offered by the Wano for Dani women and includes axes and pigs.

[4] Polishers are made of sandstones which have a mutually exclusive distribution from the rocks used for making blades. Just as exchange networks ensure that everyone can have at least two stone blades, so too polishers (8–15 kg in weight) are intensively exchanged though rarely mentioned in the literature. Beyond their existence, we learn nothing about the traders or their commercial relations.

control the length of blades exchanged with outside peoples. Stone blades are required elements of payments made in bridewealth, blood money, and funeral transactions, and the western Dani tend to keep the largest for themselves. Whereas among Wano living near the quarries the modal length is in the 20–30 cm range, among the western Dani polishers of Mulia there are two modes, at 10–20 cm and 30 cm and above. Among Dani "close users" a short distance to the east, the mode is in the 10–20 cm range, but there are also some blades in the 1–10 cm range, often broken pieces reworked and rehafted to serve as adzes. Further to the south and east, among the Baliem Dani, "distant users," pieces 10 cm or less in length outnumber blades in the 10–20 cm range. These long-time ax users have now learned to use the adz, while far to the west Kapauku and other groups in the Paniaï basin have innovated by devising new hafting methods to accommodate ever smaller ax blades.

Some long ax blades do reach Baliem but south of the Yamo river they are rare and used only for splitting wood; the main woodworking tool is the short-bladed adz. The large blades kept by the western Dani are fixed in massive decorated hafts and are used for tree cutting but also as symbols. They are typical of an area in which a certain kind of bridewealth is practiced that extends in an arc to the east, south, and west of the Yeleme quarries. Blades of other materials also attain symbolic significance. The Wano and western Dani exploit thin slabs of relatively soft green schist from which large blades are roughed out by flaking or sawing before being polished. Amongst them and the Moni this raw material is mainly used for functional purposes, but throughout the zone peripheral to the quarries flat green schist blades are kept in men's houses in order, once consecrated, to house the spirits of dead ancestors and to confer invulnerability on their owners. Among Toli and Baliem Dani and some northern Yali, axes of green schist receive special treatment, being greased with pork fat, and appear in their dozens in ritual exchanges. In the Baliem valley they are associated with sewn bands of cowrie shells, paralleling the cowry currency of the Kapauku. In this populated region the exchange of signs – here green schist blades, there cowries – contributes to the limitation of warfare, highly ritualized in Baliem but hard to control among the western Dani.

In contrast, in the Mumyeme area basalt blades are distributed only up to about 90 km away from their quarries. Distribution is between trading partners, reciprocal exchanges taking place over distances of several days' walk and, on the occasion of important ceremonies, in considerable numbers, with care being given to avoid giving back more than one has received as this would be regarded as a form of aggression. Here too reciprocal dependencies may function to limit warfare. Unlike in the area served by the Yeleme quarries, in this region blades are not selected for length or quality but are rather regarded as functional parts of everyday tools. Thus Mumyeme blades reaching Yali territory five to six days' walk to the west have essentially the same characteristics as those remaining near the quarries or at the sites of previous exchanges. Why it is that big basalt adz blades are not used as prestige goods remains unclear, but it is a fact that in New Guinea only polished axes are subject to symbolic elaboration.

The Pétrequins' work demonstrates the complexity of the factors that can underlie systems of production and exchange. In this instance the existence – which must be accepted as a given – of two ancient traditions of polished tool use combines with a number of other factors to produce a highly variable distribution of forms over the very large area of study. The pattern is generated by the interaction of differing raw materials, chaînes opératoires, technical innovations, environments and economic adaptations, population numbers and densities, and social and ideational factors. These last include contrasting modes of distribution and exchange in the eastern and western parts of the area, and the presence of symbolic elaboration only in one. Rather than passing this off as a cautionary tale, we should remember (see chapter 6) that there is a correlation between blade length and environment that is both processually pleasing and evidence that, given sufficient ingenuity in their hafting, axes and adzes are isochrestic. More generally, there is much to be learned from comparisons of regional ethnoarchaeologies, between, say, New Guinea, the Lake Baringo region, and the Mandara mountains. We are not yet very good at conceptualizing differences in patterns of regional variation.

Ceramic change and exchange among the Kalinga

When Longacre returned to the Kalinga with his team in 1987 after a decade of interruption due to political unrest he found major changes. There had been fighting between the army and communist guerillas; a dam, threatened but never built, had resulted in road building that greatly improved access to the wider world, especially for Dalupa.[5] Developments in gold mining and forestry, while reducing Kalinga access to land and forestry products, provided jobs for Kalinga men, and movement into the area of people of diverse origins offered potters new markets (Longacre and Skibo 1994). These events profoundly altered the production and exchange of Kalinga pottery in ways documented by Miriam Stark (1992, 1994) and Stark and Longacre (1993).

From October 1987 to June 1988 Stark focused on two communities, Dalupa and Dangtalan, in that part of the Pasil river basin, only some 13 km from east to west and 8 from north to south, that constitutes the Pasil municipality. She used structured and open-ended interviews and collected observational data that include remarkable pottery exchange logs for 60 potters, maintained by assistant Josephine Bommogas for three months after her departure (Fig. 12.2). These track the movement of almost 2800 vessels over the course of a year (1994: 172) both within and beyond the municipality. She also had access to

---

[5] The reader is referred to chapter 7, note 12, for discussion of Kalinga settlement units.

Fig. 12.2 Miriam Stark (*right*) and field assistant Josephine Bommogas interview a Kalinga potter in Dalupa (Luzon, Philippines), 1987. Such interviews provided information on household economics, personal histories, and learning frameworks.

data gathered by Longacre and worked up by Graves (see chapter 7) from a period when most women in Dangtalan and Dalupa potted to provide for their own households and for limited exchange with people in nearby villages. Since in earlier times women in other communities had also made pottery we infer a long-term, but irregular and punctuated, increase in specialization through time. By 1987 many fewer Dangtalan women were potting and those who did had become part-time specialists producing most of their pots during periods of rice shortage. Meanwhile in Dalupa, pottery manufacture had become a village industry, with women organized into work groups on the basis of kin and other social relations, and even one or two men getting involved. A wide range of new forms – including water jars, ashtrays, flower pots, and the water buffalo equivalent of piggy-banks (some of good quality but the "toys" or souvenir types generally very poor) – was being manufactured by techniques derived from the old, and there were changes in surface treatment – less resin, a forest product – and in decoration, with less time-consuming techniques being favored and some new designs developed to attract a varied clientele. Because dealers were buying up Chinese porcelain that had long been traded into the region as prestige items, potters began to make substitute wares.

In the 1970s movements of pottery, at that time entirely utilitarian, had been largely limited to the Pasil municipality and its immediate surroundings, and involved primarily barter and some gifting. By the late 1980s there were major changes: a considerable volume of pottery was being traded beyond the municipality; there was increased use of fictive kinship to establish long-term trading partnerships (suki) with non-locals, and, like the Wandala ironmongers discussed above, a few women were becoming engaged as intermediaries between potters and consumers. Nonetheless conditions remained far from those of the anonymous market. Stark found that

Social relations . . . play an important role in potters' selection of consumer [communities]. Within the Pasil Municipality, producers and their customers often have a direct relationship that is reckoned by kin ties, no matter how distant. Where possible, a potter relies on established social relations who, by Kalinga custom, are obligated to provide food and lodging during her barter visits . . . These hosts often receive gifts of pots in return for their hospitality. Relationships between potters and hosts can endure through generations of producers and consumers. (1992: 141)

Ceramics are often exchanged for perishable goods, such as rice, condiments, tobacco, rattan, clothing, and medicine. Indeed the notional but in fact varying former price of a pot was the amount of rice it could hold. Straight-line distances between communities involved in such exchanges are mostly less than 10 km or three hours' walk (1994: 187), but the rugged terrain and limited availability of motorized transport make for journeys that are often arduous. Movement of pottery beyond the Pasil municipality is more often characterized by monetary transactions than the barter more typical between Pasil communities, but kinship continues to play key roles in the spatial distribution of ceramics (see CK's Rajasthani research below for a comparable finding relating to subcastes). Stark argues (1992: 148) that the "Dalupa example indicates that nonhierarchical systems may also be characterized by multicentric economies," elaborating on this point in a later work (1994) in which, unlike other ethnoarchaeologists who have discussed exchange, she also records seasonal variation in the movement (as opposed to simply the production) of pots.

The research of Stark and Longacre exemplifies the benefits of long-term studies and is eloquent testimony to the ability of "traditional artisans" to respond effectively to changed circumstances and new opportunities and to develop or adopt new mechanisms of trade and exchange while continuing to maintain the old. Stark and Longacre (1994) also suggest that some changes are "top down," which is to say that some successful potters can afford the risk of innovating, while others are "bottom up" in the case of the potters who are so poor that they have nothing to lose by experimentation. In summary, the study is of relevance to the question of how, by whom, and under what circumstances innovation takes place. It supports the proposition that as production intensifies, manufacturing steps will tend to decrease and products become more standardized. It also indicates that while potters are not by nature conservative

– as Foster (1965: 49) opined years ago – the basic technology of production changes less easily than either the organization of work or the forms and styles of the ceramics produced. Motor habits and procedures learned early are hardest to change.

Trade and verticality in the Andes

Two important studies of ceramic distribution in the Peruvian Andes must be noted here. Both document the myriad mechanisms by which ceramics move across space, and both pay particular attention to ecological constraints that affect the movement of commodities, as well as to the complex relationships among potters and vendors. Karen Mohr Chavez, discussing the organization of production and distribution in southern Peru (1991), documents the production of different ceramic types by men and women, as well as the differing ways in which men and women purvey their wares. Men are itinerant vendors; women occupy specific places in weekly markets. Unlike the case described by Dean Arnold (1993), most of the pottery in Mohr Chavez's area is utilitarian.

In the Raqch'i area (southwest of Cuzco), both men and women are potters, but they make different forms, using different techniques (men turntables, women press-molds); male and female members of potters' households comple-ment one another and form a single productive unit. As elsewhere in Latin America, pottery is distributed by a variety of mechanisms: through individual relationships on a local basis, at (daily or weekly) periodic markets at varying distances from production localities, and on pilgrimages and at religious festi-vals. Production of specific ceramic forms is not only tied to potters' genders but (while Mohr Chavez is somewhat skeptical) possibly also to the raw ma-terials (particularly tempers) used for vessels with specific functions. Traditionally, localization in the production of specific forms made with par-ticular clays resulted in complementarity between vessels usually exposed to fire or heat that were produced at higher elevations, and others, designed to serve, store, carry, and ferment, made at lower elevations. Another form of complementarity has to do with relationships between settlements and markets at different elevations in the Andes, particularly important because barter of foodstuffs for ceramics, rather than exchange of currency for commod-ities, is essential in that region. However, she notes that in her research area John Murra's concept of an Andean "vertical archipelago," in which a single ethnic group occupies strongly articulating lowland and montane commu-nities, is not always appropriate.

Dean Arnold (1975a, 1983), who worked in the Ayacucho area before the radical Shining Path (Sendero Luminoso) movement rendered fieldwork tem-porarily impossible, has a number of interesting observations about ceramic production and distribution. Like Mohr Chavez, he notes that the production and distribution of utilitarian earthenwares have a seasonal aspect, wet and cold weather having an inhibiting effect on both activities. Intermediaries or middlemen play a crucial role in the distribution of ceramics from potters to consumers. In both of these Peruvian cases, the tourist industry is important, and, in the case of the Quinua center in particular, ceramic models of churches and houses can be found far from the local center, Ayacucho, and even in New York and London. Some of these items were, in the late 1980s, made by Quinua potters who had moved (with their clays) to Lima.

Rajasthani markets and scalar effects

As in the Western hemisphere, a variety of mechanisms is responsible for ceramic distribution in the Old World. In West Africa, these have been documented in ethnoarchaeological work by, among others, Crossland and Posnansky (1978), Gallay *et al.* (1996), and Nicklin (1981). Dietler and Herbich's (1994) discussion of the implications of the Luo ceramic production and market systems for stylistic variation in the archaeological record was touched on in chapter 7. One of the more complex systems of distribution documented in ethnoarchaeological research is in north India. Here, numerous means of exchanging goods are examined in a study focusing on the potter caste (Kramer 1997). Following a pilot survey in 1980, CK did research during two five-month periods (August through December, 1982 and 1983) among urban potters in the cities of Jodhpur and Udaipur in Rajasthan, whose communities of potters did not interact. In this region, wheel-thrown pottery is made by men, and distributed within and beyond both rural and urban settlements where it is made. Vessels are moved on foot, on animals' backs, in carts, and, rarely, by truck; small quantities are carried by purchasers on bicycles or in trains. The variety of transport mechanisms, combined with less extreme topographic challenges in these two districts, suggests that the scale (distances, as well as number of vessels moved) of ceramic distribution would likely be far greater than it is in, say, Luzon. One of the questions guiding this work centered on the extent to which scalar differences between settlements (in area, population, function, and administration) might be reflected in differing numbers of vessels in shops, different numbers of ceramic types, numbers of places from which vessels are imported to urban centers, and distances from which such imports derive. Ceramic variability on the surfaces of contemporaneous archaeological sites within a single region might reflect differences other than their areal disparities. A second question was whether sociological links between potters and vendors within large centers are related to and possibly affect the exchange of utilitarian earthenwares. After collecting detailed genealogical data, interviewing over 200 potters and vendors, and counting more than 200,000 vessels in about 150 censused shops, CK found that Jodhpur's areally, demographically, functionally, and administratively larger size (Fig. 12.3) is indeed expressed in ceramic contrasts with Udaipur.

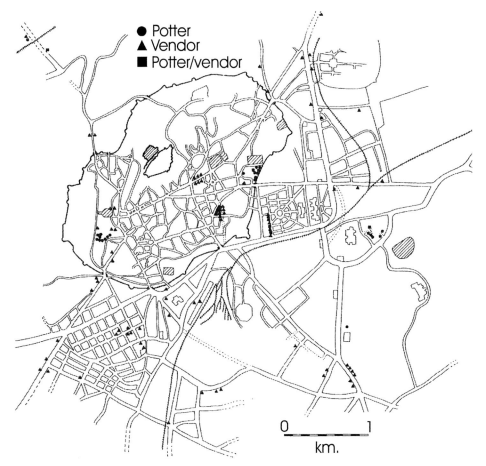

Fig. 12.3 Plan of Jodhpur, Rajasthan, India, showing remains of the medieval city wall and some of the original gates, and neighborhoods that have grown up around the densely settled walled center. Locations of potters and vendors of pottery in the early 1980s are indicated. Hatched areas are reservoirs ("tanks") built for a variety of uses. The locations of these features were recorded by CK and the plan created using several Government of India maps drawn to different scales. Obtaining reliable plans, maps, and aerial photographs in timely fashion is often a challenge to ethnoarchaeologists.

Jodhpur potters' clays come from a larger catchment, the city has more neighborhoods with shops, and those shops are owned by vendors representing more castes than are found among Udaipur's shopkeepers. Jodhpur imports pottery from more settlements, whose average distance exceeds that of external sources represented in Udaipur's shops (Fig. 12.4). Jodhpur's shops have more pots, and more vessel types, than do those of Udaipur. In addition, examination of exchange within these cities suggests biases not typically assumed by

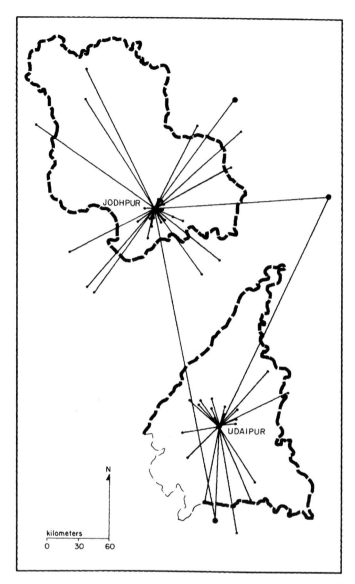

Fig. 12.4 Distribution of external sources supplying Jodhpur (pop. 506,345)
and Udaipur (pop. 232,588) with utilitarian earthenwares in the
early 1980s. Heavy dashed lines indicate district boundaries; the
lighter dashed line the state border with Gujarat. The larger city's
ability to attract more pottery from greater distances is apparent,
although the effects of modern means of transport should be borne
in mind.

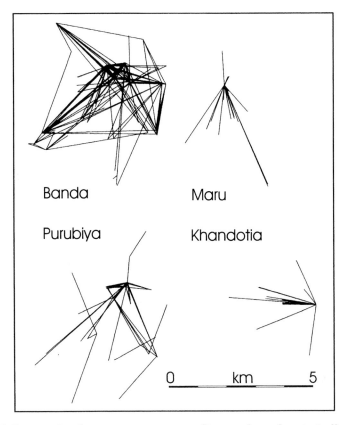

Fig. 12.5 Interaction between pottery suppliers and vendors in Jodhpur, broken down by potter (Kumhar) subcaste. Lines connect points representing potters and vendors. There are more Banda subcaste suppliers in more neighborhoods than any other subcaste, and they have the most complex exchange network. The few Khandotia potters are seasonal visitors from neighboring Haryana state (see Kramer 1997: 122ff.).

archaeologists. In this cultural setting, in which caste and subcaste affiliations are crucial in organizing diverse relationships and participation (or not) in a range of activities that includes exchange transactions, the spatial distribution of various goods is to some extent a function of sociological relationships. This Rajasthani research demonstrates that in some cases archaeologists' assumption that interaction is typically driven by spatial proximity, while inuitively appealing, is not necessarily correct. In both Jodhpur and Udaipur, CK found that even where potters are in comparative proximity to vendors, they often sell their wares to vendors at greater distances if their caste relationships are closer (Kramer and Douglas 1992) (Fig. 12.5). Like Miller's Dangwara potters, these also participate in the *jajmani* system, which accounts for other aspects of ceramic distribution in the two cities. CK also observed that particular settlements are recognized in market centers as identified with specific vessel types even though those settlements' potters make far more extensive and sometimes rather comparable inventories, designed for distribution in villages in their own hinterlands, rather than for urban sale or exchange. This form of specialization reduces the risk of competition between donor communities within the larger urban context, and also results in different vessel types being distributed at differing spatial scales. Thus scalar and social effects both influence material culture distributions, and Zipf's (1949) comforting principle of least effort does not always hold up under ethnoarchaeological scrutiny.

Concluding remarks

While the ethnoarchaeological literature on trade and exchange is limited in volume, the five case studies presented demonstrate its substantial contribution to the documentation of the range of institutions and mechanisms responsible for the exchange and distribution of artifactual materials. They also speak to processes of change and innovation, some of which, even when they occur in societies that are too often regarded as tradition-bound, can be very rapid and geared to social and economic factors operating at a national or international scale.

While ethnoarchaeologists commonly point out the significance of their findings for archaeological studies of exchange and trade, their publications are widely dispersed. There is certainly now sufficient material for a synthesis that would render such work more readily available to a potentially eager archaeological audience. Vossen's (1984) attempt at model building based on Spanish and Moroccan data deserves emulation. In the meantime there is a lot to be learned from ethnographic, ethnological, and ethnohistorical sources (e.g., Allen 1984; Féblot-Augustins and Perlès 1992).

Further reading

Ethnoarchaeological sources focusing on exchange and distribution are limited in number although information on such matters can be found in a variety of books and monographs. Margaret Nelson's (1987b) paper on the manufacture and marketing of manos and metates in the Maya Highlands takes us away from ceramics, while Scott MacEachern's (1993) "Selling the iron for their shackles" links metallurgy to exchange. Janet Chernela (1992), a sociocultural anthropologist writing for archaeologists, provides a fascinating if problematic account of exchange of craft items between language groups in affinal relationships among the Wanano-Tukano and their neighbors near the borders of Brazil and Colombia.

Another approach to scale of ceramic distribution is taken by Gallay *et al.* (1996), who describe an ethnographically complex situation in the inland Niger delta (Mali), where ethnic diversity is reflected in ceramics. In the absence of extensive documentation, but benefiting from long-term multi-disciplinary archaeologically oriented observation, this summary volume describes not only the range of mechanisms by which utilitarian earthenwares move across the (partly riverine) landscape, but also the ways in which ethnicity and marriage practices contribute to ceramic diversity in particular localities. The radius of approximately 50 km within which pottery is distributed approximates that of potters' moves when they marry and take up residence in their husbands' communities.

CHAPTER 13

MORTUARY PRACTICES, STATUS, IDEOLOGY, AND SYSTEMS OF THOUGHT

That the dead do not bury themselves may seem obvious and banal.
(Michael Parker Pearson 1993: 204)

The Tarahumara are not afraid of death or the dead, and soliciting information from informants about burial caves is no more exasperating than inquiry into other aspects of their daily life.
(Allen Pastron and C. William Clewlow 1974a: 310)

While rarely devoid of information on people's beliefs and ways of thinking about the world and their place in it, few ethnoarchaeological studies probe this aspect of culture and its expression in material things. Usually such research involves semiotic analysis of material culture and other behaviors, and employs a hermeneutic approach;[1] however some research on the disposal of the dead is not of this kind at all, but rather seeks patterning in mortuary practice that relates to social structure and status. While some authors are concerned to understand systems of thought, others emphasize ideology in the narrower sense of assertions underlying a political program. However, inasmuch as elements of the former are politicized and incorporated into the latter, it is often difficult to maintain a distinction between the two concepts, this depending largely upon the attitude of the researcher to her or his material. Linda Donley(-Reid)'s (e.g., 1982, 1990b) papers on the houses of the Swahili elite and on their uses of porcelain, beads, and utilitarian pottery are explorations of systems of thought. But they also reveal the part that material culture played in constituting the hegemony that maintained elite males' dominant position *vis-à-vis* elite women, other inhabitants of the coast, and foreign traders. Despite or rather because of its concern with symbolism Donley-Reid's work has very practical archaeological implications, as for example regarding the dating of coral rag houses (and what not to do on survey!).

In this chapter we discuss first the ethnoarchaeology of mortuary practices, especially as these relate to status and ideology, and then papers that deal with ideology, domination, and resistance. We conclude by examining examples of

---

[1] Semiotic analyses are concerned with signs and systems of signs and the way these are combined into messages and codes. Hermeneutics is discussed in chapter 2.

ethnoarchaeology's contribution to understanding the relationship between technology and systems of thought, and the implications for archaeology and ethnoarchaeological practice.

Mortuary practices, status, and ideology

Archaeologists are intimates not of death but of the dead, and there is a considerable literature regarding the ways in which mortuary rites relate to societal structure and culture. The modern period of theorizing on the topic began with the publication of a paper by Binford (1971).[2] He surveyed and, supporting his argument with cross-tabulations of traits in a worldwide sample of 40 societies, dismissed several propositions regarding the determinants of mortuary practices offered by anthropologists of the culture-historical school. He concluded that variability in mortuary practices is related to variability in society, and in particular to the social persona of the deceased and the composition and size of the group to which he or she is socially related. This theory was applied to archaeological data, elaborated and developed. During the Recent period archaeologists have become progressively more aware that the determination of mortuary practices by societal factors not only is mediated by belief systems and ideologies, but that these themselves influence aspects of mortuary behavior. In 1982 Brad Bartel argued for "the incorporation of structuralist theory and examinations of the entire trajectory of death-related behavior." Christopher Carr's (1995b) study, influenced by the anthropologists Huntington and Metcalf (1979), whose *Celebrations of death* resurrected the ideas of Robert Hertz (1907), is significantly titled "Mortuary practices: their social, philosophical-religious, circumstantial and physical determinants."

Like his predecessors Carr begins his lengthy paper with a discussion of archaeological approaches to the study of mortuary practices and of previous Human Relations Area Files (HRAF) surveys before embarking on a more ambitious one of his own which, for the first time, takes philosophical-religious beliefs into consideration. Files on 31 non-state societies, each from a different world sampling province, were searched for 28 traits pertaining to mortuary behaviors and rituals and no less than 67 relating to beliefs and world view. Forty-six practices and 29 possible causes were coded and cross-tabulated to answer the questions listed below, to which we have appended much abbreviated answers.

> 1 *Are mortuary practices and remains, as symbolic behaviors and forms, arbitrarily related to their determining causes/referents cross-culturally and within societies?* Clearly not.

[2] Arthur Saxe's (1970) Ph.D. thesis, "Social dimensions of mortuary practices," was never published commercially but is widely recognized as the other foundational text of modern mortuary archaeology. Virtually contemporary, Maurice Bloch's (1971) *Placing the dead*, a study of social identity and mortuary practice among the Merina of Madagascar, is arguably the ethnographic source that has most influenced archaeology.

2 *What are the most common associations observed cross-culturally between particular mortuary practices and particular determinants?* Energy expenditure and vertical social position; grave furniture and personal identity/beliefs about the soul/the afterlife/the soul's journey; body preparation and beliefs about the soul; grave form and vertical social position; grave furniture and gender.

3 *With what relative frequencies do social, philosophical-religious, circumstantial, physical, and ecological categories of variables determine mortuary practices?* Philosophical-religious beliefs were found to do so 1021 times, social position 727 times, and the remainder much less frequently.

4 *Are there certain mortuary practices that reflect social factors more often than philosophical-religious ones, and vice-versa?* Within cemetery location, number of burial types, of individuals per grave, and overall energy expenditure, including for grave goods, more often reflect social factors. Funeral celebrations, body position, and arrangement of grave furniture are among the practices that more commonly reflect beliefs.

5 *Are there certain kinds of mortuary practices that cross-culturally are determined by only one of a limited number of solely philosophical-religious or social organizational factors?* The answer, supported by a lengthy table, is, alas, that "most mortuary practices are determined cross-culturally by multiple, common factors" (p. 160).

6 *Does the balance of the different determinants of mortuary practices vary with sociopolitical complexity?* Social and philosophical-religious variables are far more influential than other kinds, but the importance of the latter decreases from 1.92 times the former in band-level hunter-gatherers to 0.84 in petty hierarchies before rising again to 1.53 in paramount chiefdoms.[3]

Carr has performed a service in documenting the range of factors that influence mortuary practices, but the problems associated with such an approach are manifold, including:

1 the assumption that "tribes" or "cultures" are comparable entities that can be described by a list of characteristics,

2 missing data and differential inadequacies of the original observations,

3 problems in coding inherent in the double distancing of the analyst from the original behavior and in the difficulty of recognizing similar and dissimilar material in decontextualized datasets,

4 problems in classification (Is "petty hierarchy" a valid taxon? To what extent are social, philosophical-religious, and other variables analytically separable?),

5 problems relating to the equivalence of associations (e.g., correlations of "vertical social position" with "energy expenditure" may be variously related to other factors),

[3] The figure given is "the number of observations of philosophical-religious factors determining any . . . mortuary practice divided by the number of social factors determining any . . . mortuary practice."

6 inference of causality (determination) on the basis of such data is problematical, and

7 neither last nor least, since the societies for whom files exist constitute neither a random nor a demonstrably representative sample of human societies, probabilistic extrapolation to other, and in particular past, societies is fraught with uncertainty.

These and other difficulties are presumably responsible for such things as Carr's and Binford's samples producing fundamentally different results regarding the association of "body orientation" with "horizontal social position," once again raising questions as to the validity of a method that has been repeatedly challenged – without adequate response – since the 1950s (Holy 1987: 3). Edmund Leach's (1964: 299) fundamental objections and forthright declaration that George Peter Murdock "is producing tabulated nonsense" even deny the method's utility as a means of raising research questions. He is certainly right that it does not and cannot answer them (even when buttressed by statistical correlations). Fragmentation of ethnographies into traits almost inevitably precludes understanding (at least by those using the files) of the dynamics of particular cultures or of patterns existing at larger, regional or areal, scales. Archaeological theorists have made good use of a variety of more or less esoteric sources but only exceptionally have ethnographers devoted significant attention to the links that relate disposal of the dead to society and culture. This is why, even though they will no more provide a manual for the archaeological interpretation of disposals than Carr's cross-tabs, archaeologists need ethnoarchaeological studies of mortuary behavior.

Why then can substantive ethnoarchaeological writings on mortuary practice be numbered on the fingers of two hands – and that with an overly generous interpretation of ethnoarchaeology? The answer relates both to the short time generally spent by ethnoarchaeologists in the field and to the perceived difficulty of dealing with (what Westerners regard as) a sensitive topic. Thus not only is the researcher likely to observe only a few deaths and funerals, but he or she may well hesitate to investigate the subject in the first place. Such uneasiness is by no means always justified, though the study of mortuary practices will generally be easier when it forms part of a broader program of research, and exceptional circumstances may force the fieldworker to renounce or abort work in this area, as happened during CK's analysis of the cemetery of Aliabad (Kramer 1982a: 76–80). What then has ethnoarchaeological research on death to contribute to archaeology?

The transformed worlds of Aliabad and Cambridge

Although two papers by Allen Pastron and C. William Clewlow from 1974 claim to be ethnoarchaeological they are in fact papers on recent archaeology interpreted in the light of information provided by Rarámuri villagers. It is not until 1982, the first year of the Recent period, that we have the first ethnoar-chaeological studies, two forming parts of monographs by CK and Hodder, the third a paper by Michael Parker Pearson, a pupil of the latter. CK's study of Aliabad documents variation in economic status between households and its expression in material culture, and it is from this perspective that she began her analysis of the cemetery. Before the six sudden deaths – in fact a mass murder – that interrupted her work she had accumulated enough data to inves-tigate some of the relationships between social structure and mortuary prac-tice suggested by Binford and others.

In ideologically egalitarian Aliabad, differential mortuary treatment is accorded individ-uals along lines of age and sex . . . At the same time cadavers are apparently treated the same way regardless of age, sex, or group affiliation . . . Finally, some juveniles and adult women are accorded the burial marker that is both most costly and numerically least common . . . Villagers' awareness of status differences may be reinforced by the morpho-logical variations among grave markers. (Kramer 1982a: 80)

Although Binford's (1971: 17) contention that peculiar circumstances sur-rounding death may alter survivors' acknowledgment of the social persona of the deceased finds dramatic confirmation in the treatment accorded the murder victims, in other respects this is at best a partial confirmation of his thesis. In Aliabad, the range of variation in mortuary treatment is limited (being less by far than, for example, in any French Catholic village), the cost of the most expensive inscribed headstone representing 0.7 percent of the estimated wealth of the median village household and 0.45 percent of that of a household at the bottom of the top quartile. This is largely because Islam, by equating equality in mortuary practice with equality before God, conceals and misrepresents social relations – this being one of the three ways in which, according to Giddens (1979: 193–7), ideology operates. The tendency to isomorphism between mortuary practice and social status is affected by religious beliefs both in terms of the presence or absence of differentiation and, where there is diffe-rentiation, in its nature and scale. CK also shows that despite a stated prefer-ence for family plots, limitations of space and human memory inhibit the aggregation of graves of members of horizontal social groupings. Expression of social structure is in this respect an unrealized ideal. These themes reappear in other treatments of death.

   CK's processualist approach to Aliabad led her to results that are not at var-iance with the postprocessualist view that disposal of the dead also involves a conceptual transformation of living society, with the corollary that the differ-ent ideologies found in societies worldwide must imply the existence of a variety of transformational rules. Parker Pearson (1982) advocates this position in a study of changing mortuary practices in Cambridge (England). Writing from a practice theory perspective and fashionably overconcerned with power rela-tions, he argues that "in death ritual it is not necessarily the case that the actual relations of power are displayed" (p. 101). Parker Pearson interviewed

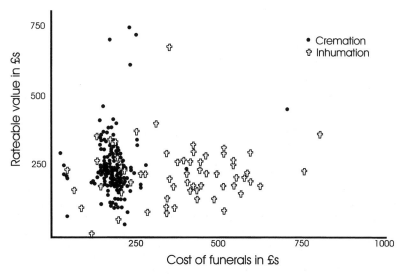

Fig. 13.1 The cost of funerals in Cambridge, England, in 1977 as compared
with the rateable (property tax) value of residential property
occupied by the deceased (redrawn from Pearson 1982: Fig. 1).

Cambridge undertakers to develop a stratified random sample of 270 deaths
that occurred in 1977, visited Cambridge cemeteries, and used historical
sources to place his field data in the context of the changing treatment of the
dead in Britain over the previous 150 years. Although class, religious affiliation,
and ethnicity are expressed in the 1977 data in subtle ways, there is a lack
of correlation between "rateable value of residential property," a measure of
the deceased's wealth and status, and "cost of funerals," inhumation being
generally significantly more expensive than cremation (Fig. 13.1). In the city's
cemeteries, which contain only inhumations, there is somewhat more differentiation along ethnic-religious lines, but, here and elsewhere, it is the grave monuments of a group consisting of English Gypsies[4] and often related showmen,
socially marginal but often cash-rich, that are most notable for their size, flam-
boyance, and expense (Fig. 13.2). Whether this symbolizes that group's resistance to hegemonic structures of the larger society, intra-group competition, or
indeed intra-group cooperation, is left unstated. However, there is no overall
correlation of wealth and funerary splendor.

The Cambridge data should be seen in the context of historical trends such
as an increase in the number of cremations so steady that even the 1963 lifting
of a Roman Catholic ban on this means of disposal resulted in no change of
slope in the rising curve of cremation frequency. Spatial patterning within
cemeteries, once "a visual representation of the emerging [nineteenth-century]

---

[4] As they prefer to be known, rather than as Roma or Romany.

Fig. 13.2 Grave monuments of English Gypsies in part of Norwich cemetery, England, December 1999. Note careful maintenance and the well-tended lawn.

hierarchy" is of ever decreasing importance, as is the use of monuments that, by reference to Classical and other ancient themes, once claimed legitimation of the social order in terms of prevailing representations of those values (p. 107). Whereas in the mid-nineteenth century "[t]he funeral was a conspicuous display of wealth consumption, and the expenditure was closely graded according to one's social position . . . No longer is the context of death a platform for overt self-advertisement between family groups" (p. 109). The causes of these changes are complex, involving population density, conceptions of hygiene, the carnage of the First World War, and other factors, all of which result in a "changing relation to the dead [that] can be explained in terms of the replacing of traditional agencies of social control, notably religion, by the new agencies of rationalism, science and medicine within the framework of modern capitalism" (p. 110).

While one may not accept every detail of Parker Pearson's analysis, the propositions that he advances in conclusion are worth quoting in full:

(1) The symbolism of ritual communication does not necessarily refer to the actual relations of power but to an idealised expression of those relations.
(2) Relations between living groups must be seen as relations of influence and inequality where deceased individuals can be manipulated for purposes of status aggrandise-

ment between those groups. Ideology as manifested in mortuary practices may mystify or naturalise those relations of inequality between groups or classes through the use of the past to legitimise the present.

(3) The relationship between living and dead should be integrated in studies of mortuary practices; in particular the new role of the deceased individual and the context of death as a platform for social advertisement must be accounted for.

(4) Social advertisement in death ritual may be expressly overt where changing relations of domination result in status re-ordering and consolidation of new social positions. (p. 112)

Later, Sarah Tarlow (1992) was to take Parker Pearson roundly and rightly to task for emphasizing power relations to the exclusion of other dimensions of death, and Aubrey Cannon (1989) has argued for the importance of cyclical change in mortuary display ostentation, but Parker Pearson's main thesis remains influential. Social structure cannot be directly read from mortuary practices, and the latter must be studied in the context of the culture as a whole, the world of the dead representing a transform of living society. No longer could or can Binfordian "mortuary sociologists" regard "differential aspects of the social system" as merely passing through a series of filters in the process of becoming "isolatable archaeological patterning" (O'Shea 1981: 40, Fig. 2).

Dirt, women, and burial among the Nuba

But just how and using what materials are such transforms achieved? While much more difficult to establish in cultures other than one's own and in the absence of a rich historical record, the approach remains the same. In a chapter on the Nuba hill peoples of southern Kordofan in central Sudan, Ian Hodder (1982a: 125–84) considers burial practices in the context of broader concerns regarding the generation of cultural patterning. The Moro and Mesakin, whose primary affiliation is with their community settlement rather than "tribe," number respectively about 30,000 (in 1971) and 8000 (in 1978) and both practice agriculture, most intensively in and around their hill settlements, and raise cattle, pigs, sheep, and goats. Besides having some limited ethnographic and linguistic reports available to him, Hodder and his team, working during a period of unspecified but short duration over an area of approximately 650 km^2, visited 73 compounds in one mixed, four Moro, and two Mesakin communities, and collected a range of information on economic and material culture, inter-community relations, eating habits and avoidances, refuse, and burial practices. They did not observe any burials but visited several cemeteries, planning one in some detail.

Hodder searches hard for themes that underlie contrasts between Moro and Mesakin communities (see Table 13.1) and their material cultures, finding them in sets of rules relating to pollution, boundedness, and categorization. To both Moro and Mesakin are attributed a "strong sense of purity and cleanliness," a

Fig. 13.3 Mesakin Qisar compound interior showing appliqué and painted decoration, and the small round entrance to the granary, above which are hung calabashes and mandibles, probably of goats, Nuba Hills, Sudan, 1978.

major source of impurity being menstrual blood. Fear of impurity through contact with women affects, among other things, attitudes to grain. Pigs, associated with women, are opposed to cattle, associated with men, and pigs and their products, including bones, are kept more or less strictly apart. Whereas the Moro emphasize cleanliness and the physical separation of pigs from men, the Mesakin allow their animals to circulate and excrete in their compounds, males achieving "their sense of freedom from pollution by a more ritual and less practical division between them, their cattle and women and pigs" (p. 159). The hanging of animal bones in (Moro) and around (Mesakin) granaries is seen in this light as an expression of a Nuba tendency for "the boundary surrounding an area or object [the grain in this case] over which there is great concern . . . [to be] 'ritualised' with signs of death, generosity and wealth, the better to preserve it" (p. 156). What seem to be opposed Moro and Mesakin practices are at a deeper level the same: "purity and fertility can be assured either by safeguarding the entrance to the granary with the clean, or by confronting impurity with the unclean" (p. 157), as the Mesakin do also by means of painted and modeled decoration (Fig. 13.3). Hodder invokes Mary Douglas's (1966) views on pollution to explain why

Table 13.1 *Some contrasting characteristics of Moro and Mesakin communities and cultures (data from Hodder 1982a: 125–84)*

MORO	MESAKIN
Patrilineal	Matrilineal (though some inheritance through males)
Little migration between communities	Some migration between communities
Stated community openness to Mesakin	Communities closed to Moro
Agglomerated settlements	Isolated homesteads
Relatively open compounds	Tightly enclosed compounds
Pigs kept separate from humans	Pigs and humans share compound space
Clean compound interiors	Dirty compound interiors
No decoration in central courtyard	Decorated central courtyards (and elsewhere)
No decorated calabash spoons	Young men decorate calabash spoons
Pig head bones hung out of sight in granary	Pig, cattle, and goat head bones displayed in front of granaries
Pigs part of marriage payment	Cattle and goats, but not pigs, part of marriage payment

the Mesakin, amongst whom there is some contradiction between male dominance and female power, should have the stronger sex pollution concepts.

How does all this relate to burial? Graves are circular in plan with narrow entrances widening to a chamber below; over the entrance the backdirt is piled to form a mound usually delimited with a kerb of stones. Cemeteries are located near settlements and horizontal social groups are segregated between and within them. As is evident in Table 13.1, burials express a certain amount of variation between genders, ages, and communities, and between the Moro and Mesakin. Noting that the association of cemeteries with the hill communities emphasizes inherited rights to land improved by the ancestors, Hodder proceeds to argue that the burials evidence a "clear relationship between death, grain and fertility" (p. 168). This is expressed in (a) explicit similarities in the forms of graves and granaries, (b) the use of pots to cover the entrance to graves and Moro granaries, (c) an earlier report of bodies of another Nuba group being wrapped in pig skins, and (d) the use of ash to cover mourners and for other uses during the burial ceremony, ash being "intimately associated with fertility and strength" and "a symbol of strength and continuity" (p. 168). The breakage on the grave of items associated with the deceased is said to remove the impurity of the dead, and release the rest of the inheritance. Among the Mesakin the competition between potential matri- and patrilateral inheritors that leads to uncertainty regarding inheritance (and increased fear of pollution) is expressed in a greater display of goods on graves. "Thus," Hodder concludes,

Nuba burial is about the handing on of Nuba assets within family lines. The continuity of the society is stressed not only in the inheritance procedures and in the grouping of graves into community cemeteries, but also in the rites concerned with the fertility of grain. To any such conception of continuity and fertility, death is a threat – the reversal of sequence. The threat is removed by purifying or breaking the items associated with the dead, by sacrificing in order to remove the guilt of inheritance from the dead, and by confronting and surrounding the dead with symbols of grain and fertility. (p. 170)

For a number of reasons this interpretation is less than persuasive. The central role attributed to men's supposed fear of pollution is not well established (nor are we made aware of the women's response). It seems unlikely, for example, that ash, so often in Africa and elsewhere a symbol of the absolutely used up, is in fact "used explicitly to ensure the fertility of the grain" (p. 136). If "men and women cover themselves in ash at various stages in the harvesting and handling of sorghum grain" (p. 156), this may well be because this prevents itching from exposure to the chaff, which is why Fulbe told ND that they rub it over themselves while threshing. (Sometimes a cigar is just a cigar.) Apart from their small circular entrances, the graves are morphologically unlike the silos of the Moro or the granary rooms of the Mesakin, and on page 163 burial chambers are described as sealed with stones rather than pots. We are told nothing of Nuba beliefs in an afterlife, nor is it clear that they consider death a "reversal of sequence."[5] Is it not possible that, rather than being *confronted* with symbols of grain, the dead are being *supplied* with food and drink, seeds and utensils for use in a Nuba afterlife? Does breakage of items on the grave really remove impurity? On these and other matters we need more evidence.

Whether or not Hodder's interpretation is in fact overinterpretation and an imposition of Western, and specifically Mary Douglas's, ideas on Nuba data cannot be resolved without further fieldwork. While we appreciate Hodder's hermeneutic aims, we are convinced that success in their achievement requires the kind of knowledge of the culture(s) involved that can only be attained by lengthy and intensive fieldwork.

Meanwhile what can be said of the relationship between the Nuba worlds of the dead and of the living? The data summarized in Table 13.2 suggest that they are remarkably similar. Age, gender, and status distinctions seem generally to be reproduced in burial, although whether the common lack of differentiation of men and women by burial position throws doubt on men's fear of impurity or whether it is an example of ideology concealing contradictions is a matter for debate – if not anyone's guess. We entirely agree with Hodder's Binfordian statement regarding the main cemetery at Tosari, that it "clearly maps out the pattern of local dependencies and ties in socio-economic relations" (p. 167). It

---

[5] Hodder nowhere discusses Moro and Mesakin beliefs and behavior in relation to their religion, to Islam, and to Christianity.

Table 13.2 *Variations by Moro and Mesakin communities in body position and items placed in and on grave*

	Male burial position (ext = extended)	Female burial position	Items placed in grave	Items deposited on grave	Other observations
MORO					
Lebu	ext on r side, head to E	ext, side varies by clan, head to E	sorghum, sesame, pots	clothes, shoes, pots, tools	
Kerbej	ext, looking E	as men	no information	pots, beds	even babies accorded burial
Nua	crouched or ext on l side	as men	none	clothes, shoes, pots, calabashes	
Anderri	ext on l side	ext on r side	no information	broken pots, calabashes, knife blades, damaged teapots	some reuse of graves for patrilateral kin
MESAKIN					
Tuwia	ext on l or r side acc. to locality	as men	cooked meat, sorghum, water, alcohol in pots; + beads (woman); painted body designs (young man)	man: spears, tools woman: walking sticks, straw head rings, broken pots	some reuse of graves for matrilateral kin
Reikha	ext on r side looking E	as men	food, including groundnuts, beans, sesame in pots; ornaments, clothes, field tools	dependent upon age man: broken spear shafts, calabashes, fighting trophies; woman: adzes, walking sticks, calabashes, head rings, water pots, shell harvesting tools	sesame seeds sometimes placed in grave mound
Tosari	ext on l or r side according to section, looking E	ext on r side, looking E	sorghum flour and seeds, sesame, alcohol, water, meat	objects used during life, often broken, types differentiated by gender; number relates to age and status; very large storage jars with broken bases often over water jars	

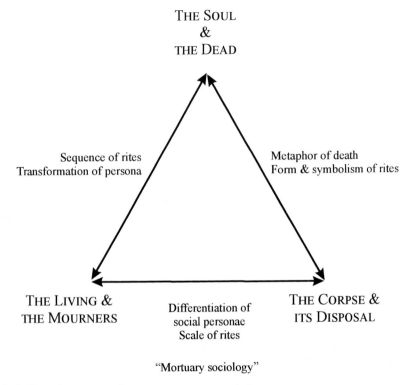

Fig. 13.4 A Hertzian view of mortuary practices (after David 1992b: Fig. 1).

would seem probable that – to offer a candidate law – the extent of transformation of the world of the dead is positively correlated with overall social complexity.

The Hertzian triangle and Mandara ways of death

Huntington and Metcalf (1979: 66, Fig. 2) represented Hertz's tripartite explanation of the fear of the dead in diagrammatic form. This is modified and generalized in ND's (1992b) regional study of traditional Mandara deathways in order to conceptualize different aspects of mortuary practices (Fig. 13.4). The relationship between the "living and mourners" and the "corpse and its disposal" determines the scale of the rites and the differentiation of social personae. It is this mortuary sociology aspect with which archaeologists were almost exclusively concerned through the 1970s. Little or no attention was then paid to the relationship between the "soul and the dead" and the "corpse and its disposal." This is apprehended through metaphor that is developed into the symbolism of the rites (e.g., sleep with awakening to resurrection, germination – even fermentation). The third dyad, relating "living and mourners" to the "soul and the dead," accounts for the sequence of rites as the social persona is transformed or extinguished. ND argues that because the three pairs of relationships are all interdependent expressions of the same ideological system, no one of the relationships can be understood in isolation. This renders suspect, since they ignore the left-hand side of the triangle, attempts such as that of Shanks and Tilley (1982) to interpret the ideological significance of arrangements of bones in European Neolithic tombs. But how are archaeologists to determine what aspects of mortuary practice express which of the operations of ideology identified by Giddens (1979: 193–7)? These are:

> 1 the representation of the interests of dominant sections of society as universal,
> 2 the denial or transmutation of contradictions, that is to say the concealment or misrepresentation of social relations, and
> 3 the naturalization of the present, by which is meant that social constructs are represented as part of the natural order of things.

With these questions in mind ND proceeds to survey the disposal of the dead in the Mandara mountains. He focuses on seven groups in the area around Mokolo whose practices are known primarily from data collected by himself and members of his team (see Fig. 7.9). At the time of writing, team members had been present at only three burials and several funeral ceremonies. These and others later observed at Sukur by ND and Sterner were frequently accompanied by disagreements about practice, that is to say the active negotiation of norms, reminding us that data, especially on rarely visited groups and on those known only from the literature, must – despite the efforts of ethnographers – emphasize the ideal at the expense of the actual.[6]

We will not summarize here the materials collected but rather consider the nature of the variation they exhibit from a regional perspective. First, the sequence of rites is everywhere similar. Elders – persons whose own parents are deceased, who have children, and who therefore qualify as ancestors – receive full mortuary treatment: some form of lying in state, a burial within a few days, to be followed some time later by more or less protracted funeral ceremonies. While their deaths are celebrated, those who die before achieving elder status are mourned and buried in sadness with abbreviated rites. In most casted groups ceremonies are directed by smiths, and otherwise by affines, and especially sisters' sons, real or classificatory. There is a strong element of display in the very public funerals of elders, to which both kin and the deceased's sons-in-law and daughters-in-law and their families contribute. The motivation here seems to be, rather than to establish rights to inheritance, to celebrate the deceased in ways that magnify his or her kin group and those allied to it by marriage.

Most people are buried near kin in small graveyards but both male and female elders may express a preference to be buried elsewhere; at Sukur a tomb with a

---

[6] Insights gained during ND's and Sterner's subsequent fieldwork in Sukur are incorporated in the following discussion.

view is a popular choice. Migration down to the plains from rocky massifs has, over much of the region, weakened links between people and clan cemeteries. An ideal distribution of graves within a cemetery can be elicited, little varying by group, and based upon age, gender, relationship to founding ancestor, the incorporation of wives, and other factors relating primarily to circumstances of death. However, it is doubtful whether this was ever realized in practice. Post-funeral ritual in this region focuses on pottery shrines, kept in the house but potentially mobile (Sterner 1992), rather than on graves, which in at most a few generations are no longer visible on the surface. A position at either end of the status scale is often expressed in burial outside the cemetery; infants and small children are commonly interred behind the house (as are placentas); "strangers," lepers, and chiefs receive different kinds of special treatment.

The preparation and clothing of the body for burial are characterized by much variation on a limited number of themes. These include the anointing of the body, usually with ochreous oil, and the sewing of goat or sheep skins over parts of the body (most commonly loins and face). An element of display, most marked in the case of male elders and chiefs, is evident in the clothing of the body. Burial structures also exhibit above and below ground variability. Tombs have a (sub-)circular opening and a subterranean chamber while graves are sub-rectangular trenches. The latter probably existed in precolonial times but were then reserved for low-status burials; with the spread of Islam and Christianity they have become more common. The variety of excavated structures in these Mandara mountain societies is remarkable and speaks to age, role, status distinctions, and circumstances of death (Fig. 13.5). Tombs and their superstructures are richly symbolic, variously referring to the womb, an inverted granary, a compound or house, a room, and a gateway. The dead are thought to lead lives underground similar to those they have left above. A concern that the earth should not come directly into contact with the deceased is general, as indeed it is in many other parts of the world – whence the impact of the epitaph for Sir John Vanburgh, architect of Blenheim Palace in England:

Lie heavy on him, Earth! for he
Laid many heavy loads on thee!

Widespread belief in an after-life under the ground, to which the deceased presumably awakens, may explain why the body is so often placed in a position that mimics that of sleep (cf. Tarlow 1995). While extension versus degree of flexure of the body seems of little significance, the difference between left and right is generally symbolically charged though of variable specific meaning. Important personages are often buried seated, a pose that emphasizes their consequence. The special treatment, involving burial seated on an iron stool and in charcoal, of Wula, Mabas, and Sukur chiefs, is likely borrowed from peoples further to the west, but the symbolism, evoking the permanence of chiefly responsibilities, is entirely familiar. A concern with orientation in relation to the rising or setting sun is universal but so variously expressed as to be archaeologically unreconstructible. The reuse of tombs is not uncommon, expressing

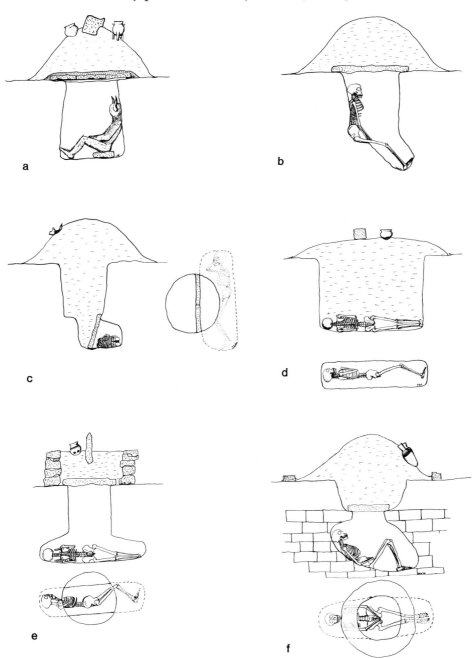

Fig. 13.5 Tombs and graves, Mandara mountains, northern Cameroon, 1980s: (a) Mafa male elder sewn into a bull's hide; (b) Cuvok chief or victim of violence; (c) Hide male; (d) Mafa female; (e) Wula woman with at least one child; (f) Gemjek male (a twin). The orientation of the bull's horns on the Mafa elder should be forward, and at least within the past century he would have been dressed in one, or more probably several, gowns. (David 1992b: Fig. 5.)

the continuity of kin groups, though different bones of previous occupants may or may not be removed. Similarly, within communities and sometimes ethno-linguistic groups, standard aspects of the social persona of the deceased are often quite precisely expressed in the goods placed in and left on the grave, but once again local codes differ.

In conclusion, ND's study shows that the vast majority of the material aspects of disposal of the dead are intimately linked with ideas, values, attitudes, and themes that repeat in many different aspects of the lives of these societies. Also apparent is the great variability in the data and the fact that the seven groups studied emphasize different aspects of their common cultural heritage in differing ways and in different dimensions of mortuary practice (Table 13.3). However if, instead of looking at specific practices, we look more generally at the sorts of ways whereby different categories of person are differentiated in death, we find more in common between the groups. Thus, although details differ, women are very commonly differentiated from men by their burial position, and strangers from those properly of the community by burial location. On a yet more general level the widely shared metaphor for the process whereby the deceased becomes ancestor is that of gestation/germination in the uterus/granary/tomb. All the groups studied, including Sukur, draw on the same symbolic reservoir (see chapter 7), with historical factors operating at various scales responsible for both differentiation and convergence of group practices.

How does ideology structure the data in larger ways? ND argues that male elders use mortuary practices, including positioning within cemeteries and type of grave, to support their dominant position and to represent their sectional interests as fundamental to the functioning of society. However, it is the size and duration of the funeral wakes (that leave no significant archaeological residue) that constitute the main forum for the display and reinforcement of status, rather than the burial and grave goods, the latter expectably skimpy in a world where there is little social surplus and there has existed no "big man" institution to compete with the principle that access to land depends on clan affiliation and seniority. It is noteworthy that, except in the western part of the region, chiefs are in death very little differentiated from other elders. Rites for women elders tend to approximate those of the men. A prime message is that the welfare of society as a whole depends upon the periodic restatement and acceptance by society at large of the traditional values that the male elders – and to an extent their wives – hold in trust for the group from the ancestors whom they, for the moment, embody. Their claim is presently being challenged by a younger, modernizing, generation, the product of schools and of world religions, who are coming more and more to control the springs of power, wealth, and influence. Many of the mortuary practices described seem unlikely to survive for long unless reappropriated by the young.

The denial or transmutation of contradictions is the second way identified

Table 13.3 *Differentiation of categories of persons in various dimensions of Mandara mortuary practices by ethno-linguistic group*

Differences are expressed as variation from treatment of male elders. As complete information on each category is often lacking, absence of information does not necessarily mean absence of differentiation.

Key: l = location of burial outside cemetery
c = preparation and ritual clothing of the body
t = type of tomb/grave
p = position/orientation in tomb/grave
f = burial furnishings and goods (excluding pots on graves)
– = no distinction made
? = no data on this category
( ) = parentheses are indicative of intra-group variability in the character.

Thus in the Mafa column we see that Mafa males who are not elders are sometimes differentiated from elders in being buried outside a cemetery, and regularly differentiated by the type of tomb/grave, and by their position/orientation within it.

Category	Mafa	Sirak	Cuvok	Hide	Mabas	Wula	Gemjek
Women elders	–	c	p	p	p	tpf	cpf
Other males	(l)tp	tp	?	t	–	–	f
Other females	(l)tp	tp	p	tp	p	tp	cpf
Infants/small children	lct	lctp	lt	ltp	ltp	ltp	–
Chief	(l)f	l	tp	l	(l)pf	pf	p
Twins (or parents)	c	c	–	–	c	–	cf
Smith–potters	c	–	–	–	–	–	–
Wealthy men	c	c	c	c	?	?	?
Victims of:							
violence	–	–	tp	–	–	c	–
smallpox	ctf	?	?	–	?	?	–
leprosy	(l)	lctf	t	(l)	–	lc	lt
"Strangers"	l	l	l	?	?	l	?

by Giddens in which ideology operates. Here the lack of mortuary differentiation of the smith-potter caste must forcibly strike any observer who knows the Mandara region. In death, smith-potters and farmers return to mythical brotherhood. In Giddens's (1979: 194) view, "It is normally in the interests of dominant groups if the existence of contradictions is denied or their real locus is obscured." This case may be an exception in that it is by no means clear that the farmers constitute a dominant group. ND's view is that both parties believe they have the best of the deal, and that the denial of contradiction reflects an unacknowledged conspiracy between them.

As to the naturalization of the present, these are societies characterized by what Douglas (1970) describes as strong grid and group, in which persons during their lifetimes proceed through a series of statuses that depend primarily upon their sex/gender, physiological age and genealogical seniority, and in which freedom of the individual to depart from role expectations is severely constrained. Although men may become relatively wealthy, great warriors (in the past), diviners or priest-chiefs, and women mothers of many living children or respected midwives, the extent of their material differentiation from the mass is not great. Thus, although achieved status is recognized in mortuary practices, it is the "God-given" categorization of "natural" statuses: infant versus fully human, man versus woman, elder versus socially immature, that most clearly and regularly structures the data. The orientation of burials to cardinal points is also a form of naturalization of social distinctions. At a funeral the celebrants are reminded of the status of the deceased in the course of a powerful affect-laden ceremony, while their regular attendance – and funerals are among the most dramatic performances available to them – must imprint upon them the nature of that structure and a feeling for its inevitability. The pots left on the graves, or their absence, remain to be read and to remind the living of that structure.

Thus in mortuary practices ideology can and does operate in all three of the ways identified by Giddens. Given the tendency for ideology to reinforce social structure, and given the importance of disposal of the dead as a dramatic institutional framework, it is inevitable that this will always be the case. The main problem facing the archaeologist is then to determine which elements of mortuary practices are operating in which way. To this there can be no general answer, particularly as, since the denial of contradiction seems likely in most instances to imply a *lack* of material differentiation, its identification requires especially full contextual knowledge of other aspects of the culture.

For the archaeologist wishing to interpret a body of mortuary data, there are further implications of the preceding sections. The theory and practice of mortuary sociology are supported in that the scale and complexity of funeral rites and associated material culture are correlated with dimensions of the deceased's social persona, but it is also clear that the correlation is far from perfect and in any case only part of a larger and richer story told in ideological translation. Second, whereas it is inconceivable that mortuary practices not be imbued with ideology, human groups drawing on the same symbolic reservoir may express themselves so variably that only a broad contextual approach to the decipherment of symbols is likely to be productive. Lastly, whereas archaeologists should no doubt continue to develop sources for analogy (e.g., Dillehay 1995; J. A. Brown 1995), ethnoarchaeologists must continue to inform interpretation, not with the intent of enabling archaeologists to infer the precise meaning of specific archaeological features, but rather to assist them towards a more sophisticated understanding of the range of factors likely to be structuring their databases. It is to be hoped that much of this work will be carried out in societies intermediate in complexity between Mafa and Cambridge.

Ideology, domination, and resistance in other areas

A concern with power relations was particularly characteristic of British and especially Cambridge archaeology and ethnoarchaeology in the 1980s. We have already noted Parker Pearson's work on disposal of the dead and Donley-Reid's research on the Swahili. Where there is dominance, there we may expect resistance, but this is not a feature of either study. Women's resistance to male dominance is more evident in Alice Welbourn's (1984) "Endo ceramics and power strategies," and in Mary Braithwaite's (1982) "Decoration as ritual symbol: a theoretical proposal and ethnographic study in southern Sudan." Both are stimulating and perceptive but less than convincing sketches by authors intoxicated by the vistas opened by interpretive ethnoarchaeology. Alas, the comprehensively documented and argued accounts that were awaited never appeared. Henrietta Moore's (1986) *Space, text and gender*, on the other hand, is an extended and sophisticated work in this genre, a classic of gender studies, but it is, as its subtitle makes clear, a (social) anthropological rather than ethnoarchaeological work. It is an examination, undertaken among the Endo Marakwet of Kenya, of the construction and maintenance of the dominant male-centered ideology of gender and of women's situating of themselves in relation to it. While it takes as its starting point an analysis of domestic space that is of the Hodderian interpretive school,[7] it soon distances itself from the material. "Space considered as a text does not take as its object real social and economic conditions, but rather certain ideological representations of the real" (p. 152). Moore's theoretical approach, founded upon practice and literary theory (Bourdieu and Ricoeur) and applied to her materials on space, the nature of Endo knowledge, and men's and women's lives and rituals, leads to profound insights into the human condition and relations between genders.

Diane Lyons (1998) offers a valuable ethnoarchaeological complement to Moore's work in her study of "Witchcraft, gender, power and intimate relations . . ." among the Mura of Déla (Doulo), a multiethnic community in northern Cameroon. The patrilineal and patrilocal Mura, of montagnard origin, are characterized by a male-dominant ideology of gender more extreme than that of the Endo, and which represents women, who are denied control of productive resources, as antisocial and consuming strangers, in contrast to males who are portrayed as being social providers. In reality men depend upon women for

---

[7] Although the intellectual history of that school remains to be written (but see Giles *et al.* 1997), it is apparent that Moore was a significant contributor. Compare for example her (presumably anterior) treatment of ash in her (1986) monograph to Hodder's in his (1987a) "Meaning of discard" paper.

their labor in the fields and in the home, and for their fertility and care of children. The tension between ideology and reality contributes to a very high divorce rate (approaching serial polyandry for many women) and fears of witchcraft/sorcery, expressed especially by males but also by co-wives in relation to each other. This situation has non-trivial material correlates. Men protect themselves by a variety of supernatural means that often involve the burial of bones and other substances, and, in compounds already structured by the ideology of gender, the anticipated impermanence of wives' stay is expressed in the less substantial buildings constructed by men to house them. For fear of the sorcery it might contain, no new wife would consent to occupy a divorced predecessor's abandoned room. Thus solid, often rectangular, coursed daub brick buildings relating to males and children of the patriline are found in the (at least notionally) higher, front part of the compound, while round huts with thinner walls of daub, mud-mortared stone, or vegetal material, house the wives in its lower rear parts. Lyons concludes by noting the dialectic relationship that holds between those with more and with less power.

> While Mura men own and inherit all that is socially valuable, it is women's labour, fertility and co-operation that underpins the success of these resources . . . Mura women do not just represent themselves more positively within the dominant ideology as suggested by Moore for the Endo. Instead they actively manipulate the negative associations placed on women including witchcraft, mobility and impermanence to their own advantage . . . [A] dialectic of gender relations means that a dominant ideology cannot wholly be the product of one gender. (pp. 358–9)

Thus objects buried in the front of the compound and unwillingness to reoccupy women's rooms are forms of acknowledgment of women's power. While the archaeologically recognizable indicators of Mura gender differentiation are likely to be characteristic of only a small number of related cultures, Lyons has provided some important clues as to how archaeologists might approach such questions.

Decorated mugs: the interpretive and the materialist positions

We conclude this section with a discussion of two articles written from opposing viewpoints. Hodder's (1991) "The decoration of containers: an ethnographic and historical study," written (in a vein and style similar to Moore's) after further fieldwork among the Ilchamus in January–March 1983, takes up themes raised in earlier publications (1982a, 1985, 1987b). The passionately negative response it provoked from Alan Osborn (1996) serves to highlight differences between the interpretive and materialist schools. The question Hodder asks is why certain calabashes, especially those used by Ilchamus mothers to give milk to their children, are decorated while other containers are not. His answer takes a poststructuralist approach that takes account of historical context, considering structural oppositions in the light of practice theory. He shows how a series of oppositions between male and female, blood and milk, outside and inside, wild and domestic, etc., are variously manipulated to produce meaning in different contexts by different actors: "the structures are not determining or fixed. They exist only in the practices of daily life" (Hodder 1991: 93). The calabashes are decorated by women, usually for their own use. Dark on the inside (when not filled with milk), the outside is polished red and pyroengraved with designs that symbolically link women with young men of the warrior age-grade.[8] Mothers use the calabashes to give milk to their children, who soon recognize their own vessels, and brides and mothers-in-law exchange them as gifts. They advertise a wife's well-being to her husband and others, and that, should she be dependent on neighbors' milk, she is a responsible and deserving recipient who will in due course repay. Hodder provides statistics in support of his statement that: "Generally, it is the large, rich families, with many cattle, with many wives and children, and with middle-aged husbands trying to build up their family size, that have a larger proportion of decorated calabashes" (p. 85). In this patriarchal society in which men frequently beat wives "openly and cruelly," "The decoration draws attention to and marks out an area of limited female control – the care of milk and children" (p. 88). But they are also in Hodder's view a part, along with songs, proverbs, and other behaviors, of women's resistance to male domination. They constitute a silent, covert mode of discourse that expresses their solidarity with the warriors whose own advancement to marriage and full adult status is held back by the gerontocracy, and with whom the women often cooperate in opposition to the elders.

While the paper could have been strengthened by analyses of the designs on particular calabashes in particular contexts – are there for example patterned differences in the designs on boys' and girls' calabashes, or on ones decorated by mothers-in-law? – Hodder builds a case made more convincing by an extension of his argument to show that "'modernizing' women not only may continue to decorate calabashes but also may extend the same principles to other spheres" (p. 91). He achieves his aim of situating calabashes

as fully as possible into their own context of meanings. [The method] involves discovering the multidimensional networks of meaning in which [calabashes] play their role . . . looking for similarities and contrasts along varied dimensions of meaning . . . suggesting ways in which the dimensions of meaning are structured at various levels . . . above all, it involves breaking down the notion that [calabashes] implies one category with a single meaning. (p. 72)

Or does he? Materialist Alan Osborn (1996) does not think so. He accuses Hodder of giving "precedence to the structure and dynamics of ideation within relatively closed cultural systems that operate independently of their biophysical environment" (p. 108) and of ignoring the "biophysical and socioecological

---

[8] Hodder is inconsistent on the association of designs with men or women (cf. Hodder 1991: 78, 88) but clear as to the symbolic linkage through designs of "wild" warriors with fertile women married to older men.

factors that create the adaptive contexts for symboling and stylistic behavior and, in turn, account for their appearance, variation, and disappearance" (p. 109). Osborn proposes "that symbols affixed to certain Il Chamus material culture reduce the uncertainties of food allocation within pastoralist compounds" (p. 109), thus increasing reproductive fitness. He develops evidence from these, Great Rift Valley, and other African pastoralists to show that milk is a scarce, critical, and seasonally variable resource for which calves are competing with humans, and that amongst the Ilchamus milk consumption and household income are positively correlated (p. 116 and Fig. 7). Next, using cross-cultural evidence, he argues that in Ilchamus homesteads, characterized by non-sororal polygyny, there is likely to be competition regarding food distribution, and that "Such conflicts within polygynous residential groups can best be understood with respect to genetic distance and resulting disparities in reproductive interests" (p. 121). He "expects" that there are frequent conflicts over food allocation affecting children, and especially foster children, during the dry season and droughts.

The preceding sets up his hypothesis that as cow's milk is an essential, limiting resource:

pastoralists might attempt to reduce the risks associated with household milk allocation and sharing by means of symbols. Nutritional stress for children during the dry season . . . could be lessened by means of a carefully monitored allocation system . . . Child-specific symbols are, then, used to link an individual to a specified quantity of food in an unambiguous fashion. Symbols are primarily used on milk calabashes in order to transmit information and to facilitate food distribution in households characterized by resource competition and conflicting reproductive interests. (p. 123)

Support for this hypothesis is claimed in a reformulation of Hodder's statistics[9] to show that the percentage of decorated calabashes per compound

1 increases with the numbers of children and of co-wives, with the mean number of cattle per compound, and with regional herd size (though this last statistic is of dubious significance since it includes non-Ilchamus with different attitudes to decoration), and
2 decreases as a woman's children age and she completes her reproductive career.

Do these data in fact support Osborn's position? Surely not; the numbers of wives, children, and cattle in a compound are positively correlated, and under (a) above he has merely shown that there are proportionately more decorated calabashes in wealthier compounds where there is likely to be *least* stress related to nutrition. The statistics supposedly supporting his point (b) fail to do so and in fact contradict his argument. The highest proportion of decorated cal-

---

[9] Hodder's statistics exasperate. We are not informed as to how many compounds, children, wives, or cattle we are dealing with, nor with the incidence of polygyny. In some cases the number of co-wives presumably includes both the wives of the head of the household and those of sons (see Hodder 1985: 151). The total number of calabashes in the Ilchamus sample appears to be 115 decorated and 346 undecorated (Hodder 1991: 86, Table 4.3).

abashes (31 percent) are owned by women aged "20"; women of ages 21–30 possess 22 percent decorated calabashes and women of 31–40 have slightly fewer (19 percent). The women whose age is given as 20 actually own 31.2 percent of *all* the calabashes, yet these can hardly be the women with the most children or access to the largest number of cattle. Other factors, most probably and importantly including the treatment of brides, are influencing the distribution of calabashes, decorated and undecorated. Second, we question Osborn's premise regarding competition and conflict amongst co-wives. It is noteworthy that, in another paper written (before the 1983 fieldwork) on the topic of calabashes, Hodder (1985: 151) emphasizes the cooperation of Ilchamus wives "against the male-centered line that has brought them together," while among the Tugen, where there may be more jealousy and quarreling between co-wives – a stated reason for at least older co-wives sometimes to live in separate compounds – there are fewer cattle, less milk, presumably more stress regarding it, and yet *less* decoration of calabashes. Surely Osborn's theory, developed cross-culturally, should apply cross-culturally? Third, Osborn's theory fails to explain why other containers related to food should be undecorated, while Hodder (1991: 80) adduces other evidence to argue that it is because agriculture and its products are perceived as being of low value, whereas "Everything to do with cattle is beautiful" and thus worthy of beautification. Fourth, are we really expected to believe that labeling kids' mugs improves a mother's reproductive success?

Tarlow (1992: 137) reminded us that to reduce "the meaning of the material culture of death to the manipulation of relations of domination and power cheapens and degrades the profundity of the human response to death." While Osborn is right to insist that cultural behavior cannot be explained without reference to the biophysical environment, he has fallen into the similar error of attempting to explain symbolic behavior in terms of adaptive fitness. Such reductionism is unlikely ever to account for complex human behaviors, and in this case interpretive ethnoarchaeology provides a more satisfying construction of the facts than materialist socioecology.

Linking technologies, objects, and social representations

Very few ethnoarchaeological studies, and those almost all written in the last decade and on African topics, reveal how native beliefs about the world and humanity constitute a substrate upon and in terms of which technologies and material cultures develop. These works are of importance to archaeologists in that they may reveal the derivation of apparent anomalies and the arbitrariness of choices that Lemonnier (1992: 66–77) has shown characterize even such high-tech areas as airplane design. While necessarily selective in our coverage, it is our concern in this section to consider some of these studies and their relevance to archaeology. It should be emphasized that such research is by no means the preserve of ethnoarchaeology, and that archaeologists have much to learn from the writings of ethnologists and others. Joseph Bastien's (1995) study of "The mountain/body metaphor expressed in a Kaatan funeral" is a case in point, and leads to the conclusion that to interpret Andean tombs it is necessary to identify the dominant metaphors from clues such as "the pictographs on weavings and ceramics, the placement of bodies and body parts, and ... the architectural setting" (p. 375). Comparable ethnoarchaeological studies are limited to metallurgy.

Back to iron working

Van der Merwe and Avery (1987) concluded from their research on Cewa and Phoka iron making (see chapter 11) that there is only limited metaphorical linkage between the technical and magical aspects of making iron, smelting and human reproduction being perceived as similar processes. Michael Rowlands and Jean-Pierre Warnier (1993) disagree, arguing (in a study that is more ethnohistorical than ethnoarchaeological) that in the case of the "magical production of iron in the Cameroon Grassfields" the question

of whether the production process could be successfully performed if its "ritual" aspect (defined as technically useless) were to be dispensed with ... is meaningless, because every step in the production process, whether technically required or not, is perceived in terms of the symbolic code. The true question is: how does such a symbolic code or such "magic" allow the workers to achieve technical success in iron production? (p. 538)

They argue that in the Grassfields iron making was bound up with "a conception of 'production' that is ideologically [in the broader sense of the word] constrained by the belief that it is part of a larger natural process of transformation of persons and things in either reversible or irreversible time" (p. 541). Thus the system of Grassfields thought links smelting, pregnancy and delivery, and death and rebirth, and "[s]melters and smiths appear to have regarded themselves as facilitators in what we would call a *natural process* by which certain materials in nature transformed themselves into a substance which could be adapted to culturally useful ends" (p. 541).

However, Rowlands and Warnier do not address the further question of interest to archaeologists and metallurgists as to whether there are more specific mutually informative linkages between what we categorize as technical and magical processes. Of course there are linkages. One is the effective proscription in most, though not all, cases of women's labor in smelting. Another, inadequately studied, is the influence of beliefs on the spatial attributes of smelting, as regards both the location of furnaces and the layout of furnace sites (David in press). A third linkage, emphasized by Schmidt and of considerable import to both scientists and anthropologists, concerns site formation processes and in particular the treatment of the byproducts of iron manufacture. Slag is frequently recycled, whether, as in the Haya and Barongo cases, for furnace construction, or for building material, pottery temper, fertility charms, and medicine. Indeed one may wonder whether the use of crushed slag in pottery and especially in forge tuyères is not itself a practice influenced at least as much by beliefs in the powers of slag as by any utilitarian superiority of slag over grog temper. A fourth kind of linkage involves practice modeled on metaphor. In the Hausa case not only does the master smelter conceive of the reduction process in terms of gestation, but certain of his actions predicated upon these beliefs, such as the way he charges the furnace, have practical effects on the course of the smelt (Echard 1983).

In the examples just cited, social representations influence objects and processes. In contrast, Schmidt's (1996a) discussion of the Barongo case would seem to indicate that their conception of menses not as waste but as intimately involved in the production of children may well be correlated with a smelting process that involves the production of iron-rich slag that is then resmelted to produce blooms. Here it would seem likely that metallurgical practice has led to a reassessment of human physiology, and not vice versa.[10]

Another area of linkage that has been far too little studied is that of the animal, vegetable, and mineral medicines used in smelting. Van der Merwe and Avery (1987: 160) astutely recognized several groups of medicines used in the more traditional Phoka smelt. These included (a) medicines against witchcraft, epidemics, and venereal diseases (likely caused by the attacks of jealous humans and of spirits, ancestor and others), (b) some that promote fertility and plenty, and (c) a group that "symbolizes the desired qualities of strength, toughness, hardness, wiliness and speed – qualities one wishes to impart to the smelting and its product." Working with Dokwaza, ND found a similar range of medicines, and was in many cases able to elicit their specific intended functions (David in press). These fall into four groups and a miscellaneous category. There are medicines that provide protection against magical and supernatural attack, others that promote overall productivity; a third group encourages slag formation, and the fourth the production of iron, the metaphor in the last two groups being the teaching of the personified furnace to consume, digest, and excrete its food while forming a bloom mass/baby with specified characteristics in its shaft/belly. One of the last group is worth special mention. Dokwaza introduced into the furnace via the tuyère a plant medicine, *madzaf nngurlele,* consisting of fleshy roots forming adjoining white nodules. It was only later that ND learned that *nngurlele* is the Mafa term for the droplets of *cast* iron that Killick and Wayman identified as one constituent of the heterogeneous bloom mass (David *et al.* 1989). Here then the reduction of metal from ore is perceived as a natural process akin to digestion. The linkage of object and representation informs upon technical process and the smelters' intentions.

---

[10] Unfortunately the argument seems largely founded on analogy with practices and beliefs of the Nyakyusa. They live some 650 km to the south and were studied by Monica Wilson, who is not to be relied on in metallurgical matters (e.g., Wilson 1959: 153, cited by Collett 1993: 504).

The metaphorical assimilation of smelting and gestation has been emphasized by several workers; so too has the personification of the furnace as the bride of the iron makers, providing a ready explanation of the widespread prohibition of sexual intercourse during smelting (Collett 1993; Goucher and Herbert 1996). We suspect that, while there is a substantial measure of truth in these constructions, they oversimplify the complexity of symbolic relationships and the interpenetration of metaphorical assimilations, for example of reduction to gestation, warfare, cooking, and hunting (cf. Moñino 1983). Moreover, Stefan Bekaert (1998), who had done field research in Zaïre (Democratic Republic of the Congo) on Sakata smithing, has shown in a study of multiple levels of meaning in the iron technology of Bantu Africa that even when conceptions of, say, the relationship between woman and furnace are identical, behavioral consequences may be very different – as is evident in the following diagram.

Woman and furnace	Must go together	Do not go together
Are the same	Possible option	Sakata option
Are opposites	Possible option	Possible option

Thus other groups might likewise recognize that women and furnaces are somehow the same but conclude the opposite, that they should be associated as closely as possible. (However, we know of no women's smelting teams in Africa, nor of orgies around the furnace!)

The benefits of in-depth study can be briefly demonstrated by reference to a thesis on the Bulsa of northern Ghana. Roland Apentiik (1997), himself a Bulsa, consciously maintains a dual viewpoint, of the native and of the Western-trained ethnoarchaeologist, in order to document the embedding of ceramic and iron working technologies in the matrix of Bulsa cosmology and ideology. His research leads, amongst other things, to a more thoroughgoing explanation of sexual taboos associated with metallurgy, for the "furnace as jealous bride" interpretation fails to explain how, in societies that forbid polyandry, the furnace can be the bride of several husbands.

Three principles of Bulsa thought can be inferred to underpin social representations in the social and technological domains.

1 *Things and behaviors that are out of place are fraught with danger.* Dirt, *dangta* in Buli, is matter out of place and "offends against order." What we define as pollution the Bulsa also call *dangta*, an offensive quality of behavior out of place that is sanctioned because "the ideal order of society is guarded by dangers that threaten transgressors" (Douglas 1966: 2–3). To the Bulsa adultery is sex out of place, while menstrual blood or that from a wound is blood out of place and therefore dirty/polluting. *Dangta* angers gods, bringing misfortune, sickness, and other evils.

2 *Symbolic and magical action has physical effects.* A sorcerer sticks a needle into food and calls the name of his victim; the victim eats food and dies. Through magic, humans, to paraphrase Lévi-Strauss (1966: 20, cited in Rowlands and Warnier 1993: 513) intervene in natural determinism, completing or modifying its course. Thus the rituals and

taboos of potting and iron working are conceptually inseparable from physical techniques and part and parcel of production.

3 *Metaphorically similar things act on each other metonymically*. There is a pervasive thermodynamic metaphor regarding heat and cold. The ideal for people is to be neither too hot nor too cold. Polluting behavior causes people to become hot. Certain activities, warfare, hunting, giving birth, and iron working, are also considered as hot, inherently dangerous, associated with blood and pain (though not necessarily bad in themselves), and they transmit these qualities to those who participate in them. Persons involved in them require special protection, as do people of certain ages or in certain states, for example fertile women who, being at risk, should avoid hot things. Thus when a woman is giving birth (seen as engaging in a good form of warfare, defending life), other potential mothers should not be present. Nor should women see animals giving birth.[11]

This third principle – rather than the hypothesis of symbolic adultery – offers the primary reason why fertile women should not be present during smelting. It also explains why fertile women are forbidden, on pain of blindness or barrenness, to manufacture pots for ritual purposes, since these are used for sacrifices in which blood is spilled. At the level of systems of thought, the two technologies, metallurgical and ceramic, are linked in this and many other ways. The thermodynamic metaphor goes further: since "hot" and "cold" things have additive and subtractive metonymic effects, two things classed as hot should not be brought into contact as too much heat will be generated. In the *heat* of the forge, the smith should not pronounce *hot* words (i.e., discuss sex or become angry). The union of smiths *hot* during smelting and women puts both at risk, and also the smith's work, especially if the woman is *cold* from menstruation.[12] Similarly, amongst the Dogon balm "cools" wounds, and should therefore not be brought near the furnace (Huysecom and Agustoni 1997).

Apentiik's thesis, of which only a small part is presented above in abbreviated and simplified fashion, is hopefully the first of many publications by natives (of Third and Other Worlds) that explore from an ethnoarchaeological perspective the systems of thought that underlie technologies and reveal the relationships between them.

Conclusions

In this chapter we have shown that while ethnoarchaeology cannot provide a manual for the interpretation of mortuary practices it has significantly contributed to the theorizing of this aspect of culture. Remembering the lessons of

---

[11] We suspect that chickens laying eggs are regarded as cool, and therefore no danger to women because the process is so easy. Among the Bulsa, as elsewhere, the egg is a powerful symbol.

[12] It should be emphasized that Bulsa and other peoples' concepts of metaphorical heat and cold vary widely; for Bulsa, cold-moist, which has many metaphorical connotations, is differentiated from chilled, the latter a primarily physical state. A menstruating woman is cold-moist. While putting two hot things together increases heat, and putting a cold-moist thing with a hot thing cools the hot thing, putting two cold-moist things together has no additive effect.

Hertz, archaeologists should not focus uniquely upon the ultimate disposal of the body but consider such practices in broader context. Disposal of the dead involves a transformation of the world of the living, but it would seem that, in simpler societies especially, transformation tends more to naturalize the present than to conceal or misrepresent social relations. This is not to deny that there will always be difficulty in differentiating between the various operations of ideology in particular contexts. But even though the symbolism of rites may be hard to read, the differentiations expressed in disposal practices seem, if allowance is made for circumstances of death, likely on the whole to correspond to those of social personae in the living society. There is more to hide in complex societies. Once again ethnoarchaeology contributes to the explanation of why processualists so often get things right. On the other hand the nature of symbolic expression implies that trait counting and comparison are inadequate to reveal the relationships within and between cultural blocks, and that it is necessary rather to search for underlying themes that may be variously expressed in material terms.

There is a very real danger that ethnoarchaeologists, whose stay in foreign cultures is typically too short to approach anything like immersion, may become intellectual fashion victims, tempted to project extraneous ideas on to the societies they study. The overconcern with power relations characteristic of Cambridge ethnoarchaeologists of the 1980s is a case in point, which is not to deny that their work and that of those who have followed them has advanced the discipline, not least in emphasizing the significance of gender in structuring the material record. While researchers of the interpretive school may have underestimated the role of environmental factors, some historically informed explanations of symbolic behavior in terms of psychosocial factors are preferable to reductionist socioecological accounts. Ethnoarchaeology is beginning to develop guides to recognition in the archaeological record of some of the larger-scale patterns that have been identified.

Studies of systems of thought have concentrated, not surprisingly in view of its exotic ritual and magical aspects, on African smelting. In 1993 Eugenia Herbert's *Iron, gender, and power* brought one era to an end by synthesizing the available ethnographic, historical, and other evidence relating to the beliefs underlying metallurgy and other transformative activities, including pottery making and the investiture of chiefs. A degree of oversimplification and a tendency to generalize too widely from a small number of cases are already being recognized in her and other publications of the time. Generalizations at the regional, areal, and continental scales depend upon field research that is focused on particular communities and groups, though hopefully on a wider range of technological and behavioral domains. We follow the lead of Herbert and other scholars whose work has been discussed above in making four methodological points:

1 In order to understand the workings of systems of thought in any group, in-depth study of its manifestations is required; this involves the search for parallels in a variety of practices in order to elucidate underlying metaphors, analogies, and theories of how the world works.

2 The practice of patching interpretive holes with questionably relevant material from other peoples, even neighbors, must be abandoned unless such data have been subjected to "source- and subject-side strategies for establishing relevance" by "expanding the bases of interpretation and elaborating the fit between source and subject" (Wylie 1985: 100–1).

3 Apparent conflicts and inconsistencies in data should be actively sought, and then followed up, preferably in the field.

4 Researchers should seek validation of their work in a number of ways, by showing that their interpretations in one area are consistent with and can explain behavior in others, by citing informants' statements relevant to their interpretations, and by submitting their inferences to the criticism of intellectuals of the groups studied.

But whatever the intrinsic interest of such research, and however carefully conducted, is it of any relevance to archaeologists? Is it still ethnoarchaeology or is it cultural studies? We will answer these questions by reference to another case study. Herbich and Dietler (1994) have shown how the layout of the Luo extended family homestead is "a spatial representation of the principle of complementary opposition" between sets of wives and between generations, and they insist that this is not "a fanciful etic construct imposed upon the data, but a feature clearly recognized by the Luo themselves" (p. 28). However, actual expression of ideal structure is complicated by the cycle of family development and decay, by cycles of rebuilding of individual houses, by the varying size and composition of the families that make up the extended family, and by the accommodation of other relatives. Thus:

The reconstruction of those rules is a bit like trying to reconstruct the rules of chess from a random sample of fifty chess boards at various stages of different games. If one knows the rules from the start, one can perhaps imagine how the pieces arrived at their present position in each case. However to move [as archaeologists must] in the other direction, to define the rules on the basis of the static position of pieces late in the game is virtually impossible, and particularly so if one uses only the pieces of one board at one stage of a single game. (p. 31)

If the board is the site, then the archaeologist may be able to recover a few of the previous moves, but to reconstruct the rules would require applying the perspective of "settlement biography" to numerous related sites, "a daunting task of uncertain feasibility," and one that would certainly never result in precise reconstruction of the "shared ideal model" claimed (perhaps rather too optimistically) by the authors to exist.

This is a very common state of affairs in the application of ethnoarchaeological results to archaeology, one that leads some archaeologists to deny the relevance of such information and to restrict their attention to topics on which they believe they can generate "reliable" knowledge. But this is sticking one's head in the sand; surely one becomes a better archaeologist by informing oneself of as many of the factors and kinds of factors that may be structuring the archaeological record as possible. As time goes by archaeologists recover more and more chessboards, permitting the kind of interpretive synthesis that Hodder (1990b) attempted in his *Domestication of Europe*.[13] Archaeologists are in for the long haul; what they excavate today may not be understood for a few hundred years.

That is one reason why we need more research into the ways in which systems of thought underpin and link technologies. However, we have reached the point where, especially but not uniquely in metallurgy, the complexity of the subject matter exceeds the capabilities of any two scholars to unravel it, even while the addition of further members to research teams must of itself affect the behavior of the observed. There are some partial solutions to this dilemma. The advantages of long-term fieldwork and exposure to the culture(s) studied are very evident. It is not always necessary that team members be in the field at the same time. Finally, for purposes of both discovery and valida-tion, there must be much more participation of native scholars who, like Apentiik, are trained in ethnoarchaeology, or who, like Edwin Okafor (e.g., 1993) have other, in his case archaeometallurgical, skills. They, at least among their own people, are unlikely to become lost in Shanks and Tilley's "third hermeneutic."

Further reading

On the topic of HRAF-style cross-cultural analyses, the *Current Anthropology* treatment of Raoul Naroll's (1964) paper "On ethnic unit classification" still makes instructive reading. David, Sterner, and Gavua's (1988) paper "Why pots are decorated" argues for an assimilation between pots and people in the Mandara region that is locally expressed in forms that reify many important social constructs, and that, in its broad lines, appears to be and to have been expressed in many parts of the world where household industry is or used to be responsible for ceramic production. Claudia Chang's (1992, 1993a 1993b) papers on pastoralism in the Grevena region of northern Greece argue that transhumance constitutes a social ideology, and are relevant to understanding the incorporation of pastoralists into early states.

---

[13] Trigger's (1998: 28–9) critique has points of similarity to ours on Hodder's Nuba work.

CHAPTER 14

CONCLUSIONS: ETHNOARCHAEOLOGY IN CONTEXT

> The study of material culture may be most broadly defined as the investigation of the relationship between people and things irrespective of time and space. The perspective may be global or local, concerned with the past or the present, or the mediation between the two. Defined in this manner, the potential range of contemporary disciplines involved in some way or other in studying material culture is effectively as wide as the human and cultural sciences themselves.
>
> *(Daniel Miller and Christopher Tilley 1996: 5)*

As ethnoarchaeology is an approach rather than a true discipline we should not expect overall progress of the kind observed in a subject like physics where research leads to ever deeper understandings of matter and energy and to applications of that knowledge. But neither is it, as in painting, a matter of the invention and perfection of techniques and the creation of masterworks that are not bettered but rather overtaken by new developments, technical and conceptual, in new historical contexts. Like other social sciences, ethnoarchaeology advances not on its own but in partnership with its disciplinary siblings, archaeology and ethnography, and within the larger context of social science and its philosophy. Early classic studies retain value but, unlike a Rembrandt masterpiece, their imperfections and lacunae (and not merely their differences) become apparent through developments in and beyond ethnoarchaeology. On the other hand, just as art students copy old masters, so too can we imbibe knowledge and know-how by analyzing earlier studies. Reconceptualization and the broadening range of subject matter, the growing sophistication of research design and implementation, the development of new techniques, and the increasing scales, synchronic and diachronic, of ethnoarchaeological projects all constitute and render possible advances in the understanding of the relationships between material culture in the systemic context and culture as a whole, and of the transformation of these relationships as material culture becomes part of the potential and actual archaeological record. A factor in these advances is widening range of authors to include substantially more women and persons originating from outside Europe and North America.[1]

---

[1] In 1956–67 women authors of ethnoarchaeological publications constituted 25 percent of the total of twelve, in 1995–8 43 percent of 86, and in that period a respectable but still too small proportion (19 percent) of authors were of neither European nor North American origin.

Ethnoarchaeology as contributor to archaeological theory and practice

This volume provides ample evidence of the broad spectrum of ethnoarchaeo-logical contributions of immediate relevance to archaeological interpretation – remember Robert Janes's 77 expectations (chapter 10)! A summary would be both tedious and pointless, though it is worth reminding ourselves of three areas in which ethnoarchaeology has played a critical and leading role in the advancement of archaeological theory: the development of middle range theory, style theory, and the reconceptualization of material culture that, in conjunction with largely French social theory, was influential in the emergence of postprocessual archaeology. In our view, however, ethnoarchaeology's con-tributions to specific topics of archaeological relevance are of lesser importance than the influence it has exerted on archaeological thinking in two main areas. Especially in Europe and other parts of the world where archaeology is taught separately from cultural anthropology, but also in North America, ethnoar-chaeology has increased the amount of ethnography, and pertinent ethnogra-phy at that, to which students are exposed. ND's (1992a: 353) remarks of some years ago remain apposite.

Ethnoarchaeology's primary *service* mission is still the raising of the analogical con-sciousness of archaeologists, sensitizing them to dimensions of variability and the rich-ness of the relationship between humans and their artifacts, including their own bodies. Many archaeologists have, after all, chosen their discipline because they prefer their culture dead. They need, if only vicariously, to experience cultural realities other than their own to combat the ethnocentrism that colors arguments and distorts inferences.

Second, ethnoarchaeology has proven itself responsive to new analogical needs resulting from changes in archaeological research design and methods, and its evidence and argument have become, almost across the board, an integral part of archaeological theorizing. There are 18 ethnoarchaeological references in the introductory sections to Preucel and Hodder's (1996) reader *Contemporary archaeology in theory*, amounting to almost 4 percent of those cited. Moreover they are dispersed, occurring in six of their nine introductions. In earlier chap-ters we have mentioned archaeological papers that depend on ethnoarchaeolog-ical data: Varien and Mills's (1997) research into rates of accumulation, Boyle's (1993) application of Binfordian concepts and approaches to studies of paleo-lithic fauna – and the list could be almost indefinitely extended to the archae-ology of all places, times, and degrees of complexity, although it is generally the case that the archaeology of complex societies relies more on epigraphy and ethnohistory than ethnoarchaeology. The proceedings of the Antibes confer-ence organized by Françoise Audouze (1992), *Ethnoarchéologie: justification, problèmes, limites*, directly address ethnoarchaeological theory and its archae-ological applications, as do papers in other ethnoarchaeological collections (e.g., Gamble and Boismier 1991; Longacre 1991a). It is perhaps as significant that ethnoarchaeological contributions now regularly appear in volumes of collected papers on a wide range of topics (e.g., in Farrington 1985; Conkey and Hastorf 1990a; Hudson 1993a).

The penetration of ethnoarchaeology into archaeological interpretation is evident – even if the eighth edition of Brian Fagan's (1995) *People of the earth* contains precisely two explicitly ethnoarchaeological references in 27 pages of bibliography, and the second edition of David Phillipson's (1993) *African archaeology* only two of 744 references. Examples could be multiplied; expository syntheses do not necessarily make apparent the foundations upon which their interpretations are built. In textbooks of method and theory we find more explicit mention of ethnoarchaeology. Of some 850 references in the ninth (1997) edition of Fagan's *In the beginning*, 21 are to ethnoarchaeology – as against a mere two in the first edition of 1972. So not only is it clear that ethnoarchaeology is contributing over a broad spectrum, but we also suspect that many archaeologists are now paying ethnoarchaeologists the ultimate compliment of *not* citing their work but treating parts of it as received wisdom, building it into research designs and incorporating it into analyses. Investigation of the extent to which the design of archaeological surveys and excavation in particular culture areas has been affected by expectations derived from ethnoarchaeology would be of interest.

Career passages and the centrality of ethnoarchaeology

Whereas ethnoarchaeology is indeed contributing to archaeology and more broadly to anthropology, it has not achieved the status of an institutionalized subdiscipline. There are still very few researchers – ND, Kent, CK, and Longacre – whose records would justify their categorization as career ethnoarchaeologists; few if any younger scholars seem likely to devote themselves principally to ethnoarchaeology.[2] A much larger number, including the authors of most of the case studies discussed in this book, have had a "bout with ethnography," as Susan Kus (1997: 209) put it, on one or more occasions, and no doubt they and others will continue to do so, although it is puzzling why, after the heady early 1980s, ethnoarchaeology appears to have fallen out of fashion in Britain. A large majority of practitioners come from and return to archaeology, though several possess other or additional forms of expertise; Aurenche, for example, was trained as an architect, and Childs and Killick as materials scientists. Ethnoarchaeology is, then, a discipline practiced for the most part by archaeologists, usually with a particular archaeological problem set in mind, as for example Binford among the Nunamiut, DeBoer in the upper Ucayali, Roux among the potters of New Delhi, and the Pétrequins in Bénin and Irian Jaya.

---

[2] Dean Arnold belongs in the career category, but his allegiance seems to be primarily to cultural ecology. Other younger scholars, for example Miriam Stark, are certainly qualified to specialize as career ethnoarchaeologists but we have conducted no inquiries as to their intentions. Olivier Gosselain, with Ingrid Herbich perhaps the most likely candidate, denies such aspirations (pers. comm. to ND 2000).

Their projects completed, they turn to application of their results, or to fresh fields of endeavor. Sociocultural anthropologists rarely if ever undertake ethnoarchaeological research, though they do on occasion write for archaeologists, as in Heider's (1961) cautionary tale and Eder's (1984) problematization of mobility and sedentism.

Another important if often transient category of ethnoarchaeological researchers comprises doctoral and, to a lesser extent, masters' students, many carrying out their research under the aegis of a larger project. Later in this chapter we consider some of their contributions in relation to the future of the discipline. The low cost of ethnoarchaeological fieldwork compared to its archaeological counterpart will no doubt sustain this research approach so long as universities and research institutes remain underfunded.

While most who do ethnoarchaeology move back and forth between it and archaeology, they also gain access to other areas. Several one-time students of ethnoarchaeology have moved in other, sometimes new, directions. Of Hodder's Cambridge postgraduate ethnoarchaeologists of the early 1980s only Parker Pearson has remained in archaeology (Giles *et al.* 1997), with a recent excursion into the ethnoarchaeology of food among the Androy of Madagascar (Parker Pearson 1999). While some left academe, Miller was instrumental in developing the anthropology of consumption and material culture studies, and is a founding editor of the *Journal of Material Culture*. Henrietta Moore (e.g., 1995) has become a figure in social, and especially feminist, anthropology. Many others who have undertaken ethnoarchaeological research have found that the consequent extension of their competences, experience, and range of contacts has opened doors, allowing them to contribute in new ways to anthropology *sensu lato*, including to applied anthropology. We have not researched the non-ethnoarchaeological, non-archaeological writings of ethnoarchaeologists, and do not propose to support this statement more than anecdotally. Polly Wiessner, together with Akii Tumu, has recently (1998) produced a *magnum opus* of Papua New Guinea regional ethnohistory. Susan Kent's (1996a) edition of a non-ethnoarchaeological volume entitled *Cultural diversity among twentieth century foragers: an African perspective* is an outgrowth of her ethnoarchaeological experience, as is, at least in part, Yvonne Marshall's co-edition with Chris Gosden of a number of *World Archaeology* devoted to the cultural biography of objects (Marshall and Gosden 1999). Steven Brandt's and his American and Ethiopian colleagues' (Brandt, Spring, *et al.* 1997) multidisciplinary study of enset, an ancient highland domesticate and important famine buffer that had received little scientific attention, was stimulated by the first author's ethnoarchaeological research. Examples could be multiplied.

In short, while ethnoarchaeology's practitioners, even including researchers of the anthropology of techniques school, are too few in number to be able to claim that they play an integrative role in modern anthropology, they certainly occupy a central position within it, even if they have not as yet exploited this to its full potential. As Ann Stahl wrote to ND in a message dated 3 February 1998:

Ethnoarchaeologists have great potential to contribute to . . . broader discussions [of social theory and] of recontextualization of imported objects, of the role of objects in social reproduction and transformation, and so on. By and large, these have not been foremost on the agenda, in part I suspect because ethnoarchaeologists tend to define their mission in relation to archaeology, rather than in relation to [sociocultural] anthropology . . . So I urge you to conclude this chapter with some imaginative possibilities, cajoling people to define their research objectives against a broader canvas.

We are cajoled by Stahl's vision, and hope that others will be encouraged by it to redefine their work in broader anthropological terms.

Lack of institutionalization, increasing maturity

Given its practitioners' penchant for disciplinary transhumance, it should be no surprise that, while ethnoarchaeology is taught, usually as a course component rather than on its own, in undergraduate programs in many European and North American universities, in Australia and no doubt elsewhere, no university boasts an ethnoarchaeology section comparable in status (even if not in size) to archaeology or cultural anthropology. Most teaching takes place at the graduate level and outside formal courses, in workshops, in field situations where the student obtains advice from the project director or – perhaps only erratically and at a distance – from his or her supervisor, and during thesis writing. We can remember no advertised position for which a specialization in ethnoarchaeology was the essential requirement. While many areal and topical journals, notably the *Journal of Anthropological Archaeology*, welcome ethnoarchaeological contributions, there is no journal devoted to it.

Absence of institutionalization is no bad thing. An ethnoarchaeology that lost contact with archaeology would soon either become a sterile pursuit, irrelevant to the discipline it was created to complement, or lose the archaeological component of its identity and become something else. Such effects have indeed contributed to the rejuvenated study of material culture. Neither is lack of institutionalization and a cadre of full-time professional ethnoarchaeologists incompatible with increasing disciplinary maturity. In chapter 1 we suggested that "maturity may be characterized by progressive incorporation into the discipline of a variety of viewpoints within a broadly agreed philosophical framework, a range of lively approaches to diverse subject matter, and the appearance of second-generation studies that group and synthesize individual case studies." Henrietta Moore's (1996) statement in her introduction to a collection on the future of anthropological knowledge, that "Anthropology is no longer a singular discipline, if it ever was, but rather a multiplicity of practices engaged in a wide variety of contexts," applies also to ethnoarchaeology. This is evident in the coexistence of processual and postprocessual ethnoarchaeology, in the large numbers of studies that combine presentation of data with development of theory, and in

1 comparative studies such as "Researching ambiguity: frames of reference and site structure" (Binford 1987a), "Man the hunted: determinants of household spacing in desert and tropical foraging societies" (Gould and Yellen 1987), and "Ethnoarchaeology and the concept of home: a cross-cultural analysis" (Kent 1995b),

2 regional studies that, while involving a comparative element, take very different perspectives, as for example "Kalinga ceramics and new technologies: social and cultural contexts of ceramic change" (Stark and Longacre 1993), "Mortuary practices, ideology and society in the Central Mandara Highlands, northern Cameroon" (David 1995), and *Hier et aujourd'hui: des poteries et des femmes. Céramiques traditionelles du Mali* (Gallay *et al.* 1996),

3 other contributions that, while deriving from ethnoarchaeological research, clearly go beyond the discipline's primary engagement with material culture, for example Hodder's (1982a: 105–24) chapter on the Lozi kingdom of the Upper Zambezi, Dietler and Herbich's (1993) "Living on Luo time: reckoning sequence, duration, history, and biography in a rural African society," and David and Sterner's (1999) "Wonderful society: the Burgess Shale creatures, Mandara chiefdoms and the nature of prehistory,"

4 feedback from ethnoarchaeologically informed archaeology to ethnoarchaeology, for example Steven Simms and Kathleen Heath's (1990) call to end the "discontinuity between what ethnoarchaeologists investigate and record and what prehistoric archaeologists *can* investigate and record," which they suggest can in part be achieved by carrying out the "standard analyses in archaeology [that] are still rare in ethnoarchaeological investigations of site-formation processes" (p. 811), and

5 the beginnings of an applied ethnoarchaeology, as exemplified by Dawson's (1995) examination of Inuit responses to the changing nature of the built environment, which has as one of its aims to "educate and challenge Euro-Canadian architects and planners to design and construct dwellings that strengthen rather than diminish the values, customs, traditions, and social relations of contemporary Inuit families" (p. 79).

In addition, practitioners are, as is demonstrated in preceding chapters, meeting the challenges of carrying out effective research in complex societies (e.g., Chang 1993a, 1993b; Kramer 1997). If the concepts of agency and structuration are not always explicit in their analyses, the native is no longer seen as the passive vehicle through which culture expresses itself. Nor is it still believed that by avoiding modernizing subjects, or by stripping off a veneer of modernity, we can recover a pristine version of their culture. The lessons of debates of the 1980s over analogy, and hopefully also of Stahl (1993), have been internalized. And, besides catching change on the wing (e.g., Sargent and Friedel 1986), ethnoarchaeologists are escaping the tyranny of the ethnographic present by tracking change over decades, and using early ethnographic, ethnohistoric, historical, and even archaeological sources in order to document and explain change over the long-term (e.g., Marshall 1987; Schmidt 1997). On this evidence, and on that of this book as a whole, it can be claimed that ethnoarchaeology is an established and reasonably mature subdiscipline of anthropology.

The future

In an earlier section we quoted Ann Stahl to the effect that ethnoarchaeology has as yet unrealized potential to contribute to social theory. Will this be fulfilled? Will ethnoarchaeology remain the handmaiden of archaeology, or is it developing in other directions, as an ethnography that privileges things, or as a branch of cultural studies? Ethnoarchaeologists have not been communicative on the future of their discipline. In 1996 Susan Kent predicted that "three domains of inquiry will dominate African ethnoarchaeology for the next decade at least: (1) gender, (2) political and social power and inequality, and (3) culture change" (1996b: 24). She also sees more long-term projects, a wider range of data collection techniques, more projects with broad anthropological perspectives, more cross-cultural comparison, and some ethnoarchaeology being applied in the area of development. A gender conscious perspective is indeed becoming progressively incorporated into a wide variety of topical areas, often in the context of the long-term, regional research programs; there will almost inevitably be more cross-cultural comparison, and, hopefully, more ethnoarchaeology applied beyond archaeology to assist, for example, in Third World development through incorporation of an appreciation of traditional knowledge and practice into what are only too often imposed programs that draw authority from culturally uninformed Western science.[3]

We can predict the future of ethnoarchaeology over the next few years by observing its recent trajectory as expressed in theses written during the 1990s.[4] Of the score of Ph.D. theses known to us, eight are on Africa with the remainder widely distributed. Perhaps most striking about the ensemble is the expanding behavioral range covered. This includes fishing (Belcher 1998) and shell fishing (Msemwa 1994) besides plant-gathering (Ertuğ-Yaraş 1997), and Reddy's ethnobotanically oriented research discussed in chapter 5. Site structure, activity areas, and architecture remain popular topics (e.g., Kneebone 1991; Plimpton 1994; Dore 1996), and it is evident here and elsewhere (e.g., Kuznar [1990] on Andean pastoralism) that more sophisticated statistical treatments are being used than in the past, and that authors are reading widely to find theory relevant to their interests. Other studies of architecture (e.g., Lyons

---

[3] The "applied" ethnoarchaeology of Huysecom (1992) refers to its application to the archaeological record.

[4] We have not conducted an extensive search but have made use of the ProQuest Digital Dissertations catalog (http://wwwlib.umi.com/dissertations). Our knowledge of MA theses is both casual and limited.

1992) focus on gender and symbolic aspects. A restrained postprocessual concern with ideology and meaning is also evident in Randi Barndon's (1992) Ph.D. candidacy thesis on Fipa iron working, and several from the University of Calgary, including Charles Mather's (1999) analysis of Kusasi shrines in Ghana, and, at the MA level, R. A. (Caesar) Apentiik's (1997) study of technology and systems of thought among the Bulsa in the same area. Kodzo Gavua (1990) studied the expression of style across classes of material culture among the Mafa of northern Cameroon. Pottery, often approached with questions of social identity in mind (e.g., Gosselain 1995; Guèye 1998), continues to attract ethnoarchaeological attention. In theses emanating from the Kalinga project, Stark (1993b) approaches ceramics from an economic, Neupert (1999) from a political, and Kobayashi (1994) from a form/function perspective.

The combination of ethnoarchaeological and other approaches evident in Reddy's work is also to be found in Gregory Laden's (1992) thesis on Efe Pygmy foraging and land use ecology, and in Claire Allum's (1997) study of Chachi land use in Ecuador. A similar engagement with ethnohistory is evident in Scott MacEachern's (1990) thesis on ethnogenesis in the Mandara mountains, in Sohkna Guèye's (1998) research in Senegal, and in a master's thesis by Claire Bourges (1996) on the ceramics present and past of the inhabitants of an inselberg within the precolonial Wandala state in northern Cameroon and Nigeria. The two last-named authors apply, as does Kuznar (1990), their results directly to the archaeological record, Bourges indeed testing the hypothesis that ceramic change is correlated with important political changes and finding that the latter may have far less effect on the artifactual inventory than archaeologists might suppose.

It is noteworthy that, while certain theses address ideology and meaning, none is cast in a postprocessual mode antithetical to processualism, and the majority are essentially naturalist in their approach, though most of those of which we have personal knowledge lack the formal testing of hypotheses characteristic of earlier processual studies. This is indeed generally true of the writing of ethnoarchaeology. The archaeological stamp and framing of studies are often obvious. There is a lack of experimentation even in antinaturalist works that contrasts with Tringham's (1991) "Households with faces . . .," Shanks's (1993) reflections on a proto-Korinthian perfume jar, or Joyce's (1994) hypertextual study of "Dorothy Hughes Popenoe: Eve in an archaeological garden." Not that the social science thesis is a genre in which literary experimentation is encouraged; rather the styles observed generally concord with the mind sets of their supervisors, who include several well-known ethnoarchaeologists, ND, Gallay, Gould, Longacre, and Watson among them, and some anthropological archaeologists, including Mark Aldenderfer, Pierre de Maret, J. Scott Raymond, and, on the technological side and supervisor of James Skibo's (1990) thesis on the use alteration of pottery, Michael Schiffer. Also worth mentioning since it goes to the issue of institutionalization is that, to the best of our knowledge, no recent PhD is employed as an ethnoarchaeologist, and that, while several though by no means all have found jobs in academe, most are employed first and foremost as archaeologists.[5]

These theses indicate that ethnoarchaeology is expanding its topical range to provide broader analogical support to archaeology, and sharpening its analytical tools. Application of Geographic Information Systems approaches to the ethnoarchaeology of landscapes would be a natural progression. While cohabitation of processual and postprocessual approaches is evident in the collection as a whole, the mind sets and methods involved are so different that it is quite unlikely that naturalist and antinaturalist research will ever be carried out simultaneously by single researchers. But hopefully, since the perspectives have much to offer each other, larger projects will be able to incorporate both within their confines. The rule of increasing division of labor applies. Teamwork will test whether synthesis and vigorous hybrid results are possible – with students, we suspect, undertaking the processual aspects of the study.

The thesis set also indicates that disciplinary boundaries will continue to be productively transgressed as, in Clifford Geertz's (1980) terms, genres are increasingly blurred. Lemonnier's (1986) anthropology of technology among the Anga has much in common with Hodder's and others' research on style and ethnicity. The ethnoarchaeologists may be less concerned with technology *per se*, but they frequently have better historical control. Other examples could be drawn from work on fauna and foraging – that of Hawkes and O'Connell and their colleagues (e.g., Hawkes *et al.* 1991) grading into optimal foraging theory and social biology. And similarly in several other areas including ethnohistory and material culture studies – though a survey of articles in the *Journal of Material Culture* suggests not that ethnoarchaeologists are moving into cultural studies but rather that researchers in that area have learned from ethnoarchaeology.

The growth of ethnoarchaeological studies has implications for the future. In some parts of the world, and especially Africa, their number, and in a few regions density, are such that they are becoming foundational elements of areal studies of the past, very much on the model of Schmidt's (1997) *Iron technology in East Africa*, or as Harappan studies benefit from the research of Kenoyer, Roux, Kramer, and others. Another inevitable development is that ethnoarchaeologists will find themselves increasingly impelled to involve themselves in and to contribute to the ongoing critique of comparison in anthropology (see Holy 1987; Gallay 1992a, 1992b; Sterner 1998).

Where are the obvious gaps to be filled? More studies should be undertaken in complex societies; and we need more long-term projects, whether sustained or taking the form of returns to the field after a period of years or decades. As

---

[5] William Belcher works as a forensic anthropologist at the US Army Central Identification Laboratory in Hawai'i but remains active in Harappan studies. Gosselain holds a research post and is working as much in sociology as ethnoarchaeology.

to topics: we have as yet very little on cooking and other domestic processing of materials, only half a dozen substantial studies of mortuary practices, practically nothing on politics, not nearly enough on production and distribution – in large part a function of the small scale of most studies in the past – and far too little on chaînes opératoires and the embedding of technology in society and systems of thought. Indeed the intellectual trend that perhaps promises most for the future is towards a growing together of ethnoarchaeology and the anthropology of techniques.

Sociological changes in membership of the ethnoarchaeological workforce will impinge upon these and other trends and developments. The first generation of ethnoarchaeologists, roughly those who began publishing before 1975, are either retired or nearing retirement. While some will continue publishing for some years, their influence on graduate students is on the wane. Ethnoarchaeology, in part because of inequities in the awarding of funds for archaeological fieldwork, has always been characterized by a more equal representation of genders than archaeology. While this has not, as Diane Gifford-Gonzalez (1993) has noted, prevented considerable androcentrism, responsible for example for the lack of studies of domestic processing noted above, the increasing numbers of feminist authors (of whatever sex) should redress the balance in future years. Similarly, the now better represented non-Euro-American authors, so long as they are neither cut off intellectually by lack of funding for fieldwork, libraries, and conferences, nor strait-jacketed by Western modes of thought (and these are huge ifs), have the opportunity to play a vital role in exploring the embedding of material culture in society and thought, thereby linking ethnoarchaeology to an anthropology in which the study of things is at last reclaiming the attention it once had and always deserved.

And what of future constraints? Geopolitics will continue to shuffle ethnoarchaeologists around the globe, but although one regrets lost opportunities, others are created in the process. For instance, Paul Jordan, a postgraduate student at Sheffield, has been working in western Siberia among the Khanty, becoming the first ethnoarchaeologist in Central Asia (Zvelebil and Jordan 1999). Other constraints – are they not in fact opportunities? – were sketched in chapter 3 and include, especially in North America and Australia, changes in access to and control over field data as Indian Tribes, First Nations, Aboriginal Associations, and their legal equivalents elsewhere take control over their cultural heritage. We will say nothing about funding as, whether in the First World or elsewhere, support of ethnoarchaeology is scarcely to be distinguished from that of anthropology in general.

Reflexivity

In chapter 2 we noted that all research and writing has sociopolitical content and implications. We end this book by asking what impact we are having on our students and on our "subjects." We shall be brief since with regard to the former our effect is scarcely distinguishable from that of social and cultural anthropology, and, regarding the latter, we have only anecdotal evidence.

In a recent paper on "anthropology, pedagogy and personhood," Coleman and Simpson (1999) point out that while anthropology is a reflexive discipline, "we have been insufficiently aware of the fact that anthropology is not only a discipline or form of knowledge, it is also a kind of culture in itself" (p. 3), one that students appropriate as instrumental knowledge (as a means to gain a degree), for purposes of "spiritual bricolage" (building anthropological knowledge into their own spirituality), and as a "bridge to personal development." This last is surely true of ethnoarchaeologists for whom research, and especially participant observation, "provides an inherent challenge to the separation of the observer and the observed" (p. 5), and we would hope that our students gain vicariously from our and others' experiences. However, this is not necessarily the case. Rather than liberating, anthropology may instead purvey middle-class assumptions. "The image of their lives that is reflected back to students through anthropology can be a disturbing one, revealing not so much a world of new possibilities as simply an alternative form of personal displacement and disempowerment" (p. 6). Our own experiences of teaching ethnoarchaeology lead us to believe that this is a rare effect; the vast majority of our students come, through ethnoarchaeology, to look at the world around them with new eyes and a greater appreciation of the social life and meanings of things (Appadurai 1986; Hodder 1989b).

With regard to our relationship to the societies we study, Chris Gosden (1999: 9) roundly accuses us of immorality:

I feel that ethnoarchaeology is immoral, in that we have no justification for using the present of one society simply to interpret the past of another, especially as the present is often seen as a latter-day survival of stage [*sic*] passed elsewhere in the world, for instance where hunter-gatherer groups from Africa or Australia are used to throw light on the European Palaeolithic.

Although readers of this book may prefer to regard this statement as a merely silly rather than mischievous misrepresentation, we should counter it for the record. First, no ethnoarchaeologist ever studies a society "simply to interpret the past of another" or without producing documentation of enduring historical value for the society concerned. Second, the Kalahari Bushman Debate evidently passed Gosden by; for who now sees any living society as "a latter-day survival" of an earlier stage of human development? Third, the statement is illogical. Why should it be immoral for Gorecki to study Papuan ethnoarchaeology but (presumably) moral for Gosden to study Papuan archaeology? Was it immoral for CK to study Aliabad to aid in interpreting its inhabitants' own prehistory? Fourth, the statement is offensive in implying that some societies are mere sources of analogy, whereas in our view all human societies past and present can mutually throw light upon each other. May a Hadza not benefit from

Fig. 14.1 Judy Sterner, on return to Sirak, northern Cameroon, in 1989, shares pictures of Canada with Gobway, an expert potter, Ndarne, her granddaughter, and her husband, Dzevay, a smith (all seen in *Vessels of the spirits* [David 1990]).

knowledge of the Neolithic of China? Fifth and lastly, it is naively paternalistic to suppose that societies cannot resist exploitation by ethnoarchaeologists.

We believe empowerment rather than disempowerment to be our impact on the societies we study. The very fact that outsiders come to observe and question people about the mundane details of their daily lives may lead them to revalue things and behaviors that the spread of meretricious modern (Western and other) values and fashions has tended to diminish in their estimation. This is especially the case when the outsider is regarded as prestigious and utilizes prestigious media. ND remembers as a high moment of his ethnoarchaeological life the showing of the video *Dokwaza: last of the African iron masters* (David and Le Bléis 1988) to a Mafa audience in Mokolo. Dokwaza was himself present and responded vigorously to questions from young Mafa men, *évolués* who, at first critical of what they regarded as primitive and uncivilized, quite clearly found themselves reassessing their attitudes to a magical technology. None of ND's team, on the other hand, had left the smelt without a feeling of awe and of having been uniquely privileged to participate in the alchemical transmutation of dust into steel. Surely many of us have had similar experiences. One cannot, for example, imagine that, quite apart from the considerable inflow of cash and other material benefits, the impact of Longacre and his team has not benefited the Kalinga socially, educationally, and in other ways, and similarly with Schmidt and his colleagues and the Haya. At Sukur in Nigeria, the creation of a Sukur District is locally believed, rightly or wrongly, to have been expedited by the presence of ND and Judy Sterner, and they composed much of the citation that resulted in Sukur being named in 1999 as Nigeria's first UNESCO World Heritage Site. Time will tell whether this is of advantage to its residents. And, as a person born and brought up in Cambridge, ND gained new understanding of his home town from Parker Pearson's (1982) study of its deathways.

Even when the ethnoarchaeologist works on her or his own with little in the way of funding, there is a human interchange, a cultural reciprocity, that it is surely not sentimental to regard as valuable in itself (Fig. 14.1). "Only connect," as E. M. Forster urged, and let us make certain that, after we return from the field, we remain connected, and that the communities in which we work and the larger societies in which they are set receive as much in the way of benefits as we are capable of offering.

BIBLIOGRAPHY

Adams, J. L. 1993. Toward understanding the technological development of manos and metates. *The Kiva* 58: 331–44.
  1996. *Manual for a technological approach to ground stone analysis*. Tucson: Center for Desert Archaeology.
Adams, R. M. 1965. *Land behind Baghdad*. Chicago: University of Chicago Press.
  1981. *Heartland of cities*. Chicago: University of Chicago Press.
Adams, R. M. and H. J. Nissen. 1972. *The Uruk countryside*. Chicago: University of Chicago Press.
Adams, W. Y. 1973. An ethnoarchaeological study of a rural American community: Silcott, Washington, 1900–1930. *Ethnohistory* 20: 335–46.
Adams, W. Y. and E. W. Adams. 1991. *Archaeological typology and practical reality: a dialectical approach to artifact classification and sorting*. Cambridge: Cambridge University Press.
Agorsah, E. K. 1982. Spatial expression of traditional behavior: an ethnoarchaeological study. *Archaeology at UCLA* 2: 1–4.
  1985. Archaeological implications of traditional house construction among the Nchumuru of northern Ghana. *Current Anthropology* 26: 103–15.
  1988. Evaluating spatial behavior patterns of prehistoric societies. *Journal of Anthropological Archaeology* 7: 231–47.
  1993. Archaeological considerations on social dynamics and spatial pattern development of traditional settlements. In *Spatial boundaries and social dynamics: case studies from food-producing societies*, A. F. C. Holl and T. E. Levy (eds.), pp. 7–24. Ann Arbor: International Monographs in Prehistory.
Agrawal, B. B., K. K. Prasad, G. I. S. Chauhun, P. K. Chaudhuri, and S. M. Aeron 1998. Evaluation of earlier ironmaking processes and their relevance in Indian context. In *Archaeometallurgy in India*, V. Tripathi (ed.), pp. 218–27. Delhi: Sharada Publishing House.
Aiyedun, K. D. 1995. Aesthetic, domestic, and nutritional use of plant resources in Niger state: an ethnoarchaeological study. *Nyame Akuma* 43: 28–34.
Allchin, B. (ed.). 1994. *Living traditions: studies in the ethnoarchaeology of South Asia*. New Delhi: Oxford and IBH Publishing Co. Pvt. Ltd.
Allen, H. 1996. Ethnography and prehistoric archaeology in Australia. *Journal of Anthropological Archaeology* 15: 137–59.
Allen, J. 1984. Pots and poor princes: a multi-dimensional approach to the role of pottery trading in coastal Papua. In *The many dimensions of pottery: ceramics in archaeology and anthropology*, S. van der Leeuw and A. A. Pritchard (eds.), pp. 407–63. Amsterdam: University of Amsterdam.
Allum, C. 1997. An ethnoarchaeological study of Chachi land-use in northwestern tropical lowland Ecuador. Ph.D. thesis, University of Calgary.
Anderson, P. C. (ed.). 1999. *Prehistory of agriculture: new experimental and ethnographic approaches*. Institute of Archaeology Monograph 40. Los Angeles: Institute of Archaeology, University of California.

Anderson, S. and F. Ertuğ. 1998. Fuel, fodder and faeces: an ethnographic and botanical study of dung fuel use in Central Anatolia. *Environmental Archaeology* 1: 99–109.

Annis, M. B. 1985. Resistance and change: pottery making in Sardinia. *World Archaeology* 17: 240–55.

1988. Modes of production and the use of space in potters' workshops in Sardinia: a changing picture. *Newsletter of the Department of Pottery Technology, Leiden* 6: 47–78.

Apentiik, R. A. 1997. Bulsa technologies and systems of thought. M.A. thesis, University of Calgary.

Appadurai, A. (ed.). 1986. *The social life of things: commodities in cultural perspective*. Cambridge: Cambridge University Press.

Ardener, E. 1978. Some outstanding problems in the analysis of events. In *The yearbook of symbolic anthropology*, vol. I, E. Schwimmer (ed.). London: Hurst.

Arnold, D. E. 1970. The emics of pottery design from Quinua, Peru. Ph.D. thesis, University of Illinois.

1971. Ethnomineralogy of Ticul, Yucatan potters: etics and emics. *American Antiquity* 36: 20–40.

1972. Mineralogical analyses of ceramic materials from Quinua, Department of Ayacucho, Peru. *Archaeometry* 14: 92–101.

1975a. Ceramic ecology of the Ayacucho basin, Peru: implications for prehistory. *Current Anthropology* 16: 183–206.

1975b. Ecological variables and ceramic production: towards a general model. In *Primitive art and technology*, J. S. Raymond, B. Loveseth, C. Arnold, and G. Reardon (eds.), pp. 92–108. Calgary: University of Calgary Archaeological Association.

1983. Design structure and community organization in Quinua, Peru. In *Structure and cognition in art*, D. K. Washburn (ed.), pp. 56–73. New York: Cambridge University Press.

1984a. Social interaction and ceramic design: community-wide correlates in Quinua, Peru. In *Pots and potters: current approaches in ceramic archaeology*, P. M. Rice (ed.), pp. 133–61. Institute of Archaeology Monograph 24. Los Angeles: University of California.

1984b. The ethnoarchaeology of pottery production. *Reviews in Anthropology* 11: 12–19.

1985. *Ceramic theory and cultural process*. Cambridge: Cambridge University Press.

1993. *Ecology and ceramic production in an Andean community*. Cambridge: Cambridge University Press.

Arnold, D. E., H. Neff, and R. L. Bishop. 1991. Compositional analysis and "sources" of pottery: an ethnoarchaeological approach. *American Antiquity* 93: 70–90.

Arnold III, P. J. 1991. *Domestic ceramic production and spatial organization: a Mexican case study in ethnoarchaeology*. Cambridge: Cambridge University Press.

Aronson, M., J. M. Skibo, and M. T. Stark. 1994. Production and use technologies in Kalinga pottery. In *Kalinga ethnoarchaeology: expanding archaeological method and theory*, W. A. Longacre and J. M. Skibo (eds.), pp. 83–111. Washington, DC: Smithsonian Institution Press.

Asboe, Walter. 1946. Pottery in Ladakh, western Tibet. *Man* 46 (Jan.–Feb.): 9–10.

Ascher, R. 1961. Analogy in archaeological interpretation. *Southwestern Journal of Anthropology* 17: 317–25.

   1962. Ethnography for archaeology: a case from the Seri Indians. *Ethnology* 1: 360–9.

   1968. Time's arrow and the archaeology of a contemporary community. In *Settlement archaeology*, K.-C. Chang (ed.), pp. 43–52. Palo Alto: National Press.

Aschmann, H. 1949. A metate maker of Baja California. *American Anthropologist* 51: 682–6.

Atherton, J. 1983. Ethnoarchaeology in Africa. *The African Archaeological Review* 1: 75–104.

Audouze, F. (ed.). 1992. *Ethnoarchéologie: justification, problèmes, limites.* Rencontres Internationales d'Archéologie et d'Histoire d'Antibes, 12. Juan-les-Pins: Editions APDCA.

   1999. New advances in French prehistory. *Antiquity* 73: 165–75.

Aurenche, O., M. Bazin, and S. Dadler. 1997. *Villages engloutis: enquête ethnoarchéologique à Cafer Höyük (vallée de l'Euphrate).* Travaux de la Maison de l'Orient Méditerranéen 26. Lyons and Paris: Maison de l'Orient Méditerranéen/Diffusion de Brocard.

Avery, D. H., N. J. van der Merwe, and S. Saitowitz. 1988. The metallurgy of the iron bloomery in Africa. In *The beginning of the use of metals and alloys*, R. Maddin (ed.), pp. 261–82. Cambridge, MA: MIT Press.

Babbie, E. 1998. *The practice of social research* (8th edn). Belmont, CA: Wadsworth Publishing Company.

Bahn, P. 1989. *Bluff your way in archaeology.* Horsham: Ravette Books Ltd.

Balfet, H. 1965. Ethnographical observations in North Africa and archaeological interpretation. In *Ceramics and man*, F. R. Matson (ed.), pp. 161–77. Viking Fund Publications in Anthropology 41. New York: Wenner-Gren Foundation for Anthropological Research.

Barkindo, B. M. 1989. *The Sultanate of Mandara to 1902.* Stuttgart: Franz Steiner Verlag.

Barley, N. 1983. *The innocent anthropologist: notes from a mud hut.* London: British Museums Publications Ltd.

Barndon, R. 1992. Traditional ironworking among the Fipa: an ethnoarchaeological study from southwestern Tanzania. Cand. Phil. thesis, University of Bergen.

   1996a. Fipa ironworking and its technological style. In *The culture and technology of African iron production*, P. R. Schmidt (ed.), pp. 58–73. Gainesville: University Press of Florida.

   1996b. Mental and material aspects of iron working: a cultural comparative perspective. In *Aspects of African archaeology. Papers from the 10th Congress of the PanAfrican Association for Prehistory and Related Studies*, G. Pwiti and R. Soper (eds.), pp. 761–71. Harare: University of Zimbabwe Publications.

Barreteau, D. and H. Jungraithmayr. 1993. Calculs lexicostatistiques et glottochronologiques sur les langues tchadiques. In *Datation et chronologie dans le bassin du Lac Tchad (Actes du Séminaire du Réseau Méga-Tchad, ORSTOM-Bondy, 11–12 septembre 1989)*, D. Barreteau and C. von Graffenried (eds.), pp. 103–40. Paris: Editions ORSTOM.

Bartel, B. 1982. A historical review of ethnological and archaeological analyses of mortuary practice. *Journal of Anthropological Archaeology* 1: 32–58.

Barth, F. 1961. *Nomads of South Persia: the Basseri tribe of the Khamseh confederacy*. Boston: Little, Brown and Co.

    1987. *Cosmologies in the making: a generative approach to cultural variation in inner New Guinea*. Cambridge: Cambridge University Press.

Bartram Jr., L. E. 1993. Perspectives on skeletal part profiles and utility curves from eastern Kalahari ethnoarchaeology. In *From bones to behavior: ethnoarchaeological and experimental contributions to the interpretation of faunal remains*, J. Hudson (ed.), pp. 115–37. Occasional Paper 21. Carbondale: Center for Archaeological Investigations, Southern Illinois University.

Bastien, J. W. 1995. The mountain/body metaphor expressed in a Kaatan funeral. In *Tombs for the living: Andean mortuary practices*, T. D. Dillehay (ed.), pp. 355–78. (A symposium at Dumbarton Oaks: 12th and 13th October 1991.) Washington, DC: Dumbarton Oaks.

Bauxar, J. J. 1957a. Yuchi ethnoarchaeology, Part I: some Yuchi identifications reconsidered. *Ethnohistory* 4: 279–301.

    1957b. Yuchi ethnoarchaeology, Parts II–IV. *Ethnohistory* 4: 369–437.

Beavitt, P. 1989. The ethnoarchaeology of sacrifice: some comments on the visible and invisible with respect to human contact with the spirit world in Borneo. *Anthropozoologica* (3e numéro spécial: Animal et pratiques religieuses: les manifestations matérielles): 173–80.

Beck, L. 1978. Women among Qashqa'i nomadic pastoralists in Iran. In *Women in the Muslim world*, L. Beck and N. Keddie (eds.), pp. 352–73. Cambridge, MA: Harvard University Press.

Beck, W., R. Fullagar, and N. White. 1988. Archaeology from ethnography: the Aboriginal use of cycad as an example. In *Archaeology with ethnography: an Australian perspective*, B. Meehan and R. Jones (eds.), pp. 137–47. Canberra: Department of Prehistory, RSPacS, Australian National University.

Behura, N. K. 1978. *Peasant potters of Orissa*. Delhi: Sterling Publications.

Bekaert, S. 1998. Multiple levels of meaning and the tension of consciousness: how to interpret iron technology in Bantu Africa. *Archaeological Dialogues* (Leiden) 5 (1): 6–29.

Belcher, W. R. 1994. Multiple approaches towards reconstruction of fishing technology: net-making and the Indus Valley Tradition. In *From Sumer to Meluhha: contributions to the archaeology of Southwest and South Asia in memory of George F. Dales*, J. M. Kenoyer (ed.), pp. 129–41. Wisconsin Archaeological Reports 3. Madison: University of Wisconsin.

    1998. Fish exploitation of the Baluchistan and Indus Valley traditions: an ethnoarchaeological approach to the study of fish remains. Ph.D. thesis, University of Wisconsin-Madison.

Bellamy, C. B. 1904. A West African smelting house (with an appendix "Analyses of specimens" by F. W. Harbord). *Journal of the Iron and Steel Institute* 64–5: 99–126.

Benco, N. L. 1988. Morphological standardization: an approach to the study of craft specialization. In *A pot for all reasons: ceramic ecology revisited*, C. C. Kolb and L. Lackey (eds.), pp. 57–72. Philadelphia: Laboratory of Anthropology, Temple University.

Bender, B. (ed.). 1993. *Landscape: politics and perspectives*. Providence, RI: Berg.

Berg, B. L. 1998. *Qualitative research methods for the social sciences* (3rd edn). Boston: Allyn and Bacon.

Bernard, H. R. 1994. *Research methods in anthropology: qualitative and quantitative approaches* (2nd edn). Thousand Oaks, CA, London and New Delhi: Sage Publications.

Bienkowski, P. 1985. New caves for old: Bedouin architecture in Petra. *World Archaeology* 17: 149–60.

Binford, L. R. 1962. Archaeology as anthropology. *American Antiquity* 28: 217–25.

    1965. Archaeological systematics and the study of culture process. *American Antiquity* 31: 203–10.

    1971. Mortuary practices: their study and their potential. In *Approaches to the social dimensions of mortuary practices*, James A. Brown (ed.), pp. 6–29. Memoir 25 of the Society for American Archaeology (*American Antiquity* 36 (3)).

    1973. Interassemblage variability – the Mousterian and the "functional" argument. In *The explanation of culture change: models in prehistory*, C. Renfrew (ed.), pp. 227–53. London: Duckworth.

    1976. Forty-seven trips: a case study in the character of archaeological formation process. In *Stone tools as cultural markers*, R. V. S. Wright (ed.), pp. 24–36. Canberra: Australian Institute of Aboriginal Studies.

    1977. General introduction. In *For theory building in archaeology*, L. R. Binford (ed.), pp. 1–10. New York: Academic Press.

    1978a. *Nunamiut ethnoarchaeology*. New York: Academic Press.

    1978b. Dimensional analysis of behavior and site structure: learning from an Eskimo hunting stand. *American Antiquity* 43: 330–61.

    1979. Organization and formation processes: looking at curated technologies. *Journal of Anthropological Research* 35: 255–73.

    1980. Willow smoke and dogs' tails: hunter-gatherer settlement systems and archaeological site formation. *American Antiquity* 45: 4–20.

    1981a. *Bones, ancient men and modern myths*. New York: Academic Press.

    1981b. Behavioral archaeology and the "Pompeii" premise. *Journal of Anthropological Research* 37: 195–208.

    1982. The archaeology of place. *Journal of Anthropological Archaeology* 1: 5–31.

    1983a. *In pursuit of the past: decoding the archaeological record*. New York: Academic Press.

    1983b. Long-term land-use patterning: some implications for archaeology. In *Working at archaeology*, L. R. Binford (ed.), pp. 379–86. New York: Academic Press.

    1983c. *Working at archaeology*. London: Academic Press.

    1984. An Alyawara day: flour, spinifex gum, and shifting perspectives. *Journal of Anthropological Research* 40: 157–82.

    1986. An Alyawara day: making men's knives and beyond. *American Antiquity* 51 (3): 547–62.

    1987a. Researching ambiguity: frames of reference and site structure. In *Method and theory for activity area research: an ethnoarchaeological approach*, S. Kent (ed.), pp. 449–512. New York: Columbia University Press.

    1987b. Data, relativism and archaeological science. *Man* 22: 391–404.

    1989. Styles of style. *Journal of Anthropological Archaeology* 8: 51–67.

    1991. When the going gets tough, the tough get going: Nunamiut local groups, camping patterns and economic organization. In *Ethnoarchaeological approaches to mobile campsites*, C. S. Gamble and W. A. Boismier (eds.), pp.

25–138. Ethnoarchaeological Series 1. Ann Arbor: International Monographs in Prehistory.

Binford, L. R. and J. B. Bertram. 1977. Bone frequencies and attritional processes. In *For theory building in archaeology*, L. R. Binford (ed.), pp. 77–153. New York: Academic Press.

Binford, L. R. and S. R. Binford. 1966. A preliminary analysis of functional variability in the Mousterian of Levallois facies. *Recent Studies in Paleo-Anthropology, American Anthropologist* 68: 238–95.

Binford, L. R. and J. F. O'Connell. 1984. An Alyawara day: the stone quarry. *Journal of Anthropological Research* 40: 406–32.

Binford, S. R. and L. R. Binford (eds.). 1968. *New perspectives in archaeology.* Chicago: Aldine.

Bintliff, J. 1993. Why Indiana Jones is smarter than the post-processualists. *Norwegian Archaeological Review* 26 (2): 91–100.

Blanton, R., S. Kowalewski, G. Feinman, and J. Appel. 1993. *Ancient Mesoamerica: a comparison of change in three regions* (2nd edn). Cambridge: Cambridge University Press.

Blier, S. P. 1987. *The anatomy of architecture: ontology and metaphor in Batammaliba architectural expression.* Cambridge: Cambridge University Press.

Bloch, M. 1971. *Placing the dead: tombs, ancestral villages, and kinship organization in Madagascar.* London and New York: Seminar Press.

Bocock, R. 1993. *Consumption.* London and New York: Routledge.

Borgstedt, J. A. M. 1927. *Dime (Nordost-Afrika, Süd-Äthiopien) – Eisengewinnung.* Film, 16 mm (8 mins.). Göttingen: Institut der Wissenschaftlichen Film.

Bourdieu, P. 1973. The Berber house. In *Rules and meanings*, M. Douglas (ed.), pp. 98–110. Harmondsworth: Penguin.

   1977. *Outline of a theory of practice.* Cambridge: Cambridge University Press.

Bourges, C. T. 1996. Ceramic ethnoarchaeology and historical process: the case of Gréa, northern Cameroon. M.A. thesis, University of Calgary.

Bowen, E. S. (Laura Bohannan). 1954. *Return to laughter.* Garden City, NY: Anchor Books.

Boyle, K. V. 1993. Upper Palaeolithic procurement and processing strategies in southwest France. In *Hunting and animal exploitation in the later Palaeolithic and Mesolithic of Eurasia*, G. L. Peterkin, H. M. Bricker, and P. Mellars (eds.), pp. 151–62. Archaeological Papers of the American Anthropological Association 4. Washington, DC: American Anthropological Association.

Bradley, R. 1984. *The social foundations of prehistoric Britain: themes and variations in the archaeology of power.* London: Longman.

Brain, C. K. 1967. Hottentot food remains and their bearing on the interpretation of fossil bone assemblages. *Scientific Papers* 32: 1–11.

   1969. The contribution of the Namib Desert Hottentots to an understanding of Australopithecine bone accumulations. *Scientific Papers* 39: 13–22.

Braithwaite, M. 1982. Decoration as ritual symbol: a theoretical proposal and ethnographic study in southern Sudan. In *Symbolic and structural archaeology*, I. Hodder (ed.), pp. 80–8. Cambridge: Cambridge University Press.

Brandt, S. A. 1996. The ethnoarchaeology of flaked stone tool use in Southern

Ethiopia. In *Aspects of African archaeology. Papers from the 10th Congress of the PanAfrican Association for Prehistory and Related Studies*, G. Pwiti and R. Soper (eds.), pp. 733–8. Harare: University of Zimbabwe Publications.

Brandt, S. A., A. Spring, *et al.* 1997. *The tree against hunger: enset-based agricultural systems in Ethiopia*. Washington, DC: American Association for the Advancement of Science.

Brandt, S. A. and K. J. Weedman. 1997. The ethnoarchaeology of hide working and flaked stone tool use in southern Ethiopia. In *Ethiopia in broader perspective: Papers of the 13th International Conference of Ethiopian Studies*, vol. 1, K. Fukui, E. Kurimoto, and M. Shigeta (eds.), pp. 351–61. Kyoto: Shokado Book Sellers.

Brears, P. D. C. 1970. *The Farnham potteries*. Farnham.

Breuil, H. 1913. Les subdivisions du paléolithique supérieur et leur signification. In *Congrès internationale d'anthropologie et d'archéologie préhistoriques, Compte rendu de la XIVe session*, pp. 165–238. Geneva: Imprimerie Albert Kündig.

Briggs, J. 1986. Kapluna Daughter. In *Women in the field* (2nd edn), P. Golde (ed.), pp. 19–44. Berkeley: University of California Press.

Brooks, A. S. and J. E. Yellen. 1987. The preservation of activity areas in the archaeological record: ethnoarchaeological and archaeological work in northwest Ngamiland, Botswana. In *Method and theory for activity area research: an ethnoarchaeological approach*, S. Kent (ed.), pp. 63–106. New York: Columbia University Press.

Brown, J. 1995. *Traditional metalworking in Kenya*. Cambridge Monographs in African Archaeology 38. Oxford: Oxbow Books (Oxbow Monograph 44).

Brown, J. A. 1995. Andean mortuary practices in perspective. In *Tombs for the living: Andean mortuary practices: a symposium at Dumbarton Oaks: 12th and 13th October, 1991*, T. D. Dillehay (ed.), pp. 391–405. Washington, DC: Dumbarton Oaks.

Brown, M. F. 1998. Can culture be copyrighted? *Current Anthropology* 39: 193–222.

Brumfiel, E. M. 1992. Breaking and entering the ecosystem – gender, class, and faction steal the show. *American Anthropologist* 94: 551–67.

Bunn, H. T. 1993. Bone assemblages at base camps: a further consideration of carcass transport and bone destruction by the Hadza. In *From bones to behavior: ethnoarchaeological and experimental contributions to the interpretation of faunal remains*, J. Hudson (ed.), pp. 156–68. Occasional Paper 21. Carbondale: Center for Archaeological Investigations, Southern Illinois University.

Bunn, H. T., L. E. Bartram Jr., and E. M. Kroll. 1988. Variability in bone assemblage formation from Hadza hunting, scavenging, and carcass processing. *Journal of Anthropological Archaeology* 7 (4): 412–57.

Bunn, H. T., E. M. Kroll, and L. E. Bartram Jr. 1991. Bone distribution on a modern East African landscape and its archaeological implications. In *Cultural beginnings: approaches to understanding early hominid life-ways in the African savanna*, J. D. Clark (ed.), pp. 33–54. Mainz: Römisch-Germanisches Zentralmuseum.

Butler, A., Z. Tesfay, A. C. D'Andrea, and D. E. Lyons. 1999. The ethnobotany of *Lathyrus sativus* L. in the highlands of Ethiopia. In *The exploitation of plant resources in ancient Africa*, M. van der Veen (ed.), pp. 123–36. New York: Kluwer Academic/Plenum Publishers.

Byrd, B. 1994. Public and private, domestic and corporate: the emergence of the Southwest Asian village. *American Antiquity* 59: 639–66.

Cameron, C. M. 1993. Abandonment and archaeological interpretation. In *Abandonment of settlements and regions: ethnoarchaeological and archaeological approaches*, C. M. Cameron and S. A. Tomka (eds.), pp. 3–7. Cambridge: Cambridge University Press.

Cameron, C. M. and S. A. Tomka (eds.). 1993. *Abandonment of settlements and regions: ethnoarchaeological and archaeological approaches*. Cambridge: Cambridge University Press.

Campbell, J. M. 1968. Territoriality among ancient hunters: interpretations from ethnography and nature. In *Archaeological anthropology in the Americas*, E. J. Meggers (ed.), pp. 1–21. Washington, DC: Anthropological Society of Washington.

Cane, S. B. 1988. Written on stone: a discussion on ethnographic and Aboriginal perspection of stone tools. In *Archaeology with ethnography: an Australian perspective*, B. Meehan and R. Jones (eds.), pp. 88–93. Canberra: Department of Prehistory, RSPacS, Australian National University.

Cannon, A. 1989. The historical dimension in mortuary expressions of status and sentiment. *Current Anthropology* 30: 437–58.

Cardew, M. 1952. Nigerian traditional pottery. *Nigeria* 39: 188–201.

Carneiro, R. L. 1979. Tree felling with the stone ax: an experiment carried out among the Yanomamö Indians of Venezuela. In *Ethnoarchaeology: implications of ethnography for archaeology*, C. Kramer (ed.), pp. 21–58. New York: Columbia University Press.

Carr, C. 1995a. A unified middle-range theory of artifact design. In *Style, society and person: archaeological and ethnological perspectives*, C. Carr and J. E. Neitzel (eds.), pp. 171–258. New York: Plenum Publishing Corporation.

   1995b. Mortuary practices: their social, philosophical, religious, circumstantial and physical determinants. *Journal of Archaeological Method and Theory* 2: 105–200.

Castel, G. 1984. Une habitation rurale égyptienne et ses transformations: chronique d'une famille. In *Nomades et sedentaires: perspectives ethnoarchéologiques*, O. Aurenche (ed.), pp. 11–18. Paris: Editions Recherches sur les Civilisations.

Chaix, L. and H. Sidi Maamar. 1992. Voir et comparer: la découpe des animaux en contexte rituel: limites et perspectives d'une ethnozooarchéologie. In *Ethnoarchéologie: justification, problèmes, limites*, F. Audouze (ed.), pp. 269–92. Rencontres Internationales d'Archéologie et d'Histoire d'Antibes, 12. Juan-les-Pins: Editions APDCA.

Chance, J. K. 1996. Mesoamerica's ethnographic past. *Ethnohistory* 43: 379–403.

Chang, Claudia 1981. Herding site locations in a contemporary Greek village: a ring model for spatial analysis. Paper presented at the 46th Annual Meeting, Society for American Archaeology, San Diego, CA.

   1992. Archaeological landscapes: the ethnoarchaeology of pastoral land use in the Grevena province of north Greece. In *Space, time and archaeological landscapes*, J. Rossignol and L. Wandsnider (eds.), pp. 65–89. New York and London: Plenum Press.

   1993a. Pastoral transhumance in the Southern Balkans as a social ideology: ethnoarchaeological research in Northern Greece. *American Anthropologist* 95: 687–703.

1993b. Ethnoarchaeological survey and pastoral transhumance sites in the Grevena region, Greece. *Journal of Field Archaeology* 20: 249–64.

Chang, K.-C. 1958. Study of the Neolithic social grouping: examples from the New World. *American Anthropologist* 60: 298–334.

Chernela, J. M. 1992. Social meaning and material transaction: the Wanano-Tukano of Brazil and Colombia. *Journal of Anthropological Archaeology* 11 (2): 111–24.

Childe, V. G. 1951. *Man makes himself.* New York: New American Library.
  1958. *The prehistory of European society.* Harmondsworth: Penguin.

Childs, S. T. 1991. Style, technology, and iron smelting furnaces in Bantu-speaking Africa. *Journal of Anthropological Archaeology* 10: 332–59.

Childs, S. T. and W. J. Dewey. 1996. Forging symbolic meaning in Zaire and Zimbabwe. In *The culture and technology of African iron production,* P. R. Schmidt (ed.), pp. 145–71. Gainesville: University Press of Florida.

Childs, S. T. and D. J. Killick. 1993. Indigenous African metallurgy: nature and culture. *Annual Review of Anthropology* 22: 317–37.

Childs, S. T. and P. R. Schmidt. 1985. Experimental iron smelting: the genesis of a hypothesis with implications for African prehistory and history. In *African iron working: ancient and traditional,* R. Haaland and P. L. Shinnie (eds.), pp. 121–41. Oslo: Universitetsforlaget AS.

Clark, J. D. and H. Kurashina. 1981. A study of the work of a modern tanner in Ethiopia and its relevance for archaeological interpretation. In *Modern material culture: the archaeology of us,* R. A. Gould and M. B. Schiffer (eds.), pp. 303–21. New York: Academic Press.

Clark, J. E. 1991. Flintknapping and debitage disposal among the Lacandon Maya of Chiapas, Mexico. In *The ethnoarchaeology of refuse disposal,* E. Staski and L. D. Sutro (eds.), pp. 63–78. Anthropological Research Papers 42. Tempe: Arizona State University.

Clark, J. G. D. 1952. *Prehistoric Europe: the economic basis.* London: Methuen.
  1954. *Excavations at Star Carr.* Cambridge: Cambridge University Press.

Clarke, D. L. 1968. *Analytical archaeology.* New York: Columbia University Press.

Clifford, J. and G. E. Marcus (eds.). 1986. *Writing culture: the poetics and politics of ethnography.* Berkeley: University of California Press.

Cline, W. 1937. *Mining and metallurgy in Negro Africa.* Menasha, WI: George Banta Publishing Co.

Cohen, R., L. L. Langness, J. Middleton, V. C. Uchendu, and J. W. VanStone. 1970. Entrée into the field. In *A handbook of method in cultural anthropology,* R. Naroll and R. Cohen (eds.), pp. 220–44. New York: Columbia University Press.

Coleman, S. and B. Simpson. 1999. Unintended consequences? Anthropology, pedagogy and personhood. *Anthropology Today* 15 (6): 3–6.

Coles, J. 1973. *Archaeology by experiment.* New York: Charles Scribner and Sons.

Collett, D. P. 1993. Metaphors and representations associated with precolonial iron-smelting in eastern and southern Africa. In *The archaeology of Africa: food, metals and towns,* T. Shaw, P. Sinclair, B. W. Andah, and I. A. Okpoko (eds.), pp. 499–511. London and New York: Routledge.

Conkey, M. W. 1990. Experimenting with style in archaeology: some historical and theoretical issues. In *The uses of style in archaeology,* M. W. Conkey and C. A. Hastorf (eds.), pp. 5–17. Cambridge: Cambridge University Press.

Conkey, M. W. and C. A. Hastorf (eds.). 1990a. *The uses of style in archaeology.*
    Cambridge: Cambridge University Press.
    1990b. Introduction. In *The uses of style in archaeology*, M. W. Conkey and
    C. A. Hastorf (eds.), pp. 1–4. Cambridge: Cambridge University Press.
Connah, G. 1985. Agricultural intensification and sedentism in the firki of N.E.
    Nigeria. In *Prehistoric intensive agriculture in the tropics*, vol. 2, I. S.
    Farrington (ed.), pp.: 765–85. BAR International Series 232. Oxford: British
    Archaeological Reports.
Costin, C. L. 1991. Craft specialization: issues in defining, documenting, and
    explaining the organization of production. *Journal of Archaeological Method
    and Theory* 3: 1–56.
Coudart, A. 1992a. Sur l'analogie ethnographique et l'ethnoarchéologie et sur
    l'histoire des rapports entre archéologie et ethnologie. In *La Préhistoire dans
    le monde*, J. Garanger (ed.), pp. 248–63. Nouvelle Clio: L'Histoire et ses
    Problèmes. Paris: Presses Universitaires de France.
    1992b. Entre Nouvelle-Guinée et Néolithique européen. De la correspondance
    entre les variations de l'architecture domestique, la durabilité culturelle et la
    cohésion sociale du groupe. In *Ethnoarchéologie: justification, problèmes,
    limites*, F. Audouze (ed.), pp. 409–46. Rencontres Internationales
    d'Archéologie et d'Histoire d'Antibes, 12. Juan-les-Pins: Editions APDCA.
Crabtree, D. E. 1968. Mesoamerican polyhedral cores and prismatic blades.
    American Antiquity 33: 446–78.
    1972. *An introduction to the technology of stone tools.* Occasional Papers 28.
    Pocatello, ID: Idaho State College Museum.
Crader, D. C. 1984. The zooarchaeology of the storehouse and the dry well at
    Monticello. *American Antiquity* 49: 542–58.
Cribb, R. L. D. 1991a. *Nomads in archaeology.* Cambridge: Cambridge University
    Press.
    1991b. Mobile villagers: the structure and organisation of nomadic pastoral
    campsites in the Near East. In *Ethnoarchaeological approaches to mobile
    campsites*, C. S. Gamble and W. A. Boismier (eds.), pp. 371–93.
    Ethnoarchaeological Series 1. Ann Arbor: International Monographs in
    Prehistory.
Crossland, L. B. and M. Posnansky. 1978. Pottery, people and trade at Begho,
    Ghana. In *The spatial organization of culture*, I. Hodder (ed.), pp. 770–89.
    University Park: University of Pittsburgh Press.
Crown, P. 2001. *Engendering ancient cultures: a case study from the Prehispanic
    Southwest.* Santa Fe: School of American Research Press.
Cushing, F. 1886. A study of Pueblo pottery as illustrative of Zuni culture growth.
    In *Bureau of American Ethnology Fourth Annual Report*, pp. 467–521.
    Washington, DC.
D'Andrade, R. 1995. Moral models in anthropology. *Current Anthropology* 36:
    399–408.
D'Andrea, A. C., D. E. Lyons, M. Haile, and A. Butler. 1999. Ethnoarchaeological
    approaches to the study of prehistoric agriculture in the highlands of
    Ethiopia. In *The exploitation of plant resources in ancient Africa*, M.
    van der Veen (ed.), pp. 101–22. New York: Kluwer Academic/Plenum
    Publishers.
David, N. 1971. The Fulani compound and the archaeologist. *World Archaeology*
    3: 111–31.

1972. On the life span of pottery, type frequencies and archaeological inference. *American Antiquity* 37: 141–2.

1973. On upper palaeolithic society, ecology and technological change. In *The explanation of culture change: models in prehistory*, C. Renfrew (ed.), pp. 277–304. London: Duckworth.

1990. *Vessels of the spirits: pots and people in North Cameroon*. Video recording (50 mins.). Calgary: Department of Commmunications Media, University of Calgary.

1992a. Integrating ethnoarchaeology: a subtle realist perspective. *Journal of Anthropological Archaeology* 11: 330–59.

1992b. The archaeology of ideology: mortuary practices in the central Mandara highlands, northern Cameroon. In *An African commitment: papers in honour of Peter Lewis Shinnie*, J. A. Sterner and N. David (eds.), pp. 181–210. Calgary: University of Calgary Press.

1995. *Black Hephaïstos: exploring culture and science in African iron working*. Video recording (48 mins.). Calgary: University of Calgary, Department of Communications Media.

1996. A new political form? The classless industrial society of Sukur (Nigeria). In *Aspects of African archaeology. Papers from the 10th Congress of the PanAfrican Association for Prehistory and Related Studies*, G. Pwiti and R. Soper (eds.), pp. 593–600. Harare: University of Zimbabwe Publications.

1998. The ethnoarchaeology and field archaeology of grinding at Sukur, Adamawa State, Nigeria. *African Archaeological Review* 15: 13–63.

In press. Lost in the Third Hermeneutic? Theory and methodology, objects and representations in the ethnoarchaeology of African metallurgy. *Mediterranean Archaeology.*

David, N., *et al.* 1999. Keyword bibliography of ethnoarchaeology and related topics. URL: http: //www.acs.ucalgary.ca/~ndavid.

David, N., K. B. Gavua, A. S. MacEachern, and J. A. Sterner. 1991. Ethnicity and material culture in North Cameroon. *Canadian Journal of Archaeology* 15: 171–7.

David, N., R. Heimann, D. J. Killick, and M. Wayman. 1989. Between bloomery and blast furnace: Mafa iron-smelting technology in North Cameroon. *African Archaeological Review* 7: 183–208.

David, N. and H. Hennig. 1972. *The ethnography of pottery: a Fulani case study seen in archaeological perspective*. McCaleb Module in Anthropology 21. Cambridge: Addison-Wesley.

David, N. and Y. Le Bléis. 1988. *Dokwaza: last of the African iron masters*. Video recording (50 mins.). Calgary: University of Calgary, Department of Communications Media.

David, N. and I. G. Robertson. 1996. Competition and change in two traditional African iron industries. In *The culture and technology of African iron production*, P. R. Schmidt (ed.), pp. 128–44. Gainesville: University Press of Florida.

David, N. and J. A. Sterner. 1995. Constructing a historical ethnography of Sukur, part I: demystification. *Nigerian Heritage* 4: 11–33.

1996. Constructing a historical ethnography of Sukur, part II: the "classless industrial" society. *Nigerian Heritage* 5: 11–33.

1999. Wonderful society: the Burgess Shale creatures, Mandara chiefdoms and the nature of prehistory. In *Beyond chiefdoms: pathways to complexity in*

Africa, S. K. McIntosh (ed.), pp. 97–109. Cambridge: Cambridge University Press.

David, N., J. A. Sterner, and K. B. Gavua. 1988. Why pots are decorated. *Current Anthropology* 29: 365–89.

David, N. and D. Voas. 1981. The societal causes of infertility and population decline among the settled Fulani of North Cameroon. *Man* 16: 644–64.

Davidson, I. 1988. The naming of parts: ethnography and the interpretation of Australian prehistory. In *Archaeology with ethnography: an Australian perspective*, B. Meehan and R. Jones (eds.), pp. 17–32. Canberra: Department of Prehistory, RSPacS, Australian National University.

Davis, W. 1990. Style and history in art history. In *The uses of style in archaeology*, M. W. Conkey and C. A. Hastorf (eds.), pp. 18–31. Cambridge: Cambridge University Press.

Dawson, P. C. 1995. "Unsympathetic users": an ethnoarchaeological examination of Inuit responses to the changing nature of the built environment. *Arctic* 48 (1): 71–80.

de Maret, P. 1980. Ceux qui jouent avec le feu: la place du forgeron en Afrique Centrale. *Africa* 50: 263–79.

  1985. The smith's myth and the origin of leadership in Central Africa. In *African iron working*, R. Haaland and P. L. Shinnie (eds.), pp. 142–63. Oslo: Norwegian University Press.

Deal, M. 1982. Functional variation of Maya spiked vessels: a practical guide. *American Antiquity* 47: 614–33.

  1985. Household pottery disposal in the Maya highlands: an ethnoarchaeological interpretation. *Journal of Anthropological Archaeology* 4: 243–91.

  1994. Foreword. In *Kalinga ethnoarchaeology: expanding archaeological method and theory*, W. A. Longacre and J. M. Skibo (eds.), pp. vii–xi. Washington, DC: Smithsonian Institution Press.

  1998. *Pottery ethnoarchaeology in the Central Maya highlands*. Salt Lake City: University of Utah Press.

DeBoer, W. R. 1974. Ceramic longevity and archaeological interpretation: an example from the Upper Ucayali, Peru. *American Antiquity* 39: 335–44.

  1975. The ontogeny of Shipibo art: variations on a cross. Paper presented at the 74th Annual Meeting of the American Anthropological Association, San Francisco.

  1984. The last pottery show: system and sense in ceramic studies. In *The many dimensions of pottery: ceramics in archaeology and anthropology*, S. van der Leeuw and A. A. Pritchard (eds.), pp. 527–68. Amsterdam: University of Amsterdam.

  1990. Interaction, imitation, and communication as expressed in style: the Ucayali experience. In *The uses of style in archaeology*, M. W. Conkey and C. A. Hastorf (eds.), pp. 82–104. Cambridge: Cambridge University Press.

  1991. The decorative burden: design, medium and change. In *Ceramic ethnoarchaeology*, W. A. Longacre (ed.), pp. 144–61. Tucson: University of Arizona Press.

DeBoer, W. R. and D. W. Lathrap. 1979. The making and breaking of Shipibo-Conibo ceramics. In *Ethnoarchaeology: implications of ethnography for archaeology*, C. Kramer (ed.), pp. 102–38. New York: Columbia University Press.

Dennell, R. W. 1974. Botanical evidence for prehistoric crop processing activities. *Journal of Archaeological Science* 1: 275–84.

Dhavalikar, M. K. 1994. Chalcolithic architecture at Inamgaon and Walki: an ethnoarchaeological study. In *Living traditions: studies in the ethnoarchaeology of South Asia*, B. Allchin (ed.), pp. 31–52. New Delhi: Oxford and IBH Publishing Co. Pvt. Ltd.

Di Piazza, A. 1990. Jardins enfouis de Futuna: une ethno-archéologie de l'horticulture. *Journal de la Société des Océanistes* 91 (2): 151–62.

Dickins, J. 1996. Change and continuity in Central Australian graphic systems. *Journal of Anthropological Archaeology* 15: 20–40.

Dietler, M. and I. Herbich. 1989. Tich matek: the technology of Luo pottery production and the definition of ceramic style. *World Archaeology* 21: 148–64.

    1993. Living on Luo time: reckoning sequence, duration, history, and biography in a rural African society. *World Archaeology* 25: 248–60.

    1994. Ceramics and ethnic identity: ethnoarchaeological observations on the distribution of pottery styles and the relationship between the social contexts of production and consumption. In *Terre cuite et société: la céramique, document technique, économique, culturel*, pp. 459–72. Rencontres Internationales d'Archéologie et d'Histoire d'Antibes 14. Juan-les-Pins: Editions APDCA.

    1998. Habitus, techniques, style: an integrated approach to the social understanding of material culture and boundaries. In *The archaeology of social boundaries*, M. T. Stark (ed.), pp. 232–69. Washington, DC and London: Smithsonian Institution Press.

Dillehay, T. D. 1995. Mounds of social death: Araucanian funerary rites and political succession. In *Tombs for the living: Andean mortuary practices: a symposium at Dumbarton Oaks: 12th and 13th October, 1991*, T. D. Dillehay (ed.), pp. 281–314. Washington, DC: Dumbarton Oaks.

Dillon, B. D. 1984. Island building and villages of the dead: living archaeology in the Comarca de San Blas, Panama. *Journal of New World Archaeology* 6 (2): 49–65.

    1988. Meatless Maya? Ethnoarchaeological implications for ancient subsistence. *Journal of New World Archaeology* 7 (2–3): 59–70.

Dobres, M.-A. and C. R. Hoffman. 1994. Social agency and the dynamics of prehistoric technology. *Journal of Archaeological Method and Theory* 1: 211–58.

    1999. Introduction: a context for the present and future of technology studies. In *The social dynamics of technology: practice, politics, and world views*, M.-A. Dobres and C. R. Hoffman (eds.), pp. 1–19. Washington, DC and London: Smithsonian Institution Press.

Donley, L. W. 1982. House power: Swahili space and symbolic markers. In *Symbolic and structural archaeology*, I. Hodder (ed.), pp. 63–73. Cambridge: Cambridge University Press.

    1987. Life in the Swahili town house reveals the symbolic meaning of spaces and artefact assemblages. *African Archaeological Review* 5: 181–92.

Donley-Reid, L. W. 1990a. The power of Swahili porcelain, beads and pottery. In *Powers of observation: alternative views in archaeology*, S. M. Nelson and A. B. Kehoe (eds.), pp. 47–59. Archaeological Papers of the American Anthropological Association 2. Washington, DC.

    1990b. The Swahili house: a structuring space. In *Domestic architecture and use of space,* S. Kent (ed.), pp. 114–26. Cambridge: Cambridge University Press.

Donnan, C. B. and C. W. Clewlow (eds.). 1974. *Ethnoarchaeology.* Institute of Archaeology Monograph 4. Los Angeles: University of California.

Dore, C. D. 1996. Built environment variability and community organization: theory building through ethnoarchaeology in Xculoc, Campeche, Mexico. PhD thesis, University of New Mexico.

Douglas, M. 1966. *Purity and danger: an analysis of the concepts of pollution and taboo.* London: Routledge and Kegan Paul.

1970. *Natural symbols.* London: Routledge and Kegan Paul.

Dozier, E. P. 1966. *Mountain arbiters: the changing life of a Philippine hill people.* Tucson: University of Arizona Press.

Draper, P. 1977. !Kung women: contrasts in sexual egalitarianism in foraging and sedentary contexts. In *Toward an anthropology of women,* R. Reiter (ed.), pp. 77–109. New York: Monthly Review Press.

Dunnell, R. C. 1991. Methodological impacts of catastrophic depopulation on American archaeology and ethnology. In *Columbian consequences,* vol. 3, *The Spanish borderlands in Pan-American perspective,* D. H. Thomas (ed.), pp. 561–80. Washington, DC: Smithsonian Institution Press.

Earle, T. K. 1981. Comment on P. Rice, "Evolution of specialized pottery production: a trial model." *Current Anthropology* 22: 230–1.

Echard, N. 1968. *Noces du feu.* Film (32 mins.). Paris: Centre Nationale de la Recherche Scientifique/Comité du Film Ethnographique (Musée de l'Homme).

1983. Scories et symboles: remarques sur la métallurgie hausa du fer au Niger. In *Métallurgies africaines: nouvelles contributions,* N. Echard (ed.), pp. 209–24. Mémoires de la Société des Africanistes 9. Paris: Société des Africanistes.

Eder, J. F. 1984. The impact of subsistence change on mobility and settlement pattern in a tropical forest foraging economy: some implications for archaeology. *American Anthropologist* 86: 837–53.

Eggert, M. K. H. 1991. Ethnoarchäologie und Töpfereiforschung, eine Zwischenbilanz. In *Töpfereiforschung – Archäologisch, Ethnologisch, Volkskundlich. Beiträge des Internationalen Kolloquiums 1987 in Schleswig,* H. Lüdtke and R. Vossen (eds.), pp. 39–61. Töpferei- und Keramikvorschung 2. Bonn.

1993. Vergangenheit in der Gegenwart? Überlegungen zum interpretatorischen Potential der Ethnoarchäologie. *Ethnographisch-Archäologische Zeitschrift* 34 (2): 144–50.

Embree, L. 1987. Archaeology: the most basic science of all. *Antiquity* 61: 75–8.

Emerson, A. M. 1993. The role of body part utility in small-scale hunting under two strategies of carcass recovery. In *From bones to behavior: ethnoarchaeological and experimental contributions to the interpretation of faunal remains,* J. Hudson (ed.), pp. 138–55. Occasional Paper 21. Carbondale: Center for Archaeological Investigations, Southern Illinois University.

Enloe, J. G. 1993. Ethnoarchaeology of marrow cracking: implications for the recognition of prehistoric subsistence organization. In *From bones to behavior: ethnoarchaeological and experimental contributions to the interpretation of faunal remains,* J. Hudson (ed.), pp. 82–97. Occasional Paper

21. Carbondale: Center for Archaeological Investigations, Southern Illinois University.

Erickson, C. L. 1985. Applications of prehistoric Andean technology: experiments in raised field agriculture, Huatta, Lake Titicaca 1983. In *Prehistoric intensive agriculture in the tropics*, vol. 1, I. S. Farrington (ed.), pp. 209–32. BAR International Series 232. Oxford: British Archaeological Reports.

Ertuğ, F. 1996. Contemporary plant gathering in Central Anatolia: an ethnoarchaeological and ethnobotanical study. In *Plant life in Southwest and Central Asia (Proceedings of the IVth Plant Life of Southwest Asia Symposium)*, pp. 945–62. Izmir: Ege Universitesi Yayinlari.

Ertuğ-Yaraş, F. 1997. An ethnoarchaeological study of subsistence and plant gathering in Central Anatolia. Ph.D. thesis, Washington University in St Louis.

Estioko-Griffin, A. and P. B. Griffin. 1975. The Ebuked Agta of northeastern Luzon. *Philippine Quarterly of Culture and Society* 3: 237–44.

    1981. Woman the hunter: the Agta. In *Woman the gatherer*, F. Dahlberg (ed.), pp. 121–51. New Haven: Yale University Press.

Fagan, B. M. 1995. *People of the earth: an introduction to world prehistory* (8th edn). New York: HarperCollins College Publishers.

    1997. *In the beginning: an introduction to archaeology* (9th edn.). New York: Longmans.

Fardon, R. O. 1987. African ethnogenesis: limits to the comparability of ethnic phenomena. In *Comparative anthropology*, L. Holy (ed.), pp. 168–88. London: Basil Blackwell.

    1996. "Crossed destinies": the entangled histories of West African ethnic and national identities. In *Ethnicity in Africa: roots, meanings and implications*, L. de la Gorgendière, K. King, and S. Vaughan (eds.), pp. 117–46. Edinburgh: Centre of African Studies, University of Edinburgh.

Farrington, I. S. (ed.). 1985. *Prehistoric intensive agriculture in the tropics* (2 vols.). BAR International Series 232. Oxford: British Archaeological Reports.

Féblot-Augustins, J. and C. Perlès. 1992. Perspectives ethnoarchéologiques sur les échanges à longue distance. In *Ethnoarchéologie: justification, problèmes, limites*, F. Audouze (ed.), pp. 195–210. Rencontres Internationales d'Archéologie et d'Histoire d'Antibes 12. Juan-les-Pins: Editions APDCA.

Fernández Martínez, V. M. 1994. Etnoarqueología: una guía de métodos y aplicaciones. *Revista de Dialectología y Tradiciones Populares* 49: 137–69.

Fewkes, J. W. 1900. Tusayan migration traditions. *Bureau of American Ethnology, Annual Report* 19: 577–633.

Fischman, J. 1992. Hard evidence. *Discover* 13 (2): 44–51.

Fisher Jr., J. W. 1993. Foragers and farmers: material expressions of interaction at elephant processing sites in the Ituri forest, Zaire. In *From bones to behavior: ethnoarchaeological and experimental contributions to the interpretation of faunal remains*, J. Hudson (ed.), pp. 247–62. Occasional Paper 21. Carbondale: Center for Archaeological Investigations, Southern Illinois University.

Fisher Jr., J. W. and H. C. Strickland. 1989. Ethnoarchaeology among Efe Pygmies, Zaire: spatial organization of campsites. *American Journal of Physical Anthropology* 78: 473–84.

Flannery, K. V. 1968. Archaeological systems theory and early Mesoamerica. In *Anthropological archaeology in the Americas*, B. J. Meggers (ed.), pp. 67–87. Washington, DC: Anthropological Society of Washington.

1972. Summary comments: evolutionary trends. In *Social exchange and interaction*, E. N. Wilmsen (ed.), pp. 129–35. Museum of Anthropology, Anthropological Papers 46. Ann Arbor: University of Michigan.

1982. The golden Marshalltown: a parable for the archaeology of the 1980s. *American Anthropologist* 84: 265–78.

Flannery, K. V., J. Marcus, and R. G. Reynolds. 1989. *The flocks of the Wamani: a study of llama herders on the punas of Ayacucho, Peru*. San Diego, CA: Academic Press.

Folorunso, C. A. and S. O. Ogundele. 1993. Agriculture and settlement among the Tiv of Nigeria: some ethnoarchaeological observations. In *The archaeology of Africa: food, metals and towns*, T. Shaw, P. Sinclair, B. W. Andah, and I. A. Okpoko (eds.), pp. 274–88. London and New York: Routledge.

Foster, G. M. 1960a. Archaeological implications of the modern pottery of Acatlán, Puebla, Mexico. *American Antiquity* 26: 205–14.

1960b. Life expectancy of utilitarian pottery in Tzintzuntzan, Michoacan, Mexico. *American Antiquity* 25: 606–9.

1965. The sociology of pottery: questions and hypotheses arising from contemporary Mexican work. In *Ceramics and man*, F. R. Matson (ed.), pp. 43–61. New York: Wenner-Gren Foundation.

Frank, B. E. 1998. *Mande potters and leather-workers: art and heritage in West Africa*. Washington, DC and London: Smithsonian Institution Press.

Freide, H. and R. Steel. 1980. Experimental burning of traditional Nguni huts. *African Studies* 39: 175–81.

Friedman, J. and M. J. Rowlands (eds.). 1977. *The evolution of social systems*. London: Duckworth.

Gabrilopoulos, N. 1995. Ethnoarchaeology of the Tallensi compound (Upper East Region, Ghana). M.A. thesis, University of Calgary.

Gallagher, J. P. 1977. Contemporary stone tools in Ethiopia: implications for archaeology. *Journal of Field Archaeology* 4: 407–14.

Gallay, A. 1992a. A propos de la céramique actuelle du delta intérieur du Niger (Mali): approche ethnoarchéologique et règles transculturelles. In *Ethnoarchéologie: justification, problèmes, limites*, F. Audouze (ed.), pp. 67–90. Rencontres Internationales d'Archéologie et d'Histoire d'Antibes, 12. Juan-les-Pins: Editions APDCA.

1992b. L'ethnoarchéologie en question? In *Ethnoarchéologie: justification, problèmes, limites*, F. Audouze (ed.), pp. 447–52. Rencontres Internationales d'Archéologie et d'Histoire d'Antibes 12. Juan-les-Pins: Editions APDCA.

Gallay, A. and E. Huysecom. 1989. *Ethnoarchéologie africaine*. Documents du Département d'Anthropologie et d'Ecologie, 14. Geneva: Université de Genève.

Gallay, A., E. Huysecom, A. Mayor, and G. de Ceuninck (eds.). 1996. *Hier et aujourd'hui: des poteries et des femmes. Céramiques traditionelles du Mali*. Geneva: Département d'Anthropologie et d'Ecologie, Université de Gèneve.

Gamble, C. S. and W. A. Boismier (eds.). 1991. *Ethnoarchaeological approaches to mobile campsites*. Ethnoarchaeological Series 1. Ann Arbor: International Monographs in Prehistory.

Gardi, R. 1954. *Der schwarze Hephästus*. Bern: Privately published.

1955. *Eisengewinnung bei den Matakam (Mandara-Bergland) (with sections by G. Spannaus and H. Thede)*. Göttingen: Institut für den Wissenschaftlichen Film.

Gavua, K. B. 1989. Goat skins versus wax prints: an analysis of Mafa costume. In *Cultures in conflict: current archaeological perspectives (Proceedings of the 20th Annual Chacmool Conference)*, D. C. Tkaczuk and B. C. Vivian (eds.), pp. 293–6. Calgary: The Archaeology Association of the University of Calgary.

1990. Style in Mafa material culture. Ph.D. thesis, University of Calgary.

Geertz, C. 1980. Blurred genres: the refiguration of social thought. *The American Scholar* 49 (2): 165–79.

Gell-Mann, M. 1994. *The quark and the jaguar: adventures in the simple and the complex*. New York: W. H. Freeman and Co.

Gero, J. M. and M. W. Conkey (eds.). 1991. *Engendering archaeology: women and prehistory*. Oxford: Basil Blackwell.

Gibbon, G. 1989. *Explanation in archaeology*. Oxford: Basil Blackwell.

Giddens, A. 1979. *Central problems in social theory*. London: Macmillan.

1982. *Profiles and critiques in social theory*. London: Macmillan.

Gifford, D. P. 1981. Taphonomy and paleoecology: a critical review of archaeology's sister disciplines. *Advances in Archaeological Method and Theory* 4: 365–438.

Gifford-Gonzalez, D. P. 1993. Gaps in the zooarchaeological analyses of butchery: is gender an issue? In *From bones to behavior: ethnoarchaeological and experimental contributions to the interpretation of faunal remains*, J. Hudson (ed.), pp. 181–99. Occasional Paper 21. Carbondale: Center for Archaeological Investigations, Southern Illinois University.

Giles, M., J. Winters, and K. Denning. 1997. Recantation, reflection, revision . . . (Mike Parker Pearson on the class of '79). URL: http://www.shef.ac.uk/~assem/2/2rrr.html.

Giligny, F. and H. Sidi Maamar. 1990. Simulation archéologique à partir de l'étude ethno-archéologique des flèches de Ye Ineri (Irian Jaya – Indonésie). *Histoire et Mesure* 5 (1–2): 145–62.

Godelier, M. 1977. *Perspectives in Marxist anthropology*. Cambridge: Cambridge University Press.

Golde, P. (ed.). 1986. *Women in the field: anthropological experiences* (2nd edn). Berkeley: University of California Press.

Golson, J. 1982. The Ipomoean revolution revisited: society and the sweet potato in the Upper Wahgi valley. In *Inequality in New Guinea highlands societies*, A. Strathern (ed.), pp. 109–36. Cambridge: Cambridge University Press.

Golson, J. and A. Steensberg. 1985. The tools of agricultural intensification in the New Guinea highlands. In *Prehistoric intensive agriculture in the tropics*, vol. 1, I. S. Farrington (ed.), pp. 209–32. BAR International Series, 232. Oxford: British Archaeological Reports.

González-Jacomé, A. 1985. Home gardens in central Mexico. In *Prehistoric intensive agriculture in the tropics*, vol. 2, I. S. Farrington (ed.), pp. 521–37. BAR International Series 232. Oxford: British Archaeological Reports.

Goodenough, W. H. 1964. Introduction. In *Explorations in cultural anthropology*, W. H. Goodenough (ed.), pp. 1–24. New York: McGraw-Hill.

Goody, J. (ed.). 1971 [1958]. *The developmental cycle in domestic groups*. Cambridge Papers in Social Anthropology 1. Cambridge: Cambridge University Press.

Gordon, R. B. and D. J. Killick. 1993. Adaptation of technology to culture and environment: bloomery iron smelting in America and Africa. *Technology and Culture* 34: 243–70.

Gorecki, P. P. 1985a. Ethnoarchaeology: the need for a post-mortem inquiry. *World Archaeology* 17: 175–91.

1985b. The conquest of a wet and dry territory: its mechanisms and its archaeological consequences. In *Prehistoric intensive agriculture in the tropics*, vol. 1, I. S. Farrington (ed.), pp. 321–45. BAR International Series 232. Oxford: British Archaeological Records.

Gosden, C. 1999. *Anthropology and archaeology: a changing relationship.* London: Routledge.

Gosselain, O. P. 1992a. Technology and style: potters and pottery among Bafia of Cameroon. *Man* 27: 559–86.

1992b. Bonfire of the enquiries. Pottery firing temperatures in archaeology: what for? *Journal of Archaeological Science* 19: 243–59.

1994. Skimming through potters' agendas: an ethnoarchaeological study of clay selection strategies in Cameroon. In *Society, culture and technology in Africa*, S. T. Childs (ed.), pp. 99–107. MASCA Research Papers in Science and Archaeology, Supplement to Volume 11. Philadelphia: MASCA.

1995. Identités techniques. Le travail de la poterie au Cameroun méridional. Description des chaînes opératoires (2 vols). Thèse de Doctorat en Philosophie et Lettres, Université Libre de Bruxelles.

1998. Social and technical identity in a clay crystal ball. In *The archaeology of social boundaries*, M. T. Stark (ed.), pp. 78–106. Washington, DC and London: Smithsonian Institution Press.

Gosselain, O. P. and A. L. Smith. 1995. The ceramics and society project: an ethnographic and experimental approach to technological choices. *KVHAA Konferenser* (Stockholm) 34: 147–60.

Gosselain, O. P. and P.-L. van Berg. 1991–2. Style, individualité et taxonomie chez les potières Bafia du Cameroun. *Bulletin du Centre Genèvois d'Anthropologie*: 99–114.

Goucher, C. L. and E. W. Herbert. 1996. The blooms of Banjeli: technology and gender in West African iron making. In *The culture and technology of African iron production*, P. R. Schmidt (ed.), pp. 40–57. Gainesville: University Press of Florida.

Gould, R. A. 1967. Notes on hunting, butchering and snaring of game among Ngatatjara and their neighbors in the west Australian desert. *Kroeber Anthropological Society Papers* 36: 41–66.

1968a. Chipping stones in the outback. *Natural History* 77 (2): 42–9.

1968b. Living archaeology: the Ngatatjara of Western Australia. *Southwestern Journal of Anthropology* 24: 101–22.

1969. Subsistence behaviour among the Western Desert Aborigines of Australia. *Oceania* 39: 253–74.

1974. Some current problems in ethnoarchaeology. In *Ethnoarchaeology*, C. B. Donnan and C. W. Clewlow (eds.), pp. 29–48. Institute of Archaeology Monograph 4. Los Angeles: University of California.

1978a. Beyond analogy in ethnoarchaeology. In *Explorations in ethnoarchaeology*, R. A. Gould (ed.), pp. 249–93. Albuquerque: University of New Mexico.

1978b. The anthropology of human residues. *American Anthropologist* 80: 815–35.

(ed.). 1978c. *Explorations in ethnoarchaeology.* Albuquerque: University of New Mexico Press.

1978d. From Tasmania to Tucson: new directions in ethnoarchaeology. In

Explorations in ethnoarchaeology, R. A. Gould (ed.), pp. 1–10. Albuquerque: University of New Mexico.

1980. *Living archaeology*. New York: Cambridge University Press.

1981. Brandon revisited: a new look at an old technology. In *Modern material culture: the archaeology of us*, R. A. Gould and M. B. Schiffer, pp. 269–81. New York: Academic Press.

Gould, R. A., D. Koster, and A. Sontz. 1971. The lithic assemblage of the Western Desert Aborigines of Australia. *American Antiquity* 36: 149–69.

Gould, R. A. and P. J. Watson. 1982. A dialogue on the meaning and use of analogy in ethnoarchaeological reasoning. *Journal of Anthropological Archaeology* 1: 355–81.

Gould, R. A. and J. E. Yellen. 1987. Man the hunted: determinants of household spacing in desert and tropical foraging societies. *Journal of Anthropological Archaeology* 6: 77–103.

1991. Misreading the past: a reply to Binford concerning hunter-gatherer site structure. *Journal of Anthropological Archaeology* 10: 283–98.

Graham, M. 1993. Settlement organisation and residential variability among the Rarámuri. In *Abandonment of settlements and regions: ethnoarchaeological and archaeological approaches*, C. M. Cameron and S. A. Tomka (eds.), pp. 25–42. Cambridge: Cambridge University Press.

1994. *Mobile farmers: an ethnoarchaeological approach to settlement organization among the Rarámuri of northwestern Mexico*. Ethnoarchaeological Series, 3. Ann Arbor: International Monographs in Prehistory.

Gramsci, A. 1971. *Selections from the prison notebooks of Antonio Gramsci*, Q. Hoare and G. Nowell-Smith (eds.). London: Lawrence and Wishart.

Graves, M. W. 1981. Ethnoarchaeology of Kalinga ceramic design. Ph.D. thesis, University of Arizona.

1982. Breaking down ceramic variation: testing models of White Mountain Redware design style development. *Journal of Anthropological Archaeology* 1: 304–45.

1985. Ceramic design variation within a Kalinga village: temporal and spatial process. In *Decoding prehistoric ceramics*, B. A. Nelson (ed.), pp. 9–34. Carbondale: Southern Illinois Press.

1987. Review of D. Miller's "Artefacts as categories." *Journal of Asian Studies* 46: 193–5.

1991. Pottery production and distribution among the Kalinga: a study of household and regional organization and differentiation. In *Ceramic ethnoarchaeology*, W. A. Longacre (ed.), pp. 112–43. Tucson: University of Arizona Press.

1994. Kalinga social and material culture boundaries: a case of spatial convergence. In *Kalinga ethnoarchaeology: expanding archaeological method and theory*, W. A. Longacre and J. M. Skibo (eds.), pp. 13–49. Washington, DC: Smithsonian Institution Press.

Greaves, T. 1994. *Intellectual property rights for indigenous peoples: a sourcebook*. Oklahoma City: Society for Applied Anthropology.

Griffin, P. B. 1984. Forager resource and land use in the humid tropics: the Agta of northeastern Luzon, the Philippines. In *Past and present in hunter-gatherer studies*, C. Schrire (ed.), pp. 95–122. New York: Academic Press.

1985. *Ethnoarchaeology and ethnography of Agta foragers*. Weston, CT: Pictures of Record.

Griffin, P. B. and W. G. Solheim. 1988–89. Ethnoarchaeological research in Asia. *Asian Perspectives* 28: 145–62.

Gronenborn, D. 1995. Ethnoarchäologische Untersuchungen zur rezenten Herstellung und Nutzung vom Mahlsteinen in Nordost-Nigeria. In *Experimentelle Archäologie: Bilanz 1994*, pp. 45–55. Archäologische Mitteilungen aus Nordwestdeutschland, 8. Oldenburg: Isensee Verlag.

Gubser, N. J. 1965. *The Nunamiut Eskimos: hunters of caribou*. New Haven: Yale University Press.

Guèye, N. S. 1998. Poteries et peuplements de la moyenne vallée du fleuve Sénégal du XVIe au XXe siècle: approches ethnoarchéologique et ethnohistorique (2 vols.). Thèse de Doctorat en Lettres et Sciences Humaines, Université de Paris X-Nanterre.

Guyer, J. I. and S. M. Eno Belinga. 1995. Wealth in people as wealth in knowledge: accumulation and composition in equatorial Africa. *Journal of African History* 36: 91–120.

Gyamfi, K. E. 1980. Traditional pottery technology at Krobo Takyiman (Techiman), Ghana: an ethnoarchaeological study. *West African Journal of Archaeology* 10: 103–16.

Haaland, R. and P. L. Shinnie (eds.). 1985. *African iron working: ancient and traditional*. Oslo: Universitetsforlaget AS.

Hahn, H. P. 1991. *Die materielle Kulture der Bassar (Nord-Togo)*. Arbeiten aus dem Seminar für Völkerkunde der Johann Wolfgang Goethe-Universität 24. Stuttgart: Franz Steiner Verlag.

1996a. Materielle Kultur und Ethnoarchäologie. Zur Dokumentation materieller Kultur anhand von Untersuchungen in Nord-Togo. *Ethnographische-Archäologische Zeitschrift* 38: 459–78.

1996b. *Die materielle Kultur der Konkomba, Kabyè und Lamba in Nord-Togo*. Westafrikanische Studien: Frankfurter Beiträge zur Sprach- und Kulturgeschichte 14. Cologne: Rüdiger Köppe Verlag.

Hammond, G. and N. D. C. Hammond. 1981. Child's play: a distorting factor in archaeological distribution. *American Antiquity* 46: 634–6.

Hanks, C. C. 1983. An ethnoarchaeological approach to the seasonality of historic Cree sites in central Quebec. *Arctic* 36: 350–5.

Hardin Friedrich, M. A. 1970. Design structure and social interaction: archaeological implications of an ethnographic analysis. *American Antiquity* 35: 332–43.

Hardin, M. A. 1977. Individual style in San José pottery painting: the role of deliberate choice. In *The individual in prehistory*, J. N. Hill and J. Gunn (eds.), pp. 109–36. New York: Academic Press.

1979. The cognitive basis of productivity in a decorative art style: implications of an ethnographic study for archaeologists' taxonomies. In *Ethnoarchaeology: implications of ethnography for archaeology*, C. Kramer (ed.), pp. 75–101. New York: Columbia University Press.

1983a. The structure of Tarascan pottery painting. In *Structure and cognition in art*, D. K. Washburn (ed.), pp. 8–24. New York: Cambridge University Press.

1983b. Applying linguistic models to the decorative arts: a preliminary consideration of the limits of analogy. *Semiotica* 46 (2/4): 309–22.

1984. Models of decoration. In *The many dimensions of pottery: ceramics in archaeology and anthropology*, S. van der Leeuw and A. A. Pritchard (eds.), pp. 573–607. Amsterdam: University of Amsterdam.

Harris, E. C. 1979. *Principles of archaeological stratigraphy*. London: Academic Press.

Harris, M. 1968. Comments. In *New perspectives in archaeology*, S. R. Binford and L. R. Binford (eds.), pp. 359–61. Chicago: Aldine.

Harstrup, K. 1978. The post-structuralist position of social anthropology. In *The yearbook of symbolic anthropology*, vol. 1, E. Schwimmer (ed.). London: Hurst.

Harvey, D. 1989. *The condition of postmodernity*. Oxford: Basil Blackwell.

Hawkes, K., K. Hill, H. Kaplan, and A. M. Hurtado. 1987. A problem of bias in the ethnographic use of scan sampling. *Journal of Anthropological Research* 43 (3): 239–45.

Hawkes, K., K. Hill, and J. F. O'Connell. 1982. Why hunters gather: optimal foraging and the Aché of eastern Paraguay. *American Ethnologist* 9: 379–98.

Hawkes, K., J. F. O'Connell, and N. G. Blurton Jones. 1991. Hunting income patterns among the Hadza: big game, common goods, foraging goals and the evolution of the human diet. *Philosophical Transactions of the Royal Society, Series B* 334: 243–51.

1997. Hadza women's time allocation, offspring provisioning, and the evolution of long postmenopausal life spans. *Current Anthropology* 38: 551–77.

Hawkes, K., J. F. O'Connell, and L. Rogers 1997. The behavioral ecology of modern hunter-gatherer and human evolution. *Trends in Ecology and Evolution* 12: 29–32.

Hayden, B. 1976. Curation: old and new. In *Primitive art and technology*, J. S. Raymond, B. Loveseth, C. Arnold, and G. Reardon (eds.), pp. 47–59. Calgary: University of Calgary Archaeology Association.

1977. Stone tool functions in the Western Desert. In *Stone tools as cultural markers: change, evolution and complexity*, R. V. S. Wright (ed.), pp. 178–88. Canberra: Australian Institute of Aboriginal Studies.

(ed.). 1979a. *Lithic use-wear analysis*. New York: Academic Press.

1979b. *Paleolithic reflections: lithic technology and ethnographic excavations among Australian Aborigines*. Canberra: Australian Institute of Aboriginal Studies.

1984. Are emic types relevant to archaeology? *Ethnohistory* 31 (2): 79–92.

(ed.). 1987a. *Lithic studies among the contemporary Highland Maya*. Tucson: University of Arizona.

1987b. Introduction. In *Lithic studies among the contemporary Highland Maya*, B. Hayden (ed.), pp. 1–7. Tucson: University of Arizona Press.

1987c. Traditional metate manufacturing in Guatemala using chipped stone tools. In *Lithic studies among the contemporary Highland Maya*, B. Hayden (ed.), pp. 8–119. Tucson: University of Arizona Press.

1987d. Past to present use of stone tools and their effects on assemblage characteristics in the Maya highlands. In *Lithic studies among the contemporary Highland Maya*, B. Hayden (ed.), pp. 160–234. Tucson: University of Arizona Press.

1993. *Archaeology: the science of once and future things*. New York: W. H. Freeman and Company.

Hayden, B. and A. Cannon. 1983. Where the garbage goes: refuse disposal in the Maya highlands. *Journal of Anthropological Archaeology* 2: 117–63.

1984a. *The structure of material systems: ethnoarchaeology in the Maya highlands*. SAA Papers 3. Washington, DC: Society for American Archaeology.

1984b. Interaction inferences in archaeology and learning frameworks of the Maya. *Journal of Anthropological Archaeology* 3: 325–67.

Hayden, B. and R. Gargett. 1991. Site, structure, kinship and sharing in Aboriginal Australia: implications for archaeology. In *The interpretation of archaeological spatial patterning*, E. M. Kroll and T. D. Price (eds.), pp. 11–32. New York: Plenum.

Hayden, B. and M. C. Nelson. 1981. The use of chipped lithic material in the contemporary Maya highlands. *American Antiquity* 46: 885–98.

Hegmon, M. 1992. Archaeological research on style. *Annual Review of Anthropology* 21: 517–36.

Heider, K. G. 1961. Archaeological assumptions and ethnographic fact: a cautionary tale from New Guinea. *Southwestern Journal of Anthropology* 23: 52–64.

Herbert, E. W. 1993. *Iron, gender, and power: rituals of transformation in African societies*. Bloomington: Indiana University Press.

Herbich, I. 1987. Learning patterns, potter interaction and ceramic style among the Luo of Kenya. *African Archaeological Review* 5: 193–204.

Herbich, I. and M. Dietler. 1991. Aspects of the ceramic system of the Luo of Kenya. *Töpferei- und Keramikforschung* 2: 105–35.

1994. Space, time and symbolic structure in the Luo homestead: an ethnoarchaeological study of "settlement biography" in Africa. In *Proceedings of the 12th International Congress of the International Union of Pre- and Protohistoric Sciences*, pp. 26–32. Nitra: IUPPS.

Hertz, R. 1907. Contribution à une étude sur la réprésentation collective de la mort. *Année Sociologique* 10: 48–137.

Hester, T. R. and R. F. Heizer. 1980. *Making stone vases: ethnoarchaeological studies at an alabaster workshop in Upper Egypt*. Malibu: Udena Publications.

1981. Making stone vases: contemporary manufacture of material-culture items in Upper Egypt. In *Modern material culture: the archaeology of us*, R. A. Gould and M. B. Schiffer (eds.), pp. 283–302. New York: Academic Press.

Hietala, H. (ed.). 1984. *Intrasite spatial analysis in archaeology*. Cambridge: Cambridge University Press.

Hill, J. N. 1968. Broken K Pueblo: prehistoric social organization in the American Southwest. In *New perspectives in archaeology*, S. R. Binford and L. R. Binford (eds.), pp. 103–42. Chicago: Aldine.

Hill, J. N. and R. K. Evans. 1972. A model for classification and typology. In *Models in archaeology*, D. L. Clarke (ed.), pp. 231–73. London: Methuen.

Hill, J. N. and J. Gunn. 1977. *The individual in prehistory*. New York: Academic Press.

Hillier, B. and J. Hanson. 1984. *The social logic of space*. Cambridge: Cambridge University Press.

Hinderling, P. 1955. Schmelzofen und Eisenverarbeitung im Nord-Kamerun. *Stahl und Eisen* 75: 1263–6.

Hitchcock, R. K. 1982. The ethnoarchaeology of sedentism: mobility strategies and site structure among foraging and food producing populations in the Eastern Kalahari Desert, Botswana. Ph.D. thesis, University of New Mexico.

1987. Sedentism and site structure: organization changes in Kalahari Basarwa residential locations. In *Method and theory for activity area research: an ethnoarchaeological approach*, S. Kent (ed.), pp. 374–423. New York: Columbia University Press.

Hodder, I. 1977a. A study in ethnoarchaeology in western Kenya. In *Archaeology and anthropology: areas of mutual interest*, M. Spriggs (ed.), pp. 117–41. BAR Supplementary Series 19. Oxford: British Archaeological Reports.

1977b. The distribution of material culture items in the Baringo district, western Kenya. *Man* 12: 239–69.

1978. The maintenance of group identities in the Baringo district, west Kenya. In *Social organization and settlement*, D. Green, C. Haselgrove, and M. Spriggs (eds.), pp. 47–73. BAR International Series (Supplementary) 47, part 1. Oxford: British Archaeological Reports.

1979. Economic and social stress and material culture patterning. *American Antiquity* 44: 446–54.

1982a. *Symbols in action: ethnoarchaeological studies of material culture.* New York: Cambridge University Press.

(ed.). 1982b. *Symbolic and structural archaeology.* Cambridge: Cambridge University Press.

1985. Boundaries as strategies: an ethnoarchaeological study. In *The archaeology of frontiers and boundaries*, S. W. Green and S. M. Perlman (eds.). New York: Academic Press.

1986. *Reading the past.* Cambridge: Cambridge University Press.

1987a. The meaning of discard: ash and domestic space in Baringo, Kenya. In *Method and theory for activity area research: an ethnoarchaeological approach*, S. Kent (ed.), pp. 424–48. New York: Columbia University Press.

1987b. The contextual analysis of symbolic meanings. In *The archaeology of contextual meanings*, vol. 1, I. Hodder (ed.), pp. 1–10. Cambridge: Cambridge University Press.

(ed.). 1987c. *The archaeology of contextual meanings.* Cambridge: Cambridge University Press.

1989a. This is not an article about material culture as text. *Journal of Anthropological Archaeology* 8: 250–69.

(ed.). 1989b. *The meanings of things: material culture and symbolic expression.* London: Unwin Hyman.

1990a. Style as historical quality. In *The uses of style in archaeology*, M. W. Conkey and C. A. Hastorf (eds.), pp. 44–51. Cambridge: Cambridge University Press.

1990b. *The domestication of Europe: structure and contingency in Neolithic societies.* Oxford: Blackwell.

1991. The decoration of containers: an ethnographic and historical study. In *Ceramic ethnoarchaeology*, W. A. Longacre (ed.). Tucson: University of Arizona Press.

Hodder, I., M. Shanks, A. Alexandri, *et al.* (eds.). 1995. *Interpreting archaeology: finding meaning in the past.* London and New York: Routledge.

Hole, F. 1978. Pastoral nomadism in western Iran. In *Explorations in ethnoarchaeology*, R. A. Gould (ed.), pp. 127–67. Albuquerque: University of New Mexico Press.

1979. Re-discovering the past in the present: ethnoarchaeology in Luristan, Iran. In *Ethnoarchaeology: implications of ethnography for archaeology*, C. Kramer (ed.), pp. 192–218. New York: Columbia University Press.

1980. The prehistory of herding: some suggestions from ethnography. In *L'archéologie de l'Iraq du début de l'époque néolithique à 333 avant notre ère: perspectives et limites de l'interprétation anthropologique de documents*, M. T. Barrelet (ed.), pp. 119–27. Paris: CNRS.

Holl, A. F. C. 1987. Mound formation processes and societal transformations: a case study from the Perichadian plain. *Journal of Anthropological Archaeology* 6: 122–58.

  1993. Community interaction and settlement patterning in northern Cameroon. In *Spatial boundaries and social dynamics: case studies from food-producing societies*, A. F. C. Holl and T. E. Levy (eds.), pp. 39–61. Ethnoarchaeological Series 2. Ann Arbor: International Monographs in Prehistory.

Holl, A. F. C. and T. E. Levy (eds.). 1993. *Spatial boundaries and social dynamics: case studies from food-producing societies*. International Monographs in Prehistory. Ann Arbor: University of Michigan Press.

Holy, L. (ed.). 1987. *Comparative anthropology*. Oxford: Basil Blackwell.

Honigmann, J. J. 1970. Sampling in ethnographic field work. In *A handbook of method in cultural anthropology*, R. Naroll and R. Cohen (eds.), pp. 266–81. New York: Columbia University Press.

Horne, L. 1982. The household in space. *American Behavioral Scientist* 25: 677–85.

  1983a. Recycling in an Iranian village: ethnoarchaeology in Baghestan. *Archaeology* 36 (4): 16–21.

  1983b. The brasscasters of Dariapur, West Bengal. *Expedition* 29 (3): 39–46.

  1994a. *Village spaces: settlement and society in northern Iran*. Washington, DC: Smithsonian Institution Press.

  1994b. Itinerant brasscasters of eastern India. In *Living traditions: studies in the ethnoarchaeology of South Asia*, B. Allchin (ed.), pp. 265–80. New Delhi: Oxford and IBH Publishing Co. Pvt. Ltd.

Horsfall, G. A. 1987. A design theory perspective on variability in grinding stones. In *Lithic studies among the contemporary Highland Maya*, B. Hayden (ed.), pp. 332–77. Tucson: University of Arizona.

Hosler, D. 1996. Technical choices, social categories and meaning among the Andean potters of Las Animas. *Journal of Material Culture* 1: 63–92.

Howell, N. 1990. *Surviving fieldwork*. American Anthropological Association Special Publication 26. Washington, DC: American Anthropological Association.

Hudson, J. 1991. Nonselective small game hunting strategies: an ethnoarchaeological study of Aka pygmy sites. In *Human predators and prey mortality*, M. C. Stiner (ed.), pp. 105–20. Westview Special Studies in Archaeological Research. Boulder: Westview Press.

  (ed.). 1993a. *From bones to behavior: ethnoarchaeological and experimental contributions to the interpretation of faunal remains*. Occasional Paper 21. Carbondale: Southern Illinois University, Center for Archaeological Investigations.

  1993b. The impacts of domestic dogs on bone forager camps: or, the dog-gone bones. In *From bones to behavior: ethnoarchaeological and experimental contributions to the interpretation of faunal remains*, J. Hudson (ed.), pp. 301–23. Occasional Paper 21. Carbondale: Southern Illinois University, Centre for Archaeological Investigations.

Hunter-Anderson, R. L. 1977. A theoretical approach to the study of house form. In *For theory building in archaeology*, L. R. Binford (ed.), pp. 287–315. New York: Academic Press.

Huntington, R. and P. Metcalf. 1979. *Celebrations of death: the anthropology of mortuary ritual*. Cambridge: Cambridge University Press.

Hurtado, A. M., K. Hawkes, K. Hill, and H. Kaplan. 1985. Female subsistence strategies among the Aché hunter-gatherers of Eastern Paraguay. *Human Ecology* 13: 1–27.

Huysecom, E. 1992. Vers une ethnoarchéologie appliquée: exemples africains. In *Ethnoarchéologie: justification, problèmes, limites*, F. Audouze (ed.), pp. 91–102. Rencontres Internationales d'Archéologie et d'Histoire d'Antibes 12. Juan-les-Pins: Editions APDCA.

Huysecom, E. and B. Agustoni. 1997. *Inagina, l'ultime maison du fer*. Video recording (52 mins.). Geneva: Huysecom, Agustoni, and PAVE.

Ingold, T. 1999. Foreword. In *The social dynamics of technology: practice, politics, and world views*, M.-A. Dobres and C. R. Hoffman (eds.), pp. vii–xi. Washington, DC and London: Smithsonian Institution Press.

Isaac, G. Ll. 1967. Towards the interpretation of occupation debris – some experiments and observations. *Kroeber Anthropological Society Papers* 37: 31–9.

    1983. Review of L. R. Binford's "Bones: ancient men and modern myths." *American Antiquity* 48: 416–19.

Jameson, F. 1991. *Postmodernism, or, the cultural logic of Late Capitalism*. Durham: Duke University Press.

Janes, R. R. 1983. *Archaeological ethnography among Mackenzie basin Dene, Canada*. Technical Paper 28. Calgary: Arctic Institute of North America.

    1989. An ethnoarchaeological model for the identification of prehistoric teepee remains in the Boreal forest. *Arctic* 42 (2): 128–38.

Johnson, A. 1978. *Quantification in cultural anthropology*. Stanford: Stanford University Press.

Jones, G. 1983. The ethnoarchaeology of crop processing: seeds of a middle-range methodology. *Archaeological Review from Cambridge* 2 (2): 17–26.

    1984. Interpretation of archaeological plant remains: ethnographic models from Greece. In *Plants and ancient man: studies in paleoethnobotany*, W. V. Zeist and W. A. Casperie (eds.), pp. 43–61. Rotterdam: Balkema.

Jones, K. T. 1984. Hunting and scavenging by early hominids: a study in archaeological method and theory. Ph.D. thesis, University of Utah.

Jones, R. and N. White. 1988. Point blank: stone tool manufacture at the Ngilipitji Quarry, Arnhem Land, 1981. In *Archaeology with ethnography: an Australian perspective*, B. Meehan and R. Jones (eds.), pp. 51–87. Canberra: Deptartment of Prehistory, RSPacS, Australian National University.

Jouaux, C. 1989. Gudur: chefferie ou royaume? *Cahiers d'Etudes Africaines* 114 (29–2): 259–88.

Joyce, A. A. and S. Johannessen. 1993. Abandonment and the production of variability at domestic sites. In *Abandonment of settlements and regions: ethnoarchaeological and archaeological approaches*, C. M. Cameron and S. A. Tomka (eds.), pp. 138–53. Cambridge: Cambridge University Press.

Joyce, R. A. 1994. Dorothy Hughes Popenoe: Eve in an archaeological garden. In *Women in archaeology*, C. Claassen (ed.), pp. 51–66. Philadelphia: University of Pennsylvania Press.

Kamp, K. A. 1982. Architectural indices of socio-economic variability: an ethnoarchaeological case study from Syria. Ph.D. thesis, University of Arizona.

Kanté, N. (with the collaboration of Pierre Erny). 1993. *Forgerons d'Afrique noire: transmission des savoirs traditionels en pays malinké*. Paris: Editions L'Harmattan.

Keller, C. M. and J. D. Keller. 1996. *Cognition and tool use: the blacksmith at work*. Cambridge: Cambridge University Press.

Kelley, J. H. and M. P. Hanen. 1988. *Archaeology and the methodology of science*. Albuquerque: University of New Mexico Press.

Kelley, K. B. 1982. Ethnoarchaeology of the Black Hat Navajos: historical and ahistorical determinants of site features. *Journal of Anthropological Research* 38: 45–74.

　1986. *Navajo land use: an ethnoarchaeological study*. New York: Academic Press.

Kelly, R. F. 1995. *The foraging spectrum: diversity in hunter-gatherer lifeways*. Washington, DC: Smithsonian Institution Press.

Kemp, B. J. 1989. *Ancient Egypt: anatomy of a civilization*. London: Routledge.

Kempton, W. 1981. *The folk classification of ceramics: a study of cognitive prototypes*. New York: Academic Press.

Kenoyer, J. M., M. Vidale, and K. K. Bhan. 1991. Contemporary stone beadmaking in Khambat, India: patterns of craft specialization and organization of production as reflected in the archaeological record. *World Archaeology* 23: 44–63.

　1994. Carnelian bead production in Khambhat, India: an ethnoarchaeological study. In *Living traditions: studies in the ethnoarchaeology of South Asia*, B. Allchin (ed.), pp. 281–306. New Delhi: Oxford and IBH Publishing Co. Pvt. Ltd.

Kent, S. 1984. *Analyzing activity areas*. Albuquerque: University of New Mexico.

　1987. Understanding the use of space: an ethnoarchaeological approach. In *Method and theory for activity area research: an ethnoarchaeological approach*, S. Kent (ed.), pp. 1–62. New York: Columbia University Press.

　1993a. Models of abandonment and material culture frequencies. In *Abandonment of settlements and regions: ethnoarchaeological and archaeological approaches*, C. M. Cameron and S. A. Tomka (eds.), pp. 54–73. Cambridge: Cambridge University Press.

　1993b. Variability in faunal assemblages: the influence of hunting skill, sharing, dogs and mode of cooking on faunal remains at a sedentary Kalahari community. *Journal of Anthropological Archaeology* 12: 325–85.

　1995a. Unstable households in a stable Kalahari community in Botswana. *American Anthropologist* 97: 297–312.

　1995b. Ethnoarchaeology and the concept of home: a cross-cultural analysis. In *The concept of home: an interdisciplinary view*, D. Benjamin and D. Stea (eds.), pp. 163–80. London: Avebury.

　1996a. Cultural diversity among African foragers: causes and implications. In *Cultural diversity among twentieth century foragers: an African perspective*, S. Kent (ed.), pp. 1–18. Cambridge: Cambridge University Press.

　1996b. The future of African archaeology: ethnoarchaeology. *African Archaeological Review* 13: 23–6.

　1999a. Sharing: the adhesive that binds households in the Kalahari together. In *At the interface: the household and beyond*, D. B. Small and N. Tannenbaum (eds.), pp. 113–26. Monographs in Economic Anthropology, 15. Lanham, New York, and Oxford: University Press of America.

　1999b. The archaeological visibility of storage: delineating storage from trash areas. *American Antiquity* 64: 79–94.

　1999c. Egalitarianism, equality, and equitable power. In *Manifesting power: gender and the interpretation of power in archaeology*, T. L. Sweely (ed.), pp. 30–48. London and New York: Routledge.

Kent, S. and H. Vierich. 1989. The myth of ecological determinism – anticipated mobility and site spatial organization. In *From hunters to farmers: the causes and consequences of food production in Africa*, J. D. Clark and S. A. Brandt (eds.), pp. 96–130. Berkeley: University of California Press.

Khan, F. 1994. The potential of ethnoarchaeology with special reference to recent archaeological work in Bannu district, Pakistan. In *Living traditions: studies in the ethnoarchaeology of South Asia*, B. Allchin (ed.), pp. 83–99. New Delhi: Oxford and IBH Publishing Co. Pvt. Ltd.

Killick, D. J. 1990. Technology in its social setting: the ironworkers of Kasungu, Malawi, 1860–1940. Ph.D. thesis, Yale University.

  1991. The relevance of recent African iron-smelting practice to reconstructions of prehistoric smelting technology. In *Recent trends in archaeometallurgical research*, P. D. Glumac (ed.), pp. 47–54. MASCA Research Papers in Science and Archaeology 8, pt I. Philadelphia: MASCA, University Museum, University of Pennsylvania .

Killion, T. W. 1990. Cultivation intensity and residential site structure: an ethnoarchaeological examination of peasant agriculture in the Sierra de los Tuxtlas, Veracruz, Mexico. *Latin American Antiquity* 1 (3): 191–215.

Kirk-Greene, A. H. M. 1969. *Adamawa past and present: an historical approach to the development of a Northern Cameroons province* (2nd edn). London: I.A.I. (1st edn, Oxford University Press, 1958).

Kleindienst, M. R. and P. J. Watson. 1956. Action archaeology: the archaeological inventory of a living community. *Anthropology Tomorrow* 5 (1): 75–8.

Knauft, B. M. 1996. *Genealogies for the present in cultural anthropology.* New York and London: Routledge.

Kneebone, R. R. 1991. Energy flow, spatial organization and community structure at Matacapan, Veracruz. Ph.D. thesis, University of New Mexico.

Kobayashi, M. 1994. Use-alteration analysis of Kalinga pottery: interior carbon deposits of cooking pots. In *Kalinga ethnoarchaeology: expanding archaeological method and theory*, W. A. Longacre and J. M. Skibo (eds.), pp. 127–68. Washington, DC: Smithsonian Institution Press.

Koch, C. P. (ed.). 1989. *Taphonomy: a bibliographic guide to the literature.* Orono, MN: Center for the Study of the First Americans.

Koelz, W. N. 1983. *Persian Diary, 1939–1941*. Museum of Anthropology, Anthropological Papers 71. Ann Arbor: University of Michigan.

Koopsman, T. C. 1951. *Activity analysis of production and allocation.* Cowles Foundation Monograph 13. New York: John Wiley.

Kosso, P. 1991. Method in archaeology: middle range theory as hermeneutics. *American Antiquity* 56: 621–7.

Kramer, C. (ed.). 1979a. *Ethnoarchaeology: implications of ethnography for archaeology.* New York: Columbia University Press.

  1979b. Introduction. In *Ethnoarchaeology: implications of ethnography for archaeology*, C. Kramer (ed.), pp. 1–20. New York: Columbia University Press.

  1980. Estimating prehistoric populations: an ethnoarchaeological approach. In *L'archéologie de l'Iraq du début de l'époque néolithique à 333 avant notre ère: perspectives et limites de l'interprétation anthropologique de documents*, M. T. Barrelet (ed.), pp. 315–34. Paris: CNRS.

  1982a. *Village ethnoarchaeology: rural Iran in archaeological perspective.* New York: Academic Press.

1982b. Ethnographic households and archaeological interpretation. *American Behavioral Scientist* 25: 663–75.

1985. Ceramic ethnoarchaeology. *Annual Review of Anthropology* 14: 77–102.

1986. Review of D. Miller's "Artefacts as categories." *Man* 21: 750–1.

1996. Ethnoarchaeology. In *Encyclopedia of Cultural Anthropology*, D. Levinson and M. Ember (eds.), pp. 396–9. New York: Henry Holt and Co.

1997. *Pottery in Rajasthan: ethnoarchaeology in two Indian cities.* Washington, DC and London: Smithsonian Institution Press.

Kramer, C. and J. E. Douglas. 1992. Ceramics, caste and kin: spatial relations in Rajasthan, India. *Journal of Anthropological Archaeology* 11: 187–201.

Krause, R. A. 1978. Toward a formal account of Bantu ceramic manufacture. In *Archaeological essays in honor of Irving B. Rouse*, R. A. Dunnell and E. S. Hall (eds.), pp. 87–120. Mouton: The Hague.

1984. Modeling the making of pots: an ethnoarchaeological approach. In *The many dimensions of pottery: ceramics in archaeology and anthropology*, S. van der Leeuw and A. A. Pritchard (eds.), pp. 615–98. Amsterdam: University of Amsterdam.

1985. *The clay sleeps: an ethnoarchaeological study of three African potters.* Alabama: University of Alabama Press.

Kus, S. M. 1997. Archaeologist as anthropologist: much ado about something after all? *Journal of Archaeological Method and Theory* 4 (3/4): 199–213.

Kusimba, C. M. 1996. Social context of iron forging on the Kenya coast. *Africa* 66: 386–410.

Kuznar, L. A. 1990. Economic models, ethnoarchaeology, and early pastoralism in the High Sierra of the south central Andes (2 vols.). Ph.D. thesis, Northwestern University.

1994. *Awatimarka: the ethnoarchaeology of an Andean herding community.* Fort Worth, TX: Harcourt Brace.

Kvamme, K. L., M. T. Stark, and W. A. Longacre. 1996. Alternative procedures for assessing standardization in ceramic assemblages. *American Antiquity* 61: 116–26.

Laden, G. T. 1992. Ethnoarchaeology and land use ecology of the Efe (Pygmies) of the Ituri rain forest, Zaïre. Ph.D. thesis, Harvard University.

Larick, R. 1985. Spears, style and time among Maa-speaking pastoralists. *Journal of Anthropological Archaeology* 4: 206–20.

1986. Age grading and ethnicity in the style of Loikop (Samburu) spears. *World Archaeology* 18: 268–83.

1987a. The circulation of spears among Loikop cattle pastoralists of Samburu District, Kenya. *Research in Economic Anthropology* 9: 143–66.

1987b. Men of iron and social boundaries in northern Kenya. In *Ethnicity and culture. Proceedings of the Eighteenth Annual Chacmool Conference*, R. Auger, M. Glass, A. S. MacEachern, and P. McCartney (eds.), pp. 67–75. Calgary: University of Calgary Archaeological Association.

1991. Warriors and blacksmiths: mediating ethnicity in East African spears. *Journal of Anthropological Archaeology* 10: 299–331.

Lathrap, D. W. 1983. Recent Shipibo-Conibo ceramics and their implications for archaeological interpretation. In *Structure and cognition in art*, D. K. Washburn (ed.), pp. 25–39. New York: Cambridge University Press.

Layton, R., (ed.). 1989. *Conflict in the archaeology of living traditions.* London: Unwin Hyman.

Leach, E. R. 1964. Comment on Narroll's "On ethnic unit classification." *Current Anthropology* 5: 299.

 1976. *Culture and communication*. Cambridge: Cambridge University Press.

Lechtman, H. 1977. Style in technology – some early thoughts. In *Material culture: styles, organization, and dynamics of technology*, H. Lechtman and R. S. Merrill (eds.), pp. 3–20. Proceedings of the American Ethnological Society (1975). St Paul, MN: West Publishing.

Lee, R. B. 1965. Subsistence ecology of !Kung Bushmen. Ph.D. thesis, University of California.

 1971. Eating Christmas in the Kalahari. In *Conformity and conflict: readings in cultural anthropology*, J. P. Spradley (ed.), pp. 7–14. Boston: Little, Brown.

Lee, R. B. and I. DeVore (eds.). 1968. *Man the hunter*. Chicago: Aldine.

Lefebvre, H. 1991. *The production of space*. Oxford: Basil Blackwell.

Lemonnier, P. 1976. La description des chaînes opératoires: contribution à l'analyse des systèmes techniques. *Techniques et Culture* 1: 100–51.

 1986. The study of material culture today: toward an anthropology of technical systems. *Journal of Anthropological Archaeology* 5: 147–86.

 1992. *Elements for an anthropology of technology*. Anthropological Papers of the Museum of Anthropology 88. Ann Arbor: University of Michigan Press.

 1993. The eel and the Ankave-Anga of Papua New Guinea: material and symbolic aspects of trapping. In *Tropical forests, people and food: biocultural interactions to development*, C. M. Hladik, A. Hladik, *et al.* (eds.), pp. 673–82. Man and the Biosphere Series 13. Paris: UNESCO and The Parthenon Publishing Group.

Leone, M. P. 1982. Some opinions about recovering mind. *American Antiquity* 47: 742–60.

Leone, M. P. and P. P. Potter Jr. 1992. Legitimation and the classification of archaeological sites. *American Antiquity* 57: 135–45.

 1996. Archaeological Annapolis: a guide to seeing and understanding three centuries of change. In *Contemporary archaeology in theory: a reader*, R. W. Preucel and I. Hodder (eds.), pp. 570–98. Cambridge, MA and Oxford: Blackwell.

Leroi-Gourhan, A. 1943. *Evolution et techniques*, vol. I. *L'homme et la matière;* vol. 2, *Milieu et techniques*. Paris: Albin Michel.

Leroi-Gourhan, A. and M. Brézillon. 1972. *Fouilles de Pincevent: essai d'analyse ethnographique d'un habitat magdalénien* (2 vols.). Paris: CNRS.

Lévi-Strauss, C. 1963. *Structural anthropology*. New York: Basic Books.

 1966. *The savage mind*. London: Weidenfeld and Nicholson.

Linares, O. F. 1976. "Garden hunting" in the American tropics. *Human Ecology* 4: 331–49.

London, G. A. 1991. Standardization and variation in the work of craft specialists. In *Ceramic ethnoarchaeology*, W. A. Longacre (ed.), pp. 182–204. Tucson: University of Arizona Press.

Longacre, W. A. 1968. Some aspects of prehistoric society in east-central Arizona. In *New perspectives in archaeology*, S. R. Binford and L. R. Binford (eds.), pp. 89–102. Chicago: Aldine.

 1970. *Archaeology as anthropology: a case study*. Anthropological Papers of the University of Arizona 17. Tucson: University of Arizona Press.

 1974. Kalinga pottery making: the evolution of a research design. In *Frontiers of anthropology*, M. J. Leaf (ed.), pp. 51–67. New York: Van Nostrand Company.

1978. Ethnoarchaeology. *Reviews in Anthropology* 5: 357–63.

1981. Kalinga pottery: an ethnoarchaeological study. In *Pattern of the past: studies in honour of David Clarke*, I. Hodder, G. Ll. Isaac, and N. D. C. Hammond (eds.), pp. 49–66. Cambridge: Cambridge University Press.

1985. Pottery use-life among the Kalinga, northern Luzon, the Philippines. In *Decoding prehistoric ceramics*, B. A. Nelson (ed.), pp. 334–46. Carbondale: Southern Illinois University Press.

(ed.). 1991a. *Ceramic ethnoarchaeology*. Tucson: University of Arizona Press.

1991b. Ceramic ethnoarchaeology: an introduction. In *Ceramic ethnoarchaeology*, W. A. Longacre (ed.), pp. 1–10. Tucson: University of Arizona Press.

1991c. Sources of ceramic variability among the Kalinga. In *Ceramic ethnoarchaeology*, W. A. Longacre (ed.), pp. 95–111. Tucson: University of Arizona Press.

1992. The perfect marriage: the essential joining of ethnoarchaeology and experimental archaeology. In *Ethnoarchéologie: justification, problèmes, limites*, F. Audouze (ed.), pp. 15–24. Rencontres Internationales d'Archéologie et d'Histoire d'Antibes 12. Juan-les-Pins: Editions APDCA.

1999. Standardization and specialization: what's the link? In *Pottery and people: a dynamic interaction*, J. M. Skibo and G. M. Feinman (eds.), pp. 44–58. Foundations of Archaeological Inquiry. Salt Lake City: University of Utah Press.

Longacre, W. A., K. L. Kvamme, and M. Kobayashi. 1988. Southwestern pottery standardization: an ethnoarchaeological view from the Philippines. *The Kiva* 53 (2): 110–21.

Longacre, W. A. and J. M. Skibo (eds.). 1994. *Kalinga ethnoarchaeology: expanding archaeological method and theory*. Washington, DC: Smithsonian Institution Press.

Longacre, W. A. and M. T. Stark. 1992. Ceramics, kinship and space: a Kalinga example. *Journal of Anthropological Archaeology* 11: 125–36.

Lupo, K. D. 1994. Butchering marks and carcass acquisition strategies: distinguishing hunting from scavenging in archaeological contexts. *Journal of Archaeological Science* 21: 827–37.

1995. Hadza bone assemblages and hyena attrition: an ethnographic example of the influence of cooking and mode discard on the intensity of scavenger ravaging. *Journal of Anthropological Archaeology* 14: 288–314.

1998. Experimentally derived extraction rates for marrow: implications for body part exploitation strategies of Plio-Pleistocene hominid scavengers. *Journal of Archaeological Science* 25: 657–75.

Lynott, M. J. and A. Wylie, (eds.). 1995. *Ethics in American archaeology: challenges for the 1990s*. Special Report, Society for American Archaeology, Washington, DC.

Lyons, D. E. 1989. Deliver us from evil: protective materials used in witchcraft and sorcery confrontation by the Mura of Doulo, northern Cameroon. In *Cultures in conflict: current archaeological perspectives (Proceedings of the 20th Annual Chacmool Conference)*, D. C. Tkaczuk and B. C. Vivian (eds.), pp. 297–302. Calgary: The Archaeology Association of the University of Calgary.

1992. Men's houses: women's spaces. An ethnoarchaeological study of gender and household design in Dela, North Cameroon. Ph.D. thesis, Simon Fraser University.

1996. The politics of house shape: round versus rectilinear domestic structures in Déla compounds, northern Cameroon. *Antiquity* 70: 351–67.

1998. Witchcraft, gender, power and intimate relations in Mura compounds in Déla, northern Cameroon. *World Archaeology* 29: 344–62.

MacEachern, A. S. 1990. *Du kunde*: processes of montagnard ethnogenesis in the northern Mandara mountains of Cameroon. Ph.D. thesis, University of Calgary.

1992. Ethnicity and stylistic variation around Mayo Plata, northern Cameroon. In *An African commitment: papers in honour of Peter Lewis Shinnie*, J. A. Sterner and N. David (eds.), pp. 211–30. Calgary: University of Calgary Press.

1993. Selling the iron for their shackles: Wandala-montagnard interactions in northern Cameroon. *Journal of African History* 34: 247–70.

1994. "Symbolic reservoirs" and cultural relations between ethnic groups: West African examples. *African Archaeological Review* 12: 203–22.

1996. Foreign countries: the development of ethnoarchaeology in sub-Saharan Africa. *Journal of World Prehistory* 10: 243–304.

1998. Scale, style and cultural variation: technological traditions in the northern Mandara mountains. In *The archaeology of social boundaries*, M. T. Stark (ed.), pp. 107–31. Washington, DC and London: Smithsonian Institution Press.

McIntosh, R. J. 1974. Archaeology and mud wall decay in a west African village. *World Archaeology* 6: 154–71.

1977. The excavation of mud structures: an experiment from West Africa. *World Archaeology* 9: 185–99.

1989. Middle Niger terracottas before the Symplegades gateway. *African Arts* 22 (2): 74–83.

McIntosh, S. K. and R. J. McIntosh. 1980. *Prehistoric investigations in the region of Jenne, Mali: a study in the development of urbanism in the Sahel. Part 2: The regional survey and conclusions.* BAR International Series 89 (2) (Cambridge Monographs in African Archaeology 2). Oxford: British Archeological Report.

Marsh, P., E. Rosser, and R. Harré. 1978. *The rules of disorder*. London: Routledge.

Marshall, F. 1993. Food sharing and the faunal record. In *From bones to behavior: ethnoarchaeological and experimental contributions to the interpretation of faunal remains*, J. Hudson (ed.), pp. 228–46. Occasional Paper 21. Carbondale: Center for Archaeological Investigations, Southern Illinois University.

1994. Food sharing and body part representation in Okiek faunal assemblages. *Journal of Archaeological Science* 21 (1): 65–77.

Marshall, J. and A. Miesmer. 1982. *N!ai, the story of a !Kung woman*. Film (59 mins.). Watertown, MA: Documentary Educational Resources.

Marshall, L. 1965. The !Kung Bushmen of the Kalahari desert. In *Peoples of Africa*, J. L. Gibbs Jr. (ed.), pp. 241–78. New York: Holt, Rinehart and Winston.

Marshall, Y. 1987. Maori mass capture of freshwater eels: an ethnoarchaeological reconstruction of prehistoric subsistence and social behavior. *New Zealand Journal of Archaeology* 9: 55–79.

Marshall, Y. and C. Gosden (eds.). 1999. *The cultural biography of objects. World Archaeology* 31 (2).

Martin, J.-Y. 1970. *Les Matakam du Cameroun: essai sur la dynamique d'une société pré-industrielle*. Mémoires ORSTOM 41. Paris: ORSTOM.

Martin, M. 1987. Production strategies, herd composition, and offtake rates: reassessment of archaeological models. *MASCA Journal* 4 (4): 154–65.

Martin, M. and L. McIntyre (eds.). 1994. *Readings in the philosophy of social science*. Boston: MIT Press.

Mather, C. M. 1999. An ethnoarchaeology of Kusasi shrines, Upper East Region, Ghana. PhD thesis, University of Calgary.

Matson, F. R. 1965. Ceramic ecology: an approach to the study of the early cultures of the Near East. In *Ceramics and man*, F. R. Matson (ed.), pp. 202–17. Viking Fund Publications in Anthropology 41. New York: Wenner-Gren Foundation for Anthropological Research.

Mauss, M. 1935. Les techniques du corps. *Journal du Psychologie* 32 (3–4): 271–93.

Mayor, A. 1994. Durées de vie des céramiques africaines: facteurs responsables et implications archéologiques. In *Terre cuite et société: la céramique, document technique, économique, culturel*, pp. 179–98. Rencontres Internationales d'Archéologie et d'Histoire d'Antibes 14. Juan-les-Pins: Editions APDCA.

Miller, D. 1982a. Artefacts as products of human categorisation processes. In *Symbolic and structural archaeology*, I. Hodder (ed.), pp. 17–25. Cambridge: Cambridge University Press.

1982b. Structures and strategies: an aspect of the relationship between social hierarchy and cultural change. In *Symbolic and structural archaeology*, I. Hodder (ed.), pp. 89–98. Cambridge: Cambridge University Press.

1985. *Artefacts as categories*. Cambridge: Cambridge University Press.

1987. *Material culture and mass consumption*. Oxford: Blackwell.

1998. *A theory of shopping*. Cambridge, UK and Ithaca, NY: Polity Press and Cornell University Press.

Miller, D. and C. Tilley. 1996. Editorial. *Journal of Material Culture* 1 (1): 5–14.

Miller, G. 1979. An introduction to the ethnoarchaeology of the Andean camelids. Ph.D. thesis, University of California.

Miller, T. O. 1979. Stonework of the Xêtá Indians of Brazil. In *Lithic use-wear analysis*, B. Hayden (ed.), pp. 401–7. New York: Academic Press.

Mindeleff, C. 1900. Localization of Tusayan clans. *Annual Report of the Bureau of American Ethnology* 19: 635–53. Washington, DC.

Miner, H. 1956. Body ritual among the Nacirema. *American Anthropologist* 58: 503–7.

Mohr Chávez, K. L. 1991. The organization of production and distribution of traditional pottery in south highland Peru. In *Ceramic production and distribution: an integrated approach*, G. J. Bey III and C. A. Pool (eds.), pp. 49–92. Boulder: Westview Press.

Moñino, Y. 1983. Accoucher du fer: la métallurgie gbaya (Centrafrique). In *Métallurgies africaines: nouvelles contributions*, N. Echard (ed.), pp. 281–309. Mémoires de la Société des Africanistes 9. Paris: Société des Africanistes.

Moore, H. L. 1982. The interpretation of spatial patterning in settlement residues. In *Symbolic and structural archaeology*, I. Hodder (ed.), pp. 74–9. Cambridge: Cambridge University Press.

1986. *Space, text and gender: An anthropological study of the Marakwet of Kenya*. Cambridge: Cambridge University Press.

1995. *A passion for difference: essays in anthropology and gender*. Bloomington: Indiana University Press.

(ed.). 1996. *The future of anthropological knowledge*. London: Routledge.

Msemwa, P. J. 1994. An ethnoarchaeological study on shellfish collecting in a complex urban setting. PhD thesis, Brown University.

Müller-Kosack, G. 1991. Zur Siedlungsstruktur der Mafa (Nord-Kamerun). *Paideuma* 37: 105–40.

1996. The Dughwede in NE-Nigeria: montagnards interacting with the seasons. In *Berichte des Sonderforschungsbereichs 268*, vol. 8, P. Breunig (ed.), pp. 137–70. Frankfurt-am-Main: Johann Wolfgang Goethe-Universität.

Murdock, G. P. and C. Provost. 1973. Factors in the division of labor by sex: a cross-cultural analysis. *Ethnology* 12: 203–25.

Nabhan, G. P. 1985. *Gathering the desert*. Tucson: University of Arizona Press.

Naroll, R. 1964. On ethnic unit classification. *Current Anthropology* 5: 283–312.

Nava, M. 1998. The cosmopolitanism of commerce and the allure of difference: Selfridges, the Russian Ballet and the tango of 1911. *International Journal of Cultural Studies* 1.

Nelson, B. A. 1981. Ethnoarchaeology and paleodemography: a test of Turner and Lofgren's hypothesis. *Journal of Anthropological Research* 37: 107–29.

1991. Ceramic frequency and use-life: a highland Maya case in cross-cultural perspective. In *Ceramic ethnoarchaeology*, W. A. Longacre (ed.), pp. 162–81. Tucson: University of Arizona Press.

Nelson, M. C. 1987a. Site content and structure: quarries and workshops in the Maya Highlands. In *Lithic studies among the contemporary Highland Maya*, B. Hayden (ed.), pp. 120–47. Tucson: University of Arizona Press.

1987b. Contemporary specialization and marketing of manos and metates in the Maya Highlands. In *Lithic studies among contemporary Highland Maya*, B. Hayden (ed.), pp. 148–59. Tucson: University of Arizona.

Netting, R. M. 1968. *Hill farmers of Nigeria: cultural ecology of the Kofyar of the Jos plateau*. Seattle: University of Washington Press.

Neupert, M. 1999. Pottery and politics: factions and the organization of ceramic production in Paradijon, the Philippines. Ph.D. thesis, University of Arizona.

Neupert, M. A. and W. A. Longacre. 1994. Informant accuracy in pottery use-life studies: a Kalinga example. In *Kalinga ethnoarchaeology: expanding archaeological method and theory*, W. A. Longacre and J. M. Skibo (eds.), pp. 71–82. Washington, DC: Smithsonian Institution Press.

Nicholson, P. T. and H. L. Patterson. 1991. The Ballas Pottery Project: ethnoarchaeology in Upper Egypt. In *Ceramic production and distribution: an integrated approach*, G. J. I. Bey and C. A. Pool (eds.), pp. 25–47. Boulder: Westview Press.

Nicklin, K. 1981. Pottery production and distribution in southeast Nigeria. In *Production and distribution: a ceramic viewpoint*, H. Howard and E. Morris (eds.), pp. 169–86. BAR International Series 120. Oxford: British Archaeological Reports.

O'Connell, J. F. 1974. Spoons, knives and scrapers: the function of *yilugwa* in central Australia. *Mankind* 9: 189–94.

1987. Alyawara site structure and its archaeological implications. *American Antiquity* 52: 74–108.

1993. Discussion: subsistence and settlement interpretations. In *From bones to behavior: ethnoarchaeological and experimental contributions to the interpretation of faunal remains*, J. Hudson (ed.), pp. 169–78. Occasional Paper 21. Carbondale: Southern Illinois University, Center for Archaeological Investigations.

1995. Ethnoarchaeology needs a general theory of behavior. *Journal of Archaeological Research* 3: 205–55.

O'Connell, J. F., K. Hawkes, and N. G. Blurton Jones. 1988a. Hadza scavenging: implications for Plio-Pleistocene hominid subsistence. *Current Anthropology* 29: 356–63.

1988b. Hadza hunting, butchering, and bone transport and their archaeological implications. *Journal of Anthropological Research* 44: 113–62.

1990. Reanalysis of large mammal body part transport among the Hadza. *Journal of Archaeological Science* 17: 301–16.

1991. Distribution of refuse producing activities at Hadza residence base camps: implications for analyses of archaeological site structure. In *The interpretation of archaeological spatial patterning*, E. M. Kroll and T. D. Price (eds.), pp. 61–76. New York: Plenum Press.

1999. Grandmothering and the evolution of *Homo erectus*. *Journal of Human Evolution* 36: 1–25.

Okafor, E. E. 1993. New evidence on early iron-smelting from southeastern Nigeria. In *The archaeology of Africa: food, metals and towns*, T. Shaw, P. Sinclair, B. W. Andah, and I. A. Okpoko (eds.), pp. 432–58. London and New York: Routledge.

O'Neill, P. and F. Muhly. 1988. *The tree of iron*. Film (57 mins.). Watertown, MA: Documentary Educational Resources.

Orme, B. 1974. Twentieth-century prehistorians and the idea of ethnographic parallels. *Man* 9: 199–212.

Ortner, S. B. 1984. Theory in anthropology since the sixties. *Comparative Studies in Society and History* 26: 126–66.

Osborn, A. 1996. Cattle, co-wives, children and calabashes: material context for symbol use among the Il Chamus of west-central Kenya. *Journal of Anthropological Archaeology* 15: 107–36.

O'Shea, J. 1981. Social configurations and the archaeological study of mortuary practices: a case study. In *The archaeology of death*, R. Chapman, I. Kinnes, and K. Randsborg (eds.), pp. 39–52. Cambridge: Cambridge University Press.

Oswalt, W. H. 1974. Ethnoarchaeology. In *Ethnoarchaeology*, C. B. Donnan and C. W. Clewlow (eds.), pp. 3–14. Institute of Archaeology Monograph 4. Los Angeles: University of California.

Oswalt, W. H. and J. W. VanStone. 1967. *The ethnoarchaeology of Crow village, Alaska*. Bulletin 199. Washington, DC: Bureau of American Ethnology.

Parker Pearson, M. 1982. Mortuary practices, society and ideology: an ethnoarchaeological study. In *Symbolic and structural archaeology*, I. Hodder (ed.), pp. 99–113. Cambridge: Cambridge University Press.

1993. The powerful dead: archaeological relationships between the living and the dead. *Cambridge Archaeological Journal* 3: 203–29.

1999. Eating money: a study in the ethnoarchaeology of food. Paper presented at the Archon Conference "From calorie to culture," Leiden.

Parkington, J. and G. Mills. 1991. From space to place: the architecture and social organisation of southern African mobile communities. In *Ethnoarchaeological approaches to mobile campsites*, C. S. Gamble and W. A. Boismier (eds.), pp. 355–70. Ethnoarchaeological Series 1. Ann Arbor: International Monographs in Prehistory.

Parsons, J. 1971. *Prehistoric settlement patterns in the Texcoco region, Mexico*. Museum of Anthropology Memoirs 3. Ann Arbor: University of Michigan.

Pastron, A. G. 1974. Preliminary ethnoarchaeological investigations among the

Tarahumara. In *Ethnoarchaeology*, C. B. Donnan and C. W. Clewlow (eds.), pp. 93–114. Institute of Archaeology Monograph 4. Los Angeles: University of California.

Pastron, A. G. and C. W. Clewlow Jr. 1974a. The ethno-archaeology of an unusual Tarahumara burial cave. *Man* 9: 308–10.

   1974b. Ethnoarchaeological observations on human burial decomposition in the Chihuahua Sierra. In *Ethnoarchaeology*, C. B. Donnan and C. W. Clewlow (eds.), pp. 161–73. Institute of Archaeology Monograph 4. Los Angeles: University of California.

Peacock, D. P. S. 1982. *Pottery in the Roman world: an ethnoarchaeological approach*. London: Longman.

Pelegrin, J., C. Karlin, and P. Bodu. 1989. Chaînes opératoires: un outil pour le préhistorien. In *Technologie préhistorique*, J. Tixier (ed.), pp. 55–62. Notes et Monographies Techniques 25. Paris: CNRS.

Perkins, D. and P. Daly. 1968. A hunter's village in Neolithic Turkey. *Scientific American* 219 (5): 97–106.

Pétrequin, A.-M. and P. Pétrequin. 1984. *Habitat lacustre du Bénin: une approche ethnoarchéologique*. Mémoire 39. Paris: Editions Recherches sur les Civilisations.

   1990. Flèches de chasse, flèches de guerre: le cas des Danis d'Irian Jaya (Indonésie). *Bulletin de la Société Préhistorique Française* 87 (10–12): 484–511.

Pétrequin, P. and A.-M. Pétrequin. 1990. Haches de Yeleme, herminettes de Mumyeme. *Journal de la Société des Océanistes* 91 (2): 95–113.

   1992. De l'espace actuel au temps archéologique ou les mythes d'un préhistorien. In *Ethnoarchéologie: justification, problèmes, limites*, F. Audouze (ed.), pp. 211–38. Rencontres Internationales d'Archéologie et d'Histoire d'Antibes 12. Juan-les-Pins: Editions APDCA.

   1993. *Ecologie d'un outil: la hache de pierre en Irian Jaya (Indonésie)*. Monographie du CRA 12. Paris: CNRS Editions.

Pettit, P. 1975. *The concept of structuralism: a critical analysis*. Dublin: Gill and MacMillan.

Pfaffenberger, B. 1992. Social anthropology of technology. *Annual Review of Anthropology* 21: 491–516.

Phillipson, D. W. 1993. *African archaeology* (2nd edn). Cambridge: Cambridge University Press.

Piaget, J. 1971. *Structuralism*. London: Routledge and Kegan Paul.

Picon, M. 1992. Ethnoarchéologie et recherches en laboratoire: le cas des techniques céramiques. In *Ethnoarchéologie: justification, problèmes, limites*, F. Audouze (ed.), pp. 115–26. Rencontres Internationales d'Archéologie et d'Histoire d'Antibes 12. Juan-les-Pins: Editions APDCA.

Pike, K. L. 1954. Emic and etic standpoints for the description of behavior. In *Language in relation to a unified theory of the structure of human behavior, part 1*, Preliminary edition, K. L. Pike (ed.), pp. 8–28. Glendale: Summer Institute of Linguistics.

Plimpton, C. L. 1994. Ethnoarchaeology of vernacular dwellings and domestic use of space in Egypt. Ph.D. thesis, Washington State University.

Politis, G. G. 1996. Moving to produce: Nukak mobility and settlement patterns in Amazonia. *World Archaeology* 27: 492–511.

Potts, R. 1984. Home bases and early hominids. *American Scientist* 72: 338–47.

Preucel, R. W. 1991. The philosophy of archaeology. In *Processual and postprocessual archaeologies: multiple ways of knowing the past*, R. W. Preucel (ed.), pp. 17–29. Occasional Paper 10. Carbondale: Center for Archaeological Investigations, South Illinois University.

1995. The postprocessual condition. *Journal of Archaeological Research* 3: 147–75.

Preucel, R. W. and I. Hodder (eds.). 1996. *Contemporary archaeology in theory: a reader*. Cambridge, MA and Oxford: Blackwell.

Rathje, W. L. 1978. Archaeological ethnography: because sometimes it is better to give than to receive. In *Explorations in ethnoarchaeology*, R. A. Gould (ed.), pp. 49–76. Albuquerque: University of New Mexico Press.

1985. The Garbage Project. In *Anthropology: contemporary perspectives*, D. Hunter and P. Whitten (eds.), pp. 71–8. Toronto: Little, Brown and Co.

Raymond, J. S., W. R. DeBoer, and P. G. Roe. 1975. *Cumancaya: a Peruvian ceramic tradition*. Occasional Papers 2. Calgary: Department of Archaeology, University of Calgary.

Reddy, S. N. 1991. On the banks of the river: opportunistic cultivation in South India. *Expedition* 33 (3): 18–26.

1997. If the threshing floor could talk: integration of agriculture and pastoralism during the Late Harappan in Gujarat, India. *Journal of Anthropological Archaeology* 16: 162–87.

1999. Fueling the hearths in India: the role of dung in paleoethnobotanical interpretation. *Paléorient* 24 (2): 61–70.

Redman, C. L. 1978. Mesopotamian urban ecology: the systemic context of the emergence of urbanism. In *Social archeology: beyond subsistence and dating*, C. L. Redman, *et al.* (eds.), pp. 329–47. New York: Academic Press.

Renfrew, C. 1994. Towards a cognitive archaeology. In *The ancient mind: elements of cognitive archaeology*, C. Renfrew and E. B. W. Zubrow (eds.), pp. 3–12. Cambridge: Cambridge University Press.

Renfrew, C. and E. B. W. Zubrow (eds.). 1994. *The ancient mind: elements of cognitive archaeology*. Cambridge: Cambridge University Press.

Rice, P. M. 1987. *Pottery analysis: a sourcebook*. Chicago: University of Chicago Press.

Ringrose, T. J. 1993. Bone counts and statistics: a critique. *Journal of Archaeological Science* 20: 121–57.

Robertson, I. G. 1992. Hoes and metal templates in northern Cameroon. In *An African commitment: papers in honour of Peter Lewis Shinnie*, J. A. Sterner and N. David (eds.), pp. 231–40. Calgary: University of Calgary Press.

Roe, P. G. and P. E. Siegel. 1982. The life history of a Shipibo compound: ethnoarchaeology in the Peruvian Montaña. *Archaeology and Anthropology* 5 (2): 94–118.

Rosen, S. A. 1997. *Lithics after the Stone Age: a handbook of stone tools from the Levant*. Walnut Creek, London, and New Delhi: AltaMira.

Rossignol, J. and L. Wandsnider (eds.). 1992. *Space, time and archaeological landscapes*. New York and London: Plenum Press.

Roux, V. 1985. *Le matériel de broyage: étude ethnoarchéologique à Tichitt, Mauritanie*. Mémoire 58. Paris: Editions Recherches sur les Civilisations, ADPF.

1989 (with the collaboration of Daniela Corbetta). *The potter's wheel: craft specialization and technical competence*. New Delhi: Oxford and IBH Publishing Co. Pvt. Ltd.

1990 (with the collaboration of Daniela Corbetta). *Le tour du potier:*

spécialisation artisanale et compétences techniques. Paris: Editions du CNRS.

Roux, V., B. Bril, and G. Dietrich. 1995. Skills and learning difficulties involved in stone knapping: the case of stone-bead knapping in Khambhat, India. *World Archaeology* 27: 63–87.

Roux, V. and P. Matarasso. 1999. Crafts and the evolution of complex societies: new methodologies for modeling the organization of production, a Harappan example. In *The social dynamics of technology: practice, politics, and world views*, M.-A. Dobres and C. R. Hoffman (eds.), pp. 46–70. Washington, DC and London: Smithsonian Institution Press.

Rowlands, M. J. and J.-P. Warnier. 1993. The magical production of iron in the Cameroon Grassfields. In *The archaeology of Africa: food, metals and towns*, T. Shaw, P. Sinclair, B. W. Andah, and I. A. Okpoko (eds.), pp. 512–50. London and New York: Routledge.

Rupert, M. forthcoming. Fordism. In *The Cold War: an encyclopedia*, S. Burwood (ed.). New York: Garland Brothers.

Ryan, K., K. Munene, S. M. Kahinju, and P. N. Kunoni. 1991. Cattle-naming: the persistence of a traditional practice in modern Maasailand. In *Animal use and culture change*, P. J. Crabtree and K. Ryan (eds.), pp. 91–6. Philadelphia: MASCA, The University Museum of Archaeology and Anthropology.

  1999. Ethnographic perspectives on cattle management in semi-arid environments: a case study from Maasailand. In *The origins and development of African livestock*, K. C. MacDonald and R. Blench (eds.). London: University College London.

Rybczynski, N., D. P. Gifford-Gonzalez, and K. M. Stewart. 1996. Ethnoarchaeology of reptile remains at a Lake Turkana occupation site, Kenya. *Journal of Archaeological Science* 23: 863–7.

Rye, O. S. 1976. Keeping your temper under control: materials and manufacture of a Papuan potter. *Archaeology and Physical Anthropology in Oceania* 11 (2): 106–37.

Rye, O. S. and C. Evans. 1976. *Traditional pottery techniques of Pakistan: field and laboratory studies*. Smithsonian Contributions to Anthropology 21. Washington, DC: Smithsonian Institution Press.

Sackett, J. R. 1977. The meaning of style in archaeology: a general model. *American Antiquity* 42: 369–80.

  1982. Approaches to style in lithic archaeology. *Journal of Anthropological Archaeology* 1: 59–112.

  1985. Style and ethnicity in the Kalahari: a reply to Wiessner. *American Antiquity* 50: 154–9.

  1990. Style and ethnicity in archaeology: the case for isochrestism. In *The uses of style in archaeology*, M. W. Conkey and C. A. Hastorf (eds.), pp. 32–43. Cambridge: Cambridge University Press.

Salmon, M. H. 1976. "Deductive" versus "inductive" archaeology. *American Antiquity* 41: 376–81.

  1978. What can systems theory do for archaeology? *American Antiquity* 43: 174–83.

Saltman, C., C. L. Goucher, and E. W. Herbert. 1986. *The blooms of Banjeli: technology and gender in West African ironmaking*. Film (28 mins.). Watertown, MA: Documentary Educational Resources.

Sanjek, R. 1990. A vocabulary for fieldnotes. In *Fieldnotes: the makings of anthropology*, R. Sanjek (ed.), pp. 92–121. Ithaca: Cornell University Press.

Sapir, E. 1949. The status of linguistics as a science . In *Selected writings of Edward Sapir*, D. G. Mandelbaum (ed.), pp. 160–6. Berkeley: University of California Press. (Originally published in *Language* 5 (1929): 207–14.)

Sargent, C. F. and D. A. Friedel. 1986. From clay to metal: culture change and container usage among the Bariba of northern Benin, West Africa. *African Archaeological Review* 4: 177–95.

Sassoon, H. 1964. Iron smelting in the hill village of Sukur, north eastern Nigeria. *Man* 64: 174–8.

Savelle, J. M. 1995. An ethnoarchaeological investigation of Inuit Beluga whale and narwhal harvesting. In *Hunting the largest animals: native whaling in the Western Arctic and Subarctic*, A. P. McCartney (ed.), pp. 127–48. Studies in Whaling, 3. Edmonton, AB: Canadian Circumpolar Institute.

Saxe, A. A. 1970. Social dimensions of mortuary practices. Ph.D. thesis, University of Michigan.

Scheper-Hughes, N. 1995. The primacy of the ethical: propositions for a militant anthropology. *Current Anthropology* 36: 409–20.

Schiffer, M. B. 1976. *Behavioral archaeology*. New York: Academic Press.

1978. Methodological issues in ethnoarchaeology. In *Explorations in ethnoarchaeology*, R. A. Gould (ed.), pp. 229–47. Albuquerque: University of New Mexico Press.

1987. *Formation processes of the archaeological record*. Albuquerque: University of New Mexico Press.

Schiffer, M. B. and J. M. Skibo. 1997. The explanation of artifact variability. *American Antiquity* 62: 27–50.

Schiffer, M. B., J. M. Skibo, T. C. Boelke, M. A. Neupert, and M. Aronson. 1994. New perspectives on experimentation archaeology: surface treatments and thermal response of the clay cooking pot. *American Antiquity* 59: 197–217.

Schmidt, P. R. 1980. Steel production in prehistoric Africa: insights from ethnoarchaeology in West Lake, Tanzania. In *Proceedings of the 8th Pan-African Congress of Prehistory and Quaternary Studies*, R. Leakey and B. A. Ogot (eds.), pp. 335–40. Nairobi: International L. S. B. Leakey Memorial Institute.

1996a. Rhythmed time and its archaeological implications. In *Aspects of African archaeology. Papers from the 10th Congress of the PanAfrican Association for Prehistory and Related Studies*, G. Pwiti and R. Soper (eds.), pp. 655–62. Harare: University of Zimbabwe Publications.

1996b. Reconfiguring the Barongo: reproductive symbolism and reproduction among a work association of iron smelters. In *The culture and technology of African iron production*, P. R. Schmidt (ed.), pp. 74–127. Gainesville: University Press of Florida.

1997. *Iron technology in East Africa: symbolism, science and archaeology*. Bloomington: University of Indiana Press.

Schmidt, P. R. and R. J. McIntosh. 1996. *Plundering Africa's past*. Bloomington: Indiana University Press.

Seamon, D. 1980. Body-subject, time-space routines, and place-ballets. In *The human experience of space and place*, A. Buttimer and D. Seamon (eds.), pp. 148–65. New York: St. Martin's Press.

Seignobos, C. 1982. *Nord Cameroun: montagnes et hautes terres*. Roquevaire: Edition Parenthèses.

1991. Les Murgur ou l'identification ethnique par la forge (Nord-Cameroun). In

Forges et forgerons (Actes du 4e Colloque Méga-Tchad, 1988), Y. Moñino (ed.), pp. 43–225. Paris: Editions ORSTOM.

Sept, J. M. 1992. Was there no place like home? A new perspective on early hominid archaeological sites from the mapping of chimpanzee nests. *Current Anthropology* 33: 187–208.

Shanks, M. 1993. Style and design of a perfume jar from an Archaic Greek city state. *Journal of European Archaeology* 1: 77–106.

Shanks, M. and C. Tilley. 1982. Ideology, symbolic power and ritual communication: a reinterpretation of Neolithic mortuary practices. In *Symbolic and structural archaeology*, I. Hodder (ed.), pp. 129–54. Cambridge: Cambridge University Press.

  1987. *Re-constructing archaeology.* Cambridge: Cambridge University Press.

  1989. Archaeology into the 1990s (with comments and response). *Norwegian Archaeological Review* 22 (1): 1–54.

Sharp, L. 1952. Steel axes for stone-age Australians. *Human Organization* 11: 17–22.

Shennan, S. J. 1996. Cultural transmission and cultural change. In *Contemporary theory in archaeology: a reader*, R. W. Preucel and I. Hodder (eds.), pp. 282–96. Oxford: Blackwell.

Shepard, A. 1956. *Ceramics for the archaeologist.* Publication 609. Washington, DC: Carnegie Institute.

Shott, M. J. 1989. On tool-class uselives and the formation of archaeological assemblages. *American Antiquity* 54: 9–30.

  1998. Status and role of formation theory in contemporary archaeological practice. *Journal of Archaeological Research* 6: 299–329.

Sidi Maamar, H. 1989. Le sacrifice du mouton pour la fête musulmane de l'Aïd el-kébir en Algerie: cas et essai d'interpretation techno-symbolique. *Anthropozoologica* (3e numéro spécial: Animal et pratiques religieuses: les manifestations matérielles): 157–62.

Silberbauer, G. B. 1972. The G/wi Bushmen. In *Hunters and gatherers today*, M. G. Bicchieri (ed.), pp. 271–326. New York: Holt, Rinehart and Winston.

Silvestre, R. 1994. The ethnoarchaeology of Kalinga basketry: a preliminary investigation. In *Kalinga ethnoarchaeology: expanding archaeological method and theory*, W. A. Longacre and J. M. Skibo (eds.), pp. 199–207. Washington, DC: Smithsonian Institution Press.

Simms, S. R. and K. M. Heath. 1990. Site structure of the Orbit Inn: an application of ethnoarchaeology. *American Antiquity* 55: 797–813.

Sinopoli, C. M. 1988. The organization of craft production at Vijayanagara, South India. *American Anthropologist* 90: 580–97.

  1991. Seeking the past through the present: recent ethnoarchaeological research in South Asia. *Asian Perspectives* 30 (2): 177–92.

Skibo, J. M. 1990. Use-alteration of pottery: an ethnoarchaeological and experimental study. Ph.D. thesis, University of Arizona.

  1992. *Pottery function: a use-alteration perspective.* New York: Plenum.

  1999. *Ants for breakfast: archaeological adventures among the Kalinga.* Salt Lake City: University of Utah Press.

Sluka, J. A. 1990. Participant observation in violent social contexts. *Human Organization* 49 (2): 114–26.

Smith, A. and N. David. 1995. The production of space and the house of Xidi Sukur. *Current Anthropology* 36: 441–71.

Smith, A. B. 1996. The Kalahari Bushmen debate: implications for archaeology of southern Africa. *South African Historical Journal* 35: 1–15.

Smith, A. L. 2000. Processing clay for pottery in northern Cameroon: social and technical requirements. *Archaeometry* 42 (1): 21–42.

Smith, J. N. L. 1993. The identification and evaluation of use-wear signatures on pottery vessels: an ethnoarchaeological case study from eastern Zaïre, Africa. M.A. thesis, University of South Carolina.

Smith, S. 1980. The environmental adaptation of nomads in the west African Sahel: key to understanding prehistoric pastoralists. In *The Sahara and the Nile: Quaternary environments and prehistoric occupation in northern Africa*, M. A. J. Williams and H. Faure (eds.), pp. 467–87. Rotterdam: A. A. Balkema.

Solecki, R. S. 1979. Contemporary Kurdish winter-time inhabitants of Shanidar Cave. *World Archaeology* 10: 318–30.

Solheim, W. G. 1952. Oceanic pottery manufacture. *Journal of East Asiatic Studies* 1 (1): 1–40.

Spencer, P. 1965. *The Samburu: a study of gerontocracy in a nomadic tribe.* Berkeley: University of California Press.

Speth, J. D. 1983. *Bison kills and bone counts: decision making by ancient hunters.* Chicago: University of Chicago Press.

Spooner, B. 1986. Weavers and dealers: the authenticity of an oriental rug. In *The social life of things: commodities in cultural perpective*, A. Appadurai (ed.), pp. 195–235. Cambridge: Cambridge University Press.

Srinavasan, N. R. 1998. Revival of rural ironmaking in Orissa. In *Archaeometallurgy in India*, V. Tripathi (ed.), pp. 228–40. Delhi: Sharada Publishing House.

Srinavasan, S. 1998. High tin bronze working in India: the bowl makers of Kerala. In *Archaeometallurgy in India*, V. Tripathi (ed.), pp. 241–50. Delhi: Sharada Publishing House.

Stahl, A. B. 1993. Concepts of time and approaches to analogical reasoning in historical perspective. *American Antiquity* 58: 235–60.

Stanislawski, M. B. 1977. Ethnoarchaeology of Hopi and Hopi-Tewa pottery making: styles of learning. In *Experimental archaeology*, D. T. Ingersoll, J. E. Yellen, and W. MacDonald (eds.), pp. 378–408. New York: Columbia University Press.

    1978a. If pots were mortal. In *Explorations in ethnoarchaeology*, R. A. Gould (ed.), pp. 201–28. Albuquerque: University of New Mexico Press.

    1978b. Pots, patterns and potsherds: ethnoarchaeology of Hopi and Hopi-Tewa pottery making and settlement. *Discovery* 15: 15–25.

Stark, M. T. 1991. Ceramic change in ethnoarchaeological perspective: a Kalinga case study. *Asian Perspectives* 30: 193–216.

    1992. From sibling to suki: social relations and spatial proximity in Kalinga pottery exchange. *Journal of Anthropological Archaeology* 11: 137–51.

    1993a. Re-fitting the "cracked and broken facade": the case for empiricism in post-processual ethnoarchaeology. In *Archaeological theory: who sets the agenda?*, N. Yoffee and A. Sherratt (eds.), pp. 93–104. Cambridge: Cambridge University Press.

    1993b. Pottery economics: a Kalinga ethnoarchaeological study. Ph.D. thesis, University of Arizona.

    1994. Pottery exchange and the regional system: a Dalupa case study. In

Kalinga ethnoarchaeology: expanding archaeological method and theory,
W. A. Longacre and J. M. Skibo (eds.), pp. 169–97. Washington, DC:
Smithonian Institution Press.

1995. Economic intensification and ceramic specialization in the Philippines: a
view from Kalinga. *Research in Economic Anthropology* 16: 179–226.

(ed.). 1998a. *The archaeology of social boundaries*. Washington, DC and
London: Smithsonian Institution Press.

1998b. Technical choices and social boundaries in material culture patterning:
an introduction. In *The archaeology of social boundaries*, M. T. Stark (ed.),
pp. 1–11. Washington, DC and London: Smithsonian Institution Press.

Stark, M. T. and W. A. Longacre. 1993. Kalinga ceramics and new technologies:
social and cultural contexts of ceramic change. In *The social and cultural
contexts of new ceramic technologies*, W. D. Kingery (ed.), pp. 1–32.
Ceramics and Civilization 6. Westerville, OH: The American Ceramic
Society.

Staski, E. and L. D. Sutro (eds.). 1991. *The ethnoarchaeology of refuse disposal*.
Anthropological Research Papers 42. Tempe: Arizona State University.

Sterner, J. A. 1989. Who is signalling whom? Ceramic style, ethnicity and
taphonomy among the Sirak Bulahay. *Antiquity* 63: 451–9.

1992. Sacred pots and "symbolic reservoirs" in the Mandara highlands of
northern Cameroon. In *An African commitment: papers in honour of Peter
Lewis Shinnie*, J. A. Sterner and N. David (eds.), pp. 171–80. Calgary:
University of Calgary Press.

1998. The ways of the Mandara mountains: a comparative regional approach.
Ph.D. thesis, University of London, School of Oriental and African Studies.

Sterner, J. A. and N. David. 1991. Gender and caste in the Mandara highlands:
northeastern Nigeria and northern Cameroon. *Ethnology* 30: 355–69.

In press. Transformers transformed: aspects of caste and iron technology in the
Mandara mountains. In *Transformations, technology and gender in African
metallurgy*, S. Ardener and I. Fowler (eds.). Oxford: Berg.

Stewart, K. M. and D. P. Gifford-Gonzalez. 1994. Ethnoarchaeological
contribution to identifying hominid fish processing sites. *Journal of
Archaeological Science* 21: 237–48.

Stiles, D. 1977. Ethnoarchaeology: a discussion of methods and applications. *Man*
12: 87–103.

Stocking Jr., G. W. (ed.). 1983. *Observers observed: essays on ethnographic
fieldwork*. History of Anthropology 1. Madison: University of Wisconsin
Press.

Stoller, P. and C. Olkes. 1987. *In sorcery's shadow: a memoir of apprenticeship
among the Songhay of Niger*. Chicago: University of Chicago Press.

Stone, G. D. 1991. Settlement ethnoarchaeology: changing patterns among the
Kofyar of Nigeria. *Expedition* 33 (1): 16–23.

1992. Social distance, spatial relations, and agricultural production among the
Kofyar of Namu District, Plateau State, Nigeria. *Journal of Anthropological
Archaeology* 11: 152–72.

1993a. Agricultural abandonment: a comparative study in historical ecology. In
*Abandonment of settlements and regions: ethnoarchaeological and
archaeological approaches*, C. M. Cameron and S. A. Tomka (eds.), pp. 75–81.
Cambridge: Cambridge University Press.

1993b. Agrarian settlement and the spatial disposition of labor. In *Spatial
boundaries and social dynamics: case studies from food-producing societies*,

A. F. C. Holl and T. E. Levy (eds.), pp. 25–38. Ethnoarchaeological Series 2. Ann Arbor: International Monographs in Prehistory.

1994. Agricultural intensification and perimetrics: ethnoarchaeological evidence from Nigeria. *Current Anthropology* 35: 317–24.

1996. *Settlement ecology: the social and spatial organization of Kofyar agriculture*. Tucson: University of Arizona.

Sumner, W. M. 1979. Estimating population by analogy: an example. In *Ethnoarchaeology: implications of ethnography for archaeology*, C. Kramer (ed.), pp. 164–74. New York: Columbia University Press.

1989. Population and settlement area: an example from Iran. *American Anthropologist* 91: 631–41.

Tajfel, H. (ed.). 1982. *Social identity and intergroup relations*. European studies in social psychology. Cambridge/Paris: Cambridge University Press/Editions de la Maison des Sciences de l'Homme.

Tamari, T. 1991. The development of caste systems in West Africa. *Journal of African History* 32: 221–50.

Tani, M. 1994. Why should more pots break in larger households? Mechanisms underlying population estimates from ceramics. In *Kalinga ethnoarchaeology: expanding archaeological method and theory*, W. A. Longacre and J. M. Skibo (eds.), pp. 51–70. Washington, DC: Smithsonian Institution Press.

Tarlow, S. 1992. Each slow dusk a drawing-down of blinds. *Archaeological Review from Cambridge* 11 (1): 125–40.

1995. What dreams may come: metaphors of death in Orkney. *Scottish Archaeological Review* 9–10: 110–14.

Thery, B., P. Pétrequin, and A.-M. Pétrequin. 1990. *Langda, l'herminette de pierre polie en Nouvelle Guinée*. Video recording (26 mins.). Paris: JVP Films–CNRS Audiovisuel–CRAVA.

Thompson, R. H. 1958. *Modern Yucatecan pottery making*. Memoirs of the Society for American Archaeology 15. Washington, DC: Society for American Archaeology.

1991. The archaeological purpose of ethnoarchaeology. In *Ceramic ethnoarchaeology*, W. A. Longacre (ed.), pp. 231–45. Tucson: University of Arizona Press.

Thomson, D. F. 1939. The seasonal factor in human culture, illustrated from the life of a contemporary nomadic group. *Proceedings of the Prehistoric Society* 5: 209–21.

Tilley, C. (ed.). 1990. *Reading material culture*. Oxford: Blackwell.

Tixier, J. 1980. Expériences de taille. *Publications de l'U.R.A. – Unités de Recherches Archéologiques du C.R.A.* 28 (1): 47–9.

1984. Débitage par pression. *Préhistoire de la Pierre Taillée* 2: 57–70.

Tobert, N. 1988. *The ethnoarchaeology of the Zaghawa of Darfur (Sudan): settlement and transience*. BAR International Series 445 (Cambridge Monographs in African Archaeology 30). Oxford: British Archaeological Reports.

Todd, J. A. 1979. Studies of the African Iron Age. *Journal of Metals* 31 (November): 39–46.

1985. Iron production by the Dimi of Ethiopia. In *African iron working: ancient and traditional*, R. Haaland and P. L. Shinnie (eds.), pp. 88–101. Oslo: Universitetsforlaget AS.

Tomka, S. A. 1993. Site abandonment behavior among transhumant agro-pastoralists: the effects of delayed curation on assemblage composition. In *Abandonment of settlements and regions: ethnoarchaeological and archaeological approaches*, C. M. Cameron and S. A. Tomka (eds.), pp. 11–24. Cambridge: Cambridge University Press.

Tomka, S. A. and M. G. Stevenson. 1993. Understanding abandonment processes: summary and remaining concerns. In *Abandonment of settlements and regions: ethnoarchaeological and archaeological approaches*, C. M. Cameron and S. A. Tomka (eds.), pp. 191–5. Cambridge: Cambridge University Press.

Tong, E. 1990. *Zhongguo xinan minzu kaogu lunwenji (Ethnoarchaeological essays on the ethnic groups of southwest China)*. Beijing: Wenwu.

Tosi, M. 1984. The notion of craft specialization and its representation in the archaeological record. In *Marxist perspectives in archaeology*, M. Spriggs (ed.), pp. 22–52. Cambridge: Cambridge University Press.

Toth, N. P. 1985. The Oldowan reassessed: a close look at early stone artifacts. *Journal of Archaeological Science* 12: 101–20.

Toth, N. P. and K. D. Schick. 1986. The first million years: the archaeology of protohuman culture. *Advances in Archaeological Method and Theory* 9: 1–95.

Trigger, B. G. 1990. Monumental architecture: a thermodynamic explanation of symbolic behaviour. *World Archaeology* 22: 119–32.

   1993. *Early civilizations: Ancient Egypt in context*. Cairo: American University in Cairo Press.

   1998. Archaeology and epistemology: dialoguing across the Darwinian chasm. *American Journal of Archaeology* 102: 1–34.

Tringham, R. E. 1991. Households with faces: the challenge of gender in prehistoric architectural remains. In *Engendering archaeology*, J. M. Gero and M. W. Conkey (eds.), pp. 93–131. Oxford: Blackwell.

Tripathi, V. and A. Tripathi. 1994. Iron working in Ancient India: an ethnoarchaeological study. In *From Sumer to Meluhha: contributions to the archaeology of Southwest and South Asia in memory of George F. Dales*, J. M. Kenoyer (ed.), pp. 241–51. Wisconsin Archaeological Reports 3. Madison: University of Wisconsin.

Trostel, B. D. 1994. Household pots and possessions: an ethnoarchaeological study of material goods and wealth. In *Kalinga ethnoarchaeology: expanding archaeological method and theory*, W. A. Longacre and J. M. Skibo (eds.), pp. 209–28. Washington, DC: Smithsonian Institution Press.

Upham, S. 1987. The tyranny of ethnographic analogy in southwestern archaeology. In *Coasts, plains and deserts: essays in honor of Reynold J. Ruppé*, S. W. Gaines (ed.), pp. 265–79. Tempe: Arizona State University.

van der Leeuw, S. 1977. Towards a study of the economics of pottery making. In *Ex horreo*, B. L. van Beek, R. W. Brant, and W. Gruenman van Watteringe (eds.), pp. 68–76. Cingula 4. Amsterdam: A. E. van Giffen Instituut voor Prae- en Protohistorie, University of Amsterdam.

   1991. Variation, variability, and explanation in pottery studies. In *Ceramic ethnoarchaeology: expanding archaeological method and theory*, W. A. Longacre (ed.), pp. 11–39. Tucson: University of Arizona Press.

   1993. Giving the potter a choice: conceptual aspects of pottery techniques. In *Technological choices: transformation in material cultures since the Neolithic*, P. Lemonnier (ed.), pp. 238–88. London and New York: Routledge.

van der Merwe, N. J. and D. H. Avery. 1987. Science and magic in African technology: traditional iron smelting in Malawi. *Africa* 57: 143–72.

VanPool, C. S. and T. L. VanPool. 1999. The scientific nature of postprocessualism. *American Antiquity* 64: 33–53.

Varien, M. D. and B. J. Mills. 1997. Accumulations research: problems and prospects for estimating site occupation span. *Journal of Archaeological Method and Theory* 4 (2): 105–39.

Vaughan, J. H. 1964. The religion and world view of the Margi. *Ethnology* 3 (4): 389–97.

   1973. Engkyagu as artists in Marghi society. In *The traditional artist in African societies*, W. L. d'Azevedo (ed.), pp. 162–93. Bloomington: Indiana University Press.

Vaughan, J. H. and A. H. M. Kirk-Greene (eds.). 1995. *The diary of Hamman Yaji: chronicle of a West African Muslim ruler*. Bloomington and Indianapolis: Indiana University Press.

Veit, U. 1997. Tod und Bestattungssitten im Kulturvergleich. Ethnoarchäologische Perspektiven einer "Archäologie des Todes." *Ethnographische-Archäologische Zeitschrift* 38: 291–313.

Vidale, M., J. M. Kenoyer, and K. K. Bhan. 1993. Ethnoarchaeological excavations of the bead making workshops of Khambhat: a view from beneath the floors. In *South Asian archaeology 1991. Proceedings, International Conference of the Association of South Asian Archaeologists in Western Europe*, vol. 9, pp. 273–87. Stuttgart: Franz Steiner Verlag.

Vincent, J.-F. 1991. *Princes montagnards du Nord-Cameroun: les Mofu-Diamaré et le pouvoir politique*. Paris: Editions L'Harmattan.

Voigt, M. M. 1983. *Hajji Firuz Tepe, Iran: the Neolithic settlement*. Philadelphia: The University Museum.

Vossen, R. 1984. Towards building models of traditional trade in ceramics: case studies from Spain and Morocco. In *The many dimensions of pottery: ceramics in archaeology and anthropology*, S. van der Leeuw and A. A. Pritchard (eds.), pp. 339–97. Amsterdam: University of Amsterdam.

   1992. Ethnoarchäologie: über die Entstehung und Zielsetzung einer neuen Wissenschaft. *Ethnographische-Archäologische Zeitschrift* 33: 3–13.

Wahome, E. W. 1989. Ceramics and history in the Iron Age of northern Cameroon. M.A. thesis, University of Calgary.

Wakin, E. 1992. *Anthropology goes to war: professional ethics and counterinsurgency in Thailand*. Monograph 7. Madison: University of Wisconsin Center for Southeast Asian Studies.

Wallaert, Hélène 1998a. Apprenticeship with style: the impact of manual lateralisation on teaching and learning procedures and its influence on strategies toward style duplication. A case study from Cameroon. Paper presented at 14th Biennial meeting, Society of Africanist Archaeologists, May 20–24, 1998, Syracuse, NY.

   1998b. Ethnoarchéologie et apprentissage de la poterie. *Nyame Akuma* (50): 2–9.

Wallerstein, I. 1974. *The modern world-system*. New York: Academic Press.

Warnier, J.-P. and I. Fowler. 1979. A nineteenth-century Ruhr in central Africa. *Africa* 49: 329–51.

Washburn, D. K. and A. Petitto. 1993. An ethnoarchaeological perspective on textile categories of identification and function. *Journal of Anthropological Archaeology* 12: 150–72.

Washburn, S. (ed.). 1961. *Social life of early man*. Viking Fund Publications in Anthropology 31. Chicago: Aldine.

Watson, P. J. 1966. Clues to Iranian prehistory in modern village life. *Expedition* 8 (3): 9–19.

1979a. *Archaeological ethnography in western Iran*. Viking Fund Publications in Anthropology 57. Tucson: University of Arizona Press.

1979b. The idea of ethnoarchaeology: notes and comments. In *Ethnoarchaeology: implications of ethnography for archaeology*, C. Kramer (ed.), pp. 277–88. New York: Columbia University Press.

Watson, P. J. and M. Fotiadis. 1990. The razor's edge: symbolic-structuralist archaeology and the expansion of archaeological inference. *American Anthropologist* 92: 613–29.

Watson, P. J., S. A. LeBlanc, and C. L. Redman. 1971. *Explanation in archaeology: an explicitly scientific approach*. New York and London: Columbia University Press.

Weingarten, S. 1990. *Zur materielle Kultur der Bevölkerung des Jos-Plateaus*. Arbeiten aus dem Seminar für Völkerkunde der Johann Wolfgang Goethe-Universität 22. Stuttgart: Franz Steiner Verlag.

Welbourn, A. 1984. Endo ceramics and power strategies. In *Ideology, power and prehistory*, D. Miller and C. Tilley (eds.), pp. 17–24. Cambridge: Cambridge University Press.

Weniger, G. C. 1992. Function and form: an ethnoarchaeological analysis of barbed points from northern hunter-gatherers. In *Ethnoarchéologie: justification, problèmes, limites*, F. Audouze (ed.), pp. 257–68. Rencontres Internationales d'Archéologie et d'Histoire d'Antibes 12. Juan-les-Pins: Editions APDCA.

Werner, D. (with C. Thuman and J. Maxwell). 1992. *Where there is no doctor: a village health care handbook*. Palo Alto: Hesperian Foundation.

Whallon, R. 1978. Review of J. Yellen "Archaeological approaches to the present." *Science* 200 (7 April): 43.

White, J. P. 1967. Ethno-archaeology in New Guinea: two examples. *Mankind* 6: 409–14.

1968. Ston naip bilong tumbuna: the living stone age in New Guinea. In *La préhistoire: problèmes et tendances*, pp. 511–16 (and plates I–III hors texte). Paris: CNRS.

White, J. P., N. Modjeska, and I. Hipuya. 1977. Group definitions and mental templates: an ethnographic experiment. In *Stone tools as cultural markers*, R. V. S. Wright (ed.), pp. 380–90. Canberra: Australian Institute of Aboriginal Studies.

White, J. P. and D. H. Thomas. 1972. What mean these stones? Ethnographic taxonomic models and archaeological interpretations in the New Guinea highlands. In *Models in archaeology*, D. L. Clarke (ed.), pp. 275–308. London: Duckworth.

White, R. 1993. Introduction. In *Gesture and speech*, A. Leroi-Gourhan (ed.), pp. xiii–xxii. Cambridge, MA: MIT Press.

Wiessner, P. 1977. Hxaro: a regional system of reciprocity for reducing risk among the !Kung San. Ph.D. thesis, University of Michigan.

1982a. Risk, reciprocity and social influences on !Kung San economics. In *Politics and history in band societies*, E. Leacock and R. B. Lee (eds.), pp. 61–84. Cambridge: Cambridge University Press.

1982b. Beyond willow smoke and dogs' tails: a comment on Binford's analysis of hunter-gatherer settlement systems. *American Antiquity* 47: 171–8.

1983. Style and social information in Kalahari San projectile points. *American Antiquity* 48: 253–76.

1984. Reconsidering the behavioral basis for style: a case study among the Kalahari San. *Journal of Anthropological Archaeology* 3: 190–234.

1985. Style or isochrestic variation: a reply to Sackett. *American Antiquity* 50: 160–6.

1997. Seeking guidelines through an evolutionary approach: style revisited among the !Kung San (Ju/'hoansi) of the 1990s. In *Rediscovering Darwin: evolutionary theory and archaeological explanation*, C. M. Barton and G. A. Clark (eds.), pp. 157–75. Archaeological Papers of the American Anthropological Association, 3. Washington, DC.

Wiessner, P. and A. Tumu. 1998. *Historical vines: Enga networks of exchange, ritual, and warfare in Papua New Guinea*. Washington, DC: Smithsonian Institution Press.

Wilk, R. R. 1983. Little house in the jungle: the causes of variation in house size among modern Kekchi Maya. *Journal of Anthropological Archaeology* 2: 99–116.

Willey, G. R. 1953. *Prehistoric settlement patterns in the Virú Valley, Peru*. Washington, DC: Bureau of American Ethnology Bulletin 155, Smithsonian Institution.

Willey, G. R. and P. Phillips. 1958. *Method and theory in American archaeology*. Chicago: University of Chicago Press.

Williams, E. 1994. Organización del espacio doméstico y producción cerámica en Huáncito, Michoacán. In *Contribuciones a la arqueología y etnohistoría del Occidente de México*, E. Williams (ed.), pp. 189–225. Michoacán: El Colegio de Michoacán.

1995. The spatial organisation of pottery production in Huáncito, Michoácan, Mexico. *Papers From the Institute of Archaeology* 6: 47–56.

Wilson, D. C., W. L. Rathje, and W. W. Hughes. 1991. Household discards and modern refuse: a principle of household resource use and waste. In *The ethnoarchaeology of refuse disposal*, E. Staski and L. D. Sutro (eds.), pp. 41–51. Anthropological Research Papers 42. Tempe: Arizona State University.

Wilson, G. L. 1917. *Agriculture of the Hidatsa Indians: an Indian interpretation*. Bulletin of the University of Minnesota, Studies in the Social Sciences 6. Minneapolis: The University of Minnesota.

Wilson, M. 1959. *Communal rituals of the Nyakyusa*. London: Oxford University Press.

Wobst, H. M. 1977. Stylistic behavior and information exchange. In *Papers for the Director: research esays in honor of James B. Griffin*, C. Cleland (ed.), pp. 317–42. Michigan Anthropological Papers 61. Ann Arbor: Museum of Anthropology, University of Michigan.

1978. The archaeo-ethnography of hunter-gatherers or the tyranny of the ethnographic record in archaeology. *American Antiquity* 43: 303–9.

1999. Style in archaeology or archaeologists in style. In *Material meanings: critical approaches to the interpretation of material culture*, E. S. Chilton (ed.), pp. 118–32. Salt Lake City: University of Utah Press.

Wright, K. I. 1992. A classification system for ground stone tools from the prehistoric Levant. *Paléorient* 18 (2): 53–81.

1994. Ground-stone tools and hunter-gatherer subsistence in southwest Asia: implications for the transition to farming. *American Antiquity* 59: 238–63.

Wright, M. K. 1993. Simulated use of experimental maize grinding tools from southwestern Colorado. *The Kiva* 58 (3): 345–55.

Wylie, A. 1982. An analogy by any other name is just as analogical: a commentary on the Gould–Watson dialogue. *Journal of Anthropological Archaeology* 1: 382–401.

1985. The reaction against analogy. *Advances in Archaeological Method and Theory* 8: 63–111.

1989. The interpretive dilemma. In *Critical traditions in contemporary archaeology*, V. Pinsky and A. Wylie (eds.), pp. 18–27. Cambridge: Cambridge University Press.

1992. The interplay of evidential constraints and political interests: recent archaeological research on gender. *American Antiquity* 47: 15–36.

1994. Evidential constraints: pragmatic objectivity in archaeology. In *Readings in the philosophy of social science*, M. Martin and L. McIntyre (eds.), pp. 747–65. Boston: MIT Press.

Yellen, J. E. 1977a. *Archaeological approaches to the present*. New York: Academic Press.

1977b. Cultural patterning in faunal remains: evidence from the Kung bushmen. In *Experimental archaeology*, D. T. Ingersoll, J. E. Yellen, and W. MacDonald (eds.), pp. 271–331. New York: Columbia University Press.

1991a. Small mammals: !Kung San utilization and the production of faunal assemblages. *Journal of Anthropological Archaeology* 9: 1–26.

1991b. Small mammals: post-discard patterning of !Kung San faunal remains. *Journal of Anthropological Archaeology* 9: 152–92.

Yoffee, N. and A. Sherratt. 1993. Introduction: the sources of archaeological theory. In *Archaeological theory: who sets the agenda?*, N. Yoffee and A. Sherratt (eds.), pp. 1–9. Cambridge: Cambridge University Press.

Zipf, G. K. 1949. *Human behavior and the principle of least effort*. Cambridge, MA: Addison-Wesley Publications.

Zvelebil, M. and P. Jordan. 1999. Hunter fisher gatherer ritual landscapes: questions of time, space, and representation. In *Rock art as social representation*, J. Goldhahn (ed.), pp. 101–27. BAR International Series 794. Oxford: BAR.

INDEX

469